Flak

Flak

German Anti-aircraft Defenses 1914–1945

Edward B. Westermann

University Press of Kansas

Published by the University Press of Kansas (Lawrence, Kansas 66045), which was organized by the Kansas Board of Regents and is operated and funded by Emporia State University, Fort Hays State University, Kansas State University, Pittsburg State University, the University of Kansas, and Wichita State University

Library of Congress Cataloging-in-Publication Data

Westermann, Edward B.
Flak : German anti-aircraft defenses, 1914–1945 / Edward B. Westermann.
p. cm.—(Modern war studies)
Includes bibliographical references and index.
ISBN 978-0-7006-1136-2 (cloth: alk. paper)
ISBN 978-0-7006-1420-2 (pbk: alk. paper)
1. Air defenses—Germany—History—20th century. 2. World War, 1939–1945—Antiaircraft artillery operations. 3. World War, 1939–1945—Antiaircraft artillery operations. I. Title. II. Series.
D757.53 .W47 2001
358'.13'09430904—dc21 2001002318

British Library Cataloguing in Publication Data is available.

Printed in the United States of America

10 9 8 7 6 5 4 3

The paper used in this publication meets the minimum requirements of the American National Standard for Permanence of Paper for Printed Library Materials Z39.48–1984.

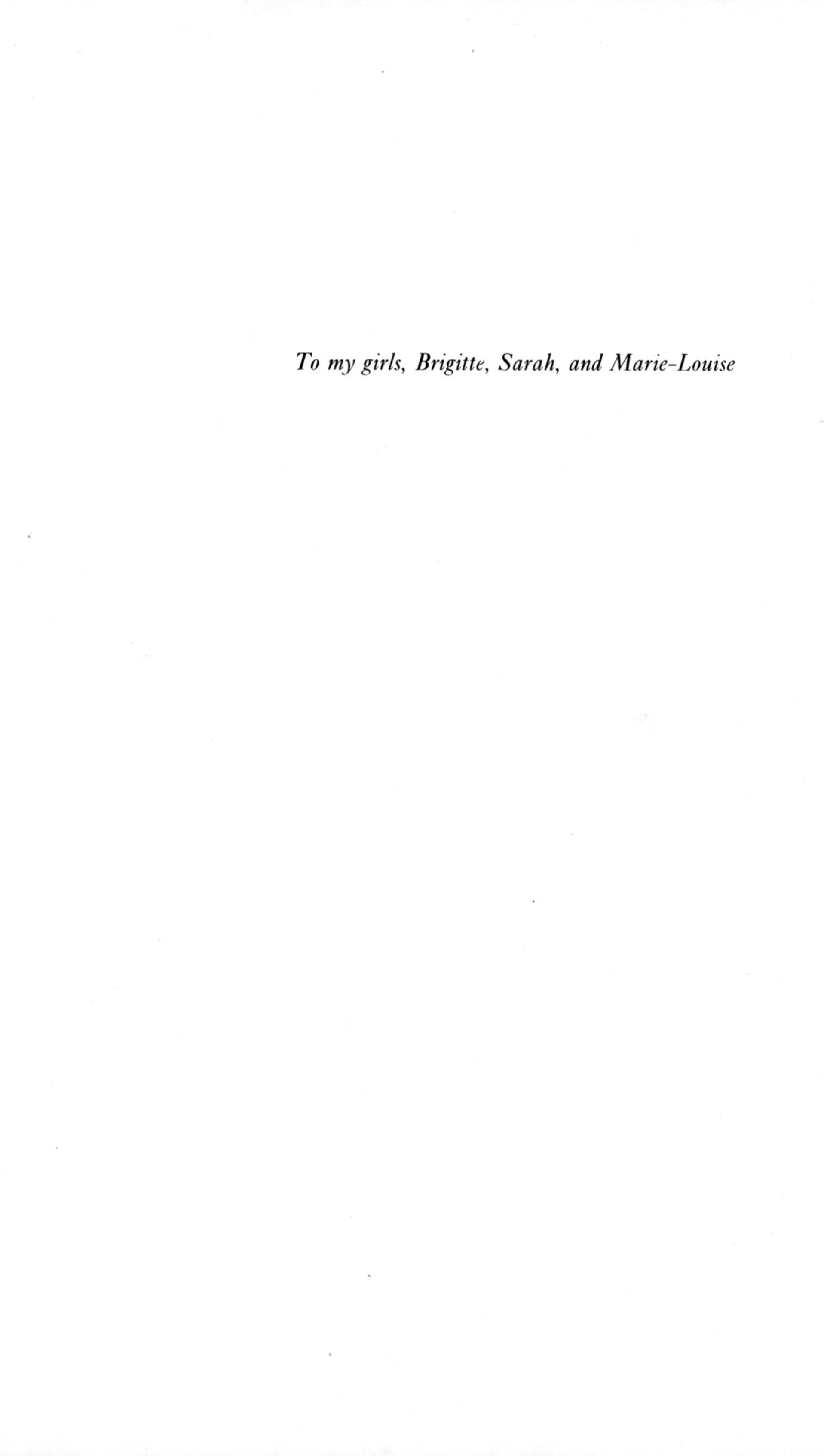

To my girls, Brigitte, Sarah, and Marie-Louise

Contents

Tables and Illustrations

Tables

Illustrations (following page 138)

Abbreviations

AA	Anti-aircraft
ADGB	Air Defence of Great Britain
AFHRA	Air Force Historical Research Agency
AHB	Air Historical Branch
BAK	*Ballonabwehrkanone*
BA-Koblenz	German Federal Archive
BA-MA	Military Archive of the German Federal Archive
BBSU	British Bombing Survey Unit
Flak	*Flugabwehrkanone*
FuMG	*Funkmeßgerät* (radar)
IWM	Imperial War Museum
MAAF	Mediterranean Allied Air Force
MGFA	Military History Research Office of Germany
NARA	National Archives and Records Administration
NSDAP	National Socialist German Workers' Party
ORS	Operational Research Section
PFF	Pathfinder Force
PRO	Public Records Office
RAF	Royal Air Force
USAAF	United States Army Air Forces
USSBS	United States Strategic Bombing Survey
USSTAF	United States Strategic Air Forces

Acknowledgments

I am indebted to numerous persons and organizations for their assistance and support in the preparation of this manuscript. First and foremost, I would like to thank the members of my dissertation committee, Tami Davis Biddle, Melissa Bullard, Konrad Jarausch, and Alex Roland, for their instruction and assistance throughout my graduate career. The combined programs at the University of North Carolina and Duke offered me a rewarding journey along the roads of early modern European, modern German, and military history. I especially would like to thank my *Doktorväter*, Richard Kohn and Gerhard Weinberg, for their meticulous attention to detail and expert advice in the preparation of this manuscript. I am profoundly grateful to both for sharing their insights, professional expertise, and friendship.

I would like to thank the German Academic Exchange Service (DAAD) for a research grant to examine archival and library holdings in Freiburg and Potsdam. While I was in Freiburg Horst Boog and Wilhelm Deist were both gracious hosts and stimulating discussion partners. Horst Boog also graciously agreed to read and comment on the finished version of this manuscript. Likewise, the staffs of the Bundesarchiv-Militärarchiv, the Bundesarchiv-Hauptarchiv, and the Militärgeschichtliches Forschungsamt provided me with friendly and expert assistance during my stay in the Federal Republic. Similarly, during a research visit to the United Kingdom, I benefited from the helpful and knowledgeable advice of the staffs of the Public Records Office, the Imperial War Museum, and the Air Historical Branch. In the case of the last, I am indebted to Sebastian Cox for sharing his insights, many cups of tea, and several hours from his busy schedule. In addition, special thanks are due to Steve Chiabotti and Rob Owen of the School of Advanced Airpower Studies for their support of my graduate studies. I also owe many thanks to the staffs of National Archives II and the USAF Historical Research Agency for their assistance during my visits to both locations. I also would like to thank the League of World War I Aviation Historians for honoring the first chapter of this work with its 1999 essay award. Likewise, I am grateful to the *Journal of Military History* for selecting the first chapter of this work for publication and allowing me to reprint it here. Jack Atwater, Bill Gaddes, and Mark Swartzburg also helped me answer questions or find materials during my research efforts.

Special thanks are due to Jim Corum not only for his helpful comments in the preparation of this work but also for his generous loan of materials from his personal collection. In addition, I would like to thank Dennis Showalter for his comments, suggestions, and encouragement throughout my brief career as a historian. Clio could not have provided me with a better mentor, role model, or friend. Finally, I would like to thank my wife, Brigitte, for all her support and patience. Her editorial comments and her excellent proofreading skills were invaluable.

Introduction

United States Army newsreel footage of the devastated landscapes of German cities provides one of the most enduring images of World War II. The pictures of gutted buildings and rubble-filled streets offer a stark testament to the ultimate failure of the Luftwaffe in protecting the German homeland from aerial attack. In the course of the war, the Royal Air Force (RAF) and the United States Army Air Forces (USAAF) obliterated entire sections of major German industrial and population centers under a hail of high explosive and incendiary bomb loads. Operating largely at night, the RAF launched its "bomber streams" against Germany's major industrial and urban centers in a strategy of area bombardment designed to "dehouse" the German people and break their will to fight. In 1943, the USAAF joined the RAF in raids against Germany by focusing on a strategy of daylight "precision" bombardment aimed at the heart of German industrial production. During the course of the air campaign against the Third Reich, tens of thousands of British and American bombers pounded targets within Germany with over 1.2 million tons of bombs.[1] In the end, Allied bombing within Germany killed an estimated 300,000 civilians, wounded an additional 780,000 persons, and destroyed 3.6 million dwellings.[2]

In the wake of this aerial Armageddon, countless monographs and articles have examined the efficacy of strategic bombing in World War II. With few exceptions, these accounts have focused on the contributions of either the Royal Air Force or the Army Air Forces to the defeat of Germany. The majority of Anglo-American accounts have emphasized the perspective of Allied military planners and the crews in the cockpit. When examining Germany's air defense network, most historians have concentrated on the role of the Luftwaffe's day and night fighter forces in the battle for control of the skies over Europe.[3] In contrast, the development and operations of German ground-based air defenses have been examined only briefly, if not completely ignored, in the standard histories of the Luftwaffe.[4]

The standard historical analyses of German ground-based air defenses have tended to dismiss the contribution of the anti-aircraft forces using one, or a combination, of the following three arguments. First, many historians accepted the postwar testimony of leading figures within the Luftwaffe that ground-based air defenses, in particular the Luftwaffe's anti-aircraft or flak forces, had achieved limited success in destroying Allied bombers. Field Marshal Erhard

Milch, the head of the Luftwaffe's Air Armaments Program and the second in command of the Air Ministry, was the most prominent official to make this argument. After the war, the British Bombing Survey Unit (BBSU) also adopted this line of reasoning. The BBSU severely underrated the importance of the Luftwaffe's anti-aircraft gun defenses by describing them as "plentiful" but not "very lethal."[5] A second widespread criticism of the flak centered on the contention that the ground-based air defenses cost too much in terms of both fiscal and personnel outlays. This argument found its initial expression in both the United States Strategic Bombing Survey (USSBS) and the report of the BBSU. Both reports contended that the production of flak guns and flak ammunition prevented the transfer of these resources to more critical areas, including the manufacture of regular artillery pieces. The resource argument also has been applied to the number of men and women employed in the anti-aircraft arm. In this context, the argument holds that the hundreds of thousands of German men and women employed in these defenses could have been employed more effectively in other military or industrial tasks.[6] The third and final argument associated with the flak is closely related to the previous criticism. Both American and German postwar historians averred that the resources spent in the buildup of the anti-aircraft arm could have been more efficiently used in the construction of more fighters.[7] Milch, the most ardent contemporary proponent of this argument, repeatedly contended that fighters were up to five times more effective versus the bombers than the flak and therefore constituted the first, and best, resort for the defense of the skies over Germany.[8] The preceding arguments concerning the Luftwaffe's anti-aircraft forces have some merit, but they are beset by problems related to their limited scope and their failure to incorporate contemporary contextual factors.

The first argument concerning the limited effectiveness of the flak is patently false. During the course of the war, German anti-aircraft defenses destroyed a high proportion of American and British fighter and bomber aircraft. For example, German flak accounted for at least half of American aircraft combat losses during the war.[9] Likewise, the official RAF history of the air war estimated that German flak accounted for 1,229 out of 3,302, or 37 percent, of Bomber Command's missing aircraft during night raids between July 1942 and April 1945.[10] Furthermore, this argument ignores, or minimizes, the effect of flak defenses in forcing aircraft to drop their bombs from higher altitudes, thus reducing bombing accuracy. This argument also neglects the damage caused by flak defenses that often facilitated the ability of Luftwaffe fighters subsequently to bring down wounded bombers. It is apparent from the statistical analyses of the British and American operational research sections, as well as the personal memoirs of innumerable veterans, that German flak defenses proved a lethal and oftentimes effective adversary.

The second criticism of the flak arm concerns the anti-aircraft arm's supposed diversion of critical matériel and personnel resources away from other areas of the German war machine. This argument is only partially correct. Admittedly, German ground-based air defense forces did absorb one-third of the output of the optical industry and between one-half and two-thirds of the production of radar and signals equipment.[11] However, in the latter case, a high percentage of radar and communications devices supported both flak and fighter operations. In addition, the Air Reporting Service (Luftnachrichtentruppe), which was not a part of the flak arm, consumed the lion's share of the resources devoted to communications. In contrast to auxiliary equipment, the question of resource diversions to flak artillery weapons and ammunition is decidedly less convincing. In its report entitled *The Effects of Strategic Bombing on the German War Economy*, the Economic Effects Division of the USSBS team found that "since earlier limitation of output was largely the result of deliberately restricted demand, it cannot be said that investment in anti-aircraft prior to 1943 represents a cost in terms of other weapons and ammunition."[12] Furthermore, the contention that the anti-aircraft program robbed the fighting front of available artillery is only partially correct. In a meeting with the Luftwaffe's Fighter Staff on August 1, 1944, Albert Speer, the Reich minister of armaments, remarked that "today our artillery programme is far beyond the target originally set us by the Fuehrer. . . . we have again achieved production records in July which, in the case of all the important weapons types, is approximately equivalent to 8–10 times the figures for 1941."[13] In addition, those who argue that flak weapons and ammunition production resulted in lower production of these items for the field armies often fail to take into account the important contribution of Luftwaffe flak forces in support of the ground combat operations during the Wehrmacht's campaigns on all fronts. In fact, the Luftwaffe's flak arm played a critical role in support of army ground operations in the invasion of both France and the Soviet Union and in the campaign in North Africa. The use of the flak in a variety of roles besides air defense refutes the simplistic calculus that holds that one flak gun was one fewer artillery piece available for the German army. With regard to personnel, the flak did indeed require a large contingent of men, and later women, to successfully perform its mission. However, contentions that the anti-aircraft network robbed the Wehrmacht of men who might have been better used in hundreds of new divisions are also spurious. Clearly, anti-aircraft defenses did involve large numbers of personnel. In 1940, there were 528,000 men serving with the flak arm alone; however, this number had increased to only 573,000 by November 1944 as a result of the mobilization of factory workers, young men and young women, and even prisoners of war. In fact, from the fall 1944 these auxiliaries constituted from one-third to one-half of all persons serving in the flak arm. In addition, in 1945, over one-third of those persons serving in the flak came from older age-groups or were unfit for military service because of medical disabilities.[14] By 1944, the flak force constituted not a pool of the Wehrmacht's "lost divisions" but rather a catchall force largely composed of those persons less able to serve on the front lines.

Finally, arguments that the Luftwaffe should have favored fighters at the expense of the flak are also only partially persuasive. In truth, Luftwaffe doctrine never viewed air defense as a question between either fighters or ground-based air defenses. At the start of the war, Hitler and Göring undoubtedly saw anti-aircraft defenses as the primary means of homeland air defense; however, Luftwaffe doctrine emphasized that flak and fighters were complementary means for ensuring the protection of Germany from air attack. Likewise, Field Marshal Albert Kesselring, a leading commander of German forces during World War II, argued, "The view of wartime economists that one should have abandoned the flak artillery based on resource grounds and instead built more fighters must be contradicted, even with a full acknowledgment of the performance of the fighters. Organic defense of the troops and the homeland by the flak [was] indispensable."[15] Furthermore, those who argue that the emphasis on anti-aircraft production resulted in decreased aircraft output often fail to consider important contextual information. For example, as early as 1942, the Luftwaffe experienced significant problems in training sufficient numbers of pilots to fly available aircraft. The ever more critical lack of aviation fuel combined with increasing losses of pilots led to the reduction in the pilot training program from 240 flight hours in 1942 to a mere 120 flight hours by the middle of 1944.[16] By the fall of 1944, thousands of airframes stood rusting in supply depots and aircraft parks because of a shortage of pilots and gasoline. The introduction of American fighter escorts in late 1943 and 1944 was also another key factor that changed the nature of the air war to the detriment of the Luftwaffe's fighter force and in favor of anti-aircraft defenses. Likewise, the advocates of the "fighters for anti-aircraft defenses argument" tend to ignore the important role played by searchlights and flak gun batteries in assisting Luftwaffe fighters in bringing down Allied aircraft. In 1941, searchlights assisted night fighters in the destruction of 325 bombers versus only 50 shot down by night fighters under nonilluminated conditions.[17] Likewise, throughout the war, Luftwaffe fighter pilots often concentrated their efforts against aircraft damaged by flak and thus rendered less maneuverable or separated from the relative safety of the formation. One Luftwaffe pilot remarked, "That was the old fighter pilot's trick. The successful ones built up their scores in this way."[18] In addition, the memoirs of American aircrews are replete with descriptions of the dangers experienced by aircraft damaged by flak and subsequently forced to "straggle" behind the main bombing force.[19] In the end, the fighter-versus-flak argument ignores the manifold interactions and contextual factors that shaped the operations of the Luftwaffe's air defenses during World War II.

The debate surrounding the fighter-versus-flak question also encompasses a more profound issue involving the widespread underestimation of the overall performance of the broad range of Luftwaffe ground-based air defenses in World War II. Both contemporary Luftwaffe leaders and postwar historians failed to appreciate the holistic nature of Germany's air defense network. The overwhelming tendency to focus solely on the numbers of Allied aircraft destroyed by flak and/or fighters provides only one piece of the air defense mosaic and has led to a widespread underappreciation of the contributions of other organizations within the Luftwaffe's air defenses. For example, the activities of the Luftwaffe's dummy installations *(Scheinanlagen)* and measures used to decoy bombers away from their intended targets have received scant attention in the majority of histories. The dummy installations and decoy measures experienced varying degrees of success throughout the conflict, but at times they proved instrumental in luring a high percentage of RAF and USAAF aircraft away from their intended targets. As mentioned earlier, the searchlight batteries also played a key role during specific periods of the war in supporting both flak and fighter operations. Finally, smoke generator companies and barrage balloon units achieved isolated success in the battle against the Allied air forces. In the final analysis, a myopic focus on flak and fighters has resulted in a profound underestimation of the contributions of all elements of the ground-based air defense system.

A second aspect that contributed to the general underestimation of the performance of the flak arm during the war involved the psychological reaction of the Luftwaffe's leadership to the "failure" of anti-aircraft defenses to prevent the destruction of the cities and factories of the Reich from the Allied aerial assault. In an oft-repeated and now famous boast, Hermann Göring exclaimed, "If an enemy bomber reaches the Ruhr, my name is not Hermann Göring. You can call me Meier."[20] While often cited as but one example of Göring's penchant for pompous proclamations, his boast clearly reflected his belief that the strength of the Luftwaffe's air defenses would make Germany largely invulnerable to attacks from the "third dimension," the heavens above the battlefields and homes of the combatants. In truth, Göring's belief was not based on simple delusion. At the start of the conflict, Germany did in fact posses the most extensive and capable ground-based air defense system in the world. However, it was certainly true that the Luftwaffe's high expectations were founded on erroneous assumptions. For example, prewar flak studies estimated that one 88-mm anti-aircraft projectile exploding within thirty-three yards of an attacking aircraft would bring the bomber down.[21] The technological advances made in aircraft design, defensive armament, and propulsion in the early stages of the war soon gave lie to these prewar expectations. In a meeting of October 1943, Göring caustically reminded the Luftwaffe's flak commanders of their prewar promise that enemy aircrews flying between 6,500 and 13,000 feet had better have their wills prepared because they would not get a second chance. Likewise, he noted that the estimate of thirty-three yards for a lethal hit had plummeted to a mere thirteen yards, and even an explosion at this distance was not guaranteed to bring down a four-engine bomber. It was at this point that the commander of the Luftwaffe's flak forces, General of the Flak Artillery Walther von Axthelm, grudgingly confessed, "At the moment we [the flak arm] are the supporting arm to the fighters."[22] Axthelm's disillusionment with his command would be shorter-lived than the memories and recollections of other Luftwaffe leaders after the war. Ultimately, extreme disappointment and a tendency to denigrate the accomplishments of the Luftwaffe's flak forces proved to be the price for the failure to meet the high expectations of the prewar period.

The following work examines the organization and operations of German ground-based air defenses in the period between 1914 and 1945. In the battle for control of the skies over Europe, technology played a critical role in shifting the balance between the defenders and the attackers during the course of the war. Likewise, resource limitations and economic considerations affected the manner in which the war could be waged. Finally, military doctrine and political decision making played an important role in determining the Luftwaffe's response to the Allied bombing campaign. In short, the development of the Luftwaffe's ground-based air defense system aptly demonstrates the linkage between economics, technology, military doctrine, and political decision making in the age of modern industrialized warfare. The evolution of German ground-based air defenses also tells a story of the role of expectations and perceptions in the formation of military strategy and illustrates the military and political consequences engendered by the failure to fulfill these expectations.

In preparing this work, it was soon apparent that, in order to tell the story of ground-based air defenses fully, an accompanying discussion of the Luftwaffe's fighter forces and the development of strategic bombardment was necessary to place the Luftwaffe's earthbound efforts in context. While not intended to be a comprehensive history of either the Luftwaffe's fighter forces or strategic bombardment, this work integrates a discussion of both throughout the narrative to provide a framework for a trenchant evaluation of the development and contributions of the Luftwaffe's ground-based air defenses throughout the period.

Before proceeding to a discussion of the organization of this work, it is also necessary to address briefly the nature of the sources used in the preparation of this manuscript. One of the major problems for historians studying the Luftwaffe involves the widespread destruction of air force records in the closing stages of the war. The loss of these records often results in documentary gaps for specific periods or the absence of information for individual organizations within the Luftwaffe. Despite these gaps, a great deal of evidence remains that allows for a reconstruction of the activities of German ground-based air defenses, including wartime German records, postwar interrogation reports, and the personal papers and memoirs of Luftwaffe commanders. In addition, the contemporary records and reports assembled by the intelligence and flying organizations of the RAF and the USAAF often allow the historian to bridge many of the holes created by the destruction of German records. Furthermore, the use of Allied records and memoirs broadens the work by providing perspectives from the ground and from the air, as well as from Berlin, High Wycombe, and Bushy Park. Likewise, for periods when documentation exists from both German and Anglo-American sources, one can compare the accuracy of both Allied and Axis estimations, a crucial step in determining the relationship between reality and perception.

With regard to Allied sources concerning aircraft losses, the Operational Research Section (ORS) of Bomber Command began compiling detailed reports on night raids only in February 1942. Furthermore, these reports did not attempt to analyze the cause of individual aircraft losses until July 1942. The figures from July 1942 onward, however, have a high degree of reliability because losses were credited to flak, fighters, accidents, and so forth only when "strong evidence" could be produced to establish the specific cause of the aircraft's destruction.[23] In contrast, USAAF reports of flak losses and flak damage tended to underestimate the effects of anti-aircraft fire until the middle of 1944. In fact, standardized reporting procedures concerning aircraft damage due to all causes were not implemented for USAAF bombers in the United Kingdom until the end of February 1943. Despite these procedures, one report by the Eighth Air Force's Loss and Battle Damage Subsection found at the end of 1943 that "it is probable that the importance of flak has been grossly underestimated."[24] Likewise, it was not until January 1945 that monthly flak conferences were organized to attempt to come to grips with the ever-increasing problems of flak losses and flak damage within the USAAF[25] In spite of the limitations found within German and Allied sources, it is still possible to piece together a story of the role played by the Luftwaffe's ground-based air defenses during the cataclysmic years between 1939 and 1945.

Chapter 1 examines the growth and performance of ground-based air defenses in the Great War. Chapter 2 traces the largely theoretical debates concerning the form and nature of air defense that occupied German military and civilian theorists in the period between 1919 and 1932. Chapter 3 details the initial expansion of the Luftwaffe's flak arm in conjunction with German rearmament after the National Socialist "seizure of power" in 1933. Chapter 4 follows the development and performance of the flak arm in 1939 and 1940 as Germany embarked upon a campaign of European conquest. Chapter 5 outlines the evolution of ground-based air defenses in the face of the modest British bombing effort throughout 1941. Chapter 6 describes the high point of the effectiveness of the Luftwaffe's flak forces in defending the Third Reich from an increasingly more lethal assault from the air. Chapter 7 depicts the dramatic reversal of fortune experienced within the German air defenses as radar jamming, a chronic lack of personnel, and the combined Allied bombing effort turned the tide in favor of the bomber offensive. Chapters 8 and 9 trace the reaction of German air defenses in the face of a massive aerial assault that eventually overwhelmed the Luftwaffe's air defenses and left millions of tons of bricks and rubble strewn across the Third Reich as a visible reminder of one man's mad vision of world conquest.

CHAPTER ONE

The Great War and Ground-based Air Defenses, 1914–1918

The Great War witnessed a dramatic, if overly romanticized, battle between the forces of the Allied and the Central Powers for control of the "third dimension." In their accounts of the air war, most historians have focused on the role and performance of the flying crews and their aircraft. The battle for the skies over Europe was not waged, however, in the air alone. During the conflict, German ground-based air defense systems began a slow but steady evolution in an effort to control the heavens from the earth below. In the face of a positional stalemate, the steadily expanding performance of aircraft led to an increasing awareness among the German political and military leadership of the need for viable and effective air defenses, both at the fighting front and on the home front. The ultimate contribution of ground-based air defenses to the overall German war effort was relatively modest. However, an evaluation of these defenses offers a story that clearly demonstrates the interrelationship between technology, resources, and doctrine in warfare. It is also a story that enriches and expands the contemporary understanding of "the first air war."

Origins of German Ground-Based Air Defenses in the Prewar Period

The origins of German anti-aircraft efforts reach back to the Franco-Prussian War of 1870–1871. The use by the Communards of hot air balloons to escape from the besieged city of Paris resulted in an urgent request by the German army for an effective weapon with which to engage the French balloons.[1] The Krupp armament works quickly began efforts to produce a 36-mm antiballoon gun (*Ballonabwehrkanone,* or BAK) mounted on a mobile cart. However, hitting a balloon and damaging it sufficiently to bring it down proved more difficult than originally envisioned. Of the sixty-six balloons known to have left Paris during the siege, the Germans succeeded in bringing down only one, the *Daguerre,* on November 12, 1870.[2] In fact, the technological and mechanical problems associated with targeting balloons, airships, or aircraft would remain the primary obstacle to the successful engagement of aerial targets by anti-aircraft guns throughout the next three-quarters of a century. For example, German gunners relied on mobility and dispersion to cover the area around the French capital. Still, by the end of 1870, the German army had only six of these guns to cover the entire perimeter of the city. Even when fire could be brought to bear on a balloon, the 36-mm metal slugs, although capable of puncturing the balloon's skin, often inflicted insufficient damage to bring it down. In any event, the French simply began making flights at night, thus minimizing the threat posed by the guns.[3] The ultimate capitulation of the French in 1871 resulted in a thirty-five-year hiatus in the field of German air defense research and development.

The introduction of airships and aircraft at the turn of the century led to an increasing realization of the potential military significance of both lighter-than-air and heavier-than-air aircraft for the conduct of reconnaissance and artillery spotting.[4] In the years before World War I, the Germans invested significant resources in the construction of dirigibles. Count Ferdinand von Zeppelin recognized the high costs of these aircraft but assured the military that an airship could provide the movements of enemy forces to German generals and admirals "in any weather, by day and by night."[5] Zeppelin successfully marketed his airships to both the military and private investors. In the latter case, the zeppelin fleet achieved commercial success by transporting approximately 34,000 people throughout Germany between 1910 and 1914. The "zeppelin craze" had, however, a darker side and triggered a series of zeppelin bombing scares in England and France evocative of the naval scares of the same period.[6] While German schoolchildren in Bremerhaven were being admonished that "Der Fisher kommt!" (Admiral Fisher's [fleet] is coming!), their English and French counterparts feared the specter of a surprise German air raid. In conjunction with its own advanced progress in airship design and manufacture, German industry embarked upon a program to develop antiaircraft guns designed to shoot down these lighter-than-air platforms, a fact evident in the German use of the term *Ballonabwehrkanone*. In 1906, the Artillery Proving Commission (Artillerie-Prüfungs-Kommission) of the War Ministry warned of French advances in balloon technology.[7] In an order dated January 29, 1906, General Sixt von Arnim cautioned that measures must be taken to combat the potential French threat. He therefore ordered the artillery schools to study the problem and prepare a report for the commission.[8]

German industry also responded to the perceived need for an air defense gun by constructing several prototypes. At the Berlin Auto Exhibition of 1906, the German firm Rheinische Metallwaren- und Maschinenfabrik (later Rheinmetall) displayed a 50-mm gun mounted on a lightly armored car for use in antiairship defense. In 1908, the armaments works of Krupp produced a 65-mm gun mounted on slewable wheels that afforded a 360-degree field of traverse and an elevation range of 60 degrees.[9] During the Frankfurt International Exhibition of 1909, both Krupp and Rheinmetall reexhibited these air defense guns. In addition to its 65-mm gun, Krupp introduced a

75-mm gun mounted on a motorized vehicle and a 105-mm gun for maritime air defense. A unique feature of several of these guns was their use of armor plating to protect the gun crews, a feature that some viewed as superfluous based on the perceived inability of balloons and airships to threaten the gun crews.[10] These initial designs aroused curiosity but few procurement orders from European military circles.

Still, the German army's burgeoning interest in the subject of air defense led to several tests to evaluate the use of standard army weapons against aerial targets. In 1907, the army employed conventional field artillery pieces fired at a balloon towed by a motorboat. The results of the trial were less than satisfactory and led to the finding that conventional artillery was not suited for combating aerial targets.[11] A second firing trial to evaluate the effect of standard infantry weapons on balloons took place at the Infantry School at Jüterborg in May 1909. This test involved two detachments of infantry and a 50-foot-long tethered balloon flying at an altitude of approximately 4,000 feet. The first infantry squad fired 4,800 rounds of rifle ammunition without apparent effect. The second group then fired 2,700 rounds from several Maxim machine guns, again without visible effect. The balloon was brought back to earth, and despite an examination that revealed seventy-six punctures, the balloon was still flight-worthy. This test clearly demonstrated not only the importance of being able to hit the target (slightly more than 1 percent of all rounds punctured the balloon's fabric) but also the importance of the type of munitions used. Based on these abysmal results, the German army concluded that infantry weapons were largely ineffective against balloons and acknowledged the need for a more suitable artillery projectile.[12]

The difficulties associated with firing on canvas-covered balloons extended beyond the physical shape and composition of the projectile itself. The fuse type used to detonate the projectile proved an equally thorny technical challenge. The light resistance offered by a balloon's soft fabric required an extremely sensitive contact fuse, which then offered the potential catastrophic consequences of premature detonation during firing from the gun's tube.[13] In addition, an even more troublesome problem was the difficulty of tracking the shell in flight. For regular artillery fires, the physical impact point of the projectile allowed for an adjustment of range and azimuth through the use of artillery spotters. In combat against aerial targets, however, this was impossible. Some other method was necessary for discerning the flight path of the projectile in order to adjust the fires. Once again, the engineers of Krupp provided a solution by designing a shell that carried an incendiary in the forward half of the projectile and a smoke-producing substance in the rear. Once fired, the shell trailed a black plume of smoke, allowing for improved flight path tracking with a corresponding improvement in fire adjustment.[14] However, the difficulty in discerning the point at which the shell burst in relation to the intended target remained a problem. The technical challenges associated with types of munitions, projectiles, and fuses were key obstacles in later efforts to create an effective anti-aircraft system.

By 1910, German army leaders clearly recognized the necessity for an air defense weapon. The type and construction of the gun became, however, a subject of debate. In January 1910, a report prepared for the Artillery Proving Commission recommended the construction of standard artillery guns on a wheeled carriage capable of being drawn by horses. A special report, dated February 14, 1910, questioned the conclusions reached in the January report. The authors of this dissenting opinion, Major Merlack, Captain Kraut, Captain Schmitt, and Captain Schneider, made a number of recommendations concerning the development of antiballoon artillery. First, the report called for the development of motorized guns. The authors argued that a gun mounted on an open truck bed was superior to a wheeled carriage because it could be fired immediately, without the delay associated with the entrenchment of wheel-mounted guns. They also highlighted the motorized gun's greater mobility, which allowed for more flexibility both in responding to airship attack and in the *pursuit* of enemy airships. Second, the report called for the construction of a "purpose-built" artillery piece with the contention that "according to the present state of technology, there is no doubt that a purpose-built gun *[Spezialgeschütz]* is always a better solution than a regular artillery gun."[15] Finally, the authors identified the need for special-purpose munitions designed specifically for use against airships. The report raised a number of fundamental issues associated with air defense weapons that would dominate the debate concerning the technical requirements of air defense in the following years.

The German army's senior leadership also acknowledged the growing importance of defense against airship attack. In a memorandum of March 14, 1910, General Helmuth von Moltke, chief of the General Staff, discussed the threat posed by French airships. Moltke advocated the arming of German airships but cautioned, "We must be, however, in the position to destroy the enemy's airships from the ground." Moltke rejected the request for purpose-built guns and urged the expeditious conduct of long-planned anti-aircraft firing trials in the Bay of Danzig "despite all of the difficulties standing in the way [of these tests]."[16] Moltke concluded his memorandum by requesting a report on air defense capabilities with specific details on the gun crews' ability to track and measure the range of maneuvering airships.

Moltke's personal involvement produced the desired results. During the annual army maneuvers of 1910, the army tested two weapons platforms for organic air defense. The first was a 75-mm gun mounted on the open bed of a truck. In addition, the army mounted an infantry machine gun on the open bed of a second truck.[17] Both concepts clearly improved the mobility of the guns, but simply mounting a field artillery piece on the back of a truck engendered numerous problems for the operators and the vehicle. The recoil of the weapon had a substantial impact on the truck's chassis, and the lack of space made the loading and aiming of the weapon cumbersome, to say the least.[18] Most important, the lack of a fire control system severely degraded the effectiveness of the gun. The use of unaided optical aiming required in effect more luck than skill. In contrast, the mounting of the machine gun offered a more promising solution. The greater ease in manipulating the gun into various firing positions, its higher rate of fire, and its reduced space and crew demands were definite advantages. The primary disadvantage with the machine gun centered on its relative lack of range, a significant handicap that allowed for unrestricted aircraft operations at a height above the machine gun's reach.[19]

In the years prior to World War I, it became clear that not only airships but also heavier-than-air aircraft constituted an emerging threat. The German General Staff recognized that advances in aircraft technology had significant implications for future military operations. The Italian campaign in Libya between 1911 and 1912 and the use of aircraft in the Balkan War of 1912 demonstrated the emerging potentialities of aircraft.[20] Closer to home and of more concern to the General Staff were the successful French aviation trials involving the bombing of point targets.[21] In his postwar memoir, General Ernst von Höppner, the commander of the German Air Service, remarked:

> As early as in March 1911 the General Staff had gained the impression from the performance of airships and aviators during the imperial manoevers [*sic*], from artillery practice against aircraft, and through information relative to the advances made by France in military aeronautics, that aviation material should be assembled and that the role of aircraft as a means of reconnaisance [*sic*] be taken up and further developed.[22]

According to Höppner, insufficient funding and a general shortage of qualified officers and enlisted troops combined to retard the growth of both German aviation and air defense in the years prior to the war.[23] Höppner's assessment was perhaps too pessimistic. In fact, between 1911 and 1914, the German army conducted numerous tests involving guns and searchlights, as well as towed and stationary aerial targets. In April 1911, the Special Commission on the Combat of Air Vehicles delivered a report on ground-based air defenses to the War Ministry. The commission warned that the capabilities of air defense continued to lag behind those of modern airships; it also noted the threat posed by smaller and more maneuverable aircraft. Recommendations to strengthen ground-based air defenses included the construction of a purpose-built gun, as well as increased and more realistic training for the gun crews.[24]

A War Ministry report of April 5, 1912, concerning the "combat of aerial vehicles" provided ambiguous support for the commission's findings of the previous year. The War Ministry recommended increasing the number of drills and exercises under live fire conditions, as well as advocating the broader dissemination of air defense procedures among the troops. In addition, the report identified the need for an accurate, reliable range-finding device. However, in contrast to the commission's findings, the War Ministry contended that traditional field and foot artillery was perfectly "suitable" for combating aerial vehicles.[25] The reluctance to abandon this position was underscored further in the first aviation manual issued by the German army in March 1913, "Guidelines for Instructing Troops About Aircraft and Means of Combating Aircraft." The manual provided a detailed discussion of ground-based air defense procedures, but it still advocated the use of standard field and foot artillery pieces to combat airships and airplanes.[26]

In early 1914, the senior leadership of the army turned to the topic of air defense with renewed interest. In a directive of April 9, 1914, von Moltke emphasized the importance of an effective air defense against the "increasing employment possibilities of aircraft," and he ordered the commitment of the necessary resources for ground-based air defense as soon as possible. He then added, "I believe that the time has come that we take extensive measures and address the organizational regulation of this question."[27] In accordance with earlier suggestions, he ordered the acquisition of thirty-two motorized anti-aircraft guns, four for each of the German numbered armies (AOKs). He noted that army trials at the infantry school at Jüterborg during the previous years demonstrated the importance of denying one's adversary the ability to conduct aerial reconnaissance. In the four years since 1910, von Moltke also had changed his opinion concerning the necessity for a purpose-built gun, perhaps in response to the report from the Field Artillery School in May 1913 that promoted the design of such guns.[28] Additionally, the Imperial war maneuvers of 1912 and the test firings of the Krupp and Rheinmetall prototypes in the Baltic Sea in 1913 and 1914 finally helped to convince the General Staff of the necessity for a purpose-built anti-aircraft gun.[29] In any event, von Moltke now advocated the need for an artillery piece specifically designed for the air defense mission. At the organizational level, von Moltke directed the establishment of one anti-aircraft battery alongside the existing regular artillery batteries of each division. But he strictly prohibited the conversion of existing field artillery batteries into anti-aircraft batteries because this would only "weaken" the division's organic artillery firepower. Moltke concluded by stating his intention to notify the kaiser's cabinet of these decisions and by remarking on the "great importance" that he had always placed on air defense. Finally, he called for extensive tests involving air defense systems during the army maneuvers for the fall of 1914.[30]

The fall maneuvers planned for 1914 would take place not in Germany but on the battlefields of France and East Prussia. Still, the German army continued to experiment with air defense concepts in the months preceding the start of the war. For example, the army conducted anti-aircraft trials in April 1914 at a test range in Swinemünde. The tests included firing modified artillery pieces at imaginary targets in the air, a practice not designed to engender advanced levels of proficiency among the gun crews.[31] With the outbreak of war only a few months away, the German effort appeared as a case of too little and too late. The technical limitations of the early anti-aircraft guns combined with a somewhat belated recognition of the rapid development of aviation technology contributed to a general atmosphere of increasing discussion but slow-paced modernization within the anti-aircraft arm.

The apparent neglect of ground-based air defenses in the years directly preceding the Great War appears paradoxical in light of the stated opinions of the War Ministry and the senior army leadership. However, a comparison between Germany's air defense efforts and those of its European neighbors at this time offers the clearest benchmark for evaluating German progress. N. W. Routledge, a historian of British air defenses, noted that the British army lagged behind Germany and France and remarked that prior to 1914 "no [British] Army AA organisation existed."[32] In contrast, the French army had commenced anti-aircraft trials already in 1906 and had experimented with mobile guns as early as 1910; however, the French army's willingness to experiment was not reflected in a corresponding outlay of funds for the acquisition of air defense weapons.[33] This brief comparison indicates that, despite the limited scope of German ground-based air defenses in 1914, the German army still was at the forefront of air defense developments within Europe. In addition, the German navy had pursued its own program of research and development of flak guns in this period, producing some of the finest anti-aircraft guns of the war.[34]

A report from the Prussian War Ministry of February 25, 1914, clearly demonstrated the realization of the practical necessity for a viable air defense network. The report, entitled "Measures for the Protection of Important Structures Against Enemy Aircraft Operations," detailed the need for defensive measures to protect key bridges, airship factories and hangars, and train stations. In fact, the practice of defending specific sites or key complexes *(Objektschutz)* remained a central doctrinal tenet of German home defense through World War II.[35] The report provided a number of trenchant suggestions, including the recommendation for active versus passive defense measures, the centralization of all air defense assets under one commander, and the close coordination between air defense and the early-warning system.[36] On the whole, however, German experience with ground-based air defenses prior to the war advanced little beyond theoretical discussions and limited trials despite the rhetoric of the army leadership.

The general state of air defenses was not surprising given the type of conflict envisioned by the General Staff in the German war plan. As has been noted often, Germany's military blueprint for World War I, the Schlieffen Plan, sought to avoid the perils of a two-front war by first defeating France in a six- to eight-week campaign and then turning east to confront the Russian "colossus."[37] An army of historians has dissected and debated the deficiencies in the plan's conceptualization and execution. With respect to the issue of air defense, however, the limited time horizon of the Schlieffen Plan explained in great part the belated German emphasis on air defense within the army. The widespread belief that the war would be a brief affair much like the Franco-Prussian War of 1870–1871 also helped to explain the almost complete neglect of German homeland air defense in 1914. Military forces acquire arms and equipment for the war they intend to fight, not for a struggle they either wish to avoid or fail to foresee. At the outbreak of World War I, German military planners anticipated a war of movement *(Bewegungskrieg)* and not the meat grinder of positional war *(Stellungskrieg)*. In the final analysis, German military planners recognized the potential value of a limited air defense capability, but air defenses did not rate among the army's top priorities in the first half of 1914.

Ground-Based Air Defense in the Great War

At the outbreak of World War I, German air defenses consisted of only 6 motorized guns and 12 horse-drawn 77-mm guns. The available guns were well below the forecast strength envisioned in prewar plans. In fact, mobilization plans called for each numbered army to receive four motorized guns and each division a horse-drawn battery.[38] In the opening days of the conflict, the 6 available motorized guns accompanied various army corps during the initial German advance, while the horse-drawn guns protected key bridges along the Rhine and airship hangars within Germany.[39] During the early days of the war, the Germany military and political leadership largely ignored the problems of air defense associated with the protection of important industrial sites and urban areas. The commander of the German Air Service, General von Höppner, explained this oversight with the contention that "the need for the defense of cities was not anticipated."[40] In any event, early Allied bombing raids and the failure to achieve a quick victory led to an increasing realization of the need for more air defense weapons. Likewise, it soon became apparent that the limited number of available anti-aircraft guns precluded the establishment of any comprehensive system for the defense of the German homeland. Initial efforts to expand Germany's air defense forces included the confiscation of anti-aircraft guns being made for foreign countries by the German armaments industry. Even with these confiscated weapons, the number of guns totaled only 36 by October 1914.[41] By the summer of 1915, the situation had improved only slightly with the army's modification of 175 field artillery guns for the air defense of the front lines and of Germany proper. By this time it was also clear that standard artillery pieces were completely unsuited to the air defense role. In fact, General Erich von Falkenhayn, the chief of the General Staff, remarked in a report of May 26, 1915, that "the combat of enemy aircraft by artillery fire has been up to this point generally accompanied by only very limited success, even with large expenditures of ammunition."[42] The shortage of flak artillery pieces also led to the reboring of captured French artillery for German use, a widespread practice also followed during World War II. In 1915 alone, the German army designated approximately 1,000 captured French, Russian, and Belgian artillery pieces for use in air defense, and by the end of the war, captured foreign artillery pieces constituted almost half of all German flak guns.[43]

By the end of 1914, the realization of the need for increased air defense measures to protect German forces and military installations led to the creation of an anti-aircraft section within the artillery branch. Höppner declared, "Its [the anti-aircraft section's] role was clear and simple—to prevent hostile air reconnaissance, aerial observation for hostile artillery fire, bombing attacks on important localities and to assist the escape of our own combat planes . . . [and] in a critical situation it was to cooperate in the infantry struggle."[44] These hastily formed units suffered, however, from want of training and an almost complete lack of understanding of their role. Fritz Nagel, a reserve officer in a BAK battery, remarked:

> We were one of the very first anti-aircraft batteries formed, but nobody knew much about firing at airplanes and we had no idea what our future role would be. The letters B.A.K. stood for Ballonabwehrkanon [*sic*]—balloon defense canon—and we therefore presumed the protection of our observation balloons would be our main jobs. . . . It was obvious that we needed special training to fire our French guns. On February 25, 1915, we were shipped to the Krupp target range at Tangerhuette where Krupp engineers instructed us. We were shooting at kite balloons and became quite efficient.

Nagel's experience was not unique, and the performance of the German flak defenses in the early stages of the war proved abysmal. In fact, Nagel contended that German army headquarters circulated a directive expressing the opinion that "flak (BAK) units in the army had proven useless."[45]

The technical limitations associated with the guns and their munitions compounded the organizational and training problems experienced by the nascent air defense forces. For example, the 77-mm gun, although mobile, generated an insufficient muzzle velocity that resulted in relatively long flight times for its projectiles.[46] Larger guns such as the navy's 88-mm achieved higher muzzle velocities and reduced projectile flight times but proved too heavy for mobile operations. In contrast, improved engines allowed Entente aircraft to operate at increasingly higher altitudes, thus escaping the lethal envelope of the anti-aircraft guns. The higher operating ceilings, in turn, meant even longer projectile flight times and generated additional problems for calculating fuse burn times in an increasingly oxygen-poor environment. Standard artillery shrapnel munitions also proved less effective than predicted in damaging canvas-covered aircraft. Finally, the absence of sophisticated fire directors remained a critical weakness in the ability of gun crews to successfully track their aerial targets. Despite continued research efforts in the area of fire director computers, this problem plagued the army and the Air Service throughout the war.[47]

The Entente powers wasted little time in taking advantage of the deficiencies within the German air defenses. By the fall of 1914, the British Royal Naval Air Service (RNAS) launched its first bombing strikes against targets within Germany. In an attempt to preempt zeppelin attacks against the British Isles, the RNAS launched raids against zeppelin hangars in Cologne and Düsseldorf on September 22 and October 8. British aircraft also bombed German dirigible sheds at Friederichshafen and Ludwigshafen on November 21.[48] The physical effects of these raids were slight, although the one on October 8 resulted in the destruction of one zeppelin. During the attacks, flak defenses proved largely ineffective and accounted for the destruction of only one aircraft during the raid on Friederichshafen. It was, however, a strike against the city of Freiburg in December 1914 that brought about a rapid change in the existing attitude concerning the air attacks. In the wake of the city's bombing, German civilians began to demand better air defenses and an improved warning system to notify them of an impending attack.[49] By the spring of 1915, it became apparent that the protection of Germany required an organized air defense system, including an effective warning system and sufficient numbers of anti-aircraft guns.

Organizing for the Front Lines and Home Air Defense

One of the major deficiencies of the German home defenses concerned the various agencies exercising authority within the nation. These agencies included the state governments *(Länder)*, bureaucratic and police agencies, local army headquarters, and local military bases.[50] The first attempt to streamline and rationalize this chaotic and inefficient system occurred with the selection by the War Ministry of an officer, Major Hugo Grimme, to inspect and coordinate improvements in the air defenses of the German homeland, the western frontier, and the Western Front on May 1, 1915.[51] Later, on July 10, the German army high command created the position of inspector of the anti-aircraft artillery for both the operational areas and home defense. In addition, the staffs of each of the numbered armies added a position of an anti-aircraft officer.[52]

As the inspector of the anti-aircraft artillery, Major Grimme was assigned to the general headquarters of the German army and directly subordinated to the chief of the General Staff. Grimme was responsible for the assignment of personnel and the disposition of anti-aircraft guns throughout the army. He oversaw the administration of the anti-aircraft schools, as well as the writing of air defense regulations. However, Grimme's influence within the army proved circumscribed, and in the spring of 1916, despite his objections, the chief of army ordnance assumed control of the anti-aircraft guns. The chief of ordnance promptly dispersed the horse-drawn guns within the divisions and assigned the motorized guns to the anti-aircraft staff officers within the numbered armies.[53] The ability of the chief of ordnance to wrest control away from Grimme demonstrated both the continuing power of more traditionally minded army generals and the superficial nature of the first air defense organizational reforms.

In addition to reorganization efforts, the army also focused on the material shortcomings within the German air defenses. The Allied air attacks against the German homeland resulted in the diversion of some flak guns destined for the front to the defense of Germany proper. In March 1915, the War Ministry warned, "The desire for the increased supply of flak to troop units must for the time being take second place."[54] This move was desperately needed to bolster the flimsy state of the home defenses. By June 1915, home area flak defenses consisted of a mere 150 guns, compared with 270 at the front. In addition to expanding the number of guns for home defense, the army also created five air defense districts stretching in an arc from Hamburg in the north to Munich in the south.[55] Based on the limited range of Entente bombers, the Germans enjoyed the advantage of being able to concentrate their air defense forces on the western border with France. In conjunction with the establishment of the air defense districts, the year 1915 also witnessed the creation of a unified Air Warning Service (Flugmeldedienst) under the command of the inspector of the flak in the homeland.[56] The Air Warning Service provided a critical link in the air defense structure. Advance warning of the strength and direction of an enemy attack proved crucial in scrambling interceptors and alerting ground-based defenses prior to the bombing raids. The use of aerial observers manning parallel lines along Germany's western border, later combined with observation posts throughout the country, helped identify impending attacks, but the system itself remained hampered by an unsophisticated and inefficient communications network.[57]

The most significant measure concerning the reorganization of German air and ground-based defenses involved the appointment of General Ernst von Höppner to the newly created position of commander of the Air Service on October 8, 1916.[58] Born in 1860, von Höppner began his career as a cavalry officer, attended the War Academy in Berlin, and served on the Great General Staff. At the start of the war, he was the chief of staff of the Third Army and eventually went on to command the 75th Reserve Division on the Eastern Front prior to his appointment as commander of the Air Service.[59] As the chief of Germany's nascent air arm, von Höppner was tasked with "the uniform development, assembly, and employment of the military resources" of the German air force.[60] This reorganization consolidated the German Air Service, the flak forces, and the Flying Signals Service under his command. The kaiser's order creating the German Air Service proclaimed, "The increasing importance of the air war requires the unification of the entire air and air defense resources of the army at the front and in the homeland."[61] In his retrospective on the war, von Höppner reflected on his assigned tasks:

> The Chief of Aviation was constantly looking ahead to provide against hostile air attacks against our frontiers, coasts, harbors, and positions of military importance in the zone of the interior. Our means of defense had been makeshifts improvised as the war went on and were devoid of any methodical plan. A series of military authorities shared the responsibility of protecting the Empire against aerial attack—the War Ministry, the Chief of Aviation, Inspector of the Anti-Aircraft at [the] Great General Headquarters, Inspector of Anti-Aircraft in the Zone of the Interior, local commanding officers, various offices under the control of the navy. To secure results from all these, unity had to be obtained.[62]

Clearly unity could emerge only with the rationalization and centralization of the ground-based air defenses.

Höppner's appointment underscored the need for a single commander to direct all aviation activities and constituted a major step toward the more efficient employment of German aviation and air assets in both an offensive and a defensive role. In short, the kaiser's order effectively centralized control over all aviation-related activities, including the organization and training of the Air Service, logistics, flak, and civil defense measures under von Höppner's command.[63] The move had the added benefit of rationalizing the system of aviation procurement and technical development. Prior to his appointment, the army and the navy had pursued their own programs independently. This dual system of development and procurement led to higher costs, excess personnel, and wasted material, and there was no mechanism for the services to share their advances.[64] Höppner's appointment also allowed for the incorporation of the more than 400 heavy naval anti-aircraft guns protecting the harbors and sea approaches to Germany into the homeland defense system.[65] Despite the reorganization, the Air Service did not become a separate and independent service, but rather an independent branch of the German army (analogous to the position enjoyed by the U.S. Army Air Forces during World War II).

Prior to the establishment of the Air Service, the army had initiated some modest steps to increase the effectiveness of its air defense forces. One measure involved the creation of a training school for officers of the anti-aircraft branch at Ostende, Belgium, in 1915. The two-week course included both theoretical and practical instruction, including a live-fire final exam in a prepared anti-aircraft position a few miles north of Ypres. Crews destined for duty at the front and those stationed in Germany received their training at Ostende until 1917, when, at the navy's request, the school was moved twelve miles north to the coastal town of Blankenberge. The army recognized the importance of expert instruction, and the school's faculty consisted of officers with extensive experience at the front.[66] The army also conducted air defense training for officers at other sites, including the Air Service's training center at Valenciennes.[67]

The consolidation of the flak forces under the Air Service resulted in increasing emphasis on the integration of ground-based air defense artillery and searchlights with the German fighter forces. In fact, the German army experimented with searchlights as early as 1912. In initial trials, the searchlights served the dual purpose of blinding the pilot and exposing the attacking airship to anti-aircraft fire.[68] In response to the increasing number of nighttime aerial raids, the army introduced improved searchlights and sound detectors in 1915.[69] These early searchlights allowed for the illumination of attacking aircraft at altitudes up to 11,000 feet, and later versions increased the range to 19,500 feet.[70] The sound detectors complemented the searchlights by using the sound of the aircrafts' engines to detect enemy planes at greater distances at night or during the periods of reduced visibility due to rain, fog, or cloud cover that were common in Europe. The primary benefit associated with searchlights concerned the gun crews' method of firing. The illumination of attacking aircraft allowed for a shift from barrier fire to aimed fire during nighttime attacks, thus reducing the number of rounds expended per aircraft shootdown. The growing importance of searchlights was evidenced by a dramatic rise in the number of available systems, increasing from 132 in June 1916 to 718 in November 1918. The unconventional tactic by Entente pilots of "cutting their motors" and gliding on the final run-in to the target was one indication of the apparent success achieved by the German defenses when combining sound detectors, searchlights, and flak.[71]

After more than two years of war, the home defenses experienced an additional administrative reorganization. A War Ministry order, dated December 8, 1916, confirmed the growing value placed on homeland defense. The order established a commander of home defense directly subordinate to the commander of the Air Service, General von Höppner. The commander of home defense received responsibility for "all arrangements and measures which are necessary for the defense of the homeland against air attacks."[72] He was tasked with coordinating air defense measures with state authorities, city administrations, and industrial leaders. Most important, the order centralized the entire spectrum of air defense activities under the commander of the home defense, including all home flak and fighter-interceptor forces and the early warning system.[73] The organizational centralization of the home air defenses also coincided with several other reform initiatives.

By the spring of 1917, German anti-aircraft defenses both at home and on the front had evolved into an increasingly effective and more capable force integrating both interceptor and ground-based systems.[74] This improvement within the air defense system occurred as a result of modest technological advances, increasing numbers of guns and equipment, organizational restructuring, and doctrinal refinements. Early in the war, the German army concentrated anti-aircraft positions in areas along the front lines frequented by Entente pilots. In these areas, the gun crews established anti-aircraft barriers *(BAK-Sperren)*. Still, the paucity of trained crews and the limited number of guns allowed for only partial coverage of the front. The army also employed anti-aircraft guns to protect some vital areas such as headquarters and supply depots. By 1917, the increasing mobility provided by motorization and the greater numbers or anti-aircraft guns began to allow for more effective coverage of the front.[75]

Technological Obstacles to Effective Air Defense

The primary limitation of the guns remained, however, technological. The difficulty associated with tracking a target in three-dimensional space and coordinating the fire of the guns still proved a formidable challenge. This technological obstacle often led to the adoption of inefficient and wasteful "barrier fire."[76] This concept essentially involved an attempt by the gun crews to create a wall of shells between the attacking aircraft and the target, forcing the attacking aircraft either to break off the attack or to risk flying through this curtain of steel. Obviously, the primary disadvantages concerning the use of barrier fire involved the high expenditure of munitions, the close coordination necessary for covering various altitudes, and the low probability of shooting down the attacking aircraft. In addition, ammunition shortages and the lack of replacement parts for the guns and other equipment effectively militated against the barrier fire concept until the resolution of the supply crisis with the establishment of reserve depots in 1917.[77] To achieve optimal results from the German ground-based systems, an effective method of "directed fire" was absolutely essential.

In the last years of the war, a number of technological and armament improvements succeeded in increasing the effectiveness of the ground-based air defense system. For example, the introduction of a better range finder *(Entfernungsmeßgerät)* in 1917 enhanced the accuracy in determining target distance for computing firing solutions.[78] These range finders were essentially a type of advanced stereoscopic binocular employing trigonometric principles to obtain the slant range distance to the target. The devices consisted of a crossarm mounted on a tripod assembly. The operator looked into the instrument, and two mirrors then reflected his vision at ninety degrees to the ends of the tube, where a second set of mirrors reflected the operator's vision toward the target. In effect, the operator's two eyes achieved a practical separation equal to the length of the crossarm, with a corresponding improvement in depth perception. For example, the 4-meter device increased the effective distance between the operator's eyes to 13 feet. A superimposed crosshair could then be manipulated with respect to the target, allowing for the calculation of the slant range.[79] Although certainly an improvement over unaided optical firing procedures, these devices required daytime, clear visibility, or illuminated conditions. They also had to be close to the flak guns in order to be effective.

Technological advances in armaments and munitions also played a role in improving effectiveness. In 1917, the Germans introduced an artillery piece designed specifically for anti-aircraft defense, the forerunner of the famous 88-mm gun of World War II fame.[80] The increased muzzle velocity offered by the 88-mm gun resulted in a shorter flight time for the shell, which, in turn, allowed for increased rates of fire and a more rapid estimation of necessary firing corrections.[81] The introduction of mechanically timed fuse munitions, shells capable of being set to explode after a given flight time, also enhanced the effectiveness of flak defenses.[82] The marriage of the optical range finder and the mechanical timed fuse allowed gun crews to set the shells to explode at a point in the projectile's flight corresponding to the estimated distance to the target. Although an improvement, the timed fuse had to be set manually, and the gun crews now needed to compensate for the distance traveled by the aircraft during the delay that resulted from setting the fuse and loading the gun. In turn, the length of this delay depended on the proficiency of the individual gun crew. The relatively slow speeds achieved by early aircraft and their modest operational altitudes allowed for some success using this technique, which by World War II became essentially unworkable with increasing aircraft speeds and higher operational ceilings. A brief comparison of aircraft performance in World War I and World War II clearly demonstrates the increasing complexity associated with aircraft targeting. The top speed of the famous Fokker DR.1 triplane was 103 mph and that of the Sopwith Camel, 116 mph. A shell fired at a muzzle velocity of 2,250 feet per second required four seconds to reach a target at a distance of 9,000 feet. During those four seconds the DR.1 had traveled 604 feet and the Sopwith Camel, 680 feet. In contrast, the Boeing B-17 of World War II had a top speed of 290 mph and a normal operational ceiling of approximately 25,000 feet. The same artillery shell required eleven seconds to reach this altitude. In those eleven seconds the aircraft traveled 4,678 feet. This example aptly illustrated the growing targeting complexity associated with aircrafts' higher operational altitudes and their increasing speed, barring corresponding increases in projectile velocity.

The rationalization of the command structure and the initiation of a designated training program slowly began to produce results. In September 1915, German anti-aircraft crews accounted for approximately 25 percent of all Allied aircraft shot down on the Western Front.[83] By the fall of 1917, the German army began introducing more motorized flak units (*Kraftwagenflak*, or K-flak) consisting of a 77-mm gun mounted on the bed of an open truck.[84] The mobility of these guns allowed for more rapid employment along the front lines. In fact, the primary mission of these guns involved the combat of low-flying Allied aircraft near the front.[85] The modest technical innovations and the expansion in air defense artillery produced some encouraging results. Flak defenses shot down 322 Entente aircraft in 1916 and an additional 467 aircraft in 1917.[86]

By the spring and summer of 1918, Allied air attacks against Germany proper offered a nominal preview of the impact of airpower in attacks aimed at the civilian population. During the last year of the war, Allied aircrews conducted 353 missions against German targets and dropped 7,117 bombs. These attacks resulted in 1,187 casualties and damages estimated at $3.6 million.[87] The effects of the attacks were, in fact, negligible when compared with the casualties experienced in the trenches and the costs of fighting a positional war on two fronts. Still, they forced the Germans to devote significant resources to protecting the home front. Commanders of anti-aircraft forces operated out of command posts in eleven major cities extending on a line from Hamburg in the north to Munich in the south.[88] These central command posts coordinated the actions of additional command posts located in the surrounding area. For example, the commander of the Munich area coordinated the defense of Munich, Augsburg, and Ingolstadt, while the commander of the Cologne area supervised the operations of command posts in Cologne, Koblenz, Schlebusch, Troisdorf, Trier, Aachen, Dormagen, Grevenbroich, and Bergheim. The expanded communications network and clearer lines of command led to greater efficiency and better coordination between the early warning service and the active air defense forces, but this system was also resource intensive.[89]

Moving Toward a Combined-Arms Approach

By the end of 1917, the air defenses within Germany proper included a mix of ground-based and fighter interceptor forces. The ground-based defenses consisted of 104 heavy motorized flak guns, 112 light motorized flak guns, 998 horse-drawn and fixed flak guns, and 416 searchlights.[90] The Air Service continued to employ flak and searchlights in the point defense of key industrial facilities and critical transportation hubs. In the last years of the war, searchlights assumed a more important role due to the steadily increasing number of Allied night bombing missions. General von Höppner, contended that the expanded employment of searchlights in the beginning of 1917 "greatly strengthened" night defenses, allowing for the "more effective" individual targeting of attacking aircraft versus indiscriminate barrier fire.[91] By the end of the war, searchlights operating with flak were credited with 76 kills; searchlights acting alone received credit for 4 kills as a result of blinding the pilot, leading to the crash of the aircraft.[92]

In conjunction with flak and searchlight defenses, in January 1917 the Air Service introduced tethered balloons to act as low-level barriers to aircraft attacks. Plans included the establishment of eight balloon barrier battalions of fifty balloons each.[93] The balloons were raised on steel cables by electrically driven winches to altitudes between 6,000 and 9,000 feet. In addition to the anchor cable, the Germans attached a number of free-hanging cables to improve the coverage area or connected several balloons to create an aerial fence.[94] These balloon barriers proved effective in the defense of industrial targets within the Saar basin. General von Höppner remarked, perhaps too optimistically, that the "systematic cooperation between flak [and balloons] led . . . to the creation of an almost impenetrable zone" during night operations.[95]

In addition to active defense, the Germans adopted a number of passive defense measures, including blackouts for cities and industrial centers, the construction of dummy targets, and the expansion of civil bomb shelters.[96] Each of these measures complicated Allied bombing efforts and helped save civilian lives. For example, in the summer of 1916, German blackouts prevented Entente pilots from finding their intended targets in raids aimed against Trier and Ludwigshafen.[97] The German experience in the war led to an appreciation of the value of passive defense measures, which remained a focus of German civil defense efforts into World War II. Although important, passive defense measures could not sweep the sky of attacking aircraft. To achieve a truly effective defense, the Air Service required active measures that united aircraft and ground-based assets in an integrated network. In addition to flak, searchlights, and balloons, the Air Service reserved nine fighter squadrons for the role of home defense.[98] Initially, the interceptor aircraft, like flak, were responsible for the protection of specific objects. By the spring of 1917, however, the Air Service reduced the number of aircraft for point defense in favor of allowing aircraft to intercept and pursue Entente bombers on their way to targets within Germany.[99]

The employment of both ground-based and interceptor (pursuit) forces was significant because it demonstrated an understanding within the Air Service that air defense required a combined-arms approach. As early as 1915, the army leadership recognized the need for both anti-aircraft guns and fighter-interceptors in the conduct of air defense, especially in the vicinity of important industrial installations.[100] According to von Höppner, "It had been demonstrated that artillery defense against air attacks was not sufficient to drive away or to destroy attacking aviators. Therefore, some units with single seater combat planes were placed at the disposal of the home defense commander."[101] The cooperation of flak and fighters even extended to the tactical level, with the interceptors receiving active guidance from the ground-based air defenses in locating enemy bombers. For example, flak units fired short bursts to guide interceptors in the direction of their target, the explosions of the shells being "visible for some distance."[102]

The German appreciation of the combined-arms approach to air defense did not involve tremendous foresight or operational acumen. Indeed, the question was not whether to allocate resources either to flak or to interceptors, but rather in what proportion available resources should be divided between the two. This question, although pertinent during the Great War, also emerged as a dominant issue in the air defense of the Third Reich between 1939 and 1945.

Evaluating the Effectiveness of German Ground-based Air Defenses

The last year of the war offered a promising portent for German ground-based air defenses. Indeed, flak defenses achieved their greatest success in 1918. By November, the Air Service operated 2,770 anti-aircraft guns, of which approximately 30 percent served in the defense of Germany.[103] The introduction of rudimentary fire directors *(Kommandogeräte)* in 1917 and 1918 transferred some of the burden for computing targeting solutions from individuals using a fire control table to a mechanical computer.[104] These initial fire directors still relied on the accuracy of inputs from human operators. The firing solutions these devices generated also were based on the so-called flak hypothesis, which essentially assumed that an aircraft's speed, altitude, and direction would remain constant during the entire period from the initial computation of the firing solution to the arrival of the projectile at the projected impact point, an assumption that guided fire direction through World War II. Despite the limitations associated with the fire directors, the increased speed they offered for solving firing solutions resulted in both greater rates and more accurate fire. Only sixty of these fire directors reached operational service during the war, but the idea of computer-assisted targeting became a central concern for future ground-based defense systems.[105]

The marriage of fire directors with timed-fuse munitions also coincided with the growing numbers of Allied aircraft that appeared in the skies over Germany and the front lines in the last year of the war. Therefore, technological improvements and increasing numbers of targets resulted in more aircraft destroyed with fewer rounds expended. For example, the number of artillery shells per aircraft destroyed decreased from 11,500 in 1914 to 5,040 in 1918.[106] In the period between January 1 and October 31, 1918, flak alone accounted for 748 enemy aircraft destroyed.[107] In fact, German anti-aircraft crews achieved their most dramatic results in the last two months of the conflict, with the destruction of 132 Allied aircraft in September and another 129 in October.[108] During the four years of the war, German anti-aircraft fire brought down a total of 1,588 aircraft, which exceeded the combined total of 500 achieved by the French, 129 tallied by the Italians, and the approximately 300 shot down by British gun crews throughout the empire.[109] In addition to aerial engagements, German flak guns occasionally assisted army forces during ground combat operations during the war. In the most notable example, German flak guns played a major role in halting the British tank breakthrough at Cambrai in 1917.[110] During the final year of the war, it was in the air and not on the ground that the flak forces proved their greatest worth. In the first ten months of 1918 alone, German flak accounted for 47 percent of the total Allied aircraft losses, with over 16 percent of Allied wartime losses occurring in the last two full months of the conflict. In comparison with flak, German aircraft accounted for 6,811 Entente/Allied aircraft destroyed, or a 4.3 to 1 ratio in favor of aircraft.[111] The fact that German flak destroyed 19 percent of Allied aircraft shot down in combat despite the technological limitations offered strong evidence that ground-based air defenses could be ignored neither on the battlefield nor in the homeland. The belated success of flak in the last year of the war allowed for guarded optimism with respect to the future viability of ground-based air defenses during the interwar period.

By the end of the war, German air defense forces totaled 2,770 guns and 718 searchlights manned by 2,800 officers and 55,000 enlisted personnel.[112] In addition, tens of thousands of men in the observer force and the signal corps supported the air defense effort. The total losses and damages experienced in Germany as a result of Allied bombing attacks between 1914 and 1918 included 746 persons killed and 1,843 wounded, with damages estimated at 25,035,000 reichsmarks (RM).[113] In contrast, German zeppelin and aircraft attacks against Great Britain killed approximately 1,400 persons and resulted in about 3 million pounds of damage.[114] The number of those killed and the damages incurred by bombing raids paled in comparison to the overall casualties experienced as a result of the ground war. Still, the Great War marked a decisive end to the era of limited war. The bombing of cities and industrial infrastructure coincided with the beginning of mass industrialized warfare, in which a nation's armed forces and its civilian population both became objects of attack. In this way, the abiding legacy of the bombing raids rested on the population's profound psychological response to aerial attack, despite the relative insignificance of the physical results of the raids.[115] In the final analysis, the psychological and physical implications of airpower's destructive potential combined to shape the nature and course of debate on air defense in the interwar period.

CHAPTER TWO

A Theory for Air Defense 1919–1932

After World War I, the appreciation of the need to protect one's civilian population from aerial attack led to a debate concerning the various alternatives for defending the nation. These included reliance on an interceptor force designed to prevent an adversary's aircraft from reaching their targets, a ground-based active and passive air defense system to protect urban and industrial areas, or a combination of the two. For Germany after the war, this debate remained largely theoretical because the restrictions of the Treaty of Versailles prohibited the German army from maintaining an air force and effectively eliminated its ground-based air defense forces. In the end, the issues surrounding the organization and performance of German ground-based air defenses in the Great War shaped the subsequent discourse concerning the development of German air defenses in the interwar period.

Versailles and the State of German Air Defenses

The Versailles treaty of 1919 dramatically reduced the size and offensive capabilities of the German armed forces. Article 160 of the treaty limited the maximum size of the German army to 100,000 men, including 4,000 officers and 96,000 enlisted men. The treaty also effectively eliminated German anti-aircraft artillery by restricting their number to seven batteries of obsolescent 77-mm truck-mounted guns, with one battery of twenty-four guns for each of the Reichswehr's seven infantry regiments. These guns proved practically worthless in the air defense role due to required modifications that restricted their range of elevation.[1] In addition, Article 167 of the treaty limited the ammunition allowance for each gun to 1,500 rounds. Furthermore, Article 169 stipulated that "German arms, munitions, and war material, including anti-aircraft material, . . . in excess of the quantities allowed, must be surrendered to the Governments of the Principal Allied and Associated Powers to be destroyed or rendered useless."[2] The Allies later eased these restrictions somewhat by allowing the army to maintain a sixteen-gun fixed anti-aircraft emplacement in Königsberg (East Prussia) and permitting the German navy to operate a small number of fixed guns on its ships and a few gun sites in fixed coastal defense positions.[3] The proscribed reduction in German air defenses, however, should not be seen in isolation from the actions taken by the other belligerents. For example, Great Britain, the main target of German bombing raids during the war, reduced its anti-aircraft defenses from 48 companies, 225 sections, and 3 mobile brigades in November 1918 to a single gun brigade and a single searchlight battalion by the end of 1919.[4]

Early Arguments on Air Defense in the Interwar Period

Nonetheless, the restrictions placed on the German armed forces by the Versailles treaty precluded further technological or material development of flak artillery in the initial years after the war. But the lack of available physical resources did not prevent attempts by retired and active-duty military officers as well as academic specialists to study the "lessons" of the war. During the interwar period, German military planners and civilian strategists recognized the potential significance of new weapons such as the tank and the airplane on the future of warfare.[5] The appraisal of the value of ground-based air defenses in the aftermath of the Great War proved less definitive. In his postwar analysis, General Erich Ludendorff, deputy chief of staff of the German army, complained that "in spite of the efforts of the General Staff in peace-time, we had begun the war with insufficient air weapons."[6]

Ludendorff, however, recognized the improvements made in German air defenses during the war. He remarked that "anti-aircraft armament was perfected and increased in supply, and defensive arrangements at the front and at home were organized on the most complete scale." He also offered a caveat to his generally positive evaluation of the development of the anti-aircraft defenses during the war by reflecting that these improvements in air defenses "cost us men and material, which the front had to do without."[7] In fact, the German manpower shortage became so acute by the summer of 1918 that Ludendorff ordered the extraordinary step of replacing physically qualified males in the signal corps with women, sending the men to serve in frontline units and the women to take over communication duties.[8] Although the end of the war prevented the implementation of the plan, this initiative offered one indication of the severity of the manpower crisis facing the German army in 1918.[9] Indeed, the extensive personnel requirements associated with manning the air defense system would pose the same problem for the Luftwaffe during World War II. Furthermore, Ludendorff's observations illustrated the dilemma faced by the army involving the question of allocating resources between the fighting front and the home front.[10] The issue of resource diversion and allocation for ground-based air defenses would also confront Ludendorff's successors some thirty years later.

Höppner proved decidedly more optimistic than Ludendorff in his evaluation of the performance of German air defenses in the war:

> A comparison between the rapid development of anti-aircraft and its ever-increasing list of victories is its best claim to glory, and it showed that its technical development and tactical employment were based on sound principles. Its success is due chiefly to the devotion of its officers, non-commissioned officers, and men in the performance of a task that was difficult and unfamiliar. It is due to them that anti-aircraft grew from small beginnings to what was at the end of the war—the best means of ground defense against aerial attacks.[11]

Höppner's appraisal highlights the difficulties encountered by the men of the anti-aircraft forces but also the substantial progress made by the air defense forces during the course of the war. But with the signing of the Versailles treaty, Germany's ground-based air defenses once again reverted to the dismal condition of the antebellum period.

One historian characterized the state of British anti-aircraft defenses between 1919 and 1935 as the "fallow years."[12] Likewise, the material state of German ground-based air defenses proved barren throughout the 1920s. Still, in spite of the physical restrictions placed on the German army, the condition of the theoretical discussion of air defense proved remarkably vibrant. General Hans von Seeckt, the head of the Reichswehr Truppenamt (de facto General Staff), promoted a frank evaluation of the performance of each branch of the German armed forces during the war. Seeckt, a proponent of airpower, demonstrated an "open-minded" attitude toward the issues of aviation and air defense.[13] In a letter to the Truppenamt in December 1919, he remarked, "It is absolutely necessary to put the experiences of the war in a broad light, and to collect this experience while the impressions won on the battlefield are still fresh, and the major proportion of the experienced officers are still in leading positions."[14] Seeckt's stance promoted theoretical discussions concerning the role of airpower and air defense in the years following the war.[15] He also ordered the establishment of numerous committees to consider the following questions:

A. What new situations arose in the war that had not been considered before the war?
B. How effective were our prewar views in dealing with the above situation?
C. What new guidelines have been developed from the use of new weaponry in the war?
D. Which new problems, put forward by the war, have not yet found a solution?[16]

In 1919, using these guidelines, the former Air Service chief of staff, Lieutenant Colonel Wilhelm Siegert, supervised more than twenty officers in a study of homeland defenses. Likewise, three additional committees studied various aspects of air defense, including the employment of air and ground-based defenses.[17]

The question concerning the most effective method for defending both the armed forces and the homeland also received attention in the professional literature of the interwar period. In 1921, an article entitled "Flak" appeared in the primary German military weekly, the *Militärwochenblatt*. The author, a Captain Seydel, reviewed both the strengths and the weaknesses of flak during the war. A major weakness discussed by Seydel was the poor standardization of the flak artillery that had resulted in the use of twenty-five different models of guns. He also noted the need for a more efficient communications system for relaying and coordinating air defense efforts. Looking toward the future, Seydel mentioned that, despite the success of flak in the latter stages of the war, rapid advances in aircraft technology demanded a corresponding improvement in flak guns and munitions to counter the anticipated high-altitude operations of the bombers of tomorrow.[18] Foreshadowing later events, he also recognized the value of anti-aircraft artillery in a ground defense role versus tanks.[19] In a later article, Seydel made his position on the importance of the flak force as an independent arm perfectly clear. He remarked that "the flak is not exclusively an auxiliary weapon to the [fighter] aircraft and can never be allowed to be falsely marked as such."[20]

Lieutenant Colonel (retired) von Keller, the former inspector of the flak in the homeland in 1915, offered a contrasting opinion. In a forty-page book entitled *The Present Defenselessness of Germany in the Light of Its Defense Against Aerial Attacks in the War of 1914/18*, von Keller argued that recent advances in aircraft technology and performance had outpaced the ability of ground-based air defenses to provide adequate protection against aerial attacks. As a result, he insisted that under the present circumstances the fighter airplane *(Fliegerwaffe)* was the primary instrument for air defense. As a former flak commander, von Keller provided a stern reminder of the existing limitations of anti-aircraft defenses.[21]

The questions surrounding air defense found expression not only in unofficial military literature but also in the doctrine of the German armed forces. By 1921, the principal tactical regulation of the Reichswehr, *Army Regulation 487*, included a detailed discussion of flak defenses and required that "each army unit be responsible for its own air defense, and set up an aircraft spotter system." Seeckt and his military planners devoted their attention to both flak defenses and the role of aircraft. Indeed, von Seeckt favored the employment of aircraft in an offensive rather than a defensive role. In his view, offensive operations would take the battle for air superiority to the enemy, hopefully destroying aircraft before they could be used against German forces or the German homeland.[22]

Military Education and the Topic of Air Defense

The German military education system of the 1920s also placed considerable emphasis on the role and future significance of air defense. The professional education of the 4,000-man officer corps focused largely on the role of technology and combined arms. Airpower and air defense were two areas that relied heavily on technology and complemented the concept of combined arms. With respect to air defense, the curriculum for officer professional education in the cavalry, infantry, artillery, and engineers directed that "the importance of air defense is to be emphasized by all faculty in all military history subjects."[23] In fact, officer candidate training included one hour per week of theoretical instruction on the subject of air defense during the first and second years of training, constituting 4 percent of the weekly theoretical curriculum for the first year and 8 percent for the second year.[24] Other organizational initiatives included the study of airpower issues relating to doctrine, theory, and technology as a requirement for all officers attending the general staff course. For example, in the late 1920s general staff candidates received one hour every two weeks of instruction specifically devoted to the topic of air defense. The discussion of airpower and air defense also took place outside the classrooms of the military education system. In the field, individual divisions held exercises and classes involving air defense, and each division was responsible for conducting an annual air defense study.[25]

In 1925 and 1926, the Reichswehr conducted operational training classes in the area of air defense. From October 3 to November 3, 1925, thirty-four officers from the artillery branch underwent anti-aircraft training at Königsberg using the flak guns of the old fortress town. In addition, seven engineering officers received training in the employment of searchlights and related air defense equipment during a ten-week course in early 1926. By 1928, the searchlight course had been discontinued, but three officers from each army division were selected to undergo a four-week course in fortifications and flak weapons.[26] The few courses offered and the modest number of participants reflected more manpower and resource restrictions than lack of interest in air defense. The willingness to devote resources to air defense training should therefore be considered in relation to the overall situation of the German army and should not be based on the absolute number of those taking part in these courses.

Manpower restrictions also affected the technical development of the Reichswehr in the 1920s. Indeed, technological and matériel shortages circumscribed the degree to which theory could be converted into practice. Limited manpower forced the consolidation of numerous technical development offices and a reduction in the number of technical and engineering officers. In 1919, the Reichswehr combined a number of offices, including that of the

Artillery Proving Commission, into the Inspectorate for Weapons and Equipment, eliminating the existing subsection for anti-aircraft artillery and further stunting the material development of air defense systems in the interwar period.[27] The shortage of qualified officers with technical degrees also remained a point of concern and a continuing weakness within the German armed forces in the years prior to World War II.[28]

Despite the restrictions placed upon its own program, the German army closely watched developments involving air defenses in other countries.[29] During the 1920s, the Intelligence Section of the Truppenamt (T-3) compiled extensive information on the organization, training, doctrine, and technological advances within foreign air forces.[30] This intelligence also found its way into the professional literature of the period. In May and September 1925, the *Militärwochenblatt* published articles on two U.S. Navy trials involving fleet-based anti-aircraft defense. The September article reported that the results of the test were "unsatisfactory" despite the firing of 16,000 rounds at a towed target trailed at 3,000 feet, an unrealistic altitude for combat operations. The article concluded by stating that the American air service regarded these results as "renewed confirmation for the correctness of their contention that ground-based air defense is not capable of fulfilling its mission."[31]

The Debate Continues

Some German writers also doubted the effectiveness of ground-based air defenses. In a 1926 work entitled *The Air War,* Captain Hans Ritter, a former General Staff officer, reflected on the performance of German flak during World War I. Ritter felt that the success of German ground-based defenses was minimal. He argued that the figure of 748 aircraft destroyed in 1918 constituted an effective shoot-down percentage of only one-eighth of 1 percent of the total of 600,000 Allied sorties open to engagement by German flak crews during the period. He therefore concluded that "with respect to flak one can hardly speak of an effective defense."[32] Despite this gloomy appraisal, Ritter did allow that flak hampered Allied aircraft from successfully reaching and attacking their objectives.

Unlike Ritter, other German military and academic writers maintained a more optimistic opinion concerning the performance of ground-based air defenses in the war. In the monograph *Danger from the Air and Air Defense,* Dr. Heinrich Hunke provided his own analysis of the influence of the nascent German air defense network during the Great War. Hunke contended that "without these air defenses life in the cities would have soon become completely impossible, factories would have stopped production, and the German army would have had to capitulate due to lack of supplies." He also highlighted the important role played by flak in affecting the "morale" of Allied pilots and forcing Allied aircraft to fly at higher altitudes, thus reducing bombing accuracy. In addition, Hunke praised the advances made in air defenses during the war, especially the cooperation between flak and fighter-interceptors. He noted, however, that this cooperation proved most effective at the front, as in the Flanders campaign of 1917, as opposed to the protection of Germany.[33] Hunke's point concerning the cooperation of ground-based defenses and fighters represented a major "lesson" learned by the German Air Service during the war, supporting Höppner's contention that "results could be had only through cooperation with aviation, for the development of anti-aircraft was fundamentally linked with air activities."[34] In turn, the concept of flak and fighter cooperation under a unified command emerged as a recurrent theme within the specialist literature during the interwar period.[35]

Another writer, Major (retired) Großkreutz, responded to conclusions made by a French military writer concerning the role of flak in an edition of the journal *La France Militaire.* In his article "The Significance of Air Defense Artillery," published in the March 1926 issue of the *Militärwochenblatt,* Großkreutz contended that press reports, military exercises, inspections, and the posting of officers reflected a trend to minimize the importance of flak. He warned that this bias could have grave consequences for Germany in a future war. He argued for a clear differentiation between the roles of air defense at the front and in the homeland. The protection of the latter required a strong flak force in order to defend "the moral strength of the nation" as well as the centers of industrial production and supply for the armed forces. Großkreutz criticized his French counterpart for focusing solely on flak artillery and noted that flak guns were only one element of a larger air defense system that included fighter-interceptors, balloons, searchlights, flak machine guns, and the weather service. He added that these elements of air defense were "dependent" on the Air Warning Service. Großkreutz concluded by stressing the need for large-scale practical exercises incorporating all the elements of air defense.[36] Großkreutz's advocacy of air defense measures was not coincidental. In fact, he was a member of the Organization of Former Flak Members (Flakverein e.V.) and an editor of and regular contributor to the organization's monthly newsletter.[37]

In the interwar discussions, flak's roles in the defense of the homeland and the protection of frontline troops were often presented as two separate issues. Großkreutz addressed the latter issue in the April 4, 1926, edition of the *Militärwochenblatt* in an article entitled "State and Employment of Flak Defense Artillery with Special Consideration in Mobile Warfare." Großkreutz's article responded to an award-winning paper published in the *Journal of the Royal Artillery* by Captain K. M. Loch. According to Großkreutz, Loch's paper provided an important addition to the understanding of the tactical use of flak in a future war of movement. Großkreutz's penultimate sentence revealed the contemporary state of discussion with respect to ground-based air defense. He observed that "this study will offer numerous ideas to the general public in the little-known area of air defense and will bring clarity to the perceptions concerning the employment of this weapon [flak] in mobile warfare."[38]

Großkreutz's comment raised the issue of the role of public opinion and public perception concerning the issue of air defense. In the early 1920s, organizations emerged within Germany that devoted themselves entirely to this concern. One, the Air Defense League (Luftschutzliga), which had tens of thousands of members by the early 1930s, organized lectures on air defense and also published an influential journal, *The Siren.* In addition, it joined forces with the Flakverein to promote the topic of air defense within government circles and among the public.[39] By 1927, other groups composed mostly of policemen, municipal employees, Red Cross workers, and firemen began organizing in support of active and passive civil defense measures.[40] In addition to *The Siren,* other journals and magazines devoted to the topic of air defense appeared in the 1920s and early 1930s, including the *Air Defense Newsletter, Gas Mask,* and *Gas- and Air Defense* beginning in 1923, 1929, and 1931, respectively.[41]

Air defense, much like the issue of early-twentieth-century naval scares, also became the object of sensationalism. A typical example was a work published in 1932 under the alarming but expressive title *Germany!! Are You Sleeping?? Air Danger Threatens! In 1 Hour! Fliers! Bombs! Poison Gas! Over Berlin! Your Cities! Your Industrial Areas! What Are Your People Doing? How Are They Protecting Themselves? Act! An Educational Book for All!!* In the 1920s, some writers, apparently influenced by the work of the Italian airpower theorist Giulio Douhet, prophesied the apocalyptic vision of massed bomber formations raining high-explosive death down upon the heads of German women and children.[42] For these writers, the issue of air defense was a question of national survival in which only careful preparation might prevent catastrophe. Pursuing an agenda designed to prepare the German people for war, the National Socialist government played upon the public fear of air attack to create the Reich Air Defense League (Reichsluftschutzbund).[43] Hermann Göring, the World War I fighter ace and future head of the Luftwaffe, led the initiative and was the league's official founder in April 1933. Eventually numbering over 16 million members, or approximately one in five persons within the German population, the league proved especially adept at stimulating public interest in air defense.[44] In addition to public exhibitions and civil defense exercises, it also sponsored essay contests such as one in 1935 concerning the topic "Air Defense—A Question of Germany's Destiny."[45] German military planners could find a twisted satisfaction in the public's anxiety. Indeed, a pervasive belief in the potential danger of aerial attack would help stimulate support for active and passive measures to defend the German homeland.

The implications of strategic bombing and air defense were not lost on the staff officers of the Truppenamt. In 1926, Helmuth Wilberg, the famous World War I pilot who headed the air section, issued a thirty-nine-page doctrinal outline concerning strategic bombing and air defense entitled *Directives for the Conduct of the Operational Air War.* The *Directives* provided a formal discussion of the organizational, targeting, and operational issues associated with strategic bombardment. The authors of the document envisioned a dual organizational structure for the employment of air assets. One portion of the force would support the theater commander's ground or naval objectives. The second, which remained under the control of the high command, would attempt to destroy targets within the adversary's homeland. One of the unique aspects of this document was the recognition of the continued importance of one's own air defenses. German military planners realized that the weakness of one's adversary might also constitute one's own weakness. They therefore stressed the importance of anti-aircraft defenses for the operational forces as well as the German homeland.[46]

The Practice of Air Defense

The appreciation of the role of aviation and air defense found expression not only in Reichswehr doctrine but also in the military exercises of the interwar period. Commenting on the Reichswehr's fall maneuvers of September 1926, a U.S. military intelligence report noted, "The assumption of the presence of both friendly and hostile air forces was made in every maneuver witnessed during the year, which assumption the umpires never failed to bring home to the commanders of every grade by constantly giving them an assumed air situation."[47] In fact, during the exercises, the aviation advisers attached to the division stood ready to evaluate the reaction of commanders and their troops after the alarm, "Attention! Aircraft!" The expected response was for the exposed troops to immediately seek cover and position machine guns to engage the imaginary enemy.[48]

The legal limitations and the material and personnel restrictions faced by the Reichswehr in the years immediately after World War I essentially precluded the development of a ground-based air defense system. Still, the lessons learned as a result of the war and the postwar discussions demonstrate that the topic of air defense was not a dead letter. The physical revival of the German air defense force, however, could not occur through theoretical discussions alone. The Allied decision to withdraw the Inter-Allied Military Control Commission in late 1926 combined with the blossoming Soviet-German relationship allowed the Reichswehr to concentrate on the practical aspects of rearmament.[49]

Rappallo and the Road to Rearmament

By the middle of the 1920s, the evolution of German military doctrine was no longer solely a function of theoretical discussions and war games but also a product of practical experience gained as a result of Soviet-German cooperation. On April 16, 1922, in a move that sent shock waves through European diplomatic circles, the Weimar government signed the Treaty of Rappallo with the Soviet Union. The treaty included a German agreement to withdraw demands for reparations for German-owned properties nationalized by the Communists and formalized reciprocal trade agreements between the two European "outcasts."[50]

The popular belief that the Rappallo treaty contained secret military clauses was incorrect. In fact, the first substantive meetings on German and Soviet military cooperation had occurred already in 1921.[51] These secret negotiations between the Reichswehr and the Red Army thus preceded the official governmental agreement reached at Rappallo. In any event, the treaty certainly promoted an atmosphere conducive to increased military cooperation between the two countries. Covert military discussions in 1923 and 1924 resulted in a number of secret agreements between the Reichswehr and the Red Army. For example, one of these military accords led to the creation of a joint German and Russian flight school at Lipetsk in 1924. Lipetsk was not only a valuable school for training German and Russian pilots but also an equally important flight test center for evaluating the technical and operational performance of German aircraft prototypes.[52] In addition to joint flight training, a German aviation company, Junkers, built a factory at Fili near Moscow. Further agreements also led to a short-lived gas production facility at Samara, a tank school and testing center at Kazan, and three munitions plants under the administration of the German armaments giant Krupp at Tula, Leningrad, and Schlüsselberg.[53] Clearly, Soviet-German military cooperation advanced the development of the Reichswehr's air and armored forces during the interwar period.[54] General Ernst von Köstring, a former German military attaché to Moscow, remarked that Hermann Göring's chief of staff credited the development and training programs at Lipetsk with allowing the Luftwaffe to reach the high state of proficiency it had achieved by 1939.[55]

In contrast to the advances made in German aviation, the German-Soviet agreements did little to benefit the development of the Reichswehr's ground-based air defenses. In 1928, Soviet representatives approached the firm of Krupp for assistance in the production of high-grade steel and artillery, including anti-aircraft guns. After showing some initial interest, Krupp decided against the venture, and as a result the Soviets subsequently turned to the firm of Rheinmetall in January 1930.[56] One of the Soviets' main objectives in its negotiations with Rheinmetall was to reach agreement on the construction of armaments factories for the production of artillery. The negotiations eventually led to an understanding by the summer of 1930 and the delivery of some flak artillery pieces;[57] however, the end of Russo-German military cooperation was already on the horizon.[58] In the final analysis, the significance of the cooperation between the Reichswehr and the Red Army centered on the experience gained by the aviation and tank trainees and the knowledge obtained by German industry. However, the advances in aviation technology and the lack of any cooperative agreements in the area of air defense helped contribute to a path of "differential development" between the two branches during the 1920s. By 1930, the technical and matériel advances within German aviation greatly exceeded the results achieved by aviation's ground-based air defense counterpart.[59]

Technological and Organizational Initiatives

While German aviation firms analyzed and tested new airframes and power plants in the 1920s, German industry also undertook a series of modest technological initiatives concerning ground-based air defense systems. The most pressing technological problem was the need for accurate targeting, which required a device capable of rapidly computing firing solutions. The interwar advances in aviation technology witnessed dramatic improvements in aircraft performance. These new commercial and military prototypes flew considerably higher and faster than their World War I counterparts. The greater speeds and higher operational ceilings achieved by aircraft vastly complicated anti-aircraft targeting and essentially rendered unaided optical targeting obsolete. In 1925, the firm of Carl Zeiss in Jena received a development contract for an optical range finder. The following year, Zeiss also began work on a fire director system, and this prototype underwent testing with the cooperation of the German navy and students from the technical college. The first operational fire director *(Kommandogerät P 27)* entered active service with the army's anti-aircraft forces at Königsberg, the anti-aircraft site that the Inter-Allied Military Control Commission allowed the Reichswehr to maintain after World War I. Live fire field tests conducted against targets towed by aircraft in 1928 led to the subsequent order for ten of the P 27 fire directors.[60] The requirement for ten fire directors resulted from the Reichswehr's secret conversion of the mobile artillery guns allowed under the original terms of the Versailles treaty to anti-aircraft guns. In 1928, these mobile artillery units received 75-mm anti-aircraft guns built by Krupp for foreign export and then transshipped to the German army.[61] Zeiss subsequently delivered the ten fire directors in 1930 and 1931.[62] Originally, the German army sought to outfit each battery with two fire directors, but the high cost of these devices prevented any additional purchases. Instead, the Germans began development of a less expensive auxiliary director to supplement the primary fire director.[63]

In addition to technical initiatives, the military also pursued an organizational restructuring of the German army. On June 30, 1927, the Truppenamt published a top secret mobilization plan, entitled Disposition Plan of the Wartime Military (the A-Plan), that outlined the responsibilities of the Reichswehr in the event of war.[64] The plan signified the intention of the army's senior leadership to formulate a comprehensive strategy for the military defense of Germany. It also required coordination between the various branches of the army, including the aviation branch, and the preparation of detailed personnel and matériel requirements. In 1928, Major (later Field Marshal) Albert Kesselring, the Reichswehr's efficiency expert, proposed the creation of a separate air inspectorate in order to centralize organizational, training, and acquisition issues relating to aviation. The army leadership rejected this proposal but did appoint a more senior officer, Brigadier Hilmar Ritter von Mittelberger, as the head of the Training Inspectorate (In 1) on October 1, 1929. The Training Inspectorate became the central office for all German aviation activities, including training, administration, budget, personnel, technology, meteorological services, and air defense.[65] In addition, the increasing importance attached to air defense found expression in the establishment of an anti-aircraft training staff attached to the Artillery Inspectorate on February 1, 1930.[66] The most significant step involved the Training Inspectorate's role in coordinating the aviation annex to the overall A-Plan. This annex, the Air Service-A-Program, dealt with the aviation requirements needed to support the general mobilization plan.[67] Not surprisingly, the initial plans developed by the inspectorate focused predominantly on the employment of aircraft in support of the army.

The Training Inspectorate, however, did not ignore the issue of air defense. In December 1930, it issued *Guidelines for the Training of the Reichswehr in the Field of the Air Force.* The draft copy of the *Guidelines* discussed the improvements made in the training of the army in airpower and air defense issues but cautioned that further progress was necessary. In fact, the "primary task" of the division's special air adviser was the education of the division's officers and enlisted men in the areas of aviation capabilities and air defense. In addition, the *Guidelines* mandated the participation of the divisional-level special air advisers in annual air defense exercises and encouraged their involvement in live fire exercises conducted by the mobile flak units.[68]

Visions of Future Warfare

By 1930, some senior officers within the Reichswehr began devoting their attention to the role of the strategic bomber in a future war. Helmuth Felmy, an air staff officer with the Training Inspectorate, and Wilhelm Wimmer, an officer in the Weapons Office, asserted that strategic bombers would play the "primary" role in the next war. Felmy's advocacy for strategic bombardment coincided with the air staff's publication of *Principles for the Employment of Air Forces* in 1930. In the *Principles*, the air staff maintained the need for a centrally controlled bomber force that could strike at "the military and economic sources of power of the enemy." The *Principles* also recognized that the contest for air superiority necessitated the cooperation and participation of both fighters and strong ground-based air defenses.[69] The standard historical response to the air staff's discussions of strategic bombardment has focused on Germany's "missed" opportunity and has highlighted the death of Walter Wever in 1936 as the point at which the Luftwaffe abandoned any ambitions of becoming a strategic force.[70] Often overlooked in this discussion, however, was the German reaction to strategic bombing arguments in the area of air defense.

By 1929 and 1930, the professional military literature began devoting increasing emphasis to the topic of air defense. In the period between October 1929 and March 1930, the *Militärwochenblatt* published a number of articles dealing specifically with the issue of air defense and anti-aircraft weapons.[71] These articles ranged from strategic analyses of the vulnerability of German industry to aerial attack to the tactical description of the Vickers .5-inch machine gun. In an article of October 18, 1929, entitled "Air Defense of German Industry," W. Hofweber, an engineer, played upon the anxieties of the German people and the military. Hofweber described Germany as a "disarmed Fatherland" and argued that "only dreamers believe in eternal peace, defenseless peoples have always been the desired object of attack."[72] He maintained that massive air fleets represented the most important weapons of the day and that these fleets, utilizing ongoing technological advances, possessed the capability "to drive Germany rapidly to her knees." Hofweber offered a number of suggestions designed to protect German industry from the "danger of annihilation," including the use of smoke generators to hide key industrial sites, the acquisition of searchlights to blind the pilots of attacking bombers, the establishment of an effective early-warning system, the construction of bombproof shelters and facilities, and the training of factory workers in emergency first aid and firefighting.[73] In credit to Hofweber's foresight, the Luftwaffe eventually pursued each of these measures prior to the end of World War II.

On October 25, an unsigned article, entitled "Air Defense from a French Perspective," appeared in the *Militärwochenblatt*. The article was, in fact, a two-page discussion and review of a book, *Preparations for Anti-Aircraft Defense*, written by the French general A. Niessel. The reviewer praised Niessel for his thoroughness and expertise. He also lamented the fact that in Germany, "where the question of air defense is especially vital, . . . one can only wish that in the near future a similar work in German might appear."[74] Niessel identified the central problem associated with air defense as "the spiritual preparation of the entire population" in the face of air attack—a point of view shared by the German reviewer. Ironically, the implication that spiritual preparation might inure one's population to aerial bombardment was in some respects reminiscent of Ardant du Picq's statements on the power of élan to overcome the physical and material advantages of an adversary, a theory seemingly laid to rest on the fields of Verdun and Ypres years before.[75]

Still, Niessel's discussion did not neglect the role played by physical forces. He examined several topics, including the nature and methods of air attack, objectives and possibilities of air attack, active and passive air defense measures, and the organization of air defenses; however, the reviewer chose to focus exclusively on Niessel's discussion of passive air defense measures. The reviewer agreed with Niessel's suggestions concerning the utility of using searchlights to blind pilots during nighttime attacks and the necessity for gas masks for the entire civilian population. He also concurred with Niessel on the limitations of smoke generators and camouflage for protecting large areas, as well as the need for air raid shelters in the vicinity of important industrial sites and communications facilities.[76] The review ended with the plaintive appeal that Niessel's book might serve as a "wake-up call" for the German people on the subject of air defense.[77]

On January 18, 1930, an article by A. Weiß, an engineer, entitled "Air Defense Through Reinforced Concrete Layers," presented a plan for protecting Germany's civilian population from aerial bombardment. Specifically, Weiß proposed the use of reinforced concrete in the construction of houses and apartments in the vicinity of industrial sites. He correctly observed that defense measures such as smoke generators or the use of interceptors during an enemy air attack would result in a number of bombs missing the intended target and landing among the civilian population. He therefore argued for construction standards that offered protection to noncombatants in these areas.[78]

The significance of the three articles mentioned here is twofold. On the one hand, they are indicative of a wave of literature dealing with air defense issues that began appearing in the late 1920s and early 1930s.[79] These articles and books warned of an aerial apocalypse and provided a multitude of solutions to the threat posed by air raids. On the other hand, the authors of these articles largely limited their discussion of air defense to *passive* measures, or those not related to the active engagement of attacking aircraft. The reluctance to discuss active defense measures most probably stemmed from three factors. First, the prohibitions placed on German anti-aircraft defenses by the Versailles treaty still remained in force. Second, the Reichswehr's active ground-based air defenses could be described as modest at best. Finally, the military may have discouraged contemporary discussions of active defense measures to prevent focusing attention on its own aviation and air defense initiatives in the late 1920s and early 1930s.

In contrast, articles did address developments in active defense outside of Germany. For example, an article in the December 25, 1929, issue of the *Militärwochenblatt* examined the organization, operation, and equipment of anti-aircraft units assigned to the U.S. Army. It presented illustrations of tactical dispositions for both day and night defense, including the integration of fire directors, range finders, searchlights, and listening devices.[80] Finally, in the edition of March 18, 1930, the newspaper published an article evaluating the newest anti-aircraft machine guns produced by the firm of Vickers.[81]

Air Defense and Rearmament

Renewed interest in air defense issues in the late 1920s and early 1930s was probably not coincidental. By the late 1920s, army planners included projections for between forty and fifty flak guns for each ground division.[82] However, a more concrete initiative in the sphere of aerial rearmament occurred in the wake of the so-called Second Rearmament Plan of September 30, 1930. The Truppenamt viewed this plan as an integral step in the systematic and coordinated rearmament of the German army. Although clearly favoring traditional army weapons systems, the plan also contained provisions for a substantial increase in the size of flak forces attached to the field armies, including the creation of twenty-eight light flak batteries and twenty-seven heavy flak batteries. The plan called for the provisioning of light flak batteries armed with 6 20-mm or 37-mm guns and heavy flak batteries armed with 4 75-mm or 88-mm guns. In addition, the rearmament plan addressed the need for the defense of the German homeland through the acquisition of 132 heavy machine gun companies, fifteen platoons of 37-mm flak guns, six batteries of 75-mm guns, twenty-four batteries of 88-mm guns, and two batteries of 105-mm guns. Under this plan, the total number of weapons devoted to home defense included 792 heavy machine guns, 30 37-mm guns, 24 75-mm guns, 48 88-mm guns, and 4 105-mm guns.[83]

The Second Rearmament Plan demonstrated the Reichswehr's determination to increase the size of the army despite the existing prohibitions of the Versailles treaty. The plan identified the necessity of providing air defense both to forces in the field and to the homeland. Not surprisingly, the plan did highlight a continuing bias within the army favoring the troops at the front as indicated by the allocation of 108 heavy guns (75-mm and above) and 168 light guns (37-mm) for the former compared with 76 heavy guns and 30 light guns for the latter.[84] However, the plan was essentially a "wish list" whose fulfillment would not be attained until after 1933. Still, the Weimar government's allocation of 484 million RM, or $115.2 million, to the Reichswehr in 1930, including 110 million RM for aircraft and equipment procurement as well as additional millions for active and passive air defense measures provided a starting point for military planners.[85]

The Flak Gets a Theorist

On February 1, 1930, Lieutenant Colonel Günther Rüdel assumed command of the anti-aircraft training staff. Born in Metz in 1883, Rüdel entered the army in July 1902 as an officer candidate with the 3rd Bavarian Field Artillery Regiment. During World War I, he was attached to the Prussian War Ministry as a member of the Artillery Proving Commission. He later commanded the anti-aircraft training school at Ostende. After the war, he served in the Reichswehr in a number of training and staff positions before being named head of the Flak Artillery Training Staff on February 1, 1931.[86]

As commander of this section, Rüdel was responsible for the secret reorganization and equipping of the flak forces. He also became the single most important individual responsible for creating and shaping German ground-based air defenses in the period between 1930 and 1941. By December of 1930, he had produced an initial top secret plan for reequipping the Reichswehr's flak forces. In the Development Program of December 13, 1930, Rüdel outlined three fundamental precepts shaping his plans for the future. First, he proposed that priority must be given to only the most essential equipment. Second, he remarked on the immediate need for the acquisition of equipment for supporting the army's mobilization plans. Third, he emphasized the necessity of keeping future plans within the boundaries of fiscal resources even if this entailed renouncing "the most desirable and most capable [weapons systems]."[87]

In the development program, Rüdel closely coordinated the needs of air defense with the planned requirements of the Army Ordnance Office.[88] As an army officer and following the intent of the Second Rearmament Plan, it was understandable that priority be given to the protection of frontline forces. Rüdel's report presented six specific tasks that he viewed as being "particularly important and urgent":

1. Completion of an automatic AA [anti-aircraft] gun for fight against low-level planes.
2. Completion of the new 8.8 cm AA gun *or* the improved 8.8 cm Army-AA gun 18.
3. Creation of an auxiliary director for remote control aiming.
4. Creation of a new instrument for location and firing by sound.

5. Creation of an efficient sound locator.
6. Speed computer . . . for range-finding training garrisons.

He finished the report with the statement that *"All other tasks are at present less urgent and can if necessary be set aside."*[89]

Rüdel's proposed development program was in several respects keenly insightful. He argued for the acquisition of an 88-mm gun as the smallest caliber for the heavy flak guns due to its better performance compared with the obsolescent 75-mm.[90] Based on the rapidly improving capabilities of aircraft during the interwar period, Rüdel recognized that only a gun with a sufficiently high muzzle velocity would be effective at the increasing altitude achieved by these aircraft. In addition, he justified the emphasis on listening devices, which seemed on the surface odd, on the expectation that "the combat of night bomber attacks is the most important task of the air defense."[91] Why not then concentrate on searchlights? In partial explanation, Rüdel mentioned that the range of the 75-mm and 88-mm guns exceeded the effective range of the current 110-cm searchlights, a fact supported by another senior flak general's contention that "no important preparatory work was done for a future anti-aircraft artillery searchlight prior to 1932."[92] Even more critical to Rüdel's future plans, however, was the acquisition of a remotely operated fire director. He went so far as to contend that "the air defense at night rises and falls with the direction finder."[93] The appreciation of the need for effective night defenses was prescient as this was indeed the primary battle faced by German flak crews in the early years of World War II, prior to the large-scale entry of the U.S. Army Air Forces in 1943. Despite its limited ambitions, Rüdel's program established the initial framework for the rearmament of the flak defenses in the early 1930s.[94]

Fighters versus Flak?

In February 1932, Lieutenant Colonel Helmuth Felmy released a study that detailed the Reichswehr's force projections for the period from 1932 to 1938. The study was essentially an airman's vision for the organization and force structure of German military aviation. Felmy projected a final strength of 1,056 aircraft of varying types, including 216 fighters and 504 bombers. He also separated air defense requirements into two categories: army air defense forces and German home air defense. According to this plan, army air defense forces were to include ten motorized flak regimental staffs with assigned signal units, 25 motorized flak detachments with 75-mm guns, 16 motorized flak detachments with 88-mm guns, 16 flak batteries with 105-mm guns, 16 searchlight batteries, 22 motorized anti-aircraft detachments armed with 20-mm machine guns,

25 motorized medium batteries armed with 37-mm guns, and, finally, 16 motorized platoons equipped with barrage balloons. The home air defense force was decidedly less impressive, with plans for seven regimental staffs, 6 batteries armed with 75-mm guns, and 14 anti-aircraft detachments armed with 88-mm guns.[95]

Felmy's study offered two important insights into the Reichswehr's thinking about air defense prior to the National Socialist "seizure of power" in January 1933. First, the air staff appreciated the need for mobile flak forces to support the advance of the army. Second, Felmy's projections for home air defense were clearly inadequate for achieving the effective protection of the nation's industrial and urban centers, all the more puzzling in light of his own advocacy of strategic bombardment and the high level of popular and professional discussion of air defense in the late 1920s and early 1930s. Perhaps Felmy simply sought to satisfy the army's desire for organic air defenses in order to obtain the numbers and types of aircraft that he truly desired. In any event, by 1932 Felmy and the other leaders of German military aviation became embroiled in a controversy concerning who should command ground-based air defenses. The World War I precedent argued for Air Service control, while the army leadership steadfastly opposed any initiative to detach air defense from its domain.[96] Already in April 1931, the chief of the Truppenamt, General Wilhelm Adam, rejected plans for the consolidation of the aviation and flak forces into a separate service independent of direct army control.[97] The outcome of this struggle for the control of Germany's ground-based air defenses would not be decided until 1935.

The Development Program of 1932

In December 1932, Rüdel, now a colonel and the chief of the army's air defense branch, compiled a secret report, entitled "Development Program of Army AA Weapons." Like Felmy's earlier plan, Rüdel's report placed a distinct emphasis on army support. It listed four primary tasks for anti-aircraft weapons: reducing hostile air reconnaissance of any sort, prevention of hostile artillery range finding with air observation, defense against air raids on ground targets, and support of own air forces in accomplishment of their tasks. The report also reflected two other important aspects of German air defense doctrine, the need for a combined-arms approach and the appreciation of air defense against strategic attack. Under "Tasks of AA Weapons," it remarked, "AA has the task either alone or in cooperation with the Air Force to protect all vital installations for the protection of the homeland as well as to protect the troops in the field from attacks from the air."[98] According to the report, the primary aim of the anti-aircraft defenses was "always the destruction of the hostile planes, . . . [although] their actual and morale effect, [*sic*] will hinder the enemy at least in the execution of his tasks or force him to abandon his activities altogether." In addition, the air defense planners realized that the number of guns would be limited, but they felt that mobility could "compensate for numerical weakness."[99]

Beyond the overview of the task and aims of air defense, the report focused on the forecast requirements of the air defense branch in the immediate future. In fact, the report presented a prioritization of air defense needs. The programs deemed "urgent" priorities were the 88-mm gun, the 20-mm and 37-mm medium flak guns, searchlights, radio locators including listening devices, barrage rockets, fire directors, and infrared tracking. In addition, the report identified barrage balloons as an "important" priority and remote-controlled anti-aircraft guns as "not urgent."[100] The plans for barrage rockets and infrared tracking of aircraft constituted two major innovations. The former of these proposals might seem overly ambitious based on the limited size and fiscal resources of the Reichswehr in 1932. It is important to note, however, that Wernher von Braun started his doctoral work on liquid-fueled rocketry at the Technical University of Berlin in December of the same year.[101] Rocket development had the additional advantage of not being covered under the restrictions of the Versailles treaty, and the army was therefore technically within its rights to pursue defensive rocket systems.[102]

This report also reversed Rüdel's earlier position concerning the utility of searchlights in nighttime air defense, a fact explained by new plans that envisioned searchlights with ranges of twelve kilometers. However, the most striking aspect of the 1932 Development Program was that it identified all the essential elements of the future German air defense system in World War II. It also presaged the employment of larger-caliber guns but cautioned that this "would be governed by the weight of a mobile AA gun. . . . Calibers over 88 mm could be used only for static or RR [railroad] AA because of weight restriction."[103]

From a doctrinal standpoint, Rüdel's identification of the "destruction" of hostile aircraft as the primary goal of anti-aircraft forces, as opposed to preventing or hampering a successful attack, was highly significant. The adoption of this position established a standard for judging the future effectiveness of the flak arm essentially based on one narrow parameter. This was an iron measure that in many respects shaped the subsequent expectations of the Luftwaffe leadership concerning the anticipated performance of the flak. During World War II, Rüdel and the rest of the flak arm would have repeated opportunity to question this premise, but it was never abandoned.

The practical results of these early plans proved far less dramatic than they appeared on paper. Still, progress was being made despite the crippling after-effects of the "Great Slump" engendered by the worldwide fiscal crisis in the fall of 1929. For example, by October 1932 the army found enough funding to convert the existing flak units from horse-drawn to fully motorized units. Already in 1931, individual batteries participated in two-week-long training courses involving live fire exercises at the training range at Döberitz and Pillau. These drills stressed the use of fire directors in gunnery trials, and commanders were urged to place "exactness before speed."[104] Additionally, these batteries conducted firing exercises on the Schilling peninsula in the summer and fall of 1932. The slow movement from theory toward practice offered a welcome break from the largely notional instruction of the late 1920s.[105]

The development plans assembled in 1932 by Felmy and Rüdel were important steps along the road to German rearmament. Germany's ground-based air defense forces admittedly were modest, but Rüdel and the members of his staff had sketched the broad outlines of the air defense force that would eventually enter the crucible of war in 1939. In fact, the Reichswehr's rearmament plans of 1930 and 1932 clearly demonstrated that it was not the National Socialists but the political and military leadership of the Weimar Republic who initiated the plans for large-scale German rearmament.[106] It was a process that Hitler and senior military leaders were only too happy to support and intensify in the years between 1933 and 1939.

CHAPTER THREE

Converting Theory into Practice 1933–1938

The ascension to power of Adolf Hitler and his National Socialist German Workers' Party (NSDAP) proved auspicious for the Reichswehr's plan of expansion and modernization. Soon after his appointment as chancellor, Hitler described the armed forces as "the most important institution in the State" and pledged his support for a comprehensive rearmament program.[1] Already in 1928, Hitler had remarked that "the first task" of German domestic policy was to provide the German people with "a military organization suitable to its national strength."[2] In Hitler's mind, the creation of a strong military included the means by which to protect the German homeland from an aerial attack. Indeed, Hitler noted the vulnerability of Germany to an attack through the air and warned that "with the present situation of German borders, there is only a very small area of a few square kilometers which could not be visited by enemy aircraft within the first hour." He then continued, "At the present time the military countermeasures Germany could take against the employment of this weapon, all in all, [are] quite nil."[3] In 1928, Hitler could only write impotently about the state of German air defenses, but by 1933 he was in a position to take concrete measures.

It is clear that Hitler's new government took a great deal of interest in both active air defense and civil defense measures. A strong ground-based air defense system became an idée fixe in Hitler's mind during the life of the twelve-year Reich.[4] Hitler's belief in the importance of ground-based air defenses most probably arose from his own experience in World War I, a contention supported by his declaration that "whoever has himself had to put up with the effects of an enemy air attack in the field knows especially well how to appraise the moral effects resulting therefrom."[5] In any event, it is clear that German ground-based air defenses underwent a rapid expansion in the years between 1933 and 1939.

The "Driving Sections"

In 1933, the army began a process of reorganizing its seven existing *Fahrabteilungen* (literally driving sections). The use of the term "driving section" was a veiled attempt to disguise the fact that these units were actually motorized flak units.

The reorganization was in truth a direct result of the Conversion Plan of November 1932 and the Reichswehr leadership's desire to increase the size of the army, and in particular the size of anti-aircraft, signal, and artillery units.[6] The army created the flak units from sections of motorized guns that previously had been attached to various artillery regiments. By May 1, 1933, the *Fahrabteilungen* were grouped into Observation Departments located in Königsberg, Jüterborg, Munich, Landsberg am Lech, and Berlin-Lankwitz. The units were composed of four batteries each, including two batteries for support of mountain operations located in Landsberg.[7]

The total of seven air defense units for the support of the army and the protection of the Reich was clearly inadequate for defending Germany in the event of a war. Yet, compared with the efforts of other major powers, the Reichswehr's endeavors were quite good. In Great Britain, fiscal austerity and the "ten-year rule" coupled with the maintenance of a far-flung empire led to the relegation of anti-aircraft defenses to the forces of the Territorial Army. The creation of a new command in 1925, Air Defence of Great Britain (ADGB), resulted in several committee studies dealing with air defense but few practical advances. In the words of one historian, the financial crisis of 1929–1930 "reduced training exercises to farcical unreality through shortage of equipment and restrictions on fuel, ammunition and cost."[8] If the state of British ground-based air defenses was modest, then that of the United States can only be described as abysmal. In a speech in 1935, Colonel George C. Marshall, the future chief of staff of the army, observed, "Our air service is far better developed or equipped than any other portion of the army. But our air resisting weapons, anti-aircraft machine guns and cannon equipment is [*sic*] sadly deficient."[9] In this light, German efforts prior to 1933 appear entirely adequate.

A closer examination of the organization and activities of the *Fahrabteilungen* provides a framework for evaluating the effectiveness of these units in the early 1930s. In March 1933, Fahrabteilung 3 at Berlin-Lankwitz was composed of a staff including medical, weather, and signal sections as well as one searchlight battery and one battery of four 88-mm guns. The staff included 9 officers, 3 civil servants, and over 130 noncommissioned officers (NCOs) and enlisted members. Likewise, the searchlight battery consisted of 6 officers, 3 officer candidates, 31 NCOs, and 130 enlisted men, and the gun battery was composed of 6 officers, 3 officer candidates, 26 NCOs, and 112 enlisted men.[10] By October 1933, the army increased the size of the unit by adding two additional gun batteries, including a battery of four 75-mm guns and another battery of four 88-mm guns.[11]

The beginning of 1933 also witnessed an acceleration in the number and scale of air defense training activities. The still-secret anti-aircraft training staff initiated a major effort to increase the proficiency of the individual flak units. In March 1933, Colonel Rüdel issued a comprehensive report, "Comments on Training for 1933," which described the training program planned for 1933 and highlighted areas requiring further improvement. A key emphasis was the training of the optical range-finding personnel. In fact, the range finders operating the optical sighting devices were perhaps the most critical members of the gun crews. The initial distance-to-target measurement provided the foundation for all subsequent calculations and played a key role in any successful engagement of the target. Rüdel remarked on the wide disparity in the proficiency of various units. Furthermore, he cautioned that experience had shown that the level of proficiency even among highly qualified crews "dropped dramatically" as soon as regular training was interrupted or discontinued for a longer period. The training and proficiency of the range-finding crews would remain a major concern of air defense commanders through 1945.

A second point of concern noted by Rüdel was the need for battery commanders to remain in constant communication with their units. This remark seems odd at first glance, but not when one considers the fact that the motorized flak units often were expected to be on the move in support of the army in the field. In turn, the battery commander was responsible for finding suitable areas to emplace his forces and the gunnery equipment. Finally, Rüdel turned his attention to the question of firing drills. He stated that the standards associated with live fire trials were to be raised to include more realistic battlefield conditions, but noted, that not all units would be able to participate in night firing exercises.[12] Rüdel's final comment on night firing exposed a serious weakness in the flak arm in 1933. The lack of night gunnery practice would return to haunt the Luftwaffe in the opening years of World War II. Despite the deficiency in night gunnery, Rüdel's report still highlighted the increased emphasis on training and improved standards for ground-based air defense forces beginning in 1933. Indeed, a look at the training regimen of specific units in early 1933 supports this view.

Practical and Theoretical Training

The activities of Fahrabteilung 3 from March to May 1933 revealed the increased pace of training exercises experienced by the flak units. In March, the unit received orders to conduct field trials three times a week, combining searchlights and sound detectors. These exercises were intended to serve as preparation for the war games scheduled in the summer. In April, the unit was to continue the weekly drills but was expected to conduct them under simulated battlefield conditions. In May, the battle exercises continued and integrated a two-week-long live fire trial at the gunnery range in Schillig, followed by another week of searchlight and combat trials involving new recruits.[13]

By the summer of 1933, the increased level of training began producing tangible results as evidenced by several performance evaluations. In the case of sound detectors, a report to the Reichswehr Ministry of July 1933 outlined the difficulties associated with aural range finding in areas close to cities, industrial areas, railroads, and highways. The high ambient sound in these areas complicated the task of the crews. Still, the report observed that in time of war the ambient noise conditions would be even worse, and therefore it was important to continue to train crews in such conditions. The report also mentioned that the best crews were not those who could provide highly accurate tracking at short and medium ranges but those who were most proficient on average at extreme range. In fact, it asserted that the training of the crews at the limits of the sound detectors' range constituted the "most important task" in the course of instruction. The report also emphasized cooperation between the sound detector personnel and the searchlight crews in training for engaging bombers at night. In sum, it demonstrated a realistic appraisal of the limitations associated with sound detection and an equally pragmatic approach to future training exercises.[14]

Important practical experience also was being gained with respect to the use of searchlights. In the interwar period, the overall perception of the efficacy of searchlights was decidedly pessimistic, and as a result the efforts dedicated to searchlight development were modest. Field trials in the early 1930s offered a more optimistic appraisal, with one commander arguing that the actual ranges of the 110-cm and especially the 150-cm searchlights were being continually underestimated.[15] In turn, operational trials generated a number of specific tactical recommendations. A report in August 1933 from the commander of Fahrabteilung 3, Lieutenant Colonel Hubert Weise (later commander of Air Region, Center) to the air defense office in the Reichswehr Ministry offered three specific recommendations. First, Weise argued that the peacetime organization involving three platoons of two searchlights allowed only for coverage of specific sectors around the protected object. Furthermore, he stated that this led to aircraft having to follow closely prescribed routes in order for the crews to successfully engage them. He insisted on the reequipping of each platoon with four searchlights and described this as an "urgent and nonnegotiable demand." Second, Weise requested that a motorized communications section be attached to each platoon to decrease response times and enable the platoons to conduct mobile operations. Finally, he concluded by stating that "even more than the flak batteries, the searchlight batteries require a realistic training target." In this respect, Weise noted the problems in using single-engine sport planes that flew lower and slower than military bombers. He then observed that unless realistic training targets could be provided, the "entire training [of the crews] would remain at the present level."[16]

If at times the practical elements of flak training proved less than ideal, the same could not be said concerning the effort and attention devoted to theoretical training. In the fall of 1933, Fahrabteilung 3 announced preparations for the conduct of two large-scale planning exercises for December 1933 and

February 1934. The former involved an exercise in homeland air defense centered around the city of Berlin, while the latter focused on the employment of flak forces in support of mobile army operations.[17] Other theoretical training included forty hours of instruction for air defense officers in the subjects of flak artillery and searchlight employment, aircraft tactics, and motor recognition; the last subject taught them to identify the distinctive sound made by specific types of aircraft engines. In addition, individual officers offered a series of twelve oral presentations on an impressive array of topics, ranging from doctrinal tenets and operational measures to tactical procedures, such as "Thoughts on the Conduct of Modern Air Warfare"; "Defense in Low-Level Attacks by Dive-Bombers"; "What Is the Minimum Number of Guns and Searchlights for Flak Batteries?"; "Smoke Production in Air Defense"; "Flak-Measuring Instruments and Their Importance in Firing Operations"; and "Activities of Air Forces and Air Defenses in the Sino-Japanese War."[18] Indeed, the thorough theoretical training of air defense forces should not be overly surprising; it merely continued a tradition of excellence established by the Prussian and German armies in this area.[19]

Nevertheless, the broad scope and intensity of the theoretical instruction resulted in some complaints from the field. One officer in his after-action report complained that attempts at conducting theoretical training during live fire exercises constituted an attempt to do too much in too short an amount of time. Major Eugen Weißmann, a future lieutenant general of the Flak Artillery, wrote that "theoretical training of the participants through the use of presentations during the live fire periods is impossible." He argued that "the burden on the participants engendered by the presentations, homework, and firing tasks was very great, [and] just within bearable limits for the purpose of the training course."[20] Weißmann surely was not alone in the belief that events were moving too quickly, a phenomenon that also applied to the organizational restructuring of the "driving sections."

In October 1933, the flak and searchlight forces included Fahrabteilung 3 (Berlin-Lankwitz), Fahrabteilung 1 (Königsberg), Fahrabteilung 2 (Stettin), Fahrabteilung 4 (Dresden), Fahrabteilung 5 (Ludwigsburg), Fahrabteilung 6 (Wolfenbüttel), and Fahrabteilung 7 (Fürth).[21] The separation of the units across a wide geographic area coincided with the existing army districts *(Wehrkreise)*. This geographical separation also helped to mask German air defense activities from the other European powers. The latter consideration was a very real concern, as evidenced by an order of October 7, 1933, by Rüdel, now inspector of Air Defense Forces, that no information or photographs concerning exercises, weapons, or equipment should be allowed to appear in the press.[22]

The prohibition concerning the release of information on weapons and equipment pointed to a further area of development within the air defense forces by the end of 1933. In the late 1920s, the firms of Rheinmetall and Krupp developed a number of designs for light and heavy flak guns, and by December 1933 some of these guns had reached the production stage.[23] For example, members of Fahrabteilung 3 gathered in December to view the 37-mm Flak/18, the 88-mm Flak/18,[24] and the 150-cm searchlight.[25] The new 37-mm gun proved somewhat of a disappointment and would require extensive modification; by contrast, the 88-mm gun and the 150-cm searchlight offered a substantial increase in performance over their predecessors. In particular, the 88-mm gun offered a dramatic improvement over the 75-mm gun, with an absolute ceiling of 33,000 feet and an effective ceiling of 26,000 feet. The former term refers to the highest altitude that a shell could theoretically attain; the latter term denotes the highest altitude at which a successful engagement could be conducted before atmospheric conditions and physical forces began to influence the trajectory of the projectile to a significant extent. The new 88-mm gun also incorporated direct transmission of firing solutions from the fire director to the gun itself, a feature that significantly decreased firing times.[26] In addition, the renewed focus on searchlights demonstrated the recognition by the air defense leadership of the dangers posed by nighttime aerial attack—a lesson learned in the night raids of World War I.

By the end of 1933, the investments in training and equipment for air defense forces began paying noticeable dividends. In 1934, the *Fahrabteilungen* experienced a 50 percent expansion in size with the formation of four new units. In addition, the army expanded the air defense unit at Döberitz through the creation of a flak training school.[27] This expansion, however, engendered a serious personnel shortage within the "driving sections."[28] In establishing the new units, the army simply drew batteries from existing organizations and reconstituted them as independent units. By August 1934, the shortage of qualified officers became especially pressing and led to the creation of 150 officer candidate positions for air defense and 70 officer candidate positions for the Air Reporting Service.[29] Despite the problems associated with the rapid growth of the flak forces, substantial progress had been achieved by the end of 1934.

Rüdel in Charge

On October 1, 1934, General Rüdel received the title of "inspector of the Flak Artillery and head of the Air Defense Office." In this capacity, Rüdel assumed the position of the senior ranking officer in matters relating to the training, organization, and equipping of the burgeoning air defense forces, a position he would retain until February 1939. In a report of November 1934, entitled "Observations on Training for 1934," Rüdel liberally praised the progress made by the air defense units. He started by remarking on the firing proficiency of the flak crews as "altogether good" and highlighted the efforts of range-finding personnel in making this success possible. He did note, however, the need to conduct future training firing drills under more realistic combat conditions. In reference to the improvements in aircraft technology, Rüdel observed, "The speed of aircraft has increased to the point that the effective coverage area of the flak is quickly crossed." In light of these developments, he ordered that "in addition to the highest level of precision, training must also achieve the *highest level of speed* in every task." He also argued for a timely concentration of fire from all guns to increase the "moral effects" of the flak defenses. In this respect, although continuing to emphasize the use of directed, or aimed, fires, using a fire director, Rüdel also mentioned the "usefulness" of barrage fire in the absence of a reliable acoustic procedure for locating aircraft in poor weather and at night. Finally, he mentioned the "considerable advances" made by searchlight crews in the performance of their duties but again warned that the training of these crews required more realistic combat conditions.[30]

Rüdel's analysis clearly showed the progress that had been made by the air defense forces by the end of 1934. It also demonstrated Rüdel's recognition of the impact of improved aviation technology on the conduct of air defense operations. His response to the danger posed by modern aircraft essentially focused on improved training through increased speed, precision, and knowledge. Finally, Rüdel's remarks concerning the use of barrier fire procedures provided an unintended insight into the flak arm's absolute reliance on sound detectors for locating aircraft flying in or above the clouds. The reliance on aural detection procedures would prove to be a major weakness within the air defense force in the opening stages of the coming war.

In the conclusion to his report, Rüdel declared that the commanders of the air defense units needed to master not only the regulations concerning their own systems but those of the fighter aircraft, as well. In fact, he argued for a detailed "understanding of the tactics and weapons capabilities" of these aircraft, as well as the need to take advantage of every opportunity to work together with fighters during planning exercises and field trials.[31] Rüdel's decision to finish his yearly evaluation on the flak force with a discussion of the need to increase cooperation with fighter forces was hardly coincidental. On the one hand, he recognized the importance of combined operations in the field of air defense. His remark also reflected his own thinking that air defense was not an either-or proposition between flak and fighters; for Rüdel, both played an important role. On the other hand, he was certainly aware that the coming year held a number of major organizational changes for the air defense forces.

The Bureaucratic Battle for Control of the Flak Arm

Since 1930, the army had resisted efforts to remove air defense forces from its command. In the Weimar period, the army had consistently won every battle against the advocates of forming an independent air arm with control over both aviation and air defense forces.[32] The need to keep aerial rearmament secret and the small size of both the nascent German air force and the flak forces were factors in keeping these forces under army control. However, in 1933 changes within the power structure of the Third Reich coupled with Hitler's grandiose plans for increasing the size of the armed forces led to the first of a number of organizational changes with respect to both aviation and air defense forces. Leading these efforts was Hermann Göring. Göring, a fighter ace in World War I and the last commander of the famed Richthofen flying circus, was an ambitious political opportunist whose appetite for the finer things in life was exceeded only by his desire for political power. He was Hitler's self-professed "truest paladin," and his political fortunes were inextricably tied to those of the Führer.[33]

When Hitler became chancellor of Germany in January 1933, he appointed Göring as a minister without portfolio in his cabinet. Hitler also acceded to Göring's desire for a leading role in the expansion of German military and civil aviation and on February 3, 1933, selected him to head the Reich Commission for Aviation. On April 27, 1933, Reich President Hindenburg changed the commission's name to the Reich Air Ministry, thereby elevating the organization to ministry status. The Air Ministry now was subordinated to the defense minister and commander of the Wehrmacht, General Werner von Blomberg.[34] On May 1, von Blomberg ordered the transfer of the Air Defense Office to the Air Ministry under the control of Göring and his second in command, State Secretary for Aviation Erhard Milch, a move that elevated Göring to a ministerial position equivalent to that of the defense minister.[35] Subsequently, on September 16, 1933, von Blomberg created the position of an "inspector of air defense forces" who was responsible in turn to Göring on matters concerning the organization, training, augmentation, and equipping of air defense forces. The inspector's "primary duty" was the "standardized coordination of all military and civil preparedness measures for air defense in the field and in the homeland as well as the systematic continued development of air defense tactics and technical matters."[36] Despite Göring's apparent victory, the army fought a successful rearguard action by retaining control over the operational activities of the inspector and the air defense forces, a position the army officially maintained until April 1, 1935.

Even prior to his official acquisition of the ground-based air defense forces, Göring played an influential role in driving the personnel and matériel expansion of the flak forces. In August 1934, Göring's office released a secret plan for the procurement of 2,000 heavy flak guns, 510 medium flak guns, 3,560 light flak guns, 1,500 150-cm searchlights, 1,000 sound detectors, and 510 fire predictors by 1938. In addition, the plan called for the acquisition of 6.4 million rounds of heavy flak ammunition, 4.3 million rounds of 37-mm ammunition, and 61 million rounds of 20-mm ammunition.[37] Göring's proposal constituted a blueprint for the planned expansion of the air defense forces, an expansion he would soon be in a position to lead.

By the spring of 1935, Hitler and the National Socialist Party had been able to consolidate their hold over German government and society. Likewise, Göring was now in a position to replace his de facto authority over military aviation and air defense forces with de jure control. March 1935 proved an important month for the German military in two respects. First, on March 1, Hitler ordered the creation of the Reichsluftwaffe as an independent and co-equal partner to the army and the navy under Göring's command. Second, on March 16, Hitler's government announced the reintroduction of conscription, amounting to the open renunciation of the Treaty of Versailles. The former measure provided the opening for the Luftwaffe to gain full control over the air defense forces; the latter guaranteed the necessary manpower base for a major increase in the size of the armed forces. In the first case, Göring moved quickly to bring flak forces under his command. In a directive dated April 1, 1935, he greeted the subordination of the flak forces under his command with the following words:

> I welcome this combat-tested force into our [Luftwaffe] ranks. Henceforth, this force will fulfill its important duties shoulder to shoulder with flyers and signal corps. . . . Powerful air fleets in many countries will bring a new face to future warfare. For their protection, the Wehrmacht and the German people demand a strong flak arm, armed with the best technology, well trained in peace but always ready for action.[38]

To be sure, Göring was well known for his bombastic proclamations throughout the life of the Third Reich. The question to be answered, then, is how did he evaluate the utility and effectiveness of ground-based air defenses between 1933 and 1945? Göring followed Hitler's lead concerning the air defense of the Third Reich by emphasizing flak, searchlights, and sound detectors as the first line of protection against aerial attack. He, like Hitler, believed that ground-based anti-aircraft defenses could create a formidable barrier around important urban and industrial centers, as well as along the borders of the Third Reich. A concrete manifestation of both men's esteem for flak forces found expression at the Nuremberg party rally of 1935 with the selection of anti-aircraft crews to conduct an air defense exercise complete with firing drills on the *Zeppelinfeld*.[39] One must be careful, however, to not overdraw this point. Clearly both men placed great store in flak forces; however, it is highly unlikely that a Luftwaffe run by a close circle of fighter pilots like Göring, Helmuth Felmy, Ernst Udet, Karl Bodenschatz et al. would completely neglect the necessary role of fighters in air defense, and indeed they did not.

The Doctrine of Air Defense

Luftwaffe doctrine in the period prior to the start of World War II did not envision home defense as solely a task for ground-based defenses. *Luftwaffe Regulation 16,* entitled *The Conduct of Aerial Warfare,* appeared in 1935 and served as the primary blueprint for Luftwaffe operations until the end of the war.[40] It offered a series of basic doctrinal precepts in its opening paragraphs:

> 1. The war in the air, in attack and defense, will be carried out by the Luftwaffe. The Luftwaffe consists of aerial forces: bombers, reconnaissance and fighters; anti-aircraft artillery; and the air force communication troops.
> 2. From the start of the conflict, the air forces bring the war to the enemy. . . .
>
>   The anti-aircraft artillery directly protects the homeland. Its primary mission is the defense of the homeland in cooperation with the fighter force. . . .
>
>   The air reporting service is a support for leadership and battle in the defense. In cooperation with the air warning service, it enables the rapid deployment of the civil air defense.
>
>   The civil air defense fulfills the aerial defense. It limits the effect of enemy air attacks against the people and their homes.
> 3. The leadership and battle of the Luftwaffe are decisively influenced by technology. Aircraft models, weapons, munitions, radios, et cetera, are in constant development. The means of attack are in constant competition with the means of defense.
>
>   During the course of a war, discoveries and improvements in materiel can have an enormous effect upon the state of hostilities.[41]

This introductory material offers a number of important insights into the Luftwaffe's approach to aerial warfare. First, the Luftwaffe defined itself as a combined-arms force incorporating the elements of attack and defense. Second, the Luftwaffe clearly placed an emphasis on *offensive* operations.[42] Third, anti-aircraft forces received the primary task of protecting the homeland; however, it was a responsibility that involved "cooperation with the fighter force." Fourth, the Air Reporting Service, with its lines of observation posts (later radar sites) and communications stations, played an important role in providing an overview of the air situation, as well as passing this information along to military and civil defense authorities.[43] Finally, *Regulation 16* highlighted the importance of technology in the dialectic competition between the attack and the defense.

A subsection of *Regulation 16,* entitled "The Defense," offered a number of more specific guidelines for air defense operations, including the organization of fighters and anti-aircraft artillery under a unified commander, as well as the close cooperation of night fighters with both flak and searchlights units. Further evidence of the commitment to combined operations appeared in paragraph 273:

> Cooperation between fighter and anti-aircraft forces requires the most thorough liaison. Simultaneous attack by anti-aircraft weapons and fighters against the same enemy formation will normally not be carried out owing to the danger to our own fighters.
>
> Fighters should engage the enemy before he enters the anti-aircraft zone: an attack at the right moment can disperse the bombing formation and create favorable conditions for anti-aircraft defense.

Paragraph 273 also cautioned that fighters wishing to press an attack within the flak zone did so at their own peril. The regulation further mentioned the extreme difficulty of coordinating fighter and flak operations at night and argued for a separation of engagement areas. The doctrinal precepts in *Regulation 16* included ideas from the Luftwaffe's best and brightest officers, and it clearly demonstrated a commitment within the air force for combined air defense operations involving fighters, flak guns, searchlights, sound detectors, and barrage balloons.[44]

War Games

The doctrinal tenets of the Luftwaffe did not remain relegated to the written page. Indeed, the Luftwaffe conducted several war games in which theory was put to the test of practice. The Luftwaffe General Staff conducted its war game exercise for the winter of 1934–1935 in November and December 1934. The scenario presumed a French surprise attack in response to German rearmament efforts involving a French ground offensive into Germany accompanied by "heavy air attacks" within German territory. The scenario also highlighted the strength of French flak forces established in two lines along the border, as well as heavy flak and searchlight concentrations protecting the major industrial and urban centers of Lorraine, Briey, Diedenhofen, Nancy, and Paris. Furthermore, a simulated German aerial attack against Paris ran into an "exceptionally strong defense by flak and fighters" and avoided heavy losses only because of cloud coverage over the target. The description of the French air defenses is interesting in two respects. On the one hand, the French air defenses mirrored the Luftwaffe's own vision of German defenses, a common assumption made by military forces when creating their own war plans. On the other hand, the French air defenses included the cooperation of fighters and flak, with flak being viewed as an effective instrument for preventing the penetration of German attacks and protecting important industrial and urban centers.[45]

This war game scenario also assumed a significant German air defense capability, encompassing anti-aircraft units with the Luftwaffe, the army, and the navy. In accordance with air defense doctrine, military planners divided flak and searchlight forces between the army and the air districts. The plan called for twenty-seven heavy flak batteries of between four and eight 88-mm guns and nine medium flak batteries of six 37-mm guns, as well as two searchlight batteries to support mobile army operations in the field. In contrast, the plan designated one fighter regiment, thirty flak batteries, and three flak machine gun companies for the defense of the Ruhr, the main objective of the French attack. In addition, planners detailed one fighter regiment, twenty flak batteries, and two flak machine gun companies to the protection of troop assembly areas. Finally, naval flak forces received the task of protecting cities along the coast, as well as the critical commercial port facilities in Hamburg.[46]

The winter exercise of 1934 and 1935 confirmed the necessity of strong air defense forces, a lesson drawn from the Wehrmacht exercise of the previous year.[47] The exercise also established the essential blueprint for the employment of German air defense forces in 1934 and 1935, with motorized flak forces acting as a mobile shield for advancing army forces while flak forces in the homeland cooperated with fighter forces in protecting key industrial and urban areas. A report, entitled "Observations of the Commander in Chief of the Air Force concerning the Training and Exercises in 1935," reinforced these points exactly, including the importance of establishing close personal contacts between flak personnel and army commanders, as well as the necessity for close cooperation between flak forces and fighters. The report also reintroduced a tactic employed in World War I by advocating the use of flak bursts to guide fighters to their targets. Finally, the report remarked that "rapid engagement and full use of available munitions is the best method for taking advantage of flak batteries versus aircraft formations."[48] In this case doctrinal advice was simply a restatement of the obvious, as early identification of enemy aircraft and a rapid rate of fire offered the greatest probability of success.

The Costs of Air Defense

By the end of 1935, the Luftwaffe had experience with both theory and practice. In modern military establishments, however, funding levels provide the ultimate expression of a military's priorities, and the Wehrmacht was no exception. The Luftwaffe was a major recipient of the National Socialist government's largesse in the area of rearmament. In his study of Luftwaffe rearmament, the American historian Edward Homze noted that "more than any other, the aircraft industry was a child of the Nazis. . . . the aircraft industry was controlled, directed and financed by the government to a degree unparalleled by any other major industry."[49] Like its aviation sibling, air defense forces benefited from increased budget allocations during the 1930s.

In October 1934, the technical office of the Luftwaffe (LC III) completed a study of initial budget projections for continued development and testing of air defense weapons, munitions, and equipment. The study, signed by Rüdel, proposed the outlay of 3,362,200 RM, or $1,344,880, for development and testing in 1935. Major areas of planned investment included 1,542,200 RM for range-finding equipment and fire directors; 575,000 RM for radar and communications systems; 496,000 RM for explosives and ballistics; 225,000 RM for flak weapons; 200,000 RM for 20-mm light flak guns; and 51,000 RM for searchlights. These totals excluded additional funding provided by the army for several of these areas, including explosives and ballistics, flak weapons, and range-finding equipment. The most expensive items included developmental funding of 410,000 RM for fire directors; 200,000 RM for radar; 170,000 RM for automatic tracking for flak guns; 165,000 RM for range finders; 138,000 RM for flak rockets; and 120,000 RM for heavy flak guns. In contrast, the plan set aside only 51,000 RM for searchlight testing and development.[50] The program's emphases are instructive in several respects. First, the concentration on fire directors, gun radar, and range finders demonstrated the recognition within the flak forces of the need for improved equipment for tracking targets and computing firing solutions, the most difficult technical challenge of the period. Second, the expenditure for flak rockets also indicated that air defense measures included some innovative ideas. In fact, the concept for the employment of flak rockets was twofold. One proposal included the development of powder-based explosive rockets capable of bringing down aircraft at altitudes of almost 23,000 feet.[51] The second proposal involved using the rockets to carry steel wires into the air, thus creating an aerial barrier against enemy bombers during an attack.[52] Finally, the nominal expenditure with respect to searchlights reflected the sound performance achieved by the existing 150-cm system.

In total, the amounts allocated for systems development and testing were perhaps modest. In contrast, the initial proposed funding for production preparations in fiscal year 1935 was substantial, totaling 152.6 million RM, or $61,040,000. The individual production funding included 40 million RM for explosives; 27 million RM for gun tubes and gun bases; 27 million RM for fuses and fuse-setting devices; 21.6 million RM for shell casings; 8.5 RM for projectiles; 8 million RM for fire predictors and optical range finders; and 7 million RM for searchlights, sound detectors, and trucks.[53] In the course of 1935, a number of requests for increased funding came into the Technical Office, including 3 million RM for production costs of the 20-mm gun; 9 million RM for the acquisition of 88-mm guns; and an additional 3 million RM for fire directors.[54] This last request came from the Zeiss company and arose from the higher costs associated with the plan to increase the production of fire directors to eighteen per month by the summer of 1936.[55] Despite a warning by Milch in March 1935 that no extra funding could be expected due to the "pressures of the financial situation," in August 1935 air defense forces received an unexpected windfall of 50 million RM.[56] The additional money raised the final budget total for the air defense forces in 1935 to 261,040,200 RM, or $104,416,080, and included the 9 million RM requested for the 88-mm guns and over 40 million RM for munitions.[57] The Luftwaffe's investment in air defense compared favorably with the early investment in aircraft development, testing, and production. For example, the Technical Office estimated the initial budget for this area at 87.6 million RM, or $26,280,000, at the start of 1933, but actual requirements ballooned to 150.9 million RM, or $45,270,000, by July.[58]

Expanding the Luftwaffe's Ground-based Air Defense Force

Not surprisingly, a dramatic increase in the size of the air defense forces followed in the wake of higher expenditures. By November 1935, Erhard Milch, the state secretary of aviation and the second in command in the Air Ministry, drafted a plan for the proposed expansion of air defense forces for the period between 1936 and 1939. Milch had served as an artillery officer and aerial observer during World War I and later became the director of Germany's civil airline, Lufthansa, in the interwar period. Because of Göring's lack of enthusiasm for administrative duties, the mundane task of day-to-day administration of the Air Ministry fell to Milch. In the course of the Third Reich, he emerged as a major figure in organizing and preparing the Luftwaffe for war.[59] A student of Guilio Douhet's theory of strategic bombardment, Milch participated in the creation of the Luftwaffe's aviation force and the implementation of air defense and civil defense programs.[60] Already in the summer of 1933, he ordered the commencement of an extensive air-raid shelter construction program in Berlin. In 1934, he studied an idea involving the use of smoke screens to protect key areas within the Ruhr valley and investigated the feasibility of Hitler's request for "'special towers for flak, heavily armoured, rearing 100 feet above a city's skyline as a protection against low-level attack.'"[61]

The draft organizational program approved by Milch on November 11, 1935, envisioned a large-scale expansion of both the regular and the reserve air defense forces. For example, between 1935 and 1938, the number of flak regiment staffs was to increase from 9 to 28; the total of regular 88-mm batteries from 40 to 114; and the number of regular 37-mm batteries from 10 to 38. The program also included plans for the organization of three railroad-based flak battalions to be operated by regular Luftwaffe personnel. In addition, it projected a rise in the number of regular 150-cm searchlight batteries from 12 to 38, while the total of 60-cm searchlights experienced a modest augmentation from 8 batteries in 1936 to 19 batteries by 1938. Finally, the plan called for increasing the number of staff batteries, signal units, and firing ranges. The "flak battalion" *(Flakabteilung)* remained the building block of the flak forces, composed of 3 to 4 regular gun batteries, 1 searchlight battery with sound detectors, and 1 replacement battery. In turn, one heavy and one light flak battalion constituted a "flak regiment," whereas two heavy battalions formed a "heavy flak regiment."[62]

A closer examination of the flak battalions at this time shows not only an increase in numbers but also an improvement in equipment. For example, a heavy flak battalion included 3 batteries of four 88-mm guns and two 20-mm guns each, 1 battery of six 37-mm guns, 1 battery of nine 150-cm searchlights and six sound detectors, and 1 replacement battery.[63] In other words, a heavy flak regiment had twenty-four 88-mm guns, twelve 37-mm guns, twelve 20-mm guns, eighteen 150-cm searchlights, twelve sound detectors, and 2 replacement batteries. In contrast, a regular Flak regiment substituted one heavy flak battalion for a light flak battalion, including 3 batteries of twelve 20-mm guns, a battery of twelve 60-cm searchlights, and a replacement battery, for a total strength of twelve 88-mm guns, six 37-mm guns, eighteen 20-mm guns, nine 150-cm searchlights and twelve 60-cm searchlights, six sound detectors, and 2 replacement batteries.[64] The "new" flak battalions clearly possessed an improved capability and vastly increased firepower in comparison to their predecessors, the "driving sections" of 1933.

In the fall of 1935, fifteen heavy flak battalions and three light flak battalions were spread throughout the Reich's air defense districts, a number that was clearly too small to provide anything but the most limited coverage. However, by the fall of 1936, the air defense forces had doubled in size to twenty-nine mixed (a combination of heavy and light guns) and eight light flak battalions. The ground-based air defense forces now consisted of 87 heavy flak gun batteries, 53 light and medium flak gun batteries, and 29 searchlight batteries.[65] The personnel requirements necessary to fuel the increasing number of batteries were substantial. For example, the allotted personnel strength for each heavy and light battery was 143 and 179 men, respectively, and ranged from cooks to gunners.[66] This rapid expansion of the force could not be accomplished through the organization of active-duty full-time units alone. Indeed, the mobilization and training of reserve air defense forces proved critical, with twice as many reserve heavy and medium flak batteries planned and equal numbers of searchlight batteries divided between the active and reserve force. The Luftwaffe undertook a number of steps to facilitate the mobilization of these forces in the event of a crisis. One measure involved the selection of personnel from recruiting districts in the vicinity of the mobilization areas. A second entailed the concentration of weapons, equipment, and munitions at specific collection points within the mobilization area.[67] A final measure emphasized organizing motorized reserve air defense units.[68] In conjunction with the ongoing expansion of the flak arm, the mobility of ground-based air defense forces remained a primary point of emphasis. Motorization of the reserve units offered two major advantages to the Wehrmacht. First, motorized units could be moved more quickly to sites throughout the Reich in the event of war. Second, the Luftwaffe's commitment to the protection of army forces in the field required a highly mobile force to keep pace with ground forces conducting offensive operations.

In July 1936, the Command Section of the Air Ministry issued a revised organizational program for the flak artillery that essentially recapitulated the major points in the program of November 1935. The revised program did provide details, however, concerning the specific organizational structure of the railroad battalions and also introduced a new element into the Luftwaffe's ground-based air defense force with the planned establishment of barrage balloon batteries.[69] In February 1936, Rüdel directed the formation of barrage balloon test units to determine the effectiveness of balloon barriers for air defense. The army weapons office was responsible for monitoring the balloon trials.[70] The objective of the balloon barriers was fourfold:

a. Destroy the enemy aircraft in a collision with the balloons' wire anchor.
b. Force the enemy aircraft to fly around the barrier and thereby obstruct bomb delivery.
c. Force the enemy aircraft to greater heights and thereby reduce bombing accuracy.
d. Employ mobile balloon barrier units to unsettle enemy aircrews for a morale effect.[71]

In October 1936, the Luftwaffe was satisfied with the results of the initial trials and ordered further tests. Prior to 1939, the balloon barriers appeared to be too effective, constituting a significant hazard for Luftwaffe aircraft and leading to several accidents. These mishaps involving German aircraft resulted in restricted training heights for balloon operations.[72] The outbreak of the war caught the experimental balloon barrier units largely unprepared for operational employment; however, these units quickly adapted to the changed circumstances and eventually constituted an important element in the defense of point targets from low-level attack.[73]

In 1936, the German aircraft industry experienced a "monetary pinch" due to lack of foreign exchange, increased domestic spending, and interservice competition for defense funds. By the last quarter of 1937, the situation had worsened following severe fiscal and raw materials restrictions that forced a decrease in production.[74] In contrast, the growth of air defense forces continued to accelerate. Already in November 1935, the Command Section of the Air Ministry, responding to higher industrial manufacturing capacity, substantially raised production target levels for the period between October 1, 1936, and April 1, 1937. Table 3.1 shows the forecast procurement goals for 1936 and 1937.[75] An analysis of the procurement goals reveals only one area in which acquisition was scheduled to be reduced. The decrease in demand for 60-cm searchlights resulted in part from a move to switch resources from its production to the manufacture of the more capable 150-cm searchlight. In September 1936, the Technical Office released 24 million RM, or $9,600,000, for the acquisition of 361 150-cm searchlights.[76]

The rapid expansion of the flak force in the mid-1930s resulted in problems for some air force agencies. In a letter of October 12, 1936, the Luftwaffe's chief of supply, General Karl Kitzinger, complained about the growing difficulty in adequately supplying the various organizations within the air force. He noted that, in the twelve-month period between October 1, 1935, and October 1, 1936, the Luftwaffe had increased in size by over 5,000 aircraft and that the total number of regular and reserve flak gun and searchlight batteries had quintupled, from 86 in 1935 to 449 in 1936. Despite the fivefold expansion of the flak, Kitzinger still expected a dramatic improvement in the delivery of flak equipment and munitions by April 1, 1937.[77]

The production targets for the flak arm were not the result of the Luftwaffe's wishful thinking. These goals proved both realistic and attainable despite the fiscal and resource restrictions that slowed industrial production throughout 1937. Table 3.2 provides a comparison of the 1937 forecast goals with actual force strengths as of January 1, 1938, and May 1, 1938.[78] Despite the fiscal crisis of 1937, the acquisition of major air defense weapons systems and equipment con-

Table 3.1 Flak Procurement Goals

	October 1, 1936	April 1, 1937
20-mm flak guns	1,200	1,950
37-mm flak guns	450	550
88-mm flak guns	1,110	1,400
Fire directors	286	330
150-cm searchlights	734	854
Sound detectors	556	702
60-cm searchlights	530	480

Table 3.2 Flak Procurement Goal versus Actual Strength

	Procurement Goal April 1, 1937	Actual Strength January 1, 1938	Actual Strength May 1, 1938
20-mm flak guns	1,950	2,117	2,284
37-mm flak guns	550	517	668
88-mm flak guns	1,400	1,900	1,984
Fire directors	330	363	390
Sound detectors	702	764	927
150-cm searchlights	854	998	1,070
60-cm searchlights	480	244	267

tinued to climb steadily. In contrast, in the area of munitions production, the resource crisis led to a significant shortage in the production of flak ammunition by the spring of 1938.[79] For example, in April 1938 the German armaments industry had produced only 2.7 million of a requested 5.3 million 88-mm shells, or 50 percent of the target. Likewise, the armaments industry's output of 37-mm rounds was only 3 million of the requested 5.7 million, or 53 percent of the target. Even worse, the Luftwaffe inventory showed only 33.5 million 20-mm rounds compared with the forecast of 78.8 million rounds, or 43 percent of the inventory goal.[80] Despite these shortfalls, the Luftwaffe still estimated that its reserves of 88-mm and 37-mm shells would last for 52 and 53 days, respectively, while the reserve of 20-mm ammunition was expected to hold out for 121 days.[81]

The Development Plan of 1937

Despite some production delays, German ground-based air defense forces had undergone a manifold expansion and made significant progress since 1932. By 1938, the Luftwaffe's air defense force was arguably the finest in the world. Rüdel, now a major general, continued to play a key role in the development of Germany's air defense system. In August 1937, he released a report, entitled "Development Program for the Flak Artillery, 1937," in which he updated the development program of 1932. In the second paragraph of the document, Rüdel provided a short synopsis of air defense doctrine:

> The flak artillery has the task, alone or in cooperation with our fighters, to protect every vital infrastructure of the state against aerial attack including the Wehrmacht, the economy, cities, the population, as well as the fighting forces of the army and the navy. In order to do this air defense forces must be in a position to effectively combat enemy aircraft and the crews

> [of these aircraft] through moral and material effects from successfully carrying out their designs.[82]

Rüdel's brief doctrinal discourse recognized that ground-based air defense units could conduct operations either as an independent force or in cooperation with Luftwaffe fighters. His comments also indirectly addressed a major debate within the air defense forces stemming from World War I. On the one side, some Luftwaffe officers, like Milch, viewed the primary objective of flak forces as the destruction of the attacking aircraft. On the other side, many flak commanders believed that the standard of success was forcing attacking aircraft to break off their bomb run or impeding their aim during the final run-in to the target. Rüdel's Flak Development Program of 1932 seemed to favor the adoption of the former standard, while his formulation in 1937 appeared to favor the latter position. Despite the implications of this debate for future expectations regarding the flak arm, the question remained unresolved. Would the measure of effectiveness lie in the number of aircraft brought down, or would it be found in the more indeterminate standard associated with success in protecting the bomber's intended target from damage?

A handbook published prior to the war by the Air Defense League entitled *Air Defense: Guidelines for Everyone* also addressed the issue of measures of effectiveness for the general public. The league's handbook identified three primary duties for ground-based air defense forces in the event of hostilities. The first was to keep an enemy air force at an altitude that would prevent precise bombing. The second task was "if at all possible to shoot down the aircraft, or at least to force it to break off the attack." The final duty was to force enemy reconnaissance flights to the "highest altitude possible."[83] Clearly, the handbook favored using a measure of effectiveness tied to preventing enemy bombers from being able to hit the intended target. In turn, the destruction of the attacker constituted a desirable, but secondary, objective. In addition, the author of the handbook provided a caveat to his discussion of ground-based air defenses by asserting that "the best air defense will always be attack-ready fighters."[84] In contrast to this position, Major Wolfgang Pickert (later the Luftwaffe's last inspector of the Flak Artillery) argued in 1937 that both flak and fighters were key elements of the air defense system, but that fighters would essentially "support" the flak in a future conflict.[85] These two positions set the boundaries of the Luftwaffe's doctrinal discussion concerning the relative merits of flak versus fighters, a debate that would continue throughout the war years.

The Development Program of 1937 was designed to prepare the air defense units for a coming conflict. The program also demonstrated Rüdel's appreciation of the impact of technology on both offensive and defensive operations. He remarked on the necessity for developments in air defense systems to keep pace with advances in aviation technology. He noted that this was especially important because the development and production of new aircraft required less time than that of flak artillery and associated defense systems. In this respect, Rüdel identified five "special factors" that needed to be taken into account in the development of Germany's air defense system. First, he called for weapons capable of engaging aircraft at an altitude of between 33,000 and 39,000 feet traveling at speeds of up to 375 mph. Second, he commented on the necessity for finding effective methods to engage aircraft operating in instrument conditions (aircraft flying in or above the clouds) and aircraft using quieter engines. Finally, he identified the use of increased protective armor in contemporary aircraft and described the associated difficulty in shooting down these aircraft.[86]

In some respects Rüdel proved prescient in his ability to forecast aircraft performance improvements and future air defense requirements. In the case of airspeed and service ceiling,[87] his projections proved to be at the limits of Allied aviation technology during World War II. For example, the RAF's fastest operational aircraft, the plywood Mosquito, attained a maximum speed of 380 mph and a service ceiling of 34,500 feet, making it almost impervious to the Luftwaffe's air defenses during nighttime "nuisance" raids over Germany. In contrast, each of the mainstays of the Allied bomber forces—the Avro Lancaster, the Boeing B-17 Flying Fortress, and the Consolidated B-24 Liberator—was limited to a maximum speed of approximately 290 mph. The Lancaster had a service ceiling of 24,500 feet, the Flying Fortress, 35,000 feet, and the Liberator 28,000 feet.[88] However, B-24s and B-17s with a full bomb load were limited to ceilings of 24,000 feet and 30,000 feet, respectively.[89] Furthermore, U.S. Army Air Force bomber crews rarely conducted operations above 30,000 feet because of the physiological dangers associated with high-altitude operations and the equipment problems experienced in conditions of extreme cold.[90]

Rüdel's discussion of the need for a system to track and engage aircraft operating under instrument conditions was, on the other hand, a tribute to his ability to discern the nature of an evolving threat. Likewise, the introduction of quieter or muffled engines would complicate the work of the sound-detector crews during the war, while improved armor protection such as that enjoyed by the Flying Fortress would allow it to absorb a great deal of punishment and keep on flying. In fact, by 1945 the ability of the Flying Fortress to endure massive damage was legendary. For example, in a raid against Berlin a flak shell hit one B-17, blowing a three-foot hole in the top of the fuselage, but the crew were still able to bomb the target and return home.[91] Rüdel's analysis of future needs demonstrated his own foresight as an operational planner, as did his suggestions for specific systems development. In the end, however, foresight must be married to both resolve and resources; otherwise, like Cassandra's fate, the ability to foresee future developments remains a prophecy unheard or unheeded.

The Development Program of 1937 was an ambitious plan for matching expectations of future warfare with the acquisition of weapons and equipment needed to counter the emergent aerial threat. A major emphasis of the program was improving the performance of the various flak guns, for example, by increasing the muzzle velocity of all flak guns to decrease projectile flight times and raise engagement altitudes. One initiative in this area included the development of a new 105-mm heavy flak gun for the defense of important sites within Germany. Initial development of the 105-mm began in 1933, with the first guns reaching operational production in the spring of 1938.[92] The 105-mm had a muzzle velocity of 2,891 feet per second and an effective ceiling of 31,005 feet, compared with the 88-mm's muzzle velocity of 2,690 feet per second and effective ceiling of 26,248 feet.[93] When considering these effective engagement altitudes, it is important to keep in mind that as late as 1939 the U.S. Army Air Corps experienced problems with engine synchronization when flying the new B-17 Flying Fortress at altitudes above 25,000 feet.[94] It is also worth noting that the Reich Air Defense League closely followed the development of American aviation in the period and featured the YB-17B prototype on the front cover of a November 1937 issue of *The Siren.*[95] By raising the effective engagement altitude to over 30,000 feet, the 105-mm flak gun offered a clear example of the flak arm's recognition of advances in aviation technology and the commitment to remain a step ahead in the defensive arena.

Technological Improvements

In a further effort to increase the reach of ground defenses and despite the improved performance offered by the 105-mm, the Luftwaffe had also initiated development of both a 128-mm and a 150-mm flak gun in 1936. The Luftwaffe tested a prototype of the first 128-mm gun in the second half of 1937, with excellent results. The effective engagement altitude of the 128-mm gun was slightly over 35,000 feet, with a maximum firing altitude of an astounding 48,559 feet. In contrast to the 128-mm gun, efforts to construct a 150-mm flak gun proved less promising. Both Krupp and Rheinmetall developed prototypes in 1938, but the modest performance improvements offered by the guns combined with substantial resource requirements led to their cancellation in early 1940. The project for a 150-mm was the first step in the development of a "supergun," but it would not be the last. The main problem with guns above the caliber of 105-mm was their size and weight. For example, the 128-mm gun was almost twenty-six feet long and weighed over twenty-six tons.[96] Not only did these guns consume vast amounts of resources in their production, but their size also restricted their use to fixed sites or rail cars. In any event, neither would be available for operational use prior to the start of the war.[97]

By the summer of 1937, Rüdel clearly was attempting to extend the technological envelope of the flak guns. Likewise, he identified a second priority, the development of either an infrared or a radar tracking system, as "urgent and of critical importance." In fact, he went so far as to describe the question of nonoptical tracking measures "as a question of life and death for the flak artillery based on the development of instrument flying."[98] These systems would allow air defense crews to acquire and engage aircraft operating at night or in the clouds. The German navy had pioneered the development of radar within the German military and had conducted initial tests in the summer of 1933. The army quickly became interested in the possibilities and by 1934 commenced initial development of radar and infrared tracking devices.[99] At the end of 1936, Colonel Wolfgang Martini, later commander of the Luftwaffe's Air Reporting Service, observed radar tests that allowed for the identification of aircraft at a range of up to eight kilometers. Martini left the test impressed with radar, but he saw its primary use as a landing aid for aircraft rather than a system with which to identify incoming enemy aircraft.[100] Almost two years later, on November 23, 1938, Göring also witnessed tests using both radar and infrared tracking devices.[101] Clearly, the senior leadership was aware of the advances in radar, but the Luftwaffe proved ambivalent in its pursuit of this new technology, most likely a result of its demonstrated penchant for weapons with offensive rather than defensive applications.

By 1939, German commercial firms had constructed three different test models: the A-1 or Freya radar developed by Gema, the A-2 developed by Lorenz, and Telefunken's A-3. The Freya was a general search radar with a range of between twenty-four and forty-five miles and an accuracy of plus or minus 2,200 to 4,400 yards for range finding and plus or minus five to ten degrees in target location. However, it could not provide altitude information. The A-2 and A-3, although capable of locating aircraft at maximum ranges of only 6 to 7.5 miles, were considerably more precise with a range-finding error of plus or minus 110 yards and an accuracy of 3 to 4 degrees for the former and only .25 degrees for the latter.[102] The Freya allowed for initial target acquisition; the A-2 and especially the A-3 provided the accuracy needed to guide flak and searchlight batteries onto the target. The Luftwaffe, however, proved somewhat slow in recognizing the importance of radar systems for air defense applications and halting in its pursuit of their development. In the end, radar would not be the only area in which the Luftwaffe would pay for its technological foot-dragging.

The Development Program of 1937 also called for the introduction of a 200-cm searchlight to be used in fixed positions as well as on railcars. The emphasis on the use of railcars for both heavy-caliber flak guns and searchlights highlighted the importance that the Luftwaffe assigned to the mobility of the air defense forces. The emphasis on mobility reflected in part the requirement to support advancing forces, as well as the recognition that mobile forces allowed for a flexible defense of urban and industrial targets within Germany. Rüdel's program concluded by calling for the completion of barrage balloon barriers, including increasing their maximum altitudes as well as their effective coverage. He also emphasized the employment of balloon barriers as a means for protecting against low-level aerial attacks.[103] Likewise, the discussion of the development needs of the barrage balloon force reflected Rüdel's satisfaction with the progress made by the experimental barrage balloon units.

The Debate Concerning the Command of the Luftwaffe's Air Defenses

The Development Program of 1937 clearly demonstrated the Luftwaffe's commitment to ground-based air defenses. This commitment was not based, however, merely upon the foresight of one man. The general staff of the Luftwaffe examined the issue of air defense operations in a series of studies and presentations between 1936 and 1938. In October 1936, Major Paul Deichmann, an officer in the General Staff and later a lieutenant general, organized a presentation on the Luftwaffe's role in a future war. All Luftwaffe group commanders, flak regiment and battalion commanders, and air force schools received a copy of the presentation. In addition, only Luftwaffe officers were cleared to view the top secret study. Deichmann's "Fundamentals for the Operational Conduct of Air Warfare" discussed the common misperception within the Luftwaffe that one had simply to completely destroy every industrial center within an enemy's homeland and the war would be over. He observed that this view was fallacious and noted that there were 2,359 important armaments targets in Germany alone, including aircraft assembly plants, munitions factories, and storage depots. He therefore contended that the Luftwaffe's mission needed to focus on the destruction of a "few decisive" targets, a view similar to the U.S. Army Air Corps Tactical School's "industrial web" theory. Deichmann remarked that although the Luftwaffe was well schooled in working with the army, its ability to conduct independent operational warfare was much less well developed.[104]

Although Deichmann's discussion of German offensive aerial operations was important, the most interesting aspect of the study was his discussion of the air defense of Germany, a subject that constituted one-half of the entire presentation. The air defense portion of the study emphasized the protection of the German homeland in general and defense of the Ruhr industrial region in particular. Deichmann highlighted the need for flexibility in employing flak forces, fighters, *or both* in the defense of specific areas or sites. He also addressed a prickly issue involving command and control of air defense forces in the various air districts. He explicitly stated that the Luftwaffe rejected the creation of a position known as higher commander of flak forces within each air district on the level of the Luftwaffe pilot commanders of the air district during wartime.[105] This point reflected a debate within the Luftwaffe that centered on the opposition of operational pilots to the appointment of flak artillery officers to command positions in air units. In 1935, the Luftwaffe leadership did appoint a senior flak commander to coordinate the training and operations of air defense forces within each air district; however, this position was strictly limited to control over flak units.[106] Deichmann's statement was a further attempt to define the exact role, or more appropriately to limit the authority, of these commanders in the event of war. He again emphasized the importance of a centralized organization in which a flying officer exercised command over all air units and flak forces within his district. He then stated, "The [Luftwaffe] leadership views the combination of offensive and defensive forces *in a single hand* as the strength of our air defense system."[107]

After establishing the importance of centralized command of air defense forces, Deichmann moved on to a discussion of the proposed employment of the air defenses in the event of war. He began with the curious analogy that "a clever man takes his umbrella with him and opens it if it threatens to rain, rather than waiting to go get it [only after it has started to rain]." Deichmann contended that this was the principle guiding the peacetime organization of the Luftwaffe's own active-duty and reserve flak forces and the effort to establish an air defense catalog of vital installations. The catalog provided a complete listing of all installations and structures that would or could require air defense forces in the event of war. These installations included vital armaments and production centers, critical transportation hubs, and important military installations. Deichmann noted that the number of these installations was too great to protect them all. He then introduced a three-tiered priority system:

Category I: Contains political, military, or economic installations of decisive importance to the war effort that must be adequately protected under all circumstances. Without exception, these [installations] receive protection by the creation of flak artillery bases in their vicinity during peacetime that are responsible for providing initial defense without delay [in the event of war].

Category II: Contains political, military, or economic installations of essential importance for the prosecution of the war that require continuous protection, unless the situation makes this unnecessary. After the creation of the reserve flak units, these [installations] will receive protection from the reserve forces and equipment stationed in the specific region.

> Category III: This category contains all installations that under specific circumstances could require protection, whether due to heightened threat from a neighboring state, due to a planned or actual operation of the army, the navy, or the air force, or due to the actual destruction of similar facilities.[108]

This three-tiered system for organizing air defense priorities provided a viable framework for allocating the Luftwaffe's ground-based air defenses.

Deichmann's study made it clear that despite the rapid expansion of the active-duty and reserve forces, flak artillery still could not cover every potential object of attack, a fact indicated by his remark that the majority of installations fell within category III. The continued shortage of air defense assets was somewhat ironic based on the fact that by the fall of 1937 there were 115 heavy flak gun batteries, 69 light flak gun batteries, 14 permanent training batteries, and 37 searchlight batteries, an overall increase of 28 percent in the size of the regular flak arm since 1936.[109] In this respect, the study presented the most profound paradox confronting Germany's ground-based air defenses. The more resources that were invested in creating an industrialized economy geared to conduct of war, the more air defenses were needed to protect the steadily expanding number of critical industrial and military sites throughout the Reich.

With respect to ground-based air defense doctrine, the Deichmann study essentially focused on the conduct of point defense *(Objektschutz),* an area of emphasis since the first days of the Great War. In fact, Luftwaffe exercises throughout 1936 featured the practice of employing flak forces in point defense. In 1936, air defense forces had sufficient opportunity to test theory through practice as the Luftwaffe participated in three major regional exercises, as well as joining army forces in a five-day joint maneuver in Hessen. The Luftwaffe also held exercises to test the air defenses and the civil defense preparations of major cities, including Dresden.[110] In addition, individual flak sections conducted small-scale exercises such as a two-day field trial in October involving a single searchlight battery from Flak Regiment 12.[111] As in the previous year, the Air Ministry released its annual evaluation of the lessons learned during the 1936 exercises. In this report, the air staff identified several areas of suggested improvement for air defenses, emphasizing the need for centralized control of all ground-based air defense forces active in the defense of a particular installation or area. The report noted that the centralization of command was especially important because of the large numbers of less trained reserve forces that by implication required more control than their regular force counterparts. In addition, numerous observations concerned improving the cooperation between the flak and army forces. Finally, the report called for the greater participation of fighter aircraft in exercises held by the Air Reporting Service in order for pilots to be in a position to thoroughly evaluate aerial reporting procedures.[112]

In 1937, the Luftwaffe continued putting theory into practice through the largest series of war games and exercises involving air and ground forces during the interwar period. The Wehrmacht maneuver held in September was viewed by Hitler and the Wehrmacht leadership and included all three services in an exercise that stretched across the North German Plain.[113] The Luftwaffe contributed 62,000 air force personnel, 1,337 aircraft, 639 flak guns, 160 searchlights, and 9,720 vehicles alone to the exercise.[114] In total, this force included seventeen bomber groups, seven fighter groups, one dive-bomber group, aerial reconnaissance units, and six flak regiments. One objective of the exercise was to test the state of the German civil defense system. Between September 20 and September 25, "red" and "blue" air forces traded attacks against major urban centers. On September 20, the red air force simulated a daylight attack on Hamburg and a night attack on Hannover; the blue air force struck Berlin in a morning bombing raid. Further attacks followed, including a raid against oil storage facilities in Stettin during which the defending forces employed smoke generators in an attempt to shield the target.[115]

The Luftwaffe learned a number of valuable lessons during the fall exercise. For example, one evaluation described the system for passing orders within the air defense network as "too slow and bureaucratic." The postexercise appraisal also noted the need to improve the speed of communications within the Air Reporting Service. In addition, the attempt at creating a smoke screen over Stettin was judged a failure as a result of commencing the operation too early, leading to the dissipation of the smoke before the bombers reached the area. Despite the areas noted for improvements, the overall exercise evaluation concluded that both flak and fighter forces had performed well over the course of the maneuvers.[116]

The Luftwaffe's War in Spain

In the late 1930s, the Luftwaffe gained practical experience not only from field maneuvers but also in actual combat operations. The Spanish civil war (1936–1939) provided a golden opportunity for a limited number of Luftwaffe personnel to gain firsthand experience in the art and science of warfare. It also presented a chance for the Luftwaffe's flak forces to test their doctrine, their equipment, and themselves in the crucible of war. When Hitler decided to support Franco and his Nationalist rebellion at the end of July 1936, one of the first German ships dispatched from Hamburg carried both German "volunteers" and equipment, including twenty 20-mm flak guns. A corporal of the flak artillery accompanied the guns and received the task of training Spanish forces in the use of the weapons. The corporal, however, could not speak Spanish, and as a result Lieutenant Hajo Herrmann, a transport pilot and the future innovator of German night fighter tactics, delivered evening training sessions in French on the use of the guns after his daily ferry flights between North Africa and the Iberian Peninsula. Herrmann's training course also included live firing drills at hot air balloons as they drifted over the Rio Guadalquivir. The Nationalist troops quickly completed the ad hoc training course, and the guns were sent to several sites throughout Spain.[117]

The establishment of the Condor Legion in October 1936 escalated German support. The Condor Legion included some 5,000 Luftwaffe personnel, 100 aircraft, and one flak section of eight gun batteries. In turn, one of these batteries was designated as a training unit for Nationalist forces; the remaining five 88-mm batteries and two 20-mm and 37-mm batteries constituted the legion's operational ground-based air defense force.[118] General Hugo Sperrle, commander of the Condor Legion, divided his mobile flak forces between positions along the front lines and sites at German airfields.[119] In the first stages of the conflict, the modest nature of the aerial threat posed by Republican forces and the Nationalists' own shortage of artillery resulted in the extensive use of the heavy flak guns in the role of ground artillery.[120] In fact, during one period of 277 days, flak guns participated in 377 engagements, but only 31 of these were in the air defense role. Baron Wolfram von Richthofen, chief of staff of the Condor Legion, remarked in his diary on this role reversal, noting that "the flak, to the horror of experts in Berlin, has consistently been used as the backbone of the ground artillery."[121] In fact, throughout the conflict German flak guns provided their most valuable contributions in the role of ground artillery.

By 1938, the Republican aerial threat had increased, and the German crews achieved some remarkable success such as one engagement where a flak unit scored two "confirmed" kills and one "probable" with the expenditure of only thirty-six rounds. While this claim appears somewhat unlikely, such reports did serve to raise future expectations with respect to the flak arm.[122] By the end of the war in early 1939, the Luftwaffe "volunteers" of the Condor Legion had shot down 386 Republican aircraft of which 59 had fallen to flak guns, or a little over 15 percent of the total.[123] Taking into account the circumstances surrounding the use of flak guns in the civil war and the small size of the force, the fact that flak units accounted for 15 percent of the legion's total is impressive. However, flak forces also experienced some problems, as when flak batteries failed to engage Republican aircraft successfully during night bombing raids on Vinaroz and Bernicalo because of the absence of searchlights.[124] By the end of the war, the flak forces of the Condor Legion had acquitted themselves well in the fighting, and the experience they had gained in Spain soon would be put to use on battlefields across Europe.

The experience of the flak gun batteries in Spain provided the Luftwaffe with some valuable experience for future operations. On the one hand, the gun batteries clearly demonstrated the effectiveness of the 88-mm gun in support of ground combat operations.[125] In Spain, the Luftwaffe modified its standard square configuration in favor of a diamond configuration that allowed three batteries to engage targets along the front lines while the fourth battery provided anti-aircraft cover.[126] On the other hand, the failure of the flak batteries in night operations resulted from the lack of searchlights and highlighted the need for improving the flak's capabilities during periods of darkness. In the final analysis, however, the overall performance of the flak in Spain confirmed the faith of the Luftwaffe in the flak as a jack-of-all-trades *(Mädchen für alles)* capable of performing a variety of missions from air defense to artillery support.[127]

Not only the Luftwaffe but also foreign observers of the war began drawing lessons from the conflict. The president of the French senatorial commission for aviation, Paul Bénazet, viewed the war as testament to modern flak artillery. In an essay for the *Petit Parisien,* Bénazet argued that the operations in Spain showed that the speed and altitudes attained by modern bombers diminished the effect of fighters. Furthermore, he proposed improving French civil defense measures as well as increasing the number of flak gun batteries throughout France. Lutz Hübner, the German correspondent reporting the story for the Air Defense League, remarked that, although debatable, Bénazet's conclusions were worthy of consideration for Germany.[128]

The Years 1933–1938 in Review

In the period between 1933 and 1938, Luftwaffe flak forces experienced an unprecedented expansion. In 1933, the personnel strength of the "driving sections" numbered slightly in excess of 5,100. By October 1, 1937, the air defense force included 1,013 officers and 46,500 enlisted personnel, and by the end of 1938 there were over 70,000 men serving in the flak, searchlight, and barrage balloon batteries of the Luftwaffe.[129] By November 1938, the number of air defense batteries totaled 372, with 160 heavy gun batteries, 140 light gun batteries, and 72 searchlight batteries.[130] In addition, extensive exercises and improvements in training and instruction throughout the flak and searchlight forces accompanied the twelvefold increase in personnel during this five-year period. Already in 1936, the growth of the flak arm led to a redistribution of existing firing ranges between the army and the Luftwaffe.[131] Furthermore, in 1937 the Luftwaffe redesignated the flak artillery school at Rerik as the Flak Artillery Training and Experimental Battalion, and on April 1 the Luftwaffe attached one flak regiment consisting of a heavy and light gun battalion and a searchlight battalion to the Luftwaffe Training Division (Luftwaffen-Lehrdivision).[132]

In addition to the personnel and material expansion experienced within the air defense force, the combined efforts of the Flak Inspectorate and the Army Weapons Office promoted significant technological progress from gun tubes to range finders. In contrast to the general atmosphere within the Wehrmacht, where each individual service competed in the fiscal counterpart of a Darwinian contest of the survival of the fittest, the flak arm had a historic and friendly relationship with the army's armament office.[133] In the early 1930s, Rüdel and the chief of the Army Armament Office, General Karl Becker, maintained a close personal and professional relationship that allowed them to work together effectively in the development of flak guns and equipment.[134] This working arrangement helped the air defense forces in some respects to avoid the wasteful and costly competition for resources occurring between the services in other areas. The activities of the flak forces in support of ground operations in Spain also highlighted the value of the flak arm in ground combat, a lesson that the army leadership would take to heart after the campaign against France and the Low Countries in 1940.

In November 1938, the Luftwaffe abolished the existing six air districts *(Luftkreise)* and replaced these with four numbered air regions *(Luftflotten)* and ten new air districts *(Luftgaukommandos)*. The new air districts received noncontinuous roman numerals coincidental with the existing army districts throughout the Reich. The new air districts included the annexed areas within Austria and the Sudetenland. Although subordinated to the commander of an air region, the commanders of each air district exercised authority over all Luftwaffe flying and ground units within their areas and were responsible for coordinating the actions of fighters and flak forces in air defense.[135] In addition, the Luftwaffe created Air Defense Commands (Luftverteidigungskommandos) to increase protection to areas particularly threatened by aerial attacks such as the cities of Hamburg and Berlin or the industrial area within the Ruhr valley.[136] The reorganization into air districts essentially created ten independent air defense areas with defined geographic boundaries within the Reich. Time would tell if this system would meet the demands placed on it by modern air warfare.

During the prewar military buildup, Hitler and Göring had lavished substantial sums on the creation of the finest ground-based air defense force in the world. Only two questions remained to be answered: Would these forces be used in anger? And, if so, would they be effective? By 1939, Hitler had long since laid his plans for conquest, and the threatening clouds of war began to take shape on the European horizon.[137] If some European political and military leaders failed, or refused, to see the indications of the gathering storm, they at least recognized that in the next war, aerial warfare would play a key role in determining the victor. British prime minister Stanley Baldwin's oft-cited observation that "the bomber will always get through" offered one viewpoint on the efficacy of defending against aerial attacks.[138] In contrast, Hermann Göring's exclamation "If an enemy bomber reaches the Ruhr, my name is not Hermann Göring. You can call me Meier" provided a more sanguinary view of the ability of air defenses to protect Germany successfully against attacks from the "third dimension."[139] By 1939, it was clear that both men could not be right. The course of the looming war would provide the arena for testing the idea of strategic bombardment and the effectiveness of Germany's air defenses, a test of decided importance to both sides.

CHAPTER FOUR

First Lessons in the School of War 1939–1940

By the beginning of 1939, one of the most grandiose construction projects in the history of the Third Reich was beginning to take shape. The erection of a line of concrete fortifications stretching from Germany's border with Switzerland to the North Sea reflected Hitler's own "Maginot mentality" and his belief in the efficacy of air defenses.[1] The Air Defense Zone, West sought to create an aerial barrier upon which waves of French and British bombers would break against fortified flak positions and swarms of fighters. Prior to the Luftwaffe's involvement, the army began building an interlocking line of defensive positions along Germany's western border, the West Wall. In June 1938, State Secretary of Aviation General Erhard Milch ordered the creation of an Air Defense Zone, West involving the construction of a secondary line of fortifications, including positions for flak guns, searchlights, and sound detectors to be integrated with the West Wall defenses.[2] The Air Defense Zone was not intended to constitute an impenetrable barrier; rather, it was envisioned as a type of "reception line" designed to disperse enemy aircraft or drive them to higher altitudes.[3] The air defense forces of the West Wall would engage enemy air forces as they attempted to penetrate German airspace and once again as they attempted to leave. In this respect, the defenses of the West Wall formed an adjunct to the air defenses, protecting important urban and industrial areas within the Reich by forcing attacking aircraft to fight their way into and out of Germany on their way to the target.[4]

Building an Aerial Barrier

The initial emphasis on the construction of air defenses centered not surprisingly on the border west of the industrial Ruhr valley. On October 22, 1938, the General Staff of the Luftwaffe ordered a buildup of the defenses to the north and the south of the Ruhr. In addition, the directive set the deadline for completion of the Air Defense Zone as October 1, 1939.[5] The selected date of completion hardly seems coincidental when one takes into account the fact that by October 1938 Hitler's brinkmanship had led Europe to the edge of war but had gained the Sudetenland for the Third Reich. Still, by the fall of 1938, Hitler's ambition was far from satiated, and the army and air defense positions along the West Wall provided a jumping-off point for German forces in the planned war against France and Britain. Likewise, when Hitler decided to attack Poland first, these fortifications also could serve as a bulwark to protect Germany's back as Hitler turned his attentions to the east.[6]

In February 1939, a general staff officer, Major Freiherr von Hanstein, delivered a presentation on the western ground and air defenses. Hanstein remarked that "in itself the Air Defense Zone–West is completely a matter for the Luftwaffe." He described the defenses as being composed of two lines, the first consisting of 20-mm and 37-mm light flak guns, and the second consisting of heavy flak guns. Hanstein then observed:

> The purpose of the Air Defense Zone–West is to create an aerial barrier. The enemy formations will be forced to an altitude between 19,500 feet and 26,000 feet. This means at once a loss of time and increased fuel consumption during the initial penetration and a corresponding decrease in the range of action. Furthermore, the necessity of having to climb to a higher altitude will limit the weight of the bomb load and finally flying at such heights means an extraordinary strain on the flying crews.

Hanstein then addressed an added benefit offered by the West Wall:

> In order to bomb point targets the aircraft must descend and then climb again to 26,000 feet on the return flight. In the meantime, the fighters are also in the air. Whichever aircraft are now badly damaged or for any reason are unable to reach the safe altitude of 26,000 feet, will again be the prey of the A.D.Z. [Air Defense Zone]. And so one can imagine, that the existence alone of the A.D.Z., so to speak an "A.D.Z. in being," is in any event not conducive to enemy aerial attacks.[7]

Military planners calculated that enemy bombers would require up to five minutes to cross the zone, which varied in width from as little as twenty kilometers in the north to fifty kilometers west of the Ruhr.[8] Likewise, construction plans called for flak sites to be situated within the zone to allow each aircraft to be engaged by three to five batteries.[9] The total number of positions completed by the fall of 1939 was 197 sites for heavy flak guns and 48 sites for light flak guns, at a cost of 400 million RM, or $160 million. These defenses allowed for the employment of 788 88-mm or 105-mm guns and 576 20-mm or 37-mm guns, with three batteries to engage any single target flying at an altitude of up to 22,750 feet.[10]

In point of fact, the West Wall was also one of the very first attempts to construct an integrated air defense network for coordinating the operations of ground-based air defenses with an interceptor force along a broad front. The ground-based defenses consisted of the entire spectrum of air defense assets, including flak guns, searchlights, sound detectors, and barrage balloons, and relied heavily on timely warning from the Air Reporting Service.[11] Again, it should be noted that the Luftwaffe did not view the West Wall as an independent and stand-alone system for the defense of Germany against aerial attack but as an adjunct to the prevailing emphasis on point defenses. In addition, the West Wall maintained the doctrinal focus on the cooperation of fighters and air defense forces. In an essay written before the war, Colonel Alfred Schlemm, the chief of staff to the commander of the Air Defense Zone, West, made exactly this point with his observation that "the effect of the [flak] batteries will be supplemented by the fighters, the barrage balloons, and the searchlights."[12]

On March 1, 1939, Göring boasted: "Since the 1st March, 1935, I and my colleagues, carrying out the Führer's intentions, had created at high speed the most modern air force which any nation could possess. I am proud that the German Luftwaffe can serve as a powerful instrument of the Führer's creative statesmanship. . . . Fear of our invincible air squadrons and our ultramodern, splendidly trained flak artillery has given many a hate-filled warmonger abroad bad dreams."[13] Göring's penchant for hyperbole aside, the Luftwaffe and the forces of the flak artillery had improved dramatically from the modest beginnings of 1932. The Air Defense Zone, West was but one further step in this process of modernization, and not merely a gigantic edifice to self-delusion.

After the war, General of the Flak Artillery Walther von Axthelm remarked simply that "the Air Defense Zone, West did not meet the expectations associated with it."[14] In this case, von Axthelm's remark was somewhat misleading, as the Air Defense Zone must be seen in the context of the times. For example, British doctrine throughout the 1930s called for the daylight bombing of targets from approximately 10,000 feet; from this altitude, the flak forces of the ADZ would have been highly effective in either engaging these aircraft or forcing them to higher altitudes. The RAF simply chose to ignore the danger posed by anti-aircraft fires at an altitude of 10,000 feet and relied on the speed of the aircraft to get it through the flak zone quickly.[15] Ironically, this was an assumption shared by the U.S. Army Air Corps, as evidenced in a remark by an instructor at the Air Corps Tactical School, Captain Lawrence S. Kuter, that "anti-aircraft may be annoying but should be ignored."[16] If some within the RAF and the Army Air Corps underestimated the effect of flak, it is equally true that both Hitler and Göring overestimated the effectiveness of flak in the years prior to the war. However, they had undertaken substantive measures in creating the most modern ground-based air defense force in the world. Ultimately, the foundations of the West Wall were built in equal measures on high expectations concerning anti-aircraft effectiveness and an underestimation of rapidly developing aircraft capabilities, but the cornerstone of air defense did not rest upon sand.

Creation of the Luftwaffe Commission

On February 1, 1939, Göring appointed General of the Flak Artillery Rüdel to the position of president of the Luftwaffe Commission. In this post, Rüdel was directly subordinated to Göring and was responsible for the evaluation of "special topics" relating to the Luftwaffe, especially those concerning the flak artillery and air defense in general. The president of the commission essentially functioned in the role of an inspector general accountable for assessing the current capabilities of the air defense force and offering suggestions for improvements in equipment, manning, doctrine, and organizational matters.[17] The creation of the post most likely occurred for two reasons. First, the organizational structure of the Luftwaffe in 1939 divided the country into four "air force regions" (*Luftflotten,* formerly named *Luftkreise*) and ten "air districts" *(Luftgaukommandos).* A pilot officer commanded each air force region, and each of the air force regions also encompassed several air districts. In this system, Rüdel was too senior an officer to exercise operational command over any organization below an air force region; however, command of these regions was in practice essentially restricted to flying officers.[18] Second, the choice of Rüdel and the establishment of the post of president of the Luftwaffe Commission demonstrated Göring's continued interest in developing German ground-based air defenses.

In the months prior to the outbreak of World War II, the commission tackled a number of issues related to air defense. For example, it conducted a study dealing with replacement and training measures for reservists; explored methods by which to reduce the number of personnel required to operate rangefinding and fire director systems; evaluated the need for a radar or infrared aircraft-tracking system; and analyzed the use of flak guns against bunkers and fortified positions. One of the most important tasks Rüdel attacked involved a forecast for the peacetime and wartime organization of the air defense force. On May 11, 1939, the commission released a report, entitled "War- and Peacetime Organization of the Flak Artillery," which differentiated between flak requirements for army forces in the field and flak forces needed for the defense of Germany proper. The commission calculated that 220 heavy flak, 205 light flak, and 30 searchlight batteries would be needed to support the operations of a ground force composed of 150 divisions. The number of air defense assets totaled 880 88-mm guns, 675 37-mm guns, 1,530 20-mm guns, and 270 searchlights. Likewise, for homeland air defense the study estimated the need for 75 105-mm flak batteries, 650 88-mm flak batteries, 40 37-mm flak batteries, 700 20-mm flak batteries, and 200 150-cm searchlight batteries. The latter force included a total of 320 105-mm guns, 2,800 88-mm guns, 500 37-mm guns, 9,000 20-mm guns, and 1,900 searchlights, a force over four times the size of that recommended for the support of army operations in the field.[19]

Table 4.1 offers a comparison of the commission's total requirements with the forecast strength of air defense forces for April 1, 1939, compiled in the fall of 1938.[20] The commission's calculations, although strictly limited to flak guns and searchlights, demonstrated that there was a major disparity between planned and projected strength in the area of heavy flak guns alone. In July 1939, Hitler reacted to the deficit in heavy flak guns by ordering increased production of the 88-mm flak gun, as well as accelerated production of all equipment associated with the operation of the heavy flak batteries.[21] As a result, on August 3, Göring raised production of heavy flak guns by 150 per month.[22] Hitler's intervention again demonstrated the continuing importance he placed upon the development of German ground-based air defenses, as well as his continued personal involvement in issues related to the flak arm.

By September 1, 1939, the total flak and searchlight forces available included 657 heavy flak batteries, 560 light flak batteries, and 188 searchlight batteries with a numerical strength of 2,628 88-mm and 105-mm flak guns, 6,700 20-mm and 37-mm flak guns, 1,692 150-cm searchlights, and 2,052 60-cm searchlights.[23] The air defense forces also consisted of three railroad flak gun battalions and three battalions of barrage balloons, as well as seven naval flak battalions for the defense of important ports along the German coast.[24] These figures show that although the Luftwaffe failed to reach the desired force strength established in the years before the war, the size of the force was still impressive. A comparison with other major powers supports this contention. For example, at the outbreak of the war the anti-aircraft forces of the British ADGB consisted of approximately 1,296 heavy flak guns, an eclectic assortment of some 1,200 light flak guns, and over 2,500 searchlights. The leading historian of the British anti-aircraft forces remarked:

> It would be unreal for anyone to suppose that the 1939 ADGB deployment to war stations, brought into immediate being a force fit for battle; the effects of the recent rapid expansion and the lack of equipment were too powerful. Many of the new regiments had done little more than learn the basic

Table 4.1 Luftwaffe Commission Flak Requirements for Wartime Operations versus Forecast Strength for April 1939

	Commission Requirements	Forecast Strength
105-mm/88-mm flak guns	4,000	3,090
37-mm flak guns	1,175	1,154
20-mm flak guns	10,530	11,756
150-cm/60-cm searchlights	2,170	3,404
Fire directors	—	710
Sound detectors	—	1,821

> gun and instrument drills and all were devoid of any practical experience of applying tactical procedures, of using the raid reporting system, of manning positions under war conditions, of the identification of hostile aircraft or of practising formal unit movement.[25]

Likewise, the anti-aircraft forces of the U.S. Army even trailed behind those of their British counterparts. Although the army had conducted a number of exercises and trials involving anti-aircraft and searchlight defenses during the 1930s, the fiscal limitations of a peacetime budget restricted acquisition of flak guns and equipment to a bare minimum.[26] Furthermore, army leaders like General George C. Marshall recognized the value of anti-aircraft defenses but emphasized the high cost of these systems and argued instead for using these funds to build up the army's ground forces.[27] Finally, an examination of the French air defense forces in September 1939 reveals that the French army controlled an anti-aircraft force comprising a diverse collection of 1,261 artillery pieces and some 1,800 machine guns.[28]

Civil Defense Measures

If by 1939 the Luftwaffe controlled the most modern air defense network in the world, then, too, Germany enjoyed the best civil defense system in existence at the time.[29] The main purpose of civil defense forces was limiting the number of casualties and minimizing the destruction to urban and industrial areas caused by bombing raids. During the period between 1933 and 1939, the National Socialist government exerted prodigious efforts in the area of civil defense. The Reich Air Defense League acted as the primary organization for directing all passive air defense initiatives. The league continued to publish its twice-monthly magazine, *The Siren,* and organized exhibitions and essay contests throughout the Third Reich. By the end of 1938, the number of dues-paying members had risen to almost 13 million women and men, with over 630,000 persons acting as league officials.[30] The majority of these officials were house or block wardens responsible for ensuring that occupants of homes and apartments followed blackout guidelines and that mandatory fire-fighting equipment, including the ubiquitous pails of sand, was available in all buildings.[31] By July 1940, the league's membership expanded to 16 million, or approximately one of every five citizens.[32]

Although not a focus of this study, a brief examination of civil defense preparations is important for three reasons. First, the creation of an extensive system of passive air defense measures gives lie to the contention that Germany's senior political and military leadership did not expect bombers to reach targets within the Third Reich. Clearly, the government recognized the importance of civil protection and undertook extensive measures to prepare the German population against aerial attack. Second, the civil defense system augmented the efforts of the active defense forces by lessening the impact of bombing efforts in both urban and industrial areas. Finally, as in the case of the Air Defense Zone, the major effort in promoting civil defense measures demonstrated the regime's desire to protect its citizens from the physical and psychological effects of aerial attack.

The Flak Arm Goes to War

With the outbreak of the war, Germany's active and passive defense networks were both put to the acid test of combat. It is clear that the senior political and military leadership held extremely high expectations concerning the effectiveness of Germany's air defense network. In the case of Hitler and Göring, these expectations were especially lofty for the flak arm, which in turn received primary responsibility for homeland air defense.[33] On the first day of the war, Göring published a daily order to the flak forces in which he exclaimed, "Every round from your barrels will guarantee the lives of your wives, mothers, and children and the safety of the entire German people."[34] Likewise, in 1938, Rüdel optimistically had prophesied that "the flak artillery will be the decisive factor in the air war of the future."[35] Despite the hyperbole and dramatic pronouncements, Rüdel and other Luftwaffe leaders, like General (later Field Marshal) Albert Kesselring, recognized that flak and fighters were two sides of the same coin and intrinsically inseparable.[36] Undoubtedly, Luftwaffe leaders expected ground-based air defenses to carry the lion's share of the air defense effort, but in the end the events of the war would demonstrate the point at which perception and reality diverged.

By the fall of 1939, the Luftwaffe was in a position to begin evaluating the initial results of the air defense network. On October 12, 1939, Rüdel presented a report on nighttime air defense to the Luftwaffe general staff. In his report, Rüdel once again demonstrated his ability to discern the direction of aerial warfare, as well as his open-minded approach to air defenses. He observed:

> Air defenses (fighters and flak) have shown themselves to be very strong during the day. *At the present,* our fighters and attack aircraft are clearly superior to the British and French bombers with respect to speed and armaments. It is therefore to be expected that the British and French will favor the nighttime for bombing raids against targets deep within Germany.[37]

Rüdel continued by explaining that either night fighters or flak forces could conduct operations during periods of darkness. However, he cautioned that the use of both at the same time required "careful preparation" and was possible only under certain conditions. He also remarked on the key role played by searchlights in nighttime operations, whether used in conjunction with flak or fighter forces. He even went so far as to state that flak crews were "dependent" on the searchlights.

In a telling aside, he declared that "at the moment the most capable air defense asset for night operations is without a doubt night fighters, just as the fighter should be considered the best weapon during the day." He provided a caveat to the latter contention by stating that this was true only "when they [day fighters] are available in sufficient numbers at both the right time and place." However, he then cautioned that "these relationships may change, if attacking aircraft become faster, better armed, and less vulnerable." Finally, Rüdel argued that "air defense cannot be permitted to become too methodical or rigid, it must be elastic and responsive in employing the possible means together, independently, or in turn according to the given conditions."[38] Rüdel's report demonstrated a clear grasp of the nature and course of the developing air war, and his remarks clearly dispelled any notions that Germany's highest-ranking and most influential flak officer was the slave to an immutable belief in his own weapons branch.

Rüdel's report is also important in another regard. At the start of the war, the Luftwaffe did not possess a designated night fighter force despite discussions concerning the need for one as early as 1936.[39] Shortly after the outbreak of hostilities, the Luftwaffe created two squadrons of Bf-109 aircraft specifically as a night fighter force at Bonn-Hangelar and at Heilbronn.[40] Göring initially opposed the establishment of such a force, probably for two reasons. First, he clearly placed a great deal of faith in the ability of the flak batteries operating with searchlights and sound detectors to counter the nighttime raids. Second, his own experience in World War I, in which German fighters only began conducting night interceptions late in the war, most probably colored his thinking on the subject.[41] In any event, it was only after the German victory in France in June 1940 that Göring ordered the creation of two wings of dedicated night fighters.[42] The lack of a large, well-trained night fighter force ipso facto placed the burden of night engagements on the backs of the ground-based air defense forces in the first years of the war.

In addition to evaluating the evolving air war over Germany, the Luftwaffe initiated a study to draw lessons from the campaign against Poland (September 1 to October 6). Since World War I, flak doctrine had stressed the importance of providing protection to army units on the ground. The transfer of the air defense forces to Luftwaffe control in April 1935 had not altered this presumption; rather, it only shifted the responsibility for this mission from organic army assets within the Wehrmacht to the air defense units of the air force. During operations against Poland, the Luftwaffe attached anti-aircraft forces to each of the numbered German armies (AOK), the highest organizational echelon of the German army. As a result of the rapidity of the campaign and the fact that flak forces were held too far in the rear, these forces were often not available at the front or in areas where they were needed most.[43]

During the five-week campaign, the twenty mixed flak battalions and the nine light flak battalions attached to the army accounted for thirty-nine aircraft shot down.[44] At first glance, this figure seems insignificant; the number seems more impressive when one takes into account the fact that the total operational strength of the Polish air force was approximately 500. Furthermore, the Luftwaffe destroyed a large percentage of Polish aircraft at airfields on the ground during the opening weeks of the invasion. In any event, the rapid destruction of the Polish air force led the Luftwaffe to begin withdrawing fighter units already by the middle of September.[45] The small size of the Polish air force and the success achieved by the German military in the early stages of the attack resulted in a low threat of aerial attacks and conversely limited the actions of the flak forces. But there were other tasks for the flak forces as they became reacquainted with the mission of ground combat. During the campaign, flak forces participated in direct ground actions in several instances, renewing the precedent established in Spain.[46]

In an analysis of the role of air defense forces in the Polish campaign, Rüdel offered three suggestions for improving future performance. First, he maintained that flak command centers and flak forces needed to be moved from the numbered army level to a lower echelon and forward to the front lines. Second, he noted that flak forces could be used effectively in support of direct ground combat when the aerial situation permitted. Finally, he recommended that the number of guns in the mixed battalions be increased with the justification that future opponents would have more capable air forces.[47] One concrete measure taken by Göring as a result of the experience in Poland was the establishment of Flak Corps I and Flak Corps II in October 1939.[48] On the one hand, the flak corps were seen as a method for improving responsiveness in support of army operations. On the other hand, they allowed for greater flexibility in the employment of the flak in a variety of roles, from air defense to ground combat and even as coastal gun batteries.

The "Phony War"

The performance of the air defenses in Poland provided only a partial framework for evaluating the effectiveness of German flak forces. Indeed, the first major test of these forces occurred over German skies in the face of French and British bombing raids. The Royal Air Force did not wait long to start operations against Germany. On September 4, 1939, fourteen Wellingtons and fifteen Blenheims took off on a daylight raid against German warships in the vicinity of Brunsbüttel and Wilhelmshaven. Upon locating their targets, the bombers conducted low-level individual attacks with predictable results. In the face of heavy anti-aircraft fire, five Blenheims and two Wellingtons were shot down while inflicting only superficial damage against their intended targets. It was hardly an auspicious beginning for the men and machines of Bomber Command.[49]

In contrast to the early RAF raids against German shipping, the French air force concentrated on nighttime reconnaissance flights and propaganda missions that included the dropping of millions of leaflets. Night flights hardly seemed to offer the best conditions for success in spotting German military positions, but, in truth, the French suffered from a shortage of modern aircraft, especially long-range, or even medium-range, bombers.[50] By the end of November, the French air force had flown 700 reconnaissance and 300 observation missions, losing twenty-five aircraft in the process. Unable to establish air superiority over the skies of Germany, the French air force reacted by confining flights to depths less than 20 kilometers inside the German border.[51] In the end, the lack of adequate aircraft for offensive operations forced the French air force to assume a defensive stance, a decision that saved pilots and aircraft for a future day, but one that simply postponed the destruction of the air force until May and June 1940.

According to the official RAF history of the air offensive against Germany, three engagements in December 1939 shaped the course of RAF strategy for the next years of the war. On the morning of December 3, twenty-four Wellingtons attacked German ships in the vicinity of Helgoland. The bombers came under fighter and flak attack, with flak damaging two of the aircraft, but all twenty-four returned to England. On December 14, twelve Wellingtons conducted an armed patrol aimed at German shipping in the Schillig Roads. Poor weather forced the aircraft down at times to as low as 200 feet. The formation then came under coordinated attack from anti-aircraft fire and German fighters and lost five aircraft. The RAF ascribed these losses to anti-aircraft, not to the German fighters, and ordered bombers subsequently to attack their targets from altitudes above 10,000 feet. In the final engagement of December 18, twenty-four Wellingtons launched another attack against shipping targets along the German coast. German radar identified the force and alerted fighter and ground-based air defense units. German flak guns forced the bombers to 13,000 feet and loosened the formation, allowing fighters to press home their attacks. The RAF lost twelve bombers on this raid, correctly attributing the majority of losses to the German fighters.[52]

The events of December shook the RAF's faith in daylight raids by large bomber formations. Furthermore, the primary lesson drawn by the British air planners was that fighters were superior to bombers in daylight operations.

From the German perspective, it should have been clear that with sufficient warning time provided by radar identification, flak forces operating in coordination with fighters increased the effectiveness of both. In contrast, the official battle report of the Luftwaffe Fighter Group 1 concerning the December 18 engagement claimed thirty-four Wellingtons (out of twenty-four) shot down by fighters and credited only one aircraft to flak.[53] The first number is a testament to the Luftwaffe fighter pilots' penchant for overestimating their own victories, while the second offers an indication of their underestimation of the flak. In retrospect, these engagements offered two clear lessons concerning air defenses. First, the effectiveness of flak at low and medium altitudes made bombing attacks from these heights prohibitive during daylight. Second, any standard for judging the effectiveness of flak forces needed to extend beyond the number of aircraft brought down to include the second-order effects produced by the flak forces. By damaging bombers or loosening the bomber formation, the flak was creating opportunities for the fighters to bring their attacks to bear. Throughout the war, many within the Luftwaffe leadership, like Field Marshal Erhard Milch, ignored the importance of these second-order effects in their evaluation of the contributions of ground-based air defenses by focusing on the numbers of aircraft destroyed alone.

In the early stages of the war, the overall scope of the RAF bombing campaign was extraordinarily limited. The *Sitzkrieg*, or phony war, existed not only on the ground but also in the air. Indeed, in the period between September 1, 1939, and May 9, 1940, the flak positions along the West Wall accounted for a mere eleven aircraft destroyed, a prorated cost of over 36 million RM, or $9 million, per shootdown.[54] However, one must take into account the fact that the RAF did not drop its first bombs on the German mainland until the night of May 10, and the War Cabinet only authorized bombing east of the Rhine in a meeting of May 15, 1940.[55] In fact, besides the attacks on German shipping, in the early stages of the war the British pilots were dropping leaflets, not bombs, on German cities. The commander in chief of Bomber Command, Air Marshal Sir Charles Portal, in a letter to the deputy chief of air staff, Air Marshal Sir Sholto Douglas, of May 19, 1940, aptly described the condition of the British bomber force early in the war:

> The difficulty has been twofold. First that we had not enough bombers to justify the casualties that would have been incurred if we had sent formations into Germany while the Germans had nothing much else on their hands. . . . The second point is that our present Heavy Bombers are either terribly slow because of the protection they have been given, or else they have inadequate defensive arcs of fire and are therefore extremely vulnerable to beam attacks.[56]

Perhaps the most telling evidence with regard to the initial difficulties experienced by the British bomber crews came from the accounts of the crew members themselves. One RAF pilot recounted his first bombing mission against a railway station in Düsseldorf. He explained that when the crew reached the target area, German blackout procedures prevented them from identifying the station whereupon they began to conduct a "square search" of the area; after a while, they simply dropped their bombs into the darkness below. This pilot then went on to complain that "such objectives were pointless when so many [crews] found difficulty in even locating the cities in which they were situated."[57] This anecdote evokes several interesting points. First, it clearly shows the navigational problems experienced by the British bomber crews early in the war. Even on clear nights, objects such as roads and small villages could only be identified from below 6,000 feet, and to discern individual structures such as factories pilots needed to fly below 4,000 feet, well within the range of both light and heavy flak guns.[58] Second, it was not a glowing testament to the strength of German nighttime air defenses when a pilot had the time and inclination to conduct a laborious "square search" pattern over a major industrial area. Finally, it aptly demonstrated the effectiveness of German civil defense measures and the success of blackout procedures. Ironically, during the initial stages of nighttime air war, both the Luftwaffe and the RAF were figuratively and literally groping in the dark.

The low level of British and French air activity offered a welcome but unexpected interregnum for the Luftwaffe. In fact, the headquarters of Air District VII (Munich) warned air defense units to expect immediate aerial attacks against major cities such as Munich, Stuttgart, and Augsburg and their surrounding industrial installations with the entry of the Western powers into the war.[59] Paradoxically, despite the vast amount of resources the Luftwaffe had devoted to air defenses, these forces quickly found themselves stretched thin due to the loss of units for the campaign in Poland and the need to protect a wide variety of targets. In Air District VII, the shortages required setting priorities including the protection of major cities, major industrial sites, important transportation hubs, primary supply sources, and airfields and military supply points.[60] The call-up of the flak reserves helped in part to alleviate the shortage and raised the number of flak battalions by about one-third, from 80 to 115,[61] but the mobilization of the reservists proved to be a two-edged sword. On the one hand, the increased number of units allowed for greater air defense coverage of sites within Germany. On the other hand, the rapid mobilization exacerbated existing equipment shortages within the air defense forces, and training deficiencies among the reservists quickly became apparent.[62] In the case of the former, one example included the Air Defense Zone, West, where only 50 percent of the batteries had fire directors.[63] In the case of the latter, one Luftwaffe study remarked that the reserve units led to a qualitative "weakening" of the homeland air defenses.[64] In one respect, the shortage of fire directors was a mixed blessing because each of the Model 36 devices required thirteen persons to operate it.[65] Despite the equipment shortages, the Luftwaffe's air defense forces maintained a healthy surplus in one critical area, munitions. Table 4.2 details the number of rounds of ammunition used and the total number of available rounds for the first three months of the war.[66] These numbers indicate the minimal amounts of flak munitions required in the campaign against Poland and in the defense of the Reich proper during the initial months of the war. In fact, the quartermaster general made exactly this point when he wrote that "no conclusion on ammunition requirements for the flak artillery can be drawn from the Polish campaign."[67] In a similar report, General Hans Jeschonnek, chief of the Luftwaffe General Staff, went even further and cautioned that the Luftwaffe should expect an "exceptionally high" requirement for ammunition in a future campaign in the west.[68] It is also clear from the surplus of ammunition that, despite a number of bottlenecks in flak munitions production, flak forces maintained a ready supply of ammunition should it be required.[69] In this respect, the minimal activity by RAF and French aircraft provided the air defense forces with a substantial cushion of available munitions. By March 1940, the excess ammunition also had the added benefit of allowing for the use of either barrier fire procedures or fire based on aural detection techniques despite the high wastage involved in both procedures.[70]

If by the end of 1939 there was sufficient ammunition for the flak forces, there was still a serious shortage of available gun batteries and searchlights.[71] In Air District VII, there were only three heavy gun batteries available to protect 41 airfields and military sites at the start of the war.[72] The scarcity of batteries led to a decision to provide flak defenses only to the most important airfields and to limit the protection of these fields to a single battery each. By March 1940, the primary concentration for the air defense batteries centered on the protection of industrial installations.[73] On May 1, the headquarters of the air district conducted a dramatic volte-face by ordering priority protection for Luftwaffe airfields and ground installations with a minimum of two

Table 4.2 Flak Ammunition Totals (1,000s), September–November 1939

	September Used	Total	October Used	Total	November Used	Total
105-mm	.027	85.87	.039	96.23	.021	96.21
88-mm	23.24	5,541	15.01	5,359	1.87	5,639
37-mm	66.3	4,532	72.9	5,017	16.17	5,092
20-mm	296.8	64,053	48.2	65,597	338.59	67,677

heavy batteries each. Furthermore, the order stated that the "aerial attacks against cities are not expected in the near future" and called for the withdrawal of all extra flak defenses from the cities for the protection of air force installations.[74] The Luftwaffe's sudden concern for airfields and ground installations was easy to explain. The Wehrmacht was only nine days short of launching its campaign against France.

The Campaign in the West

German flak forces played an important role in the operations against the Low Countries and France between May 10 and June 22, 1940. The flak corps established by Göring at the end of September 1939 became involved in a variety of combat missions. If the Polish campaign had provided the flak forces' baptism by fire, then the French campaign constituted a sanguinary confirmation ceremony. Twenty-four mixed flak battalions and eleven light flak battalions participated in the war in the west, a force only slightly greater than that used in Poland. However, casualties among the flak forces, including those listed as dead, wounded, or missing, totaled 60 officers and 890 enlisted men, a number almost four times greater than the casualties taken in the east. Still, during the campaign the flak forces gave as well as they received, accounting for the destruction of 503 aircraft, 152 tanks, 151 bunkers, thirteen forts, and over twenty warships and naval transports.[75] In addition, the flak forces played a key role in assisting the army in breaking the French positions along the Maginot line.[76]

The excellent performance of the flak forces in the initial operations soon led to a demand from army commanders for more air defense units. In one case, the Seventh Army "pressed for the accelerated formation of flak units" to support army operations. In response, on June 9, Air District VII created Flak Brigade Veith (named after its commander), a unit consisting of four mixed flak battalions and two light flak battalions. On June 20, Flak Brigade Veith moved east of the Rhine in support of the Seventh Army's Operation Little Bear. The brigade had two primary missions: offering direct ground support to the army and providing air defense to the bridges along the upper Rhine. With the armistice literally hours away, the brigade succeeded in destroying twenty bunkers and numerous French defensive positions at a loss of seven killed, forty-one wounded, and five missing.[77]

At the end of the campaign, army commanders praised the support they had received from air defense units. General Heinz Guderian, one of the Wehrmacht's leading tank commanders, personally recognized the efforts of Flak Regiment 102 in support of his forces by noting, "Eighteen days of hard fighting lie behind us. Flak Regiment 102 including the light flak battalions performed inestimable services for the army corps and contributed in an outstanding manner to [the corps'] success." He continued:

> It was shown that flak is a weapon that can be successfully employed in a variety of ways. . . . Against heavy tanks, bunkers, fortresses it [the flak] fought with remarkable success. The regiment put even destroyers, torpedo boots, and troop transports out of commission. The men of the flak were always on the spot when the moment came to help their comrades from the army.[78]

In addition to its success against ground and shipping targets, Flak Regiment 102 scored 243 aerial kills, almost half the total for all flak forces during the campaign.

In a meeting with army commanders on July 2, Hitler also praised the performance of the flak, especially in the destruction of bunker fortifications. However, he prohibited the official publication of these results until the end of the war to prevent Germany's enemies from taking countermeasures.[79] The performance of the air defense units in the west in support of army forces clearly followed the doctrinal precept of combined operations established in World War I and emphasized during the interwar period. However, it is necessary to note that only through the creation of a large air defense force was this level of participation at the front lines possible. In fact, if the size of the flak forces prior to the war had been half as great, this level of participation would have been impossible without literally stripping the air districts of their anti-aircraft forces to support the field campaigns. In any event, the flak forces played a substantial role in the German victory, and every aircraft destroyed in the skies over France was one fewer aircraft that could be sent to Germany.

One of the most immediate effects of the victory over the French involved the deactivation of the Air Defense Zone, West. With the front line between British and German forces now on the Channel coast, the Air Defense Zone had lost much of its raison d'être. As a result, the Luftwaffe moved its air defense forces into the occupied western territories to provide protection to key military and industrial installations.[80] In the final analysis, the Air Defense Zone provided a perfect illustration of the high expectations of the Third Reich's political and military leadership concerning air defenses. In one respect, it was also an extraordinary undertaking on the part of a military that continually emphasized the offense at the expense of the defense. From a technological standpoint, improved aircraft performance and the move to nighttime operations would soon have made the concept obsolete. From a material standpoint, the fortified defensive positions along the zone required too much manpower and too many resources to complete. From a military standpoint, the deterrence effect constituted the zone's greatest value. Still, the Air Defense Zone was never really put to the test, and had the campaign in France failed, then the positions of the West Wall would certainly have remained crucial to the defense of Germany proper.

At the beginning of June 1940, Air District VII evaluated the performance of its air defenses in the first nine months of the war. The report provided a telling snapshot of the air war. In the initial months of the war, the majority of Allied missions concentrated on reconnaissance flights along the border in the vicinity of the upper Rhine. Table 4.3 lists the Allied missions into Air District VII in the period between September 1939 and May 1940.[81] Allied air activity increased substantially by the spring of 1940, and later missions included flights as far as Munich and Vienna. Still, for the entire period an estimated 75 to 80 percent of all flights were reconnaissance missions along the borders that intruded upon German airspace "only for a few minutes."[82] The number of night missions also rose dramatically, with 80 percent of the entire number of night flights for the period being conducted between March and May.

The report also noted that, in general, planes immediately turned toward the west after coming under flak fire. In addition, Allied aircraft began flying above 19,000 feet after their first encounters with German fighters. Besides an isolated attack against Freiburg on October 5, the first bombing raids in Air District VII did not occur until June, with missions against Munich, Ulm, Memmingen, and the Black Forest. The success of German air defenses was modest. Between September 1939 and June 1940, fighters accounted for seven "kills," while flak forces also received credit for seven shootdowns. The low number of aircraft brought down resulted primarily from the limited penetration of most flights into German territory. However, the report's most telling comment concerned the fact that not one aircraft had been shot down during night operations.[83]

Table 4.3 Allied Sorties into Air District VII

	Total Flights	Night Flights (% of total)
September 1939	25	0 (0)
October	20	2 (10)
November	75	6 (8)
December	25	3 (12)
January 1940	25	9 (36)
February	25	3 (12)
March	60	22 (37)
April	55	10 (18)
May	100	25 (25)
Total	410	70 (17)

Problems with Night Fighting

In the summer of 1940, the Achilles' heel of the German air defenses was in fact the lack of an integrated night-fighting network. In a visit to Air District VII in March, Rüdel addressed this issue in a meeting with flak commanders. He observed, "Due to the changing situation at the present time one must count on a majority of night attacks." He then directed that training efforts focus on the conduct of night combat.[84] In his postwar memoir, Marshal of the RAF Sir Arthur Harris noted that the RAF quickly realized that German night defenses were "rudimentary." Likewise, the official RAF history correctly described weather, not German air defenses, as the main threat to British bombers operating at night.[85] As mentioned previously, it was only by the summer of 1940 that Göring accelerated plans for the creation of night fighter units. In fact, only after bombing raids against Munich on the nights of June 4 and 5 did the Luftwaffe establish a night fighter zone around the city. These zones posed a major problem for ground-based air defenses because it was very difficult to distinguish between German fighters and British bombers during night engagements using sound detectors. In visual conditions, the primary method involved the fighter's using its landing light to identify itself as a friend, a tactic that was quickly copied by RAF bombers. The creation of a protected night fighter zone around Munich provoked the following response from the air district: "This suggestion by the air region supposes the exclusion of the entire flak artillery in the vicinity of Munich. . . . The defense against enemy aircraft during the night by flak artillery is then put into question."[86]

Radar and Air Defense

In truth, the main limitation preventing the flak forces from operating more effectively at night was technological. The sound detectors used by the Luftwaffe to detect British bombers proved unsuited for several reasons. First, the altitudes at which the aircraft flew and the high ambient noise levels associated with combat tested the limits of the crews. Second, weather conditions, including humidity, adversely affected aural detection. Finally, as in World War I, bomber pilots routinely changed the operating pitch of the engines and glided down from altitude on the final run-in to the target in order to confuse the crews of the sound detectors.[87] As the majority of the British bombing effort shifted to the hours of darkness, it became clear to the commanders of the flak forces that a new and improved tracking system was needed.[88]

At the start of the war, the German military had only eight Freya radar systems in operation along the northern coast of Germany, but these stations had proved their worth by providing warning of impending British attacks in the first months of the war.[89] Already in early 1939, the Luftwaffe Commission had scheduled the operational testing of the Freya devices using units of the navy, the signal corps, and the flak artillery. The Freya proved capable of identifying approaching aircraft at distances of up to 120 kilometers, but it did not provide the altitude of the target or suitably precise position values for anti-aircraft gun operations. The commission had planned trials on improved systems for early 1940 to test Lorenz's A-2, Telefunken's A-3, and Telefunken's new Würzburg radar.[90] By the summer of 1940, the pressures within the air defense forces for a more effective means by which to engage British night bombers led to a demand for the immediate delivery of experimental radar test devices to operational units as well as technical personnel from the manufacturing firms.[91] In addition, Göring, in his position as chairman of the Reich Defense Council, raised gun-laying radar to the highest production priority on July 18, 1940.[92]

In the case of gun-laying radar, necessity proved to be the mother of compromise. In operational tests during the summer of 1940, the Lorenz device (Funkmeßgerät 40L or FuMG 40L) demonstrated a range of between fifteen and twenty-four miles and an accuracy under ideal conditions of plus or minus twelve to fifteen yards, making it highly suitable for anti-aircraft gun targeting. In contrast, Telefunken's Würzburg radar had almost double the range of the Lorenz device but was less accurate. However, the Air Reporting Service already had placed orders for the Würzburg system and began receiving shipments of the devices in August 1940. This latter point tipped the scales in favor of the Würzburg device despite the need to upgrade its accuracy for radar gun-laying operations.[93] Essentially, Telefunken won the contract because its product was more readily available than that of Lorenz. In any event, the Würzburg underwent a series of modifications in the course of the war designed to make it more effective as a gun-laying radar. By the summer of 1941, the Würzburg device was the Luftwaffe's standard gun-laying radar, and the model FuMG 39T(C) incorporated improvements that made it effective for aircraft targeting.[94] By December, the Luftwaffe introduced the FuMG 39T(D), which remained the standard flak control radar through the end of the war.[95]

The failure of the Luftwaffe to pursue more energetically the development of radar seems somewhat paradoxical considering the attention devoted to ground-based air defenses in general. This oversight appears even more pronounced when one takes into account Rüdel's comments in the Development Program of 1937 that the design of a nonoptical tracking system was "urgent and of critical importance." Likewise, his caution that this would become "a question of life and death for the flak artillery" should an adversary air force commence flights in instrument conditions seemed prophetic by the summer of 1940.[96] Equally puzzling is the fact that Göring had personally observed radar tests in November 1938, as had Hitler at the test base in Rechlin in July 1939.[97]

Why, then, did the senior leadership of the Luftwaffe fail to pursue radar technology more energetically? Without a doubt, Göring saw the Luftwaffe as an offensive weapon designed to attack, and his own grasp of intellectual matters proved as limited as his attention span during technical discussions.[98] Furthermore, it is reasonable to assume that his own experience in World War I, when daylight visual operations were the standard, probably led him to expect that aerial operations in World War II would follow the same course. Luftwaffe fighter ace General Adolf Galland described this mind-set in his postwar autobiography: "The old fighter pilots from World War I, who were now sitting 'at the joy stick' of the supreme command of the Luftwaffe with Göring at their head, had a compulsory pause of 15 years behind them, during which they had probably lost contact with the rapid development of aviation."[99] Each of these factors certainly played a role in decisions relating to radar, as did fiscal considerations and bureaucratic rivalries. One historian of military technology identified rivalry between the Luftwaffe and the navy, as well as the Luftwaffe's penchant for emphasizing offensive weapons systems as the primary factors inhibiting acquisition of radar systems.[100] In any event, by the fall of 1940, the Luftwaffe was forced to play a game of catch-up with the systems on hand.

Expanding the Flak Arm and the Economic Costs

In July 1940, Hitler intervened in several issues related to air defense. First, he ordered an increase in the production of 88-mm ammunition to 1 million shells per month. He also raised production targets for 20-mm flak guns and ordered the use of captured flak guns in the defense of the Reich.[101] On August 19, 1940, the air defense forces received an added boost when Hitler ordered an additional increase in the size of the flak forces in response to the increased penetration of RAF bombing raids.[102] Hitler's personal involvement proved successful in raising the monthly production of 88-mm guns from 48 per month in the fourth quarter of 1939 to 108 per month by the third quarter of 1940. In contrast, the monthly consumption of 88-mm guns due to excessive wear or destruction averaged a mere 10 guns throughout 1940. However, the production of 88-mm ammunition would not exceed 1 million rounds until the middle of 1941.[103] In any event, the overall strength of the flak forces had risen substantially in the first ten months of the war. By June 1, 1940, the flak arm had 3,095 heavy guns (88-mm and 105-mm), compared with 2,628 in September 1939. In the same period, the number of light flak guns (20-mm and

37-mm) increased from 6,700 to 9,817, while the number of searchlights (60-cm and 150-cm) grew from 3,000 to 4,035. In addition, the flak arm operated over 2,000 sound detectors and 502 fire directors.[104] By the summer of 1940, the Luftwaffe had raised the total of heavy flak guns by 15 percent, light flak guns by 32 percent, and searchlights by 25 percent. In addition, ammunition reserves stood at 5.9 million 88-mm rounds, 5.4 million 37-mm rounds, and 78.2 million 20-mm rounds.[105] By August, the continued expansion of the flak arm required the services of 528,000 men to operate the broad range of ground-based air defense weapons and equipment.[106]

A comparison of the expansion of the air defense forces with the Luftwaffe Commission's 1939 forecast for wartime requirements reveals that the flak forces had reached projected strengths in all but two areas. Light flak guns were at only 76 percent and fire directors at 70 percent of the forecast.[107] The latter shortage was most significant because the fire director provided the "brain" for mechanically calculating firing solutions, and the absence of sufficient quantities of these devices reduced the overall level of accuracy achieved by the gun batteries. By 1940, the lack of fire directors and the need to cover gaps in the homeland air defenses led the Luftwaffe to organize a number of "barrage barrier" batteries *(Sperrfeuerbatterien)*. These units were outfitted mostly with captured Czech, Belgian, and French flak guns and optical range-finding equipment. Their primary function involved throwing a curtain of steel into the air surrounding a protected object, either to force a bomber to abandon the attack or at the very least to disrupt the crew's aim during the bomb run. According to one Luftwaffe study, the use of barrier fire also had the added advantage of breaking up the bomber formations and thus making them more vulnerable to fighter attacks.[108]

The employment of barrier fire procedures resulted in far fewer aircraft destroyed compared with optically directed fire using a fire director.[109] The use of barrier fire also wasted ammunition and significantly increased the costs per aircraft destroyed. In regard to this latter point, the ammunition costs of the flak arm as a percentage of the total Wehrmacht budget were relatively modest. Table 4.4 offers a comparison of the distribution of ammunition production for each branch of the armed forces as a percentage of the total Wehrmacht munitions budget for the year.[110] The anti-aircraft's weapons budget averaged approxi-

Table 4.4 Flak Ammunition Production as Percentage of Budget, 1940 (by quarter)

	Army	Navy	Luftwaffe	Flak
1st	58	9	15	18
2nd	52	7	30	11
3rd	53	6	33	8
4th	44	9	33	14

mately 15 percent for the entire year. Despite the significant expansion of the flak arm in the first years of the war, the Wehrmacht was in fact spending a modest amount of its budget on anti-aircraft defenses at this point in time.

Decoys and Deception in Air Defense

Ironically, despite the increasing buildup in the size of the flak force, one of the greatest successes achieved by the ground-based air defenses in the early stage of the war was the construction of numerous dummy installations *(Scheinanlagen)* throughout the Reich. These installations have received very little attention in the historical literature, and far less than they deserve. In early July, the commander of Air Region 3, General (shortly thereafter Field Marshal) Hugo Sperrle, ordered the construction of industrial dummy installations throughout his command. Furthermore, he directed the building of these installations "without consideration to personnel, materials, and capital expenditure."[111] The idea of using mock installations and facilities to simulate their operational counterparts was not new. In fact, the German military considered building dummy industrial structures in World War I, and the Luftwaffe introduced dummy installations as a measure to protect their air force during war game simulations against the French in the winter of 1934–1935.[112] The Luftwaffe's objective was to build dummy installations that looked similar to and were located close enough to existing industrial sites to confuse British bomber crews. By mid-July, construction crews finished building one of the first dummy installations in the vicinity of Augsburg.[113] Soon thereafter others appeared outside of Stuttgart and Karlsruhe. By the end of the year, there were eleven dummy installations in the vicinity of Hamburg alone.[114] Nine installations were in operation in Air District VII by the first week of August, including sites in the vicinity of Karlsruhe, Söllingen, Stuttgart, Augsburg, and Göppingen.[115]

Luftwaffe construction teams went to great lengths to deceive the RAF pilots into believing that these were actual targets. They constructed replica buildings, factory facilities, railway stations, and even streetcar lines, including devices to simulate the electric sparks generated in the overhead lines by the passage of a streetcar.[116] They also placed flak guns and searchlights around the targets. To lure RAF crews to the phony target, the facilities were poorly lighted to make it appear as if the lighting was a product of sloppy blackout procedures. In addition, flak guns commenced firing and searchlights scanned the skies upon the approach of British aircraft to divert their attention from the actual target toward the fake. The Luftwaffe also detonated pyrotechnics at the fake sites to simulate bombs bursts in a further effort to divert approaching aircraft to the site.[117]

On August 6, Air District VII headquarters released several guidelines for the operation of the dummy installations. First, the directive emphasized that the flak batteries and the searchlight units should conduct their activities in such a manner as to convince the bomber crews that they were protecting a vital installation. The second guideline called for flak forces to change their positions at regular intervals in an effort to exaggerate their true strength; however, the directive cautioned that the flak forces should not overdo it lest the bombers choose to avoid the area. Finally, the guidelines discouraged flak operations during the day because the chance of duping the bomber crews in daylight conditions was dramatically less than at night.[118]

At first, RAF crews appeared adept at distinguishing between the real and the fake installations. In one respect, flak batteries apparently tipped their hand through a too-obvious display of gunnery. German interrogations of British prisoners of war found that several remarked on the "extraordinary firing displays" in the vicinity of the dummy installations. In the period between July 26 and August 9, British aircraft flew over several of the installations, in some cases even releasing flares, but not their bomb loads.[119] By the middle of August, however, RAF bombers increasingly began bombing the phony sites, leading the Luftwaffe to believe that the deception was working.[120] By the middle of September, the improved success of the dummy installations led to the construction of several new sites. However, the effectiveness of the dummy installations proved to be a two-edged sword, as was the case for a small town in the vicinity of one site whose mayor complained that these deceptive measures increased the risk of collateral damage to his village. The mayor's request to have the site relocated was denied, but the Luftwaffe noted that it was important to provide small communities near the sites with timely air raid warnings.[121]

It is not surprising that the mayor's protest fell on deaf ears as interest in the deception scheme could be found at the highest levels of the Luftwaffe leadership. In fact, both Göring and Milch suggested improvements to the operations. Milch ordered that only captured flak pieces be used at the sites, a measure that prevented the further dilution of German air defense resources and saved the best flak guns for operational positions.[122] The level of interest in the dummy installations ultimately rested on their effectiveness. In August and September, the Luftwaffe calculated that the RAF had dropped 415 high-explosive bombs, 1,607 incendiaries, and 376 flares on targets in Air District VII. Of this total, 60 high-explosive bombs, 219 incendiaries, and 77 flares fell on dummy installations, or 14 percent of high-explosive bombs and incendiaries and 20 percent of flares.[123]

The initial results seemed promising, and by mid-November the success achieved through the use of the sites resulted in praise from the Reich minister of propaganda Josef Goebbels. Writing about the effect of British bombing, Goebbels noted in a diary entry of November 14 that "it is apparent that the English have been duped by fake installations to the greatest extent."[124] Likewise, Sperrle lauded the performance of the sites:

> The great significance of the established dummy installations in the course of the last weeks especially and distinctly stands out. They [the sites] have completely fulfilled their purpose and mandate. This is satisfying proof for the intelligent and skillful balanced solution, under very difficult planning questions and construction execution, in the correct tactical employment [of the sites] and adroit service [by the crews].[125]

Sperrle's commendation followed in the wake of a highly effective week for the dummy installations. Between November 4 and 10, British bombers released 172 high-explosive and 355 incendiaries over targets within Air District VII. Dummy installations absorbed 58 of the bombs and 183 of the incendiaries of the entire RAF effort, or a total of 34 percent and 51 percent, respectively.[126] In Augsburg, on the night of November 6, the fake sites alone received 33 percent of the high-explosive bombs and 70 percent of the incendiaries dropped by the RAF bombers. Similarly, in Stuttgart on the night of November 8, the numbers were almost reversed, with 65 percent of the high-explosive bombs and 38 percent of the incendiaries hitting the dummy installations. In contrast, the totals for Munich and Augsburg on the night of November 8 proved to be a disappointing 12 percent of the of high-explosive bombs and only 8 percent of the incendiaries. The Luftwaffe rationalized the low percentage in these areas as a product of too few dummy installations (Munich had only one) and noted that further construction was under way.[127]

The success of the dummy installations in the early stages of the war offers another example for gauging the overall effectiveness of the *entire* ground-based air defense system. Although these sites were not bringing down British bombers, they were achieving the desired effect of substantially diluting the impact of the RAF attacks. Furthermore, the existence of the dummy installations offers a tantalizing insight that helps in part to explain the results presented in later RAF studies concerning the general inaccuracy of British bombing operations early in the war.

In any event, the impact of the phony sites needs to be considered in any equation for calculating the costs and benefits associated with the ground-based defense network. They required few resources and very little effort to maintain. In addition, Milch's order to use only captured flak guns meant that the guns and, to some extent, the munitions were also an expendable resource. Furthermore, these sites offered an excellent live fire training ground for inexperienced gun and searchlight crews, as well as recently mobilized reservists.

During the course of the war, the installations gradually lost some of their effectiveness as the RAF crews became better trained in recognizing them and as electronic navigational procedures improved.

Barring the Sky with Balloons

In addition to the dummy installations, the Luftwaffe experimented with other measures designed to improve the effectiveness of its passive defenses, including the expanded employment of barrage balloons. At the beginning of the war, there were still some lingering doubts about the utility of balloon defenses, but the Luftwaffe soon realized the effectiveness of barrage balloons in deterring low-level attacks. As a result, it began assembling between 60 and 100 balloons in a ring or checkerboard pattern around port installations and important industrial sites.[128] These defenses consisted primarily of two types of fabric-covered, hydrogen-filled barrage balloons, including a 200-cubic-meter-capacity balloon capable of flying at an altitude of between 6,000 and 8000 feet as well as a smaller 77-cubic-meter balloon flown at altitudes below 3,000 feet.[129] By September 1940, the Luftwaffe had more than tripled the number of barrage balloons available, from 108 at the start of the war to 380.[130] In general, barrage balloons proved most effective at night for the protection of discrete objects, including dams, oil refineries, and bridges. This last point was of critical importance as the Luftwaffe's flak arm struggled in its early efforts to engage successfully British bombers in their nighttime raids against the Reich.

Firing Blind

Unfortunately for Luftwaffe air defense commanders, not every element of their defense system worked as well as the dummy installations. By the fall of 1940, flak batteries were still deficient in night firing operations. In a particularly egregious example, searchlight batteries "coned" a British bomber for almost eleven minutes while flak batteries engaged the aircraft,[131] firing 123 rounds without success.[132] The incident highlighted both the difficulties in hitting the target and a relatively low rate of fire. In the case of the latter point, already in August, flak gun batteries received instructions to engage enemy aircraft with all available guns "without consideration of ammunition expenditure."[133] With respect to aircraft shot down, the performance of Air District VII flak batteries proved abysmal in early 1940, with only two credited kills from January through June. In addition, flak gunners failed to shoot down any British aircraft in August or September while expending 30,893 88-mm rounds, 11,663 37-mm rounds, and 44,258 20-mm rounds in the two-month period.[134]

One Luftwaffe report addressed the difficulty in shooting down aircraft by reminding flak commanders that the tactic of sudden massed fires could be used to break up enemy formations and drive attacking aircraft to higher altitudes. Still, the report emphasized that "the ultimate goal remains [achieving a] shootdown."[135] This ambiguity went to the heart of the debate concerning measures of effectiveness. Indeed, simply using the number of aircraft shot down as the measure of success for the flak batteries at best minimized, and at worst ignored, the deterrent effect of flak fires in diverting crews away from targets or disrupting their aim. For example, flak batteries employing barrier fire procedures successfully diverted British bombers away from the center of Munich during a raid on the night of November 8, 1940, the seventeenth anniversary of the failed "beer hall putsch."[136]

The poor performance in night firing operations was the result of several factors. First, accuracy suffered in part from the large influx of inexperienced reservists and hastily trained replacements, as well as a shortage of fire directors.[137] The large influx of older reservists also resulted in an unbalanced age distribution and concerns within the air defense units of the effects of this imbalance on future performance.[138] Second, the gun crews experienced some problems with the flak rounds themselves, including numerous misfires and premature detonations.[139] Third, flak commanders complained about the lack of suitable aircraft for aerial target towing and aural detection training at night.[140] Fourth, poor weather, a common trait in central Europe especially in the late fall and winter, complicated targeting and often rendered searchlights completely ineffective. Fifth, the demands of night operations, whether for ground-based air defense units or fighter pilots, required a high level of training to reach basic proficiency. It was and remains a truism today that an excellent gun crew or pilot in daytime conditions might perform poorly when thrust into night actions without specialized training. Finally, the continued absence of suitable gun-laying radar proved the primary obstacle to improved gunnery performance.

The limited effectiveness of the flak batteries in nighttime operations did not go unnoticed by the high command of the Luftwaffe. On November 24, Göring complained that "the shootdown success of the flak artillery has considerably abated in comparison to [the results] during the time of the offensive in the west." He then ordered his flak commanders to "take all measures" to improve "gunnery against aerial targets at night."[141] In an effort to devise an effective procedure for tracking aircraft at night barring the introduction of gun-laying radar, one solution involved using two sound detectors at different positions to provide firing solutions for several batteries. This procedure for "aural intercept" plotting proved, however, little better than existing methods.[142] In fact, some flak batteries increasingly resorted to the ammunition-intensive procedure of either firing based on aural detection or simply using barrier fire procedures. Despite Göring's complaint, the flak batteries in Air District VII again failed to bring down a confirmed kill in November, even though they had fired 16,472 88-mm rounds, 3,393 37-mm rounds, and 47,478 20-mm rounds.[143] The situation led an exasperated Field Marshal Sperrle to demand that night firing procedures be improved at all costs and under all conditions to rectify this deficiency.[144]

Göring's ire was due to two factors. On the one hand, RAF raids within Germany, and especially on Berlin, had embarrassed Göring profoundly. Throughout Germany jokes circulated in various forms concerning Reich Marshal "Meier."[145] Göring may have been the first victim of his own propaganda, but he was not the only one. For example, one Luftwaffe war diary expressed surprise that civilians had complained of aircraft flying over their towns at night. The aircraft had not dropped bombs, but the mere fact that they were there provided cause enough for complaint.[146] These complaints provided at least one indication of the psychological effect of the mere presence of enemy aircraft on one's civil population. Apparently, Göring's Luftwaffe now was reaping the fruits of its own planting, as expectations exceeded the Luftwaffe's existing capabilities. On the other hand, the fact that in September, October, and November RAF bombers began visiting Berlin in force for the first time in the war presaged the future course of the air war and served as a warning concerning the danger posed to urban areas.

German defenses around the Reich capital at the end of August included twenty-nine heavy flak batteries, fourteen light flak batteries, and eleven searchlight batteries. The RAF raids on the nights of September 23 and October 7 killed 60, wounded 154, and left over 2,000 inhabitants of the capital without shelter. As part of a continuing expansion of air defense forces and in recognition of the increased threat posed by the British bombers, the forces surrounding Berlin ballooned to forty-five heavy flak batteries, twenty-four light flak batteries, eighteen searchlight batteries, and two night fighter squadrons by the middle of October.[147]

In an effort to improve the defenses surrounding Berlin, in November the Luftwaffe consolidated Air District III and Air District IV under the command of General Hubert Weise.[148] During a visit to an air-raid-warning center, Goebbels listened to a presentation by Weise and subsequently described the air defense network as "a miracle of system and organisation."[149] The beefed-up flak forces around Berlin achieved their first dramatic success against a British raid of some thirty aircraft on the night of November 15 by downing seven aircraft. The secret to this success involved the use of a prototype gun-laying radar and again demonstrated the future potential of these tracking systems if they could be acquired in sufficient numbers.[150] Interrogations of captured RAF crews also showed that they had gained a new respect for the defenses around the capital.[151] In general, November proved to be a successful month for Luftwaffe air defenses, with a total of thirty-seven aircraft destroyed.[152]

Evaluating the Effectiveness of the Flak

An overview of the activities of ground-based air defenses at the end of 1940 offered several measures for evaluating the performance of these forces. Despite problems in tracking aircraft, flak batteries had downed 1,489 enemy aircraft by the end of the year. In one respect, the performance of the flak forces in Air District VII was disappointing; on average each shootdown required 2,412 heavy flak rounds and 4,598 light flak rounds. Additionally, the earlier success achieved in the campaign against France and the Low Countries skewed the overall average. In December alone, German flak forces accounted for 31 aircraft destroyed, at an average expenditure of 7,058 heavy flak rounds and 20,604 light flak rounds per aircraft. But these results tell only part of the story; heavy flak accounted for 6 aircraft, light flak for 12 aircraft, and a combination of the two for 13 aircraft destroyed.[153] In addition, directed fire led to the destruction of 23 of these aircraft, while barrier fire procedures resulted in the destruction of only 1 aircraft.[154]

An analysis of the December totals allows for some conclusions concerning air defense operations in the period. For example, all eleven of the daylight and twenty-eight of the total shootdowns occurred in the occupied western territories.[155] There were two reasons for the high number of aircraft destroyed by flak in the west. First, the RAF conducted numerous attacks on port facilities and airfields in the occupied territories, normally in the late afternoon against troop and supply concentrations and German ships preparing for the planned cross-Channel invasion.[156] The strong flak defenses of some of these areas made them particularly dangerous targets. The description of one RAF pilot in an attack on the port of Saint-Nazaire provided a vivid view from the cockpit:

> Here we go on the run up, the sight is terrific. Searchlights come from nowhere. We are at 9,000 feet. We weave violently towards the [target] markings. Flak is coming up more now. I see a PFF [Pathfinder Force] A/C coned below and to port and they are giving him merry hell, however he escapes—good show! Now we are almost there. Never have I experienced such a feeling of tense excitement such as this. The whole sky is lit up with weird lights—just like ten times glorified Henley Night. Bombs burst with vivid white flashes. Flak is all around, and light flak, like snakes, comes up to meet us in long red streams. We steady up for the bombing run. It seems ages. One feels like a sitting pigeon, so exposed or like a man walking across

> Piccadilly with no trousers on would feel. At length the bombs go, and the crate shudders as they leave the carriers. Away we go again weaving violently with much power on. We narrowly miss being caught in the fork of two probing searchlights, as we run out of the target.[157]

This passage offers a gripping description of the fear and chaos experienced by bomber crews during night attacks in the face of German ground-based air defenses.

Second, the Luftwaffe pushed numerous flak and searchlight batteries forward to the coast after the victory in the west, forcing British bombers to cross these defenses first en route to targets in Germany. Göring's appointment of Colonel Josef Kammhuber in the summer of 1940 to lead the Night Fighter Division led to the creation of the famous "Kammhuber line," a twenty-mile-wide defensive line stretching from Denmark in the north, then south along the border between Germany and the occupied western territories. The Kammhuber line consisted of a series of geographic boxes employing radar, night fighters, flak, and searchlights in an integrated air defense system.[158] The radar and signal crews tracked approaching aircraft and alerted searchlight batteries to begin scanning the skies to provide illumination for the night fighters to press home their attacks.[159] One veteran of Bomber Command described his impression of the system during a raid in early 1941:

> The only lighting was masses of blinding searchlights stretching along the Dutch and German coastline and strategically placed along the German/Dutch border and surrounding all major cities and towns. Accompanying the searchlights were batteries of heavy calibre anti-aircraft guns and light flak guns. The latter were to prevent flying attacks and were "hosepiped" into the sky.

He then remarked that night fighters loitered "near the cones of the searchlights, so any British bomber caught in them was 'easy meat.'"[160] The system, although certainly not impenetrable, obviously earned the respect of British bomber crews. The searchlight batteries also were critical in assisting German night fighters, a point often overlooked in discussions of the effectiveness of ground-based air defenses during the war. Third, the December totals highlighted the success enjoyed by the light flak batteries whether alone or in combination with heavy flak guns. Indeed, these guns were effective at altitudes between 5,400 and 6,500 feet and posed a significant threat to RAF operations against ports and airfields. Finally, the results demonstrated the low number of kills achieved by air defense forces in Germany proper, with only three aircraft destroyed. This meager total was in large part due to poor weather, inadequate nighttime tracking systems, and the generally limited penetration range of RAF attacks.

While the Luftwaffe's flak arm experienced difficulties, so, too, did Bomber Command during this period. On October 28, 1940, Air Vice Marshal Sir Richard Peirse, Portal's replacement as commander in chief of Bomber Command, informed Air Marshal Douglas that, by attempting to cover a broad range of targets, "we have already reached the stage when the Bomber Force is becoming a jack of all trades and a master of none, and unless we concentrate more on a smaller number of objectives, our attacks will degenerate into nothing more than harassing and nuisance raids." Peirse continued: "The small size of the disposable bomber force, coupled with progressively restricting weather conditions now being encountered, emphasises this. My recent experience has been that of aircraft detailed about one in five reaches a long distance objective, and one in three a medium distance objective, in present weather conditions."[161] Peirse's comments demonstrated that poor weather was a sword that cut both ways, for those defending as well as those attacking. Furthermore, the continued small size of Bomber Command's force meant that little real damage could be inflicted on German industry or the civil population. In fact, the RAF dropped a mere 9,000 tons of bombs on German targets in 1940, less than 1 percent of the total weight of bombs that fell on Germany by May 1945.[162]

The Years 1939–1940 in Review

By the end of 1940, German ground-based air defenses could look back upon some significant achievements. For example, the role of flak forces in the campaign in the west had demonstrated how effective these units could be in supporting ground combat operations. Likewise, the construction of numerous dummy installations successfully decoyed a substantial portion of the RAF bombing effort away from its primary targets at various times throughout the year. In addition, the Luftwaffe began pursuing another promising measure by testing a device capable of creating artificial fog to blanket factories and installations with smoke.[163] Finally, the searchlight batteries had acted as important adjuncts to both the flak and the burgeoning night fighter force. In contrast to these accomplishments, operations during 1940 exposed a major weakness in the Luftwaffe's air defense system. The marginal performance of the sound detectors and the lack of an operational gun-laying radar had allowed the RAF to focus on nighttime attacks without the fear of substantial losses. Still, the deficiency in night gunnery was not crippling or even profound because the level of RAF bombing raids into Germany remained at an extremely low level.

This state of affairs led Prime Minister Winston Churchill to complain that the tonnage of bombs dropped on Germany was "at present lamentably small," a situation he described as a "scandal."[164] The Luftwaffe was given a grace period in which to address the problems associated with its air defense network. The only question that remained was whether the Luftwaffe leadership possessed the inclination and foresight to do so.

Ironically, at the same time that Göring was castigating his flak commanders in November, Hitler delivered a speech to workers in the armaments industry in which he proudly exclaimed, "We in Germany today have a flak defense, like no other country in the world possesses."[165] Hitler was certainly right in his contention that Germany possessed the most extensive ground-based air defense network in the world. By the end of 1940, the numerical strength of the flak arm included a half million men, 791 heavy flak batteries, and 686 light flak batteries.[166] Despite his infatuation with flak defenses, Hitler was not blind to the problems being experienced. In fact, he remarked that in the near future barrier fire procedures would continue to play a significant role in flak operations, and he remained an unswerving advocate of "a massive flak arm with a great deal of ammunition."[167] But barrier fire seemed a poor choice for extended anti-aircraft operations, and the question remained whether Hitler's vision of the air defense of the Reich was the most effective method for protecting Germany's cities, industry, and armed forces. Only the future would tell.

CHAPTER FIVE

Winning the Battle, 1941

By the end of January 1941, despite the problems experienced by the air defense units, Göring still boasted that "the air defenses in the homeland and in the occupied territories stood like iron. They achieved it that the enemy air missions produced no military damage and hardly any other damage worth mentioning."[1] Göring's optimistic assessment of the situation did not prevent him, however, from reversing his earlier position on the utility of night fighters. In the first week of the New Year, he forwarded a directive to the commanders of the air regions and the air corps requesting "the best bomber and reconnaissance aircrews to volunteer for the night-fighter defence of the Reich."[2] In truth, the success achieved by the night fighters throughout 1940 had been modest. Specifically, the Luftwaffe's night fighters received credit for the destruction of forty-two British bombers. In an attempt to improve night fighter success, the Luftwaffe coupled gun-laying radar to searchlights in September 1940.[3] It was increasingly apparent that gun-laying radar held the key to improving the performance of both the flak and the night fighter force. However, the slow infusion of these systems continued to hamper night operations throughout early 1941.

Improving Performance and Sharing Lessons

The technological deficiencies in aircraft tracking systems did not prevent the air defense forces from pursuing a number of organizational and training measures designed to increase the effectiveness of flak forces. For example, a directive in Air District VIII (Silesia/Protectorate) ordered the creation of future flak regiments and batteries around existing regiments and batteries to prevent the problems associated with creating new units from whole cloth. By maintaining a core cadre as the nucleus of new units, the flak forces hoped to maintain a degree of expertise in all units and to increase the level of proficiency throughout the air defense arm. In recognition of the disparate level of gunnery training within the various regular and reserve units, the Luftwaffe extended the gunnery training of the 8th Officer Replacement Year Group at the flak artillery schools in Rerik and Stolpemünde. In addition, Göring ordered the regular rotation of air defense personnel between the front lines and units within Germany.

The rotation of personnel not only offered flak personnel a chance to return to Germany but also, and more important, provided a greater number of crews with combat experience in the more active western theater.[4]

In a further effort to improve performance, the office of the inspector of the flak artillery began publishing the *Flak Newsletter* in January 1941. The Luftwaffe intended the *Flak Newsletter* to serve as a vehicle for disseminating information to all officers and senior NCOs within the flak arm. The newsletter provided extracts from important orders, directives, situation reports, guidelines, and decrees. Furthermore, it offered a forum for feedback from operational units in matters relating to all aspects of air defense.[5] The senior leadership of the flak artillery also continued to emphasize the importance of theoretical instruction in preparation for active combat. For example, air defense units conducted war-gaming exercises focusing on the appropriate selection of firing procedures as well as the integration of gun-laying radar into gunnery operations.[6]

Sound Detectors versus Radar

The air defense leadership also focused on improving practical instruction. The shortage of radar sets forced the air defense units to continue their search for, and training of, personnel for service with the sound detectors. The Luftwaffe also conducted trials to determine the most effective method of aural detection by evaluating three procedures to locate the British bombers. First, they continued to use two separate sound detectors to plot an aural intercept from both devices. Second, crews tried locating the sound detectors at sites away from the guns in order to decrease the ambient noise level. In contrast to the second method, as a third approach, some sound detector crews operated within the battery position itself to determine if better results could be obtained in direct proximity to the guns. General von Renz stated that the last of these procedures achieved the greatest level of success. In addition, he asserted that "success through surprise fire was possible particularly when a unit had moved into a new firing position, or when an enemy unit was on a constant course directed by beam radio. Sudden fire under such circumstances, with no preliminary warning of searchlights and so forth repeatedly produced astonishingly good results."[7]

The primary weakness in aural detection attempts involved "sonic lag," which was the distance traveled by the aircraft in the time it took the noise generated by the aircraft engines to reach the sound detector crews. The influence of meteorological conditions further complicated locating the aircraft's position and computing a firing solution. In addition, the RAF tactic of using tightly bunched attacks coupled with the increased speed of British aircraft exacerbated these problems and marginalized the performance of the sound detectors.[8] Despite the problems plaguing aural detection efforts, there were still over 5,500 sound detectors in use within the Luftwaffe in August 1944.[9]

By early 1941, the answer to the difficulty associated with nonoptically aimed fires appeared to be at hand. The steady infusion of radar equipment raised hopes throughout the flak forces. In one specific example, gun-laying radar repeatedly acquired and successfully relayed the position of RAF bombers to the gun batteries of Flak Regiment 25, resulting in one possible aircraft shot down during the night of February 10.[10] In other cases, results did not match expectations, as evidenced in a report compiled at the end of February:

> The flak batteries awaited the introduction of the radar gun-laying equipment with much enthusiasm and optimism. Because the training state of the crews was poor and the equipment often had technical troubles, at first every success remained out of reach, so that the mood gradually threatened to turn around in the opposite direction. In the last weeks of February, however, we have overcome these deficiencies through increased usable target representations, and the batteries and the gun-laying radar equipment are on the best course in the second half of February to attain the good results that are possible with this equipment.

The report then ended with the telling observations that "the air defense units are in any event extraordinarily thankful that they henceforth possess a device that can lead to success in night gunnery."[11] The introduction of gun-laying radar quite literally provided the flak batteries with eyes to see at night.

Ammunition and Artillery

By the spring of 1941, the increased performance offered by radar was becoming important for an additional reason. The Luftwaffe's use of barrier fire procedures, although successful in deterring the attacks of RAF bombers and reducing their bombing accuracy, resulted in a large expenditure of ammunition. In March, Göring reacted to a growing shortage of flak ammunition by ordering the accelerated procurement of 88-mm flak rounds.[12] Already in January, light batteries received a directive to limit their firing to directed-fire *(Vernichtungsfeuer)* operations as a consequence of the shortage of 37-mm flak rounds. The ammunition shortage was in fact a problem largely of the Luftwaffe's own making. After the defeat of France in June 1940, production targets of 88-mm munitions were lowered to 100,000 rounds per month as Wehrmacht planners shifted resources into the construction of submarines, aircraft, and tanks.[13]

Luftwaffe planners soon recognized the need for more flak rounds and increased monthly production quotas first to 400,000, then to 1 million and eventually to over 2 million rounds.[14] In concurrence with the Reich Ministry for Armaments and Ammunition, Göring, in his position as chairman of the Reich Defense Council, created two new special classifications for priority weapons acquisition in February 1941. The designation "S," or the higher classification "SS," moved these projects to first priority for resource allocation and production. Anti-aircraft artillery and ammunition both received the "SS" designation; however, production in the closed system of a limited resource economy was not as simple as merely ordering increased production quotas.[15] For example, a number of bottlenecks existed in the production process, including shell casings, gunpowder, explosives, and timed fuses. In the case of the shell casings, the Luftwaffe counted on new production as well as recycling expended ammunition. But recycled casings needed to be cleaned before they could be used again, and the capacity of the cleaning process was limited. The gunpowder and explosives bottleneck was in part alleviated by the use of captured equipment and facilities in the occupied territories, as well as through the use of alternate explosive compounds.[16] Finally, the construction of timed fuses was a complicated process that involved precision machine tools and highly skilled workers. Despite increased emphasis, the total production of timed fuses for the Luftwaffe and the navy amounted to only 600,000 per month by the beginning of April 1941.[17]

Despite the production difficulties associated with the manufacture of 88-mm ammunition, industrial output jumped to 890,000 rounds per month in the second quarter of 1941, 1,260,000 rounds per month in the third quarter, and 1,300,000 rounds per month in the fourth quarter. In a period of nine months, the output of 88-mm ammunition increased by 710,000 rounds per month compared with first-quarter production figures.[18] In contrast, the goal of 2 million rounds per month proved beyond the capabilities of the German munitions industry, with 1,444,000 rounds per month marking the highest output of 88-mm munitions in the last quarter of 1943.

The difficulties associated with the production of munitions provide some insight into the complexity and scale of effort needed to create and maintain the air defense units. There were, however, other obstacles and problems associated with the increased consumption of munitions. The high expenditure of ammunition resulted in the need to replace the barrels of the flak guns at shorter intervals, a problem exacerbated by the fact that flak gun barrels wore out more quickly than regular artillery barrels because of the flak projectiles' higher exit velocity. Throughout 1941, the Wehrmacht lost an average of forty-one 88-mm guns per month due to excessive wear or destruction in combat, a rate four times greater than in 1940.[19] The problems associated with the shortages of replacement barrels and 88-mm ammunition even led to an order in

February to fire only on aircraft that "are considered to be attackers." Additionally, the order directed that aircraft flying in the vicinity of flak sites were to be engaged only if "favorable firing situations" existed.[20] The order limiting engagement of the enemy was rescinded two weeks later with the directive that "the enemy is always to be engaged, irregardless of when and where he is met."[21]

The high wastage rate of gun barrels and the large expenditure of ammunition were just two of the problems encountered by the gun batteries. Additionally, the flak batteries experienced a serious incidence of flak rounds exploding in the gun barrels in the spring of 1941. This was obviously a serious problem because it destroyed the barrel and endangered the entire gun crew. The causes for the mishaps proved twofold. First, poor assembly of the rounds themselves, involving the threading of projectile housings with the shell casing, caused the majority of the premature explosions.[22] Second, a defective lot of munitions proved to be the culprit in a number of other cases.[23] The former was an indication of poor training or inattention to procedures within the flak batteries themselves, a deficiency that could be rectified through better supervision and increased attention to detail. In contrast, the latter offered an example of the role of chance and friction in warfare, an inherent element in the prosecution of armed conflict.

In a situation report of February 20, 1941, General Kurt Steudemann, inspector of the Flak Artillery, commented pessimistically on the current problems within the flak forces by noting that "in the near future neither equipment nor weapons and munitions can be characterized as sufficient for the tasks to be solved."[24] Likewise, General of the Flak Artillery Rüdel complained that the crews of the gun batteries had ignored standard firing procedures in an attempt to increase the rate of fire. He reminded flak commanders that "the standardization of training and procedures is the prerequisite for mission readiness." He also admonished his subordinate commanders that "in order to bring forth the full capabilities of the flak weapons to the best effect, [it] is absolutely necessary, to use and operate them [the weapons] correctly."[25]

Searching for New Solutions: The Flak Missile

In February 1941, the growing frustration surrounding the problems of antiaircraft targeting at night led one military engineer, Major Dr. Friederich Halder of the quartermaster general's office, to propose a plan for the development of remotely controlled flak missiles.[26] Later, on May 7, Walter Dornberger, a World War I veteran of the artillery branch and one of the key figures in the Third Reich's rocket and missile program, ordered the scientific staff at Peenemünde to study the possibility of creating a liquid-fueled anti-aircraft missile capable of reaching altitudes between 50,000 and 60,000 feet. Wernher von Braun headed German missile research at the research and launch facilities of Peenemünde, the site of Germany's "vengeance weapons," or V-weapons, missile development program. Braun examined the plan to build anti-aircraft missiles, but he became convinced of a better alternative. Instead of a surface-to-air missile, von Braun favored the concept of a rocket-powered interceptor because of the massive resource requirements needed for the manufacture of anti-aircraft missiles. In July 1941, during a visit to the research complex at Peenemünde, Roluf Lucht, the chief engineer of the Technical Office, talked with von Braun and his staff and adopted the rocket scientist's suggestion for a rocket-powered interceptor despite the objections of representatives from the flak artillery.[27] Rüdel, however, remained convinced of the need for remotely controlled missiles to combat British bombers, but he could find little support within the senior leadership of the Luftwaffe for his position.[28] In the end, several years passed before the Luftwaffe received approval to pursue the program, a delay that would prove costly to the flak arm's hopes of developing an operational surface-to-air missile.

Evaluating the Success of the Flak Arm

Despite the technical difficulties, training problems, and resource deficiencies within the air defense forces, the flak and searchlight batteries did achieve a moderate level of success in the first third of 1941. Table 5.1 offers an overview of the number of aircraft destroyed by the Luftwaffe's flak units between January and April 1941, as well as the total number of rounds of ammunition used.[29] Clearly, January had been an especially poor month for the heavy and light flak forces, a situation resulting from the extended periods of heavy cloud cover and reduced number of daylight hours during this time of year.[30] In comparison, April witnessed a remarkable improvement in performance as the heavy gun batteries lowered the average number of rounds per aircraft destroyed by over 6,200 and the light flak batteries by over 29,800 rounds from the January levels. These reductions in per capita rounds expended occurred despite the fact that the number of rounds fired by the heavy batteries increased by 83 percent and the number of rounds fired by the light flak batteries increased by 6 percent. The improved accuracy of the flak forces resulted from three factors. First, increased fire discipline and the renewed emphasis on gunnery procedures reduced the wastage that occurred in normal operations. Second, better weather conditions allowed for improved optical targeting using fire directors. Finally, the slow infusion of gun-laying radar promoted increasing accuracy within the entire air defense arm, as more of these units became available to operational units throughout Germany and

Table 5.1 Flak Shootdowns, January–April 1941

		Flak Rounds		Flak Rounds/Aircraft	
	Aircraft Destroyed	Heavy Rs	Light Rs	Heavy Rs	Light Rs
January	13	154,456	499,607	11,881	38,431
February	38	234,550	391,106	6,339	10,570
March	31	317,759	476,907	10,250	15,384
April	62	282,270	529,842	4,533	8,546
Total	144	989,035	1,897,462	8,250	18,232

the occupied territories. In fact, anti-aircraft units had received almost 300 of the modified Würzburg radar sets by the middle of 1941.[31]

In the period between January and April, the flak forces continued to achieve the majority of their shootdowns in the occupied western territories. The flak forces in the occupied territories, including Norway, accounted for 115 of the 144 aircraft destroyed, or 79 percent of the total. The success of the air defenses located in the occupied western territories resulted from the high concentration of searchlights, flak gun batteries, and night fighters in the west, which provided these forces with numerous opportunities to engage British bombers both on the way to their targets and as they returned to England. Additionally, the German battleships *Scharnhorst* and *Gneisenau* arrived in Brest in March 1941, leading the RAF to devote a substantial number of sorties to attacks against both vessels in the subsequent eleven months.[32] In fact, Peirse complained to Portal that "whilst fully recognising the need for disabling these ships I regard it as strategically unsound to continue to employ the bomber force to this end. . . . We can do more for the Battle of the Atlantic and, at the same time, use the bomber force in the manner for which it was designed by attacking targets in Germany."[33] Hitler also recognized the important role played by these two capital ships in attracting British bombers. In a conference with Admiral Dönitz, the commander in chief of the German navy, the Führer remarked that "the Naval Force at Brest has, above all, the welcome effect of tying up enemy air forces, which are then prevented from making attacks against the German homeland."[34]

Despite the preponderance of shootdowns in the west, flak gun batteries in Germany proper were able to make their presence felt in April, accounting for 40 percent of the total aircraft destroyed by the Luftwaffe's anti-aircraft forces. A comparison of the success of flak units during the day and at night revealed that flak forces brought down 35 percent of the aircraft destroyed during the day and 65 percent at night. In January only 5 of 13 aircraft, or 38 percent, were brought down at night, while in April 44 out of 62 aircraft, or 71 percent, fell to night defenses. Finally, during the four month period, directed fire accounted for the overwhelming number of kills by destroying 121 out of 144 aircraft, or 84 percent.[35]

The shootdown totals are interesting in several respects. First, they provide dramatic evidence for the continuing effectiveness of the forward-based air defenses in the west. Second, the anti-aircraft forces within Germany clearly were improving as better equipment became available, and as the RAF ventured farther and more often into the Reich. Examples of increased British bombing efforts included a planned strike by 79 aircraft against Bremen on the night of February 11 and an 80-plane raid against Berlin on the night of April 9.[36] Finally, the success of night gunnery coincided with improvements in the use of directed fires, as gun-laying radar acting in combination with the flak and searchlight batteries began to make its presence felt.[37] However, the high percentage of kills achieved at night must be balanced against the inordinately high RAF concentration on night missions. The high level of night operations was an important contributor to the increased number of aircraft brought down during the hours of darkness. For example, one Luftwaffe study estimated that in the first quarter of 1941 the ratio of RAF night flights to day flights was 40 to 1.[38]

Despite the high frequency of night raids, the emphasis on directed fire operations combined with improved accuracy and the decreased number of rounds per aircraft destroyed confirmed the fact that the Luftwaffe's ground-based air defenses were learning to fight more efficiently at night. The leadership of the RAF also noticed the improvement in German air defenses in the period. At the beginning of April, Peirse commented on the difficulties being experienced with bombing "in the face of the heavy and accurate flak which the Hun seems able to put up to great heights."[39] In a letter of April 22 concerning recent Bomber Command losses, Portal raised the issue of increased losses with Peirse and questioned whether "our recent heavy casualties have been attributable mainly to the low height at which our aircraft fly over Germany."[40] The next day Peirse replied to Portal that "the over-riding factor in avoiding casualties is to fly high enough. Over 16,000 feet would appear necessary to avoid the worst danger from A.A. fire and to prevent being picked up by group searchlights working in conjunction with fighters."[41]

Peirse's remark with respect to bombing height and the cooperation of fighters and searchlights was important in two respects. First, on the same day that Peirse replied to Portal, he had received a report from his director of bombing operations, Air Commodore J. W. Baker. Baker reported that German light anti-aircraft fire appeared to be effective up to at least 12,000 feet, and possibly up to 16,000 feet, and he suggested higher flight profiles to reduce casualties due to flak. This finding was at odds with a report made by Bomber Command's anti-aircraft liaison officer suggesting that flights between 9,000 feet and 11,000 feet were safest for bombing.[42] In this case, Baker, and not the command's anti-aircraft liaison, proved correct, as subsequent operational reports indicated effective German light flak fire at altitudes up to 16,000 feet, the maximum ceiling of the early models of the 37-mm flak gun.[43] Second, Peirse's discussion of the use of searchlights in support of fighters demonstrated the importance of these ground-based air defense systems in successful fighter operations.

Flak versus Fighters?

In any event, searchlights assisted both flak and fighter operations in the first quarter of 1941. The number of Luftwaffe-confirmed shootdowns by fighters and flak in this period included 22 by fighters and 13 by flak in January; 95 by fighters and 38 by flak in February; and 84 by fighters and 31 by flak in March.[44] In total, fighters tallied 201 kills to 84 by the flak in this quarter, or an overall shootdown rate 2.4 times greater than the flak. The exceedingly poor weather of January greatly restricted fighter operations and largely accounts for the ratio of only 1.69 for the month. The comparison of the January totals raises, however, an extremely important point. Early in the war, Luftwaffe fighter pilots received no training in instrument flying; therefore, poor weather forced them to stay on the ground, a condition that would persist throughout the war.[45] In contrast, periods of fog or heavy overcast degraded the efficiency of the air defense units but never completely prevented them from engaging the RAF bombers.

The periods of poor weather affected both Luftwaffe and RAF operations alike. In a letter of February 28, Peirse informed Portal of the effects of the poor weather in preventing Bomber Command from striking German oil facilities, the RAF's primary objective at this time. Peirse noted that, between January 1 and February 27, "we only had three nights when we could go for oil exclusively. Of the six other nights when we went for industrial towns, my selection was dictated by the very limited openings presented by the weather—this applied even to Hanover. The five occasions on which the Channel ports only were attacked were again entirely due to the vagaries of weather."[46] In the end, absent radio or radar navigation equipment for the RAF and sufficient numbers of gun-laying radar for the Luftwaffe, periods of poor weather affected the attackers as well as the defenders in almost equal measure.

Organizational Initiatives in Air Defense

In the spring of 1941, the Luftwaffe high command undertook several organizational measures to improve the effectiveness of the home air defenses. A major organizational restructuring of the air defenses designed to improve the performance of the anti-aircraft forces occurred in March 1941. At the end of January, General Hubert Weise, commander of air defenses in Air District III/IV, had completed a study that addressed the reorganization of the air districts in order to enhance homeland air defenses. After the successful campaigns in Denmark, Norway, and the west, the geographic size of the air regions had grown to accommodate these territories, with the Luftwaffe adding a fifth air region covering Norway. The expansion of Air Regions 2 and 3 led to a move to consolidate the air districts within the Reich under a single command. In his study, Weise examined three possibilities for a restructured homeland air defense. The first solution involved the creation of a centralized command for all Luftwaffe units within Germany proper, entitled Air Region Homeland (Luftflotte Heimat). The second solution was to place all the air districts within the Reich directly under Göring's control, bypassing the intermediate air regions. The final solution incorporated the organization of a new command entitled Air Defense Homeland (Luftverteidigung Heimat), to be responsible only for the interceptor and ground-based air defenses within the Reich.[47]

The Luftwaffe rejected the second solution that would directly subordinate the individual air district commanders under Göring because this would in fact create a number of independent air defense areas, leading to a highly decentralized and heterogeneous network. In addition, Göring's own dislike for the mundane task of day-to-day administration and the associated greater workload for the Reich marshal made this plan essentially a dead letter. The third solution offered the advantage of unifying all units specifically tasked with air defense duties within Germany proper; however, administratively it would have bypassed the air districts while remaining dependent on them for logistics and administrative support. In the end, the first alternative seemed to offer the best solution for centralizing the Reich's air defenses, and the Luftwaffe created an air force commander, center *(Luftwaffenbefehlshaber Mitte)* on March 24, 1941.[48]

The new system provided for the centralized control of all Luftwaffe assets within the home air districts under a single commander, allowing for standardized air defense procedures and streamlining the chain of command. Significantly, Göring named Weise, an officer from the Flak Artillery branch, to head the new command. Weise had commanded Flak Corps I during the campaign in the west and later served as the commander of air defense forces in Air Districts III and IV.[49] In his position as the air force commander, center, Weise exercised operational control over all Luftwaffe units in Air Districts III (Berlin), IV (Dresden), VI (Münster), VII (Munich), XI (Hamburg), and XII/XIII (Wiesbaden) and the 1st Night-Fighter Division (Zeist near Utrecht).[50] As commander of Air Region, Center, Weise occupied a unique position in the Luftwaffe's hierarchy. In fact, Air Region, Center, enjoyed a special status at the level between an air district and a numbered air region, making Weise the senior-ranking operational flak commander within the Luftwaffe.[51]

This reorganization was not achieved, however, without some difficulties. The location of the night fighter division in Holland, hundreds of miles from Berlin, under Kammhuber's command created one problem for Weise. Most likely as a result of the pilot's traditional aversion to relinquish control to a nonflyer, Kammhuber desired to retain sole control over the night fighter force and pursued numerous efforts to retain his independence from the headquarters of Air Region, Center.[52] Field Marshal Sperrle, the commander of Air Region 3, posed a similar problem for Weise. Despite the restructuring, most of the interceptor force and a significant number of ground-based air defense units remained in the occupied western territories under Sperrle's control.[53] Likewise, Sperrle feared losing control of the flak forces in his region and proved reluctant to integrate his operations with those of Weise's new command.[54] Sperrle even successfully maintained control of both administration and personnel questions in Air Districts VII and XII/XIII, despite the fact that the forces in these areas were under Weise's operational control.[55]

In a more positive light, the reorganization of the anti-aircraft forces also led to a change in the physical disposition of the flak batteries, with the formation of air defense centers of gravity in the various air districts, much like the existing air defense commands. As a result of these measures, Category I sites, including airfields, received additional platoons of light flak guns. Furthermore, the Luftwaffe continued to emphasize the necessity for mobile reserves capable of being moved quickly into threatened areas.[56]

The Army and the Flak Arm

The centralization of air defenses within the Reich was not the only organizational battle that the Luftwaffe entered in 1941. In a letter to the chief of the Luftwaffe General Staff in early January, Rüdel noted the interest of the army in the Luftwaffe's radar program. He also remarked that the army was clearly intent on creating an organic flak force, especially in the wake of the success of Flak Corps I in ground combat operations during the campaign in the west. Rüdel warned against allowing the army to organize an independent flak arm based on the practical and morale effects that this move would have on members of the Luftwaffe's flak arm. On the one hand, he cautioned that development and cooperation between Luftwaffe flak and army flak would "completely fall apart." On the other hand, he observed that "the army will get the good and effective tasks and the Luftwaffe's flak forces will be less desirable [for potential recruits]." He continued, "The esteem and morale of the flak force will suffer greatly."[57] The army leadership was not to be put off so easily. By the early spring of 1941, the Wehrmacht was engaged in final preparations for Operation Barbarossa, the invasion of the Soviet Union. The leadership of the army recognized the massive scale of the undertaking and used it in part as a pretext to push for an independent army flak arm.

In April, General Steudemann prepared a report for Rüdel concerning his evaluation of the army's proposal for independent flak brigades. Not surprisingly, in his eighteen-page report Steudemann built a strong case against the army proposal and made a number of assertions. He argued that "from all available experience to this point, the army flak battalions will never reach a satisfactory training level. They also will not improve their training proficiency, as long as they belong to another weapons arm, e.g., army artillery." He then stated that "the air defense of the front and the homeland will only function reliably, if it is centrally controlled. . . . Only one decision has a prospect for success, army or Luftwaffe and not the compromise army and Luftwaffe."[58] Steudemann concluded his report with recommendations that the Luftwaffe retain the responsibility for operational air defense, as well as for the development, training, and equipping of the flak forces. But he agreed that Luftwaffe units should be used in support of army operations as had occurred in the campaign against France and the Low Countries.[59] In the short run, the Luftwaffe won the day. Milch briefed Hitler on May 8 concerning the army proposal, after which Hitler decided against the creation of independent army flak battalions.[60]

In the bureaucratic struggle over the flak, the army had lost a battle but certainly not the war. In actuality, the army had controlled a modest antiaircraft force since the start of the war.[61] These forces consisted mainly of units using flak machine guns. By February 1941, the army had de facto flak battalions mostly composed of self-propelled 20-mm and 37-mm guns with a few additional batteries of 88-mm guns designated for the air defense of army troop formations.[62] In addition, the Luftwaffe flak school at Rerik trained a number of army officers and enlisted men for air defense duties. The army also created approximately a half dozen motorized army flak battalions composed of a staff battery, two 88-mm flak gun batteries, and one 20-mm flak gun battery prior to the invasion of the Soviet Union. These units suffered, however, from a shortage of fire directors and advanced aircraft tracking systems, making them most suitable for ground combat operations, a situation that proved entirely amenable to the army's leadership.[63] Still, the army's appetite for organic flak forces was far from sated, and its demand for an independent flak force would ultimately be answered in the fall of 1941 with the formation of a fourth battalion for the army's motorized and armored artillery regiments, consisting of two heavy flak batteries and one light flak battery.[64]

The Flak and Ground Combat, 1941

The army's obsession with flak was in many respects completely understandable. The military campaigns in North Africa, southeastern Europe, and the Soviet Union once again demonstrated the effectiveness of flak forces in support of ground combat operations. For example, in a report to Göring, the General of the Luftwaffe attached to the army remarked that the flak forces proved to be an "indispensable antitank weapon" in the battle for control of the desert in North Africa. In fact, by the end of 1941, the two Luftwaffe flak battalions of the Africa Corps had destroyed 264 tanks and only 42 aircraft. In addition, six mixed flak battalions and nine light flak battalions disabled 13 aircraft, 7 tanks, 30 bunkers, and one tank factory in the campaign in southeastern Europe. However, it was in the east against the Russian "colossus" that the Luftwaffe's flak forces found their most impressive success. By the end of 1941, thirty Luftwaffe mixed flak battalions and eleven light flak battalions had received credit for an astounding total of 1,891 aircraft, 926 tanks, and 583 bunkers demolished in operations against the Soviet Union. The success achieved by the flak forces in these campaigns did not come cheap, with Luftwaffe casualties from these operations totaling 385 officers and 7,238 enlisted men.[65]

In a report of February 28, 1942, to Göring, the Luftwaffe liaison with the army offered the following assessment of the performance of the flak forces in the campaign in Russia:

> In the Russian campaign, next to air defense, the employment in ground combat against Russian tanks and ground targets increasingly became the primary task of flak artillery of all calibers. Often at the temporary expense of tasks in air defense, large parts of the flak artillery were employed by the army command for antitank defense, destruction of bunkers, and in infantry attacks. They [the flak units] often formed the decisive positions in the defense line [and were] the backbone of the army defense.[66]

The success of the flak forces proved a mixed blessing when the Wehrmacht failed to achieve the rapid victory expected by Hitler and his military planners. As the war in the east transformed into a battle of attrition, the army began to rely increasingly on the flak forces of the Luftwaffe, as well as its own hastily formed flak units and flak battalions established as part of the Waffen-SS in August 1940.[67] Likewise, the Russian steppes became the graveyard for ever-greater numbers of flak assets, forces that had to be diverted from the defense of the Reich.[68] In fact, the Eastern Front's insatiable hunger for manpower and matériel even led to the creation of hastily formed air defense units composed of Luftwaffe ground personnel, construction crews, the signal corps, and anti-aircraft forces.[69]

The Flak Loses Its Leading Theorist

As the Wehrmacht drove deep into Russia in the summer of 1941, the final act in a bureaucratic power play involving Göring, Rüdel, and the chief of the Luftwaffe General Staff General Hans Jeschonnek reached its denouement. At the end of May, Rüdel wrote a letter to Jeschonnek complaining that his office was being bypassed in questions concerning flak weapons testing and development. Rüdel accused the Luftwaffe General Staff of working directly with the office of the inspector of the Flak Artillery without consulting him. Furthermore, he let Jeschonnek know that he had brought the matter to Göring's attention and had received a promise of his support.[70] In truth, although his criticism of the General Staff was justified, Rüdel's position of influence in the Luftwaffe had eroded substantially by June. In an earlier letter of January 5, he bitterly remarked to Jeschonnek that he felt Göring held him personally responsible for the British raids against Berlin in September 1940 and the early failure of the air defense units in night operations. Rüdel commented that, although his relationship with the General Staff was "established and good," Göring had cut him out of the decision-making process even in questions of "very great importance" for the future of the air defense arm. Rüdel then questioned the need for his office given the existing circumstances and informed Jeschonnek that Göring had rejected his request to be relieved of his duties.[71]

On June 28, a rumor circulated that Rüdel was to be named as the flak adviser at Hitler's headquarters. Three days later Rüdel submitted a formal request to the General Staff asking for the official dissolution of his position as General of the Flak Artillery attached to the Reich minister of aviation and commander of the Luftwaffe. On July 7, Göring transferred all questions concerning the development and acquisition of Luftwaffe weapons systems to General Ernst Udet, chief of the Technical Office.[72] Although he would remain on active duty until September 1942, Rüdel had lost the battle to Udet. Thereafter, Rüdel's ability to influence decisions concerning the development of the flak arm was effectively finished. As a result, he felt compelled to resign from Göring's staff.[73] With Rüdel's fall from grace, the Luftwaffe lost one of its premier air defense theorists and strategists and a man with sufficient force of personality to challenge the air force leadership on questions related to ground-based air defenses. Both his foresight and his technical competence would be sorely missed in the years ahead.

With or without Rüdel, the air war over Germany continued, and by the midsummer of 1941 the frequency and intensity of the attacks began to increase substantially. Since April, the British Air Staff and the leadership of Bomber Command argued for more aircraft to "raise the intensity of our bomber offensive . . . to an intolerable pitch." As a result, the RAF drew up plans calling for the expansion of the medium and heavy bomber force from a strength of 388 in March to 449 by July and 569 by the end of the year.[74] Already in May, German cities began to experience the increasing weight of RAF bombing as over 100 bombers struck Cologne on the night of May 3, and 188 and 133 aircraft bombed Hamburg and Bremen, respectively, throughout the night of May 8.[75]

In the face of the heavier RAF attacks, Luftwaffe ground-based air defense units continued to work on improving their effectiveness during night operations. In May, the Luftwaffe released the results of a large-scale test of the sound detector units involving almost 2,400 flights by various German military aircraft. The report found that the sound detectors had been able to direct multiple searchlights onto the target only 2 percent of the time, while 21 percent of the time they had provided enough information for the aircraft to be located in the "scattered searchlight patterns." In addition, the tests showed that 60 percent of the sound detector crews located the target at an altitude below its actual height, while 56 percent of crews located the target at a point ahead of its actual position. The study observed that under these conditions the probability of acquiring the target "without a purposefully executed search procedure" was "very low." Finally, the report concluded that, based on the tendency to locate the position of the aircraft below its actual height, searchlights should start their patterns at higher altitudes than those reported by the sound detectors.[76] The sound detectors were clearly not the answer to the problem of nighttime gunnery, but the continued paucity of gun-laying radar made them indispensable despite their limitations.

In 1941, the Luftwaffe also had come to several conclusions concerning the searchlight batteries. A report in January 1941 noted that "experience has taught that a flak searchlight with a [horizontal] separation of four kilometers and a [vertical] spacing of eight kilometers cannot lead to success. A greater concentration of the flak searchlights is the prerequisite for success." The report then recommended a maximum horizontal spacing of three kilometers and a maximum vertical separation of four kilometers.[77] In line with the study's recommendation, General Weise, air commander, center, ordered an intensification of training for the crews of the searchlight batteries and limited the separation between searchlights to three to four kilometers. These measures apparently led to increased performance as Weise praised the actions of the searchlight crews in a daily order in April 1941.[78]

As mentioned previously, the searchlight batteries not only played a key role in the operations of the flak artillery but also contributed greatly to the success of the night fighters throughout 1941. By September, night fighters operating in cooperation with searchlights had destroyed approximately 325 aircraft versus only 50 brought down by night fighters operating solely under radar guidance in nonilluminated conditions, a ratio of 6.5 to 1 in favor of searchlight-assisted intercepts.[79] The searchlight-assisted and nonilluminated shootdown totals reflected the Luftwaffe's reliance on a dual strategy for night intercepts. On the one hand, the Luftwaffe established night fighter areas located in the occupied western territories, relying on radar interception alone without the assistance of searchlights. On the other hand, the Luftwaffe also created a second line of night fighter areas in the west and a night fighter zone ranged around the capital of Berlin.[80] In these latter areas, the searchlights provided illumination at depths of between five and twenty miles to allow Luftwaffe fighters to identify and then attack the RAF bombers.[81]

By mid-1941, night fighters operating under radar control largely relied on the Himmelbett procedure for achieving an aerial intercept. In this procedure, one night fighter flew within a specific area and worked with a ground controller who coordinated the intercept from separate radar returns received from the target and the fighter. The main weakness of this system was that only one night fighter could fly within the proscribed area at any given time. The RAF quickly took advantage of this deficiency by sending streams of bombers through the same airspace at short intervals, thus overwhelming the German defenses. In addition to ground-controlled radar intercepts, the Luftwaffe also developed an infrared tracking device *(Spanner)* for its night fighters that could detect the engine heat of the British bombers; however, the range of the device proved extremely limited. Finally, air force technicians constructed an aerial intercept radar *(Lichtenstein)* that provided pilots with three displays inside the aircraft to locate the British bombers. These devices were complicated but by August 1941 had led to some initial successes, resulting in an order for expanded production.[82] Despite the promise of improved results in nonilluminated conditions offered by ground-based and aerial radar, the assistance of the searchlight batteries continued to play a key role in nighttime intercepts. In turn, illuminated night fighter operations expanded later in the war, encompassing the defense of major urban and industrial areas as the German homeland became the site of increasing concentrations of searchlight defenses.

During the summer of 1941, the Luftwaffe's ground-based air defenses once again proved their worth both in the field and on the home front. Table 5.2 displays the results achieved by the flak artillery in the period between May and August 1941.[83] Clearly the Luftwaffe flak forces operating in the Soviet Union had achieved dramatic results in the first three months of the invasion. However, forces in the Reich and in the west also had increased their tally of aircraft destroyed. For example, the forces under the air commander, center, shot down 6 aircraft in May, 10 in June, 22 in July, and 33 in August. Likewise, flak forces in Belgium, Holland, and France destroyed 13 aircraft in May, 45 in June, 80 in July, and 70 in August. In addition, searchlight forces in

Table 5.2 Flak Shootdowns, May–August 1941

	Day	Night	Total
May	6	29	35
June (withUSSR losses)	184	22	206
June (without USSR losses)	36 (at least)	15 (at least)	58
July/Aug (with USSR losses)	1,707	98	1,805
July (without USSR losses)	89	32	121
Aug (without USSR losses)	100	44	144
Total	2,122 (at least)	242 (at least)	2,369

Belgium and northern France received credit for 2 aircraft brought down as a result of disorienting the pilots and thereby causing the aircraft to crash.[84]

The increased success enjoyed by German anti-aircraft defenses in July and August coincided with a change in the RAF's bombing emphasis. In a directive issued on July 9, Bomber Command restated the objectives of future bombing raids as "dislocating the German transportation system and destroying the morale of the civilian population as a whole and of the industrial workers in particular."[85] The RAF's decision to strike at the morale of the civilian population emerged in part in recognition of the abysmal results being achieved by its bomber crews. In August 1941, D. M. Butt released a devastating evaluation of the results of some 100 RAF bombing raids conducted between June 2 and July 25. After examining poststrike photographs of the targets, the report concluded that no more than one crew in five of all aircraft dispatched had dropped their bombs within five miles of the correct target. Furthermore, the flight crews had obtained even worse results in the heavily built-up and smog-filled Ruhr, where only one in ten bombers placed its bomb load within five miles of the target.[86]

The poor accuracy of British bombing in the first two months of the summer was the result of several factors. First, the British lacked a navigational system that would enable them to locate targets precisely. Second, German fighter and anti-aircraft defenses continued to expand while becoming more effective, as indicated by the increasing loss rate suffered by the RAF. With respect to the impact of flak defenses, the Butt report noted that only 20 percent of attacking aircraft dropped their bombs within five miles of the target in areas of "intense" anti-aircraft fire.[87] By the end of March 1941, bomber losses amounted to a mere 181 aircraft; by the end of June, this number had grown to 541 aircraft; and by the end of September, the total stood at 1,170 aircraft. Admittedly, these losses included noncombat accidents and mishaps, but German air defenses still directly or indirectly accounted for the majority of RAF losses in the period.[88]

Dummy Installations, Act 2

An additional factor that helped to explain the poor results achieved by Bomber Command was the Luftwaffe's continued use of dummy installations to decoy RAF crews away from their intended targets. For example, RAF crews dropped 55 percent of their high-explosive bombs and 69 percent of their incendiaries on dummy installations in the vicinity of Stuttgart and Karlsruhe in July. In August, Bomber Command wasted 38 percent of its high-explosive loads and 31 percent of its incendiaries on phony sites within Air District VII.[89] In another remarkable example, during a raid against Berlin in 1941, RAF crews dropped forty-three times more high-explosive bombs and forty-seven times more incendiaries on a dummy installation than on the city itself.[90] In the case of Berlin, work crews camouflaged major streets and landmarks, thus transforming the aerial view of the city's center to such an extent as to make visual identification extremely difficult for the bomber crews, especially in blackout conditions.[91]

The RAF was certainly not oblivious to the efforts of the Luftwaffe with respect to decoy and deception measures. In fact, Portal sent Prime Minister Churchill a report in October that discussed the nature of Berlin's air defenses. He informed the prime minister that "the large numbers of searchlights at Berlin are intensely dazzling and the Germans are continually improving their elaborate systems of decoys and camouflage. For these reasons, crews may take some time in determining their exact position and in deciding on the best run-in to their targets."[92] The dummy installations continued to pay a handsome dividend at relatively little cost into the fall of 1941. As a result, the Luftwaffe construction crews in Air District VII began work on two new sites at the beginning of September.[93] The percentage of all bombs dropped on fake installations in Air District VII for the three-month period included 53 percent of high-explosive and 41 percent of incendiaries in September; 37 percent of high-explosive and 28 percent of incendiaries in October; and 28 percent of high-explosive and 11 percent of incendiaries in November.[94]

The decreasing percentage of bombs dropped on the dummy installations through the fall of 1941 indicated that the RAF crews had become more adept at identifying the phony sites. A Luftwaffe after-action report in November remarked on this trend by noting "the heavy use of parachute flares over the dummy installations is once again noticeable, allowing for the presumption that the enemy is reckoning with such installations and is seeking to identify them."[95]

By the summer of 1941, the RAF was well on the way to developing a radionavigational system to improve bombing accuracy.[96] Despite these efforts, Bomber Command did not correctly identify one dummy installation constructed to simulate the Krupp works near Essen until 1943, by which time it had dropped 64 percent of all high-explosive and 75 percent of all incendiaries on the fake factory instead of its authentic counterpart. In addition, Berlin lay beyond the range of the new radionavigational devices, and the sixteen dummy sites surrounding the capital were more or less effective throughout the war.[97] The phony sites in the vicinity of Berlin also included fake airfields created in moors or on lakes replete with runway lighting.[98] All in all, the dummy installations continued to bedevil British night missions until late in the war. Reich Minister of Propaganda Josef Goebbels ruefully remarked on the success of the dummy sites in a diary entry of July 1941 by confiding, "We cannot deny the pompous declarations of success by the RAF, because they mostly concern dummy installations. The statistics mentioned by the English are totally grotesque. But perhaps they even believe them themselves. They give us a certain pause to catch our breath."[99] On September 7, Goebbels again remarked that his office would not deny British claims of bombing destruction in western and northwestern Germany because "the English are for the most part hitting dummy sites."[100] One Luftwaffe report went so far as to describe the role played by the dummy installations during the buildup of the German night defenses as "decisive."[101]

The Flak and Popular Opinion

Despite the RAF's objective to strike at the heart of civilian morale, the British bombing raids appeared to be little more than a nuisance for many among the German population even as late as August 1941. On August 21, the police president of Augsburg noted the unconcerned reaction of the city's inhabitants to a British raid. He observed, "People were indifferent to the air raid. The majority did not believe that an air alarm would be sounded during the day, let alone that an air attack would take place."[102] If the citizens of Augsburg were unimpressed by an isolated bombing raid, then the same certainly could not be said of those persons living in Berlin and Hamburg, who experienced numerous "visits" from Bomber Command. Still, even as late as 1943, crowds in Berlin gathered outside to watch the raids and even danced as the bombers released their loads.[103] To be sure, it could be a dangerous proposition to gather outdoors to watch the battle between the flak and the bombers, as exploding anti-aircraft shells produced a veritable "rain of flak splinters" that whistled down in a "shrill organ concert" over German cities.[104] These flak splinters became a favorite object of German schoolchildren but could easily wound or even fatally injure those foolish enough to venture outdoors without a helmet and protective clothing during an air raid.[105]

Despite the general success of air defense units in either preventing air attacks or ameliorating their effects, the leadership of the flak artillery proved highly sensitive to civilian complaints. A story in the November edition of the *Flak Newsletter* addressed the issue of civilian resentment toward the anti-aircraft forces. The writer complained that the "civil population often, even when it is unjustified, holds the flak artillery responsible for all damages that are caused through the effects of enemy actions throughout the Reich." The author then warned that this attitude could damage recruiting efforts for replacement personnel to the air defense branch. As a result, the flak arm was to commence a propaganda campaign to dispel the false impressions within the population concerning the flak by promoting stories highlighting the effectiveness and the "actual success of the flak artillery."[106] In April 1941, the inspector of the Flak Artillery, General Steudemann, also remarked on the existence of a sentiment casting the flak artillery as the target of popular ridicule *(Volkswitz)*. Steudemann even contended that this brand of popular humor went so far as to cause embarrassment for flak personnel when they wore their uniforms in public.[107]

To be sure, jokes concerning the flak forces did circulate during the war. One of the most biting, and hence most popular, of these anecdotes involved the tale of a soldier who had been condemned to death and given his choice of several means of execution. In the story, the apocryphal soldier chose execution by anti-aircraft fire. He was then placed in a tower surrounded by three flak batteries, which fired for a period of three weeks. At the end of this time, the soldier was found dead not from flak wounds but from starvation.[108] However, one must be careful to not overdraw the significance represented by the gallows humor of a people at war. Even after the war, when Germany lay prostrate and its cities reduced to rubble, the U.S. Strategic Bombing Survey found that 15 percent of the population described anti-aircraft defenses as "adequate," and 34 percent described them as "adequate in the beginning only."[109] The fact that 49 percent of the population found ground-based air defenses adequate in the early years of the war even as they stood upon the ruins of the thousand-year Reich is indicative of a certain level of satisfaction with the initial performance of the air defense forces.

The Pros and Cons of Barrier Fire Batteries

In the fall of 1941, the air defense forces continued to grow at a rapid pace. At this point, the flak artillery consisted of 967 heavy flak batteries and 752 light flak batteries.[110] Still, Hitler ordered a further increase in the size of the ground-based air defenses in September.[111] In the period between September 15 and October 15, 1941, air defense forces increased by 5 batteries of 105-mm heavy flak guns, 4 batteries of 37-mm light flak guns, 5 batteries of 20-mm light flak guns, 2 batteries of 40-mm captured flak guns, and 1 battery of 150-cm searchlights. In the same period, the Luftwaffe also created an additional 49 "barrier fire" batteries,[112] which provided a perfect illustration of a case where qualitative improvements did not keep pace with the quantitative expansion. These batteries lacked all but the most rudimentary optical range-finding devices and offered a clear case of quantity over quality. Still, an in-depth analysis of the pros and cons of these units allows for a more nuanced evaluation of their utility and ultimate effectiveness.

The move to create barrier fire batteries reflected the broader discussion of how to measure the effectiveness of the anti-aircraft forces. Did the number of aircraft shot down alone constitute the efficacy of the air defense branch, or was merely the ability to prevent the bombers from accurately striking their targets the measure of flak effectiveness? By the end of 1941, experience in defending against RAF attacks had clearly shown that the primary advantage of barrier fire was its use as a deterrent and its effectiveness in driving bombers to increased altitudes or disrupting their aim. Without a doubt, Hitler advocated the use of flak in this role even when faced by opposition from within the Luftwaffe.[113] In this respect, Hitler certainly recognized the civilian population's psychological need to hear German guns answering the attacks of the Allied bombers, an important but oft-understated point.[114]

In contrast, the main disadvantage of barrier fire procedures was the high rate of ammunition usage. Milch and others criticized barrier fire operations as both ineffective and a waste of limited resources. Milch, in fact, harbored a deep-seated pessimism with respect to flak artillery throughout the war and let few opportunities pass to either needle air force flak commanders or denigrate the efforts of the ground-based air defense units. Throughout the war, he consistently favored the production of more fighters at the expense of the flak.[115] It is difficult to discern the reason for Milch's attitude concerning the flak arm. However, Milch had been an artillery officer and aerial observer in World War I, and his antipathy for the flak might have simply arisen from the artilleryman's general disdain for the "bastard son" of the regular artillery and his own strong attachment to aviation.

In the final analysis, both sides involved in the argument concerning the barrier fire batteries were partially correct. These firing procedures did use large amounts of ammunition; however, the batteries must be seen in the context of the time and in light of their role and the prevailing situation. First, the vast majority of the barrier fire batteries consisted of captured French, Russian, or Czech flak guns and equipment. In this respect, the employment of these weapons did not require a major diversion of resources because the guns either could be rebored to accommodate German ammunition or could be employed using captured ammunition stocks. While either procedure required the appropriation of some resources, the investment was relatively low in comparison with the production of hundreds, or even thousands, of new German guns. Furthermore, the overall quality of the guns proved to be high. In July 1941, the Luftwaffe established a special unit, Luftwaffe Flak Staff (East), to study Russian flak equipment and evaluate these weapons and equipment for possible use by the Wehrmacht. In contrast to the Luftwaffe's expectations, these weapons proved to be of high quality, if simple design.[116] Second, a large percentage of the barrier fire batteries conducted operations at dummy installations throughout the Reich.[117] These installations required flak batteries in order to decoy British bombers successfully. In turn, the barrier fire batteries were tailor-made for these operations by providing a high volume of fire in a short period of time. In addition, these batteries provided an opportunity for training inexperienced crews in the basics of anti-aircraft operations under combat conditions. Finally, the shortage of optical aircraft tracking systems, including fire predictors and gun-laying radar, combined with the growing necessity of protecting major urban centers, led to the employment of barrier fire batteries as an adjunct to existing defenses. These batteries were available to augment the protection of cities, and, in addition to their effect on the bomber crews, they provided a certain sense of psychological comfort and protection to the citizens of these areas during the raids.[118]

The case of the barrier fire batteries aptly illustrates the many facets associated with evaluating one specific aspect of the ground-based air defense system. Like the searchlight batteries, which supported both the flak and the night fighter force, the employment of barrier fire batteries directly affected other areas of air defense, most specifically the efficacy achieved by the dummy installations. Furthermore, the Luftwaffe could distribute its own more advanced equipment and flak guns to other sites by using captured guns at the dummy installations, thus increasing the coverage available to other areas within the Reich. Finally, these batteries also offered a sense of psychological comfort to the German population in the face of British raids, an important if unquantifiable effect.

Technological Initiatives for Improving Air Defense

In the fall of 1941, the leadership of the flak forces continued to explore new measures for improving the performance of the ground-based air defenses.[119] Raising the capabilities of existing equipment and weapons offered one solution. By 1939, the higher altitudes achieved by bomber aircraft and the Luftwaffe's requirement for a more capable mobile heavy flak gun resulted in the award of a development contract to the firm of Rheinmetall for an improved version of the 88-mm gun. The engineers at Rheinmetall began work and produced a prototype weapon, the 88-mm/Model 41 (88-mm/41) in 1941. The Model 41 incorporated several new features designed to increase its effectiveness. For example, the gun employed a turntable mount that allowed it to be pivoted back and downward, providing an extremely low silhouette when used in the ground combat role. Engineers also designed a three-piece inner barrel that allowed for the differential replacement of barrel parts caused by uneven wear. Selective replacement of individual sections rather than the entire barrel led to resource savings.[120]

The most significant improvements offered by the new gun were its outstanding ballistic characteristics, which included an absolute firing altitude of 48,500 feet and an effective engagement altitude of 33,000 feet. Furthermore, the Model 41 had a rate of fire between twenty and twenty-five rounds per minute, and the exit velocity of the projectile was 3,315 feet per second.[121] The new gun thus offered a 20 percent increase in both effective engagement altitude and projectile exit velocity over the previous models of the 88-mm flak gun. In fact, it even exceeded the ballistic characteristics of the larger-caliber 105-mm gun.[122] General von Renz remarked that the performance of the Model 41 was "almost equal to the 128-mm and 150-mm." Renz, however, blamed shortsighted technical experts in Albert Speer's Ministry of Armaments for delaying the production of the gun until 1942 based on the fact that it required an extra 220 pounds of materials per gun than the existing models of the 88-mm gun. Despite these initial difficulties and nagging production delays, the Model 41 later emerged as pound-for-pound the most capable flak gun of the war.

Evaluating the Doctrine of Air Defense

In addition to attempts at improving the performance of weapons and equipment, the air defense branch began experimenting with tactical-level reorganizations that included increasing the number of guns per heavy flak battery. According to one historian, it was Göring who first suggested the formation of larger gun batteries using six, eight, or even ten guns.[123] In the fall of 1941, the Luftwaffe organized experimental flak units of eight guns per battery versus the standard four guns. The guns in this case usually were arranged in a circle of seven, with the eighth gun placed in the center.[124] According to General of the Flak Artillery Walther von Axthelm, these "double batteries" *(Doppelbatterien)* produced a "certain improvement in aircraft shot down," but not to the levels desired by the air force leadership.[125] In a similar measure, the Luftwaffe added two more guns to numerous heavy flak batteries at the end of 1941, either with the additional guns placed at opposite corners of the traditional square arrangement or with five guns formed in a circle around the sixth.[126] In one example, the Luftwaffe created several six-gun heavy flak batteries to augment the defenses around Munich in December.[127]

In 1941, the Luftwaffe remained true to the precepts of *Regulation 16* by retaining an emphasis on combined flak and interceptor operations. In a war game exercise conducted in December 1941, the scenario projected a situation for 1944 that included an Allied ground offensive in the west. One interesting feature of the exercise was the concentration on procedures involving cooperation between fighter and flak forces in a variety of situations. However, the most telling aspect of the report was that it was not an exercise prepared by the ground-based air defenses but a scenario put together by the fighter forces.[128] The exercise showed that the doctrinal emphasis on cooperation between the flak arm and the fighter forces was not merely window dressing designed to assuage the feelings of the two sides; instead, this concept of cooperation was an integral element in the planning and activities of both groups. This example also demonstrated that attempts to present air defense as an either-or situation involving fighters or flak constituted a false dichotomy. The senior leadership of the flak forces certainly recognized the necessity for cooperation, even if others, like Milch, appeared to frame their arguments concerning air defense in the terms of one or the other.

Still, by the end of 1941, the center of gravity of the Reich's air defenses undeniably rested on the ground-based flak and searchlight batteries versus their aerial interceptor counterparts. While the Luftwaffe's day fighter force was concentrated along the Eastern Front, there was only one wing of day fighters located in the Reich proper by the end of 1941.[129] In contrast, there were over 250 night fighters protecting the approaches to, and the airspace over, Germany.[130] The Luftwaffe's emphasis on night fighter forces versus day fighter forces within Germany was perfectly natural based on the RAF's concentration on night raids during the period. Between July and October 1941, the RAF conducted twice as many night raids as daylight raids on targets within Germany and in the occupied western territories.[131] In November and December, the ratio remained the same, as the RAF conducted a total of 2,589 night and 1,243 day missions.[132] In addition to the British attacks, small groups of Soviet bomber and torpedo aircraft unexpectedly raided Berlin with both leaflets and high-explosives over seventy times in August and September. The Soviet bombing raids caused little damage, but they did result in the Luftwaffe moving some air defense assets to the east of Berlin for a short time.[133]

Evaluating the Effectiveness of the Flak Arm

By the end of 1941, it was clear that the ground-based air defense units had made considerable progress in the past twelve months. Table 5.3 shows the

Table 5.3 Flak Shootdowns, September–December 1941

	Day	Night	Total
September	115	45	160
October	52	47	99
November	33	41	74
December	16	33	49
Total	216	166	382

total number of aircraft destroyed by flak forces in the Reich and the occupied western territories between September and December 1941.[134] An analysis of these figures shows the relatively constant number of aircraft destroyed by flak during the night. Furthermore, the Luftwaffe estimated that in September 3.76 percent, in October 2.51 percent, in November 4.01 percent, and in December 2.47 percent of all RAF aircraft conducting sorties were destroyed by flak.[135] In the last six months of the year, flak forces in the Reich and in the west brought down 405 aircraft during the day and an additional 242 at night for a total of 647 aircraft destroyed. In contrast, Luftwaffe night fighters brought down 421 aircraft in all of 1941.[136] In addition, these totals do not include the 1,325 aircraft shot down by Luftwaffe flak forces mostly in the east between October and December.[137]

German ground-based defenses sparked growing concern within Bomber Command. In a letter of September 23, 1941, to Portal, Peirse wrote, "I asked you yesterday afternoon whether I could be given a free hand to try out experiments over enemy territory designed to counter their searchlights and A.A. defences; defences which are having an increasingly impeding effect upon our offensive."[138] Peirse then requested that he be allowed to begin trials involving the dropping of "metallic objects" with which to confuse German gun-laying radar used to direct both anti-aircraft and searchlight batteries. In a letter of September 30, Portal replied that he had contacted Sir Henry Tizard of the Operational Research Section to study the issue. He cautioned, however, that "he [Tizard] thinks that before we can determine the form which such experiments should take, we ought to have further evidence for the view that enemy searchlights are in fact accurately controlled by R.D.F. [radio direction finding] methods. He also thinks that we should consider rather more fully to what extent the experiments would help the enemy beat our own defences."[139]

The exchange between Portal and Peirse in the fall of 1941 identified the existence of a new radar countermeasure that would later become known as "Window." Window used bundles of aluminum strips (chaff) designed to disrupt German radar by causing a blanket of radar returns, preventing the location of individual aircraft in the cloud of reflective debris. Peirse's letter also confirmed the increasing effectiveness of German ground-based air defenses by the end of 1941 and demonstrated Peirse's concern that new countermeasures were needed to slow the operational wastage being experienced in the skies over the Continent. In the end, the fear that the Germans might also use this simple but highly effective countermeasure outweighed the concerns associated with decreasing operational losses and led to a decision by the RAF's leadership to refrain from introducing Window at this time.

The improved performance of the flak forces throughout 1941 and the relatively light damage caused by the British bombing raids help to explain the paradoxical behavior of Göring, the ex–fighter pilot, and his unwillingness to increase the size of the Reich's fighter force. Already in August, General Werner Mölders, chief of the Fighter Arm, General Josef Kammhuber, chief of the Night Fighter Arm, and Jeschonnek approached Göring with suggestions to increase the size of the fighter arm in reaction to the increased loss of aircraft, especially in actions on the Eastern Front. Göring, ever the optimist, replied, "The Russians will soon be beaten. Once I get my fighters back to the west, the whole business will be different."[140] Again in October, Mölders, Kammhuber, and the fighter ace Adolf Galland argued with Göring to increase the production of day fighters to provide for the defense of the Reich proper. Once again, Göring demurred and exclaimed, "The Luftwaffe must attack and not defend. The reprisal raids on Britain ordered by the Fuehrer must be agreed to and carried out."[141] A month after this meeting, Göring's faith in his air defenses was put to a severe test.

Disaster over Berlin

On the night of November 7, 1941, Peirse organized a maximum effort aimed at Berlin and targets in Germany. A total of 169 aircraft took off in poor weather conditions to strike at the capital of the Third Reich; 21 of these aircraft, or almost 13 percent, failed to return. In addition, 55 aircraft launched a strike against Mannheim, and another 43 bombers attacked targets in the Ruhr. These forces lost 7 aircraft, or 13 percent, and 9 aircraft, or 21 percent, respectively. For the entire night, Bomber Command had suffered the loss of 37 bombers, a disastrous loss rate of 14 percent in the attacks on three German targets.[142] The fact that the Wellington and Whitley bombers were operating at the limits of their range in poor weather offers a partial explanation for the magnitude of the losses. The raid, however, also demonstrated the increasing effectiveness of German air defenses. Night fighters operating in conjunction with searchlights and radar-assisted flak batteries combined to force the British to pay a high cost for their incursions against targets deep within Germany.[143]

The most direct result of the catastrophe of November 7 was a Bomber Command order of mid-November limiting attacks to coastal targets and occasional raids on the Ruhr. In the wake of the disastrous raid, Peirse sent a letter to Portal on December 2, in response to criticisms concerning the heavy casualties experienced by Bomber Command in the mission against the German capital. Peirse wrote:

> As regards our losses on Berlin, I certainly do not regard them with complacence, but I have to deal with facts as they are, and it is certain that with our present equipment and standard of training we will incur an average loss of approximately ten per cent in such attacks. The figures for individual attacks of reasonable magnitude in the past have varied from five per cent to thirteen per cent, and in the last big attack on the 7/8th September it was nine per cent. On the night of the 7/8th November enemy fighter activity, as deduced from the number of interceptions reported, was only slightly less than normal, and a considerable amount of R/T traffic was intercepted although no "Sieg Heils" were heard. . . . Further, a very accurate anti-aircraft fire was reported over BERLIN. A loss of at least ten per cent cannot therefore be regarded as unusual or unexpected.[144]

Peirse's letter to Portal made it very clear that, at this stage in the war, deep attacks into Germany, especially those aimed at one of the most heavily defended targets in the Reich, could be conducted only at great risk and cost of life to the crews of Bomber Command. Not including numerous nuisance raids by Mosquito bombers, it would be fourteen months before a large Allied bomber force again would be seen in the skies over Berlin. Despite the restrictions on deep penetration missions, the RAF lost a further 141 aircraft in the last six weeks of the year in attacks on Hamburg, Kiel, Emden, and Essen, most of these losses resulting from German air defenses.[145] Göring's prophecy on preventing British bombing of the Reich still rang hollow; however, the Luftwaffe's air defenses had proved to be more than an equal match for the RAF in 1941. The ground-based defenses may not have fulfilled Göring's high expectations, but they had largely blunted the blows of the British bombing effort.

The Economic Costs of Air Defense

In addition to evaluating the performance of the flak arm, one must also examine the economic costs associated with the organization and maintenance of these defenses. The percentage of total funding from the entire armed forces weapons budget devoted to the flak arm rose continually throughout 1941, from 15 percent in the first quarter, to 17 percent in the second quarter, 19 percent in the third quarter, and finally 24 percent in the fourth quarter. Likewise, expenditures for flak ammunition jumped from 18 percent in the first quarter to 27 percent in the second quarter and to 34 and 35 percent in the last two quarters of 1941, respectively.[146]

The devotion of over one-third of the Wehrmacht's entire ammunition budget to anti-aircraft munitions in the last two quarters of 1941 once again highlighted the importance placed by Hitler on strengthening the Reich's ground-based air defenses. Several historians have questioned the large-scale diversion of resources to flak ammunition and flak equipment. In turn, many have argued that these resources would have been better spent on building more fighters.[147] It is important to note, however, that the United States Strategic Bombing Survey found that "since earlier limitation of output was largely the result of deliberately restricted demand, it cannot be said that the investment in anti-aircraft prior to 1943 represents a cost in terms of other weapons and ammunition."[148] In other words, the opportunity costs associated with expanding the flak arm in the first three years of the war do not appear to have negatively impacted the overall German war economy prior to 1943. Furthermore, the increased production of fighters also entailed numerous hidden resource costs, including expanded pilot training programs, increased fuel demands, and the necessity for more air bases, maintenance depots, and supporting aviation infrastructure. In short, the calculus of air defense did not allow itself to be reduced to a simple binomial equation.

The Year 1941 in Review

In December, the Luftwaffe's ground-based air defense forces could with justification look back upon 1941 with a good deal of satisfaction. The participation of the Luftwaffe's mobile flak forces in campaigns in North Africa, the Balkans, and Russia had proved highly successful. The dummy installations located throughout the Reich continued to draw a significant portion of RAF attacks away from their intended targets. Searchlight batteries played a key role in the success enjoyed by the night fighters and the flak. Finally, substantial improvement of the flak forces' performance within the Reich and the occupied western territories loomed on the horizon through the increased availability of gun-laying radar and more capable flak guns. German air defenses, both fighters and ground-based forces, had shown measurable improvement in the course of 1941. The increased allocation of both moneys and resources contributed to the continuing expansion and improvement in performance of the flak arm.

Despite these positive factors, the outlook for German air defenses was not entirely salutary. The disastrous raid on Berlin in November had cost the

RAF dearly; however, the raid was merely the culmination of a trend involving Bomber Command's ability to launch increasingly larger missions against the Reich. Likewise, December had also witnessed a portentous development for the German war effort. The entry of the United States into the war not only meant an increase in aid and assistance to the British, and by extension the RAF, but also, and more important, it signaled the appearance of a U.S. Army Air Force intent on proving its case that daylight precision bombardment held the key to victory in modern warfare.

In the face of the looming intensification of a combined Allied bombing campaign, the Luftwaffe would require increasing numbers of fighters, flak equipment, and personnel in the coming years. In regard to this last requirement, Goebbels noted in a diary entry on Christmas Day 1941 that "what we lack most of all are people. They are missing on the Eastern Front and in the homeland."[149] As the air war over Germany intensified in 1942, the lack of qualified personnel to operate flak guns, searchlights, and radar sites emerged as a nagging problem and, eventually, a critical weakness in the Reich's defensive armor.

In the end, the way in which the Luftwaffe chose to deal with the anticipated expansion of the bomber campaign, as well as the growth of its ground-based air defenses, would go a long way to determining success or failure in the coming years. In truth, at the turn of the year, the massive Allied air fleets existed only in the minds of USAAF and RAF commanders and in the projections of air staff planners. However, the German political and military leadership could ill afford to underestimate the speed by which "paper airplanes" might be transformed to finished works of aluminum and steel. For the Luftwaffe, the decisions made and the actions taken in the next twelve months, as well as the decisions left unmade and actions not taken, would determine the fate of German air defenses in the closing stages of the war. The coming year would up the ante in the high-stakes game of protecting the Reich, while Hitler continued to place his bet on the flak arm.

Motorized flak gun crew conducting direct fire operations during World War I. (James Corum)

German motorized 77-mm flak gun prior to World War I. Note crew member at left using 1-meter optical range finder. (James Corum)

Anti-aircraft gun crew with 37-mm machine gun during World War I. (James Corum)

Members of the Condor Legion operating a 20-mm flak gun in a ground combat role during the Spanish civil war. The effectiveness of flak guns against ground targets was one of the major lessons learned by the Wehrmacht during the conflict in Spain. (James Corum)

Civil defense exercise circa 1936. The National Socialist government put great store in civil defense measures prior to and during World War II. (James Corum)

Flak battery consisting of six 88-mm flak guns in prepared positions. The change from four-gun to six-gun batteries represented an initial attempt by the Luftwaffe to increase the firepower of flak batteries against Allied bombers. (BA-Koblenz)

Flak gun (88-mm) crew supporting ground combat operations on the Eastern Front in the summer of 1941. Note the four white rings on the barrel denoting the number of aircraft shot down. (BA-Koblenz)

Crew training on fire director with attached 4-meter optical range finder. Note the Würzburg gun-laying radar in the background. (BA-Koblenz)

Luftwaffe 20-mm flak gun crew practicing against a simulated target aircraft along the French coast in 1941. (BA-Koblenz)

Motorized four-barreled 20-mm flak gun in firing position. Note the markings on armor shield plate denoting the number of tanks and aircraft destroyed. (BA-Koblenz)

Destroyed 88-mm gun barrel in a position near Tobruk in 1942. These incidents usually resulted from the use of defective ammunition or firing the gun beyond the barrel's service life. (BA-Koblenz)

Flak gun (88-mm) firing on Soviet tanks during the winter of 1942. The 88-mm flak gun emerged as the most feared antitank gun of the war. (BA-Koblenz)

Flakhelfer responding to an exercise air-raid alarm. It was not unusual for classes to be conducted next to the gun batteries or for the instruction to be interrupted by practice or real air-raid alarms. (BA-Koblenz)

Flakhelfer operating a sound detector in the spring of 1943. The mobilization of these young boys for service in 1943 highlighted the personnel crisis faced by the Luftwaffe's flak forces at this stage in the war. (BA-Koblenz)

Female Luftwaffe auxiliaries cleaning a 150-cm searchlight. By the end of the war, these young women played a critical role in the German ground-based air defenses. (BA-Koblenz)

Female Luftwaffe auxiliaries preparing a barrage balloon to be raised for use against low-level attacks. (BA-Koblenz)

Crew operating a Würzburg gun-laying radar in 1943. Note the silhouettes of the bombers inside the radar dish denoting the crew's participation in the shootdown of these aircraft. (BA-Koblenz)

Four-barreled 20-mm flak gun mounted on a railcar. Railroad flak guns emerged as an important component of the Luftwaffe's flak forces in the last years of the war. (BA-Koblenz)

Railroad flak guns (105-mm) in positions near the French coast in 1942. (BA-Koblenz)

One example of the massive flak towers constructed in Berlin, Hamburg, and Vienna. These structures served a variety of purposes, including air defense headquarters, ammunition depots, air-raid shelters, and first aid stations. (BA-Koblenz)

Armor shield on an 88-mm flak gun denoting the variety of tasks for which this weapon was employed. The red stars and symbols signify the number of Soviet aircraft, tanks, bunkers, artillery, and observation posts destroyed by this gun. (BA-Koblenz)

One of the steel radar reflectors placed on wooden floats in lakes surrounding Berlin to deceive Allied H2S/H2X radar by altering the radar image of these distinctive bodies of water. (BA-Koblenz)

Flak gun battery (88-mm) in action. The crew has painted the Union Jack and the USAAF symbol on the gun barrel instead of the traditional white rings to denote the number of aircraft destroyed. (BA-Koblenz)

Twin-barreled 128–mm flak gun. These gigantic weapons were placed atop the massive concrete flak towers in Berlin, Hamburg, and Vienna and were the most capable anti-aircraft guns of the war. (BA-Koblenz)

Flak gun crew member displaying a piece of an American bomber brought down by his gun position. (BA-Koblenz)

CHAPTER SIX

Raising the Stakes, 1942

The success of German ground-based air defenses owed much to the high priority placed on increasing the size and capability of the force in the last three-quarters of 1941 and into early 1942. On January 5, 1942, in a discussion at his field headquarters, the *Wolfsschanze,* Hitler boasted to Reich Minister Fritz Todt and a group of military officers, "In 1940 the English announced to us, that the 'flying fortresses' would pulverize Germany. . . . We had to assume [that] they would quadruple their efforts in the air in 1941. In response, I undertook an increase in our Flak and, above all, our Flak munitions."[1] An analysis of German military spending clearly demonstrates that Hitler was correct in his assertion that the flak arm had benefited from a major increase in funding in 1941 and 1942. The proportion of funding from the entire armed forces weapons and ammunition budget devoted to flak systems and flak ammunition in the first half of 1942 stood at 24 percent for flak weapons and 31 percent for flak ammunition in the first quarter and at 24 percent for flak weapons and 21 percent for flak ammunition in the second quarter.[2]

The devotion of almost one-quarter of the Wehrmacht's entire weapons budget to anti-aircraft armament in the first two quarters of 1942 and the significant outlays for ammunition continued the trend begun in 1941 and once again highlighted the importance placed by Hitler on strengthening the Reich's ground-based air defenses. This emphasis continued into 1942 with Hitler's approval of the Guidelines for Armaments Production, 1942, on January 10, 1942. The overall objective of the guidelines included a continued concentration on the expansion of the Luftwaffe and the German navy in preparation "for battle against the Anglo-Saxon powers," despite the ongoing campaign in Russia. The plan called for the implementation of the aircraft acquisition program and the anti-aircraft program within the limits of the available resource allocations. Furthermore, Hitler explicitly stated that any decrease in the flak program required his express approval.[3] If one gives credence to the expression that "money talks," it was clear that by the beginning of 1942 Hitler had placed a great deal of the Wehrmacht's budget on a wager involving anti-aircraft defenses.

* * *

A New Commander for the Flak

In January 1942, Hitler not only bet on the anti-aircraft horse but also chose a new jockey to guide Germany's ground-based air defenses to the finish line. General Walther von Axthelm replaced General Steudemann as the inspector of the flak and general of the Flak Artillery on January 12, 1942. Born in the town of Hersbruck in the vicinity of Nuremburg in 1893, von Axthelm had entered the army in 1913 and served in the 8th Bavarian Field Artillery Regiment during World War I.[4] After the war, he joined the Reichswehr and held a variety of command and staff positions and even participated in a two-week exchange with the Swedish army. On April 1, 1935, he transferred to the Luftwaffe and was mentored by Rüdel during a staff tour in the Flak Artillery Inspectorate prior to the war.[5] However, it was during the campaign against the Soviet Union that von Axthelm came to the attention of Göring and the Luftwaffe leadership. When he was commander of Flak Corps I, his forces accounted for approximately 300 aircraft and 3,000 armored vehicles destroyed in the opening three months of the war in the east. As a result, von Axthelm received the Knight's Cross, the Third Reich's highest combat decoration, and his path to the pinnacle of the flak artillery forces appeared assured.[6] A proven combat leader with an extensive operational background and high-level staff postings, von Axthelm seemed the perfect choice to guide the Luftwaffe's flak forces.

Likewise, January 1942 certainly seemed like a propitious moment for a commander to take control over Germany's ground-based air defenses. The increased budgetary allocations to the flak arm resulted in steady expansion in the numbers of heavy and light flak gun batteries, as well as the total size of the searchlight force. For example, at the start of 1941 the number of flak gun and searchlight batteries, within the Reich and on the Western Front totaled 634 heavy gun batteries, 541 light gun batteries, and 209 searchlight batteries. By 1942, there were 866 heavy gun batteries, 621 light gun batteries, and 273 searchlight batteries in these areas, amounting to increases of 27 percent, 13 percent, and 23 percent, respectively. In the Reich proper, the number of heavy gun batteries increased from 537 to 744 (+28 percent), light gun batteries increased from 395 to 438 (+10 percent), and searchlight batteries expanded from 138 to 174 (+21 percent).[7]

Searchlights and the Effectiveness of the Flak

The growth in the size of the searchlight batteries was especially striking and provided direct evidence of the importance attached to these systems in support of both anti-aircraft artillery and the Luftwaffe's night fighter force. One

British Operational Research Section (ORS) report highlighted the importance of searchlights as adjuncts to anti-aircraft fire. An examination of losses in a three-month period in 1942 led to the conclusion that searchlights assisted anti-aircraft batteries in inflicting 70 percent of all flak casualties experienced by RAF bombers over German targets.[8] Another study found that the employment of searchlights increased the number of aircraft hit by flak by approximately 50 percent.[9]

The leadership of the Luftwaffe clearly recognized the critical role played by searchlights in air defense operations. In fact, Göring personally addressed the importance of increased searchlight production in a meeting of the Air Armaments Office on April 26 in which he proclaimed that "the production of searchlights must be increased under all circumstances with all available means."[10] Despite the fact that the production of searchlights, especially the 150-mm and 200-mm models, required significant amounts of scarce copper resources,[11] the output of 150-mm searchlights increased from 1,392 in 1941 to 1,610 in 1942. Furthermore, the Luftwaffe produced 250 of the new 200-mm searchlights in 1942.[12] These 200-mm mammoths, distinguished by their bluish tinge when viewed from above, acted as "master lights" to find bombers and then guide their 150-mm counterparts on to the aircraft.[13] In any event, Göring's personal support of increased searchlight production was one indication of the good results achieved by these defenses in the latter months of 1941 and in the opening months of 1942.

The RAF's Reaction to the Luftwaffe's Air Defense Initiatives

The performance of the flak arm throughout 1941 and early 1942 seemed to verify Hitler's faith in the effectiveness of the German ground-based defenses. As mentioned earlier, the high losses experienced by Bomber Command in the second half of 1941 led Prime Minister Churchill to demand that the bomber force be conserved. Churchill's order, combined with the historically poor winter weather over the Continent, resulted in an extremely limited bombing effort in the last months of 1941 and the early months of 1942. In fact, between November 10, 1941, and February 22, 1942, Bomber Command flew missions on only 54 out of 105 nights. In addition, on only four occasions did the total number of aircraft involved exceed 200 bombers.[14] At the same time that they were limiting the bombing effort, the leaders of the RAF attempted to ascertain the causes for the operational losses in the skies over Europe. In a report of January 20, 1942, designed to identify the percentage of RAF bombers lost to flak defenses in night raids, the analysts of the British ORS offered several important conclusions with respect to German flak defenses. First, the report noted, "While it is impossible to deduce the proportion of aircraft destroyed by flak, it can be said that it is greater than 20% of the total aircraft missing both by day and night." Second, the report's author noted, "Such information as available suggests that during the day sorties fighters and flak have been equally lethal."[15] This conclusion clearly lent some support to Hitler's continued belief in the viability of anti-aircraft defenses, especially during day raids, despite the pessimism expressed by Milch and others within the Luftwaffe high command concerning the efficacy of flak defenses.

By early 1942, the analysts within the ORS may have experienced difficulty in establishing the exact numbers of aircraft lost to either German fighters or German anti-aircraft defenses; however, such was not the case with respect to Bomber Command aircraft damaged in attacks over Europe. Table 6.1 displays the percentage of aircraft labeled as missing, damaged by flak, and damaged by fighters in night raids between January and May 1942.[16] These figures offer a number of important insights into the nature of night combat over Europe. First, the ratio of aircraft returning to England with flak damage versus fighter damage ranged from a high of 9.27 to 1 in April to a low of .85 to 1 in March. In the remaining months, the ratio of aircraft damaged by flak versus fighters ranged between 8 to 1 and 9 to 1 in favor of the flak defenses. In regard to flak damage, another ORS study found that up to 80 percent of flak casualties occurred over the target area, a fact easily explained by the concentration of flak guns around the target.[17]

Admittedly, one must be careful to not overdraw conclusions concerning the effectiveness of flak defenses versus fighters based on this limited sample. For example, it is conceivable that fewer aircraft returned to England with fighter damage because fighters that successfully engaged aircraft achieved a much higher number of shootdowns than their ground-based counterparts. This assumption is in part supported by an ORS report of February 17, 1943, that analyzed numbers of casualties sustained by Bomber Command aircrews returning in damaged aircraft from April 26, 1942, to November 30, 1942. This report found that total aircrew casualties as a result of flak numbered 95 and total aircrew casualties inflicted by fighters numbered 105. In turn, the pro-

Table 6.1 Aircraft Damaged by Flak and Fighters, January–May 1942

	Total Sorties	Missing (%)	Damaged by Flak (%)	Damaged by Fighters (%)
January	2,200	2.4	3.6	0.4
Febuary	1,157	1.9	2.4	0.3
March	2,224	3.5	6.0	7.0
April	3,752	3.7	10.2	1.1
May	2,699	4.3	7.0	0.8

portion of fatal aircrew casualties resulting from flak effects was 9.5 percent, while the proportion resulting from fighter attacks was 14.8 percent.[18] An additional ORS report evaluating daylight losses concluded that "damage by fighter is more often lethal than damage by flak."[19]

Much of the data collected and analyzed by the Operational Research Section offered insights into evaluating the effectiveness of German ground-based and aerial defenses, but not enough information to reach definitive conclusions. The ORS analyses often provided only one piece of a very large puzzle. For example, an aircraft damaged by flak was far more likely to fall prey to a fighter as a result of its decreased maneuverability, slower speed, or increased visibility due to smoke or engine fire.[20] In addition, the success of German night fighters in this period in many instances depended on the ability of ground-based searchlights to illuminate the bomber for the fighters. With respect to this last point, an RAF report of April 14, 1942, recognized the importance of searchlights in both flak and fighter operations by noting that "the Germans have organised their searchlights to a high state of perfection and their A.A. guns appear to rely considerably upon searchlight co-operation to obtain results. Searchlight co-operation also plays a large part in the enemy's fighter interception technique."[21] However, throughout 1942, the night fighters began to rely far less on the searchlights. The proportion of searchlight-assisted night fighter shootdowns plummeted from 15 percent in the spring to approximately 3 percent by the end of the year.[22] Likewise, an ORS report of early 1943 observed that, during the course of 1942, "the use of searchlights to illuminate bombers for the benefit of fighters has declined very considerably but their employment as an accessory to gun-fire control probably increased . . . [and] it appears possible that they may double flak losses."[23]

The importance of searchlights in the Luftwaffe's air defenses also was apparent in the postmission reports of the bomber crews. For example, a report for the night of January 22 indicated that "controlled night fighters were very busy assisted by numerous lights." In another example, after a January night raid against Bremen, crews reported, "Heavy flak intense and accurate with searchlight co-operation. Searchlights very numerous operating in cones of 20/30." Likewise, in a mission against Hamburg, aircrews recalled "searchlights very active co-operating with flak in cones of 30–60 beams" and searchlights "were intensely active though flak was moderate on the whole."[24] And these were not isolated observations. In fact, one historian of the air war has contended that being caught in the cones of searchlights was the "greatest fear" of RAF bomber crews.[25] Without doubt, the searchlight batteries continued to play a vital role in the Luftwaffe's air defense network, and the superior performance of these batteries explains their dramatic expansion throughout the war.

The Growth of Gun-laying Radar

One other factor increased the high percentage of flak damage experienced by RAF bombers during night operations. By the early months of 1942, the German flak defenses were becoming increasingly adept at employing gun-laying radar. On the one hand, a Luftwaffe study estimated that one out of every three heavy flak batteries was equipped with gun-laying radar by March 1942.[26] On the other hand, modifications to gun-laying radar improved range data and simplified handling of the equipment while increasing the radar's position-finding accuracy to between twenty-five and forty meters.[27] Despite the improved performance of gun-laying radar, these systems still did not reach the accuracy of directed fire under illuminated or optical tracking. For example, of the forty-three aircraft brought down by anti-aircraft crews in Air Region, Center, in April 1942, only eleven were shot down using gun-laying radar as the primary targeting system.[28] Still, these systems did play an important role in guiding both searchlights and anti-aircraft guns to the target in the initial phase of the attack. The Luftwaffe, however, faced a shortage of gun-laying radar throughout 1942. In turn, German industry began developing and producing an auxiliary firing system, designated as the "Malsi converter." These devices essentially could use the information obtained from a gun-laying radar set located at one site and then convert these data for use by a gun battery at a separate location.[29] The Malsi converters were far less resource intensive than complete radar sets and greatly enhanced the usefulness of the existing gun-laying radar.[30]

Despite the introduction of the Malsi converters, the senior leadership of the Luftwaffe, especially Göring, complained of inadequate numbers of radar sets and protested that the modifications to existing equipment were taking too long.[31] In response to Göring's criticism, Milch ordered the temporary transfer of engineers and skilled workers to the gun-laying radar program in order to increase production.[32] In spite of the shortage of radar sets, postmission reports of RAF bomber crews in 1942 indicated the flying crews' growing respect for radar-directed fire. For example, in a mission over Bremen on the night of January 17, crews reported "heavy flak moderate to intense on selected targets, accurate through 10/10 cloud." In a later raid against Münster on the night of January 28, crews again reported "moderate to intense heavy flak, accurately predicted through 10/10 cloud cover." This same report also noted that German aircraft were instructed to land because of "bad weather and snow."[33] These reports are notable in several respects. First, they demonstrate that, at least in certain well-defended areas, the German flak gunners were successful in targeting bombers through a full overcast using gun-laying radar. Second, the report concerning the recall of the night fighters because of poor weather again demonstrates one of the major limitations of aerial interception during the war. Lacking an all-weather interceptor and in light of the notoriously poor weather over Germany during the winter, the Luftwaffe's night fighters were at times unable to contribute to the defense of the Reich.[34] In contrast, the flak arm, despite its shortcomings and limitations, was not prevented by poor weather from engaging the bombers and affecting their ability to strike their targets. Finally, these reports did not indicate isolated achievements by the flak. The RAF's official history of the air war correctly noted that by 1942 "radar control was increasingly displacing the much less precise sound locator as a means of directing anti-aircraft fire and searchlights."[35] In recognition of the limitations of these devices, the Luftwaffe reduced the numbers of sound detectors with the searchlight batteries by one-third in 1942.[36] The authors of the RAF history also observed that "the mounting casualties which Bomber Command suffered after the resumption of its full-scale offensive in March 1942 established the reality of the new danger. Symptomatic of the changed situation was the greatly increased activity of German night fighters and the improved accuracy of the flak."[37]

Evaluating the Flak's Performance

One noted historian of the air war argued that in 1942 German interceptor and ground-based air defenses over the Reich reached their peak efficiency. This same historian also contended that improvements in Germany's night fighter force resulted in a situation in which "nearly 70 percent of British Bomber Command's night losses were due to German night fighters."[38] The former of these assertions is arguably true, while the latter contention is patently false.

A study by the ORS examined bomber losses due to fighter and flak using a sample of 95 losses due to known causes in the period between March and August 1942. The report attributed 35 losses to flak and 60 losses to fighters, or 30 percent and 51 percent of total losses for the period, respectively. Furthermore, the study concluded that in view of the limited sample and incomplete information, "all that can justifiably be said is that on the whole, the ratio of losses due to fighter to losses due to flak is not greater than 60 to 35."[39] In other words, the ratio of fighter shootdowns to aircraft destroyed by flak was 1.7 to 1. But the study examined losses during a period when European weather tends to be at its best, especially for night operations, a condition offering fighters the greatest possibility of success. Finally, the official RAF history recorded the estimated causes of losses in night raids between July and December 1942 as 169 aircraft lost to fighters and 193 aircraft lost to flak, a ratio of 1.14 to 1 in favor of the flak. Furthermore, in the same period the estimated number of aircraft damaged "beyond repair" by fighters was 11 versus 23 for flak, while aircraft damaged but repairable numbered 142 for fighters and 918 for flak.[40] These figures clearly refute the exaggerated claims attributed to night fighter success and demonstrate how the achievements of Germany's flak defenses have been underestimated in many postwar histories of the air war.

If some postwar historians failed to appreciate the effectiveness of German anti-aircraft defenses, such was not the case for contemporary RAF observers. In a report of April 14, 1942, one Royal Air Force analyst observed:

> There is every indication that in approximately the next six months the quality of our A.A. gunfire due to the introduction of new equipment will improve very considerably. Nothing is known of impending enemy improvements, but it is reasonable to suppose that progress will be made. Although our losses due to enemy A.A. gunfire at night have been small in the past, they have shown a gradual increase, and it is considered that they are likely to increase still further, unless energetic action to implement counter-measures is taken.[41]

The attempt to base projected German developments on known British advances is problematic in some respects based on the existing German material and technical superiority in this area. Still, it did indicate a feeling that progress was being achieved within the German ground-based air defense system. The report also demonstrated a measure of strategic vision intended to prepare the forces of Bomber Command for future operations.

Allocating Resources for Air Defense

The report's forecast for advances in the German ground-based air defenses proved to be prophetic even if "nothing" was known of "impending enemy improvements." For example, the "Führer Flak Program" in 1942 called for a continued increase in flak forces to achieve a strength at the end of 1943 of 900 heavy flak batteries, 750 light batteries, 200 150-cm searchlight batteries, and 25 barrage balloon batteries within the borders of the Reich proper.[42] To reach these numbers, the flak artillery branch would require a sustained allocation of substantial fiscal and material resources. The percentage of the total Wehrmacht weapons and ammunition budget devoted to the flak arm in the last half of 1942 witnessed a slight increase in the expenditures for flak weapons and a significant reduction in outlays for ammunition. Between July and September, flak weapons consumed 28 percent and flak ammunition 17 percent of the total Wehrmacht budget in the areas of weapons and ammunition. In the last three months of the year, spending for flak weapons and flak ammunition decreased slightly, to 27 percent and 15 percent, respectively.[43] In other words, the flak artillery averaged approximately one-fourth of the entire Wehrmacht weapons budget for the period, while the percentage of the Wehrmacht's ammunition budget in support of flak munitions declined by slightly more than half from the first-quarter allocation of 31 percent. The decrease in flak ammunition resulted primarily from two factors. The first involved an existing surplus in mid-1942 created by the high fiscal expenditures in late 1941 and during the early months of 1942. In fact, Milch estimated that the Luftwaffe had a surplus stock of 8 million anti-aircraft rounds and 4 million unfilled shells in early 1942.[44] In fact, German industry produced between 1.3 and 1.5 million rounds of 88-mm high-explosive ammunition in March 1942, while the maximum monthly expenditure totaled 800,000 rounds, an imbalance that, according to Milch, was causing severe problems in finding storage facilities for the ammunition surplus.[45] The second factor was the growing necessity to provide army forces with adequate supplies of ammunition as the war in the east became a black hole swallowing manpower and matériel in a spiraling battle of attrition.[46] For example, in the third quarter of 1942 the army received 54 percent, and in the fourth quarter 59 percent, of the Wehrmacht's entire ammunition budget.

By the middle of 1941, the German war economy began to experience the strains of conducting a multifront war. In June 1941, General Georg Thomas, the head of the Wehrmacht Economics and Armaments Office, notified Field Marshal Wilhelm Keitel, the chief of the Wehrmacht High Command, "I have told the Führer that this situation in which the branches of the Wehrmacht work at cross purposes is no longer viable since the economy is so over-stretched that the optimum armaments production can no longer be achieved. An office must be created which can ruthlessly override the three Commanders-in-Chief."[47] Likewise, a primary concern surrounding the Führer Flak Program for 1942 was the issue of resource allocation. The Office of Air Armament constituted the single most important Luftwaffe agency dealing with issues related to the research, testing, development, and production of air force weapons systems. Göring created the office in February 1939 and named Ernst Udet as the head of the organization. Udet proved singularly inept at controlling the vast scope of the office and committed suicide in November 1941 in the face of increasing criticism and impending removal from his post. Milch was subsequently appointed as Udet's successor and set about to rationalize the operation of the Air Armaments Office. The death of Dr. Fritz Todt, the minister of armaments, in a plane crash in February 1942 further complicated the struggle for bureaucratic control of the Third Reich's armaments complex. Hitler's subsequent appointment of Albert Speer as Todt's replacement led to a surprisingly cooperative relationship between Speer and Milch in the prosecution of a strategy for developing and producing the Luftwaffe's weapons systems.[48]

The appointment of Milch as head of the Air Armaments Office had a number of direct implications for the Luftwaffe's ground-based air defense forces.

In the words of one biographer, Milch strongly believed that "air defence rested primarily on the fighter squadrons." In fact, Milch immediately set about to boost the production of German fighter aircraft in an attempt to create "an umbrella over Germany." Meeting with Jeschonnek in late March 1942, Milch outlined a plan for increasing fighter production to 360 aircraft per month, a plan that led to Jeschonnek's memorable exclamation "I do not know what I should do with more than 360 fighters."[49] Any attempt to create an umbrella of fighters over the Reich was not simply a matter of increasing fighter production. Jeschonnek's statement was evidence not of his disdain for greater numbers of aircraft but of his recognition of the fact that the existing output of the Luftwaffe's pilot training program could not fill the cockpits of these aircraft. Indeed, Milch was forced to recognize this very point in a meeting of the Air Armaments Office on June 29, 1942, when he observed, "Everywhere there is a shortage of aircrews [and] the deficiency is continually intensifying. Something must be done immediately to increase [aircrew] training."[50]

Despite his belief in the primacy of fighter aircraft for air defense, Milch did not immediately attempt to reduce production of flak guns and associated ground-based air defense systems. He did, however, initiate steps to decrease the production of flak ammunition in an effort to redirect the aluminum used for the fuses in the projectiles toward aircraft production.[51] In truth, Milch was a skilled manager and able administrator highly attuned to the political realities of life in the Third Reich. He recognized that Hitler stood firmly behind anti-aircraft defenses and that Göring in turn would be a staunch supporter of the Luftwaffe's flak arm as well. Indeed, at one of Milch's first meetings as head of the Air Armaments Office, the issue of flak figured prominently in the day's agenda. First, Göring addressed Hitler's continued support for the Luftwaffe's flak arm. He explained that "the Führer wishes a strengthening of the flak defenses in the east. The execution [of this plan] is only possible by weakening the flak employed in the homeland."[52] The plan to increase the flak forces on the Eastern Front at the expense of those defenses in the Reich demonstrated the Wehrmacht's own penchant for robbing Peter to pay Paul, as personnel and matériel increasingly had to be shifted to the east at the expense of other theaters and the home front. Conversely, the lack of protest at this decision was not merely the result of simple acquiescence to Hitler's wishes; in part it was the product of the performance of ground-based air defenses within the Reich. Indeed, the decision to shift resources to the east did not seem to evoke concerns surrounding the potential weakening of the existing defenses within the Reich.

During the meeting on March 6, Göring also addressed the problems associated with resource allocation for the flak forces. He ordered the preparation of a "detailed calculation of materials" necessary for the implementation and execution of the Führer Flak Program. Furthermore, he remarked that some of the needed resources could be obtained from existing and as yet unfinished partially manufactured goods and materials. He also noted that supplies of chrome lay in the Ukraine but could not at present be transported to the Reich.

In response to Göring's observations, Milch made a number of points. First he noted that chrome was no longer being used in the Luftwaffe's armor plating. Despite this measure, a shortage of chrome was affecting the manufacture of artillery guns while sufficient amounts of copper were available to support artillery production. He mentioned, however, that the heavy searchlights, the 150-cm and the new 200-cm models, required a high quantity of copper, 560 kilograms and 1,410 kilograms, respectively. Göring then interjected that changes in design plans aimed at substituting other materials were needed.[53] This last point was significant because during the course of the war German industry became adept at finding substitutions for various strategic resources in the manufacturing and production process.[54] By March 1942, the Luftwaffe had introduced engine radiators free of both copper and tin.[55] Still, the high demand for copper in the searchlights pointed in part to an endemic weakness of resource allocation within the Third Reich. In a postwar interrogation, Milch made exactly this point as he described how his predecessor, Udet, calculated the need for sixteen tons of aluminum and four tons of copper per aircraft. However, when Milch toured the aircraft production factories, he found that some had stockpiled enough reserves for eight or nine months of production.[56] In other words, industrial leaders had provided inflated resource requirements in order to guarantee that they would have a safety margin for future production, a practice that is not unsurprising for an environment in which the competition for limited resources approached the economic equivalent of the survival of the fittest.

The common practice of resource hoarding present throughout the Reich has bedeviled the ability of historians even to the present to gain a clear picture of the existing economic situation within Germany during the war. Without doubt, copper was a scarce resource throughout the war. However, the problem was further complicated by the practice of each of the armed services, the army, the navy, and the Luftwaffe, to present resource demands that were vastly in excess of their actual needs, a practice intended to ensure the allocation of a sufficient percentage to cover their desired production. This system led to absurd situations such as one in which "the Wehrmacht's total demands for copper exceeded the total world production."[57] A growing realization of the need for changes in resource allocation procedures, especially noticeable in light of the continuing war in the east, led in March 1942 to the creation of a body known as Central Planning, which consisted of Speer, Milch, and a representative from Göring's Four-Year Plan Office. The Office of Central Planning was to rationalize the German war economy and squeeze out excess production from the large degree of existing slack within the industrial sector.[58]

The remarkable success achieved by both Speer and Milch in armaments production after this period can in great part be explained by their success in eliminating the inefficiencies associated with the allotment of available resources and the streamlining of production procedures.

Sir Arthur Harris at the Helm

The beginning steps on the road toward industrial rationalization in the early months of 1942 came at an important juncture in the air war. In February 1942, Air Vice Marshal Arthur Harris replaced Peirse at the head of Bomber Command. The disastrous losses incurred over Berlin in November 1941, declining morale within Bomber Command, and increasing friction between Portal and Peirse sealed the latter's fate in early 1942.[59] With the departure of Peirse, Harris profited from several new developments within the bomber force in the first months of his tenure.

First, by February over one-third of Bomber Command aircraft had been fitted with a new radio direction finding device known as GEE. The GEE devices essentially received signals from three transmitters stationed in the United Kingdom; by measuring the differences in the time taken to receive each signal, bomber crews were able to fix their positions. The main weakness with the devices was that their range was limited to between 350 and 400 miles. Still, this was sufficient to reach a number of targets within the industrial Ruhr valley, including Essen, Duisburg, Düsseldorf, and Cologne.[60] But GEE was not an aid for precision bombardment. It only allowed aircrews to reach the general target area with greater accuracy than had previously been achieved.[61]

Second, by early 1942 Bomber Command had drawn a number of lessons from its experiences early in the war concerning aircrew training. In addition to adding a designated crew position for bomber-aimers, the RAF introduced the "single-pilot" policy in March 1942, a move that cut the number of pilots per plane from two to one, thus effectively doubling the size of the pilot force. Third, a program of expanding and upgrading RAF airfields was nearing completion. Fourth, an increasing number of "heavy" bombers, such as the Avro Lancaster, with longer range and greater bomb loads, were entering the air force.[62] Finally, Harris took over Bomber Command at a time when the RAF had recently released a new bombing directive that officially sanctioned "concentrated incendiary attacks."[63] Aircrews now received instructions to aim for "built-areas" within German cities instead of specific targets, the goal being to strike at "the morale of the enemy civil population and, in particular, of the industrial workers."[64]

While clearly benefiting from good timing, Harris was equally determined to take full advantage of the situation by attempting to overwhelm the German defenses by means of a series of concentrated attacks. Harris chose the Renault truck factory, at Billancourt on the outskirts of Paris as the first major target for a new bomber offensive. On the night of March 3, over 220 bombers struck the factory, inflicting considerable damage that would affect production for almost a month.[65] The raid helped to convince the new commander of Bomber Command that concentration was the key to success. But attacks on targets within Germany offered a far different proposition than the raid against Paris. RAF planners selected the industrial town of Essen as the first German target for implementing the new strategy for nighttime area bombardment. On the night of March 8, RAF bombers using GEE devices approached Essen in three waves. The first dropped flares to mark the approach path to the target, while the second dropped incendiaries over the city's center. Then, the main force spread a mix of incendiaries and high explosives. But the results proved less successful than expected. Subsequent raids on Essen and Cologne again demonstrated that GEE helped crews find the general target area, but the device could not guarantee an accurate concentration on the target, even one as large as a city center. GEE devices also could not solve the human problem described by one RAF group commander as the tendency of "weaker brethren" to release their bombs on the outer perimeter of the target area in an effort to avoid flying into the brunt of enemy flak defenses, the "scourge" of creep-back.[66]

The March raids against the Ruhr provided continuing evidence of the success experienced by both German active and passive ground-based air defenses. Air Commodore J. Searby described the attacks using GEE in this period in the following terms: "It could take us to the Ruhr and within sight of the objective, but the precise aiming point, more often than not hidden by smoke and industrial haze, had to be discovered by visual means—an almost impossible task in the deluge of heavy flak burst and dazzling searchlights." Another pilot provided a vivid and detailed description of the approach to the target:

> Long before you reached the target area you would see ahead of you a confusing maze of searchlights quartering the sky, some in small groups, others stacked in cones of twenty or more. These often had a victim transfixed, as if pinned to the sky, their apex filled with red bursts of heavy flak. . . . The Germans liberally sprayed the ground with dummy incendiaries and imitation fire blocks in the neighbourhood of important targets, hoping to attract a share of the bombs. Gun flashes, photoflashes, bomb-bursts, streams of tracer of all colours, and everywhere searchlights—it was all very confusing, especially when the air gunners were directing the pilot to avoid flak and searchlights in all directions at the same time.[67]

These typical recollections offered two important insights into the nature of German ground-based air defenses in the Ruhr during this period. First, the searchlight and anti-aircraft batteries, especially in areas of high flak and searchlight concentrations, continued to cooperate well in defense against the bombers. Second, the experiences of these pilots demonstrated the Luftwaffe's continued employment of decoy and deception measures designed to induce RAF aircraft to release their bomb loads over dummy targets.

With respect to the first point, the RAF lost thirty-five aircraft from a total of 893 sorties, for a loss rate of 3.9 percent during the March raids on Essen. During these attacks, night fighters accounted for slightly over half of the aircraft destroyed, while flak tallied the rest. The official Canadian history of the war remarked that, despite the increasing effectiveness of night fighters, for many crews flak remained the "main worry." One crew member remembered, "The most alarming factor of the German defences was undoubtedly the searchlights. They had master beams, radar controlled, . . . once caught, every searchlight in range would fix you and, wriggle and squirm as you might, you couldn't shake them off. Then the guns joined in and filled the apex of the cone with bursts. . . . All too often the sequel was a small flame, burning bright as the aircraft fell towards the ground."[68]

Dummy Sites, Act 3

In addition to the active defensive measures taken against the bombers, the Luftwaffe also continued to conduct deception operations using dummy installations; however, by the summer of 1942, the RAF became increasingly adept at identifying these sites. In one case, British bombers overflew twenty dummy sites in Air District VII during the night of August 28 but released only a single high-explosive bomb on a site near Augsburg. Still, even as late as December, an RAF bomber dropped ten high-explosive bombs and one hundred incendiaries on one dummy site. The interrogations of two downed pilots in September produced a mixed evaluation of the sites, with one pilot remarking that the lighting of the dummy sites made them easily discernible and the other pilot describing the effectiveness of the sites, especially those northwest of Berlin.[69] In any event, the noticeable decrease in the efficacy of the dummy sites led the Luftwaffe to attempt new methods for decoying the bombers away from their intended targets. For example, the Luftwaffe constructed walled enclosures labeled by the British as "fire sites" in areas near potential RAF targets. These enclosures were filled with combustible materials and set alight prior to, or during, an actual bombing raid. At night and from a height of over 10,000 feet, the fire sites resembled burning buildings and thus were simple but extremely effective decoys. In the wake of a failed raid on Mannheim on the night of May 19, 1942, Harris berated his group commanders over the issue of bombs being released over the fire sites. In a lengthy passage, Harris showed his anger with his crews:

> It is apparent from the night photographs and from the reports of crews, that almost the whole effort was wasted in bombing large fires in the local forests, and possibly decoy fires. Nevertheless, in spite of the now incontrovertible evidence that this is what in fact occurred, the reports of the crews on their return from the raid were most definite in very many cases that they had reached the town and bombed it. . . . The cause of this failure is beyond doubt to be found in the easy manner in which crews are misled by decoy fires or by fires in the wrong place. . . . somehow or other we must cure this disease, for it is a disease, of wasting bombs wholesale upon decoy fires.[70]

An RAF study at the end of the war confirmed Harris's fear and noted that the principal type of decoy used in 1941 and 1942 had been the fire site. The study then concluded that, although these sites were often recognized in night photographs, they were still "frequently effective in diverting a considerable proportion of our attacks."[71] Despite Harris's admonition to his crews, the fire sites would continue to retain much of their effectiveness until the RAF introduced target-marking devices for the Pathfinder Force in 1943, at which time the German defenders would initiate a new series of countermeasures in an endless game of action and reaction. In any event, the fire sites demonstrated the Luftwaffe's continued success in deception operations versus the bombers and once again highlighted the importance of examining the ground-based defensive measures in a broader context beyond the simplified calculus of flak guns versus fighters.

As an adjunct to the dummy sites, the Luftwaffe also began to use smoke generators to conceal the primary target and divert the bombers to the fake installations.[72] During the latter half of 1941, smoke generators had proved highly effective in protecting the battleships *Scharnhorst* and *Gneisenau*, anchored in the harbor at Brest, from RAF bombing raids.[73] Likewise, smoke generator companies surrounding the oil refinery at Pölitz achieved a "complete success" in preventing the accurate bombing of the site in December 1942. By the end of the year, the Luftwaffe had eight smoke-generating companies consisting of 500 men each. The main drawback associated with these units was, however, their demand for 15,000 tons of smoke acid per month, a demand that German industry found impossible to meet as the number of smoke generator companies expanded to one hundred by 1945.[74] The performance of the smoke generator companies, like that of the dummy installations, provided yet another example of the effectiveness of ground-based air defenses when viewed from a holistic perspective.

Area Bombing and the Destruction of German Cities

Despite the success of early 1942, the Luftwaffe could not defend the entire Reich or decoy all RAF bombers away from their intended targets. In late March, Harris chose the picturesque Hanseatic city of Lübeck as a further test case for the emergent strategy of area bombardment. On the night of March 28, RAF bombers set out for an attack against the city. Although beyond the range of GEE, Lübeck provided an easily distinguishable target for RAF bombers because of its proximity to the Baltic coast. In his postwar memoirs, Harris reflected on the raid:

> It was not a vital target, but it seemed to me better to destroy an industrial town of moderate importance that [*sic*] to fail to destroy a large industrial city. However, the main object of the attack was to learn to what extent a first wave of aircraft could guide a second wave to the aiming point by starting a conflagration.[75]

If the object of the attack was to develop a lesson on the ability of aircraft to engender a conflagration, then the mission was a decided success. The raid devastated the ancient city center as incendiaries found ready fuel in the old wooden structures located throughout the district. In the end, the raid killed over 300 persons, inflicted over a thousand civilian casualties, and seriously damaged over 2,000 buildings in the city.[76] The National Socialist district leader *(Gauleiter)* for the Hamburg area, Karl Kaufmann, described the raid as the most severe ever experienced by a German city from the air, and initial German reports estimated the destruction to the city center at 80 percent.[77] Kaufmann was correct, but there was much worse yet to come.

The attack proved costly not only for German civilians but also for the crews of British bombers. The RAF lost thirteen bombers, or 5.5 percent of the entire force, to German defenses, a rate that, according to Harris, if continued over time, threatened to prevent the expansion of Bomber Command or at least keep its offensive from reaching its fullest intensity.[78] Despite the losses, the attack on Lübeck confirmed Harris's belief in the importance of concentration. In an official report in April 1942, one RAF analyst argued, "Great concentration of our aircraft in time and space, together with wide dispersion in height, will provide a sound counter-measure against the enemy A.A. defences by night."[79] The RAF report mirrored Harris's own thinking on the subject of future bomber operations. The attack on Lübeck and subsequent attacks against the Baltic port of Rostock proved that a large bomber force of several hundred aircraft could saturate German defenses over a lightly defended target, but Harris was determined to test his theory concerning bomber concentration on a major urban area in a massive nighttime raid.[80]

Despite the success achieved at Lübeck, Harris sought to assemble a bomber force that could "saturate the then existing defences of a major industrial town of a half million or more inhabitants." He felt that even the large raids launched up to this point in the war, with over 200 aircraft, provided too few planes to saturate the enemy air defenses and did not offer sufficient bomb concentrations over the target. An attack on the scale he envisioned would require the prime minister's approval. Harris thus approached Churchill and received permission for a "thousand-bomber" raid against a single German target, using the code name "Millennium." To assemble a thousand planes, Harris had to gather crews and aircraft not only from Bomber Command but also from operational training units and aircraft conversion units.[81] Initially, Bomber Command chose Hamburg as the primary target, but poor weather in the north of Germany sealed the fate of the alternate target, the city of Cologne, with its distinctive Gothic cathedral. On the night of May 30, thousands of seasoned operational crew members and a lesser number of inexperienced student trainees clambered aboard a diverse array of RAF bombers with instructions to strike Cologne. Over 900 aircraft reached the target and released their loads of high explosives and incendiaries with devastating effect.[82]

The raid against Cologne should not have been a great surprise to the Luftwaffe. By the end of May 1942, both the German population and the Luftwaffe began to grow accustomed to the regular RAF raids. Moreover, the Luftwaffe expected increased British efforts in the near future. In a case of extreme historical irony, Goebbels noted in a diary entry prepared the day before the attack that "the Führer also does not put very much store in the threats by the RAF. He believes, to be sure, that it is possible that the English will risk a couple of very large blows. But the necessary precautions have been taken for this [eventuality]."[83]

Air Defenses on the Ropes?

Despite Hitler and Goebbels's apparent optimism in the very shadow of the Cologne raid, previous experience had not prepared them for this type of massive attack. In fact, the size and scale of the raid clearly caught the German defenses by surprise. By entering the Continent along a relatively narrow front, the RAF bombers swamped Kammhuber's night fighter system using the *Himmelbett* procedure involving ground-controlled intercepts. The main weakness in the *Himmelbett* system was that it might be overwhelmed by a mass influx of tightly spaced aircraft. This is in fact what occurred during the raid on Cologne as only twenty-five ground-controlled intercepts could be conducted against the large force of bombers. Postmission bomber crew reports indicated a pervasive feeling that the Luftwaffe's anti-aircraft and searchlight defenses also had been swamped by the size of the bomber force, an impression most likely resulting from the fact that gun and searchlight defenses concentrated on single targets versus barrier fire procedures. In fact, the RAF lost an estimated 22 aircraft over the target—16 to flak, 4 to fighters, and 2 due to a midair collision. In addition, 116 aircraft returned to the United Kingdom with damage, with 85 damaged by flak and 12 by fighters.[84] During the Cologne raid, the RAF lost 41 aircraft, for a total loss rate of 3.9 percent; most of these aircraft fell victim to the flak defenses. Despite the losses, damage in Cologne was extensive; poststrike analysis revealed six hundred acres of complete devastation, with nearly half of the destruction covering the city's center, the object of the mission.[85] In the wake of the attack, Hitler blamed Göring for neglecting Cologne's flak forces, which in the Führer's mind explained the extent of the damage suffered by the city.[86]

In the days immediately following the attack, a strange dispute broke out between the German air staff and the district NSDAP leadership of the Cologne area concerning the number of aircraft involved. The air staff stubbornly clung to an estimate that only 70 aircraft were involved in the attack, while party officials in Cologne estimated the number at a few hundred. Both sides rejected the British claims that a thousand bombers participated in the operation as a propaganda ploy to impress the British public.[87] The air staff's interest in providing a low figure for the number of attacking aircraft most probably resulted from its own belief, or desire to believe, that the RAF had suffered over 50 percent casualties in the attack on Cologne. In any event, it was clear that, even days after the raid, the Luftwaffe and the civilian leadership still did not comprehend the size of the bomber force directed against Cologne.[88]

The raids on Lübeck, Rostock, and Cologne reinforced Harris's belief in the value of concentrated attacks and aptly demonstrated the danger posed by large incendiary raids for cities throughout Germany. In the wake of these attacks, the Luftwaffe leadership now faced more vocal demands from civilian party officials for increasing the protection of their respective towns, cities, and industrial sites. These officials insisted on the need for more anti-aircraft guns and searchlights, requests that led to the transfer of searchlights from western belts in the occupied territories to the Reich. Kammhuber subsequently labeled the latter move as "a terrible blow."[89] In turn, the Luftwaffe leadership pursued a policy of attempting to protect all targets of importance throughout the Reich.[90] Although politically expedient, in practice this strategy proved impossible. The increased range and numbers of British bombers and the ever-looming specter of American entry into the air war placed the Luftwaffe in the unenviable position of having to choose areas of concentration for its ground-based air defenses. Military commanders throughout history have recognized that seeking to protect everything was in effect a decision to protect nothing well. It was a lesson that Luftwaffe commanders were about to relearn.

The Luftwaffe Responds

Despite the manifold increase in the size of the Luftwaffe's ground-based defense forces, neither the German economy nor its manpower base could support the necessary expansion to protect every important target within Germany and the occupied territories. One response was an attempt to rely on mobility to move flak forces more quickly to threatened areas. For example, the Luftwaffe high command ordered the construction of more heavy and light railroad flak battalions capable of being moved quickly throughout the Reich.[91] The railroad batteries became the flak elite, receiving the most modern equipment and the best-trained personnel. By the end of 1942, there were fifty batteries of railroad flak.[92] Another initiative focused on accelerating the ongoing expansion of the number of weapons in each of the heavy gun batteries from four to six barrels to increase the firepower of the individual batteries.[93]

Increasing the number of guns per battery certainly offered one means of raising the volume of firepower per battery. In fact, the concept eventually led to the creation in the spring of 1942 of "superbatteries" *(Großbatterien)* that linked three batteries of four guns each to one centrally located fire director. The problems in transmitting firing data to twelve different guns at three separate sites proved "acute." However, with the introduction of the improved Würzburg gun-laying radar, the Luftwaffe largely had mastered this problem by the middle of 1942. In the superbatteries, the three flak gun batteries formed an equilateral triangle, with a gun-laying radar and three fire directors located in the center of the triangle. The radar fed the firing information to one of the directors, which then electrically transmitted these values to each of the batteries; the remaining two fire directors were kept in reserve in case of the failure of the primary device.[94]

The superbatteries offered three primary advantages for the air defense crews. First, the ability to increase the concentration of directed fire resulted in a greater probability of shooting down an engaged aircraft. Second, the consolidation of three batteries with one centrally controlled fire direction center allowed the flak units to reduce the overall number of administrative and support personnel. Finally, the superbattery also reduced the number of technical support personnel needed. However, the advantages of the superbatteries had to be weighed against several disadvantages. First, they were more vulnerable to attack and disruption due to the centralization of the fire direction function and the thousands of yards of cable and wiring needed to provide the gun batteries with firing solutions. Second, they required a great deal of space. Third, the complexity of controlling twelve guns did not allow for the coordination with fighter aircraft in the flak engagement zone. Admittedly, with single batteries this coordination proved difficult, but with three batteries it was essentially impossible. Finally, the superbatteries required extremely well trained personnel to be effective.[95]

In the final analysis, the superbatteries did improve the performance of the flak defenses. According to General von Axthelm, the superbatteries enjoyed success especially in early operations. He observed, "In the time to come these superbatteries proved themselves very well during the ever stronger and more intensive attacks in the second half of 1942."[96] It was ironic that the initial suggestion for larger gun batteries should have come from Göring, a man normally loathe to involve himself in tactical details. However, it was equally clear that the superbatteries were not meant to constitute a stand-alone air defense system but rather were intended to be part of a coordinated interceptor and ground-based defense network.

In addition to organizational initiatives, the Luftwaffe attempted to increase the performance of the flak artillery by introducing more capable guns. In this respect, the Luftwaffe leadership belatedly recognized the capability of the 88-mm/Model 41 flak gun. In his meeting with Göring on March 6, 1942, Milch described the "gratifying performance" achieved by the new weapon but also remarked on two concerns associated with the gun. The first problem was due to the design of the multisection inner barrel, which required the use of shells with copper driving bands because shells with steel driving bands tended to expand in the joints of the lower section, and the cartridge case would not extract.[97] On the one hand, this was a technical problem involved in firing the weapon. On the other hand, it constituted a resource problem because the earlier switch to steel driving bands had been intended to eliminate the need for using precious copper stores in the manufacture of anti-aircraft ammunition. Second, Milch discussed the disadvantage associated with the shorter life of the Model 41 inner barrel due to the gun's increased muzzle velocity, in comparison to the 88-mm/Model 36. This problem was mainly a result of the higher performance capabilities and hence higher muzzle velocity associated with the Model 41 that produced greater stresses on the barrel and reduced service life.[98] Finally, the 220 pounds of extra material, including aluminum, needed to manufacture the Model 41 dampened initial enthusiasm for the new weapon.

In light of the disadvantages associated with the Model 41, on March 19, 1942, Hitler restricted the production run of the guns to the forty-four already on order. As a result of production delays, the first operational models did not emerge from German factories until August 1942, whereupon Hitler ordered their immediate transfer to Rommel's forces in North Africa despite the objections of members of the flak arm. Hitler's decision apparently was influenced by the recommendation of the Flak Artillery School that the gun's low silhouette made it ideal for antitank operations despite its evident suitability for air defense duties. In any event, half the guns sent to North Africa were lost en route when Axis supply transports were sunk. In addition, the technical problems associated with all new weapons system plagued the remaining twenty guns that reached Rommel's force.[99] By the end of 1942, German industry had produced only forty-eight 88-mm/Model 41 guns, but by this time Hitler and the Luftwaffe leadership finally had recognized the weapon's potential in the air defense role and increased orders for the weapon throughout the remainder of the war.[100]

Like its 88-mm counterpart, the 128-mm flak gun was experiencing production problems despite the fact that the initial prototype had been tested in 1937.[101] By the end of 1942, only forty-five single-barreled versions of the gun and an additional ten twin-barreled versions had emerged from German factories.[102] The twin-barreled versions were designed to sit atop the enormous concrete flak towers constructed in Berlin, Hamburg, and Vienna.[103] In terms of performance, the 128-mm flak gun was undoubtedly the most capable anti-aircraft weapon of World War II. In terms of efficiency, the 128-mm gun averaged 3,000 rounds per aircraft brought down, half as many as the 105-mm guns and less than one-fifth of the totals for the older 88-mm models.[104] In a private conversation on the evening of August 28, 1942, Hitler evaluated the relative merits of the Luftwaffe's anti-aircraft guns. He remarked:

> The best [flak gun] is the 8.8 [cm]. The 10.5 has the disadvantage that it consumes too much ammunition, [and] the barrel does not hold up very long. The Reich Marshall [Göring] continually wants to build the 12.8 [into the flak program]. This double-barreled 12.8 has a fantastic appearance. If one examines the 8.8 from a technician's perspective, it is to be sure the most beautiful weapon yet fashioned, with the exception of the 12.8 [cm].[105]

The 128-mm flak gun was indeed an imposing and capable weapon. However, its length of almost twenty-six feet and weight of over 28,000 pounds made it essentially a fixed-base weapon despite the Luftwaffe's efforts to build several large transporters to make the gun mobile. By 1942, resource restrictions led to the cancellation of orders for the massive Meiller transporters, and the 128-mm guns were assigned to specially designed railroad flat bed cars, the roofs of the flak towers, or in fixed positions throughout the Reich.[106]

The Flak Arm Digs In

With respect to the last point, Milch had suggested placing the larger-caliber guns in fixed positions already in March, and by June Göring issued an order to increase the numbers of anti-aircraft in static positions, including all 128-mm guns.[107] Göring did allow some 128-mm flak guns to be sited on railroad cars to provide a mobile reserve for building up air defenses in threatened areas.[108] The decision to emplace anti-aircraft guns in fixed positions was based on two considerations. First, fixed guns required the diversion of fewer personnel and material resources. For example, by emplacing flak guns, the Luftwaffe eliminated the material expenditure associated with the production of mobile gun carriages. Furthermore, static sites greatly reduced the need for transport vehicles and trailers for moving the guns and their associated equipment and personnel, a nonmotorized heavy battery requiring fifty-three fewer persons than its motorized counterpart.[109] Second, the accuracy of the weapon could be improved to a limited degree in prepared positions, especially for flak guns of extremely large caliber. However, the main disadvantage associated with these weapons was the inability to move them to reinforce threatened areas when the sites they protected were not under attack. In the end, economic considerations outweighed tactical concerns as the Luftwaffe increasingly chose to build fixed anti-aircraft sites in place of mobile guns, a decision that would have important consequences as the fronts in the east and the west began to collapse in late 1944.[110]

The Search for Personnel

By the middle of 1942, the Luftwaffe began to feel not only the pinch of economic constraints but also the pressures of personnel shortages.[111] In truth, flak gun and searchlight batteries were manpower intensive, producing a demand for many specially trained individuals conducting a wide variety of tasks and also requiring a large number of auxiliary technical and logistics personnel ranging from cooks to electronic technicians. For example, a nonmotorized heavy flak gun battery required 129 to 143 persons, whereas a nonmotorized light flak gun battery employed 158 to 175 persons.[112] The effort to decrease the number of flak personnel had led Göring to consider several unorthodox ideas. He ordered a feasibility study to determine whether army gun crews manning shore gun emplacements could also do double duty by manning the flak guns associated with these positions. In March, Jeschonnek informed Göring that this plan was impractical because in the event of an Allied landing the crews would certainly face air opposition and would be forced to man the shore artillery positions and abandon the flak guns.[113] The rejection of this idea, however, did not end the search for ways to economize on the numbers of military members engaged in air defense duties.

By the spring of 1942, Wehrmacht forces fighting on the Eastern Front experienced an increasing number of casualties, losses that could no longer be replaced.[114] In an effort to release soldiers for duty at the front, the Luftwaffe examined the feasibility of creating Home Guard flak batteries *(Heimatflak-*

batterien). Shortly thereafter, the Luftwaffe began creating flak batteries composed of factory workers and inhabitants within industrial areas throughout the Reich. The idea of using industrial workers to protect factories was not new. In fact, the War Ministry considered the idea as early as 1915 during World War I.[115] Although workers and civilian volunteers constituted the vast majority of these units, Luftwaffe officers and senior NCOs from the flak artillery still commanded the Home Guard units.[116]

The Home Guard flak batteries were organized into platoons and were equipped with a diverse mix of older German flak weapons and captured enemy flak guns and equipment. The Home Guard units essentially worked an eight- to ten-hour shift during the day and then, after work, trained on the flak guns. During the evening, they stood on alert in the event that RAF bombers chose to conduct an attack on their factories or places of work.[117] These units were not outfitted with gun-laying radar, and most did not even possess fire directors.[118] A Home Guard heavy flak battery consisted on average of 72 men, whereas light flak batteries employed 55 men, with 30 additional men in the event that the unit operated a 60-cm searchlight.[119] In Air District VII, the Luftwaffe established both heavy and light Home Guard flak batteries, to protect individual factories and to augment the defenses of various cities throughout the command. In one case, Air District VII organized three Home Guard barrier fire batteries, each with four captured Russian 76.2-mm flak guns, to supplement the defenses of Strasbourg and Augsburg. In addition, Home Guard units using the obsolescent German 20-mm/Model 30 received the task of protecting specific factories and industrial complexes in which the members of the unit worked.[120]

By the end of 1942, the Luftwaffe had organized over 200 heavy flak batteries and more than 300 light flak batteries manned by members of the Home Guard, with a total strength of approximately 100,000 men. The Luftwaffe also used Home Guard members for manning both barrage balloon batteries and smoke generator companies.[121] These units were in perfect accord with Hitler's views on the expansion of anti-aircraft duties into the public sector. In March 1942, he exclaimed, "If this war continues for ten years, . . . in Germany every man and every woman will belong to a flak crew. If we obtain 5,000 more guns every year, every village will have its own flak."[122] The creation of these units also demonstrated the increasing manpower strains being felt throughout the Wehrmacht by the summer of 1942.[123] Still, the fact that sufficient weapons and munitions existed to arm over 500 heavy and light batteries, even if for the most part with captured weapons stores, highlighted the available stockpiles still present within the war economy by mid-1942. Finally, the lack of adequate training and the absence of gun-laying radar and fire direction equipment dictated that these units would have to rely on the ammunition-intensive practice of barrier fire. Based on the nature of the sites that the Home Guard batteries were tasked to defend and the state of the batteries' equipment, it is clear that the primary task of these units was to impede the aim of the attacking bombers and not to destroy them. In fact, the creation and duties of the Home Guard batteries provided a de facto recognition of a measure of effectiveness tied to preventing the bombers from accurately striking their targets versus that associated with the destruction of the attacking force.

The search for new measures designed to increase the size of the ground-based air defense force did not end with the creation of the Home Guard flak batteries. In August 1942, the Wehrmacht began organizing emergency flak batteries *(Alarmflakbatterien)* manned by Wehrmacht personnel, military administrators, and civilian officials.[124] These batteries were composed largely of light flak guns and were situated near military installations and government buildings. In the event of an air raid, instead of seeking shelter, the crews participated in the active defense of their bases and workplaces. During the course of the war, British intelligence identified Emergency Flak Batteries associated with naval shore installations, signal stations, police stations, and even the construction projects supervised by the Organization Todt.[125]

Without a doubt, the creation of the Home Guard flak batteries and the Emergency Flak Batteries expanded the number of persons available for manning flak defenses throughout the Reich. However, the main issue associated with the units was the level of effectiveness that could be expected from units created from whole cloth with little specialized training and minimal experience in air defense operations. These forces were in many respects the flak's equivalent of the German peoples' militia *(Volkssturm)* organized at the end of the war. Clearly, factory workers and nonspecialist military and civilian personnel could not be expected to perform at the level of specially trained and experienced flak gun crews. In fact, the large influx of auxiliaries overloaded the Luftwaffe's training system and shifted much of the training burden from the Luftwaffe schools to the units themselves.[126] Furthermore, one must certainly question the effect of flak duties on the effectiveness of factory workers who lost sleep and were deprived of rest after a full day's labor.

In the end, the decision to form the Home Guard and Emergency Flak Batteries can be evaluated from essentially two perspectives: as an act of utter desperation or as a measure designed to take better advantage of available manpower and surplus equipment in the face of increasing British bombing efforts and the looming shadow of American entry into the air war over Europe. The actual explanation appears to lie somewhere between these two interpretations. The worsening manpower crisis throughout the Wehrmacht clearly played a key role in the decision to search for alternative methods to strengthen the Reich's ground-based air defense network.[127] Seen in this light, the Home Guard and Emergency Flak Batteries essentially provided the Luftwaffe with a force that could augment existing flak units. These batteries also could provide coverage of specific areas, thus freeing regular Luftwaffe units from the responsibility of protecting these sites and potentially releasing flak batteries in the homeland for action in other theaters.

The spiraling demands for soldiers at the front also resulted in the increased mobilization of Luftwaffe women auxiliaries *(Luftwaffenhelferinnen)* for duty with the Air Reporting Service. Already during World War I, the War Ministry issued a decree calling for the mobilization of women as replacements for able-bodied men in the Signal Corps, but the rapid and unexpected end of the war prevented the implementation of this plan.[128] In contrast, during World War II women were active in the Air Reporting Service in a variety of roles. By the end of 1941, over 34,000 Luftwaffe women auxiliaries served in various communications and administrative positions throughout the Reich proper. In addition, several thousand volunteers were on duty in the occupied territories.[129] These young women were grouped in private lodgings or barracks and entered a communal environment dominated by work, sport, homemaking activities, and ideological instruction.[130] On September 1, 1942, General Wolfgang Martini, the commander of the Air Reporting Service, informed Göring that "the air communications branch is already mostly converted to young women."[131] In 1942, these young women, nicknamed *Blitzmädel* (lightning girls)[132] performed a variety of communications tasks, including duty as radio, telephone, and telegraph operators. They also assumed various duties in Luftwaffe command posts involved in coordinating daytime and nighttime air defense operations.[133] As the war progressed, these young women assumed an ever larger and more important role in the Luftwaffe's air defense system.

The lack of sufficient numbers of persons to operate ground-based air defense systems led to ever more unorthodox solutions. By the fall of 1942, not only young German women but also foreign prisoners of war were mobilized into the flak force. Plans for the employment of Russian POWs as auxiliary personnel within the flak gun batteries provided a clear indication of the extent of the personnel crisis facing the Wehrmacht.[134] With the promise of better rations, pay, and cigarettes, the Luftwaffe enticed Russian enlisted men for the physically demanding positions associated with hauling ammunition and loading the heavy flak guns.[135]

Looking into the Future: The 1942 Development Program

The search for sufficient numbers of men and women to fill the ranks of the ground-based air defenses was certainly an important issue occupying the thoughts of the Luftwaffe's senior leadership by mid-1942; however, it was the question of weapons and systems acquisition and development that constituted the most critical matter faced by the Luftwaffe that summer. In June

1942, von Axthelm forwarded a report to Göring, entitled "Review of the State of Development and Development Designs for the Flak Artillery," which was intended to provide the guidelines for the future development and acquisition of all weapons and systems related to the Luftwaffe's ground-based air defenses. Axthelm began by noting that, since 1918, the relative rate of development in aircraft technology had clearly outpaced that of anti-aircraft weapons. Furthermore, he emphasized that in the future "one must count on a considerable increase in aircraft speeds and service altitudes." In fact, von Axthelm predicted that "in the next few years aircraft speeds and flight altitudes by different aircraft types will gradually reach 625 m.p.h. and between 33,000 and 49,000 feet.[136]

In the Development Program of 1942, von Axthelm noted that increased aircraft speeds and operating altitudes would result in the decreased probability of hitting one's target. He then remarked that, in addition to improving the performance of existing guns and developing new weapons, the flak artillery needed to either reduce the lead points of the current weapons or even reject the "flak hypothesis" entirely.[137] The latter point was in many respects a bombshell. The flak hypothesis formed the foundation for calculating the path of the projectile from the moment it left the barrel until the intended impact point. The flak hypothesis used the explicit assumption that the speed, altitude, and direction of a target would remain constant from the moment of initial targeting until the projectile reached it. Without the flak hypothesis, crews or projectiles would be required to continuously calculate the change in three-dimensional space of the target's position, a task far beyond the capabilities of the rudimentary computers associated with the existing fire directors.

Axthelm certainly realized that, in light of the existing technology, his demand was unworkable. Why, then, did he make it? The answer lies in his subsequent contention that the only solution to the increasing demands of the air war was to be found in either remote-controlled projectiles or flak missiles. In fact, flak missiles emerged as the centerpiece of the Development Program of 1942. Axthelm admitted that missile development was in its "first stages." Still, he called for development to be driven forward "by degrees," including the acquisition of powder rockets compatible with existing fire directors, as well as a more ambitious program for an optically guided liquid-fueled missile that would revert to active homing in the vicinity of the target.[138]

In one respect, von Axthelm's call for the development of guided missiles was simply a restatement of demands made by Rüdel in the Flak Development Program of 1932 and a renewed attempt to gain support for the flak missile program despite continued skepticism concerning the feasibility of the project. However, von Axthelm, like his mentor and predecessor Rüdel, was a decided supporter of flak missile development. In fact, he delivered presentations to Göring and members of the General Staff in favor of anti-aircraft missile development immediately after his selection as the inspector of the Flak Artillery.[139] In addition, von Axthelm apparently supported, if not instigated, a memorandum authored by Major Dr. Friedrich Halder in May 1942 that criticized the Flak Development Division, an office moved from the Army Ordnance Office to the Air Ministry in 1940. In his memo, Halder roundly criticized the division as "a collection of out-of-touch Army traditionalists who failed to see the potential of radical new technologies like the rocket."[140]

Axthelm's energetic campaign in favor of flak missile development finally convinced Göring to support the program as part of the overall Flak Development Program of 1942, but there were a myriad of technical problems that would have be overcome, ranging from proximity fusing to optical and radar guidance systems.[141] The technical problems associated with the missiles and the belated start of the program ultimately would prevent the anti-aircraft missile program from reaching operational status during the war.[142] After the war, Albert Speer looked back with regret on the decision to pursue development of the V-2 ballistic missile and not the anti-aircraft missile. He claimed:

> To this day I think that this [anti-aircraft] rocket [*sic*], in conjunction with the jet fighters, would have beaten back the Western Allies' air offensive against our industry from the spring of 1944 on. Instead, gigantic effort and expense went into developing and manufacturing long-range rockets which proved to be, when they were at last ready for use in the autumn of 1944, an almost total failure. Those rockets, which were our pride and for a time my favorite armaments project, proved to be nothing but a mistaken investment. On top of that, they were one of the reasons we lost the defensive war in the air.[143]

Speer's contention must be tempered with a dose of skepticism. It is far from certain whether a decision to begin development in 1941 might have accelerated appreciably missile production in view of the significant technical obstacles and the existing resource limitations. If Hitler had been willing to forsake the V-2 program, a highly improbable counterfactual, the flak missile project might have reached operational status. But one still must keep in mind that it was far easier to launch a ballistic missile at a distant ground target than to coordinate a missile intercept with a target moving at 200 mph or more.

The anti-aircraft missile might have constituted the centerpiece in von Axthelm's development program, but he also recognized the necessity to upgrade the weapons and systems performance of the ground-based air defenses in several areas. The development program contained a table that demonstrated the growing concern over potential increases in the operational altitude of Allied bombers. Luftwaffe studies indicated that at 29,500 feet, the 88-mm/Model 18 and 36 had only fourteen seconds to effectively engage a target, the 105-mm had forty-nine seconds, and finally the 88-mm/Model 41 and the 128-mm each had approximately sixty-eight seconds of effective engagement time. At 36,000 feet, only the 88-mm/Model 41 and the 128-mm were able to engage a target for a period of only thirty-one seconds. Immediately after this discussion, von Axthelm noted, "At this time, the flak artillery does not dispose of any means of defense against the to be expected high-altitude aircraft."[144] Axthelm's observation was correct, but his predictions concerning the projected developments in aviation technology proved widely exaggerated. In contrast to Rüdel, von Axthelm's strategic foresight proved far less developed. For example, the Luftwaffe was well aware of American efforts to build the B-29, the technologically most advanced bomber of World War II, but even this aircraft, with a capability for cabin pressurization, had a service ceiling limited to 31,850 feet and a maximum speed of 358 mph.[145] Axthelm may not exactly have been tilting at windmills, but he could be accused of either grossly overestimating his opponent's capabilities or deliberately seeking to create an exaggerated threat in the hope of gaining more fiscal and material resources for his flak forces.

To prepare for the threat posed by aircraft operating at extremely high altitudes, von Axthelm proposed the development of a supergun with a caliber between 200-mm and 250-mm. He admitted that such a gun had several disadvantages, including intensive labor and resource requirements. Axthelm estimated that a 250-mm gun would require 120,000 labor hours and 200 tons of steel to construct, with a final weight of approximately 130 tons. Still he remarked, "Despite the considerable resource and labor expenditure, the development of the super heavy flak gun in closest cooperation with the navy must be demanded with all energy, because they [superheavy flak guns] offer the expectation of a palpable solution along tested paths when measured against the [current] development stage of new defense systems (flak missiles)."[146] Milch later took von Axthlem to task concerning the short life cycle of the barrel and the low rate of fire of such a weapon. Milch archly observed, "I don't believe in the super heavy gun with which one cannot do anymore than to shoot as [other flak guns have] to this point."[147] In fairness to von Axthelm, he was not advocating the mass production of these weapons; rather, he envisioned six batteries of twenty-four guns situated around a few important sites including Berlin, Hamburg, and the Ruhr.[148] In retrospect, von Axthelm's championing of the superheavy gun seems odd, if not bizarre. These proposed guns represented an air defense white elephant that offered minimal returns on a massive investment.

In one respect, von Axthelm's advocacy of a superheavy anti-aircraft gun merely reflected the German military's penchant for massive artillery pieces established with the use of the 380-mm Paris Gun in World War I and continued into World War II with the production of the gargantuan 812-mm Dora Gun. The latter artillery piece, which was used in the reduction of the Soviet defenses at Sevastopol in 1942, was 164 feet long and 35 feet high and weighed an incredible 1,488 tons.[149] Still, it was the British, not the Germans, who constructed the largest-caliber purpose-built anti-aircraft gun for operational use in World War II, a 5.25-inch (133-mm) flak gun.[150] Furthermore, it was the British who employed six massive 8-inch (203-mm) coastal guns against aerial targets during the war.[151] In the case of the coastal guns, firing at aircraft was clearly the only role left for these obsolescent giants and their munitions stores after the threat of a German invasion had faded. In any event, the Luftwaffe's vain pursuit of the superheavy flak gun simply expressed a traditional viewpoint that "bigger is better, and monstrous is best of all."

Axthelm's advocacy of the superheavy gun and the anti-aircraft missile lent a certain sense of unreality to the Flak Development Program of 1942. Still, the program did contain a number of important observations on the existing deficiencies within the flak forces. Axthelm noted the decreasing effect of high-explosive light and heavy flak munitions in the face of the improved armor protection of Allied aircraft. He also remarked that gun-laying radar presently provided accurate distance and position information but in the future countermeasures might make gun-laying radar susceptible to jamming. Furthermore, he bemoaned the limited range of the sound detectors that proved effective only to a height of 19,000 feet. In addition, he observed that balloon barriers were increasingly losing effectiveness due to the introduction of aircraft cable cutters and protective armor plating. Finally, he stated that the 150-cm searchlight was no longer sufficient for the existing circumstances.[152]

At the conclusion of his development program, von Axthelm offered a number of suggestions for improving the performance of ground-based air defenses. In addition to the development of anti-aircraft missiles and the superheavy gun, he called for improving the ballistic and explosive characteristics of existing ammunition, including the use of improved explosive compounds and the manufacture of cone-shaped or rocket-assisted projectiles. He also advocated the production of smoothbore and conical flak gun barrels to increase the muzzle velocities of existing weapons. At the tactical level, he argued for more fixed flak positions and for providing these sites with "special equipment" to improve cooperation with night fighters.[153] Axthelm also called for decreasing the weight of mobile guns, as well as the expanded use of railroad flak guns as a mobile reserve for employment within the homeland and the occupied territories. With respect to auxiliary systems, he mentioned the need for jam-proof gun-laying radar, fully remote-controlled 150-cm searchlights, a 300-cm searchlight, explosive charges for balloon barriers, and, finally, smoke generators capable of producing black smoke instead of light-colored smoke.[154]

Evaluating von Axthelm's Vision for Air Defense

After having more than two months to consider von Axthelm's suggestions, Göring approved the program on September 1. In his cover letter, Göring ordered that "the suggested performance improvements in the attached development program concerning the weapons and equipment of the flak artillery and the new developments, especially the flak missile and the superheavy flak gun (in close cooperation with the navy) are approved. He then remarked, *"The development efforts are to be pushed forward with the most extreme vigor."*[155] Furthermore, Göring directed that he be continuously apprised of the development progress. In retrospect, von Axthelm's development program blended a mixture of reality and fantasy. Even Hitler, the most ardent supporter of the flak forces, described it as "utopian."[156] On the one hand, it clearly envisioned a threat that lay far beyond the existing capabilities of the RAF and its American counterpart, the USAAF. Due either to his lack of a flying background or to a myopic focus on his own arm, von Axthelm failed to recognize the severe technological and physiological problems associated with flight above 30,000 feet. Furthermore, his program demonstrated a marked underestimation of the current performance of the flak forces, especially the searchlight and barrage balloon forces.[157] In turn, the proposal for a superheavy gun seemed more fanciful than realistic. On the other hand, von Axthelm's advocacy of anti-aircraft rockets and missiles seemed farsighted, despite the difficulties associated with these projects. His evaluation of the potential limitations of gun-laying radar and his call for a "jam-proof" system were equally perceptive. Finally, his demand for improving the ballistic performance of the gun barrels and the destructive capability of flak munitions offered promising solutions for increasing the effectiveness of the flak arm in the future.

On September 29, 1942, von Axthelm sent Rüdel a copy of the approved development program with a request for Rüdel's comments.[158] Rüdel responded in a letter of October 7, in which he thanked von Axthelm for the copy of the development program and expressed his pleasure that von Axthelm had embarked on a course to solve the "ever more difficult problems" faced by the flak forces. Rüdel also mentioned to his satisfaction that Göring had approved the development program personally and that it did not require clearance through the Air Armaments Office. This last point, he opined, demonstrated that his bureaucratic battle with Udet had not been in vain. Rüdel refrained from offering his opinion on any specific weapons system, but he did provide an important concluding observation. He noted that the timely recognition of available possibilities in the face of tactical and technical demands was the most decisive factor for weapons development. He also referred to the importance of training to gain maximum effectiveness from the new weapons.[159] These remarks may have been both a reminder and a caution to his former protégé, but Rüdel clearly expressed his faith in both von Axthelm and the proposed program in his closing remarks. In the end, von Axthelm's letter to Rüdel is interesting in two respects. First, von Axthelm clearly valued the judgments of his former boss and mentor and sought Rüdel's approval. Second, it is clear that von Axthelm did not seek Rüdel's assistance in the preparation of the program, nor was Rüdel apparently kept abreast of the administrative and bureaucratic relationship between the inspector of the Flak Artillery and the Air Armaments Office. Rüdel was clearly unaware of Milch's leading role in overseeing technological research and development within the ground-based air defenses.

In any event, the Flak Development Program of 1942 made immense demands on the technological and material resource base of the Third Reich. Already in a meeting of August 8, Göring admitted that neither the aircraft nor the flak program could be fulfilled under the current conditions. He then ordered Milch to brief Hitler personally on the subject.[160] Milch's meeting with Hitler apparently resulted in his temporary conversion as a believer in the flak arm. In a meeting of August 18, Milch mentioned the importance of the flak in the protection of the homeland, and he commented on the need to increase flak defenses within the Reich.[161] In a meeting of the Air Armaments Office on the same day, Milch provided a caveat to his support by remarking that with the exception of minor reductions, the flak program had been completely met, while the aircraft production program was only half complete.[162]

Despite the very real resource limitations within the German war economy, Göring's approval of the Flak Development Program of 1942, especially with its implicit demands for the consumption of even greater resources than the Führer Flak Program of January, is not surprising. The development program merely offered a blueprint for research and development and did not commit the Luftwaffe to the purchase or production of specific numbers of weapons or equipment. Clearly, approval of the plan implied the allocation of resources to specific research projects, but the scale of the research and the total allocation of funding remained to be determined in subsequent rounds of bureaucratic negotiations. Most important, the development program provided the inspector of the Flak Artillery with an opportunity to present his strategic vision concerning the needs of ground-based air defenses, as well as his priorities for the future.

Without doubt, von Axthelm's development program provided an extremely pessimistic appraisal of the overall condition of the flak forces, as well as the prospects for these forces in the future. If one were to read this document alone, it would appear that the flak was barely able to mount a credible defense. The explanation for von Axthelm's gloomy prognosis lay in the general nature and procedure for military planning, especially in wartime. Staff planners are taught to plan for "worst-case" scenarios when compiling estimates of both their own future military requirements and their forecast of enemy intentions. The use of a worst-case scenario is not merely a tool to extract increased budget allocations but rather a method designed to enable one's own military to be in a position to respond effectively should an adversary choose the strategy most threatening to one's own forces. Admittedly, worst-case planning often can lead to the creation of an enemy who is "ten feet tall." Indeed, von Axthelm apparently fell victim to this tendency, and his gross overestimation of future Allied capabilities aptly demonstrated the potential pitfalls associated with worst-case planning. In addition, von Axthelm, the trained artillery officer, displayed a surprisingly myopic focus on the flak artillery to the exclusion of a holistic view of ground-based air defenses. For one thing, he completely failed to discuss improvements to the dummy sites that had been used to such great effect in the previous two years.

Image and Reality

In an ironic twist of events, Göring met with almost the entire Luftwaffe senior leadership concerned with air defense on the very day he approved the Flak Development Program of 1942. This three-hour meeting on September 1, much more than the development program, provides an unvarnished view of the state of German air defenses by the summer of 1942. Besides Göring, those present at the meeting included the chief of the Luftwaffe General Staff, General Hans Jeschonnek; General of the Night Fighters Josef Kammhuber; the commander of Air Region, Center, General Hubert Weise; commander of the Air Reporting Service, General Wolfgang Martini; General Walther von Axthelm; and the future commander of the fighter forces, Colonel Adolf Galland. In the course of the meeting, the participants examined a diverse number of topics associated with the protection of Germany from aerial attack, and the protocol of the meeting offers a clear insight into the current state of the Third Reich's interceptor and ground-based air defenses.

Göring began the meeting by discussing the personnel shortage within the ground-based air defense forces. He informed the participants at the meeting that Hitler had approved the employment of members of the SA (storm troops), SS, Reich Labor Service, and Hitler Youth for air defense duties. Göring also declared, "We already need the military-trained youth *[militärische Jugend]*, those who are about to be called up for service, and beyond that [we] also must employ women to fill positions at switchboards, at radar sites, and in command posts."[163] In response to Göring's remarks, Generals Weise and Kammhuber both expressed reservations concerning the mobilization of high school students, a plan previously brought forward and rejected in 1939.[164] Kammhuber argued that all available young men had already been mobilized and that efforts to "sift through" the remaining youth would lead to decreasing success by the air defense units. In contrast, Weise argued for a judicial decree to establish the legal status of these recruits before any further mobilization of women into the air defense force. Kammhuber quickly agreed with this suggestion and again cautioned that current replacements were not up to the demands of their duties.[165]

Göring ignored these objections and inquired about the state of the effort to emplace flak guns in fixed sites versus the production of motorized or mobile guns. Weise replied that the switch had been made completely in the Berlin defenses, but that it had engendered disadvantages in training. Göring replied testily, "Then you [Weise] must likewise build [emplaced] flak guns at the training ranges instead of towing your entire batteries to the firing range. That is madness alone on the grounds of transportation."[166] Göring's last point is important because already in the fall of 1942 the Luftwaffe began to feel the very real effects of fuel shortages that placed increasing restrictions on the training of both pilots and personnel within the flak artillery arm. In fact, Göring warned that the lack of aircraft fuel for training purposes threatened to lead to a situation of the Luftwaffe having too many aircraft and not enough pilots by the spring of 1943, one of his few accurate prophecies during the war.[167] The specter of empty cockpits had important implications for the flak forces, as will be seen in the final year of the war. In any event, Göring reiterated his earlier order that all 128-mm guns were to be emplaced at fixed sites. Weise stated that lack of construction resources hampered the expansion of fixed sites. Göring responded that Speer certainly would rather provide the material for building fixed sites than those materials necessary for the production of gun carriages.[168]

Subsequently, Göring moved on to a related subject and asked who was responsible for the construction of the dummy installations. Jeschonnek replied that Weise coordinated these requirements with the Inspectorate of Civil Defense. Göring then recommended that these sites be moved periodically to prevent the British from discerning their locations. Weise agreed and added that experience demonstrated that flak fire improved the effectiveness of the dummy installations in decoying the bombers. Göring again changed the topic by demanding that smoke generators capable of producing dark versus white "fog" (smoke) be introduced for the protection of the hydrogenation plants "in the shortest time."[169] The hydrogenation plants produced the aviation fuel upon which the Luftwaffe was dependent and were a critical link in the Third Reich's war economy. Göring's mention of the dummy sites and the hydrogenation plants provided a strong indication of the success attained at the dummy installations and their importance to the war effort.

At this point in the meeting, Göring called Speer by telephone to ensure the delivery of sufficient building materials for completing the fixed flak sites and to investigate a claim by Weise that Speer had ordered the transfer of the Luftwaffe's second 128-mm gun battery from Berlin to Hamburg. After a short break the meeting reconvened, and Weise reported that both the Luftwaffe's 128-mm batteries would be used to defend Berlin, with additional batteries planned for the protection of Hamburg, Cologne, and Duisburg in that order. Göring then mentioned that Hitler wished to see flak towers built in Munich, Vienna, Linz, and Nuremberg, in addition to those already constructed in Berlin and Hamburg. These gigantic concrete towers provided the heavy flak with a raised platform, allowing for increased gun depression, and served a variety of functions as air defense headquarters, bomb shelters, and first aid stations.[170] According to Göring, Hitler remarked that the destruction of Nürnberg and Vienna "lay like a nightmare over his soul." Weise exclaimed that he could not defend all these sites if he did not receive additional batteries and people to man them, including the Romanians of German descent *(Volksdeutsche)* scheduled to return to the Reich.[171] Göring replied that Weise would get these persons as soon as the Wehrmacht stood south of the Caucasus. Jeschonnek then suggested the withdrawal of all flak batteries from France as "the protection of industry there is illusory at any rate," to which Göring retorted that "Paris without flak protection is not acceptable."[172]

Weise then pressed his case further by stating the need for more heavy flak gun and searchlight batteries, as well as more equipment for the Home Guard units. Obviously irritated, Göring shot back, "I am not interested in presentations all the time in which things are demanded from me, but rather I would like to hear for once how more can be accomplished with what is available." He then angrily exclaimed that at least one time he would like to hear an offer of someone prepared to give up personnel or equipment.[173] The chill in the air must have been noticeable, and the meeting was suspended for a short lunch break. The deliberations during the first part of the meeting clearly illustrated the manpower strains being experienced throughout the ground-based air defense network, from the gun and searchlight batteries to the manning of the radar sites. The comments also showed that Hitler's presence hung like a shadow across many issues related to air defense. Finally, and most interestingly, it is what is missing that proves most important. The problems raised during the meeting dealt with the need for more resources or personnel to increase performance. The absence of any complaint about the current performance of the flak artillery was like "the dog that did not bark" in the Sherlock Holmes mystery. Weise's demands for more resources were nowhere accompanied by a criticism of current performance, a strong indication of the satisfactory results achieved by ground-based air defenses up to that point in time. Clearly, the representatives from the flak artillery branch felt that more resources and persons were needed, but this did not necessarily reflect poorly on the current performance of the flak arm.

After a thirty-five-minute break, the meeting reconvened, and Jeschonnek responded to a question by Göring concerning the amount of "cushion" available in the area of flak guns. Jeschonnek informed him that "every usable gun is employed," and that there were not even any more weapons available for the barrier fire batteries. Weise then added that German industry produced the equivalent of twenty batteries every month.[174] In truth, Weise's estimate was misleading. The number of heavy flak guns produced in 1942 totaled 4,147, of which 2,828, or 68 percent, were the older 88-mm models.[175] In fact, the average monthly production figures in 1942 for light and heavy flak guns were 2,040 and 304 barrels, respectively.[176] Using the figure of 304 guns, the total monthly number of 6-gun batteries averaged almost fifty-one versus the twenty cited by Weise. However, it was certainly true that many of these guns were needed as replacements for the 148 88-mm guns per month that wore out or were destroyed during British bombing raids.[177] After Weise's comment, Jeschonnek apparently changed his evaluation by declaring that there was a cushion of approximately 300 guns, but these were not "finished" weapons. Göring replied that it was "ridiculous" for German industry to deliver unfinished guns and ordered that only finished weapons were to be delivered even if it meant a decrease in the number produced. Jeschonnek then laid the blame for this situation at the feet of the Army Ordnance Office and favorably noted Göring's decision to appoint Milch to supervise the flak production program.[178]

In only his second comment of the meeting, von Axthelm interjected that it was easier to get a complete flak gun than a single replacement barrel. Weise then asked whether he might transfer flak guns from the south to other areas, whereupon Göring rejoined, "The Führer himself must decide that." Jeschonnek suggested that captured Russian weapons be used to replace German flak guns in the east and East Prussia. Weise expressed reservations about this plan based on the raids against Danzig and Königsberg. He then observed that the "largest flak gap" was in middle and southern Germany, and that in relation to its size Berlin was insufficiently protected. He also remarked that only at this time were the Home Guard heavy flak batteries beginning to appear. Weise's comments again must be viewed with a degree of skepticism. As previously discussed, Home Guard heavy flak batteries had appeared in Air District VII already in July. In addition, his comments on the "insufficient" protection of Berlin and his overall evaluation of the lack of guns seemed to have been based on two motives. First, he was attempting to support his argument for more weapons. Second, although the capital had not been attacked in force since November 1941, Weise sought to provide himself with cover should Berlin be struck on the scale experienced in Cologne. Still, Kammhuber supported Weise's request to strengthen the Berlin defenses, and both men argued for the establishment of the 4th Fighter Division to increase the defenses around the capital.[179]

As the discussion of the flak began to wind down, Weise and von Axthelm requested the production of between four and five quadruple 150-cm searchlights per month for use as master searchlights tied to gun-laying radar. Göring then received Martini's assurance that this request would not conflict with the radar production program of the Air Reporting Service. Göring then asked, "What all is part of a [heavy gun] battery?" This would seem to be a curious question coming from the commander of the Luftwaffe three years into the war. Weise responded that, in addition to the guns and the gun-laying radar, each battery had a fire director, an auxiliary fire director, and an optical distance-measuring device. Weise added that in Air Region, Center, there were 2,800 heavy flak guns, whereupon Göring exclaimed, "No country in the world has such a strong flak artillery [arm]." Weise quickly moved to downplay expectations by wistfully observing that he could think of nothing better than to be able to protect "little England" with the forces available to him.[180]

The conference of September 1 exposed several traits exhibited by the leadership of Germany's air defenses. First, Göring remained clearly oblivious to the technical and tactical details involved with his ground-based air defense forces. Second, von Axthelm rarely contributed to the discussion despite his position as the inspector of the Flak Artillery. In fact, von Axthelm would continue this pattern of behavior in the coming years. Like his instigation of Major Halder's memorandum concerning missile developments, von Axthelm allowed others to take the point in issues surrounding air defense. He seemed content to observe from the sidelines instead of risking direct confrontation with either Göring or Milch. Finally, Weise, the commander of the Reich's air defenses, repeatedly sought to downplay expectations by noting his need for more personnel and equipment.

The atmosphere of the conference provided a striking contrast to the tone of von Axthelm's development program, one signed on the very day during which the conference took place. Indeed, the conference itself demonstrated that the flak forces were experiencing stresses and strains caused by personnel and equipment demands, but that overall these problems were neither crippling nor seriously degrading the current performance of the flak forces. It is also important to note that the conference occurred in the wake of Harris's effort to increase the pressure on the Luftwaffe's air defenses and Germany's civilian population.[181]

Bomber Command's Summer Campaign

During the summer of 1942, the RAF conducted a series of large-scale raids on cities throughout the Third Reich. Somewhat to the chagrin of Harris and Bomber Command, the thousand-plane bombing raid on Cologne had set the standard against which future missions would be measured.[182] During the summer months, Bomber Command launched a series of raids against Bremen, Hamburg, and several targets within the Ruhr valley. These raids consisted of several hundred aircraft each, but the closest that Bomber Command came to repeating the attack on Cologne was a mission against Düsseldorf during the night of July 31 involving 630 aircraft. The large number of bombers combined with a heavy concentration of bombs and incendiaries succeeded in starting over 950 fires and destroyed or damaged more than 1,500 buildings; however, losses were high, especially among the training unit crews, with 11 of their 105 aircraft being shot down.[183] Despite the increasing efforts of Bomber Command, the Luftwaffe had once again gained the upper hand in the air war over Europe. One indication of the favorable situation within the Reich can be found in Goebbels's diary entries during this period. The minister of propaganda expressed his relief concerning the lessening intensity and effects of the bombing campaign in the summer of 1942.[184] In fact, Goebbels even held hopes for a rapid German victory in the war as a result of the Wehrmacht's successes in North Africa and the Soviet Union during the summer.[185]

Night Fighters Ascendant

By August, the Luftwaffe had recovered from the shock experienced in the wake of the attack on Cologne and again had achieved growing success against RAF bombers. In fact, the overall loss rate experienced by Bomber Command Aircraft increased from 4.1 percent in June to 4.4 percent in July and to 6.6 percent in August. The Luftwaffe's success owed much to the improved performance of the night fighter force. On July 31, most of the remaining sections of the western searchlight belt were disbanded, thus completing the process that had begun earlier in the spring with the incremental withdrawal of searchlights to provide protection to cities within the Reich proper.[186] Despite the loss of the western searchlight belt, Kammhuber's night fighters enjoyed particular success in the summer months using ground-controlled intercept procedures and onboard radar *(Lichtenstein)*.[187] The latter device consisted of three cathode-ray tube displays in the cockpit that indicated the range, height, and horizontal displacement of the aircraft being tracked. Although tested operationally in August 1941, the aerial intercept radar was not readily available until the middle of 1942.[188]

The success achieved by the night fighters resulted not only from the introduction of new equipment and procedures but also from the increasing size of the force. The size of the night fighter force grew from 154 aircraft in January to 362 aircraft in December, with the number of crews almost doubling from 386 to 741.[189] In one respect, the success of the night fighters led Kammhuber to overestimate his forces and engendered a sense of false security among the Luftwaffe leadership. In his postwar memoir, Adolf Galland, the Luftwaffe's commander of the fighter forces between 1941 and 1945, observed:

> Because of the encouraging results of the night fighters we forgot at times the limits of night fighting set by present procedure. . . . The success of the German night fighters in 1942 could have been more formidable, and they could have also been more lasting. Our Command allowed the enemy to dictate the necessary defense measures instead of countering actively with original measures, planned with foresight.[190]

Galland's memoir, like those of many former Wehrmacht officers, must be viewed with a critical eye, but he is undoubtedly correct in his contention that the Luftwaffe's senior leadership, especially Göring, failed to foresee the intensity with which the air war would evolve in the coming years. In one respect, the Luftwaffe was a victim of its own success. As long as it held the upper hand, there appeared to be very little impetus to prepare for a coming air war it did not foresee, or refused to see.

Evaluating the Effectiveness of the Flak

Still, it would be inaccurate to accuse the Luftwaffe of resting on its laurels. In fact, the substantial increase in the size of the day and night fighter forces in 1942 demonstrated a recognition that the Reich's air defenses needed to be strengthened. Likewise, the continual growth in the size of the ground-based air defense forces, especially the flak and searchlight forces, provides a clear indication of Hitler's and the Luftwaffe's continuing efforts to expand the capabilities of these forces. Without doubt, the multifold expansion of ground-based air defenses strained the personnel and equipment resources of the flak arm. Despite these strains, the expansion of the flak forces continued at a rapid pace, with the Führer Flak Program for 1943 calling for a doubling of the size of the flak forces from the 1942 level.[191]

The central question associated with the expansion of the flak forces concerned the effectiveness of these forces during the period. Table 6.2 provides the RAF official history's comparison of the estimated number of RAF aircraft destroyed over Europe during night raids by fighters and flak between July and December 1942.[192] In terms of absolute losses, the Luftwaffe's flak arm held an edge of twenty-four aircraft over its fighter counterpart through the latter half of 1942. Furthermore, the modest numbers of aircraft destroyed in the last three months of the year resulted not from the decreasing effectiveness of German air defenses but from a precipitous fall in the number of sor-

Table 6.2 Flak versus Fighter Shootdowns, July–December 1942

	Total Losses	Losses to Fighter	Losses to Flak
July	171	45	51
August	142	48	36
September	169	36	55
October	89	12	24
November	53	7	9
December	72	21	18
Total	696	169	193

ties conducted by the RAF. In fact, Bomber Command night sorties totaled 3,489 in September, 2,198 in October, 2,067 in November, and a mere 1,758 in December. The reduction in the number of sorties resulted primarily from a long period of poor weather that stretched from mid-September through the end of the year. In addition, the RAF diverted a sizable number of aircraft in attacks on northern Italy in late October and November in support of the Allied landings in North Africa.[193]

Radar for the Fighters

The evaluation of RAF losses supports the view that flak forces continued to play an important role in the defense of the Third Reich throughout 1942. Without doubt, the expansion of the ground-based air defenses created a great deal of stress on the war effort, particularly with respect to personnel. Likewise, the increase in the size of the night fighter force in 1942 substantially contributed to the improved performance of the air defenses; however, it was apparent that periods of poor weather disproportionately affected the night fighters and once again demonstrated the value of the flak batteries, especially those equipped with gun-laying radar. Indeed, one of the most important improvements made in the German defense system by late 1942 involved the increasing availability of gun-laying radar. In the three-week period between August 31 and September 18 alone, the defenses surrounding Munich, Augsburg, and Stuttgart received eighteen of the most advanced gun-laying radar, the model Fu.M.G. 39 T(D).[194]

In October, despite the increasing availability of gun-laying radar, Göring appealed to Hitler for "priority for radar and communications equipment" within Air Region, Center.[195] The reason for Göring's request, however, had less to do with an increased demand for radar units in support of flak than with growing claims for radar in support of the fighter force. In a meeting with Göring and Milch on October 14, Martini pleaded for more radar sets, especially the long-range Freya systems. Martini complained that orders for the Freya devices had suffered as a result of demands by the flak arm for Würzburg gun-laying radar. Göring then chided Martini for allowing Rüdel and the flak arm to run roughshod over the signal corps in 1941 and criticized Martini for failing to provide unequivocal requirements earlier in the war. Milch also remarked that shortages in the supply of aluminum, iron, and copper would affect the construction of the devices. Still, Göring was willing to support the request, but he demanded standardization in the production of the devices, with the manufacture of one specific type versus several different models.[196]

Moving Toward a Combined Bomber Offensive

The increased availability of radar was, now as before, vital for assisting the crews of the flak gun and searchlight batteries primarily in the nighttime defense of the Reich or in periods of daytime overcast.[197] By the fall of 1942, it was clear, however, that Germany would soon face a two-pronged attack by the RAF and the bomber forces of the nascent American Eighth Air Force (Eighth Bomber Command). Despite the entry of the United States into the war in December 1941, organizing, training, and equipping American aircrews for operations from bases in the United Kingdom had taken longer than expected.[198] As the Eighth Air Force approached operational status in the summer of 1942, General Ira Eaker, the commander of the American bomber force, was determined to demonstrate the effectiveness of daylight strategic bombing despite the earlier failures experienced by the RAF.[199]

In fact, Bomber Command had attempted a daylight raid into Germany in April 1942. In an attempt to show that RAF bombers could best assist in the Battle of the Atlantic in attacks on targets within Germany instead of raids aimed at port facilities, Harris ordered an attack on the submarine engine assembly plant located in the city of Augsburg.[200] On April 17, 12 Lancasters took off on a low-level flight of over 1,000 miles. Luftwaffe fighters brought down 4 of the aircraft over France, while flak defenses in Augsburg tallied 3 more bombers and damaged the 5 remaining Lancasters.[201] The bomber force had suffered a catastrophic 58 percent loss rate on the mission. In the words of one British historian, "The main lesson of the raid, however, was in any case clear. Lancasters in 1942 could no more brave the skies of Germany in daylight without crippling losses than could Blenheims or Wellingtons in 1939 and 1940."[202]

By the end of 1942, low-level daylight missions were extremely hazardous, whether flown over Germany or the occupied western territories. An ORS report of November 1942 found that of the 403 low-level sorties flown between July 1, 1941, and October 17, 1942, the RAF had lost 61 aircraft with a further

88 damaged. The analysis concluded that "light flak at the target is by far the most serious danger to be contended with on this type of operation." In fact, German light flak defenses accounted for 70 percent of losses due to known causes.[203] As USAAF bombers entered the air war in increasing numbers, they, too, would learn the perils of low-level operations over Europe.

For General Eaker and the Eighth Air Force, the question remained as to whether B-17s and B-24s could succeed where their RAF counterparts had failed. Fittingly, the first American bombing mission took place on July 4. The mission included an attack by a joint Anglo-American force of six Boston light bombers each against aerodromes in Holland. Of the six aircraft with American crews, only two actually hit their targets, while German flak defenses brought down two bombers and severely damaged a third. In addition, the British force lost one aircraft to flak.[204] The first raid by Eighth Air Force bombers over the Continent proved an inauspicious beginning to American plans for a daylight offensive; however, the USAAF quickly learned that low-level bombing was a dangerous proposition, and medium bombers were ordered to higher altitudes.[205]

It was not until August 17 that Eaker and the Eighth Air Force launched a second raid. Escorted by RAF fighters, twelve B-17 bombers attacked the railroad marshaling yards at Rouen (France) from an altitude of 23,000 feet. The attack was a success, and the bomber force experienced no losses. The presence of a fighter escort and bombing from a relatively high altitude seemed to offer a potential recipe for success. In the wake of the raid, Harris sent the following message to Eaker: "Congratulations from all ranks of Bomber Command on the highly successful completion of the first all American raid by the big fellows on German occupied territory in Europe. Yankee Doodle certainly went to town and can stick yet another well-deserved feather in his cap."[206] Harris's hyperbole to the contrary, the raid against Rouen provided very little evidence as to whether American bombers could successfully conduct long-range daylight penetrations into Germany against heavily defended targets.

Between August 17 and October 9, the Eighth Air Force conducted a total of fourteen missions against targets mostly in France. The largest effort included a raid of 108 bombers against industrial targets in the French city of Lille. Despite heavy fighter escort, only 69 bombers succeeded in reaching the target. The American force met stiff Luftwaffe fighter opposition, with 3 B-17s and 1 B-24 destroyed during the attack; an additional 46 bombers were damaged due to fighter attack. Bombing accuracy proved disappointing, with only 9 of 588 high-explosive bombs falling within 1,500 feet of the aiming point.

According to the U.S. Army Air Forces' official history of World War II, these initial attacks persuaded American air commanders that the bombers were "more than able to hold their own against fighter attacks, even with a minimum of aid from the escorting aircraft." Furthermore, the official history stated that these early missions led air leaders to minimize the dangers of German air defenses as "at no time had they presented a serious threat to the bombers."[207] If some USAAF commanders downplayed the threat of flak, such does not appear to have been the case among the bomber crews. For example, Colonel Curtis LeMay, later commander of the 3rd Air Division, arrived in England in the fall of 1942 and queried Colonel Frank Armstrong about his combat experiences. According to LeMay, Armstrong stressed two points: that "the flak is really terrific" and that "if you fly straight and level for as much as ten seconds, the enemy are bound to shoot you down."[208]

It is not unusual for aircrews to have different perceptions of the air war than their staff counterparts. It is, however, paradoxical that the commanders of the Luftwaffe and the USAAF reached entirely opposite conclusions concerning the results of the early American raids. On the one hand, Göring dismissed the relatively light damage caused by the modest American bomber formations and promised Hitler that "there is no need for big increases in day fighters for defensive purposes."[209] Likewise, on October 20, 1942, Eaker wrote a letter to the commander of the Army Air Forces, General Henry "Hap" Arnold, contending that "[the] daylight bombing of Germany with planes of the B-17 and B-24 types is feasible, practicable and economical."[210] Eaker's assessment seems extremely optimistic for the commander of a force that had yet to strike a target within Germany and that would not bomb a target within the Reich proper until the end of January 1943. In fact, during the last three months of 1942, poor weather and the requirement to support the Allied landing in North Africa combined to restrict severely Eighth Air Force operations over Europe. The planned landings on the coast of Africa resulted in the diversion of Eighth Air Force aircraft to the Twelfth Air Force. Likewise, efforts to prevent German submarines from threatening the Allied invasion convoys led to a concentration of attacks on German submarine pens along the French coast.[211] By the end of 1942, the USAAF may have been in the war, but from a German perspective it appeared to make very little difference.

The Year 1942 in Review

The situation for the Luftwaffe at the end of 1942 constituted in many respects the calm before the impending storm. In 1942, the ground-based air defenses had performed well. The success achieved by German air defenses led the commander in chief of Bomber Command, Air Marshal Arthur Harris, to lament that "our casualty rate continually increased, to the point where, in the later months of 1942, the enemy appeared to have gained a serious degree of tactical superiority." Although recognizing the "increasingly efficient" performance of radar-assisted anti-aircraft guns, Harris attributed the lion's share of the Luftwaffe's success to the growing night fighter force.[212] In addition, an ORS report analyzing RAF losses between August 1941 and December concluded: "Losses on German targets showed a rising trend throughout 1942. During the year, losses increased by about 1% of sorties for operations against Western Germany by 2% of sorties for Northern Germany and by 3% of sorties for Southern Germany." The report then observed that "the proportion of returning aircraft reported damaged by flak or attacked or damaged by fighter has also increased during the year."[213]

At the end of the year, Göring praised flak as the "backbone" of the air defense system on all fronts.[214] Clearly, ground-based air defenses remained a key element in the Luftwaffe's air defense system. The total number of confirmed aircraft shootdowns for all theaters since the start of the war stood at 8,707.[215] Additionally, flak crews serving in the east and in North Africa achieved excellent results in combat against Soviet and British tank forces. For example, one flak division on the Eastern Front alone received credit for the destruction of 300 aircraft and 260 tanks between April 10 and November 3, 1942.[216] Likewise, Luftwaffe decoy and deception efforts continued to enjoy on occasion a high degree of success against RAF night bombing attacks. In addition, the number of flak guns and the amount of air defense equipment had increased dramatically in the course of the year. The expansion of the flak force proved to be, however, a two-edged sword, for the Luftwaffe had to employ less-qualified men and women in an attempt to keep pace with the growth of the various ground-based air defense sites. Indeed, the rapid expansion of military and civilian flak forces had produced visible cracks in the air defense edifice. From the Luftwaffe's perspective, the mobilization of men and women from the civilian sector resulted in a decrease in the quality and readiness within the air defense arm.[217] Additionally, despite the expansion of the night fighter force, the flak and searchlight batteries clearly remained the primary means for defending the Reich. Up to this point, the air defense system for the most part had worked well. RAF raids against Lübeck and Cologne had temporarily shaken many German civilians and angered Hitler and the rest of the Nazi leadership, but they had failed appreciably to affect morale or lessen support for the regime.[218] However, the critical question facing the Luftwaffe's leaders at the end of 1942 was whether they were adequately prepared for operations in the coming year.

CHAPTER SEVEN

Bombing around the Clock, 1943

January 1943 would be a fateful month for both the Third Reich and the Luftwaffe. By the beginning of the year, losses in North Africa coupled with the death throes of the German Sixth Army trapped at Stalingrad provided an ill omen for the Wehrmacht as the tide of German conquest ebbed in the face of increasing Allied pressure in the air and on the ground. Between January 14 and January 25, Franklin Roosevelt and Winston Churchill met along with the Allied Combined Chiefs of Staff in the Moroccan city of Casablanca to discuss the future direction of the war against the Axis powers. On January 21, the Combined Chiefs of Staff issued what is commonly referred to as the "Casablanca Directive." The directive provided the foundation for a joint Allied air offensive aimed at "the progressive destruction and dislocation of the German military, industrial and economic system, and the undermining of the morale of the German people to a point where their capacity for armed resistance is fatally weakened."[1]

The wording of the directive reflected perfectly the desires of Allied air leaders. Already in the summer of 1942, General Carl "Tooey" Spaatz, later commander of the USAAF strategic bombing force in Europe, envisioned a strategic bombing plan involving the use of American bombers to achieve the "systematic destruction of selected vital elements of the German military and industrial machine through precision bombing in daylight" while at the same time the RAF would conduct "mass air attacks of industrial areas at night, to break down morale." In addition to setting the broad outlines of Allied bombing strategy, the Casablanca Directive also established the following five target priorities: German submarine construction yards, the German aircraft industry, transportation, oil plants, and other targets in the German war industry.[2]

In the short term, the decisions reached at Casablanca concerning the air war proved overwhelmingly symbolic because detailed plans in support of the new strategy would not appear until June 1943. Indeed, it was not until March that the Eighth Air Force would be able to conduct missions involving more than one hundred bombers on a consistent basis.[3] The prioritization of the German submarine yards meant that the majority of Eighth Air Force missions would be thrown at the difficult task of attacking German submarines in their reinforced concrete shelters in bases along the Atlantic, North Sea, and

Baltic coasts.[4] On January 27, fifty-three Eighth Air Force bombers attacked the submarine yard at Wilhemshaven after poor weather forced them to divert from their primary target, the shipyards at Vegesack near Bremen.[5] Heavy cloud cover limited the physical effects of the first American strike at Germany, and Luftwaffe fighters claimed three bombers. Despite the psychological boost to the Allied effort experienced in the wake of the American raid, RAF commanders, to their dismay, realized that they would have to continue to bear the brunt of the bombing effort until more American aircrews and bombers reached England.[6]

Evaluating the Performance of the Flak in Early 1943

Despite the success achieved by Allied forces in North Africa, RAF aircrews were still paying a heavy price in the air war over the Continent. In fact, in the early months of 1943, only 17 percent of Bomber Command aircrews could be expected to survive thirty operational missions, and the life span of a bomber was a mere forty flying hours.[7] In his postwar memoir, Harris observed that between 1942 and early 1943, the Germans "brought their radar-assisted night fighters and anti-aircraft guns to a point of extreme efficiency."[8] Table 7.1 offers a comparison of the losses experienced by Bomber Command due to flak and fighter operations in night raids over Europe in the first quarter of 1943.[9] The losses experienced by the RAF in this period demonstrated that flak forces continued to hold an advantage over the Luftwaffe's fighter forces during the periods of traditionally poor winter weather.[10] Likewise, the number of aircraft damaged during combat operations clearly favored flak forces at a ratio of approximately 9 to 1.[11]

In early 1943, Hitler continued to champion the further strengthening of the Reich's anti-aircraft forces. In a diary entry of February 22, Goebbels noted Hitler's desire "to expand the flak to a grandiose extent," as well as the Führer's plan to "outfit the Reich with so much flak by the fall [of 1943], that any penetration of the flak belt belonged to the realm of the improbable, if not to

Table 7.1 Flak versus Fighter Shootdowns, January–March 1943

	Losses		Damage	
	Fighter	Flak	Fighter	Flak
January	10	21	23	160
February	22	23	22	179
March	64	46	36	385
Total	96	90	81	724

say, the impossible."[12] This last utterance was reminiscent of the earlier hopes pinned to the Air Defense Zone in 1939 and aptly demonstrated Hitler's continued faith in the Luftwaffe's flak forces.

At the start of 1943, the performance of the ground-based air defenses in the first three years of the war seemed to justify Hitler's confidence in Germany's flak defenses. In several respects, however, the success of German air defenses up to this point was somewhat misleading due to a number of factors. First, the intensity of the Allied bombing effort remained relatively modest. In fact, Allied bombers had dropped only 6.5 percent of the total tonnage of bombs that eventually fell on German targets.[13] Second, despite raids over the Continent, American bombers had yet to conduct a mission against a target within Germany. Third, the Luftwaffe had suffered critical aircraft losses on the Eastern Front near Stalingrad as well as in North Africa during the last months of 1942.[14] Finally, at the turn of the year, personnel shortages and resource limitations constituted a chronic and nagging problem for the entire ground-based air defense force. As the Third Reich greeted the New Year, the German population could not know that 93 percent of the Allied bombing effort lay before them, but it was clear that Allied bombing efforts would soon increase, as would the pressure on all branches of the Wehrmacht.

The National Socialist *Levée en Masse*

The setbacks experienced by the Wehrmacht in North Africa and the Soviet Union engendered a corresponding increase in the pressure felt within the antiaircraft forces. In an attempt to ease the personnel shortages within the German armed forces, the Luftwaffe leadership finally acted upon the recommendations for the mobilization of teenage boys and girls discussed in the fall of 1942. On January 13, 1943, Hitler issued a directive, entitled "Comprehensive Employment of Men and Women for Duties in the Defense of the Reich," which proclaimed, "The need for forces for duties in the defense of the Reich makes it necessary to lay hold of all men and women, whose labor capabilities are not at all or not fully utilized, and to bring their abilities to bear."[15] The stated goal of the directive was to release physically fit men for combat duty at the front. In the search for replacements, the Wehrmacht cast its net wide, including all men between the ages of sixteen and sixty-five and all women between the ages of seventeen and fifty, a National Socialist *levée en masse.* The directive did allow for some exceptions, including mothers of small children, men and women in the civil service, and men and women employed full-time in agricultural activities.[16] Hitler's directive had an immediate and longstanding impact on an entire generation of young men and women who would carry the title of *Flakhelfer* (flak auxiliaries) into the postwar period.[17]

The mobilization of men and women, the young and the old, provided dramatic evidence of the severe effects being induced throughout the Wehrmacht by the shortage of men for military duty created by escalating combat losses. The Luftwaffe acted quickly to tap the pool of women and men now made available for military service. In February, the Luftwaffe drafted its first group of young men from the 1926-year group for duty as flak auxiliaries.[18] In the city of Krefeld, approximately 150 young men between the ages of fifteen and sixteen marched into the city hall on February 15 accompanied by their parents. After a series of patriotic speeches, including one speaker's exclamation that "you are wood of our wood, flesh of our flesh," the assembled high school students took an oath to be "loyal and obedient" and "courageous and prepared."[19] By the end of May, over 38,000 young men had marched into city halls throughout the Reich and had spoken similar oaths in preparation for service with the Luftwaffe's flak arm.[20]

In addition to the mobilization of young men, young women found increasing employment in aerial observation command posts and fixed radar sites within the Reich and the occupied territories in 1943. The Luftwaffe drafted young women for service in barrage balloon and searchlight batteries, and even flak gun batteries.[21] By the summer, groups of young women from the League of German Girls (Bund Deutscher Mädel) began replacing regular Luftwaffe personnel in the searchlight units in order to free these men for combat duty at the front.[22] In 1943 alone, approximately 116,000 young women replaced Luftwaffe enlisted men employed in air defense duties.[23] Although some accounts criticized these young women as "very unreliable" and "jittery" in the face of fire, numerous other reports indicated that they performed their duties in a professional and efficient manner.[24] In fact, Milch remarked that without these young women the Luftwaffe would not have been able to maintain the Reich's air defense network.[25]

In one respect, however, the introduction of young women into Luftwaffe units under the direction of older men did present some problems. In an order of September 18, 1942, Göring issued a warning to Luftwaffe commanders in which he remarked that it had come to his attention that certain supervisors, both officer and enlisted, had "attempted to enter into love affairs" with these teenage women. He remarked that he expected supervisors to protect the honor of their female subordinates and to treat them as one would like his own sister to be treated. Finally, he threatened that any future misuse of authority in this manner would be punished with the "fullest severity under the law."[26] Likewise, Goebbels noted the "very strong" public sentiment against the drafting of female Luftwaffe auxiliaries in a diary entry of March 7.[27] Indeed, Hitler himself had deep-seated reservations about the mobilization of these young women for military duties, but pragmatism eventually vanquished ideological conviction concerning a woman's "proper" role in society.[28] Despite problems and public opposition to the move, the mobilization was necessary in the face of the need for more soldiers at the front. The drafting of young women into the signal corps and the searchlight batteries illustrates the increasing strains within the entire ground-based air defense network by the fourth year of the war.

It is difficult to judge the full impact on the readiness and performance of the air defenses caused by the employment of these male and female auxiliaries. Without doubt, many of the young men and women drafted into service approached their duties with great enthusiasm and dedication.[29] However, training courses were often abbreviated or conducted piecemeal as conditions permitted. One former flak auxiliary described the specialized training as "short and concentrated," lasting between two weeks and two months. In fact, time pressures led to some young men being assigned to flak guns after only several days of training.[30] In contrast, young women mobilized into service with the searchlight batteries received six weeks of training.[31] Still, the loss of experienced air defense crews and their replacement with hastily trained substitutes resulted in a qualitative decline in the performance of air defense forces. As in the case of the Home Guard batteries, inexperienced and undertrained high school students were not an adequate replacement for professional soldiers despite the enthusiasm and dedication they displayed in the pursuit of their duties.

In truth, the mobilized flak auxiliaries were not the only group suffering from shortened training courses in 1943. The level of instruction provided to regular soldiers at flak training schools also began a steady decline in 1943. According to von Axthelm, several factors explained the gradual deterioration in training. First, training schools began to experience a shortage of training equipment, from fire directors to flak guns, as the Luftwaffe stripped the schools of serviceable systems for employment at the front. Second, the increasing need for personnel resulted in the assignment of teaching cadre to combat units, reducing the number of available instructors and lowering the quality of training. Finally, the shortage of fuel restricted the operations of Luftwaffe target training aircraft and limited the number of live fire exercises conducted by mobile training units at test and firing ranges.[32] In the early months of 1943, the shortage of aviation fuel also indirectly affected the air defense of the Reich by slowing the training of new pilots. As a result, during a meeting on February 24, 1943, Milch informed Göring of his decision to reduce pilot training from seventy-two weeks to fifty-two weeks, primarily because of the shortage of aviation fuel.[33]

Germany's air defenses were not the only area affected by the lack of sufficient manpower. For example, the protocol of the Flak Development meeting held on January 18, 1943, noted that flak development was in a "critical state" due to the mobilization of industrial workers, a situation resulting in "unbearable time delays" in production.[34] Other areas of German industry, especially electronics manufacturing, also suffered from the growing shortage of trained men and women. At a meeting with Göring on January 21, Martini complained that he needed more skilled workers in order to continue research and development efforts and to reach production goals with respect to the radar program. He requested that Göring grant the release of 1,000 radar technicians from duty at the front and pleaded for a prohibition on the further mobilization of some 17,000 specialist workers associated with the radar industry. Attesting to the importance of these issues, Göring contacted Hitler the same day and received the Führer's permission to undertake the necessary measures to protect the program.[35] Hitler and Göring's attention produced the desired results as the radar program showed good progress by the end of April.[36]

Allocating Resources

In reaction to the intensifying Allied bomber offensive, the Luftwaffe pursued several measures related to resource allocation and the conservation of existing materials. In a meeting of the Flak Acquisition Committee on March 12, Milch attempted to get more from less by ordering a production ratio of one stationary 88-mm gun for every mobile gun. Although this measure raised gun production, in one respect it simply shifted resource demands from the area of weapons production to that of industrial construction.[37] Another initiative involved the increased employment of modified Russian artillery pieces for air defense duties. In the area of fire control equipment, results were mixed. On the one hand, production estimates for fire directors reached 180 units per month, and projections for the 1943 model Malsi auxiliary fire computers climbed to 250 units per month. On the other hand, the Luftwaffe still lacked sufficient numbers of 4-meter optical range finders for the growing number of gun batteries.[38] Furthermore, the conversion of all heavy searchlight batteries to radar control during the course of 1943 placed an added demand on limited fire control equipment.[39] One organizational measure designed to address the continuing shortage of fire control equipment involved the stepped-up creation of superbatteries throughout the year, a process that accelerated in the fall.[40] As mentioned earlier, the concentration of guns into superbatteries had the twofold advantage of increasing available firepower and decreasing the overall demand for personnel and fire control equipment.[41]

Undoubtedly, the flak arm had a voracious appetite for persons and matériel, and the German war industry was stretched to the limit to sate the Luftwaffe's hunger for flak guns and equipment. The Luftwaffe's goal of increasing the size of the flak arm combined with the loss of existing weapons due to excessive wear or their destruction during combat required a prodigious amount of resources. Still, a report prepared by Milch's office in March observed, "The fabrication of the entire Luftwaffe equipment [requirements] to this point could be executed with the available raw materials without a substantial disruption with regard to quantity and quality." The report did caution, however, that the fulfillment of the existing program would only be possible through the "*most extreme intensification of conservation measures.*"[42]

Despite the report's warning, Hitler's craving for ever-greater numbers of flak gun batteries continued unabated. On April 11, 1943, Hitler met with Admiral Karl Dönitz, the commander in chief of the German navy. Hitler responded to Dönitz's demand for a larger naval building program by remarking on the army's need for tanks and antitank guns and the Luftwaffe's need for anti-aircraft guns. Furthermore, Hitler mentioned the necessity for an immense expansion in the Luftwaffe's resources to prevent the loss of the air war.[43] From this remark, it is apparent that Hitler was not oblivious to the importance of the air war, but the question still remained, How was the Luftwaffe to maximize the resources on hand?

By April 19, Milch reluctantly agreed to consider a ratio of three stationary guns to every one mobile gun if the necessary resources were not available for one-to-one production.[44] The necessity for finding methods to save on the number of personnel and equipment within the ground-based air defense arm eventually forced Göring to order the concentration in production on stationary flak guns versus mobile guns.[45] In comparison to their motorized counterparts, each stationary battery reduced the number of people needed by almost half.[46] Despite these savings, Göring's decision would have major implications for the future ability of the Luftwaffe to shift its ground-based air defenses throughout the Reich.[47] Likewise, the Luftwaffe planners recognized the potential impact of this decision and continued to channel resources into the production of railroad flak batteries. By the end of 1943, there were one hundred heavy and twenty light railroad flak batteries operated by elite crews and deployed throughout the Reich.[48] These batteries were highly mobile, and their movement was dependent largely upon the availability of coal and not upon increasingly precious petroleum reserves.[49]

In addition to personnel and equipment concerns, the further expansion of the flak force also led to forecasts of ammunition shortages. In a meeting of the Flak Development Committee on April 19, Milch responded to a report that only 30 percent of future munitions needs could be satisfied based on current resource allocations. He directed the quartermaster general's representative to search for additional measures for saving resources throughout the entire Luftwaffe program. By the spring of 1943, Milch not only was concerned about future problems but also was faced with several existing shortages with regard to munitions. For example, the flak arm reported shortages in the areas of 20-mm high-explosive ammunition, 88-mm shell casings, and 128-mm ammunition. In addition, a lack of sufficient quantities of training rounds, especially for the 128-mm flak gun, caused delays in the training of flak gun crews throughout the Luftwaffe.[50] By the middle of September, however, Wehrmacht armaments planners estimated that production quotas for all flak munitions, with the exception of 37-mm rounds, would be reached by the end of the year.[51]

The Costs of Air Defense

The Luftwaffe's investment in its anti-aircraft forces remained substantial during the first quarter of 1943. For example, in January, Wehrmacht expenditures for the production of weapons and munitions totaled 132 million RM, or $52.8 million, including 64 million RM for army spending, 20 million RM for navy spending, 9 million RM for Luftwaffe spending on aircraft weapons and munitions, and 39 million RM for the flak force.[52] In January alone, anti-aircraft forces consumed almost 30 percent of the Wehrmacht's weapons budget. The percentage of total Wehrmacht outlays for weapons and ammunition for the entire year included 29 percent for flak weapons and 14 percent for flak ammunition in the first and second quarters; 29 percent for flak weapons and 20 percent for flak ammunition in the third quarter; and 26 percent for flak weapons and 19 percent for flak ammunition in the fourth quarter of 1943.[53] These expenditures demonstrate the relatively constant level of weapons outlays during 1943. Likewise, the fiscal spending for ammunition in the first two quarters was fairly modest, especially when one considers the fact that in the last two quarters of 1941 flak ammunition outlays constituted 34 and 35 percent of the entire Wehrmacht munitions budget.[54]

Expanding the Ground-based Air Defense Force

The increase in munitions outlays during the last two quarters of 1943 was the product of improved Allied electronic countermeasures. As will be discussed later, the introduction by the RAF of radar countermeasures during a raid against Hamburg in July 1943 temporarily blinded the crews of the Luftwaffe's gun-laying radar and forced the anti-aircraft forces to rely for a short time exclusively on optical and acoustic methods, as well as the ammunition-intensive barrier fire procedure. Additionally, there were more than 500 Home Guard flak batteries and over 200 barrier fire batteries by the end of 1943.[55] In fact, British military intelligence estimated that 125,000 Home Guard personnel operated 281 heavy flak batteries, 393 light flak batteries, and twenty barrage balloon units in May 1943.[56] The Home Guard batteries' lack of adequate fire control equipment, their lower state of training, and their general reliance on barrier fire procedures all combined to drive up ammunition expenditures.

Despite the nagging personnel problems within the flak arm, 1943 witnessed a further increase in the number of gun and, especially, searchlight batteries operating within the Reich proper and along the western approaches to Germany.[57] On January 13, 1943, there were 659 heavy and 558 light antiaircraft gun batteries defending Germany proper; by the middle of June, a mere five months later, there were 1,089 heavy flak batteries and 738 light flak batteries protecting the Reich.[58] To support this expansion, the production of heavy flak gun barrels had almost tripled between 1941 and 1943, to a total of 6,864. In 1943, German industry produced 4,416 88-mm flak guns (122 of which were Model 41 flak guns), 1,220 105-mm flak guns, 282 128-mm single flak guns, and 8 128-mm double-barreled flak guns. The growth in the number of light flak guns was equally dramatic, with the production of 31,503 20-mm flak guns and 4,077 37-mm flak guns, an increase of 9,132 and 1,941 flak guns, respectively, from the 1942 output.[59] In addition to new production, the Luftwaffe proved adept at modifying captured enemy flak guns and munitions for use in the air defense network. In January alone, the Luftwaffe salvaged 285 Russian artillery pieces and modified them for use with German flak batteries.[60] In addition, at the recommendation of Albert Speer, the Luftwaffe exchanged the 88-mm guns of 124 barrier fire batteries for captured Russian artillery pieces rebored to accommodate German 88-mm ammunition by the middle of January 1943.[61] This exchange allowed the Luftwaffe to transfer the more capable guns to units with more sophisticated fire control equipment. Between 1939 and 1944, the Luftwaffe's captured weapons section salvaged a total of 9,504 flak guns and almost 14 million rounds of flak ammunition.[62]

By the end of 1943, the number of heavy and light flak gun batteries protecting the Reich totaled 1,234 and 693, respectively. In addition, the number of searchlight batteries within Germany expanded from 174 in 1942 to 350 by the end of 1943. In the case of 200-cm searchlights, rationalization measures within German industry and the transfer of weapons resources to searchlights led to a fourfold increase in monthly production in 1943 from levels at the end of 1942, despite earlier concerns involving the large amount of copper needed by these devices.[63] Table 7.2 provides a comparison of the increase in anti-aircraft and searchlight batteries between 1942 and 1943 in the Wehrmacht's various theaters of operation.[64]

The information in Table 7.2 offers a number of interesting insights into the development of German ground-based air defenses during 1943. First, it clearly illustrates the continuing expansion of the flak gun and searchlight force in the period. Second, the reduction of searchlight batteries on the Western

Table 7.2 Flak Strength Comparison, 1943 (change from 1942, by percentage)

	Heavy Batteries	Light Batteries	Searchlight Batteries
Germany	1,234 (+65%)	693 (+58%)	350 (+100%)
Western Front: France, Belgium, and Holland	205 (+68%)	295 (+61%)	33 (–66%)
Northern Front: Norway and Finland	92 (+109%)	69 (+92%)	1 (0 in 1942)
Southeastern Front: Romania, Greece, and Hungary	61 (+2%)	39 (–17%)	8 (–11%)
Eastern Front: Russia	148 (no change)	162 (no change)	0 (no change)
Southern Front: Italy and North Africa	278 (+4,500%)	80 (+1,500%)	20 (0 in 1942)
Totals	2,132 (+86%)	1,460 (+64%)	455 (+61%)

Front resulted from the continued expansion of protection for areas within the Reich proper. This trend continued into 1943 as National Socialist district leaders clamored for more anti-aircraft defenses in their respective districts.[65] Third, the dramatic increase in anti-aircraft batteries on the Southern Front occurred as a direct result of the Allied stationing of American bombers from the Fifteenth Air Force in North Africa and later Italy. In effect, the bombers of the Fifteenth Air Force constituted a second aerial front into Europe by the fall of 1943, requiring the redistribution of the Reich's air defenses.[66] Fourth, the size of the flak forces on the Eastern Front remained constant despite the reverses experienced in early 1943. Finally, 58 percent of all heavy flak gun batteries, 47 percent of all light flak gun batteries, and an astounding 78 percent of all searchlight batteries were devoted to the defense of the Reich proper.

Improvements in Bomber Command

The continued growth of the Third Reich's ground-based air defenses was necessary to keep pace with the expanded scope of the Allied bombing campaign, especially the RAF's offensive against the Ruhr in the spring. By March, Harris and Bomber Command were prepared to embark upon a major air campaign aimed at German cities throughout the Ruhr valley. The campaign against the Ruhr witnessed the marriage of tactical and technical innovations as the RAF employed "pathfinder" aircraft to locate and mark the target while using two improved navigational aids, OBOE and H2S. Neither of these innovations was in fact entirely new.

In the summer of 1940, Portal, then commander in chief of Bomber Command, experimented with the use of flare ships to identify the objective, followed by incendiary marking of the target, but initial results had been less satisfactory than expected.[67] In November 1941, Group Captain Sydney Bufton, the deputy director of bomber operations, revived the concept and suggested the creation of a "target-finding force" composed of handpicked crews. These crews were expected to become intimately familiar with specific geographic areas within Germany so that they might lead bombing raids against targets within these areas. After Peirse's departure in early 1942, Bufton approached Harris with the idea, but Harris rejected the suggestion outright.[68] In his postwar memoir, Harris remarked that he "was entirely opposed to the idea of taking the best men from each group; the very men who were most needed to raise the general level by their example and precept. . . . the formation of a *corps d'élite* seemed likely to lead to a good deal of trouble and might be thoroughly bad for morale."[69]

Despite Harris's opposition, Bufton had a strong supporter in the person of Portal. In fact, Portal's support of the pathfinder concept proved pivotal, and in the summer of 1942 Harris was forced to accede to Bufton's plan although with some modifications, including the selection of whole squadrons versus picked crews. On August 11, 1942, the Pathfinder Force (PFF) entered official service with the RAF. A lack of equipment, support for the landing in North Africa, and poor weather, combined with the usual problems associated with training forces for a new type of mission, hampered the operations of the PFF throughout the rest of the year; however, by 1943 the force was beginning to hit its stride.[70]

Two major improvements made to the PFF by the start of 1943 included the introduction of a blind bombing aid, OBOE, and a radar navigation device, H2S. Bomber crews utilizing OBOE essentially followed a curvilinear course along a transmitted radio beam while two ground transmitters monitored the course and speed of the aircraft. When these ground stations determined that the aircraft was over the target, a special signal was transmitted to the aircraft to release its bomb load. The main disadvantage of the system was that it required crews to fly a steady course over a long distance without deviation until reaching the target.[71] Furthermore, crews needed to fly at an altitude of at least 26,000 feet in order to receive the signal in the Ruhr. Initial operational tests in Holland and the Ruhr in December 1942 proved inconclusive, with bombing errors ranging from 600 yards to one mile.[72] In addition to OBOE, the RAF introduced H2S, a device that provided a rudimentary radar map of prominent ground features in the aircraft's flight path. The H2S sets were valuable in assisting navigation, especially in areas beyond the range of OBOE, but they did not work well in areas of poor terrain relief such as the Ruhr or the North German Plain. Despite the limitations of both devices, the PFF's adoption of OBOE and H2S offered the promise of improved bombing accuracy in the spring of 1943.

The Battle of the Ruhr

The Pathfinder Force and the aircrews of Bomber Command faced their first major test of 1943 on the night of March 5 as a force of 442 bombers stood ready to strike at Essen, the largest city within the heart of Germany's industrial complex. According to Harris,

> At long last we were ready and equipped. Bomber Command's main offensive began at a precise moment, the moment of the first major attack on an objective in Germany by means of Oboe. This was on the night of March 5–6th, 1943, when I was at last able to undertake with real hope of success the task which had been given to me when I first took over the Command a little more than a year before, the task of destroying the main cities of the Ruhr.[73]

Harris achieved a decided success in his opening move in the "Battle of the Ruhr." RAF Pathfinder Mosquito aircraft equipped with OBOE flying at altitudes between 28,000 feet and 30,000 feet dropped red target indicators on the city. Additional Pathfinder Force Stirling and Halifax bombers followed up by raining green target markers onto the red target markers to ensure the visibility of the aim points during the entire raid. Finally, waves of bombers carrying loads of one-third high-explosive and two-thirds incendiary blasted the city for approximately forty minutes.

In the aftermath of the raid on Essen, 160 acres of the city, including 3,000 dwellings, lay in ruins, with an additional 450 acres severely damaged. The ostensible object of the attack, the massive Krupp factory complex, received damage to numerous buildings, but the raid failed to destroy the factory's heavy equipment or to disrupt production significantly.[74] In turn, the attack cost Bomber Command fourteen aircraft, or 3.2 percent of the force dispatched.[75] In a postmission message, Harris congratulated his crews:

> The attack on Essen has now inflicted such vast damage that it will in due course take historical precedence as the greatest victory achieved on any front. You have set a fire in the belly of Germany which will burn the black heart out of Nazidom and wither its grasping limbs at the very roots . . . and within the next few months the hopelessness of their situation will be

> borne in upon them in a manner which will destroy their capacity for resistance and break their hearts.[76]

Despite Harris's florid description, the attack on Essen did signal a new phase in the battle for control of the skies over the Third Reich.

The most significant aspects of the attack for German ground-based air defenses involved not only the size of the attacking force, but, more important, the concentration of the bombers over the target in a relatively brief period of time.[77] As the attack on Cologne in May 1942 had demonstrated previously, a tightly bunched bomber stream not only overloaded German night fighter areas in the west but also provided flak crews with less time to successfully acquire and engage their targets.[78] The concentration of bombers was in some respects analogous to the naval convoy system, which sought to provide increased protection for the group while overwhelming a submarine's ability to pick off individual vessels operating alone with great separation. In any event, Bomber Command's tactic of increasing the physical and temporal concentration of the bomber stream confronted the Luftwaffe's air defenses with a thorny problem.

The Bombing Campaign Hits Home

It did not take long for the implications of the RAF effort to become apparent to some members within the Nazi leadership. In a diary entry of March 6, Goebbels reflected on the course of the air war:

> Almost every night massive air attacks take place against some German city. These [raids] cost us much in material and morale terms. For example, reports to me from the Rhineland indicate that the population of one or another city is gradually getting somewhat weak in the knees. That is understandable. For months the working population there has had to go into air-raid shelters night after night, and when they leave they see a part of their city in flames and smoke. . . . Through our war in the east we have lost air supremacy in important sections of Europe and are now in this respect somewhat at the mercy of the English.[79]

In a bitterly ironic twist, not all Germans were disheartened by the bombing campaign. For example, Hans Rosenthal, a young German Jew who was being hidden by an elderly woman in a Berlin "garden colony," looked forward to Bomber Command raids as an opportunity to emerge from his hiding place in a cramped garden hut. For this young boy, the falling bombs evoked feelings of hope, not danger.[80] Still, for the majority of the German population, Goebbels's assessment certainly illustrated the shift in attitude that began to emerge as Harris increased the intensity of his area bombing campaign and the bombers of the Eighth Air Force began to enter the fray in slow but steadily growing numbers. In response to the raid on Essen, Goebbels remarked, "If the English continue to prosecute the air war in this way, they will prepare extraordinarily great difficulties for us." He then bemoaned the fact that Germany still did not have enough flak and that while the night fighters had achieved considerable success, they still could not force the RAF to abandon their attacks.[81]

The industrial cities of the Ruhr were not the only areas that felt the brunt of the RAF's renewed offensive. Assisted by H2S radar devices, a force of over 300 bombers struck the cities of Munich, Nuremberg, and Stuttgart during separate raids.[82] In addition, Pathfinder aircraft using H2S radar attacked Berlin with devastating effect during the night of March 1.[83] Goebbels described the raid as almost as serious as the May 1942 raid on Cologne, calling it "the most serious air raid thus far experienced by the Reich capital." The raid on Berlin claimed the lives of over 500 of the city's inhabitants, but Luftwaffe air defenses brought down 19 aircraft.[84] On the nights of March 27 and March 29, Bomber Command aircraft again launched attacks against Berlin. In the first attack, a force of almost 400 bombers dropped their bombs miles short of the city because the target markers dropped by the PFF either had burned out or had been extinguished by the time the main force arrived. In his diary, Goebbels wryly noted, "I believe in this case that the weather helped us more than the air defenses."[85] Two nights later, a second attack by 329 bombers achieved little success at the loss of 21 aircraft, or 6.4 percent of the force dispatched on the raid.[86] Goebbels's assessment of German air defenses during this raid proved more sanguine. He remarked, "Tonight, the flak fire is extraordinarily strong and effective." In fact, German flak gunners claimed to have brought down a total of 25 aircraft during the raid.[87]

During April and May, Harris's bomber force continued its assault on targets within Germany, as well as raids against the German submarine bases along the coast of France. In late April, the RAF ventured as far as Stettin and Rostock. In addition, bomber streams of over 500 aircraft struck Kiel, Frankfurt, and Stuttgart. However, Harris overplayed his hand in a raid against the Skoda armaments works at Pilsen (Czechoslovakia) on the night of April 16. Of the 327 aircraft dispatched, 36 failed to return from the mission, a disastrous loss rate of 11 percent. The Pilsen raid demonstrated that, despite Bomber Command's increasing success, the Luftwaffe's air defenses were still capable of exacting a high toll during long-range penetrations into the Reich. In contrast, RAF bombers visited Dortmund, "the forge of Germany," on the nights of May 4 and May 23 with 596 and 826 aircraft, respectively. The attacks destroyed over 3,000 buildings and killed nearly 1,300 people, including 200 prisoners of war. On the night of May 29, 719 bombers struck the city of Wuppertal-Barmen with even greater effect, destroying approximately 4,000 houses, damaging over 200 factories, and killing more than 3,400 persons.[88] In total, bombing raids between March and May killed 13,100 persons and destroyed 26,000 buildings.[89]

In the face of the increasing destruction, the German population began to display physical and psychological reactions to the Allied bombing raids. The Security Service (Sicherheitsdienst, or SD) compiled intelligence reports from throughout the Reich dealing with public opinion. According to one such report of June 17, the Allied aerial campaign was emerging as the most prevalent topic of discussion throughout Germany. The report noted the reaction of the population of the city of Wuppertal-Barmen to the ruinous RAF raid on the night of May 29:

> Up to this time, the population of Wuppertal lived with a certain sense of unconcern as the city remained spared to this point from larger attacks. Because the flak protection there also consisted entirely of several batteries of light flak, the population believed themselves safe from enemy air attacks, because they assumed that strong flak fires would only attract enemy aircraft. Many comrades [*Volksgenossen*] for their part even greeted the withdrawal of the flak from Wuppertal. Today, however, one cannot find anyone who wants to remember that he was among those who believed that Wuppertal could get by without flak. Rather, today one points out that it was wrong to leave Wuppertal without flak protection, while they [the populace] now believe that if Wuppertal had been protected by flak it would not have been possible for enemy aircraft to have destroyed the city to this extent.[90]

The case of Wuppertal-Barmen demonstrated the dilemma faced by Luftwaffe air defense planners as the air campaign against Germany expanded. The inability to cover all potential targets and the necessity of shifting guns between threatened areas meant that there would naturally be areas left unprotected at given periods. In turn, the increasing ferocity of the bombing campaign resulted in greater demands on the part of the civil population for more protective measures.

Dummy Sites and Decoys, Act 4

One initiative for improving the Reich's air defenses involved the continued employment of decoy and deception measures. In a review of bombing operations between February 1 and April 18, the ORS determined that of the twenty-nine major bombing operations carried out against German targets "only 3 have achieved complete success, 8 have been partially successful, whilst 15 have been complete failures." In other words, the ORS identified over one-half of the raids in this period as having been "complete failures." The section attributed most of the failures to problems with either OBOE or H2S equipment; however, in five cases the actions of German ground-based air defenses proved decisive. The report noted that "in at least 5 cases out of the ten which have been investigated in detail it is highly probable that the enemy has directly contributed to the failure of the operation by the use of decoys or smoke screens."[91]

The ORS report in June 1943 also noted that there was some evidence of the use of "sky marker flares."[92] For example, during an attack on Bochum in May, Bomber Command aircraft reported seeing red target markers on the ground despite the fact that PFF aircraft had failed to mark the area at the designated time. The Luftwaffe's employment of decoy markers was an issue of extreme importance for RAF bombing operations. Bomber Command first introduced red target markers for PFF aircraft in a raid against Berlin on the night of January 16. In turn, target markers greatly reduced the effectiveness of the Luftwaffe's existing decoy fire sites. The Luftwaffe, however, quickly adapted to the changed circumstances and by March had constructed decoy rocket-launching sites in the vicinity of the existing fire sites. Approximately twenty Luftwaffe personnel operated the sites in twelve-hour shifts. When an attack appeared imminent, the Luftwaffe ground crews launched decoy rockets in the general direction of the fire sites. The decoy rocket closely simulated the PFF's red target indicator, and the lighting of the fire sites offered an added measure for deceiving Bomber Command aircrews. In addition, to decoy rockets, the sites also maintained decoy ground flares in a variety of colors. The sites themselves were both easy to conceal and extremely rudimentary, consisting of wooden crates for launching rockets and concrete launchpads of a few square meters. The use of decoy target markers also took advantage of the tendency among aircrews in the bomber stream to drop on the first target markers or ground fires they encountered. This practice was a completely natural reaction of the crews to drop their bomb load and leave the target as soon as possible, but it also resulted in the continual "creep-back" of the bomb pattern from the original aim point.[93] Despite growing evidence, the RAF proved somewhat obstinate in believing reports that the Luftwaffe was employing decoy target indicators. In fact, it was not until September 1944 that military intelligence confirmed the use of such indicators.[94]

The operation of the decoy target indicator sites was important in several respects. First, the creation of decoy rocket sites married with the existing fire sites provided a further illustration of the Luftwaffe's ingenuity in the field of ground-based air defenses. Second, these sites required little maintenance, proved difficult to identify from the air, and offered high returns on a minimal investment. Even if the sites proved successful in diverting only a portion of the attacking force, they had served their purpose well. Third, the sites, although not by intent, may have played a significant role in inducing the "creep-back" phenomenon associated with many Bomber Command raids during the war. Finally, the sites demonstrated the cat-and-mouse game of move and countermove being played by both sides in the air war over Germany.

In addition to the decoy markers, the Luftwaffe also continued to rely on traditional camouflage and decoy methods. For example, British intelligence identified a "dummy town" northwest of Berlin described as "a realistic reconstruction by dummy lights, factories and marshalling yards of a nearby town or factory target."[95] In another case, the RAF verified the existence of a decoy lake at Wedel near Hamburg, altered to resemble the port city's famous Außen Alster. In this case, the deception was believed to have contributed to fooling a "large proportion" of aircraft during a raid on the night of March 3. In fact, an ORS report noted, "It seems likely that the whole village of Wedel has been made into a decoy for Hamburg, which it resembles somewhat in shape, and the possibility that such decoys exist for other German cities should not be overlooked."[96] It is unclear what opinion the citizens of Wedel held regarding these measures, but certainly their countrymen in Hamburg appreciated any attempt to provide them with some respite from RAF bombing. Despite some success, Bomber Command's increasing use of ground-mapping radar reduced the general effectiveness of sites in western Germany, leading to their deactivation at the end of 1943.[97] In the end, passive decoy measures by themselves could not prove decisive over the long term; nevertheless, these measures had constituted an important but auxiliary method for degrading the effectiveness of Allied bombing in 1941–1943.

An Air Defense Dilemma: Flak or Fighters?

By the middle of March, Hitler's frustration with the increasing strength of the Allied air campaign was clearly evident. On March 9, Goebbels traveled to the Führer's field headquarters at Vinnitsa in the Ukraine. According to Goebbels, Hitler expressed his extreme displeasure with the course of the air war and Göring's leadership of the Luftwaffe. Likewise, Hitler argued that both the Luftwaffe's bomber forces and the flak arm required further expansion. Hitler did concede, however, the difficulties caused within the flak forces due to the large-scale personnel changes, as well as those engendered by the transfer of equipment to Italy. Finally, he identified the need to pay "special attention" to the night fighter force.[98] Hitler's remarks to Goebbels demonstrated his continued belief in the effectiveness of the flak forces but also showed his recognition of the need for night fighter defenses. Additionally, Hitler's loss of faith in Göring resulted in his assuming de facto responsibility for all major decisions relating to the air war by the spring of 1943.[99]

The waxing of Göring's star made room for other Luftwaffe officers to rise to positions of increased authority within the German air force. The General of the Night Fighters, Kammhuber found his star clearly on the rise based on the success achieved by the Luftwaffe night fighter forces throughout 1942 and into 1943.[100] In March 1943, Kammhuber unveiled a plan for strengthening the Reich's air defenses. This plan consisted of several elements. First, believing that the creation of a unified region under a single commander would allow for a more effective defense of the German homeland, Kammhuber sought to unite Air Region, Center, with Air Region 3 to the west. Second, he called for the establishment of a single commander responsible for all air defense forces in this area, day fighter, night fighter, and flak forces. Finally, he argued for the strengthening of both the flak and the fighter forces. In the case of the fighter force, Kammhuber envisioned the creation of a Fighter Air Fleet, controlling 2,000 night fighters and consisting of three corps of three fighter divisions each.[101]

In essence, Kammhuber's plan called for a more than fourfold increase in the number of night fighters available for the defense of the Reich and the western occupied territories. He obviously recognized the threat posed by ever-growing numbers of British and American bombers and sought to increase the Reich's fighter defenses to meet this challenge. In February 1943, there were 535 single-engine day fighters and 430 night fighters protecting the Reich and the occupied western territories. By May 1943, the number of single-engine day fighters actually had decreased to 507, while the number of night fighters increased by only 3 aircraft to 433.[102] Kammhuber realized that there were too few fighters available to contest the intensifying American and British aerial assault. He convinced Jeschonnek, Weise, and Göring that his plan could change the balance of the air war. Kammhuber's proposals also received indirect support from Milch, who remained a steadfast advocate of increased aircraft production.[103] In the end, however, Hitler would cast the deciding vote. Kammhuber traveled to the Führer's headquarters to present his plan. Hitler, however, refused to believe Kammhuber's estimates concerning the expected production figures for the Allied bomber force and angrily dismissed his proposal.[104]

Despite Hitler's earlier comment that he wanted to pay "special attention" to the night fighter force, he was not prepared to divert resources on the scale demanded by Kammhuber to support his proposal for a fighter air fleet. Hitler was not, however, oblivious to the need to increase protection to the Ruhr. He ordered that additional flak gun batteries be sent to Germany's industrial heartland and that some factories be relocated to safer areas.[105] After his meeting with Hitler, Kammhuber's days were numbered. Kammhuber's disagreement with the Führer and his dogged refusal to modify his *Himmelbett* system for night interceptions, despite the RAF's growing success in swamping these defenses, damaged his professional reputation within the Luftwaffe and weakened his position.[106] Coincidentally, at the moment of Kammhuber's fall from grace, another young Luftwaffe pilot entered the stage with a proposal for improving the performance of the night fighter force.[107]

The Birth of the "Wild Boars"

In March 1943, Major Hajo Herrmann, a young bomber pilot serving on the Luftwaffe Air Staff, prepared a report that identified a projected shortfall of German fighters in the face of accelerated Allied bomber production. Herrmann, like Kammhuber, recognized that the German night fighter force needed to be increased; however, he did not merely call for the increased production of night fighters. In addition to increased production, he noted, "The huge shortfall in night fighters into 1944 can be remedied by operating day fighters at night, backed up with all possible technical, organisational and training support."[108] In essence, Herrmann's plan was in part a restatement of the earlier practice of using German night fighters to conduct intercepts in the illuminated searchlight belts of the occupied western territories *(helle Nachtjagd)*. The removal of most of these lights to areas within the Reich now provided the same opportunity for night operations in illuminated conditions over German cities.[109] The innovative element in Herrmann's plan involved the employment of single-engine day fighters at night to combat RAF bombers.

Despite Kammhuber's opposition to his plan, Herrmann secretly obtained permission to fly a single-engine day fighter at night out of the airfield at Berlin-Staaken.[110] In turn, he reached an agreement with the commander of the 1st Flak Division involving the cooperation of searchlight batteries in practice attempts to intercept a Luftwaffe bomber acting as a simulated target under illuminated conditions. After several training missions, Herrmann decided to test his technique under combat conditions over Berlin in April 1943. He therefore requested that Berlin's flak forces be limited to firing below 19,500 feet. General Weise flatly refused on the grounds of an existing Führer order. Herrmann was told, "'You fly if you like: we're not going to stop shooting for anyone.'" Despite Weise's refusal to restrict flak operations, Herrmann decided to test his theory over Berlin. During his first mission, he successfully intercepted an RAF Mosquito flying at an altitude of over 30,000 feet caught by searchlights and bracketed by flak. Herrmann failed to bring the bomber down, but he did land with a hole made by a flak splinter a few feet behind his cockpit headrest.[111]

Word of Herrmann's intercept of the elusive and much-hated Mosquito quickly made the rounds of the Air Staff. In a meeting with Milch, Herrmann received permission to begin training a small cadre of instructor pilots at the flying school in Brandenburg-Briest. The group of some dozen pilots trained throughout May and June but would not have an opportunity to engage in combat until early July. Herrmann's procedure became known as *Wilde Sau,* literally "wild boar" but figuratively an expression for someone run amok. In fact, many Luftwaffe and flak officers thought Herrmann and his group were crazy to fly among the tons of flak splinters present in the air above Berlin during a night bombing raid.[112] Although Herrmann's force was decidedly modest, Milch's authorization indicated the Luftwaffe leadership's willingness to pursue increasingly unorthodox solutions to combat the growing threat posed by Allied bombing raids through the spring of 1943.

Effects of the Bombing Campaign and the Effectiveness of Air Defense

By the end of May, Harris's campaign against Germany's industrial heartland had achieved a significant level of destruction, and the leadership of the Third Reich clearly recognized the danger posed by the RAF attacks. In a meeting with Dönitz on May 31, Hitler observed, "We have had very strong and systematic attacks against our industrial centers, attacks that in the long run cannot be prevented through defensive measures alone." In fact, Hitler's planned response to Bomber Command's campaign involved a renewed aerial bombing offensive against the British Isles or expanded attacks on Allied shipping.[113] When Dönitz requested more men only two weeks later, Hitler responded, "I haven't got this personnel. It is necessary to increase the flak and night fighter forces in order to protect German cities."[114] Several days thereafter, Göring ordered "special protection" for the middle German industrial area, including the increased employment of night fighters in the defense of the region.[115]

The RAF campaign against the Ruhr undoubtedly intensified the stresses on Germany's air defenses by the middle of June; however, Luftwaffe air defenses had exacted a high toll from Bomber Command crews during this period. In the second quarter of 1943, RAF night losses totaled 75 aircraft to fighters and 79 aircraft to flak in April; 131 aircraft to fighters and 76 aircraft to flak in May; and 142 aircraft to fighters and 70 aircraft to flak in June. In addition, German fighters shot down 21 aircraft in daylight conditions while the flak tallied 4 aircraft destroyed.[116] Bomber Command losses for the period provide several insights into the course of the air war by the summer of 1943. First, the fact that Bomber Command absorbed almost 600 combat losses in the period was indicative of the strong performance of German air defenses, but it also demonstrated the growing strength and size of the RAF's bomber force. Only a year earlier, losses on this scale would have crippled Harris's force.[117] Second, flak enjoyed a slight edge over fighters during night attacks in April, while night fighters attained almost a two-to-one success ratio in May and June. As in the previous years of the war, shorter nights and improved weather were important factors that favored the fighters in this period. Third, flak batteries damaged 1,496 aircraft and accounted for an additional 22 aircraft damaged beyond repair, while fighters damaged 122 and rendered another 8 aircraft completely unserviceable. Finally, Bomber Command lost 2.76 percent in April, 4.03 percent in May, and 3.64 percent in June of *all* aircraft conducting night sorties in the period.[118] The total percentage of aircraft missing for the period in raids on German targets, including those lost to accidents and unknown causes, rose to 5.3 percent of all sorties.[119]

The Hidden Effects of Flak: Evasive Maneuvers and Bombing Accuracy

In one respect, many Allied bomber crews displayed a remarkably similar tendency during the final bomb run to the target. In a meeting of April 23, 1943, Harris gathered his group commanders to discuss the tactical aspects of recent bombing missions. Harris mentioned the possibility of routing bomber aircraft at low level (altitudes below 1,000 feet) in attacks aimed at southern Germany, Italy, and to "a lesser degree when crossing Denmark." In contrast, the committee agreed that difficulties with navigation and the Luftwaffe's light flak defenses made this "impossible" over most of Germany. Likewise, Harris expressed his concern regarding the number of aircraft taking "violent avoiding action" over the target. One member at the meeting, a Dr. Dickens, "confirmed that when over heavily defended areas the concentration of flak was so great that no avoiding action, however, violent, could help." Dickens's suggestion was simply for crews to fly a straight course at maximum speed to minimize time of exposure within the flak zone. Harris then requested that an ORS report on this topic be prepared to inform the aircrews of the need to avoid violent evasive action.[120]

The issue of violent evasive maneuvers was vitally important because excessive maneuvering by the pilot over the target could significantly disrupt bombing accuracy even if the objective measured the size of a city's entire central district. In fact, the experience of Bomber Command in March indicated that only about 48 percent of aircrews placed their bomb loads within three miles of the aiming point.[121] Admittedly, evasive actions allowed aircrews to feel they had some control over their fates as they faced the deadly flak splinters blossoming suddenly and without warning around their planes. On May 24, Bomber Command issued a tactical memorandum that addressed the issue of evasive maneuvering over the target, admonishing the crews as follows:

> The enemy has put up a very great deal of effort into his A.A. defences with the result that our bombers have to face fire of considerable intensity. Much evasive action is normally taken with a view to minimising the effectiveness of this fire and bomb-aiming is in consequence rendered considerably less accurate and many bombs are wasted. The enemy is, therefore, achieving his purpose to a great extent.

The memo warned aircrews that "a large part of the evasive action at present being carried out by bomber crews is completely useless against any form of A.A. fire" and underlined the "evil effects of evasive action" on bombing accuracy.[122]

Bomber Command's Eighth Air Force counterparts also addressed this issue in the first years of American bombing operations. After taking over the 3rd Air Division, Colonel Curtis E. LeMay gathered his group commanders to discuss evasive maneuvering over the target. In theory, the bombardier using the Norden bombsight assumed control over the aircraft during the final run-in to the target from the initial point. The bombsight was linked to the autopilot, allowing the bombardier to fly the aircraft from his station. LeMay mentioned, however, that in practice pilots continued to override the autopilot during the final bomb run. He castigated his commanders by observing, "Too many times, the command pilot, who is supposed to lead a mission, is the one who causes it to fail. Every time he sees a burst of flak, he takes the wheel and swerves his plane. That causes trouble for the whole group." He continued, "If there is anything that is necessary on a bomb run it is that there be no evasive action."[123] In his memoir, LeMay described the initial bombing efforts of the Eighth Air Force as "stinko." He recounted, "It was SOP [standard operating procedure] to use evasive action over the targets. Everybody was doing it. And everybody was throwing bombs every which way."[124]

Thus flak batteries, by inducing evasive maneuvering by both the crews of Bomber Command and their American counterparts, reduced bombing accuracy. In the case of the Eighth Air Force, the effects of maneuvering to avoid flak proved even more profound based on the American doctrine devoted to the "precision bombing" of point targets. In this respect, Bomber Command's area bombing policy certainly allowed for a more widespread bomb pattern in order to be considered effective; however, in the case of the Eighth Air Force, the likelihood of hitting a point target while conducting evasive maneuvers was almost nil.

Improving Flak Defenses: The Doctrinal Approach

In addition to somewhat unorthodox solutions, like Herrmann's wild boars, the Luftwaffe also pursued more conventional methods in an effort to improve the Reich's air defenses. For example, in March 1943, the German military released a manual that dealt extensively with the question of fighter and flak cooperation. The manual made the following general observations:

> The employment of day and night fighters is the most important reinforcement of Flak protection. In areas where both fighters and Flak operate, fighters form the forward defences. Successful air defence is dependent upon close liaison between the commanders of the day and night fighters, Flak, and the early warning system. Personal liaison is necessary between commanders of fighters and flak divisions. If the command posts are not close together, liaison officers must be appointed and telephonic communication maintained.[125]

The Luftwaffe's description of combined efforts between fighters and flak clearly emphasized the physical separation between areas of fighter and flak activity. However, it recognized the importance of close cooperation and communication between fighters, flak, and the Air Reporting Service. It also mandated a liaison officer at the division level between the flak and fighter forces, a measure that was formalized through the creation of the position of "flak mission commander" at each of the fighter divisions. These individuals were selected from proven flak regiment commanders and enjoyed a status equivalent to that of a division commander.[126] Likewise, the creation of the flak mission commander and the high qualifications needed by flak officers to fill this position demonstrated the increasing importance placed on cooperation between the fighter arm and its flak counterpart.

The manual also provided additional explanation of the liaison between flak and fighters during the day and at night. For day operations, the manual offered six additional "rules":

> i. Enemy aircraft will be engaged by both fighters and Flak.
> ii. The fighter commander must advise the warning services and the Flak division or local Flak commander of take-off, position, height and landing of fighters. Flak divisions or local Flak commanders must report to the fighter commander the numbers and heights of aircraft picked up visually or by radar.
> iii. As a rule Flak will engage leading aircraft of any attacking force.
> iv. The fighter commander must decide how far into the Flak zone he will continue to attack the enemy aircraft. He must accept the danger from Flak fire, as an immediate cessation of the Flak fire is not always possible. As soon as the ground defences see that a fighter is in a position to attack, fire must be withheld.
> v. If a single enemy aircraft flies into the area, the Flak commander may, at the request of the fighter commander, order Flak not to engage.
> vi. Fighters should avoid light flak zones of engagement.[127]

These expanded guidelines clearly showed that, although military planners sought to maintain physical separation between the two arms, they also recognized that this would not always be possible. In turn, fighter pilots were given a good deal of latitude in deciding whether to enter the flak zone.

The instruction to concentrate fire on the lead aircraft was a response to the American practice of placing the best crew and lead bombardier at the front of the formation to signal the bomb release point for the rest of the formation's aircraft. The Luftwaffe's flak crews apparently achieved a good deal of success in these efforts, as reflected in the postwar memoir of General LeMay, who recalled, "Then the flak batteries united in trying to knock down the leaders." He added, "Vaguely I knew that I was losing more Lead Crews than I was producing, and that our Division would be bound to go downhill as a result. Finally, I woke up, and put a big input of crews into the Lead Crew training program."[128] The targeting of lead aircraft demonstrated the flak arm's ability to shape its doctrine and tactical procedures in response to the unique characteristics of American bombing operations.

The manual also noted that cooperation between flak and night fighters was "especially important" to "ensure that [one's] own fighter aircraft are not engaged by Flak and that maximum fire-power is directed against enemy aircraft." It specified that night fighter command posts *must* be collocated with the command post of the flak divisional commander. Furthermore, the manual established five "rules" for flak and night fighter operations:

i. The local Flak commander is alone responsible for the defence of the immediate target area; night fighters form the outer defences and have no responsibility for the defence of the particular objectives.
ii. In night fighter areas, Flak has the right to fire up to any height, and also to fly balloons at maximum heights, unless special conditions apply in the area.
iii. In areas of light Flak concentrations, the night fighter operates above 1,000 metres (3200 feet), whilst Flak may fire up to that height. The night fighter must accept the risk that some rounds will burst higher than 1,000 metres.
iv. When single enemy aircraft are flying through the area, or if night fighters are in difficulty or have lost touch with their ground control, the night fighter commander may request the Flak commander to cease fire.
v. Night fighter command posts must have a Flak liaison officer.[129]

The rules concerning night operations again clearly favored flak forces, but they did provide some room for independent action on the part of the night fighters. In addition, the emphasis on liaison personnel illustrated a continuing effort to harmonize the operations of flak forces with their night fighter counterparts.

Improving Flak Defenses: The Technological Approach

By the middle of June, the Luftwaffe's Flak Development Committee was in the midst of pursuing several technical initiatives designed to increase the performance of the flak force. One project involved the development of a 55-mm medium flak gun prototype.[130] The Luftwaffe intended the 55-mm flak gun to serve as a rapid-fire weapon designed to engage targets up to approximately 15,000 feet. Initial designs called for the construction of the 55-mm flak gun with a specially designed fire control package for a completely integrated weapons system.[131] Milch went so far as to raise the project's priority rating and to secure additional engineers and specialist workers; however, it would be at least a year before the weapon could be ready for mass production.[132] In addition to the 55-mm gun, Krupp and Rheinmetall continued work on new prototypes of the 150-mm flak gun, a project subsequently canceled in September. The Luftwaffe also began upgrading 2,000 of the Model 18 and Model 36 versions of the 88-mm flak gun to improve their performance.[133]

In the summer of 1943, research efforts also focused on experimental munitions types, including a discus-shaped projectile and an incendiary shrapnel shell. Whereas the former proved less promising than originally thought and was canceled, the latter showed potential and achieved moderate success in 1944.[134] Upon detonation, the incendiary rounds released seventy-two pellets capable of penetrating the skin of an aircraft to damage electrical or fuel systems.[135] In 1943, the Luftwaffe also introduced "aerial mines." These consisted of a projectile, roughly the size of a shoe box, fired by flak gunners to a point above the bomber formation whereupon it exploded, releasing a number of small explosive devices that descended on parachutes into the bomber formation.[136] In addition, a suggestion was put forward to modify the fuses of the 88-mm projectiles with both a timed fuse and a contact fuse. According to General von Renz, an office chief in Speer's armaments ministry rejected the idea based on the increased risks involved in transporting this type of ammunition.[137] As the events of 1945 would later confirm, this proved to be a momentous decision for the flak arm, with trials using time- and contact-fused ammunition achieving dramatic results in the last months of the war.

The Flak and the V-1 and V-2 Missiles

Ironically, the German flying bomb (V-1) project, and not flak guns and munitions, proved to be in the forefront of the thoughts of the Luftwaffe's senior flak officer, General von Axthelm, in June 1943. Indeed, retaliation, and not defensive measures, was on the minds of many of the Third Reich's leaders in the wake of the intensifying Allied bombing effort. In a private meeting on

March 9, Hitler confided to Goebbels that "the British terror attacks will be answered with terror from our side."[138] Hitler's determination to retaliate for British and American bombing raids found resonance within the German public, especially in areas devastated by Bomber Command raids.[139]

The method for bringing the war home to the British population would be the V-1 and V-2 missile programs. With Speer's backing, the Long-Range Bombardment Commission compared the two missiles in a head-to-head competition on May 26, 1943. Despite two failures by the V-1, the commission recommended pursuing both programs. By early June, Hitler viewed the missiles as the perfect weapons for retaliating against the Allied bombing campaign.[140] In a meeting of June 18, von Axthelm met with Göring to discuss the progress of the V-1 program and the flak arm's plans for the operational employment of the missile. Axthelm briefed Göring on the proposed construction arrangements for the command and supply areas, as well as for the planned ninety-six launch sites. Göring ordered that the sites proposed by von Axthelm be constructed with the "greatest urgency." Furthermore, he agreed to contact Speer and Fritz Sauckel, the Third Reich's chief of slave labor, with a request that additional workers and materials be provided for development and production. Finally, Göring remarked on his hope for the production of an astounding 50,000 missiles by the end of the development stage, as well as his intention to brief Hitler on the plans for the employment of the missiles.[141]

The development and testing of the V-1 proved important to the flak arm as the project drew away a large number of officers and men from the anti-aircraft force, a force already experiencing severe personnel shortages.[142] Oberst Max Wachtel, a flak officer, was chosen to command the V-1 unit due to his experience with other special programs, and the flak arm was selected as a means for disguising the true nature of the still-secret weapon. On August 3, 1943, the Luftwaffe established Flak Regiment 155 (W) to conduct tests in preparation for the operational employment of the flying bomb. The regiment drew its members from throughout the Luftwaffe, but mainly the flak arm, and numbered almost 7,000 men. Almost a year later, in June 1944, as the V-1 reached operational status, Wachtel made a personal request to Hitler for more men. Hitler approved that request, and an additional flak regiment, Flak Regiment 255 (W), combined with Flak Regiment 155 (W) to form the 5th Flak Division.[143] The formation of an elite flak unit for a project completely unrelated to traditional air defense duties was but one of a number of continuing demands placed on the flak arm by the middle of the war.

The association of the flak arm with the missile program was not, however, without some potential benefits. Despite the primary mission of the V-1 and V-2 as weapons of retaliation, the Luftwaffe leadership also was interested in employing a modified V-2 missile as an anti-aircraft missile. Already in December 1942, Milch ordered that a flak liaison officer be attached to the army's V-2 program. He selected von Renz to assume command of the program for flak missile development. In turn, the Luftwaffe's flak staff ventured a prognosis that, based on the army's success with the V-2, a flak missile could be available within five years.[144]

On January 16, 1943, von Axthelm met with the missile program's leading technical experts, including General Walter Dornberger, Wernher von Braun, von Renz, and several representatives from German industry. The group discussed two projects. First, the engineers of Rheinmetall proposed a powder flak rocket capable of being fired to an altitude of approximately 19,700 feet and guided by optical aiming. The second proposal involved modifying the army's liquid-fueled A-4 (V-2) surface-to-surface missile into a flak missile (code-named "Waterfall") using remote guidance via a radar data link. Despite von Braun's reservations concerning the technical difficulties associated with the latter project, the group set a target date for flight tests of the missile by the end of 1944.[145]

In the summer of 1943, high expectations for the project's success even led to forecasts for the future production of 10,000 missiles per month.[146] In this respect, von Renz played a key role in raising inflated expectations for the project in a report in which he compared the predicted effectiveness between flak missiles and existing flak guns. He predicted that two Waterfall missiles would be needed to bring down a bomber versus an average of 3,000 rounds of 88-mm or 105-mm flak. Based on this estimate, von Renz calculated the savings in explosives per shootdown at between 2.5 and 4.3 tons alone.[147] Despite his extraordinary prediction of the need for two missiles to bring down one aircraft, von Renz noted that a "tightly knit defense" could be achieved only through the use of both flak missiles and fighters. It is difficult to assess what prompted von Renz to provide such an incredibly optimistic, and illusory, prognosis concerning the flak missile program. On the one hand, his remark concerning the need to balance flak missiles and fighters, without mention of anti-aircraft guns, might be seen as an indication of his loss of faith in the flak arm. On the other hand, he might have proposed exactly the argument that he was sure would meet the approval of Milch in an attempt to strengthen his own position within the Luftwaffe's bureaucracy. In this instance at least, von Renz's unrealistic forecast certainly did not reflect well on the expertise of the flak's senior technical officer, whatever his motivation.

In any event, it soon became apparent that solving the overwhelming technical difficulties associated with missile guidance and control would require a substantial investment of research effort and considerable resources. In fact, one report estimated that the training and assembly line preparations for a production run of 5,000 missiles per month using 14,000 workers would require slightly more than 1.1 million man-hours. Furthermore, the competing claims on workers and matériel presented by the V-1 and V-2 missile programs significantly hindered any effort to accelerate the flak missile program. In fact, in June 1943,

Professor Carl Krauch, an official representative of the German chemical industry, suggested developing a flak missile before pursuing the V-1 and V-2 progams, an idea that was summarily rejected by Hitler.[148] Despite these problems, in a report of October 1943, the Flak Development Group offered Milch a plan for a Reich defense zone utilizing anti-aircraft guns and flak missiles in which the missiles would assume a key role in protecting the German homeland. By December 1943, the Flak Development Group even went so far as to provide "comprehensive recommendations" for the employment of the missiles and outlined the accompanying ground organization to support these operations.[149] In the end, the flak arm employed a small number of unguided powder rockets with little success, while the Luftwaffe's quest for an operational flak missile proved illusory.[150]

The Wild Boars Go to War

In the summer of 1943, the Luftwaffe could not afford to wait for the employment of potential "wonder weapons"; rather, it was time to use all means at hand against the massed raids of RAF bombers visiting destruction nightly upon the German homeland. By early July, Hajo Herrmann's wild boars were ready to undertake their first operational mission. On the night of July 3, Herrmann and nine of his fellow pilots assembled their fighters at an airfield in Mönchengladbach, awaiting instructions from the Air Reporting Service on the position of the approaching bomber stream. The fighters scrambled in anticipation of an attack against the Ruhr. Flying at altitudes between 20,000 and 23,000 feet, the fighters circled without fear of their own flak fire as the result of an agreement that had been reached with General Johannes Hintz, the commander of flak forces covering a large part of the Ruhr, including Essen, Duisburg, Bochum, and Düsseldorf. Herrmann's force watched as bombers exploded on the horizon, victims of night fighters operating according to the *Himmelbett* procedure in the occupied western territories. However, Herrmann's fighter force was in for a surprise as the bombers turned away from the heart of the Ruhr toward the city of Cologne.[151]

In his postwar memoir, Herrmann described the situation:

> We were not flying above General Hintz's flak but over Cologne-Mulheim, in the area of the 7th *Flakdivision,* which was illuminating bombers and fighters indiscriminately. They fired on us without paying any heed to our flashing belly and navigation lights. Searchlight beams were concentrated around us, and ahead of us we heard the thunder of our artillery. In the intoxication of that summer night's battle we forgot the countless flak splinters and other dangers that faced us, and we tore into the witch's cauldron

> hot with anger and spurred with enthusiasm. This was *Wilde Sau* pure and simple.

By the end of the night, twelve bombers had been brought down in the skies over Cologne. Herrmann claimed all twelve victories for his fighters, which resulted in some acrimony between him and the 7th Flak Division. Herrmann's fighters and the flak division subsequently received credit for six aircraft each.[152] The dispute over who should receive credit for downing the bombers is interesting in several respects. First, it was certainly to Herrmann's personal advantage to claim all the downed aircraft as a result of his "new" method for night interception. Second, in the chaos of aerial combat Luftwaffe fighter pilots (and their Allied counterparts) were known to provide inflated, if sincere, tallies of aircraft destroyed. For example, based on claims of aircraft destroyed in aerial engagements during one point in the Battle of Britain, the Luftwaffe calculated that there could be no more RAF fighters in Great Britain.[153] Third, the extremely strict guidelines for receiving a confirmed flak "kill" made Herrmann's subsequent claims less believable. Finally, even without the assistance of the flak, Herrmann still owed a large part of his unit's success to ground-based air defenses. In fact, the wild boar procedure relied completely on either searchlights or flak to provide illumination for the initial intercept, thereby allowing the fighters to press home their attacks. Admittedly, it was the fighters that finished off the bombers, but ground-based air defenses provided the necessary conditions for ensuring this outcome.

The success of the wild boars over Cologne did not go unnoticed. In Herrmann's words, "The combined battle by fighters and flak generated interest in every *Luftgau* [air district]." Weise congratulated Herrmann on the success of the operation achieved in the midst of the flak barrage. In addition, first Jeschonnek and then Göring ordered Herrmann to brief them personally on the wild boar procedure. At the first meeting, Jeschonnek placed Herrmann in charge of a night fighter wing consisting of day fighters from three separate groups.[154] At a later meeting with Milch on July 6, Herrmann outlined his objective:

> In the area of the *Flak* division in the Ruhr, where the illumination conditions are fairly good, you can expect, on average, that 80 to 140 enemy targets will be captured by the searchlight beams in the course of an air raid, and in fact will be tracked for more than two minutes. The requirement I place on crews is that every target which is tracked longer than two minutes by the searchlights will be shot down. . . . they can quite easily lose an additional 80 aircraft during the course of one night, if I get the necessary aircraft to do the job.[155]

After his promotion, Herrmann set about to improve the coordination between his night fighters and the Luftwaffe's flak and searchlight batteries. One method included the introduction of guidance flares fired by the flak batteries to indicate the direction of a British attack to night fighters circling in the skies above Germany.[156] In fact, this tactic had been used in World War I, when flak batteries fired rounds to provide fighters with the general location of attacking aircraft. Additionally, Herrmann's night fighters came to rely on searchlights for ascertaining their positions. Ground crews arranged groups of two to four searchlights in specific patterns to denote particular cities within Germany and established lanes of vertically stationed lights between airfields and important cities throughout the Reich. In fact, the use of searchlights for navigation and illumination flares fired by flak batteries emerged as the primary methods for guiding Herrmann's fighters toward their targets.[157]

Despite efforts to coordinate with the ground-based air defenses, the practice of intercepting bombers within the flak zone could not be conducted without considerable risk to the fighter pilots operating in the area. Herrmann aptly described the general confusion present during a Bomber Command raid over Berlin:

> The R/T [radio transmitter] was full of noise. Curses were flung about, against each other, against the *Flak* that was peppering the fighters with gunfire or dazzling the pilots with searchlights, against the enemy that wouldn't go down but got away: curses at their own stupidity and bad luck. The curses of the anti-aircraft crews erupted on other frequencies and so were unheard by our ears. Everything looked red.[158]

In one engagement, Herrmann closed in on an aircraft already engaged by flak. After firing his flare pistol to warn off the anti-aircraft gunners, he was chagrined to note that the gunners below either had not seen his recognition flare or had chosen to ignore it. Herrmann's disgust with the anti-aircraft gunners was balanced by his high regard for the performance of the searchlight crews, which he described as "splendid." He praised these batteries by remarking, "When they caught a bomber they didn't let it go but offered it up for sacrifice."[159] In any event, the skies over Berlin were a dangerous and crowded area for British bombers and German fighters alike.

Flak and Fratricide

Based on Herrmann's description, one might suspect that numerous Luftwaffe fighters fell victim to their own flak guns. Losses to friendly fire did in fact occur and were certainly a source of concern for the Luftwaffe, but not a major problem. Although some 229 aircraft were lost in 1943, the pilots were still over German territory and could often return to their duties, albeit with psychological, if not physical, wounds.[160] In comparison, the Luftwaffe lost 1,788 fighter pilots to all causes during the first eight months of the year alone.[161] Luftwaffe losses over the Reich in 1943 as a result of friendly fire included 54 aircraft in the first quarter, 46 in the second quarter, 85 in the third quarter, and 44 in the fourth quarter.[162] On the one hand, the relatively high losses experienced in the winter months were largely attributable to the use of either barrage fire procedures or radar-directed fire in periods of traditionally poor weather. On the other hand, the losses in July and August—29 and 35 aircraft, respectively—resulted from three factors. First, the numbers of night sorties in July and August were the highest of the year for the RAF, with 6,170 in July and 7,807 in August.[163] Second, the inauguration of the wild boar procedures placed more Luftwaffe fighter pilots in danger from their own flak forces. Finally, Bomber Command introduced a new countermeasure to the German radar network on the night of July 24 in a massive attack against the port city of Hamburg, forcing the Luftwaffe for a time to rely heavily on the use of barrier fire procedures.

The Introduction of Window and the Destruction of Hamburg

Between May 1940 and the middle of 1943, Bomber Command aircraft had struck the ancient Hanseatic city of Hamburg on almost one hundred occasions.[164] However, the series of attacks beginning on the evening of July 24, code-named Operation Gomorrah, would make these earlier efforts seem inconsequential. Almost 800 aircraft took off from bases in the United Kingdom with a bomb load that averaged 7 armor-piercing bombs, 147 high-explosive bombs, 469 phosphorous bombs, 29 jellied gasoline bombs, and 17,580 incendiary bombs per square kilometer.[165] The defenses facing the assembled British force included the Luftwaffe's night fighter forces in the Reich and those stationed forward in the occupied western territories, as well as 54 heavy flak batteries, 26 light flak batteries, 22 searchlight batteries, and 3 smoke generator batteries.[166] However, the RAF was prepared to unveil a new method for neutralizing the air defenses along the route to, and in the vicinity of, Hamburg.

While still eighty miles from the German coast, PFF and main force aircraft began to drop hundreds of bundles consisting of 2,200 twelve-inch aluminum foil strips at an interval of one bundle per minute, code-named "Window." At last the RAF had decided to use the procedure requested by Peirse two years earlier. As the bundles of foil strips descended, they expanded into a growing cloud of radar-reflective material that in effect blinded the ground-based

Würzburg radar, as well as the night fighters' built-in aerial intercept radar sets.[167] In the words of one participant, the ground-based radar operators were faced with "an indecipherable jumble of echo points resembling giant insects, from which nothing could be recognised at all." Likewise, one Luftwaffe night fighter pilot described the situation as equivalent to "fishing in the murk."[168] With their gun-laying radar out of commission, searchlight batteries wandered aimlessly across the sky while the flak gun batteries were forced to employ barrier fire tactics in the hope of hitting, or at least deterring, some of the attacking bombers.[169]

In the execution of the mission, the RAF lost twelve aircraft, for a minuscule loss rate of 1.5 percent for all aircraft dispatched. In turn, the first of the Operation Gomorrah attacks on Hamburg cost the lives of 1,500 of the city's inhabitants and left an estimated 200,000 persons without shelter.[170] Goebbels bemoaned the "devastating effects" of the raid on Hamburg's civil population and the city's armaments production. He bitterly remarked, "With this attack the illusions that many have made relative to the continued progression of the enemy's air operations will be finally destroyed." He also was critical of the small number of bombers brought down by the German defenses, a problem he in part attributed to Weise's decision to send some of Hamburg's heavy flak batteries south to Italy only two days prior to the raid.[171] The explanation for Weise's seemingly baffling decision to transfer these batteries to the south lay in events taking place in the Mediterranean at that time. The Allied invasion of Sicily on July 10 and growing indications of the Italians' widespread unwillingness to continue fighting had forced Germany to transfer substantial military reinforcements to Italy in the summer of 1943, including some of Hamburg's heavy flak batteries.[172]

The Allied invasion of Sicily may have caught the island's German defenders by surprise, but the RAF use of Window had long been expected by the Luftwaffe. In fact, the German military had tested a similar device in the winter of 1942 in a series of trials over the Baltic Sea. These trials demonstrated that if the Allies employed foil strips (chaff) cut to half the length of the radar's operating frequency, ground-based radar would be "badly affected."[173] One engineer warned Milch, "If they shower clouds of these strips out over a big city, they will remain suspended for about twenty or thirty minutes in the air, and render our 'Würzburg' radar temporarily blind."[174] The German military kept these trials absolutely secret, going so far as to prohibit work on countermeasures for fear that such measures might leak out and alert the Allies to the jamming method. In turn, the Luftwaffe began to pursue countermeasures only after the devastating raids on Hamburg.[175]

Hamburg's agony did not end with the attack on the night of July 24. During the day on July 25, despite heavy smoke still rising over the city, a force of 68 American bombers struck Hamburg's submarine yards, and another

67 bombers attacked the submarine base at Kiel. Losses were, however, high with 19 aircraft failing to return, including five bombers that reportedly fell victim to flak fire, which was reported as "at times both intense and accurate." On the following day, almost 200 American bombers again attacked targets in northwestern Germany, including Hannover, Hamburg, and other targets of opportunity. The losses for these raids totaled 24 aircraft, with 13 "kills" attributed to fighters, 7 to flak, and 4 to unknown causes.[176] In a two-day period, Eighth Air Force bombers had experienced a loss rate of over 10 percent. The daylight attacks by American bombers demonstrated that during daylight and in good weather, the Luftwaffe's fighter and flak forces could still inflict heavy losses on an attacking force with or without radar assistance. In fact, throughout the war, optical targeting procedures using a fire director remained the most effective method for tracking aerial targets. One estimate found that engagements by visual means were five times more effective than engagements using radar control.[177] In addition, despite the initial confusion and dislocation induced by the RAF's use of chaff, the German air defenses adapted themselves rapidly to the changed situation by relying on searchlights to first acquire a target or waiting for breaks in the area of chaff coverage.[178]

Despite the success of the Luftwaffe's air defenses on the previous two days, in an armaments conference of July 27, Milch complained, "We are no longer on the offensive. For the last one and a half or two years we have been on the defensive. This fact is now apparently recognized even at the highest levels of the Luftwaffe command." Milch then ruefully noted that for the last three months he had been trying without success to gain an increase in the number of fighters assigned to the defense of the Reich. He also observed that these aircraft would have made the American attacks against Hamburg and Hannover "impossible."[179] That night the RAF struck Hamburg again in force, with more than 700 bombers and over 2,300 tons of high-explosive and incendiary bombs. The bombing concentration proved exceptionally good. Dry conditions and the damage sustained in the earlier attack, including the loss of numerous water mains, combined to produce a firestorm that ravaged the city. The resulting inferno proved apocalyptic, melting asphalt streets, ripping three-foot-diameter trees up by their roots, and even burning thick wooden pilings in the city's canals down to the level of the water.[180] Approximately 40,000 persons perished in this single raid, many dying of asphyxiation as the fires literally sucked oxygen out from basements and air-raid shelters throughout the city.[181]

To complete the destruction of Hamburg, the RAF launched two subsequent raids on the evening of July 29 and again on the night of August 2. During the entire course of the "Battle of Hamburg," Bomber Command launched over 3,000 sorties and dropped more than 8,500 tons of bombs, the vast majority being incendiary devices, on the 750-year-old city. In contrast to the level of effort, losses were incredibly light, totaling a mere 87 aircraft, for a total loss rate of less than 2.5 percent of all sorties.[182] The loss rate was in fact less than half of the total of 6 percent experienced during previous raids on the city.[183] Despite the confusion caused by the use of chaff, RAF loss rates totaled 1.5 percent during the first raid, 2.2 percent on the second, 3.6 percent on the third, and 4.1 percent on the final raid on the night of August 2. In turn, flak forces accounted for approximately 25 percent of these losses, with the rest attributed to night fighters, including those assisted by searchlights.[184]

Strengthening the Reich's Air Defenses

The psychological effects of the British and American attacks against the Ruhr and Hamburg rippled throughout Germany among the civil populace. In the wake of the raids, the Security Service reported that the bombing of Hamburg had produced a "shock effect" on the "population of the entire Reich." Rumors also spread throughout Germany's western industrial area that Berlin had "written off" the Rhineland. Furthermore, a Security Service report noted that many blamed Göring for the fiasco and questioned why the Luftwaffe did not possess adequate defenses to prevent such massive attacks. Finally, increasing numbers of persons were becoming impatient with the Luftwaffe's failure to conduct the promised retaliatory strikes against Great Britain.[185] Public dissatisfaction combined with the impact of the devastating physical destruction experienced by Germany's second-largest city led to a frantic search for measures to improve the Reich's air defenses.

On July 28, in the wake of the second raid on Hamburg, Göring ordered Milch to designate the air defense of the Reich proper as the main emphasis for future Luftwaffe production. In turn, Milch ordered the accelerated development and production of an aerial intercept radar for the Luftwaffe's night fighters that would be impervious to British jamming efforts. The severe shock engendered by the destruction of Hamburg also led to additional suggestions for improving the Reich's air defenses. On July 29, Colonel Victor von Lossberg, a bomber pilot in the General Staff, proposed a new method for intercepting aircraft by infiltrating a night fighter into the bomber stream, which would then act as a radio beacon for other night fighters, a procedure known as *zahme Sau,* or "tame boar." According to von Lossberg's plan, numerous night fighters would join the bomber stream and individually engage the bombers on their own initiative without need for radar control. On the next day, Milch, Weise, Galland, and the commander of the 1st Night Fighter Wing, Major Streib, approved the plan, along with a suggestion to increase the size of Herrmann's wild boar force. In contrast, Kammhuber's objections to von Lossberg's plan fell on deaf ears.[186] It was apparent that Kammhuber's beloved

Himmelbett system was no longer effective in defending the Reich against the mass of British bombers now operating over the Continent. In a meeting with his air defense commanders on August 27, Göring complained that Kammhuber's system had become torpid and required too many support personnel.[187] Shortly thereafter, Göring promoted Kammhuber and sent him to Norway to command Air Region 5, a promotion that in truth constituted a method for removing him from his post as commander of the night fighter force.[188] Already on August 1, Göring had ordered the changes suggested by von Lossberg, as well as a further expansion of Herrmann's force, thus inaugurating a new phase in Germany's night fighter defenses.[189]

The Luftwaffe also began strengthening its day fighter forces within Germany proper by withdrawing flying units from the front for duty in the Reich. For example, the Luftwaffe withdrew two fighter groups from the Eastern Front, one fighter group from the Western Front and the Mediterranean, as well as several fighter and fighter-bomber wings from Norway, Russia, and the Mediterranean. Although these fighter forces stiffened the Reich's defenses, their withdrawal from the combat fronts in the east and the Mediterranean had profound implications for German ground forces in these areas as the Luftwaffe stripped away the army's air defense umbrellas.[190] By the end of August, the fighter defenses of the Reich included five fighter divisions consisting of 1,102 day fighters, night fighters, and fighter-bomber aircraft, or 45.5 percent of the Luftwaffe's fighter force. In addition to these aircraft, there were two fighter groups with 224 aircraft stationed in northern France. In a period of two months, the fighter defenses of the Reich had doubled in strength.[191]

In addition to changes within the Reich's fighter organization, the British and American attacks generated a number of measures designed to increase the size of the ground-based air defense forces within Germany. By the beginning of August, the Luftwaffe encountered a situation in which more equipment was being produced than could be operated by the existing numbers of personnel.[192] On the one hand, the Luftwaffe's pilot training program could not keep pace with German industry's production of aircraft, a situation that General Adolf Galland, commander of the fighter force, described as having reached "disastrous dimensions" by the fall of 1943.[193] On the other hand, the Luftwaffe continued to struggle in its attempts to find enough men and women to operate the ground-based air defenses. In fact, the number of heavy flak guns within Germany proper increased from 4,800 in June to 6,041 by the end of August, with 57 percent of the Luftwaffe's heavy flak guns protecting the Reich. In addition to these defenses, the Luftwaffe needed personnel to operate 340 searchlight batteries, 73 barrage balloon batteries, and 19 smoke generator companies within Germany.[194]

For one group of civil servants, the devastating bombing raids and the surplus of flak equipment had an immediate effect as Göring ordered the temporary mobilization of postal employees into the Home Guard flak batteries.[195] In another example, the quartermaster general of Air District XVII reported that the lack of sufficient numbers of ethnic Germans prevented the establishment of additional Home Guard flak batteries in the southeastern districts of the Reich.[196] The general manning crisis also led the leadership of this air district to authorize the employment of civilian auxiliaries, Russian prisoners of war, indigenous auxiliaries, and female air force auxiliaries, in that order of priority, in the establishment of a smoke generator company. In this case, the air district cautioned that "at the very least" the inner defense ring needed to be manned by German auxiliaries.[197]

In a report of July 31 entitled "Special Operational Experiences of the Flak Artillery," von Axthelm addressed the state of the Luftwaffe's flak arm in the wake of the British and American raids on Hamburg. He argued that the attacks provided two lessons for Germany's ground-based air defenses:

1. The formulation of the question "shootdown or deterrence" has become untenable, as the flak artillery is no longer capable of conducting a real defense against the enemy mass attacks. There remains only one possibility—by the present condition of the means available at this time—only through shootdowns [can] the enemy be weakened in the long run.
2. It has been shown that the shootdown rate with solely electrical [radar] tracking is significantly lower as compared to targets held visually by searchlights. The reason for this lies in the second place on the better firing particulars. In the first place, the success is attributable to the concentration of flak fire of many batteries against targets held in searchlight beams.

Axthelm's statement concerning the flak's objective of achieving shootdowns instead of deterring or impeding an attack clearly showed his support for measuring the effectiveness of the flak arm by the number of aircraft destroyed. Indeed, this attitude continued to dominate the thinking of the Luftwaffe's leadership throughout the war.

Axthelm also mentioned that the need for concentrated fires had led to the creation of the superbatteries, but that many operational areas had only double batteries of four guns each and still lacked superbatteries of their own. In turn, von Axthelm identified the primary obstacle to the establishment of superbatteries as the lack of available personnel. He concluded his discussion by suggesting three tactical initiatives. The first proposal involved the combined targeting by all of a battery's guns on the leading aircraft in the bombing formation. The second suggestion involved restricting flak fire to the lowest flying aircraft within the formation. The final tactical proposal advocated the use of dispersed but directed barrier fire barrages aimed at known primary approach avenues to the target.[198] From von Axthelm's comments it was apparent that he still believed that the flak could achieve results if only enough guns could be concentrated around a given object. This view was also held by one of the flak's staunchest supporters, Hitler.

As in the past, Hitler's immediate reaction to the growing devastation inflicted by the Allied aerial assault involved increasing the size and strength of the Reich's air defense forces. In a meeting with his naval leaders, Hitler optimistically predicted:

> We shall master the danger from the air through new methods, by expanding our anti-aircraft and fighter defenses. We must do this, because [the aerial threat] is an extraordinary burden on the people. . . . We shall succeed in maintaining our armaments program; the new technologically advanced defensive weapons will make the air raids too costly and will cause them to be discontinued.[199]

Apparently, Hitler had placed his faith in the promise of his rocket program and the further expansion of the Reich's air defense forces. In pursuit of the latter objective, the Luftwaffe drafted another group of young men from German secondary schools on August 16.[200] An additional measure designed to increase the personnel strength within the flak arm was Hitler's order to create 250 flak batteries to be operated by members of the Reich Labor Service on August 20.[201] The Labor Service recruits received three months of basic military training and an additional three months of specialized air defense training before assuming their duties in the flak forces of the Luftwaffe, the navy, or the Waffen-SS.[202] From September 1943 until February 1944, the number of flak batteries operated solely by Labor Service draftees reached 300, and later in the war the number exceeded 400 batteries.[203] In addition, these units achieved a great degree of proficiency based on the physical and psychological maturity of their age cohort, their high morale, and the high level of their training regimen. After the war, British military intelligence described these batteries as "one of the more successful Flak personnel experiments."[204]

Evaluating the Effects of the Battle of the Ruhr

The raids against Hamburg proved to be the last chapter in Harris's "Battle of the Ruhr," but they were also the opening phase of a bombing campaign that would leave hundreds of German cities in ruins by May 1945. This aerial assault had stretched from early March until the end of July, during which time Bomber Command had launched 14,177 sorties against cities within the Ruhr and the Rhine valleys at a total cost of 673 aircrews, or 4.7 percent of the attacking force.[205] In this five-month period, the RAF estimated that Bomber Command lost 493 aircraft to fighters and 322 aircraft to flak defenses in night raids over Europe, a ratio of 1.5 to 1 in favor of the fighters.[206] In turn, American daylight losses to flak in the attacks on Hamburg, Kiel, and Hannover lay somewhere between 28 and 37 percent of all losses. Not only Allied aircrews but also the German population had paid a high price during the five-month campaign. Allied bombing attacks killed an estimated 67,200 persons and destroyed approximately 101,800 buildings, leaving hundreds of thousands without shelter.[207]

Despite the strong performance by the Luftwaffe's ground-based air defenses in the first half of 1943, the Battle of Hamburg represented a major turning point in the air war over Germany. Without doubt, Bomber Command's employment of Window provided the RAF with a distinct, albeit temporary, tactical advantage. When used properly, Window could effectively shut down the German Würzburg radar systems in a given area; however, the Allied use of this countermeasure proved less than completely effective on a number of occasions. One postwar report by the Allied Control Commission found, "On many occasions, . . . window was laid incorrectly, or a high wind dispersed the clouds very rapidly, and radars were presented with light concentrations. . . . As a result it was frequently the case that while certain radars in a GDA [German Defense Area] were virtually useless, others could produce satisfactory data which could be used for the prediction of barrages for sites whose radars were jammed."[208] Likewise, some American crew members simply threw handfuls, or even whole boxes, of tangled foil strips out of their aircraft.[209] As a result of some of these problems, the USAAF favored combining Window or chaff with active radar jamming (Carpet), in which a device carried by lead elements of a formation disrupted German radars by transmitting a powerful electromagnetic signal designed to overwhelm the ground radar.[210] Despite the real difficulties associated with the effective employment of Window, the ORS issued a report on August 19, 1943, that noted the "marked effect" of the countermeasure in reducing the numbers of RAF aircraft hit by flak and the overall level of damage sustained. In fact, the ORS report concluded that Bomber Command's missing rate on raids into Germany had been reduced by one-third. Furthermore, it calculated that "the number of sorties damaged by flak has been reduced to about one half of its previous value."[211] In a diary entry for August 5, 1943, Goebbels apprehensively observed that "the air war is the sword of Damocles that is hanging over our heads."[212] Goebbels's words would prove prophetic, and the late summer and fall of 1943 certainly marked a low point for Germany's ground-based air defenses; however, these defenses remained a force to be reckoned with, as the events of the following months demonstrated.

The USAAF faces the Luftwaffe's Air Defenses

Unlike their British counterparts, the Americans did not introduce radar countermeasures until the fall of 1943, at which time the Eighth Air Force unveiled an active radar jammer during an attack on Bremen on October 8.[213] As a result of this delay, radar systems continued to guide Luftwaffe fighters and provide target tracking for anti-aircraft batteries into late summer during USAAF bombing missions. In turn, August proved a decidedly sanguinary month for the bomber crews of the USAAF. On August 1, German flak defenses inflicted devastating losses on a force of 176 American B-24 bombers launched from bases in North Africa with the objective of conducting a surprise low-level strike at the oil facilities at Ploesti (Romania). A navigational error led to confusion during the run-in to the target and provided the German defenses with ample warning. As a result, the fifteen heavy and twelve light flak gun batteries protecting Ploesti's complex of refineries and oil storage areas exacted a high toll on the 166 bombers that made it to their targets, downing 41 of the attacking aircraft. In addition, another 13 aircraft failed to return from the mission. In one day, the Ninth Air Force had lost 54 bombers, or almost 33 percent of the attacking force.[214] Later that month, on August 12, 243 heavy bombers from the Eighth Air Force struck targets in the heavily defended Ruhr for the first time at a cost of 25 aircraft, a loss rate of 10 percent.[215] This raid marked the one and only American mission into the heavily defended Ruhr valley during all of 1943. In fact, the strength of the flak defenses in this area resulted in a prohibition against Ninth Air Force medium bombers attacking targets in the Ruhr based on the flak threat *alone*.[216] On August 17, it was the turn of Germany's day fighter defenses to bloody Eighth Air Force bombers conducting a two-pronged attack against Regensburg and Schweinfurt. In the course of the two raids, Luftwaffe air defenses shot down a total of 60 bombers, or 19 percent, from an attacking force of 310 aircraft.[217] German fighters tallied 46 aircraft, the flak scored 5 victories, and 8 aircraft fell victim to fighters after having first received flak damage.[218] Although Luftwaffe fighters claimed the lion's share of victories, almost a third of the 203 bombers launched by the 1st Bombardment Wing returned with flak damage.[219]

More Hidden Statistics: Flak-Fighter Shootdowns and Delayed Effects

Based on the high percentage of aircraft that received damage from anti-aircraft, it is reasonable to assume that as a result of flak damage some of these aircraft proved more vulnerable to subsequent fighter attacks. The raids on

Regensburg and Schweinfurt indicated that at least eight aircraft, or 13 percent of the USAAF bombers lost on the two missions, fell prey to fighters only after first being damaged by the flak. Indeed, the number of flak-damaged aircraft that subsequently fell victim to fighter attacks is a significant hidden statistic of the air war. It remains largely hidden because of the great difficulty in ascertaining the exact cause or causes that led to the ultimate destruction of individual aircraft. It is, however, apparent that flak forces played a significant role by damaging aircraft, and thus making them more susceptible to Luftwaffe fighters. During night raids between March 5 and July 23, 1943, Bomber Command lost fourteen aircraft to German fighters after the bombers had been damaged first by anti-aircraft fire, while only one aircraft fell victim to the flak after first being damaged by fighter attack.[220] This statistical sample for a period of almost five months strongly suggests that, at night, flak gun batteries assisted their night fighter counterparts at a much higher rate than fighters assisted flak in achieving aircraft "kills." In part, this result was to be expected as in the period between March and July fighters had damaged 183 aircraft, rendering an additional 10 completely unserviceable due to extensive damage, while flak batteries damaged 2,155 aircraft and rendered another 37 unserviceable because of severe damage.[221] The ratio of flak-damaged to fighter-damaged aircraft therefore stood at 22.5 to 1 for the five-month period.

American bombers operating during daylight also experienced high proportions of flak-assisted aircraft shootdowns during the first five months of 1943. The official history of the U.S. Army Air Forces credited German flak with only 14 percent of all U.S. bomber losses in the period between January and the end of May. The authors of this history admitted, however, that "flak damage no doubt made it possible on many other occasions for enemy fighters to destroy the bomber entirely. Thus flak, while of relatively small importance as an immediate cause of bomber losses, was a major source of damage, and since a damaged plane easily became a straggler, flak often proved an important indirect cause of losses."[222] Like their RAF counterparts, the number of American bombers damaged by flak routinely exceeded 20 percent of the aircraft attacking the target, and it rose to over 30 percent, especially for missions against heavily defended targets within Germany and along the Atlantic coast. For example, 43 out of 109 aircraft, or 39 percent, from the 1st Bombardment Wing received flak damage in an attack against Bremen in April. Likewise, 29 out of 49 aircraft, or 59 percent, of the 4th Bombardment Wing were hit by flak in an attack against Hüls on June 22. In the latter case, 3 aircraft were shot down, 2 severely damaged, and 24 slightly damaged.[223]

In addition to the unknown numbers of aircraft downed by fighters as a result of flak damage, another hidden statistic associated with flak contributed to the Luftwaffe's own underestimation of the performance of its anti-aircraft forces. As mentioned previously, the nature of flak damage to aircraft fuel and engine systems often led to a delay in the time between the initial engagement and the subsequent crash of the aircraft, a delay that might allow the aircraft to fly on for several hundred miles. Between April 20 and July 14, no fewer than 12 Bomber Command aircraft crashed during the later course of their flights as a result of flak damage alone; some of these aircraft even reached Great Britain before succumbing to the delayed effects of their anti-aircraft wounds.[224] American bomber crews also experienced the delayed effects of flak hits.[225] Paradoxically, the Luftwaffe's strict guidelines for awarding a confirmed kill often meant that, absent physical evidence of a crash in the vicinity of an engaged flak battery, the flak arm rarely received credit for the destruction of these aircraft. In fact, this statistic in part helps to explain differing perceptions of flak effectiveness and discrepancies in aggregate shootdown totals between RAF, USAAF, and Luftwaffe estimates during the war.

Losing Faith in the Flak

The Battle of the Ruhr, the RAF attacks against German cities, and the increasing strength of American bomber strikes into Germany offered a glimpse into the dangers facing German industry and the civil population in the coming months. In the three months following the campaign against the Ruhr, many within the Luftwaffe leadership became increasingly disillusioned with the flak arm and began to place their hopes on Germany's fighter defenses. In contrast to the views expressed by Hitler and von Axthelm that the Luftwaffe only needed additional gun batteries to improve its defensive posture, Milch offered a decidedly more pessimistic evaluation of Germany's flak forces. For him, the attacks on Hamburg proved that the flak force could never fulfill the high expectations held by Hitler, Göring, and Jeschonnek. Even Göring began to waver by questioning the effectiveness of flak operations at night and describing night gunnery as "completely insignificant."[226]

In a meeting of the Air Armaments Office on August 20, Milch complained that "the German air force is being led by the flak arm and not the flying arm. . . . the flying arm, which has it tough, has nothing to say."[227] Although clearly an exaggeration, Milch's comment demonstrated his own view of the flak arm. Likewise, the failure of the Luftwaffe to prevent the inferno at Hamburg and the subsequent failure of German air defenses during a Bomber Command attack against the secret missile test site at Peenemünde led Jeschonnek, like his predecessor Udet, to commit suicide under the weight of mounting recrimination concerning the performance of the Luftwaffe's air defenses.[228] In turn, Jeschonnek's suicide helped to strengthen Milch's position even further.

At a conference concerning aircraft production on August 25, Milch outlined his strategy for the air war. He warned, "If we fail and the percentage of enemy aircraft shot down remains at the same level as up to the first half of July, we shall be crushed." He continued, "There is only one remedy. That is for our fighters to hit the enemy so hard day and night that he is forced to abandon the policy of destroying our arms production." Milch's plan called for a dramatic increase in the production of day and night fighters, with the "mass of fighters" going to the defense of the Reich. Using this strategy, Milch felt that the Luftwaffe could inflict an astronomical loss rate of between 25 and 30 percent on the Allied bomber force.[229] Milch's evaluation of the Luftwaffe's anti-aircraft forces proved distinctly less sanguine. He stated that flak accounted for "something over 1%" of the Allied loss rate, while fighters accounted for between 3 and 5 percent. He then argued, "You can set up five times as many A.A. batteries; it will make no difference to the figure of 1–2%. But if we put twice as many fighters in the air, the number of successes will be at least twice as high. If we have four times as many fighters, the number of successes will be at least four times as high." Milch then averred that a similar expansion of the night fighter force would lead to the end of night raids against Germany, and "[t]his would be the first step towards Germany winning the war."[230]

Milch's assessment of the Luftwaffe's air defenses was instructive in a number of respects. First, he clearly favored the creation of a large fighter force stationed within Germany. In this case, he was most assuredly correct in arguing that the Luftwaffe's fighter force needed to be expanded, and in fact these steps were already being undertaken. Second, he clearly underestimated the success achieved by the flak forces and failed to take into account the secondary effects achieved by anti-aircraft forces in assisting in the destruction of the bombers by the fighters. Finally, his simplistic calculus in which five times the number of flak guns had no effect whereas twice the number of fighters would double Allied losses is both misleading and patently false. Clearly, it was true that twice the number of fighters might have a more profound effect on aircraft losses than doubling the number of flak guns, but according to Milch's logic there essentially existed an imaginary number of flak guns after which no appreciable gains could be made in aircraft destroyed.

In his evaluation of Germany's air defenses, Milch was guilty of committing several strategic and computational errors. First, he failed to grasp the need for a balanced air defense network in which neither fighters nor flak batteries were expected to win the air war alone. In truth, Milch's denigration of the Luftwaffe's ground-based air defenses simply provides the opposite extreme to Hitler's view of the flak. Second, Milch's evaluation demonstrated a simplistic vision of aircraft and pilot production. He completely failed to address the question of where the Luftwaffe might find the necessary pilots and aviation fuel for a planned doubling, or quadrupling, of the fighter force. Third, his comments indicated a lack of appreciation for the holistic nature of German ground-based air defenses, systems ranging from the dummy sites to the actual flak batteries. Fourth, Milch used loss percentages for the flak that he himself must have realized could not be accurate. In fact, the Luftwaffe quartermaster's office calculated that fighters destroyed 676 American bombers, whereas flak accounted for 233 American bombers in 1943, a ratio of only 2.9 to 1 in favor of the fighters. Furthermore, the quartermaster noted that flak damaged 8,847 American bombers, 9.3 times as many aircraft as Luftwaffe fighters in 1943.[231] Fifth, aircraft losses cannot simply be calculated using a linear progression; rather, they involve several variables, including type of guns, availability and type of fire directors, and spacing of batteries. Finally, it was an argument that Milch did not make that seems most interesting. He did not argue, as others have, that flak production impinged on resources available for fighter production. In turn, it seems reasonable to imply that, at least at this point in the war, the oft-cited resources argument played a much smaller role than is often assumed.

The Luftwaffe Attempts to Recover

Despite the damage suffered in the attacks of the summer of 1943, Göring offered an optimistic appraisal of the current situation in a two-day meeting on September 2–3. He noted that the Luftwaffe's main priority remained the strengthening of the Reich's air defenses; however, he argued that the success enjoyed by the Luftwaffe's air defenses at Regensburg and Ploesti demonstrated that "considerable progress" had been achieved. Despite his optimistic forecast, it was clear that Göring was primarily counting on increased performance from the day and, especially, the night fighter force and not the flak arm for improving the Reich's air defenses.[232] In fact, Göring's decision to favor production of radar devices to support fighter operations at the expense of the ground-based gun-laying radar offers one clear indication of his shift in favor of the fighter force.[233] By the end of the month, Göring's optimism appeared to be well placed as he congratulated his day and night fighter forces on their recent accomplishments.[234] The change in night fighter tactics incorporating both von Lossberg's and Herrmann's suggestions appeared to be achieving results. In August and September, night fighters shot down 141 and 48 RAF bombers, respectively, and completely wrecked an additional 13 aircraft. In contrast, flak brought down 55 aircraft in August and 32 aircraft in September while damaging a further 9 aircraft beyond repair during Bomber Command night sorties over Europe.[235]

No doubt in an effort to shore up his own crumbling political position, Göring displayed a renewed interest in the tactical and operational aspects of Germany's air defense network in the fall of 1943. At a conference of September 25, he assembled the entire leadership of the Reich's air defenses, including

Milch, Weise, Martini, Galland, Kammhuber, von Lossberg, Herrmann, and General Günther Korten, Jeschonnek's replacement as chief of the Luftwaffe General Staff. The meeting covered a broad range of topics related to air defense, including a suggestion by Galland and Kammhuber that the Air Reporting Service be placed under their control to facilitate fighter operations. Göring rejected the latter proposal, but he demanded better cooperation between the two organizations, as well as the prioritization of the fighters' needs by the air-warning network. The most illuminating aspect of the conference, however, was Göring's clear interest and active participation in the discussions. He ordered Korten to prepare a war game designed to examine the prosecution of both day and night air defenses within the Reich. He also stated his intention to personally supervise the exercise. Furthermore, Göring mentioned measures for improving the cooperation between fighters and the flak arm, as well as the expansion of searchlight zones within the Reich to facilitate night fighter operations. With respect to the night fighter force, he ordered the conduct of operations over the target, in the searchlight belt, and by the infiltration of the bomber stream, as well as the full use of the *Himmelbett* procedure. Finally, he directed that day fighter recovery bases should be arranged to allow these aircraft to be refueled and rearmed so they could conduct a second sortie against the bomber formations after their initial interception.[236]

Contrary to his usual practice, Göring maintained his focus on the issue of air defense and gathered the entire leadership of Germany's flak and fighter forces for a two-day conference at Hitler's Bavarian retreat in Obersalzberg on October 7 and 8. The topic of the conference was the "Homeland Defense Program," and the subsequent typed protocol of the meeting exceeded 200 pages. This conference addressed issues across the entire spectrum of the Luftwaffe's air defenses and provided a candid snapshot of the current state of Göring's air force. Göring began the proceedings with a warning to his air defense commanders that "the Luftwaffe stands at the moment in its gravest crisis, at its lowest point." He then bitterly observed that the Luftwaffe had lost the trust of both the German people and the German fighting man. Göring continued with a description of the public's impression of the Luftwaffe:

> The crisis is concentrated above all on the fighters, and certainly with the day fighters. And it is concentrated here because the people do not know the combat tactics of the fighters. The population says: our fighters run away and come too late; the enemy mass formations fly undisturbed for hours and in parade formation [Nürnberger Formation]; that has become a slogan over our cities.
>
> Then the flak. Before they missed, and now they still miss. They are only astounded when they occasionally hit something. . . . With respect to the

flak it is said, perhaps rightly so, they can't do it, it's just not possible, when the aircraft fly so high, they just can't shoot them down. Consequently there is not a crisis [with the flak]. The flak enjoys very high regard among the population and the fighting forces namely due to their toughness and unquestionable success in ground combat.

The reputation of the night fighters has risen considerably. It is doubtless that the population views this [the performance of the night fighters] as absolute progress. But here again the leadership says: by every high estimation of the activities of the night fighters, we must reconcile ourselves to the fact that now the bad [weather] season is coming when the night fighters will not be able to do much.[237]

Characteristically, Göring's opening monologue laid the blame for the performance of the Luftwaffe's air defenses in the summer at everyone's feet but his own. However, he did identify several real weaknesses in the Luftwaffe, including the poor state of fighter pilot training, extended delays in the introduction of new weapons, and difficulties with the development and production of radar equipment. On the one hand, it was clear that Göring was parroting many of the criticisms Hitler had mentioned to him in previous conversations. On the other hand, the Reich marshal made his own disillusionment with the flak repeatedly apparent in a number of disparaging comments. For example, he mentioned a complaint by the National Socialist district leader of Frankfurt concerning the performance of the fighters in a raid against the city. Göring acidly noted that the complaint did not mention the performance of the flak, as "one expected nothing more from the flak than that they fire [their guns]."[238]

As the conference proceeded, Göring later conceded that the flak pushed the enemy bombers to higher altitudes and disrupted their aim, but he reminded his subordinates that "only shootdowns" are important, and that other results interested no one from the Führer to the smallest German child. In Göring's view, however, it was not the flak, but rather, flak missiles, that could turn the balance in the air war. He questioned von Axthelm concerning the expected date of operational deployment for the missiles. Axthelm responded that it would be at least twelve to eighteen more months before the missiles could be employed, whereupon Göring jibed sarcastically, "Have you appointed such well-chosen idiots there?" Axthelm responded that his development team included 500 of the best members of the flak arm. In this instance, von Axthelm received assistance from a somewhat unlikely corner as Milch interjected that the technical problems associated with a flak missile were "considerably more difficult" than for the A-4 (V-2) missile. Somewhat mollified, Göring exclaimed that all he needed was a projectile with an acoustical detonator that could be fired into the mass formations of American bombers.[239] This last remark once again demonstrated his lack of appreciation for the technical aspects associated with modern weapons systems, as well as his search for a quick fix to the problem of protecting Germany from aerial attack.

On October 8, the conference reconvened with a discussion of the current state of the Luftwaffe's defenses, including the status of the measures designed to negate the Allied use of chaff (Window). Kammhuber confidently reported that "anti-Window countermeasures are 100 percent effective." Kammhuber remarked that operational tests using modifications to the radar during the previous three nights had functioned flawlessly. In contrast, von Axthelm notified Göring that Window was the main difficulty facing the flak arm at the moment, but that his command was undertaking the greatest effort to produce an effective countermeasure against it. Axthelm then confessed, "At the moment, we [the flak forces] are the supporting arm *[Hilfswaffe]* to the fighters." Göring sarcastically shot back that the flak was a supporting arm that "drove away his fighters" whereupon von Axthelm reminded Göring of the important role played by searchlights and illumination flares fired by the flak in assisting the night fighters, a point seconded by Weise. Still, von Axthelm's admission graphically demonstrated the problems created for the Luftwaffe's ground-based air defenses by the introduction of Window.[240]

Evaluating the Performance of the Flak

From von Axthelm's comments it was apparent that Window had succeeded in degrading the performance of the flak. It is, however, curious that not one mention was made of actual numbers of aircraft brought down by flak and fighters at any point during the conference. In fact, the closest anyone came to citing specific figures occurred when Göring confessed that the Luftwaffe for the "one and only time" issued inflated numbers of RAF aircraft brought down in the wake of the raid on Hamburg.[241] One might expect Göring to offer an impressionistic description of the current state of the Luftwaffe, but it is surprising that neither Weise nor von Axthelm attempted to provide a broader statistical analysis of the performance of Germany's air defenses. In any event, RAF statistics for the last three months of 1943 dramatically demonstrated the falloff in the performance of the Luftwaffe's air defenses. Bomber Command aircraft lost 250 aircraft to fighters and 94 aircraft to flak defenses during night raids between October and December.[242] In addition to these losses, the flak accounted for damage to 794 aircraft, and fighters damaged a further 192 aircraft, for a damage ratio of flak to fighter of 4 to 1.

In evaluating the performance of the flak during the course of the year, one finds that the Luftwaffe's flak forces had managed to bring down 90 aircraft in 12,760 night sorties during the first quarter of 1943, compared with only 92 in 13,969 night sorties in the last quarter.[243] This decline in performance is even more telling given that, during the course of 1943, the size of the flak forces within Germany had increased from 628 to 1,300 heavy flak gun batteries, 535 to 708 light flak gun batteries, and 277 to 395 searchlight batteries.[244] In other words, despite the twofold expansion in the number of heavy gun batteries defending Germany proper, the ratio of shootdowns per night sortie was in fact decreasing, whereas the ratio of numbers of flak guns per shootdown was increasing. It should be noted, however, that the first and fourth quarters were the periods in which European weather tended to be at its worst.

Bloody Lessons for the Eighth Air Force

Despite the marked decrease in the flak's performance at night, the Eighth Air Force learned that both Luftwaffe flak and fighters could exact a terrible toll during daylight attacks, especially in good weather, over the heart of Germany. Ironically, on the same day that Göring was castigating the leadership of the Luftwaffe's air defense, a force of 357 American bombers struck targets in and around Bremen. John Comer, a crew member on board a B-17, recalled his feelings as his bomber neared Bremen on October 8: "As we approached the target the enormous field of flak ahead was unbelievable. And frightening! My thoughts were 'Good God! Can anything fly through that!'"[245] For a number of aircraft, the answer was no. Of 162 1st Bombardment Division aircraft attacking the target, 116 (71.60 percent) received flak damage and seven (4.32 percent) fell victim to the Luftwaffe's anti-aircraft defenses. Of 155 3rd Bombardment Division aircraft attacking Bremen, 110 (71.0 percent) experienced damage by flak, and the city's flak defenses brought down 5 of these bombers.[246] In total, the Eighth Air Force lost 30 bombers during the attack with flak alone, accounting for 40 percent of these losses. The mission against Bremen showed that the Luftwaffe's flak defenses could still exact a terrible toll over a heavily defended target in visual conditions.

Despite the losses over Bremen, the Eighth Air Force chose to launch one of its most ambitious raids of the year in a return visit to the ball-bearing factories at Schweinfurt on October 14. Lying deep within Germany, Schweinfurt was a daunting target with approximately twenty-three heavy flak batteries, five light flak batteries, six searchlight batteries, and a smoke generator company, making it per square mile one of the most heavily defended cities within Germany.[247] The USAAF massed 291 bombers for the mission, with 229 successfully reaching the target. The prevailing clear weather not only allowed for an excellent bomb pattern but also allowed Luftwaffe fighters and flak to inflict a crippling toll on the attacking force. In the course of the mission, fighters intercepted the bomber formations along their route of flight prior to, and after, they released their bomb loads. At the end of the day, the Eighth Air Force had lost 60 aircraft, or almost 17 percent of the force dispatched on the raid.[248] En route to Schweinfurt, German flak gunners brought down one bomber, while over the target the city's flak defenses accounted for 11 additional aircraft. On the return flight, flak defenses in the vicinity of Karlsruhe badly damaged another bomber, forcing it to crash-land in Switzerland.[249] In addition, 17 aircraft received major damage, while another 121 were damaged but reparable as a result of anti-aircraft fire.[250] All told, Luftwaffe flak defenses accounted for almost 22 percent of the aircraft brought down during the mission.

The official history of the Army Air Forces proclaimed that by the middle of October the Eighth Air Force "had reached a crisis" as a result of the month's disastrous losses. The Schweinfurt raid left the American bomber force without the physical and psychological resources to launch another raid deep into Germany for the remainder of the year.[251] In the end, it was the strength of the German air defenses combined with the traditionally poor winter weather that led the commander of the USAAF, General Henry "Hap" Arnold, to authorize the use of "blind," or instrument, bombing by Eighth Air Force crews in November 1943.[252] The switch to blind bombing proved salutary for the bomber crews, with one monthly flak report noting that attacks through a full overcast resulted in half as many flak casualties as during visual raids.[253] The Americans ended the year as they had begun it, by concentrating on the more lightly defended targets along the French Atlantic coast. In the first round of the battle between the Luftwaffe and the Eighth Air Force, German air defenses had proved a capable opponent, but the fight was still far from over.

Target Berlin

In contrast to their American counterparts, Bomber Command crews ended the year with a campaign against Berlin, the most heavily fortified target in all of Germany. Buoyed by his success against Hamburg, Harris now turned his attention to the capital of Hitler's Reich. In a letter to Churchill in November 1943, Harris predicted, "We can wreck Berlin from end to end if the U.S.A.A.F. will come in on it. It will cost between us 400 and 500 aircraft. It will cost Germany the war."[254] Despite Harris's enthusiasm, the USAAF was in no shape to attack Berlin, so the job was left to the men of Bomber Command. Berlin was indeed a formidable target, with over 700 heavy flak guns, including three mammoth concrete flak towers studded with twin-barreled 128-mm flak guns.[255] Already in early August, Weise initiated efforts to strengthen Berlin's flak and fighter defenses, and by the end of September the Luftwaffe had withdrawn German and Italian flak forces stationed in Italy into the Reich's defenses.[256] The flak area surrounding the capital was forty miles wide, and the searchlight belt extended for sixty miles. One RAF bombardier described his feeling during a mission against Berlin:

> Lying in the nose of a Lancaster on a visual bomb run over Berlin was probably the most frightening experience of my lifetime. Approaching the target, the city appeared to be surrounded by rings of searchlights, and the Flak was always intense. The run-up seemed endless, the minutes of flying "straight and level" seemed like hours and every second I expected to be blown to pieces.[257]

In anticipation of the coming offensive, the Luftwaffe also concentrated its night fighter force in the vicinity of Berlin.[258]

The battle for Berlin in the last two months of 1943 signaled Harris's most ambitious gamble yet. In a series of eight raids, 3,656 Bomber Command aircraft dropped 14,074 tons of bombs on the city at a loss of 180 bombers. The attacks cost the lives of almost 6,000 Berliners and left over 470,000 persons homeless.[259] In contrast, Bomber Command had lost almost 5 percent of its attacking force in the raids; however, unlike the situation in 1942, the RAF could now afford these losses, an ill tiding for a Luftwaffe stretched to its limits. In August, Goebbels had exclaimed, "The air war is our open wound through which we are losing more and more blood."[260] By the end of December, the bleeding had been temporarily stanched, but in the coming year the skies over the Reich would literally rain bombs as the Allied air campaign reached a new level of ferocity.

The Year 1943 In Review

Throughout 1943, the Luftwaffe's ground-based air defenses had bent but not broken despite the increasing intensity of the combined bomber offensive and the Allied employment of passive and active radar countermeasures. Still, the large-scale drafting of young men and women into the air defense force, the mobilization of postal employees and factory workers, and the use of foreign nationals led to a clear diminution in the quality of the flak and searchlight force. In fact, the drafting of Poles, Russians, Czechs, and Hungarians into the anti-aircraft force led Göring to quip, "My anti-aircraft batteries are like a League of Nations meeting."[261] Although the fiscal resources devoted to the flak arm had been substantial, the shootdowns per sortie showed a continuing decline, especially in light of the manifold expansion of the Reich's ground-based air defenses. In addition, the Luftwaffe failed to achieve the hoped-for technological breakthroughs such as the flak missile, while the production of advanced heavy flak guns, including the 88-mm/Model 41 and the 128-mm gun, remained well behind schedule.

Despite this litany of woes, ground-based air defenses proved invaluable in supporting the night fighter force with searchlights and flak illumination flares, and the dummy installations continued to achieve limited, if not spectacular, success in decoying RAF bombers away from their targets. In addition, the massed firepower of one hundred flak batteries established a "fire canopy" over the Straits of Messina that prevented effective attacks by Allied aircraft and enabled the Wehrmacht to withdraw 100,000 troops and 10,000 vehicles from Sicily in August.[262] In fact, Allied aircrews compared the flak over the straits with that of the Ruhr.[263] One Allied officer described the antiaircraft fire at Messina as "the heaviest ever encountered in the Mediterranean."[264] Although a result of unique circumstances, the flak's role in the successful withdrawal from Sicily hinted at the potential effectiveness that might be achieved with highly concentrated flak defenses surrounding point targets. Similarly, the performance of the flak in the late summer and fall had also shown that, even at the low point of flak effectiveness, the antiaircraft force could inflict high casualties when Allied bombers attacked at low level (Ploesti), in clear weather (Bremen and Schweinfurt), or against heavily defended targets (the Ruhr and Berlin). Likewise, the flak artillery continued to play an important role in ground combat both in the east and in North Africa prior to the defeat of Axis forces there.[265] By the end of 1943, it was clear that the coming year would place increased demands on both fighter and flak defenses of the Luftwaffe. The only question that remained was whether either could bear the added burden.

CHAPTER EIGHT

Escorts over the Reich January–May 1944

In his New Year's Day message of 1944 to Germany's soldiers, sailors, and airmen, Hitler praised the performance of the Wehrmacht during the past year. He also identified the need for new and improved measures to protect the Reich from the intensifying Allied aerial bombardment. Looking into the future, he remarked, "The Luftwaffe, like the army, has enormous [tasks] to perform on every fighting front. Furthermore, for the Luftwaffe comes the additional task of defending the home front. Its [the Luftwaffe's] heroism stands exalted above all others."[1] By the beginning of 1944, it was becoming clear that heroism alone would not be sufficient to hold back the gathering swarms of Allied bombers and fighters venturing into the heart of the Reich.

Bomber Command did not wait long to deliver its own New Year's message to the German populace. On the night of January 1, 421 bombers set out for a raid against Berlin. As the bombers crossed into Holland, Luftwaffe night fighters joined the bomber stream and shot down numerous aircraft, with one Luftwaffe pilot alone claiming six kills.[2] Over Berlin, Luftwaffe fighters had much less success than their counterparts along the route of flight due to heavy cloud cover that prevented all but a handful of successful intercepts and placed the burden of defense once again on the flak forces surrounding the city.[3] The poor weather also impeded bombing accuracy, and the bombers inflicted little damage to the capital. Seventy-nine of the city's inhabitants died, but the raid cost the RAF 28 aircraft, 168 aircrew killed, and 34 prisoners of war, an unwelcome balance for Bomber Command.[4]

On the following night, 383 bombers set off in poor weather for another strike at Berlin. A widely dispersed force eventually reached the city but again did little damage. In contrast, Herrmann's wild boars, operating with the searchlights, achieved a number of kills, and the RAF lost 26 bombers.[5] During this raid, the flak gun batteries achieved little success because they were prohibited from firing above 16,500 feet in order to give Herrmann's fighters free rein over the capital.[6] The firing prohibition essentially prevented the flak from engaging the majority of the bomber force and provided clear evidence of a shift in attitude within the Luftwaffe that favored night fighter operations at the expense of the flak arm.

Expanding the Luftwaffe's Air Defenses

The two raids against Berlin cost Bomber Command fifty-four aircraft and accomplished very little. These raids did show, however, that the Luftwaffe had begun to recover from the setbacks of late 1943. Despite the problems due to Allied jamming initiatives and the intensifying level of air attacks, German air defenses had effectively blunted the British and American bombing effort by the beginning of the year.[7] The Luftwaffe's improved performance in this period resulted from a number of factors, including the implementation of several offensive and defensive initiatives. On the one hand, the Luftwaffe had achieved a great deal of success in countering, or at least ameliorating, the worst effects of Allied active and passive jamming measures.[8] In addition to modifying existing gun-laying radar to overcome jamming efforts, the Luftwaffe's technical branch began to develop and test a new gun-laying radar with increased range and improved aircraft-monitoring characteristics.[9] Furthermore, the night fighter arm, employing both wild boar and tame boar procedures, became increasingly adept at bloodying Bomber Command during Harris's ongoing "Battle of Berlin."[10] By February, the size of the Luftwaffe's ground-based air defense force had swelled to a wartime high of 13,500 heavy flak guns, 21,000 light flak guns, 7,000 searchlights, and 2,400 barrage balloons.[11] Table 8.1 provides the number and geographic distribution of the Luftwaffe's flak and searchlight batteries in 1944.[12] This distribution indicated several trends. The number of the Reich's heavy flak batteries continued to expand, while the light flak batteries declined slightly. Further, the Luftwaffe was shifting flak

Table 8.1 Flak Strength Comparison, 1944 (change from 1943, by percentage)

	Heavy Batteries	Light Batteries	Searchlight Batteries
Germany	1,508 (+22%)	623 (–10%)	375 (+7%)
Western Front: France, Belgium, and Holland	412 (+101%)	425 (+44%)	32 (–3%)
Northern Front: Norway and Finland	126 (+37%)	80 (+16%)	3 (+200%)
Southeastern Front: Romania and Greece	122 (+100%)	70 (+79%)	3 (–62%)
Eastern Front: Russia	311 (+110%)	328 (+102%)	43 (0 in 1942)
Southern Front: Italy	176 (–37%)	86 (+7%)	14 (–30%)
Totals	2,655 (+25%)	1,612 (+10%)	470 (+3%)

resources to France, Belgium, Holland, and Norway in anticipation of an Allied ground invasion. Similarly, the reverses experienced by the Wehrmacht on the Eastern Front led to increasing demands from army commanders for support from the Luftwaffe's flak arm in an effort to stem the gathering Russian tide, in the air and on the ground. In the period between 1940 and 1944, the total number of heavy flak batteries had more than tripled, and the number of light flak gun and searchlight batteries had more than doubled, matching the increasing pressures on Hitler's Reich.

Reorganizing for the Air War

January 1944 also brought an important organizational change in the structure of the Reich's air defense network. In the last week of December 1943, General Hans-Jürgen Stumpff replaced Weise as the commander of Air Region, Center.[13] Stumpff had served in the army during World War I and had been a member of the Reichswehr's Truppenamt after the war. He also acted as the Luftwaffe's chief of the General Staff between June 1937 and January 1939. Before his selection to command the Reich's air defenses, he commanded Air Region 5, covering Norway and Finland, from May 1940 until November 1943.[14] Although not an aviator, Stumpff was a highly decorated combat officer and was considered an expert administrator. While he advocated a combined arms approach between the fighters and the flak, Stumpff placed a higher value on fighter operations. The restriction of flak fire to 16,500 feet over Berlin provided one expression of his views. In this respect, his strategic outlook complemented Göring's growing disillusionment with the flak arm engendered by the general decline in the effectiveness of the anti-aircraft forces in late 1943. Stumpff also had demonstrated a facility for working with National Socialist district leaders, an important consideration for any future commander of Germany's air defenses.[15] The district leaders also doubled as regional defense commissars *(Reichsverteidigungskommissare)* and were responsible for coordinating air defense measures for their districts with military officials.[16] Finally, unlike Kammhuber's practice of bypassing Weise, Stumpff had the professional standing to keep his fighter commanders under his control.[17]

A reorganization of Air Region, Center, occurred close on the heels of Stumpff's appointment with the creation of Air Region, Reich (Luftflotte Reich) on January 27, 1944.[18] As commander of Air Region, Reich, Stumpff was responsible for the coordination of all fighter and flak forces in the protection of Germany, Hungary, and Denmark. The combined forces at Stumpff's disposal included ten flak divisions and six flak brigades, with 9,359 light flak guns, 5,325 heavy flak guns, and over 5,000 searchlights, as well as five fighter divisions, with 774 day and 381 night fighters.[19] In a further effort to improve the performance of the Reich's fighter forces, Göring acceded to the earlier demands of his fighter commanders in the fall of 1943 by placing the Air Reporting Service under the command of the fighter arm in February. From this time on, the fighter division command posts became the central organizations for compiling the aerial situation report and passing this information on to the flak arm and the civil defense warning centers.[20] The reorganization of the Reich's air defenses helped to simplify command and control over the flak and the fighter arm, while the appointment of Stumpff and the reorganization of the Reich's defenses constituted another attempt to better integrate fighter and flak defenses and to streamline air defense procedures.

The Battle for Resources

Paradoxically, despite the growing shortages of personnel and material resources within Germany, the Luftwaffe's air defense forces experienced a major expansion in the first half of 1944. On the one hand, fighter production exceeded 2,000 aircraft per month for the first time in May 1944.[21] By the end of May, the Luftwaffe reported 1,517 day and night fighters serving in the defense of Germany alone.[22] Moreover, the output of heavy flak guns (all calibers) increased from 6,864 in 1943 to 8,402 in 1944, and the production of light flak guns rose from 35,580 in 1943 to 50,917 in 1944.[23] In comparison, the losses of 88-mm guns due to excessive wear and combat rose to an average of 380 guns per month in 1944, over two times greater than the rate in 1943.[24] Despite the general increase in the production of heavy and light flak weapons, the output of the newest and most capable guns, including the 37-mm/Model 43, the 88-mm/Model 41, and the 128-mm/Model 40, lagged far behind production targets.[25] In fact, British intelligence estimated that only thirty 128-mm flak guns and a mere fourteen 88-mm/Model 41 flak guns were reaching operational units every month in early 1944.[26] The British estimates were accurate. Delays and problems associated with the manufacture of these two gun types deprived the Luftwaffe of its most effective flak weapons for defending against the Allied aerial assault. These two weapons were especially critical to combat the American daylight missions because B-17 bombing altitudes generally exceeded 25,000 feet and pushed the older 88-mm and 105-mm guns to the limits of their performance.

In addition to the increased production of flak guns, the output of 150-cm and 200-cm searchlights increased from 3,180 in 1943 to 5,757 in 1944. In the case of the 200-cm searchlight, monthly production rose from 152 in January to 240 by July. Likewise, the production of 150-cm searchlights was 241 in January and increased to 338 by July.[27] The Luftwaffe's plan for the eventual production of 10,990 150-cm and 6,900 200-cm searchlights by March 1946 provides clear evidence of the continued importance it placed on the operations of the searchlight batteries.[28] The significant increase in the production of searchlights between 1943 and 1944 also bore witness to their continuing effectiveness in supporting both flak and fighter operations.

In contrast to the searchlights and the flak guns, the production of sufficient numbers of gun-laying and aircraft-tracking radar presented an ongoing problem for the Luftwaffe throughout 1944. During a conference at Hitler's headquarters attended by Speer, Milch, and Dönitz on January 1, Göring laid the blame for the shortage of radar systems on General Martini and the Air Reporting Service. The reason for the presence of the commander of the German navy was soon apparent as Göring sought Dönitz's agreement for combining the efforts of the Luftwaffe and the navy in the area of radar research-and-development.[29] This meeting represented an effort to rationalize the Wehrmacht's radar program in the hope of ameliorating the existing radar shortage. In a subsequent research-and-development conference on February 11, Milch revealed the decision to combine the Luftwaffe and the navy radar development programs, with an emphasis on the development of centimeter radar systems,[30] which allowed for a sharper concentration of the radar beam, increasing range and improving plotting accuracy.[31] The rationalization of radar development and production was essential in order to combine resources so it would be possible to pursue the latest technology and keep pace with the continued high demand for radar equipment. The German navy also clearly benefited from cooperative measures as the Luftwaffe consumed an estimated 50 to 55 percent of the existing production of radar and communications equipment in 1944.[32]

Barrage balloons constituted another area that was experiencing resource shortages in early 1944. By 1944, the Luftwaffe employed two primary types of hydrogen-filled barrage balloons: a 200-cubic-meter-capacity balloon capable of flying at an altitude of between 6,000 and 8000 feet, and a 77-cubic-meter balloon flown at altitudes below 3,000 feet.[33] By February 1944, production difficulties associated with supporting equipment for the barrage balloon units hampered their operations. Problems arose with the manufacture of the steel gas canisters used to fill the balloons, as well as with the winches used to raise and lower the balloons. Production bottlenecks also led to trials involving captured French and Italian barrage balloons as potential replacements for some existing German models.[34] In truth, the barrage balloons began to lose their effectiveness by 1944, although Hitler insisted on their continued employment through the end of the war. He even suggested stringing wires between balloons and attaching explosive mines to create a high-explosive aerial fence.[35] Still, the number of barrage balloons declined from approximately 2,400 at the start of 1944 to about half that number by the end of the year.[36]

The Luftwaffe also constructed aerial barriers consisting of steel cables strung between two sides of valleys to deter low-level attacks.[37] Eventually the Luftwaffe built valley barriers using cables, mines, and even torpedo nets to protect factories, power plants, and other important installations from the growing numbers of Allied tactical aircraft appearing in the skies over the Reich.[38] Although limited to areas with suitable topography, these barrier defenses could be left continually in place, required little maintenance, and needed only a fraction of the personnel and resources associated with a barrage balloon battery.

Without doubt, the most ominous shortage faced by the flak arm in the first half of 1944 was in the production of ammunition. In the first two quarters of the year, anti-aircraft ammunition production accounted for 17 percent and 16 percent, respectively, of the Wehrmacht's entire ammunition budget. These percentages had in fact decreased from 20 percent and 19 percent in the third and fourth quarters of 1943.[39] However, the continued expansion of the numbers of heavy and light flak guns began to outpace the ability of the German armaments industry to provide these guns with adequate supplies of ammunition. At the flak development meeting on May 8, a report noted that the ammunition supply was "extremely unfavorable" and, barring a diversion of resources from other projects, the situation would remain so for the next six months. Furthermore, the report remarked that the production of explosives constituted the primary limitation to increased production.[40] From May 1944, the specter of an ammunition shortage hung on the horizon like an approaching storm, one that would vent its full force on the flak arm in the fall of 1944.

Despite the threatening signs of growing resource shortages within Germany's armaments industry in the first half of 1944, the Reich's fighter forces and ground-based air defenses appeared to be faring well. Several historians have noted the diversion of resources to the flak arm as a major contributing factor to the reduced scope of aircraft production. Often overlooked in this argument, however, was the effect of the V-1 and V-2 missile programs with respect to the production of air defense equipment and, to a lesser extent, the drain on resources caused by the V-3 and V-4 projects.[41] Plans for the manufacture of the V-2 alone called for 200,000 skilled workers, including many from the electronics and precision instrument industry, 1,000 tons of aluminum per month, tens of thousands of tons of pure alcohol, hydrogen peroxide, and liquid oxygen. Not only did this effort draw critical resources away from aircraft production, but by January 1944, Milch recognized that the V-2 program was consuming the majority of resources that otherwise might have been used for the development of the flak's anti-aircraft missile (Waterfall).[42]

The Battle for Personnel

The further expansion of ground-based air defenses in 1944 resulted in an increase of nearly 250,000 men and women serving within the flak arm during the course of the year.[43] As during the prior two years, the growing personnel demands placed on the flak arm by the expansion of the Luftwaffe's ground-based air defense network were satisfied in large part by the increased use of auxiliaries. In January there were 244 heavy and 328 light Home Guard flak batteries serving within Germany. By the end of the year, there were 247 heavy and 273 light Home Guard flak batteries. In addition to the Home Guard batteries, a second mobilization of the Reich Labor Service took place between December 1943 and June 1944 in which almost 31,000 Labor Service personnel trained for flak duties.[44]

The growth of the flak arm also led to the expanded inclusion of young women in the air defense network. For example, in March 1944, a new office entitled "flak leader" for women was established. This position's primary responsibilities were training young women in air defense duties, leading them in political instruction, and arranging their recreational activities.[45] In the spring of 1944, some 111,000 young women were active in the air defense network of the Reich proper.[46] By the end of the year, the searchlight batteries were operated almost exclusively by female auxiliaries, and growing numbers of women were serving with the barrage balloon units. Furthermore, young women increasingly could be found operating fire control equipment, communications systems, and sound detectors within the heavy flak batteries.[47] Although uncomfortable with the mobilization of women for air defense duties, the National Socialist leadership framed the service of the female auxiliaries as a necessary and noble sacrifice. In an effort to prevent these young girls from losing their "womanly character," training discussions included slogans such as "The wooden barracks must become a home. Where women live, there is no dark, dusty corner" and "The woman in a soldier's post but still a woman."[48]

In a message to the Luftwaffe on May 22, 1944, Göring addressed the important role being played by both young men and women in the flak auxiliaries. He began his message with an evaluation of the performance of the auxiliaries:

> The employment of the Luftwaffe auxiliaries in the flak batteries has proven a success. These young people, not yet of age for [service in] the armed forces, are actively participating in Germany's victory. Through enthusiastic commitment to their duties *[begeisterte Einsatzfreudigkeit]*, courage, rapid comprehension, and good training, they have demonstrated that they are completely up to the task and to the [demands of] the positions in which they are employed and have fully taken the place of the soldiers released for fighting at the front.[49]

Göring's praise was not misplaced, as many of the flak auxiliaries continued to perform their duties even as German cities crumbled around them in the last year of the war. One youth publication suggested that the auxiliaries repeat the following oath made by the military theorist Carl von Clausewitz in 1812: "I declare and inform the world now and the world to come . . . that I am willing to find a glorious death in defense of the freedom and the worth of the homeland."[50]

It should not be surprising that German youth who had come of age under National Socialism should rally to the defense of the Reich; however, the growing enlistment of foreign volunteers and prisoners of war demonstrated the increased strain and desperation felt by the anti-aircraft forces in the never-ending search for personnel. Two of the largest groups of foreign volunteers were those from Croatia and Italy. The latter included Italian military forces that remained loyal to Mussolini despite his official removal from office in 1943.[51] In addition to these volunteers, approximately 51,000 Soviet prisoners of war were serving with the flak by August 1944.[52] An examination of the composition of the 14th Flak Division in October 1944 provides a clear indication of the diverse nature of German flak personnel by this stage of the war. The division primarily was responsible for the defense of the Leuna synthetic oil refinery and was composed of the following groups:

Regular Luftwaffe personnel	28,000
Labor Service personnel	18,000
Male Luftwaffe auxiliaries	6,000
Female Luftwaffe auxiliaries	3,050
Hungarian and Italian volunteers	900
Soviet POWs	3,600
Others	3,000
Total	62,550[53]

The diverse makeup of the 14th Flak Division was representative of the overall composition of the entire home-based flak arm by 1944. For example, a heavy flak battery within the Berlin defenses in the spring of 1944 consisted of ninety young male auxiliaries, twenty Soviet prisoners of war, and only thirty-six regular Luftwaffe personnel.[54] In addition to the use of nonmilitary personnel, the regular and reserve Luftwaffe service members employed in the flak arm were increasingly drawn from older age-groups and those medically unfit for service at the front. By the end of the war, 35 percent of the Luftwaffe personnel serving with the flak were at least forty-nine years old or previously had been medically disqualified for service in the Wehrmacht.[55] The mass influx of auxiliaries, foreign volunteers, and prisoners of wars and the large proportion of older and medically impaired Luftwaffe personnel provide an important caveat to the argument that the flak arm represented the Wehrmacht's "lost divisions." By 1944, the flak arm was not the elite formation that it had been at the start of the war, and it could no longer be seen as a major pool of replacements for frontline combat units. Still, despite the large percentage of civilians, foreign nationals, and high school students, the flak arm continued to perform its duties ably in the first quarter of 1944.

Bomber Command's Failure in the Battle of Berlin

After the initial raids on Berlin at the beginning of the year, Bomber Command visited the capital of the Reich four more times in January. Bomber Command also struck the cities of Brunswick and Magdeburg in two separate raids. The January raids on Berlin had cost Bomber Command 147 aircraft, or 5.8 percent of the force dispatched, while the other two raids resulted in the loss of an additional 95 bombers, or 8.3 percent of the force dispatched.[56] In February, Bomber Command visited Berlin on one occasion with the largest bomber force yet sent against the city. On the night of February 15, 891 aircraft set out for Berlin.[57] Despite seventy-five aborts, the remaining aircraft reached the city in a tight stream, spending a mere twenty-two minutes over the target. The compact bomber stream minimized the exposure of the bombers to the flak and searchlight-assisted night fighters over Berlin, but the force still lost 43 bombers, for a loss rate of 4.8 percent.[58] From the RAF's perspective, the mission was a decided success, with an estimated 700 persons perishing and an additional 60,000 persons left homeless.[59]

Shortly after the raid, General Erich Kreßmann took command of the city's flak defenses. Goebbels showed his own frustration with the course of the air war by mentioning his hope that Kreßmann's appointment would "finally bring the Berlin flak up to speed." On March 3, Goebbels also noted that "the air war has awakened a certain feeling of helplessness within the German population, especially in those cities that were bombed in the past week."[60] In truth, Berlin's flak defenses were hardly to blame for their lack of success in this period. The order restricting anti-aircraft fire to 16,500 feet and below severely handicapped the capital's flak defenses, a prohibition that remained in effect even after Hitler's promise to have Göring rescind this order.[61] Hitler's support of the firing limitation marked a rare break with his usual practice of supporting unrestricted flak operations and likely resulted from Göring's personal efforts to limit flak operation in an effort to clear the field for Herrmann's night fighters.[62] As a result of the firing restriction, the most important contribution made by Berlin's ground-based defenses during RAF night raids in February and March was providing illumination for the wild boars with searchlights and flares.[63]

March proved a fateful month for the crews of Bomber Command and for Harris's plan to destroy Berlin. On the night of March 24, the RAF sent 811 bombers to strike the city. Unlike during the raid in February, a strong wind dispersed the bomber stream across a wide area on its way to and from the target.[64] A low overcast lay across Berlin, an ideal situation for using searchlights and phosphorous flares to light the cloud base, thus framing the British bombers like images on a television screen for Herrmann's fighters circling overhead.[65] However, it was the night fighters using the SN-2 aerial intercept radar outside the illuminated areas that proved most successful as the bombers withdrew into a quartering headwind estimated at approximately 125 mph. The unexpectedly fierce wind blew the returning bombers into the teeth of some of the Luftwaffe's stiffest flak defenses at Magdeburg, at Münster, and in the Ruhr as the aircraft crept home.

One crew member recounted his experience as his aircraft drifted south over Magdeburg:

> The navigator and bomb aimer were exchanging comments on the heading of the aircraft. We were pointing directly towards heavy Flak and searchlights, obviously Magdeburg. The navigator said that, owing to the heavy winds, we would have to track south of Magdeburg to keep clear of those defences. Almost immediately, we were hit by Flak—CRUMP! CRUMP! CRUMP!—accompanied by the sound of tearing metal. I knew that the aircraft was mortally wounded and I switched back to intercom. Stan Wick, the pilot, said, "This is it, chaps, Bale out."[66]

This account illustrated how quickly the end might come for a crew venturing into heavy flak defenses. In another account of the same mission, the pilot of a Lancaster bomber approached the Ruhr defenses and witnessed several of his comrades' planes explode as a result of flak hits. His own aircraft was "coned" by searchlights on two occasions, forcing him to corkscrew wildly to avoid exploding flak shells. This crew proved luckier than their counterparts over Magdeburg and eventually landed safely in England, but not without first having experienced a Bomber Command crew's worst nightmare, being caught by searchlights, twice.[67]

In sum, the mission to Berlin on March 24 cost Bomber Command 72 aircraft, with an estimated 9 destroyed on the way to the city, 6 destroyed over the capital, and 57 destroyed during the flight back to England. One historian of the air war estimated that flak accounted for 12 shootdowns, or almost 17 percent of the total destroyed.[68] Another historian, however, suggested that on this raid "the majority of Bomber Command losses seems to have fallen to the *Flak* rather than the fighters, as a result of off-course bombers straying over heavily defended areas."[69] In either event, the performance of the flak was all the more impressive based on the firing restriction over Berlin, a prohibition that greatly diminished the flak's chances for success over the target area.

This raid marked a bloody end to Bomber Command's campaign against Berlin, as Harris turned away from the capital to provide reluctant support to the forthcoming invasion of France. The eight raids against the German capital in early 1944 had cost the RAF dearly, with a total of 351 aircraft destroyed, 1,787 airmen killed, and 506 crew members captured. If one takes into account the aircraft that crashed in England or were damaged beyond repair, the number rises to a staggering 606 aircraft, the equivalent of twenty-four squadrons.[70] In comparison, the series of raids against Berlin killed 3,589 of the city's residents and left over 230,000 homeless.[71] In his postwar memoir, Harris evaluated the effort against the capital:

> The Battle of Berlin cost us 300 aircraft missing, which was a loss rate of 6.4 percent. This could not be considered excessive for a prolonged assault on this distant, most difficult, and most heavily defended target. . . . But it did mean that the enemy had succeeded in reorganising his defences and finding new tactics.[72]

The official Royal Air Force history provides a much sterner judgment of the campaign by commenting, "From the operational point of view, it was more than a failure. It was a defeat."[73] Ironically, the man who had ridiculed the search for "panacea targets" such as oil or ball bearings had himself fallen victim to a similar obsession centered on the physical destruction of the Third Reich's major urban centers.

Evaluating the Effectiveness of the Flak Against the RAF

The performance of German ground-based air defenses during the first quarter of 1944 seemed to offer some cause for optimism within the Luftwaffe's flak arm. The RAF credited Luftwaffe flak defenses with the destruction of 79 aircraft during night raids in January, a total matched only once before in April 1943. An overview of the estimated number of aircraft destroyed by the Luftwaffe's flak and fighter forces in the first quarter of 1944 shows that Bomber Command lost 136 aircraft to fighters and 79 to flak in January, 70 aircraft to fighters and 50 to flak in February, and 115 aircraft to fighters and 50 to flak in March. Furthermore, German fighters damaged 245 bombers to 462 damaged by the flak during the three-month period.[74] Therefore, the ratio of Bomber Command losses due to fighters and flak was 1.72 to 1 in January, fell to 1.4 to 1 in February, and rose to 2.3 to 1 in March. For the entire period, bomber losses favored the fighters at a ratio of 1.79 to 1, while bombers damaged favored the flak by a ratio of 1.88 to 1. The latter statistic indicated a significant drop-off in the proportion of aircraft damaged by the flak from earlier periods; however, this decline can be explained by the RAF's overwhelming concentration on Berlin and the corresponding firing restrictions placed on the capital's flak defenses. In an effort to improve the performance of the Berlin flak defenses, General Kreßmann reorganized those surrounding the capital by moving batteries farther away from the city's center to expand the flak zone.[75]

At a meeting on February 23, Milch once again voiced his disappointment with the performance of the flak defenses and his preference for fighters. He remarked, "Let us not delude ourselves about the effectiveness of the flak. We know that flak is necessary and that it definitely worries the enemy a great deal, . . . [but] the enemy cannot be impeded to any appreciable extent by flak. Fighters, therefore, are the only counter-measure to come under consideration."[76] Clearly, Bomber Command did not share Milch's view. Despite the problems experienced by the Luftwaffe's flak defenses in early 1944, Bomber Command noticed an improvement in the performance of German flak defenses in the period. One ORS study reviewing Bomber Command night losses suffered in the spring observed, "In view of the technical progress in the firing and fragmentation of German A.A. shells and the results of provisional investigation of the strikes received by damaged aircraft, it is considered possible that the effectiveness of the enemy flak has increased in recent months."[77]

While the flak began to operate with increased effect, the performance of the wild boars declined, leading to the dissolution of several wild boar units in March. During the preceding months, Herrmann's force had experienced a progressive decrease in effectiveness as a result of poor weather, the loss of experienced pilots, and the introduction of inadequately trained replacements. More important, the Luftwaffe sought to stem the high loss rate experienced by day fighters during night intercept missions. This rate was exacerbated by Herrmann's instructions to his crews to remain in the air as long as there was any chance to destroy a bomber, even if this meant running out of gas and abandoning the airplane. This attitude led some conventional night fighter crews to quip that Herrmann's pilots "had more parachute jumps to their credit than kills."[78]

The introduction of day fighters cooperating with the searchlights had provided the Luftwaffe with a short-term tactical advantage. However, the high wastage rate experienced by this force because of poor winter weather and aggressive tactics, combined with the bomber crews' growing recognition of these tactics, resulted in a general decline in effectiveness of the wild boars. In addition, the restrictions on anti-aircraft fire severely limited the ability of the flak batteries to challenge RAF bombers over the target. Despite these problems, Herrmann's pilots still destroyed an estimated 330 aircraft between the introduction of the wild boar tactics in July 1943 and the general dissolution of the force in March 1944.[79]

Changing the Air Defense Equation: The Introduction of Daylight Escorts

By the beginning of 1944, the USAAF finally had emerged as a force capable of striking effectively and in growing numbers at the heart of Germany. However, it was not the increasing numbers of bombers that posed the greatest threat to the Luftwaffe's air defenses, but rather the introduction of long-range escorts that fundamentally shifted the balance of the daylight air war. Already in September 1943, American P-47 Thunderbolts had escorted Eighth Air Force bombers in a strike against Emden, successfully defending the bombers from Luftwaffe fighter attacks. At first, Göring refused to believe that American fighter escorts could reach Germany even after he was informed that several P-47s had been shot down over the Reich. Göring, always ready to demonstrate his technical ineptitude, responded to these claims by asserting that the fighters must have "glided" into Germany after being damaged over the occupied western territories. By the beginning of 1944, even Göring could no longer deny the existence of the American fighter escorts. In contrast to the Reich marshal, the leaders of the Luftwaffe fighter force quickly realized the potential impact of fighter escorts in the battle against the American bombers. The head of the Luftwaffe's fighter forces, General Adolf Galland, noted that prior to the appearance of the escorts, the Luftwaffe was losing one fighter for every bomber brought down; after the appearance of daylight escorts, the number of fighters lost per bomber rose to two or three.[80]

In the period between February 20 and February 25, the USAAF waged a campaign that would provide the acid test of the effectiveness of escorts over Germany. Known as "Big Week," American strategy involved a series of concentrated attacks aimed at the heart of the German aircraft industry. During this week, 3,300 bombers from the Eighth Air Force and another 500 from the Fifteenth Air Force dropped almost 10,000 tons of bombs, approximately one quarter of the tonnage delivered against Germany in all of 1942. The RAF supported these missions in a series of night raids by delivering an additional 9,198 tons of bombs. The cost to the bomber forces of both countries was high but not exorbitant. The USAAF lost 226 bombers and 28 fighters, while RAF losses totaled 157 heavy bombers. Although the raid set back German aircraft production, the ostensible goal of the campaign, the main effect of these missions was the attrition of the Luftwaffe's fighter forces. The authors of the official history of the USAAF argued that "there is reason to believe that the large and fiercely fought air battles of those six February days had more effect in establishing air superiority on which Allied plans so largely depended than did the bombing of the industrial plants."[81]

In many respects, Big Week marked a turning point for the Luftwaffe's fighter forces because it demonstrated that the fighters would no longer enjoy unopposed hunting in the daytime skies over Germany. Likewise, a decline in the effectiveness of the Luftwaffe's fighter forces had major implications for Germany's ground-based air defenses. Any decrease in the efficacy of the Luftwaffe's fighter defenses would force the Reich's flak defenses to shoulder an increasing share of the air defense burden. Ironically, at a point in the war when many Luftwaffe leaders had expressed growing disillusionment with the anti-aircraft forces, these defenses were gaining importance and would continue to do so throughout the remainder of 1944. To be sure, the Luftwaffe's ground-based air defenses successfully had carried the lion's share of air defense in 1939 and 1940, but the nature and ferocity of the air war in 1944 were orders of magnitude greater than the threat posed by a small and poorly equipped RAF bomber force in the early years of the war.

The USAAF Joins the Battle for Berlin

Despite the success achieved by early escort missions, it was clear by the spring of 1944 that, based on the limited range of the P-47, the USAAF required another fighter for escort missions deep into the Reich. The P-51 Mustang, fitted with external drop tanks, offered the answer to the Eighth Air Force's prayers for a fighter that could escort the bombers to Berlin and back.[82] On March 4, P-51s accompanied Eighth Air Force bombers all the way to Berlin; it was the first visit for both to the capital. The raid did not prove to be an auspicious beginning for the American effort because poor weather caused many of the 238 aircraft to turn back or to strike alternate targets. However, one wing of 30 bombers reached Berlin and dropped approximately 67 tons of bombs on the city's suburbs, albeit with little effect. In the course of five additional missions before the end of the month, 2,826 bombers delivered 6,379 tons of bombs against Berlin, at a loss of 187 aircraft and 1,870 aircrew members killed or captured. In contrast, these raids resulted in the deaths of 774 of the city's residents and left over 43,000 homeless.[83]

During the American campaign against Berlin, it soon became apparent that the Luftwaffe was increasingly unwilling, or unable, to engage escorted bomber formations. In April, Galland noted in a report concerning Luftwaffe fighter losses that "the day fighters have lost more than 1,000 aircraft during the last four months, among them our best officers. These gaps cannot be filled. . . . Things have gone so far that the danger of a collapse of our [fighter] arm exists."[84] Another Luftwaffe fighter pilot, Captain Anton Hackl, recalled, "Our older pilots were very good, but the new ones coming from the training schools could do little more than take-off and land the aircraft."[85] By the end of March, it was evident to the leadership of the Luftwaffe that the high losses within the fighter arm and the introduction of inadequately trained replacements had resulted in a major decrease in the qualitative performance of the fighter force.[86]

Despite the problems being experienced within the Luftwaffe's fighter arm, the flak defenses surrounding Berlin proved to be a worthy match for the American bombers. Philip Ardery, a B-24 pilot, described a raid against the capital in the spring of 1944:

> On we went. Berlin seemed the biggest city in the world. We flew on for terribly long minutes until finally we were passing over some large buildings almost in the middle of town. The formation was completely haywire. The flak bursts were so thick it seemed to me some of the shells must be colliding with each other. A couple of bombers I could see were already heavily hit.

Ardery continued:

> The flak was all around us, and we could see the sheets of flame in the explosion of many shell bursts. The ships kicked around in the air like canoes in a Lake Superior storm. . . . Once out of the flak, I looked around to take stock of our situation. Many airplanes showed gaping holes, many had feathered propellers marking dead engines. Some were smoking as if they were about to burst into flames, and a couple had gone down.[87]

Improving the Effectiveness of the Flak

The routine employment of escorts to protect the American bombers in the spring of 1944 shifted the burden for air defense increasingly from the Luftwaffe's fighter arm to the ground-based air defenses. By the beginning of April, the Luftwaffe had 6,387 heavy flak guns, 9,333 light flak guns, and 5,360 searchlights stationed throughout Germany.[88] In this respect, the increased number of guns, coupled with effective countermeasures to Allied jamming efforts, led to a period of improved effectiveness.[89] Likewise, the Luftwaffe took advantage of the growing size of the flak arm by further increasing the numbers of superbatteries throughout the Reich. In fact, by July the superbatteries emerged as the Luftwaffe's standard tactical flak formation.[90] One Eighth Air Force flak report described their formation as "the most intelligent thing that the Hun has done for many a day. . . . The Hun himself seems to realise this, and 'Grosskampfbatterien' [*sic*] are appearing everywhere."[91] At the same time, the Luftwaffe pursued technological initiatives to further increase its ability to mass anti-aircraft fire.

In 1944, the Luftwaffe introduced an experimental "central conversion device 44" (Zug 44). The Zug 44 was similar to the existing Malsi converter that allowed the fire control data from one gun-laying radar to be used by other batteries for computing targeting solutions. The Zug 44, however, offered a major improvement over the Malsi converter because it could provide instantaneous firing data for up to thirty-two batteries.[92] In addition, the device dramatically reduced the requirement for gun-laying radar because one or two radar sets could provide firing solutions for a large number of flak batteries equipped with the converter. Likewise, if one radar experienced problems due to jamming, then the Zug 44 could receive data from another operational radar not experiencing interference and transmit this information to the batteries affected by the jamming efforts. The latter capability led American planners to instruct aircrews that "it therefore becomes imperative to jam the total radars in the target area to render radar information useless."[93] Based on these advantages, the Zug 44 offered a perfect complement to the increased number of flak guns, if the device could be brought into production for operational use with the flak arm.

As a result of the success of the superbatteries in this period, the flak arm began trials to evaluate whether the number of guns might be increased to twenty-four per superbattery or even thirty-six. According to von Axthelm, the former required first-class training for "every person in the [gun] crew."[94] In the case of the latter, the thirty-six-gun batteries were to be known as "mammoth batteries" *(Mammutbatterien);* however, the practical complications involved in making electrical data connections between firing computers and thirty-six synchronized flak guns essentially prevented the realization of this concept.[95] Despite the failure of these efforts, the Luftwaffe did successfully establish superbatteries employing 88-mm/Model 41 and even 128-mm flak guns around especially critical facilities, including the Reich's synthetic oil plants, by the middle of 1944.[96]

The increased reliance on the massed firepower of the superbatteries was a key element in the improved effectiveness experienced by the flak arm in the spring of 1944. In a postwar study, von Axthelm described the success achieved by the superbatteries in late 1943 and throughout 1944 as "noteworthy."[97] Likewise, the official history of the USAAF noted that "by March the daylight bombing forces were facing a greatly increased volume of flak, much of which was directed with improved accuracy . . . and by the late spring of 1944 flak had come to be responsible for more of the losses sustained by AAF bomber forces than were the German fighters."[98] An additional measure introduced by the flak arm involved the employment of grooved projectiles in an effort to increase the number of flak splinters generated by the detonation of the flak round.[99]

The development of effective antijamming devices for gun-laying radar was a technical innovation that helped improve the performance of the flak arm in the first half of 1944.[100] Indeed, the marriage of technical improvements with organizational and tactical initiatives allowed the flak arm to recover in large part from the disappointing operations during the latter half of 1943. Furthermore, American bomber raids with their fighter escorts made it increasingly apparent that the Reich's ground-based air defenses were slowly emerging as the main line of defense in the face of the combined Allied bombing effort.

Evaluating the Effectiveness of the Flak in Daylight Raids

By early 1944, the flak arm had recovered from the debilitating blows it had suffered only six months earlier. The monthly reports from Eighth Air Force flak intelligence officers in the first quarter of 1944 reflected the improved performance of the German anti-aircraft defenses. By February, the 1st Bombardment Division's flak liaison officer, Major E. R. T. Holmes, remarked, "I see signs of slight improvement (long overdue) in the accuracy of flak generally, but the Hun is still very bad, fortunately for us, and continues to rely on quantity rather than quality." He continued, "However, the time may not be far distant when he shows real improvement, in which case formation bombing by day might become a very costly business."[101] One month later, Holmes reported, "Hun flak is improving slowly month by month, in spite of our chaff." He then reluctantly admitted, "If conclusions could be drawn from damage figures alone, then it might be claimed with reason that the use of Chaff is a waste of time."[102] By April, Holmes could no longer ignore the evidence of improvements in the performance of the Luftwaffe's flak arm. He stated, "There is no doubt but that the accuracy of Flak has improved considerably during the last two months, in spite of Chaff that we drop, and in spite of all the various counter measures [*sic*] that we adopt."[103] Holmes's comments indicate a somewhat grudging recognition that German anti-aircraft defenses had improved. They also provide strong evidence that the flak arm had countered the worst effects of passive and active jamming by early 1944.

An analysis of the number of aircraft losses by both the Eighth Air Force and the Fifteenth Air Force confirms Holmes's judgment concerning the improved effectiveness of the flak in this period. In the first four months of 1944, the Eighth Air Force and the Fifteenth Air Force lost 315 bombers to anti-aircraft guns, with a further 10,563 damaged by flak fire.[104] In comparison to Eighth and Fifteenth Air Force estimates of a total of 61 bombers lost to flak during the last quarter of 1943, the figures for early 1944 provide clear evidence of the growing effectiveness of the flak during the spring as tactical initiatives and improved weather worked to the advantage of the anti-aircraft batteries.[105]

The Raid on Berlin: March 6, 1944

One individual mission illustrates these trends. In the spring of 1944, the Eighth Air Force shifted its attention to Berlin, a city renowned for its awesome flak defenses. Half of the flak losses experienced by the 2nd Bombardment Division in March occurred on missions to the capital.[106] The city's flak defenses were in fact imposing, with 504 heavy guns, 220 light guns, and 420 searchlights grouped together in twenty-four superbatteries. The capital's defenses also included 12 of the formidable two-barreled 128-mm heavy anti-aircraft guns operating from the rooftops of Berlin's three massive concrete flak towers.[107] Eighth Air Force's mission to Berlin on March 6 revealed much about the performance of the Luftwaffe's air defenses and the contribution of the flak arm to the protection of the Reich at this point in the war.

The March 6 raid on Berlin involved 730 bombers, of which 672 eventually reached the target. Only at one other time during 1944 would the USAAF muster more bombers for an attack on the capital.[108] The designated targets of this attack included the Erkner ball-bearing plant, the Bosch electrical equipment plant, and a Daimler-Benz aircraft motor plant south of the capital. Despite visual bombing conditions, the bomber formations were widely scattered over their targets, resulting in confused aiming and a wide dispersion of the 1,626 tons of bombs, with few bombs landing near their intended targets.[109]

This failure was all the worse because of the terrible toll exacted by German air defenses. The Eighth Air Force lost 71 bombers destroyed, including 4 forced to land in Sweden because of combat damage. Likewise, 12 bombers returned to bases in England but were damaged beyond repair. The estimated number of aircraft lost to fighters was 50 bombers, while the flak received credit for 14 bombers. In addition, 5 bombers fell to fighters after having been damaged by flak fire, while 2 aircraft reportedly fell to flak defenses after having first been damaged by fighter attacks.[110] Furthermore, fighters received credit for damaging 4 aircraft beyond repair, while flak damaged 5 bombers beyond repair, with flak and fighters sharing credit for another 3 aircraft damaged beyond repair. A testament to the effectiveness of the capital's anti-aircraft defenses was reflected by the fact that 318 bombers (48 percent of the force) returned to their bases in England with some degree of flak damage.[111]

Flak's "Hidden Contributions"

The losses experienced by Eighth Air Force bombers on the March 6 mission provide a number of insights into the performance of the Luftwaffe's air defenses. First, estimated fighter shootdowns exceeded flak kills by a ratio of 3.6 to 1. Second, a full 10 percent of the fighter shootdowns occurred after these bombers were first damaged by flak. Likewise, an estimated 14 percent of flak kills occurred in the wake of earlier fighter attacks; however, one must keep in mind that in this period aircraft were over ten times more likely to be damaged by the flak than by fighters. In the raid on Berlin described earlier, Philip Ardery mentioned the danger posed by enemy fighters to flak-damaged aircraft. Ardery recalled:

> I did my best to keep the formation well grouped and fly it in such a manner that the cripples could stay up. Many of the cripples did manage to stay with us, but there were reports of two ships falling back. . . . We kept getting reports of attack after attack on the two that dropped back until at last their calls were heard no more. From one I picked up that familiar last call: "Ship on fire, crew bailing out."[112]

Ardery's account is but one of hundreds of similar reports by bomber crews throughout the war. The success of the flak in facilitating subsequent fighter shootdowns once again demonstrates the hidden contribution of the antiaircraft forces to many fighter victories.

Another factor that was almost as important as the number of downed aircraft was the flak's success in preventing the bombers from successfully striking their intended targets. Despite an average bombing height of 21,000 feet in visual conditions, the bombers largely failed in their attempts to hit the industrial installations. After the attack, Goebbels noted in his diary, "The industry is almost completely untouched; in any event there can be absolutely no talk of damage to our armaments production." Furthermore, Goebbels praised the cooperation of the flak and the fighters and commented that the Berlin flak defenses had claimed 20 bombers destroyed.[113] These initial flak claims were within reasonable limits when one considers the damaged aircraft that subsequently fell to fighters, as well as the 7 aircraft brought down by unknown causes. In any event, it is apparent that the city's flak defenses exacted a heavy toll and played a key role in preventing the bombers from successfully hitting their targets.

Three days after this raid, Berlin's flak forces demonstrated another advantage favoring the ground-based air defenses over their aerial counterparts. On March 9, 339 bombers of the Eighth Air Force again approached the capital. However, the weather over the city was so poor that not one fighter could be launched to oppose the attack. In turn, the city's flak defenses successfully brought down 9 bombers despite having to rely on radar-directed and barrage fire.[114] Like Berlin, Frankfurt and Munich also suffered the ignominy of having their fighter forces remain on the ground during attacks in this period. One historian of the air war correctly pointed out that "in bad weather raids the Germans were often unable to engage the American day raiders at all, owing to the risk of a high crash rate, with the consequent irreplaceable loss of skilled fighter pilots."[115] With the fighters grounded, the task of defending these cities fell completely on the shoulders of the flak arm. As had been the case from the first days of the war, in periods of poor weather, the flak arm constituted the Luftwaffe's sole line of defense.

Dummy Installations: The Final Act

Throughout 1944, the Luftwaffe continued to utilize dummy installations and decoy measures as an effective adjunct to the flak gun defenses. The growing Allied practice of relying on radar bombing during periods of poor weather led to the introduction of an ingenious countermeasure in the form of radar-reflective floats. The early versions of Allied H2S/H2X ground-mapping radar were limited in their ability to distinguish between terrain features; however, large bodies of water offered an excellent contrast with land features and provided navigators with important information to fix their positions. Berlin, a major Allied target, was surrounded by a number of lakes that greatly facilitated navigation by the bombers when the sky was overcast. To confuse Allied navigators, the Luftwaffe constructed cruciform-shaped floats and placed them in rows across lakes on the western approaches to the capital.[116] These floats in turn reflected radar energy back to Allied planes, providing an image that made one lake appear as two or more bodies of water.[117] Postwar investigation teams from the American military described this deception measure as "quite successful."[118]

Throughout 1944, the Luftwaffe also continued to employ decoy target indicators to divert Bomber Command aircraft from their objectives. An Operational Research Section report of April 14, 1944, warned that "a large volume of evidence has now been collected which shows beyond reasonable possibility of doubt that the enemy is making attempts to divert our attacks from his cities by the use of decoy T.I. markers, and that his efforts have been meeting with some degree of success." The report also remarked on the decreased effectiveness of German fire sites but cautioned that "used in conjunction with decoy TI's, and possibly smoke screens as well, they can form an effective decoy system, . . . [and] it appears probable that he [the enemy] is planning a rapid expansion of these decoy activities in the near future." Finally, to counter the German effort, the ORS report suggested the development of a new target marker that could not be easily duplicated.[119]

In addition to the decoy measures involving radar-reflective floats and decoy target indicators, the Luftwaffe constructed dummy flak batteries and dummy airfields in the vicinity of important urban and industrial targets. On the phony airfields, damaged aircraft or fabric and wood models provided effective decoys. Likewise, the Luftwaffe set up phony anti-aircraft batteries to conceal the departure of flak defenses from specific areas.[120] In the case of the dummy flak sites, one Eighth Air Force flak report observed, "It is possible that the enemy is deceiving us to some extent by leaving behind dummy equipment whenever he abandons or temporarily leaves unoccupied a gun position." This report then continued, "A possible example of this is at Bielefeld where photographs still show 10 heavy guns although no Flak has been encountered there during the past month even in visual conditions. On the same basis it is possible that some of the guns in the Ruhr have been removed."[121] By concealing the removal of flak guns from specific sites, the Luftwaffe hoped to prevent Allied flak intelligence officers from noticing the shift in gun batteries from secondary objects to the protection of high-priority areas during the last year of the war.

In conjunction with the dummy airfields and flak sites, the Luftwaffe continued to rely heavily on dummy installations throughout 1944 to divert Allied bombers from their intended targets. The worsening petroleum crisis caused by the Allied bombing of oil facilities led the Luftwaffe to focus on the construction of dummy installations in the vicinity of oil refineries and the Reich's critical synthetic oil plants. For example, the Luftwaffe constructed two separate dummy facilities near Ploesti in an effort to fool Allied bombers. These dummy sites were located approximately eight miles northwest and seven miles east of the real oil facilities.[122] In another example, decoy plants surrounding the synthetic oil plant at Leuna successfully diverted a total of 4,550 bombs away from the actual site.[123] In fact, more bombs hit the dummy sites than the real facility in seven of the first eight attacks aimed at the plant.[124] Likewise, the United States Strategic Bombing Survey team that inspected the synthetic oil plant at Meerbeck remarked that a dummy plant located some three miles from the main plant proved "very effective until May 1944." In the case of Meerbeck, the RAF dropped 23,926 high-explosive bombs and 103,743 incendiary bombs during forty-one attacks, but after the war the survey team found evidence of only 328 bomb craters within the plant area.[125] While the incendiaries would not have produced a crater, the fact that little more than 1 percent of the high-explosive bombs fell within the plant area highlighted the RAF's difficulties with night bombing accuracy against point targets and provided a strong indication of the effectiveness of the nearby dummy site.

By mid-1944, attempts to protect German industry also included extensive use of camouflage, as well as dispersing industrial facilities and moving them underground.[126] In the face of increasing aerial bombardment, the government ordered the dispersal of "vital industries" to less threatened areas in March 1944.[127] Likewise, the British raid against Peenemünde in August 1943 had started a movement to put V-2 missile production underground. By 1944, the infamous Buchenwald satellite camp, Dora, employed thousands of forced laborers and prisoners of war working and living in atrocious conditions beneath the earth.[128] Likewise, in the face of increasing American attacks on the German aircraft industry, Hitler tasked the Organization Todt with the construction of subterranean aircraft factories.[129] Camouflage, dispersal, and the movement of critical industries underground were important passive defense measures that complemented efforts associated with the dummy installations. In the final analysis, the innovative decoy and deception measures introduced by the Luftwaffe throughout the war demonstrated a continuing facility for adaptation and ingenuity within the ground-based air defense force. The success of these forces was one of the major achievements of the air defense effort.

Clouding the Sky

Throughout 1944, the Luftwaffe's ground-based air defenses expanded their use of artificial fog, or smoke screens, which were intended to hinder accurate navigation, to hide actual sites, and to decoy bombers to dummy sites.[130] A Luftwaffe study on air defenses in 1944 noted that "artificial fog proved itself as a valuable complement to the protection of objects both by day and night."[131] In fact, the number of smoke screen installations operated by the ground-based air defenses doubled to approximately seventy-five during the course of the year.[132] The expansion of the smoke generator units occurred in large part as a result of a request from Dönitz during meetings in early May with Hitler and Göring. During the discussions, Dönitz presented a demand for increased anti-aircraft and smoke screen protection for the cities of Hamburg, Danzig, and Bremen. Göring responded that "complete security could not be attained by an increase in anti-aircraft and smoke screen protection," to which Dönitz replied that "[some] smoke protection is better than no smoke at all." In this case, Hitler agreed with Dönitz and ordered Göring to take the appropriate measures to strengthen both the anti-aircraft and the smoke screen defenses of these cities.[133]

Hitler's decision provided the necessary impetus for the subsequent expansion of smoke generator units. In addition to establishing these units in port cities, the Luftwaffe stationed smoke generator units at synthetic oil plants throughout Germany. Approximately 500 chemical smoke generators and 600 ovens for smoke production were located at the synthetic oil facility at Leuna alone by fall 1944.[134] The former devices used smoke acid consisting of a mixture of sulfur trioxide and chlorosulfonic acid that was stored in cylinders and released by remote control; the latter devices produced natural smoke via combustion by burning residual tar compounds from the refining process.[135] In addition, the Luftwaffe introduced a low-tech initiative involving the use of "smoke pots" around key sites. These smoke pots were essentially like the "smudge pots" used in citrus orchards today during freezing weather. At the end of May 1944, the commander of the flak defenses at Ploesti deployed approximately 2,000 of these smoke pots around the area's oil facilities to hamper attacks by Fifteenth Air Force bombers.[136]

In practice, the local flak commander exercised operational control over the smoke generator units and gave the order concerning smoke production. The decision to produce smoke was based on several variables. Most important was the delay between the decision to commence smoke operations and the time needed to achieve coverage of the area, an interval of approximately forty minutes. This time delay essentially limited smoke operations to areas within the Reich. In addition, successful smoke operations depended on a number of climatological factors, including wind speed, humidity, and temperature. Favorable conditions included a wind speed of between 4 and 8 mph, high humidity, and a warm temperature.[137] The decision to commence smoke operations required the local flak commander to weigh several variables. First, he had to determine if his area was the object of the attack and if sufficient time was available to cover the area. Second, he needed to ascertain whether the climatological conditions favored smoke production; if not, the smoke would rise in vertical columns or gather in small clouds around the generators, betraying the position of the facility.[138]

In perhaps the most famous incident of the war, the commander of Schweinfurt's smoke defenses determined that weather conditions did not favor smoke generation during an Eighth Air Force raid in the fall of 1943 and decided against initiating smoke operations. Furious with this decision, Göring ordered that this commander be court-martialed. The situation looked ominous for the commander of the smoke unit, especially when the chief judge arrived and announced, "Today heads must roll." To Göring's chagrin, however, the subsequent investigation supported the commander's decision not to commence smoke operations based on the climatological conditions at the time of the raid.[139] An additional variable concerning whether to commence smoke operations involved the problems posed by smoke obscuring the aim of the antiaircraft batteries surrounding the site. One solution to this problem included moving the gun batteries farther away from the protected sites, but at many sites the decision to employ smoke involved a trade-off between accurate antiaircraft fire and shielding the site from visual bombing.[140]

Despite the difficulties associated with smoke production, these units did provide an effective adjunct for the defense of important sites in favorable weather conditions. For example, USAAF bombers failed to locate their targets in Wiener Neustadt during a raid in January 1944 as a result of German smoke operations.[141] In another example, Harry Crosby, a B-17 navigator, described a mission to Bremen in the spring of 1944: "We penetrated the German coast between Flensburg and Bremen, my old nemesis. We were miles from Bremen, but their gunners still aimed at us with flak and sent up a smoke screen over the city. The air was black for miles around."[142] Likewise, Leroy Newby, a B-24 bombardier, described a raid against Ploesti during which columns of smoke from dummy fires "fooled" several bomber groups, including his own, to drop over a thousand tons of bombs "into a sea of white smoke." During this raid, the reduced visibility over the target caused by the smoke coverage also led several groups to proceed to the secondary target.[143]

By 1945, approximately 50,000 people were serving in one hundred smoke generator companies, constituting an added strain on the Luftwaffe's personnel base.[144] However, it was not manpower but a crippling shortage of the chemicals necessary for the production of smoke acid that proved the main factor limiting the operation of these units throughout the remainder of the war.[145] According to one estimate, the Luftwaffe required 17,000 tons of smoke acid per month to support normal operations; however, production never exceeded 8,000 tons, and by the end of the war the output of smoke acid had sunk to 4,000 tons per month.[146] This state of affairs even resulted in situations in which generating equipment stood idle because no smoke acid was available.[147] Despite resource shortages and the problems and limitations associated with these units, the Luftwaffe's smoke defenses provided an important adjunct to the existing network of active and passive air defenses at critical installations.

Awaiting the Allies

On November 3, 1943, Hitler issued a Führer order for the strengthening of defensive positions in the occupied western territories, as well as the reinforcement of Wehrmacht forces in these areas.[148] A month later, he appointed Field Marshal Erwin Rommel to conduct an inspection tour of the "Atlantic Wall" stretching from Denmark to Spain and to report on the state of these defenses. During his tour, Rommel found many of these positions either unfinished or in a poor state of readiness. In turn, his findings led to the initiation of a major effort to improve the defensive fortifications along the Atlantic coast, including the construction of numerous fortified positions overlooking potential Allied landing sites, as well as the placement of millions of mines and obstacles along the beaches of northern France. In addition to these construction efforts, the Wehrmacht increased the number of its ground forces in the west. By the beginning of June 1944, there were a total of fifty-eight German divisions under the control of Field Marshal Gerd von Rundstedt, the commander in chief of German forces in the west, ready to face an invasion force.[149] As the Allied ground and naval armada gathered at bases and ports throughout England in the spring of 1944, it was clear that cracking the German defenses would be no simple task; however, the process of breaching "Fortress Europe" was already under way as Allied bombers shifted their sights from the Reich to France.

CHAPTER NINE

Aerial Götterdämmerung June 1944–May 1945

In preparation for the forthcoming invasion of Europe, Air Chief Marshal Sir Trafford Leigh-Mallory and Air Chief Marshal Sir Arthur Tedder presented General Dwight D. Eisenhower, the supreme commander of Allied forces in Europe, with a plan for an air campaign designed to isolate German forces stationed along the Atlantic coast from their lines of supply.[1] The plan, however, required the commitment of both Allied tactical and strategic air forces. Initially unwilling to shift the weight of their efforts from targets in Germany, both Harris and his American counterpart, Spaatz, protested against the proposed diversion of the strategic bomber force.[2] Only as a result of the political pressure created by Eisenhower's threat to resign did Harris and Spaatz reluctantly agree temporarily to subordinate the heavy bomber force to the supreme commander for operations against transportation targets.[3]

For the crews of Bomber Command, the switch in targeting to the Transportation Plan proved a welcome relief from the nighttime penetrations of the Reich's defenses as morale rose and operational tour lengths plunged.[4] In the period between April 17 and June 6, Bomber Command launched a mere thirteen main force raids into Germany in comparison with approximately one hundred missions against railroads, airfields, and coastal defense sites in France and the Low Countries. As a result of the change to more lightly defended targets in France and the Low Countries, Bomber Command losses fell to only 241 aircraft from 12,920 sorties conducted in support of the coming invasion, a minuscule loss rate of 1.8 percent in April and May.[5] In addition to providing Bomber Command with a much-needed respite, the shift in concentration to targets outside Germany reduced the pressure upon the "heart of Germany" and "provided a breathing space" to both the Luftwaffe's air defenses and German towns. According to the official RAF history of the strategic air war, the change in bombing emphasis allowed Harris to revive the psychological and physical resources of his forces at a time "when German air defences were achieving their greatest successes in the night battle over their own territory."[6] This last observation highlights the strain experienced by Bomber Command in the first half of 1944 and offers confirmation of the resurgence of the Luftwaffe's air defenses from their low point of the previous summer.

Like their Bomber Command counterparts, American bombers struck a number of targets in France and the Low Countries in April and May. Bombers from the Eighth Air Force and the Ninth Air Force plastered Luftwaffe airfields in France with almost 6,000 tons of bombs during preinvasion missions. During this period, American bombers also concentrated on the fortifications of the Atlantic Wall, as well as the Luftwaffe's radar system in the west.[7] In addition to operations in the west, Eighth Air Force bombers visited Berlin six times between March 22 and May 24. During a raid against the capital on March 22 poor weather prevented the Luftwaffe from launching fighters; however, the Eighth Air Force still lost 12 bombers, all to anti-aircraft fire.[8] In three separate raids during May, the Berlin flak defenses brought down 11 bombers and damaged an astounding 553 out of 938 (59 percent) bombers from the 1st Bombardment Division alone. In addition, 114 of the 553 aircraft hit by flak fire were listed as "seriously damaged."[9] In the six raids against the capital prior to the invasion, Luftwaffe fighters and flak batteries claimed a total of 157 bombers shot down.[10] On the one hand, the success achieved by German air defenses demonstrated the benefits of integrated fighter and flak operations. On the other hand, the losses and damage suffered by the bombers highlighted the continued effectiveness of anti-aircraft fire in areas of concentrated flak defenses.

In April and May, the German oil industry also became the target of repeated attacks by American bombers. Between April 5 and April 19, the Fifteenth Air Force conducted 5,479 effective sorties against the oil facilities at Ploesti, losing 223 bombers in the process. During the April raids, the flak accounted for 131, and fighters 56, of this total, a ratio of 2.3 to 1 in favor of the flak.[11] Between May 12 and May 29, the Eighth Air Force joined the campaign by launching three separate raids on synthetic oil production facilities throughout Germany. The Luftwaffe fighter defenses rose in force to meet the bombers and their escorts. The May raids cost the Eighth Air Force 112 bombers from a total force of 2,858 aircraft, or 3.9 percent of the force dispatched.[12] Luftwaffe flak defenses accounted for slightly over 10 percent of these losses, and anti-aircraft fire damaged more than 20 percent of the total force. In fact, flak defenses damaged 208 out of 316 (66 percent) of the 1st Bombardment Division's aircraft attacking the oil plant at Merseburg (Leuna) on May 12, including 26 bombers reported as "seriously damaged."[13] The primary lesson that could be drawn from the performance of flak defenses surrounding Berlin and the synthetic oil installations was that, in sufficient concentrations, anti-aircraft fire could exact a high toll against an attacking force, especially when used in conjunction with the fighters.

The Flak Arm in the Shadow of the Allied Landing in the West

By the end of 1943, it was apparent to Wehrmacht planners that the Allies were planning a cross-Channel invasion for sometime in the winter of 1943–1944 or the spring of 1944. On December 12, 1943, the Luftwaffe released a contingency plan entitled "Imminent Danger, West" ("Drohende Gefahr West"), which outlined the Luftwaffe's blueprint for the reassignment of combat forces to repel the expected invasion. In addition to details concerning the reorganization of fighter and bomber forces, the plan contained an annex dealing with the transfer of mobile flak formations from the Reich to France and the Low Countries to strengthen the western air defenses.[14]

By the end of February 1944, the air staff issued a revised version of the original plan with the prescient remark that "there are increasing indications that the enemy will conduct his intended landing in the west in the spring of 1944." Once the Allies began the invasion, the plan called for the transfer of two railroad flak regiments, consisting of three heavy battalions and two light flak battalions each to the invasion area. In addition to the railroad flak regiments, the plan directed the reassignment of 1 regimental flak staff, 13 heavy flak battalion staffs, 5 light flak battalion staffs, 43 heavy flak batteries, 23 light flak batteries, and 12 flak combat formations from Air Region, Reich, to Air Region 3. In the event of a simultaneous landing in Denmark and/or Norway, the force would be split into two, with half going to the west and the other half being sent to the north.[15] These flak reinforcements included approximately 11,000 flak personnel, not counting the railroad flak regiments or the motorized support forces needed to move these units from the Reich into the occupied western territories.[16] The contingency plan noted that the replacement batteries were composed mostly of young male auxiliaries, a factor resulting in the restriction that these units could participate in ground combat operations only in self-defense.[17]

In a further effort to shore up flak forces in the west prior to an invasion, the Luftwaffe created Flak Corps III on February 22, 1944, and subordinated it to the commander of Air Region 3 in the occupied western territories. The establishment of Flak Corps III provided direct recognition of the important role that Flak Corps I and II had played in earlier operations in the west and the east. The Luftwaffe intended Flak Corps III, like its predecessors, to serve as a mobile combat force capable of supporting operations against enemy aircraft as well as ground forces.[18] The formation of Flak Corps III led to the transfer of some 3,500 light and medium flak guns to positions along the Channel coast.[19]

Confronting the Invasion

When Allied forces landed at Normandy on June 6, the Luftwaffe soon realized the need to strengthen its air defenses in the region, especially in the face of the massive Allied strategic and tactical air effort supporting the landings along the French coast. The initial augmentation forces forecast in earlier contingency plans proved inadequate for the demands being placed on the German forces in the west. As a result, the Luftwaffe transferred a total of 140 heavy and 50 light flak batteries into France.[20] This transfer set an ominous precedent, as the withdrawal of flak forces from the Reich's defenses to the front lines became a common practice during the last ten months of the war, causing an eventual hemorrhage within the home front's ground-based air defenses.

As Allied armies advanced through France during the summer of 1944, American and British tactical and strategic airpower pounded German flak and armor formations in the west. After the landings, Flak Corps III moved forward to support German forces near the Normandy beaches, playing a key role in slowing the advance of Allied armored forces in June and July.[21] In initial operations, the corps claimed twenty-five aircraft destroyed while suffering "considerable" material and personnel losses. In fact, the situation on the ground forced the corps to concentrate its batteries for use in artillery barrages against advancing Allied armor forces, accounting for the destruction of approximately one hundred armored vehicles.[22] Allied forces quickly gained respect for the Luftwaffe's flak forces, especially the capabilities of the 88-mm flak gun in ground combat operations. It was, however, apparent that the Luftwaffe's flak forces provided only a temporary impediment to the Allied aerial and ground offensive. A report prepared by British military intelligence noted that "it is clear from recent reports that the losses among Flak units in the battle area, in personnel and particularly in equipment, have been very considerable."[23]

By the end of August, the Luftwaffe had suffered enormous losses to its flak forces in the west, primarily light flak guns, including the 1st and 4th Flak Assault Regiments of Flak Corps III, reported by the Luftwaffe as "almost completely destroyed."[24] These losses resulted from a combination of "extremely hard fighting" and "'indescribably heavy' air activity," while the lack of available transportation hampered the movement of flak weapons, equipment, and personnel rearward in the face of the advancing Allied ground offensive.[25] Despite the massive equipment and motor transportation losses, the Wehrmacht still succeeded in evacuating a majority of the flak personnel trapped against the Seine River. These forces, however, had to abandon 1,000 guns because of the limited availability of transport across the river.[26]

The Allied advance through France during the summer of 1944 signaled the beginning of the end for the Reich's air defense network. The Luftwaffe had lost significant amounts of equipment and matériel in opposing the invasion forces, and the forward basing of Allied tactical aircraft in Europe placed an added strain on the Reich's air defense network because British and American fighters and medium bombers could now roam throughout Germany.[27] In addition, the surrender of territory in the west corresponded with the loss of many of the Lutwaffe's forward-based early-warning radar sites, a situation with serious implications for the continued viability of the night fighter force.[28] From the summer of 1944 onward, the Reich would face an aerial assault of withering proportions.

The Luftwaffe Runs Out of Gas

Even before it was clear that the Allied landings in France had succeeded, Spaatz sought to throw the strategic bombers of the Eighth and Fifteenth Air Forces back into the battle against German oil facilities. Already on May 24, Göring warned, "What good does it do if I strengthen the entire front when the enemy continues to go after the hydrogenation plants? Then flying operations will completely stop and we can disband the Fighter Staff."[29] Likewise, Milch described the Allied prosecution of large-scale attacks on the synthetic oil plants as the "decisive moment" in the war.[30] In truth, the battle for the German oil facilities ultimately would determine the strength and form of the Luftwaffe's opposition to the growing Allied aerial armada. It was clear to both sides that the oil facilities represented a critical battleground that would decide the fate of the Luftwaffe.

To counter the expected attacks on the oil facilities, Göring ordered the creation of centers of gravity within the Reich air defense network.[31] In reaction to the Eighth Air Force raid on the oil installation at Pölitz on May 29, the Luftwaffe transferred flak batteries from the Berlin defenses to augment the plant's defenses.[32] Additionally, Göring tasked the 14th Flak Division with the protection of the oil facilities in central Germany, and both Milch and Speer visited the division commander to emphasize the importance of protecting these sites. At this time, there were approximately 374 heavy flak guns covering the area, including 104 in the vicinity of the facilities near Leuna and another 174 in the Halle-Leipzig area.[33] The Luftwaffe, however, soon realized that these defenses were not strong enough to deter the forthcoming aerial offensive. As a result, the Luftwaffe increased the number of flak guns around these sites throughout the remainder of the year.[34]

On June 8, Spaatz ordered the U.S. Strategic Air Forces (USSTAF) to concentrate on denying the German armed forces their oil supplies as the primary mission of the heavy bomber forces. Spaatz envisioned a two-pronged attack in which Fifteenth Air Force bombers operating from bases in Italy would strike at German oil facilities in southeastern Europe and Poland, while Eighth Air Force bombers would focus on oil installations in Germany proper.[35] During the next three months, the American strategic forces, with some assistance from Bomber Command, not only supported the Allied breakout from Normandy but also focused on destroying German oil production and storage facilities throughout Europe. On June 15, the Eighth Air Force's 3rd Bombardment Division opened the postinvasion oil campaign with an attack by 215 bombers on Misburg.[36] On June 20, the Eighth Air Force sent a record force of 1,361 heavy bombers and 729 fighter escorts against oil targets at Hamburg, Harburg, Ostermoor, Misburg, Pölitz, and Magdeburg.[37] On this raid, the improved flak defenses at Pölitz shot down 10 out of 267 bombers, for a loss rate of 3.7 percent, and damaged another 112 bombers, 42 percent of the force.[38] In the raid against Hamburg, the 1st Bombardment Division lost 7 out of 451 aircraft dispatched, while another 300 aircraft (66 percent) received flak damage, including "serious damage" to 86 bombers.[39] The fact that both raids occurred in clear conditions highlighted the continued efficacy of optically aimed flak fire and indicated the increased effectiveness of concentrated anti-aircraft forces. But these raids also demonstrated the need for an integrated defensive system combining flak and fighters as the growing numbers of Allied bombers began to overwhelm the Luftwaffe's air defenses.

By the end of June, the Third Reich's military and political leaders recognized that the aerial campaign against Germany's oil production constituted a grave threat to the Wehrmacht's ability to prosecute the war. On June 21, Göring ordered the further reinforcement of the flak defenses around the twelve most important synthetic oil and hydrogenation plants.[40] Likewise, Speer sent Hitler a personal letter on June 30, detailing the effects of the recent Allied raids on the synthetic oil plants. Speer informed Hitler of the "catastrophic" nature of the attacks and remarked that "aviation spirit production is at the moment utterly insufficient." In fact, production had dropped from a high of 5,845 tons per day on May 1 to a mere 1,212 tons per day by June 30. To provide improved protection to the plants, Speer pleaded with Hitler to assign more fighters to these sites. He also requested two additional measures to strengthen the ground-based air defenses surrounding these plants. He suggested:

1. A considerably increased supply of smoke units [is necessary] even at the expense of other important items. Consideration should be given to ensuring better camouflage by setting up a dummy plant with the same smoke screen as well as the white smoke which points to the existence of the actual plant.
2. In spite of the recent increase in the Flak, it should be strengthened still more, even at the expense of the protection of German towns.[41]

Speer's letter indicates the critical value of synthetic oil to the German war effort. Furthermore, his suggestions for improving these defenses also highlights the importance he placed on both passive and active ground-based air defense measures in protecting these facilities from aerial attack.

Shortly after receiving Speer's letter, Hitler met with Admiral Dönitz at his headquarters on July 9. Field Marshal Wilhelm Keitel, Hitler's senior military adviser, was also in attendance. In response to Speer's appeal, Keitel asked Dönitz to assign naval forces to the protection of the oil facilities. Keitel declared that "at this time, the continuous destruction of these plants constitutes the greatest concern for the [further] conduct of the war." He also informed the naval commander that the Luftwaffe had doubled the smoke screen protection of the plants, but that the air force resources were not sufficient to strengthen adequately the defenses at these sites. Keitel therefore requested that the navy provide its allotment of 128-mm gun production and some of its own smoke generator units for the protection of the oil facilities, a request that Dönitz agreed to consider.[42]

Speer's and Keitel's efforts provided the necessary impetus for increasing the strength of the air defenses surrounding the oil sites as the Luftwaffe shifted flak defenses to the protection of these facilities throughout the summer.[43] During the course of 1944, the defenses at the synthetic oil plant at Leuna increased to over 500 heavy flak guns, including 150 of the Luftwaffe's prized 128-mm guns.[44] In comparison, the heavy gun defenses of the hydrogenation plants at Pölitz and Böhlen rose from 26 and 24 heavy guns in March to 352 and 203, respectively, by December.[45] The growing concentration of flak defenses around the synthetic oil sites did not come without cost. Despite the effort to draw flak guns from new production, the need to augment the anti-aircraft defenses around the oil facilities eventually forced the Luftwaffe to withdraw flak units from Berlin and the Ruhr, and even to completely strip Eisenach, Weimar, Chemnitz, and Dresden of their own flak defenses.[46]

In the fall of 1944, a U.S. intelligence report noted the Luftwaffe's growing tendency to reallocate flak defenses from German cities to the oil installations. The report stated that "this policy has caused a tremendous shift in flak to all priority daylight targets," providing an example by comparing the defenses surrounding the oil facilities at Brüx with those of the city of Cologne:

> The oil installations at Brux [*sic*] are now defended bynearly 300 heavy guns while the whole city of Cologne is defended by little more than 200 heavy guns. In March of this year, Cologne's defenses totalled nearly 300 heavy guns while Brux [*sic*] was defended by only 24 guns. The result of this increased density of defense at targets which the 8th and 15th Air Forces are committed to attack has been a sharp increase in flak losses and flak damage.[47]

The shift of flak gun defenses to the oil installation proved to be a worthwhile investment. On the one hand, the high concentration of flak surrounding these sites exacted a deadly toll on Allied Bombers. Of the 82 aircraft destroyed by known causes in raids on Leuna, flak defenses accounted for 59, fighters received credit for 13, and 7 fell to accidents. In other words, flak accounted for 72 percent of known losses, a figure 4.5 times greater than the number of fighter shootdowns. On the other hand, the United States Strategic Bombing Survey team found that the flak defenses surrounding Leuna "undoubtedly contributed to inaccuracy in the bombing of the target." In fact, the survey found that only 10 percent of all bombs delivered against the target fell within the plant grounds, an area of 757 acres.[48] As in the case of the performance of the German flak during the withdrawal from Sicily, the Leuna defenses provided a strong indication that flak operated most effectively when it could be concentrated in very large numbers within a relatively small area. In these situations, massed fires could inflict significant damage and, most important, prevent accurate bombing.

The view from the cockpit confirmed the increased lethality of the flak defenses surrounding the oil facilities. Harry Crosby, an Eighth Air Force navigator, described the flak defenses surrounding Leuna during a raid on July 20 as one of the "worst flak barrage[s] until that time."[49] Likewise, Lieutenant Bill Duane, an Eighth Air Force navigator, recounted a mission against Leuna on September 28:

> The bomb run was 13 miles long. About 2½ minutes before bombs away we got intense and very accurate flak. About a minute later King, the flight engineer, was hit in both legs. He fell down into the passageway. . . . I took off my flak suit, cut open five layers of clothes [and] applied a tourniquet. All this took place in some very intense and tracking flak—and me without my helmet. . . . Three ships went down over the target after a collision. I hope that we won't see anything like this again.[50]

Duane's account highlights two physical effects of the flak. First, flak often wounded aircrew members when it did not cripple the aircraft. Second, flak damage caused some pilots to lose control of their aircraft, leading to catastrophic results for other bombers within the formation.

Aircrew members in the Fifteenth Air Force experienced much the same feelings concerning the flak as their Eighth Air Force counterparts during attacks on the oil facilities surrounding Ploesti. Leroy Newby, a Fifteenth Air Force bombardier, remarked that increased flak defenses around Ploesti had forced B-24 bombing heights up from 22,000 feet to over 24,000 feet, a profile that often required the bombers to jettison some of their bomb load to reach this altitude. Newby provided the following dramatic description of a raid against Ploesti:

> We were less than thirty seconds away from the bomb release Point. . . . As I shook the perspiration out of the chin section of my oxygen mask . . .

> there was a loud explosion just outside the nose section. A large piece of flak tore through the right side of our compartment and across, just above the eyepiece of the bombsight and out the other side. Two gaping holes told a graphic story. *If I had not lifted my head from the sight, the piece of flak would have gone right through my head—or at least would have hit my helmet.*
>
> I got back to work and refined my cross hairs at the base of the tower of black smoke that was spiraling its way toward our altitude. . . . When the bombsight released the bombs, I hollered "bombs away," closed the bomb bay doors, and peered over the sight to watch the results of my handiwork. The flak was now worse. The loud bangs were happening more frequently and the familiar sound of gravel thrown onto a tin roof never seemed to stop. Another of our sister ships peeled over on one wing and went into its death dive.[51]

Newby's description illustrates the sudden and capricious nature of exploding flak shells. It also demonstrates the danger posed by flak during the critical minutes associated with maintaining a steady course and speed on the final bomb run.

The success of the massed flak defenses around the oil installations was not achieved without cost. Stripping the flak defenses of German cities left the citizens of these areas with greatly reduced numbers of flak guns, or in some cases completely undefended. The National Socialist district leaders "barraged" Hitler with a storm of protests concerning the withdrawal of flak defenses from their cities.[52] However, these complaints fell on deaf ears as conditions within the Reich and at the fighting fronts deteriorated rapidly. By the end of the summer, this situation allowed the flak arm to respond only to the direst air defense emergencies. At this time, Goebbels complained bitterly about the "complete failure" of the Luftwaffe's fighter arm in preventing an attack in the vicinity of Hannover. He also showed his own frustration by adding, "But that of course is nothing new anymore." Furthermore, he mentioned a "certain feeling of despair" among the German population and remarked that the German people had completely lost faith in Göring and "his" Luftwaffe.[53]

By July, the Luftwaffe's flak arm was forced to prioritize the Reich's air defense requirements by further concentrating flak defenses into centers of gravity around only the most important areas. At the same time, one air staff planner remarked optimistically that close cooperation between the fighter and the flak arm had emerged as an "incontestable commandment."[54] In truth, the goal of close cooperation between the fighters and the flak constituted a theoretical ideal by the summer of 1944. In reality, the flak arm increasingly began to fire on bombers without regard for Luftwaffe fighters. In a tactical memorandum of July 15, the Training Department of the Luftwaffe High Command Operations Branch addressed the issue of fighter and flak cooperation over the target area. The memorandum urged that "the only way to ensure maximum anti-aircraft effectiveness is for every weapon to fire without any restrictions whatsoever. They should 'free fire' at all altitudes, without regard for our own fighters, by day and night." The Luftwaffe memorandum also remarked on the necessity for the "concentrated employment of all air defense weapons," as well as the immediate transfer of flak guns "from objectives that have already been destroyed or rendered less important by the course of events."[55]

With respect to the transfer of flak guns within the Reich, the slow advance by British and American forces in the west and the south, coupled with the Soviet advance in the east, revealed a serious weakness in Germany's ground-based air defenses. Göring's order in 1943 to concentrate on the construction of fixed flak sites had conserved resources, but the shortage of motorized or mobile batteries prevented the rapid transfer of these guns from their static positions as the fronts were pushed closer to Germany's borders.[56] Furthermore, worsening transportation problems hampered the movement of fixed guns from sites that had been destroyed or in areas that had lost their importance to the war effort into areas where they were now needed.[57] As a result of the problems associated with dismantling and moving the fixed guns, the railroad flak batteries emerged as an ever more important reserve based on their mobility and the high quality of their equipment and crews. In fact, British military intelligence remarked, "In view of his heavy losses in forward areas since the re-opening of land operations in the WEST, these [railway] units have now acquired an enhanced value as representing a large proportion of remaining reserves of high quality mobile flak."[58] Still, there were not enough railway units to cover the widening gaps within the Reich's air defenses. The emphasis on fixed flak guns had proved a success in the short term, but the Luftwaffe's flak arm would pay a high price in available strength for this decision in the last ten months of the war.

On July 28, Speer addressed another urgent personal letter to Hitler, highlighting the "dire consequences" of Allied air attacks on the synthetic oil plants during the month. Speer warned Hitler that if "further attacks are made on the synthetic oil plants, . . . then a planned use of the air force in September or October will be impossible." Furthermore, he remarked, "The strengthened protection of the synthetic oil plants, through A.A. and artificial fog units, did not prevent the most successful attacks in the last few days." He then complained that "the fighter protection, which is alone decisive for the protection" of these sites, had decreased in the period. In fact, the number of fighters assigned to the protection of these installations had fallen from 495 aircraft on June 1 to 255 aircraft by the end of July.[59] Speer ended his letter by once again pleading for increased numbers of fighter aircraft, anti-aircraft guns, and smoke generators with which to protect the plants. Finally, he requested that all flying operations be held to a minimum to preserve the existing supplies of aviation fuel.[60] Speer's letter demonstrated the full extent of the crisis facing Germany's air force as thousands of new aircraft lay idle throughout the Reich because of dwindling supplies of fuel and pilots.

The Costs of the Oil Campaign

Despite the dire situation faced by the Luftwaffe's air defenses by the end of the summer of 1944, ground-based air defenses continued to offer stiff resistance in the face of the intensifying Allied aerial campaign. In the three months following the invasion of Europe, Bomber Command, the Eighth Air Force, and the Fifteenth Air Force pounded tactical targets to support ground operations as well as strategic targets within the Reich. Eighth Air Force heavy bombers alone dropped 60,000 tons of bombs in June, 45,000 tons in July, and 49,000 tons in August. Paradoxically, in this period the heavy bombers experienced the vast majority of their losses not in the attack of tactical targets but during the bombing of strategic targets. For example, the July flak report of the 3rd Bombardment Division observed that "a good many tactical targets have been attacked with little or no flak opposition from relatively low altitudes. However, in attacks on strongly defended strategic targets operational altitudes have been high, 24,000 and 25,000 feet [due to flak]."[61] Likewise, the July flak report of the 2nd Bombardment Division noted that "the damage sustained on tactical targets has been exceptionally slight this month."[62] In contrast, German flak defenses inflicted considerable casualties against Allied fighters and bombers engaged in low-level bombing and strafing missions in support of the invasion of southern France in August, and the disastrous operation to capture bridges across the lower Rhine in an attempt to open the door into Germany in September (Operation Market Garden).[63]

Although the American campaign against Germany's oil facilities was effectively strangling the Wehrmacht's fuel supply, the attacks proved costly in terms of bombers lost. The official history of the USAAF remarked that "the ratio of losses was correspondingly high, notwithstanding the weakened state of the Luftwaffe, because flak was more deadly now and because bombers often went out under conditions that would have been regarded as unflyable a year before."[64] Table 9.1 provides an overview of the estimated number of Eighth and Fifteenth Air Force aircraft destroyed or damaged by flak from the beginning of June until the end of August.[65] In addition to the gross figures, it is important to mention that the number of Fifteenth Air Force aircraft suffering "major damage" due to flak in this period totaled 536, or 16 percent of all aircraft damaged. In comparison, the records of the Eighth Air

Table 9.1 Flak Losses and Damage, June–August 1944

	Eighth Air Force		Fifteenth Air Force	
	Losses	Damage	Losses	Damage
June	104.5	2,642	75	904
July	93	3,881	150	1,813
August	144	4,449	88	640
Total	341.5	10,972	313	3,357

Force's 1st Bombardment Division for this period listed 1,215 aircraft as "seriously damaged" by flak, or 22 percent of the division's aircraft damaged by flak.[66] Likewise, seriously damaged aircraft required major repairs or the replacement of critical systems that might result in their withdrawal from combat for a few days, several weeks, or even permanently. The number of "seriously damaged" aircraft or those identified as having received "major damage" as a result of flak fire constitutes another "hidden statistic" associated with flak defenses.

To provide a broader context for evaluating flak effectiveness in the summer of 1944, it is instructive to consider bomber losses due to flak in relation to total American bomber losses. According to an Army Air Force operations analysis of aircraft losses, the Luftwaffe's flak defenses emerged as the chief cause of loss of American bombers in June 1944. Furthermore, flak batteries were inflicting ten times more damage than fighter attacks at this point in the war.[67] Slowly, some German political and military leaders began to recognize the improved performance of the flak arm. In a speech of August 1 to the Luftwaffe's fighter staff, Speer praised the performance of the antiaircraft force:

> In the last few months the flak has shown that in massed raids on cities even more enemy aircraft can be shot down than had ever been believed possible. It will acquire an ever greater importance. In view of the expected shortage of aviation fuel we do not know how defence will fare both at home and against enemy aircraft at the front. However, the flak will at least force enemy aircraft up to greater altitudes and reduce their aiming accuracy accordingly.[68]

Speer's evaluation accurately reflected the contemporary state of the Luftwaffe's air defense network and demonstrated the ongoing shift toward an increased reliance on ground-based defenses alone.

Abandoning the Fighter Arm?

In mid-August, Galland telephoned Speer at his office in Berlin, seeking Speer's assistance in an attempt to reverse a Führer order transferring the Reich's fighter reserves from the defense of Germany proper to the Western Front. Galland feared that the young and inexperienced pilots from these units would be annihilated while serving no useful purpose in the west.[69] According to Galland, Speer listened to his concerns and suggested that both men should immediately fly to Hitler's headquarters in East Prussia.[70] Hitler received them and listened quietly before angrily interjecting, "Operative measures are my concern! Kindly concern yourself with your armaments! This is none of your business!" Hitler then terminated the meeting with the comment "I have no time for you."[71]

Later that evening Hitler notified both men that he desired to speak with them again on the following day.[72] In Speer's account of this meeting, Hitler flew into violent rage, shouting:

> I want no more planes produced at all. The fighter arm is to be dissolved. Stop aircraft production! Stop it at once, understand? You're always complaining about the shortage of skilled workers, aren't you? Put them in flak production at once. Let all the workers produce anti-aircraft guns. Use all the material for that too! Now that's an order. . . . A program for flak production must be set up. . . . A program five times what we have now. . . . We'll shift hundreds of thousands of workers into flak production. Every day I read in the foreign press reports how dangerous flak is. They still have some respect for that, but not for our fighters.[73]

Galland's version of the meeting, although slightly different from Speer's, also noted that Hitler became agitated and shouted:

> I will disband the fighter arm. With the exception of several advanced fighter Groups, I will carry on air defense solely with anti-aircraft defenses. Speer, I order you to immediately submit a new program. Production is to be switched from fighters to flak guns and increased immensely.[74]

Both accounts clearly highlight Hitler's resolve to increase the anti-aircraft defenses of the Reich, as well as his growing sense of frustration with the course of the air war. When subsequently faced with incontrovertible proof that his request was not feasible, Hitler reduced his demands for flak guns by half, but he still demanded a twofold increase in ammunition to be attained by December 1945.[75]

Hitler's meeting with Speer and Galland in many respects symbolized the dilemma faced by the Luftwaffe in the late summer of 1944. Without a doubt, fighters were a critical element of any integrated air defense network; however, barring sufficient quantities of fuel and adequately trained pilots, this force could hardly be utilized with great effect. One historian described the state of the Luftwaffe by September 1944 in the following terms: "Bereft of fuel, its units ravaged by the summer attrition, the *Luftwaffe* was a force that no longer exercised any influence on the conduct of either air or ground operations."[76] Although perhaps too pessimistic, this appraisal clearly highlights the difficulties faced by the fighter arm by the end of the summer of 1944. Throughout the remainder of 1944, the Luftwaffe at times was still capable of sending hundreds of fighters against the Allied bombers, but these were episodic events separated by periods of several weeks.[77]

With the fighter arm in its death throes, the Luftwaffe's anti-aircraft guns assumed the dominant role in the Reich's air defenses. One indication of the increased value placed on the flak included the appointment of a flak general, General Otto Deßloch, to command the air defenses of air region 3 in the areas still occupied by Wehrmacht forces in the west.[78] Deßloch had the distinction of being the only flak artillery officer chosen to command an air region during the war. By the end of the summer, however, it was apparent that neither flak-trained commanders nor flak defenses alone could hope to prevent Allied bombers from ravaging German cities and industry. In their favor, the flak defenses were less affected than the fighters by the growing fuel crisis, and sufficient quantities of trained crews still were available to operate the batteries at the most important sites. Still, the Allied attacks on the hydrogenation plants led to a precipitous decline not only in oil but also in nitrogen supplies that affected the Wehrmacht's entire ammunition production. The resulting shortage of explosives led to the widespread use of rock salt as an inert filler.[79] In truth, the attacks on the German chemical and oil industry, coupled with crumbling fronts in the east and the west, put the Reich's air defenses in a position from which they could no longer recover. It was no longer a question of winning the air war but rather of holding out as long as possible in the face of an impending disaster.

Battling Bomber Command at Night

In the three months following the Allied invasion, Bomber Command aircraft concentrated on providing tactical support to Allied ground forces in France. During the summer, Harris's bombers attacked transportation networks and German naval shipping in French ports, and they even conducted close air support operations for armies in the field. In addition, Bomber Command, unlike its Eighth Air Force counterparts, proved enthusiastic in its raids against V-1 launching sites in northern France.[80] The focus on tactical targets in the west resulted in a continual decline in the numbers of bombers lost to flak between June and September. For example, the estimated numbers of RAF bombers lost to both fighters and flak in this period were 128 to fighters and 55 to flak in June; 92 to fighters and 40 to flak in July; 65 to fighters and 39 to flak in August; and 27 to fighters and 14 to flak in September.[81] The marked decline in the performance of German air defenses at night occurred as a result of several factors. First, the loss of German early-warning radar in the wake of the Allied advance in France and the Low Countries effectively blinded the Air Reporting Service by reducing warning times of impending attacks to minutes. Second, Bomber Command's focus on tactical targets in the west substantially reduced the exposure of RAF bombers to both night fighters and flak.[82] Third, Allied fighters and bombers pounded the Luftwaffe's forward airfields, destroying numerous aircraft on the ground and forcing the night fighters to retreat to bases within Germany.[83] Finally, the RAF had captured the newest model of the Luftwaffe's SN-2 aerial intercept radar in July. Up to this time, the SN-2 radar had been impervious to Allied jamming efforts; however, the RAF used the captured device to modify its radar countermeasures to successfully disrupt the German onboard radar.[84]

Despite the mounting problems being experienced by the Luftwaffe's night defenses through the summer of 1944, when Bomber Command crews ventured against strategic targets within Germany, the Luftwaffe's air defenses were still able to inflict heavy casualties. For example, on the night of June 12, Bomber Command lost 17 Lancasters in an attack on the synthetic oil production plant at Gelsenkirchen, or 6 percent of the attacking force.[85] In three subsequent attacks on oil facilities within Germany, the "missing rate" was 10 percent, 6.5 percent, and a staggering 27.8 percent.[86] In this last raid on the night of June 21, Bomber Command lost 38 aircraft, mostly to night fighters, in an attack on oil facilities at Wesseling, south of Cologne.[87] On the night of July 28, four days after the first anniversary of the opening of Operation Gomorrah, Bomber Command split its force in raids against Hamburg and Stuttgart. The attack on Hamburg cost Bomber Command 22 bombers, while the raid on Stuttgart resulted in the loss of 39 bombers. In the case of the latter, a new ground-based radar, code-named "hunting lodge" *(Jagdschloß)*, stationed near Stuttgart, allowed controllers to infiltrate night fighters into the bomber stream west of the city with great success.[88]

Despite the success in protecting targets within Germany, the Luftwaffe's air defenses were up against the wall by the early autumn of 1944. In his postwar memoir, Harris stated that German air defenses "crumbled to pieces" in September 1944.[89] The commander of the RAF's strategic force was not far off the mark with respect to nighttime air defenses. In the last three months of

1944, Luftwaffe flak defenses downed an average of only 18 aircraft per month during RAF night raids. Likewise, night fighters averaged a mere 31 aircraft destroyed per month during this period.[90] In the case of the night fighters, the crippling effects of the aviation fuel shortage allowed the Luftwaffe to operate only 50 fighters per night by the end of the year despite the fact that the night fighter force totaled 980 aircraft.[91] In addition, the Luftwaffe lost 1,295 night fighter pilots in 1944, over twice as many as in the previous year.[92] By December 1944, the debilitating loss of experienced pilots and the shortage of aviation fuel allowed the RAF finally to wrest control of the nighttime sky away from the Luftwaffe.

The State of the Flak Arm

By the autumn of 1944, the ground-based air defense force numbered 1,110,900 persons, with 448,700, or 40 percent, coming from outside the Luftwaffe. The non-Luftwaffe personnel included 220,000 Home Guard, Labor Service, and male high school auxiliaries; 128,000 female auxiliaries; and 98,000 foreign volunteers and prisoners of war.[93] The fact that 40 percent of the Luftwaffe's flak arm consisted of auxiliaries indicates the extent of the personnel crisis facing the German armed forces by the last year of the war. In August 1940, the Luftwaffe's flak arm had included 791 heavy flak gun batteries, 686 light flak gun batteries, and 221 searchlight batteries operated by a total of 528,000 regular and reserve Luftwaffe personnel.[94] Four years later, the size of the flak arm had increased to 2,655 heavy flak gun batteries, 1,612 light flak gun batteries, and 470 searchlight batteries.[95] Despite the fact that the total number of batteries had almost tripled, the number of service personnel had grown by only 134,000, while civilians, high school students, foreign nationals, and prisoners of war increasingly provided the basis for the Luftwaffe's battle against Allied bombers. In fact, flak units stationed within the Reich consisted of only 10 percent fully qualified regular military personnel by the latter stages of the war.[96]

In spite of the bombing campaign and the growing personnel shortage, the production of anti-aircraft weapons and equipment in the last two quarters of 1944 exceeded that in the first six months of the year in all but one category. Table 9.2 provides the quarterly production figures for several types of flak guns and searchlights in 1944.[97] These figures clearly demonstrate the continued availability of flak weapons and searchlights to support the ground-based air defense operations throughout 1944. The decline in the production of 105-mm guns occurred as the Luftwaffe shifted resources for the production of this weapon toward the more capable 88–mm/Model 41 and the 128-mm flak guns. Despite the continued availability of flak weapons, transportation emerged

Table 9.2 Flak Equipment Production Figures, 1944 (by quarter)

	1st	2nd	3rd	4th
20-mm flak	6,437	9,051	12,881	11,669
37-mm flak	1,112	1,763	2,708	2,646
88-mm flak (all types)	1,245	1,452	1,512	1,724
88-mm/model 41	36	46	94	114
105-mm flak	311	318	310	192
128-mm flak	124	151	187	202
150-cm S/L	756	785	1,024	743
200-cm S/L	502	626	681	640

as a nagging problem as it became increasingly difficult to move finished guns, equipment, and munitions to units at the front and within the Reich.[98]

Paradoxically, the increased production occurred in the face of a relatively constant level of resource allotments to the anti-aircraft forces. The percentage of the total Wehrmacht budget allocated to anti-aircraft weapons remained between 25 and 27 percent for the entire year. Likewise, expenditures on flak ammunition expressed as a percentage of the entire Wehrmacht munitions budget were 17 percent in the first quarter, 16 percent in the second quarter, 18 percent in the third quarter, and 20 percent in the fourth quarter.[99] The total percentage devoted to weapons production remained essentially constant, with a slight rise of 2 percent in the third quarter. Despite the constant nature of these expenditures, production rose significantly for both flak guns and searchlights in the final two quarters of 1944. Similarly, the percentage of resources devoted to flak ammunition rose slightly in the first half of the year but increased by 2 percent in each of the last two quarters in direct response to the growing shortage of flak ammunition.

Despite the increased output of weapons, the flak arm faced a number of serious problems by November. Without a doubt, the most pressing was the ammunition shortage. By the fall of 1944, the Luftwaffe's consumption of flak ammunition peaked at over 3.5 million rounds of heavy flak ammunition and over 12.5 million rounds of light flak ammunition per month.[100] The shortage of flak munitions arose as a result of a number of factors. First, Allied attacks on the German chemical industry affected the overall production of explosives, especially nitrogen, leading to increased use of inert fillers in ammunition production. Conversely, the decrease in explosive force reduced the effectiveness of individual rounds, which in part explains the increase in the number of rounds per aircraft destroyed in 1944.[101] Second, the attacks by Allied tactical and strategic air forces against transportation targets led to problems in moving available stocks of ammunition to operational units. In turn, the need to protect important transportation routes, including rail lines and waterways, exacerbated this problem by forcing the reapportionment of flak defenses from industrial targets to these lines of communication. For example, the Luftwaffe shifted 500 heavy flak guns from defense of arms factories to the protection of transportation routes and diverted another 350 heavy flak guns from November production for this purpose as well.[102] In addition, the Luftwaffe established a "flak belt" along the entire course of the Rhine to protect shipping on this vital waterway, including the use of river barges as mobile platforms for 20-mm and 37-mm flak guns.[103] Finally, the increased numbers of Allied aircraft in the skies over the Reich meant more available targets and hence a greatly increased volume of fire, necessitating even more ammunition. In this respect, the collapse of the Luftwaffe's fighter force proved doubly damaging as the flak arm struggled under the weight of an ever-increasing share of the air defense burden.

In addition to the lack of ammunition, the flak arm also experienced a shortage of optical and radar fire control equipment by October 1944. This situation contributed to a further rise in the number of heavy flak guns per battery. By raising the number of heavy guns per battery, the Luftwaffe was able to raise the volume of fire, as well as reduce the need for fire control equipment.[104] It should be noted, however, that the shortage of these devices resulted from increased anti-aircraft artillery production, not a decreased output of fire control equipment. In response, Hitler ordered the expanded production of gun-laying radar and optical fire directors as part of his plan for accelerated flak weapons, munitions, and equipment production in early November.[105]

In a Führer order of November 4, Hitler once again demonstrated his unswerving commitment to Germany's flak defenses by demanding a threefold increase in the production of heavy flak guns and a severalfold rise in the output of light flak guns, with these weapons to be concentrated within the Reich.[106] Hitler's order opened with the statement "In his terror attacks against the Reich, the enemy speaks of the hell of the German flak. Many of his plans have been thwarted by our concentrated flak defenses." He continued, "In order to make full use of this psychological and tactical momentum, it is necessary to strengthen the firepower of the flak defenses in every conceivable manner." Hitler also ordered increased flak munitions production and the accelerated pursuit of research initiatives involving flak guns and flak munitions.[107] This November Führer order can be interpreted in two ways. On the one hand, it can be seen as further evidence of Hitler's continued ardent, if not irrational, commitment to anti-aircraft defenses. On the other hand, it can be interpreted as a pragmatic measure. Indeed, flak defenses seemed to offer the only alternative at a time when the bulk of Germany's fighter force lay smashed across the landscape of Europe or sat with empty fuel tanks at airfields throughout the Reich. Undoubtedly, criticism of Hitler's earlier decisions to rely on the flak force as the primary guarantor of air defense contains a good deal of truth; however, by the late fall of 1944 there appeared to be little room for choice. With the battle for control of the nighttime skies over Germany already lost, the only remaining question was how long and how effectively could the Luftwaffe's anti-aircraft forces continue to provide protection during the day to the rapidly crumbling foundation of the "Thousand Year Reich."

Losing the Day Battle

The last four months of 1944 witnessed a substantial decline in the effectiveness of Germany's anti-aircraft defenses. Throughout September, the Luftwaffe's flak defenses remained a capable force for deterring the attacks of American heavy bombers. Eighth Air Force flak reports for September remarked on the "noticeable increase" in flak damages and losses. These reports attributed the improved effectiveness in large part to the Luftwaffe's concentration of flak defenses around key targets.[108] The monthly report from the 2nd Bombardment Division warned, "There is little doubt that, in the future, opposition from Flak will become more severe."[109] By the end of October, it was apparent that these fears had been exaggerated as the bombers experienced a "sharp reduction" in the number of losses due to flak.[110] Several factors contributed to the decrease in flak efficiency, including poor weather, a shortage of ammunition, and the decline in the effectiveness of gun-laying radar. A flak report compiled by the 1st Bombardment Division aptly summarized the problems being experienced within the Luftwaffe's flak arm:

> It becomes increasingly evident that it is the visual target which appeals to the Hun, and that at times he hardly even bothers to engage targets which are flying above 10/10ths cloud. His reasoning for this state of affairs may be that he is fully aware of his inability to overcome effectively the difficulties presented by the unseen target—difficulties which are now becoming even greater owing to the many and varied counter measures employed by our formations—added to which, the necessity for conserving ammunition (accentuated by local transport difficulties) and equipment, is probably a very real factor, resulting in comparatively stringent regulations restricting the engagement of targets when conditions are such that the chances of any kind of success appear remote.[111]

Despite the difficulties being experienced in engaging "unseen" targets, a raid by Eighth Air Force bombers against Pölitz on October 7 provided a stark reminder of the effectiveness of massed flak in visual conditions. During this raid, the 1st Bombardment Division sent 143 bombers against the oil facilities near the city. The flak defenses shot down 16 bombers, seriously damaged 43 aircraft, and inflicted light to moderate damage on a further 62 bombers. In other words, the bomber force had suffered a loss rate of over 11 percent and a damage rate of 73 percent.[112] Still, the success of the flak at Pölitz proved more the exception than the rule, and the performance of the Luftwaffe's flak defenses against the Eighth Air Force continued to decline throughout the remainder of the year. For example, the number of Eighth Air Force bombers destroyed by the flak in the last four months of 1944 fell from a high of 162 aircraft in September to 66 aircraft in October, then rose slightly to 90 in November but plummeted to 44 in December. Likewise, the number of bombers damaged by the flak fell from 4,522 in September to 2,630 in October, then rose to 3,339 in November before dropping to 1,987 in December.[113] These figures clearly illustrate the overall decline in the effectiveness of German flak defenses during this period. The increase in lost and damaged aircraft for November was an anomaly and can be explained by three separate raids against oil facilities at Merseburg (Leuna), resulting in the loss of 44 bombers and damage to 1,212 aircraft. Likewise, the precipitous decline in the December totals occurred in part because of poor weather, as well as the shift of Allied bombers to support ground forces in the last week of the year to stem an attempted German ground offensive in the Ardennes.[114]

In contrast to their Eighth Air Force counterparts, the bomber crews of the smaller Fifteenth Air Force continued to face stiff flak resistance in the last four months of 1944. The Fifteenth Air Force lost a total of 285 bombers destroyed and 2,244 damaged due to flak between September and December.[115] The continued success of German flak defenses against Fifteenth Air Force bombers resulted from two factors. First, between the end of August and early November, the command's strategic bombers provided considerable support to the Russian advance in the Balkans.[116] These missions included attacks against airfields, bridges, and transportation hubs. The need for lower bombing altitudes to improve accuracy against point targets such as bridges resulted in higher losses, especially among the command's B-24 force, which suffered 83 percent of the heavy bomber losses in the period.[117] Second, the Fifteenth Air Force heavy bombers continued to attack heavily defended oil and industrial facilities within Germany, including Austria.[118] Most of these targets were located in the vicinity of Vienna, a city defended by a formidable array of 418 heavy and 383 light flak guns.[119] Missions against the oil facilities at Brüx and targets in the vicinity of Vienna and Munich encountered concentrated flak defenses that were still capable of inflicting significant damage, especially in visual conditions.

By the end of 1944, the Allies had successfully wrested control of the skies over Europe from the Luftwaffe. The ultimate expression of the Luftwaffe's demise could be found in a simple phrase contained in a growing number of postmission pilot reports: "no enemy air opposition encountered."[120] Conversely, the absence of a credible and sustained fighter threat meant that the flak arm was forced to shoulder an increasing portion of the air defense burden. The withdrawal of flak defenses from German cities, a growing ammunition shortage, and an increasing reliance on inadequately trained auxiliaries placed the Luftwaffe's ground defenses at a disadvantage from which they would never recover. The 2nd Bombardment Division's monthly flak report for December provided a stark testament to the decline in the Luftwaffe's air defenses with the comment that "during the last three months of the year, . . . contrary to expectations, the enemy Flak deteriorated rapidly both in accuracy and intensity, and in conditions of 10/10th cloud few of the enemy guns opened fire even in areas as heavily defended as the Ruhr."[121] At one time, the flak defenses of the Ruhr had induced dread into the hearts of Allied aircrews; now they stood guard as silent and impotent sentinels as the bombers passed overhead. By December, the entire Reich lay open to devastating aerial bombardment by night and by day. In the last stage of the war, the flak arm fought a battle more reminiscent of Cannae than Thermopylae, as Allied field armies in the east and the west tightened the ring around the Reich and gathered their forces for the final push into Germany.

The Year 1944 in Review

At the beginning of 1944, the Luftwaffe had recovered from the shock of the summer of 1943. Both the fighter arm and the flak forces expanded to all-time highs in the first half of the year. Likewise, the Luftwaffe had prevented Bomber Command from destroying Berlin under a hail of incendiary bombs, thus handing Harris a resounding operational defeat. However, the "Battle of Berlin" proved a Pyrrhic victory for the Luftwaffe because Bomber Command proved able to replace losses that only eighteen months earlier would have been considered disastrous. Furthermore, the Eighth Air Force and the Fifteenth Air Force emerged as capable instruments for the conduct of daylight strategic bombardment, placing added stress on the fighter and flak forces assigned to protect the Reich. The invasion of France and the campaign against Germany's synthetic oil plants marked a decisive turning point in the war as the Luftwaffe's day and night fighter arms suffered from an increasing loss of experienced pilots and a debilitating deficiency of aviation fuel.

The "defeat of the Luftwaffe" in the summer of 1944 placed an increasing burden on the Luftwaffe's ground-based air defense forces to preserve the industrial infrastructure and to protect the civil population of the Third Reich.

In the pursuit of these objectives, passive defenses, including decoy and deception measures, continued to pay handsome dividends, while smoke generator units provided an important adjunct to the passive defenses. Still, in the end, it was the active anti-aircraft defenses, and not their passive counterparts, that would determine the ultimate success of the Luftwaffe's ground-based air defense efforts. Unfortunately for the Luftwaffe, the active anti-aircraft forces suffered from a variety of chronic problems, despite increased weapons production in the last half of 1944. On the one hand, the continued dilution of the regular force with auxiliaries, foreign volunteers, and prisoners of war lowered the qualitative performance of the flak arm. On the other hand, the growing shortage of fire control equipment, and especially ammunition, presented the flak arm with a painful dilemma. Likewise, the losses sustained in opposing the Allied invasion force and the loss of 100 heavy flak gun batteries, 110 light flak gun batteries, and 16 searchlight batteries during Hitler's gamble in the Ardennes in December reduced the numbers of weapons available for the defense of the Reich.[122] These losses, coupled with normal attrition and the inability to shift static gun defenses within Germany, presaged the collapse of the flak arm. By the end of 1944, Luftwaffe flak batteries increasingly were forced to withhold their fire in all but the most favorable firing conditions, a decision that preserved precious ammunition but accelerated the devastation of German industry and urban areas.

During 1944, the Luftwaffe's fighter arm died as a result of a number of heavy blows, while the flak defenses experienced the death of a thousand cuts. Despite the growing severity of the problems experienced by the ground-based air defenses, the flak defenses of the Reich and the occupied western territories had accounted for the destruction of 6,385 Allied aircraft while inflicting damage to more than 27,000 additional aircraft throughout the course of the year.[123] At the end of December, von Axthelm prepared his New Year's message to the men and women of the flak arm. He wrote:

> Men and women of the flak,
>
> The year 1944 has imposed heavy blows and trials on our people. We have succeeded in getting through them.
>
> Men and women of the flak! In the coming year, by day and night with every shot at the enemy's aircraft think of the murdered women and children, the razed and destroyed cities and villages, the demolished cultural sites of our people. And in close cooperation with our fighters, with unsurpassed zeal, with never-tiring energy and a committed will to duty you will achieve our goal, the breaking of the enemy air terror.[124]

The men and women of the flak arm must have read von Axthelm's words with a certain degree of incredulity and bitterness. They must have questioned whether zeal and nonexistent fighter formations could be expected to defeat the mass formations of Allied bombers. In truth, von Axthelm's message sounded more like an epitaph than an exhortation, a fitting end to a disastrous year.

The Final Act

At the beginning of 1945, Allied ground forces stood on the doorstep of the Reich. In the east, Soviet forces were massing for a planned two-phase offensive with the capture of Berlin as the ultimate goal. In the west, American, British, and Commonwealth forces were clearing the bulge caused by the German attack into the Ardennes, as well as pushing Wehrmacht forces back across the Rhine.[125] The strength of the USAAF and the RAF had risen to over 10,000 bombers and more than 13,000 fighters, a force capable of inflicting vast destruction while roaming at will across the skies of the Reich.[126] In the final assault on Germany, the Allies expected the Wehrmacht to defend tenaciously the German homeland, but it was equally clear that Hitler and his Reich would soon reap the bitter bounty of a whirlwind of his own sowing.

Ironically, in the last four months of the war the Luftwaffe's anti-aircraft defenses increasingly found themselves flung against tanks and not bombers as the ring of Allied ground armies closed around Germany.[127] One indication of the changed role of the flak involved the formation of flak assault batteries *(Flak-Sturm-Batterien),* units designed specifically for ground combat operations.[128] The flak arm began the new year as it had ended 1944 by shifting flak batteries from the Reich to a fighting front, only this time flak batteries were headed toward the east and not the west. During the last week of January, the Luftwaffe transferred 110 heavy and 58 medium and light flak batteries to bolster Wehrmacht defenses attempting to slow the Soviet offensive on Berlin.[129] These reinforcements could barely keep pace with escalating losses of personnel and equipment as Flak Corps I and II alone lost 575 88-mm guns and 512 20-mm guns between January 12 and January 31 opposing the Soviet advance.[130] On February 6, in response to the escalating losses, the Luftwaffe increased the number of heavy and medium/light flak batteries ordered to the east to a total of 327 and 110, respectively.[131] These batteries alone represented 21 percent of the heavy flak guns and slightly over 16 percent of the light flak guns protecting the Reich proper.[132] In sum, the Luftwaffe transferred a total of 555 heavy and 175 medium/light flak batteries to the fighting fronts during the last eight months of the war.[133] The mass transfer of flak batteries to the combat fronts in the closing stages of the war effectively stripped entire areas within Germany of their air defenses, opening these areas to unimpeded aerial attacks.

Death Throes of the Flak Arm

As increasing numbers of flak units were thrown into the ground battle, the Luftwaffe desperately sought to maintain the defenses of key targets within the rapidly shrinking Reich. Throughout 1944, the Luftwaffe had stripped numerous German cities of their flak batteries to reinforce the defenses of the synthetic oil facilities and a few select urban areas. By the first months of 1945, the practice of robbing Peter to pay Paul now extended to the flak defenses of Berlin and Hamburg. On January 23, the Luftwaffe ordered the transfer of thirty heavy and thirteen light flak batteries from the defenses surrounding Berlin, and two weeks later the air staff disbanded the searchlight units surrounding the city to free more men for ground combat at the front.[134] Likewise, in the last week of January, the Luftwaffe withdrew flak batteries from the defense of Hamburg for duties at the front, despite the strenuous objections of the local National Socialist district leader.[135] By the middle of February, as the Soviet offensive rolled toward the Oder River, the need for artillery support even led to the weakening of flak defenses surrounding the critical synthetic oil plants.[136]

Despite the transfer of batteries to the east, the Luftwaffe's flak batteries continued to achieve good results in daylight visual conditions against Eighth Air Force bombers. The January flak report for the 2nd Air Division remarked that "the flak at most strategic targets, with few notable exceptions, has been as intense and accurate as ever whenever visual conditions existed."[137] The monthly report of the 3rd Air Division confirmed this appraisal by observing that "well defended targets continue to put up effective flak when attacked under visual conditions."[138] In addition, the Luftwaffe's night fighter force experienced a temporary resurgence by scoring 117 aircraft destroyed in January.[139] In contrast, the Luftwaffe day fighter force continued on its downward spiral despite the increased appearance of the jet fighter, the Messerschmitt 262 (Me 262). The lack of daylight fighter sorties against American bombers was due in large part to the Luftwaffe's concentration of its aircraft against Soviet forces in the east.[140] In fact, William Smith, a B-17 pilot, was amazed by the number of bomber pilots he met who told him that they had not seen a German fighter during their entire tour in the last months of the war.[141]

In February, the flak experienced its last significant aerial victories and its worst defeat. On February 3, the Eighth Air Force sent 1,003 bombers against Berlin in clear weather.[142] Luftwaffe fighters did not rise to meet the bombers and their escorts, and the city's flak batteries were left to carry the sole burden of defending the capital. In turn, these defenses threw up a "murderous" fire that claimed between 21 and 25 of the attacking bombers.[143] Likewise, in a clear-weather attack against oil facilities near Vienna on February 7, the Fifteenth Air Force lost between 19 and 25 bombers to the city's still formidable flak defenses.[144] The attacks on Berlin and Vienna proved that, even at this stage of the war, anti-aircraft defenses could exact a high toll on American bombers in attacks on heavily defended targets in visual conditions. In contrast to the successes achieved over Berlin and Vienna, a Bomber Command raid on the night of February 13 and a follow-up raid by the Eighth Air Force on February 14 devastated the city of Dresden in a firestorm reminiscent of Hamburg, leading to the deaths of an estimated 25,000 persons.[145] In one respect, the success by British bombers in achieving a tight concentration of bombs resulted from the Luftwaffe's previous decision to strip Dresden of its flak batteries to strengthen the defenses of other more important objectives. Although the presence of flak defenses might not have prevented the conflagration that arose in the ancient baroque city, it is conceivable that anti-aircraft fire might have prevented the RAF from achieving the massive concentration of incendiaries that eventually generated the devastating firestorm that engulfed the city. In any event, devoid of flak defenses, the city's inhabitants paid the ultimate price for the Luftwaffe's shell game involving the flak.[146]

As Allied ground forces advanced deep into Germany from the east and the west in March, the stresses on the Luftwaffe's ground-based air defenses reached the breaking point. Between January 12 and February 28, the Luftwaffe lost forty-one heavy and thirty-five light flak batteries alone in combat against Russian forces along the Oder front.[147] By March 11, the entire Wehrmacht, including the flak arm, suffered from a critical shortage of ammunition.[148] In a diary entry of March 21, Goebbels remarked that a large proportion of Berlin's flak forces had been sent to the front and that those flak units remaining behind had few ammunition reserves.[149] In fact, the flak arm was receiving only one-third of the ammunition it required by the last month of the war.[150]

In addition to the lack of munitions, a shortage of fuel and transportation forced the Luftwaffe to commandeer milk trucks and fire engines to shift Berlin's flak defenses within the city.[151] The fuel situation was no better for the fighter force as teams of oxen were used to pull Me-262 jet fighters to runways to conserve the fuel used by these aircraft in taxiing to their takeoff positions.[152] Another indication of the desperate state of affairs within the Luftwaffe was the training of a group of pilots for suicide ramming missions against the Allied bomber formations.[153] Recounting a meeting with Hitler, Goebbels aptly summed up the Reich's current situation in a diary entry of March 22:

> We keep returning to the same point in our discussion. Our entire military predicament can be traced back to the enemy's air superiority. In practice a coordinated conduct [of the war] is no longer possible in the Reich. We no longer have control over transportation and communications links. Not only our cities, but also our industries are for the most

part destroyed. . . . It is shortly before twelve, if the hands of the clock have not already passed midnight.[154]

One clear indication that the clock already had struck midnight was the fact that in March Bomber Command would fly more day sorties than night sorties within Germany for the first time since the opening months of the war.[155] By the end of March, the use of oxen and milk trucks lent the Luftwaffe's air defenses all the elements of an opéra bouffe; however, the final act remained to be played.

In April, the flak arm went from the farcical to the absurd as 3,000 flak personnel trapped in East Prussia were withheld from ground combat until they could be reequipped with flak weapons while fifty flak batteries composed entirely of women trained for combat.[156] Of these all-female flak batteries, only ten had sufficient time to complete the entire course of training and subsequently were employed in the Berlin defenses.[157] The organization of all-female flak gun batteries provided stark evidence of the severity of the personnel crisis within the Wehrmacht. Furthermore, these batteries represented the final sacrifice of the regime's ideological beliefs concerning the role of women in the face of a Götterdämmerung of its own making.

In the final weeks of the war, the ammunition shortage within the flak arm became acute. The critical situation led the Luftwaffe to test a projectile with a contact and timed fuse *(Doppelzünder)*, the same round that a member of Speer's ministry refused to support in 1944, based on safety considerations involved with the transportation of these munitions. During combat trials in Munich on April 9, heavy flak batteries using these rounds brought down thirteen aircraft at the cost of a mere 370 rounds per shootdown, an extraordinarily favorable ratio compared with the existing average of approximately 4,500 rounds.[158] However, more time and trials were needed to evaluate the performance of the dual-fused rounds, and time was a commodity that the Luftwaffe did not possess. Likewise, the use of the experimental Egerland radar in a gun-laying role drastically reduced the number of rounds expended per aircraft shot down to less than 300.[159] Although these results were impressive, the Luftwaffe had only two experimental Egerland radar sets by the end of the war.[160]

One indication of the Allied air forces' continued respect for German antiaircraft defense was the Fifteenth Air Force's conduct of two trial attacks against Luftwaffe flak positions on April 1 and April 19, 1945. During these attacks, flights of B-24s dropped 260-pound fragmentation bombs on flak positions from over 24,000 feet. The attacks were intended to reduce the "morale and accuracy of the gun crews" and to damage or destroy fire control equipment.[161] To be sure, these "flak-busting" missions had been attempted earlier in the war. Bomber Command crews experimented with this tactic during the raid on Hamburg in July 1943 by dropping antipersonnel bombs on anti-aircraft positions.[162] Likewise, the American tactical air forces conducted low-level attacks against flak positions using fighter-bombers and medium bombers after the Allies gained a foothold in Europe. Most pilots preferred any mission to the flak-busting sorties, and General Elwood "Pete" Quesada, the commander of the Ninth Air Force, commented that "flak-busting was like a man biting a dog."[163] Fortunately for Allied pilots, these missions proved the exception and not the rule as the war sped to a close.

On April 14, with less than a month remaining in the European war, the Luftwaffe became involved in a dispute with the army concerning control of its flak forces. In response to an army request that Luftwaffe flak forces be immediately subordinated to the Army High Command (OKH), the air staff vigorously objected to the proposed measure by arguing that the primary emphasis of the flak artillery needed to remain focused on the aerial threat versus a subordination to the army that would result in the use of the flak solely for ground combat operations.[164] In truth, ground combat and not air defense operations did constitute the primary duties of the flak arm in the remaining weeks of the war. After April 25, Eighth Air Force bombers would begin dropping food over Holland rather than bombs over Germany, while the Luftwaffe flak gun crews manning the 128-mm twin guns atop Berlin's flak towers traded artillery fire with the Red Army.[165] Ironically, at a time when Soviet forces stood before the gates of Berlin, the most heated battle involving the flak arm was being conducted between the leadership of the German army and air force. Perhaps fittingly, the final curtain call over the Reich ended as the opening act had begun, with a bureaucratic battle for control of the flak.

Conclusion

During the interwar period, active-duty and retired military members and civilian theorists debated the viability of air defenses in the age of the bomber. These analyses often included a discussion concerning the relative merits of anti-aircraft and fighter defenses. Some writers favored a reliance on fighters alone, while others argued for a concentration on flak defenses. However, the majority of participants in this debate advocated the use of a combination of flak and fighter defenses as the most effective and responsive means for protecting both industry and the German populace. With the ascension of the National Socialists to power and Hitler's grandiose plans for the rearmament of the Third Reich, the size and strength of all branches of the German military increased dramatically between 1933 and 1939. With respect to the Luftwaffe, the Wehrmacht's penchant for offensive operations resulted in the creation of an air arm best suited for the support of army operations in the field, a fact made evident in the skies over Britain in the summer of 1940.

As German tanks ground to a halt on the east coast of the English Channel in June 1940, the small RAF bombing effort proved more a nuisance than a threat, but Bomber Command raids demonstrated that the German homeland was not beyond the reach of modern aerial warfare. At the start of the war, primary responsibility for the protection of the Reich rested squarely on the shoulders of the Luftwaffe's flak arm. Hitler's unshakable faith in the efficacy of anti-aircraft defenses and Göring's patronage had resulted in the creation of the largest and best-equipped ground-based air defense force in the world by September 1939. However, it was soon apparent that the Luftwaffe's expectations exceeded the flak arm's capabilities despite the sums lavished on the creation of these forces in the years before the war.

In the first year and a half of the war, the RAF's decision to concentrate on nighttime bombing left the flak arm literally and figuratively firing in the dark. Throughout the conflict, the Luftwaffe searched for tactical, doctrinal, and technological solutions to the threat posed by the growing number of British, and later American, bombers appearing in the skies over Germany. However, despite a vast increase in numbers of people and major improvements in equipment, the flak arm would never achieve the level of success envisioned by the Luftwaffe leadership before the war. Still, the number of Allied aircraft damaged and destroyed by anti-aircraft fire, combined with the performance of other ground-based defenses, offers a persuasive case for the ultimate effectiveness of the Luftwaffe's flak arm.

Tallying the Results

The number of Allied aircraft shot down and damaged by German ground-based air defenses provides one of the most obvious benchmarks for evaluating the performance of the Luftwaffe's flak defenses during the war. Between July 1942 and April 1945, German flak defenses accounted for the destruction of an estimated 1,345 Bomber Command aircraft during night sorties, while Luftwaffe fighters brought down an estimated 2,278 Bomber Command aircraft.[1] According to these figures, Luftwaffe fighters enjoyed a 1.69 to 1 advantage over the flak arm; in other words, fighters accounted for 59 percent of Bomber Command's estimated losses, while flak accounted for the remaining 41 percent. Furthermore, between February 1942 and April 1945, Luftwaffe fighters damaged 163 bombers beyond repair, while the flak accounted for 151 aircraft determined to be damaged beyond repair, a ratio of 1.08 to 1 in favor of the fighters. In the same period, German flak defenses damaged 8,842 bombers, while fighters damaged 1,731 aircraft, a ratio of 5.1 to 1 in favor of the flak. Expressed as a percentage of all night sorties during the period, flak batteries inflicted damage on 3.5 percent of all bombers dispatched.[2] It is important to note that the actual percentage is much higher if one eliminates those aircraft that aborted their missions or failed to reach their targets.

In comparison to their British counterparts, flak defenses accounted for over half of the USAAF's combat losses during the war in Europe, downing almost 5,400 aircraft compared with the 4,300 aircraft shot down by Luftwaffe fighters.[3] The Eighth Air Force lost a total of 1,798 aircraft to flak during the war.[4] This number represents approximately 31 percent of Eighth Air Force bomber losses during the war due to all causes, including weather, accidents, mechanical malfunctions, and fighter attacks.[5] In comparison with the Eighth Air Force, estimates by the Mediterranean Allied Air Forces (MAAF) concerning the proportion of aircraft lost to flak are significantly higher for this theater. In terms of all types of aircraft (fighters, medium bombers, and heavy bombers), the MAAF lost 2,076 aircraft to flak compared with 807 brought down by enemy aircraft in the period between January 1944 and February 1945, a ratio of 2.6 to 1 in favor of the flak.[6] Specifically, the Fifteenth Air Force lost 1,046 heavy bombers to flak between its activation in November 1943 and its final bombing mission in May 1945. The heavy bombers lost to flak represented 44 percent of all Fifteenth Air Force heavy bomber losses.[7] Approximately 10 percent of these losses occurred during attacks on the oil facilities in the vicinity of Ploesti, the "graveyard of bombers," the vast majority as a result of flak.[8] In addition to the strategic air forces' loss of heavy bombers, Luftwaffe flak defenses claimed a total of 2,415 aircraft from the Ninth Air Force and the Twelfth Air Force.[9]

In comparison to Allied estimates, the official German tally of American aircraft lost to fighters and flak over Europe between August 1942 and June 1944 stands at 1,682 and 905 aircraft, a ratio of 1.86 to 1 in favor of the fighters.[10] Expressed as a percentage, this ratio equates to 65 percent for the fighters and 35 percent for the flak. Unfortunately, Luftwaffe figures are unavailable for the last nine months of the war; however, the ratio favoring fighter to flak losses certainly decreased from the summer of 1944 onward, with the emergence of anti-aircraft fire as the main threat to the bombers.[11] In the end, flak accounted for approximately 50 percent of the combat losses for American heavy bombers during the war; however, the number of flak shootdowns pales in comparison to the number of USAAF aircraft damaged by German flak defenses.

The total number of Eighth Air Force aircraft damaged by flak fire between December 1942 and April 1945 was an astounding 54,539, or slightly more than 20 percent of all sorties dispatched.[12] For Fifteenth Air Force heavy bombers, flak damaged a total of 11,954 aircraft, or 8.5 percent of all sorties dispatched.[13] Clearly a great deal of this damage was superficial and could be repaired quickly, in many cases by simply covering the hole with a piece of sheet metal. However, when one considers the percentage of aircraft designated as "seriously damaged" by flak, the effectiveness of these defenses becomes more readily apparent. For example, between May 1944 and March 1945, the 1st Bombardment Division (later 1st Air Division) recorded 4,115 aircraft as having received "serious damage" out of a total of 15,042 aircraft damaged by flak. In other words, slightly over 27 percent of all aircraft struck by flak fire were seriously damaged.[14] Assuming that this percentage of seriously damaged aircraft is representative for the entire command, the total number of "seriously damaged" aircraft between December 1942 and March 1945 was a staggering 14,889. Furthermore, if one assumes that a mere 5 percent of aircraft listed as seriously damaged were damaged beyond repair, this number comes to an additional 744 bombers destroyed by the flak, a number that is almost half as great as the estimated number of Eighth Air Force flak losses. With respect to German estimates of flak damage, it is important to point out that German sources calculated that flak damaged 20,455 American aircraft over Europe between August 1942 and June 1944. This total is in fact 5,852 less than the actual number of Eighth and Fifteenth Air Force heavy bombers damaged by flak alone, not including damage to medium bombers and fighters, and provides clear evidence of the Luftwaffe's general underestimation of the damage being done by its flak forces to the American bomber formations.[15]

Finally, in addition to British and American flak losses, the Soviet air force also suffered thousands of aircraft losses to German anti-aircraft fire on the Eastern Front. In the opening six months of the invasion of Russia, Luftwaffe flak defenses accounted for the destruction of 1,891 aircraft.[16] Likewise, estimates of Soviet losses on the Eastern Front due to anti-aircraft fire totaled more than 2,000 aircraft between January 1944 and February 1945 alone.[17] During the course of the war, the Soviets lost an estimated 17,000 aircraft to Luftwaffe, army, and SS flak defenses in the east.[18] The vast majority of the Soviet losses occurred in close proximity to forward fighting fronts; however, Soviet long-range bombers did conduct over 7,000 sorties against targets within Germany and countries aligned with the Axis between 1941 and 1945.[19]

Ground-based Air Defenses: A Holistic View

Without doubt, anti-aircraft batteries were an integral component of the Luftwaffe's ground-based air defense network; however, to focus on the flak alone is a mistake. Many in the upper echelons of the Luftwaffe leadership, including Göring, Milch, and von Axthelm, demonstrated a limited understanding of the broader outlines and effectiveness of Germany's ground-based air defenses. These men were repeatedly guilty of evaluating the performance of the Luftwaffe's air defenses using a simple binomial equation that compared flak versus fighter performance. This myopic focus led the Luftwaffe's leadership consistently to ignore or grossly underestimate the contributions of other elements of the ground-based air defenses. In fairness to the Luftwaffe, British and American intelligence officers were also guilty of underestimating the performance of German ground-based air defenses, and it was only through the efforts of U.S. and British operations analysts that these views changed by the end of the war. Still, throughout the war many Luftwaffe leaders often failed to recognize the outstanding returns achieved by decoy and deception measures at a relatively low level of investment, despite the large number of British and American bombs that fell on these sites at various times. Another example involved the critical support provided by searchlights to fighter forces at different stages of the conflict. In fact, without the Luftwaffe's considerable searchlight force, Herrmann's wild boar procedure would have been unworkable, and the success of flak gunnery at night would have been seriously diminished. In addition, both barrage balloons and smoke generator units effectively augmented the Luftwaffe's active defenses at various times. By the end of 1944, the former suffered a precipitous decline in efficacy, while the latter literally ran out of the chemicals needed to sustain "smoke" operations.

In the final analysis, any calculation of the effectiveness of the Luftwaffe's ground-based air defenses involves the consideration of a number of variables, the values of which changed over the course of the war. The inclusion of these variables in the "flak versus fighter" equation provides a far more accurate appraisal of the effectiveness of the Luftwaffe's ground-based air defenses than existing interpretations. In addition to a general failure to consider the contributions of the entire range of ground-based air defenses from the smoke generators to the searchlights, Luftwaffe leaders also ignored or underestimated the hidden effects of their flak defenses.

Flak's Hidden Effects

Those who were most disappointed by the performance of the Luftwaffe's flak defenses often failed to take into account the very real and important hidden effects of anti-aircraft fire. By far the most important of these attributes was the influence of flak on bombing accuracy. On the one hand, flak drove bombers to higher altitudes, thus decreasing bombing accuracy. On the other hand, anti-aircraft fire over the target induced British and American bomber pilots to initiate violent evasive maneuvering, a procedure that effectively prevented the bombing of point targets while significantly degrading the "accuracy" of area bombing. During early Eighth Air Force bombing operations, General LeMay complained that, as a result of evasive maneuvering on the final run-in to the target, American bombers were "throwing bombs every which way."[20] Likewise, at a conference in late March 1945, General Spaatz, the commander of the U.S. Strategic Air Forces, remarked that flak was the "biggest factor" affecting bombing accuracy.[21] A postwar Army Air Forces study concluded that 39.7 percent of the radial bombing error of American bombers occurred as a result of nerves, evasive action, and reduced efficiency due to flak. Additionally, the study attributed 21.7 percent of the radial error to increased bombing altitudes to avoid flak. In other words, 61.4 percent of American radial bombing error could be directly attributed to the Luftwaffe's flak defenses.[22] In the case of Bomber Command, flak defenses not only caused pilots to execute violent evasive maneuvering but also induced the phenomenon known as "creepback," a tendency that remained a problem for Bomber Command crews as late as March 1944.[23]

In addition to the effect of flak on bombing accuracy, aircraft damaged by flak fire often faced two additional problems caused by that damage. First, such aircraft often were unable to keep up with the bomber formation. Without the protection provided by the supporting fire from other bombers, these "stragglers" became easy prey for Luftwaffe fighter pilots, who viewed them as preferred victims for adding to their shootdown totals. In but one example, the monthly flak report for the 1st Bombardment Division of May 1943 noted that the division had lost five aircraft to flak and an additional five aircraft that were first crippled by flak and subsequently downed by fighters.[24] The USAAF's Operations Analysis section found that the experience of the bombers in the 1st Bombardment Division was far from an isolated occurrence. In a postwar report, the section noted, "It was only after interrogations of crew members of lost aircraft had begun that the true importance of flak as causing straggling with resultant vulnerability to enemy fighter attack became apparent."[25] Additionally, the fear of becoming a straggler constitutes one of the most prevalent themes in American aircrew memoirs. Although the concept of straggling did not apply readily to Bomber Command, which used "bomber streams," one still finds numerous accounts of aircraft that subsequently fell victim to fighter attack after first being damaged by flak. In this case, fires or smoke caused by flak damage helped to expose the bombers to the night fighters, while reduced maneuverability or the loss of speed as a result of flak damage provided night fighters with the nocturnal equivalent of the daytime straggler.

The second major hidden effect resulting from flak wounds involved the delayed effects of anti-aircraft damage. Most flak splinters were relatively small, often producing minor damage such as nicked fuel or oil lines.[26] The slow seepage of oil from an aircraft engine or gradual loss of fuel allowed some bombers to fly as far as their home bases before they were forced down. In contrast, numerous damaged bombers were able to fly on for only 10, 20, or 100 miles before succumbing to flak damage.[27] In many cases, stricken bombers chose Sweden and Switzerland and certain internment rather than risk a crash landing in Axis-controlled territory. In fact, almost 200 bomber crews were interned in these two countries by the end of 1944.[28] Likewise, bomber pilots often headed their damaged aircraft out over water and chose to ditch in the North Sea in the hopes of being picked up by the Royal Navy or the Air Sea Rescue Service. During the war, the RAF's Air/Sea Rescue Service saved 5,721 aircrew members alone, enough men to operate 572 B-17s or 817 Lancaster bombers.[29]

In the case of aircraft that crashed as a result of the delayed effects of flak, those that landed in neutral countries, and those that ditched in the sea, the absence of physical remains or the inability to credit a specific flak battery with a downed aircraft meant that many either were not claimed or counted as flak kills by German authorities. The existence and size of these groups point to a large number of hidden flak kills and highlight a major problem with Luftwaffe accounting procedures for aircraft destroyed by flak fire. The strict nature of German shootdown confirmation procedures provides one explanation for the disparate view of flak effectiveness between the RAF and German reports. In order to receive credit for a "confirmed" kill, Luftwaffe flak batteries were required to submit a number of items to the Luftwaffe's Shootdown Verification Commission. These included a standardized report from the flak battery claiming the shootdown, a deposition from at least one impartial witness, a sketch by the witness and the flak battery of the location of the supposed crash site, and physical remains of the wreckage.[30] In one respect, these guidelines prevented a gross inflation of claims and credit for aircraft destroyed; however, this policy placed a heavy burden of proof on the commanders of the Luftwaffe's flak batteries. This burden was even more pronounced in some air districts, such as Air District XI, which suffered disproportionately as a result of this policy. For example, the Luftwaffe proved extremely reticent in granting shootdown credit for aircraft that crashed over water, a not uncommon occurrence in Air District XI, which covered the city of Hamburg and the northern coast of Germany.[31] The rigorous guidelines for confirming shootdowns led to a situation in this air district whereby a total of 541 reported flak shootdowns were listed as "unconfirmed" as late as July 1944 based on the unavailability of sufficient supporting evidence.[32]

A final hidden effect induced by ground-based air defenses involved the psychological reactions of the aircrews forced to face flak and searchlights in their daily or nightly raids against the Reich. The constant flights into the teeth of Germany's most strongly defended areas began to take a physical and psychological toll on the crews of both Bomber Command and the United States Strategic Air Forces. The threat created by the flak batteries and the probing searchlights were two major sources of emotional stress for British airmen. Likewise, flak proved a chief source of stress for American aircrews. John Comer, an aerial engineer and gunner in a B-17, exclaimed, "Flak, while not nearly as dangerous as fighters, scared the hell out of me. When it was bursting around us I stood in my turret and cringed and shivered."[33] Another American ball turret gunner on a B-17 described his reaction to flak: "Sometimes that flak would come up and go 'whoooooomp'! It would force me right out of the seat when it burst. I'd get so mad that I'd sometimes turn the turret down toward the ground and 'boom, boom.' I'd put a few rounds down at the gunners. You weren't doing any good, of course, but it made me feel better."[34] One historian who surveyed the effects of mental and physical pressures on Allied aircrews noted, "While statistical data tended to show that German fighters actually put British and American airmen more at risk, many Allied veterans preferred to face almost anything rather than the threat of anti-aircraft guns over their targets."[35]

Without doubt, the mental stress engendered by prolonged or repeated exposure to German air defenses resulted in a wide variety of psychological reactions, both normal and abnormal. In 1943 alone, approximately 1,000 Bomber Command crew members were diagnosed with neurosis, and an additional 100 were categorized as exhibiting a "lack of moral fibre."[36] Like their RAF counterparts, American aircrews experienced many of the same physical and psychological stresses, including fighter attacks and flak barrages. American crews were spared the unique demands associated with night operations; however, the USAAF high-altitude bombing profiles, occasionally in excess of 30,000 feet, posed their own set of unique physiological demands. One psychiatric study of the experience of American aircrews between July 1942 and July 1943 noted, "In the spring of 1943 deeper penetrations were made and raids were begun against the German mainland. . . . At this point combat crews were brought face to face with the stern reality of their profession and more psychiatric casualties began to appear." The report also observed, "Watching close-in and constant enemy fighter attacks, flying through impenetrable walls of flak, seeing neighboring planes tumble out of control and at times explode in mid-air, returning with dead or seriously wounded on board and other such experiences imposed a severe and repeated stress which demanded a high degree of personal 'toughness' to tolerate."[37] Admittedly, the number of aircrew members suffering abnormal psychological reactions proved small; however, the terms "flak happy" and "Focke-Wulf jitters" became established expressions for describing those suffering from profound mental distress to those who simply displayed eccentricities or committed small errors. In the final analysis, flak was a significant, if not the only, cause of stress for Allied aircrews during their bombing raids over Europe.

Calculating the Costs of a "Kill"

The economic and matériel costs of maintaining the flak arm are often noted in much of the postwar literature as a justification for implying that the flak arm consumed a great deal of resources while providing a relatively small return. One of the most consistently cited examples of flak inefficiency is the contention that flak gunners expended an average of 16,000 rounds of 88-mm/Model 36-37 ammunition per aircraft destroyed in 1944. At a cost of 80 RM per round, this equated to 1,280,000 RM, or $512,000, per aircraft destroyed.[38] While technically accurate, using the figures for 1944 as a measure of flak effectiveness is equivalent to using share prices from the Dow Jones on October 25, 1929, the day after the infamous crash, as an indicator to track the performance of the stock market for the 1920s. A detailed analysis of the many factors that contributed to the rise in the expenditure of 88-mm ammunition in 1944 demonstrates that the figure of 16,000 rounds of 88-mm ammunition per aircraft shootdown was in many respects a statistical aberration.

The total of 16,000 rounds of 88-mm ammunition per shootdown in 1944 is biased by a number of factors. First, the overwhelming majority of German heavy flak guns in this period were 88-mm/Model 36-37.[39] These guns had an effective range of up to 26,000 feet, in excess of the B-24's average bombing altitude but near the lower limit of the B-17's normal bombing profile of between 24,000 and 27,000 feet.[40] Therefore, the Eighth Air Force's overwhelming use of B-17's over German targets in 1944 meant that the majority of Luftwaffe flak batteries were stretched to, or beyond, the limits of their effective engagement range.[41] Second, many batteries were forced to continue using guns that had been effectively degraded by firing beyond their normal operational lives.[42] This decreased firing accuracy because of excessive barrel wear and risked the danger of the guns exploding and killing or wounding the gun crews. Throughout 1944, the flak lost 380 88-mm flak guns per month as a result of excessive wear or destruction, a rate of consumption twice that of 1943 and nine times greater than in 1942.[43] In addition to the problem of limited ceilings and worn-out barrels, it is important to keep in mind that throughout 1944 there were an average 262 Home Guard heavy flak batteries operating within the Reich.[44] These units lacked sophisticated fire control equipment and were equipped only with 88-mm/Model 36-37 guns or modified 75-mm flak guns firing 88-mm ammunition. As a matter of necessity, these units used general barrage fire procedures. The number of the Home Guard batteries, combined with their relatively obsolescent equipment, also helps to explain the high number of rounds expended in 1944. Another factor was the Allied employment of improved electronic countermeasures, including the use of a "chaff-screening force," consisting of several bombers equipped with special dispensers, which improved the distribution of chaff and degraded German attempts at radar targeting.[45] Finally, the massive influx of auxiliaries into the flak arm in 1943 and 1944, combined with increasingly obsolescent weapons and equipment, degraded the qualitative performance of the 88-mm flak batteries and resulted in rising numbers of rounds per shootdown.

Perhaps the most telling example of this last point involves a comparison of the performance of the 128-mm gun with that of the 88-mm/Model 36-37. In the course of 1944, the number of 128-mm rounds per aircraft shootdown was 3,000, less than one-fifth the number expended by its 88-mm counterpart. The large disparity in shootdown per rounds expended between these flak guns was primarily a result of two factors. First, the 128-mm had an effective ceiling of 35,000 feet, well above the operational ceilings of all Allied bombers.[46] Second, and most important, regular Luftwaffe flak personnel operated every 128-mm flak gun battery and were considered the "cream" of the Luftwaffe's flak arm.[47] The performance of the 128-mm gun crews demonstrates the results that could be obtained with well-trained crews and high-quality equipment. Unfortunately for the Luftwaffe, by the end of 1944, there were only 31 two-barreled 128-mm guns and a further 525 single-barrel guns, approximately 5 percent of the total number of available heavy flak guns in the flak inventory.[48]

In contrast to the 1944 estimates of rounds expended per aircraft destroyed, the average number of rounds per shootdown over the course of the first twenty months of the war stood at 2,805 heavy flak rounds and 5,354 light flak rounds.[49] During November and December 1943, the flak arm averaged 4,000 rounds of heavy flak ammunition and 6,500 rounds of light flak ammunition per shootdown in a period in which the flak was battling to overcome the combined effects or Allied jamming efforts and poor weather.[50] Over the entire course of the war, one source estimated that the flak arm averaged 4,940 rounds of light flak ammunition and 3,343 rounds of heavy flak ammunition per shootdown. Using the latter figures, the cost of bringing down an aircraft with heavy flak totaled 267,440 RM, or $106,976, while the cost per aircraft brought down with light flak totaled 37,050 RM, or $14,820.[51] Admittedly, using flak munitions expenditures per aircraft destroyed provides only a very rough estimate of the total cost per aircraft shootdown. This estimate omits the value of the resources used in the manufacture of the weapons and their associated equipment, as well as the costs associated with training flak personnel. Likewise, it is difficult to establish a direct comparison between the cost of a fighter kill and a flak kill because there were enormous hidden costs associated with the design, production, and operation of fighter aircraft. In the case of fighters, one must take into account the infrastructure costs associated with the construction and maintenance of airfields, aircraft upkeep and repair, fuel costs, as well as the expenditure involved in pilot training with its specialized training and hundreds of flight hours.

One method by which the cost of an individual flak kill can be placed in perspective involves examining the production costs of some of the aircraft that they were intended to destroy. For example, the cost of a fully outfitted B-17 was approximately $292,000, while a fully equipped B-24 cost approximately $327,000 in 1942.[52] In comparison to the heavy bombers, the unit cost of a North American B-25 and Martin B-26 medium bomber in 1942 was $153,396 and $239,655, respectively.[53] These unit production costs for the medium bombers do not include expenditures for maintenance, ordnance, and fuel or the costs associated with training the bomber aircrews. In any event, it is apparent that a cost of $107,000 per shootdown for the heavy flak guns and $15,000 per shootdown for the light flak guns was not excessive in comparison with the costs involved in the production of these aircraft. However, the entry into the war of the United States, with its vast economic resources and massive production potential, allowed the Allies in many respects to conduct a war of financial attrition against the Axis powers, a type of war that the Luftwaffe was ill prepared to wage.

Germany's "Lost Divisions"?

In addition to the question of the cost-effectiveness of the flak, an associated criticism of the flak concerns the high personnel requirements of the flak arm. General von Axthelm estimated that ground-based air defenses employed approximately 1.2 million persons by the end of the war.[54] Without doubt, the Luftwaffe's flak and searchlight batteries absorbed a great number of people; however, the contention that these persons could have been used to establish hundreds of additional Wehrmacht divisions is flawed for several reasons. First, by April 1945, fully 44 percent of those serving with the flak arm were either civilians or auxiliaries, including factory workers, prisoners of war, foreign nationals, and high school students. Furthermore, of the regular service personnel serving with the flak, 21 percent were between the ages of thirty-nine and forty-eight, and a further 35 percent were older than forty-eight or medically exempted from combat duty.[55] Second, this "lost divisions" argument fails to consider the fact that a large proportion of the active Luftwaffe flak formations were in fact engaged in combat activities at the fighting fronts; the operations of Flak Corps I and Flak Corps II in the campaign against France and the Low Countries in 1940 offer but one example.[56] Finally, based on its geographic position and the scale of the Allied bombing effort, the Luftwaffe required a substantial ground-based air defense force within the Reich for both military and political reasons regardless of the heavy personnel demands made by the flak arm. The military simply had to defend the Reich's industrial infrastructure and urban centers, and that required a sizable ground-based air defense force. Similarly, political considerations involving public opinion dictated the presence of flak defenses, a point made explicit by the many complaints lodged by National Socialist district leaders when these defenses were withdrawn from their districts or viewed as being insufficient. Likewise, Hitler remembered the disastrous effects of the collapse of morale on the home front in World War I, and he clearly recognized the public's psychological need to see, or at least hear, German forces battling the hated Allied bombers.[57]

A variation of the "lost divisions" argument can be found in the contention that the flak arm absorbed an estimated 250,000 to 300,000 persons in the production of anti-aircraft weapons and equipment.[58] This statement, however, must be placed in context. By August 1944, Germany employed over 7.5 million forced laborers in a variety of roles, ranging from agricultural tasks to industrial production. Likewise, well over 25 percent of forced laborers worked in industries critical to armaments production.[59] It is not possible to determine the exact number of foreign nationals and prisoners of war included in the estimate of those employed in the production of flak armaments, but the total quite likely reached into the tens of thousands. Furthermore, the widespread mobilization of women into industrial production, as well as the use of men who were medically disqualified from military service, would have further reduced the number of available men from this pool who were fit for combat duties. Finally, by the end of the war, the National Socialist leadership had repeatedly combed through the pool of industrial workers in the search for Wehrmacht replacements, leaving very few able-bodied workers in all but the most critical areas.

Opportunity Costs I: Flak Artillery versus Field Artillery

If the flak arm did not rob the Wehrmacht of a vast manpower reserve, the creation of thousands of batteries of anti-aircraft artillery did have an effect on the production of field artillery by consuming resources for flak production that might have been used to manufacture artillery for German forces in the field. In his postwar memoir, Albert Speer remarked:

> Our heaviest expense was in fact the elaborate defensive measures. In the Reich and in the western theaters of war the barrels of ten thousand anti-aircraft guns were pointed toward the sky. The same guns could have well been employed in Russia against tanks and other ground targets. Had it not been for this new front, the air front over Germany, our defensive strength against tanks would have been about doubled, as far as equipment was concerned.[60]

In one respect, Speer's contention seems odd in light of his earlier statement to the Fighter Staff in August 1944 that industry had achieved "production records" with respect to the artillery program that were eight to ten times greater than the figures for 1941.[61] Still, it was true that, barring the need for flak guns, more artillery pieces could have been produced. In fact, one USSBS report estimated that "since caliber for caliber anti-aircraft equipment requires about twice as much labor as an army gun, . . . the strength of the artillery might have been almost doubled if production of heavy anti-aircraft guns had not been necessary."[62]

A more detailed comparison of flak artillery versus field artillery production reveals that in January 1943 the Wehrmacht spent 64 million RM, or $25.6 million, on army guns compared with 39 million RM, or $15.6 million, on anti-aircraft artillery, a ratio of 1.64 to 1 in favor of army weapons. By December 1944, the amount spent on army guns almost tripled to 180 million RM, or $72 million, compared with 87 million RM, or $34.8 million, for anti-aircraft artillery, a ratio of 2.07 to 1 in favor of army guns.[63] With respect to the number of guns produced, in December 1943, German industry manufactured approximately 1,020 light and heavy field artillery pieces ranging in caliber from 75-mm to 210-mm balanced against 570 anti-aircraft artillery pieces ranging from 88-mm to 128-mm. In addition, the armaments industry produced slightly more than 1,300 tank, antitank, and self-propelled guns in the same month. By December 1944, the number of heavy and light field artillery pieces produced rose to 1,360, while the output of heavy flak guns increased to 700. Likewise, the army received another 2,200 tank, antitank, and self-propelled guns in December 1944.[64] In December 1943, the army received 2,320 artillery and tank guns compared with 570 heavy flak guns, a ratio of 4 to 1 in favor of army artillery production. Twelve months later, the army obtained some 3,560 artillery and tank guns, while the Luftwaffe acquired 700 heavy flak guns, a ratio of 5 to 1 in favor of army guns.

The preceding comparison certainly does not alter the fact that more artillery pieces could have been produced had the Wehrmacht moved resources away from the production of flak guns; however, these figures show that production of artillery and tank guns clearly favored the army, even as late as December 1944, despite the emphasis on increasing the size of the flak force. In fact, one USSBS report found that Wehrmacht ground forces were better armed at the beginning of 1944 than at the start of the war against the Soviet Union, although the artillery situation, not including antitank and self-propelled guns, was viewed as "slightly poorer."[65] Furthermore, in November 1944, fully 45 percent of the Luftwaffe's 88-mm flak guns were located in the occupied western territories, in Italy, or on the Eastern Front, with a great number of these weapons being used for ground combat support instead of anti-aircraft protection.[66] Similarly, the Luftwaffe transferred 100 heavy flak batteries to support the Ardennes offensive in December 1944 and over 300 heavy flak batteries to the Eastern Front in January and February 1945 primarily for use as antitank and artillery weapons.[67] In this respect, production of flak artillery offered an added bonus, as these weapons could be used for both air and ground combat, whereas field artillery pieces were suited for ground operations alone.

In addition to production figures, it is also necessary to note that Wehrmacht doctrine favored the tank at the expense of artillery. In fact, it was mobility and not firepower that was intended to propel German ground forces to victory.[68] The doctrinal predisposition to favor armor at the expense of field artillery provides an important contextual factor that helps explain the Wehrmacht's priorities with respect to field and anti-aircraft artillery. In the end, the production of flak artillery and field artillery required the Wehrmacht to decide between competing priorities. In turn, the allocation of artillery production between the army and the Luftwaffe appears adequately to have balanced the conflicting demands between armies at the fronts and Luftwaffe forces protecting against a growing Allied aerial armada.

Opportunity Costs II: Flak Munitions versus Artillery Munitions

In the last year of the war, it was munitions and not artillery tubes that proved the greatest concern to the Wehrmacht leadership. According to one USSBS report, the Allied attacks against the synthetic oil facilities and hydrogenation plants not only affected Germany's fuel situation but also "had a profound effect on Germany's powder and explosives production." By February 1945, munitions output had dropped to approximately one-third of the level in October 1944, engendering critical shortages of both flak and field artillery ammunition.[69] At this time, it was clear that every flak round produced meant that fewer rounds of field artillery could be manufactured for the German army. Still, in the first four years of the war, flak munitions production did not appreciably detract from the manufacture of other munitions. In 1943 and 1944, the cost of heavy flak artillery ammunition represented only 9 percent of the total value of all ammunition production.[70] Likewise, between 1942 and 1944, the production of 88-mm flak ammunition remained essentially static despite a 250 percent increase in the production of 88-mm flak artillery pieces.[71] Furthermore, only about 20 percent of all ammunition (70-mm and above) produced in 1944 was used by the flak arm.[72]

According to the Economic Effects Division of the USSBS, the production of anti-aircraft weapons and ammunition did not constitute a sacrifice in terms of the manufacture of other weapons and equipment prior to 1943.[73] Admittedly, this situation had changed by 1945 as the output of flak shells was maintained at the expense of the field artillery.[74] During the last six months of the war, the devotion of munitions production to the flak arm certainly resulted in a decrease in the availability of munitions to the army, but two points must be kept in mind. On the one hand, the increasing presence and numbers of Allied aircraft over Europe by the beginning of 1945 demanded that the flak arm continued to be supported, even at the expense of the forces in the field. On the other hand, the Luftwaffe's flak forces themselves were increasingly called upon to support ground operations by employing their ammunition reserves against tanks and advancing Allied armies. As in the case of the trade-off between the flak artillery and the field artillery, it is difficult to determine the exact nature of the opportunity costs associated with the production of flak munitions during the final months of the war. However, by the end of 1944 the Wehrmacht found itself caught between the proverbial rock and a hard place, where the iron rules of production reduced the range of available options in a system teetering on the edge of economic collapse.

The High Costs of Unfulfilled Expectations

The political and military leadership of the Luftwaffe entered World War II with high expectations of the flak arm. The performance of the flak in the last year of World War I, coupled with interwar technological advances and the rapid growth of the flak arm in the late 1930s, led to the creation of an elite force by the beginning of World War II.[75] Both the growth of the flak arm and the sense of being an elite military formation owed a great deal to Hitler's ardent support of the flak and his conviction that the flak arm represented the primary element of the Luftwaffe's air defenses. In the first months of the war, the performance of flak and fighter defenses appeared to validate the Luftwaffe's concept of air defense, as these defenses soon forced the RAF and the French air force to abandon the daytime skies over Europe. But Bomber Command's shift to nighttime raids proved a mixed blessing for the Reich's air defenses because the Luftwaffe lacked a fighter force capable of operating effectively during periods of darkness at the start of the war. Additionally, the night gunnery of the flak batteries proved abysmal and remained so throughout the first year of the war. In truth, it was only the small size of the RAF's bombing effort in 1939–1940 that provided the flak arm with sufficient time to pursue technological and tactical initiatives that would greatly improve the performance of the flak batteries by the end of 1941.

Between January 1942 and July 1943, the flak arm steadily improved its performance and emerged as a capable force despite the problems engendered by a threefold expansion in size and worrying signs of a personnel crisis. At this point in the war, the Luftwaffe's decision to rely on the flak arm as the main line of air defense appeared to be paying dividends, if not the high returns that a larger fighter force might have provided. However, the growth of Bomber Command and the increasing numbers of American bombers arriving in England, combined with the use of active and passive electronic countermeasures, delivered a near-fatal blow to the Luftwaffe's flak force in the summer of 1943. The precipitous decline in the performance of the flak in the last half of 1943 resulted in a general loss of faith in the anti-aircraft arm among the Luftwaffe's leadership. Milch saw the decline in the performance of the flak as the justification of his long-held doubts concerning the effectiveness of ground-based air defenses. Likewise, Göring suddenly reversed his prior support of the flak arm and increasingly expressed his bitterness and disappointment with the flak through numerous quips and slights during his marathon sessions with his air force leaders. By October 1943, even the flak's senior general questioned the efficacy of the force under his command. By the end of 1943, the behavior of the Luftwaffe leadership betrayed the downside to high hopes: the expression of equally profound disappointment in the face of unfulfilled expectations.

During the low point of flak success in the last half of 1943, Hitler alone remained unswerving in his support for the Luftwaffe's anti-aircraft forces. The American introduction of daylight fighters capable of escorting bombers to Berlin and back, coupled with the Luftwaffe's introduction of effective antijamming measures, seemed to justify the Führer's faith in the flak by the summer of 1944. As American fighters increasingly swept the skies over Europe free of Luftwaffe fighters and as the Reich's fuel reserves fell, the flak arm found itself carrying an ever-greater share of the air defense burden as it had done in the first years of the war. However, by the middle of 1944, the British and American bombing effort had reached a scale that would have been unimaginable to Luftwaffe leaders as late as 1940; concentrated flak defenses might still be able to inflict heavy damage on an attacking force in favorable weather conditions, but by themselves they could not hope to hold back the massive British and American aerial armada nor the iron ring closing around Germany as Allied ground forces advanced in the east and the west.

Measures of Success

Perhaps the single greatest factor that prevented the flak arm from fulfilling the expectations of the Reich's political and military leadership was the standard used to determine the success of the Luftwaffe's ground-based air defenses. At the beginning of the war, the Luftwaffe evaluated the effectiveness of the flak arm primarily on the basis of the number of aircraft destroyed. Although a clear and quantifiable standard for measuring performance, this number proved an inappropriate yardstick for gauging the overall contributions of ground-based air defenses to the protection of the Reich. In comparison, the most appropriate measure for judging the efficacy of the flak was the ability of ground-based defenses to prevent the bombers from accurately striking their intended targets. This standard was, however, more ambiguous and required the consideration of numerous variables and second-order effects. For men like Milch and even von Axthelm, numbers of aircraft destroyed, and not effects, mattered. This was an iron standard that obscured the achievements of the ground-based air defenses and shaped the opinions of these men and others within the Luftwaffe leadership concerning the success of the flak arm throughout the war.

Ground-based Air Defenses: A Final Appraisal

Prior to World War II, Luftwaffe doctrine recognized that both flak and fighters were integral elements in a coordinated air defense network. Despite this doctrinal prescription, the flak arm clearly entered the war as the primary instrument *(Hauptträger)* of the Luftwaffe's homeland air defenses. With good reason, numerous participants in the air war, as well as postwar historians, have identified the failure of the Luftwaffe to increase the size of its fighter force in 1941 as the turning point in the battle for air superiority over Germany. In retrospect, it is apparent that, ceteris paribus, a decision to pursue increased fighter and pilot production in 1941 would have improved the position of the Luftwaffe in later years. However, the Luftwaffe chose instead to rely on its ground-based air defenses. As the Allied air offensive intensified in the final two years of the war, the flak arm clearly failed to meet the high expectations placed on it by the Luftwaffe leadership. In the historical record, the flak arm has paid for its failure to meet these expectations far more severely than it deserved. The myopic focus on the benefits of a fighter force has produced a literature that often fails to consider the many hidden, and admittedly often nonquantifiable, effects of the flak arm. Furthermore, a tendency to focus solely on the flak batteries has obscured the varied and important contributions of other elements within the Luftwaffe's ground-based air defenses. In the end, Hitler's vision of a flak battery protecting every German town and village proved as illusory as his quest for a millenarian empire. The Luftwaffe's ground-based air defenses, by themselves, could not prevent the devastation of Germany from the air; however, this failure should not obscure the significant contributions made by these defenses between 1939 and 1945. The events of 1939–1945 clearly demonstrated that the air war could not be won with ground-based defenses alone, but these events make it equally apparent that without these defenses, German cities and factories quickly would have been bombed into ruins. After the war, the commanding general of the USAAF, General Henry "Hap" Arnold, observed, "We never conquered the German flak artillery."[76] In the end, it did not matter because the flak arm could not change the fate of the Reich nor save German cities and industry from destruction. Nevertheless, the efforts and performance of these defenses clearly deserve more credit than they have received.

Notes

Introduction

1. USSBS, Civil Defense Division, *The United States Strategic Bombing Survey: Civil Defense Division Final Report* (Washington, D.C.: GPO, 1945), 2.

2. USSBS, Strategic Bombing Survey Team, *The United States Strategic Bombing Survey: Summary Report* (Washington, D.C.: GPO, 1945; reprint, Maxwell AFB, Ala.: Air University Press, 1987), 5–6.

3. Major works dealing with this aspect of Luftwaffe operations include Asher Lee, *The German Air Force* (New York: Harper and Brothers, 1946); Richard J. Overy, *The Air War, 1939–1945* (New York: Stein and Day, 1981); Williamson Murray, *Strategy for Defeat: The Luftwaffe, 1933–1945* (Maxwell AFB, Ala.: Air University Press, 1983); Peter Hinchliffe, *The Other Battle: Luftwaffe Night Aces Versus Bomber Command* (Osceola, Wis.: Motorbooks International, 1996).

4. One significant exception is Horst-Adalbert Koch, *Flak: Die Geschichte der deutschen Flakartillerie, 1939–1945* (Bad Nauheim: Verlag Hans-Henning Podzun, 1954). Koch provides a largely descriptive account of the German flak forces in a work augmented by one hundred pages of appendixes.

5. BBSU, *The Strategic Air War Against Germany, 1939–1945: Report of the British Bombing Survey Unit* (London: Frank Cass, 1998), 50. The BBSU was the British counterpart to the USSBS. In his introduction to the public release of the BBSU report, Sebastian Cox, the head of the Air Historical Branch, remarked that this "seems a dubious statement at best."

6. Ibid., 97–98; see also USSBS, *United States Strategic Bombing Survey: Report on the German Flak Effort Throughout the War* (n.p., 1945), 1, 4–5, collection of the Air Force Historical Research Agency. The BBSU estimated that regular artillery production might have been almost doubled if the large-scale flak program had not been pursued.

7. Stephen L. McFarland and Wesley P. Newton, *To Command the Sky: The Battle for Air Superiority over Germany, 1942–1944* (Washington, D.C.: Smithsonian Institution Press, 1991), 120; see also Horst Boog, *Die Deutsche Luftwaffenführung, 1935–1945: Führungsprobleme, Spitzengliederung, Generalstabsausbildung,* Beiträge zur Militär- und Kriegsgeschichte (Stuttgart: Deutsche Verlags-Anstalt, 1982), 212–213.

8. Charles Webster and Noble Frankland, *The Strategic Air Offensive Against Germany, 1939–1945,* vol. 4, *Annexes and Appendices* (London: Her Majesty's Stationery Office, 1961), 308.

9. McFarland and Newton, *To Command the Sky,* 54.

10. Webster and Frankland, *Strategic Air Offensive,* 4:432–433.

11. Richard J. Overy, *Why the Allies Won* (New York: Norton, 1995), 131.

12. USSBS, Economic Effects Division, *The United States Strategic Bombing Survey: The Effects of Strategic Bombing on the German War Economy* (Washington, D.C.: GPO, 1945), 187.

13. Webster and Frankland, *Strategic Air Offensive,* 4:343.

14. USSBS, *United States Strategic Bombing Survey: Report on the German Flak Effort Throughout the War,* 4–5.

15. Albert Kesselring, *Gedanken zum Zweiten Weltkrieg* (Bonn: Athenäum-Verlag, 1955), 171.

16. Wolfgang Schumann and Wolfgang Bleyer, *Deutschland im zweiten Weltkrieg,* vol. 5, *Der Zusammenbruch der Defensivstrategie des Hitlerfaschismus an allen Fronten (Januar bis August 1944)* (Cologne: Pahl-Rugenstein Verlag, 1984), 146.

17. Hinchliffe, *Other Battle,* 66. These figures are based on the period from January to September 1941. The proportion of searchlight-assisted night fighter shootdowns fell to 15 percent in 1942, largely as a result of the withdrawal of searchlight batteries from the occupied western territories to the Reich proper. See Gordon Musgrove, *Operation Gomorrah: The Hamburg Firestorm Raids* (London: Jane's, 1981), 22.

18. Martin Middlebrook, *The Schweinfurt-Regensburg Mission* (New York: Scribner's, 1983), 117.

19. Harry H. Crosby, *A Wing and a Prayer: The "Bloody 100th" Bomb Group of the U.S. Eighth Air Force in Action over Europe in World War II* (New York: HarperCollins, 1993); Gerald Astor, *The Mighty Eighth: The Air War in Europe as Told by the Men Who Fought It* (New York: Donald I. Fine Books, 1997); Geoffrey Perret, *Winged Victory: The Army Air Forces in World War II* (New York: Random House, 1993); and Philip Ardery, *Bomber Pilot* (Lexington: University Press of Kentucky, 1978). These works are but a small sampling of available literature that refers to this subject.

20. Asher Lee, *Goering: Air Leader* (London: Duckworth, 1972), 141.

21. Wilhelm von Renz, *The Development of German Anti-aircraft Weapons and Equipment of All Types up to 1945* (Maxwell AFB, Ala.: Historical Division, 1958), 259, K113.107-194, AFHRA.

22. "Besprechung beim Reichsmarschall, Thema: Heimatverteidigungsprogramm [October 7–8, 1943]," RL 3/Folder 60/Pages 666–667, BA-MA.

23. Webster and Frankland, *Strategic Air Offensive,* 4:429.

24. Charles W. McArthur, *History of Mathematics,* vol. 4, *Operations Analysis in the U.S. Army Eighth Air Force in World War II* (Providence, R.I.: American Mathematical Society, 1990), 37, 79.

25. Ibid., 286.

1. The Great War and Ground-based Air Defenses, 1914–1918

1. Melvin Kranzberg, *The Siege of Paris, 1870–1871: A Political and Social History* (Ithaca, N.Y.: Cornell University Press, 1950), 37–38. The most famous of these escapes involved Leon Gambetta, the Commune's minister of the interior, in October 1870.

2. Ian V. Hogg, *Anti-Aircraft: A History of Air Defence* (London: MacDonald and Jane's Publishers, 1978), 13. The gun could be elevated up to 85 degrees and rotated through 360 degrees.

3. Germany, Reichsluftfahrtministerium, Kriegswissenschaftliche Abteilung der Luftwaffe, *Die deutschen Luftstreitkräfte von ihrer Entstehung bis zum Ende des Weltkrieges 1918*, Text-Band, *Die Militärluftfahrt bis zum Beginn des Weltkrieges, 1914, Anlage-Band, Dokumente-Karten-Tabellen* (Berlin: E. S. Mittler und Sohn, 1941), 332.

4. Lee Kennett, *The First Air War, 1914–1918* (New York: Free Press, 1991), 18–19, 40.

5. Ferdinand von Zeppelin, *Die Eroberung der Luft* (Stuttgart: Deutsche Verlags-Anstalt, 1908), 26. This volume is part of the collection of the Military History Research Office in Potsdam.

6. John H. Morrow Jr., *The Great War in the Air: Military Aviation from 1909–1921* (Washington, D.C.: Smithsonian Institution Press, 1993), 80; see also Kennett, *First Air War*, 10–11, 16.

7. The Artillerie-Prüfungs-Kommission was established in 1809 and was tasked with evaluating the military potential of the various inventions it examined. For a more detailed discussion, see Dennis E. Showalter, *Railroads and Rifles: Soldiers, Technology and the Unification of Germany* (Hamden, Conn.: Archon Books, 1975), 143–144.

8. Germany, Reichsluftfahrtministerium, Kriegswissenschaftliche Abteilung der Luftwaffe, *Die Militärluftfahrt*, 257.

9. Renz, *Development of German Anti-aircraft*, 2, K113.107-194, AFHRA. General von Renz served as a senior officer in the Luftwaffe responsible for the evaluation, procurement, and technical development of German anti-aircraft weapons, munitions, and targeting systems during World War II.

10. Hogg, *Anti-Aircraft*, 15–16.

11. Georg Wetzell, ed., *Die Deutsche Wehrmacht, 1914–1939* (Berlin: E. S. Mittler und Sohn, 1939), 559.

12. Hogg, *Anti-Aircraft*, 17.

13. Ernst von Höppner, *Germany's War in the Air: A Retrospect on the Development and the Work of Our Military Aviation Forces in the World War*, trans. J. Hawley Larned (Leipzig: A. F. Kochler, 1921), 44. This work is held by the Air University Library at Maxwell AFB, Alabama. According to Höppner, this problem persisted into World War I.

14. Bernard Delsert, Jean-Jacques Dubois, and Christian Kowal, *La Flak, 1914–1918*, vol. 1 (Guilherand Grange: La Plume du Temps, 1999), 72–73. This is the first volume in a two-volume set by Delsert et al. Both volumes provide a wealth of detail concerning the German flak arm and should be considered the standard reference for technical questions related to German flak artillery, munitions, and fire control equipment in World War I.

15. Germany, Reichsluftfahrtministerium, Kriegswissenschaftliche Abteilung der Luftwaffe, *Die Militärluftfahrt*, 259.

16. Ibid., 260.

17. Hans Ritter, *Der Luftkrieg* (Leipzig: von Hase & Koehler Verlag, 1926), 19. The 75-mm gun could be elevated to an angle of up to 70 degrees and rotated through 270 degrees.

18. Max Schwarte, ed., *Die Technik im Weltkriege* (Berlin: E. S. Mittler und Sohn, 1920), 201.

19. Höppner, *War in the Air,* 23; see also Ritter, *Der Luftkrieg,* 57. Ritter remarks that machine guns were ineffective above 1,000 meters.

20. Kennett, *First Air War,* 18–19; see also Hogg, *Anti-Aircraft,* 26–27. According to Hogg, a Bulgarian pilot by the name of Constantin has the dubious distinction of being the first recorded casualty attributable to anti-aircraft fire. Constantin crashed and died after being struck by a rifle bullet during a reconnaissance flight along the Turkish lines.

21. Heinrich Hunke, *Luftgefahr und Luftschutz: Mit besonderer Berücksichtigung des deutschen Luftschutzes* (Berlin: E. S. Mittler und Sohn, 1933), 3.

22. Höppner, *War in the Air,* 2.

23. Ibid.

24. "Sonderkommission zur Bekämpfung von Luftfahrzeugen, Betr.: Bekämpfung von Luftfahrzeugen [April 13, 1911]," PH 9 XX *Inspektion des Militär-, Luft- und Kraftwesens*/Folder 72/Pages 26–27, BA-MA.

25. "Kriegsministerium. Allgemeines Kriegs-Departement. Nr. 490/12 [April 5, 1912]," PH 9 XX/Folder 72/Pages 319–321, BA-MA.

26. *Anhaltspunkte für den Unterricht bei der Truppe über Luftfahrzeuge und deren Bekämpfung* (Berlin: Reichsdruckerei, 1913), 15, 20, and appendixes.

27. Germany, Reichsluftfahrtministerium, Kriegswissenschaftliche Abteilung der Luftwaffe, *Die Militärluftfahrt,* 261.

28. Wetzell, *Deutsche Wehrmacht,* 559.

29. Höppner, *War in the Air,* 2.

30. Germany, Reichsluftfahrtministerium, Kriegswissenschaftliche Abteilung der Luftwaffe, *Die Militärluftfahrt,* 261–262.

31. Curt von Lange, ed., *Gegen Bomber, Bunker, Panzer* (Berlin: Verlag Scherl, 1942), 300.

32. N. W. Routledge, *History of the Royal Regiment of Artillery: Anti-aircraft Artillery, 1914–55* (London: Brassey's, 1994), 3.

33. E. Büdingen, ed., *Kriegsgeschichtliche Einzelschriften der Luftwaffe,* vol. 1, *Entwicklung und Einsatz der deutschen Flakwaffe und des Luftschutzes im Weltkriege* (Berlin: E. S. Mittler und Sohn, 1938), 182–184.

34. Delsert, Dubois, and Kowal, *La Flak,* 2:264–265.

35. Georg W. Feuchter, *Geschichte des Luftkriegs: Entwicklung und Zukunft* (Bonn: Athenäum-Verlag, 1954), 304.

36. Germany, Reichsluftfahrtministerium, Kriegswissenschaftliche Abteilung der Luftwaffe, *Die Militärluftfahrt,* 266–271.

37. James L. Stokesbury, *A Short History of World War I* (New York: William Morrow, 1981), 32.

38. Koch, *Flak,* 10–11; see also Hogg, *Anti-Aircraft,* 41. Hogg states that the six motorized guns were the original guns introduced by Krupp and Rheinmetall at the 1909 Frankfurt exhibition. See also Fritz Nagel, *Fritz: The World War I Memoirs of a German Lieutenant,* ed. Richard A. Baumgartner (Huntington, W.Va.: Der Angriff Publications, 1981), 41. Nagel, a reserve officer in the German anti-aircraft service, states that the batteries consisted of two guns, thirty horses, and forty men commanded by a lieutenant.

39. Höppner, *War in the Air,* 21. The Fifteenth Army Corps received two motorized guns, while the First, Seventh, Sixteenth, and Twenty-first Army Corps had one each.

40. Ibid., 24.
41. Ibid., 22.
42. "Chef des Generalstabes des Feldheeres, Gr.H.Q. [May 26, 1915]," RL 4 *Chef des Ausbildungswesens/General der Fliegerausbildung und Luftwaffen-Inspektionen/ Waffengenerale*/Folder 257, BA-MA.
43. Lange, *Gegen Bomber,* 301; and Curt von Lange, ed., *Flakartillerie greift an: Tatsachenberichte in Wort und Bild* (Berlin: Verlag Scherl, 1941), 127; see also Nagel, *Fritz,* 41. Nagel recalled that his battery's first gun was a rebored French 75-mm artillery piece.
44. Höppner, *War in the Air,* 22.
45. Nagel, *Fritz,* 42, 45.
46. Max Schwarte, *Die militärischen Lehren des Großen Krieges* (Berlin: E. S. Mittler und Sohn, 1920), 130. For example, the muzzle velocity of the motorized (K-Flak) 77-mm gun was only 1,522 feet per second, while the standard 77-mm gun generated a muzzle velocity of 1,673 feet per second. In contrast, the towed 88-mm flak gun had a muzzle velocity of 2,575 feet per second.
47. Höppner, *War in the Air,* 22–23, 90.
48. Morrow, *Great War,* 81. The RNAS conducted these attacks based on its responsibility for home defense. In contrast, the flying units of the Royal Flying Corps (RFC) remained largely tied to the support of the British Expeditionary Force along the front lines.
49. Höppner, *War in the Air,* 24.
50. Büdingen, *Entwicklung und Einsatz,* 55.
51. Höppner, *War in the Air,* 43. The Germans could afford to ignore the Eastern Front because the technological limitations of Russian aviation and the extended flight distances between Russia and Germany effectively precluded any organized campaigns against German forces or the German homeland. In addition, the German defeat of the Russian forces at the Battles of Tannenberg and the Masurian Lakes and the later Russian emphasis versus Austro-Hungarian forces further secured Germany's eastern flank. For a discussion of Russian aviation deficiencies, see Kennett, *First Air War,* 177–178.
52. Koch, *Flak,* 12; see also Lange, *Gegen Bomber,* 301.
53. Höppner, *War in the Air,* 43.
54. Büdingen, *Entwicklung und Einsatz,* 56.
55. Ibid., 57; see also Hunke, *Luftgefahr und Luftschutz,* 21.
56. Walter von Eberhardt, ed., *Unsere Luftstreitkräfte 1914–1918: Ein Denkmal deutschen Heldentums* (Berlin: Vaterländischer Verlag C. A. Weller, 1930), 454.
57. Hunke, *Luftgefahr und Luftschutz,* 22.
58. Hogg, *Anti-Aircraft,* 64–65; see also Koch, *Flak,* 13.
59. Richard Suchenwirth, *The Development of the German Air Force, 1919–1939* (Maxwell AFB, Ala.: USAF Historical Division, 1968), 225.
60. Hunke, *Luftgefahr und Luftschutz,* 12.
61. Koch, *Flak,* 13.
62. Höppner, *War in the Air,* 58.
63. James S. Corum, *The Luftwaffe: Creating the Operational Air War, 1918–1940* (Lawrence: University Press of Kansas, 1997), 26.

64. Höppner, *War in the Air,* 58. Germany was not the only country to experience the counterproductive effects of intraservice competition for men and aviation resources. The RFC and the RNAS also became embroiled in a battle for pilots, engines, and airframes. For more on this point, see Tony Mason, *Air Power: A Centennial Appraisal* (London: Brassey's, 1994), 21–22.

65. Delsert, Dubois, and Kowal, *La Flak,* 2:351–355.

66. Nagel, *Fritz,* 48, 51; see also Höppner, *War in the Air,* 47, 91.

67. Georg Paul Neumann, *Die deutschen Luftstreitkräfte im Weltkriege* (Berlin: E. S. Mittler und Sohn, 1920), 274; see also Corum, *Luftwaffe,* 29.

68. "XVII. A.K. Der Chef d. Gen. Stabes, Betr: Bekämpfung von Luftfahrzeugen [April 11, 1912]," PH 9 XX/Folder 73/Page 43, BA-MA.

69. Hunke, *Luftgefahr und Luftschutz,* 18–19; see also Höppner, *War in the Air,* 45.

70. Höppner, *War in the Air,* 45–46. Höppner contends that the early 60-cm and 90-cm searchlights proved inadequate, but this deficiency was overcome with the later introduction of 110-cm naval and 200-cm coastal defense searchlights.

71. Hunke, *Luftgefahr und Luftschutz,* 19, 22. In contrast to the Germans, the French employed listening devices as independent fire directors. The results were, however, poor, with 308,000 rounds expended in the shooting down of only twenty-eight aircraft, a ratio of 11,000 rounds per aircraft destroyed. Hunke stated that Allied pilots began cutting off their engines during an attack in the middle of 1916. The Germans responded by establishing balloon barriers as a deterrent.

72. Büdingen, *Entwicklung und Einsatz,* 200.

73. Ibid.

74. Hunke, *Luftgefahr und Luftschutz,* 24.

75. Höppner, *War in the Air,* 88.

76. Koch, *Flak,* 13; see also Hunke, *Luftgefahr und Luftschutz,* 17. Hunke claims that the difficulties in coordinating searchlights with listening devices led to the reliance on barrier fire.

77. Höppner, *War in the Air,* 89. The policy of German army headquarters in granting priority to the field artillery units for ammunition supply exacerbated shortages within the anti-aircraft arm. According to Höppner, the naming of an "Inspector of Material" in the winter of 1917–1918 improved the delivery of replacement parts and gun barrels.

78. Koch, *Flak,* 14. The horizontal distance of the device's crossarm determined the accuracy of the device. For example, the 2-meter device was superior to the 1-meter device.

79. Wilfred O. Boettiger, *An Aircraft Artilleryman from 1939 to 1970* (Louisville, Ky.: By the author, 26 Southwind Road, 1990), 17.

80. This was the first 88-mm anti-aircraft gun ever developed for the German army. In 1931, Krupp began work on an 88-mm predecessor that arguably became the most famous artillery piece of World War II. See Hogg, *Anti-Aircraft,* 81.

81. Germany, Reichsluftfahrtministerium, Kriegswissenschaftliche Abteilung der Luftwaffe, *Die deutschen Luftstreitkräfte von ihrer Entstehung bis zum Ende des Weltkrieges 1918,* vol. 6, *Die Luftstreitkräfte in der Abwehrschlacht zwischen Somme und Oise vom 8. bis 12. August 1918* (Berlin: E. S. Mittler und Sohn, 1942), 224.

82. Lange, *Gegen Bomber,* 301. The Germans fired a total of 100,000 timed-fuse shells on the Western Front during the last years of the war.

83. Koch, *Flak,* 13.

84. Büdingen, *Entwicklung und Einsatz,* 189, 195. For example, German motorized flak guns increased from 38 in February 1916 to 56 by May 1916. By the end of the war, the Germans had 800 motorized flak guns.

85. Nagel, *Fritz,* 69.

86. Corum, *Luftwaffe,* 43.

87. Ibid., 40. The casualties included 797 killed and 380 wounded. An unintended advantage for the historian of the German penchant for bureaucracy is the documentation of numbers and even types of bombs dropped by Allied forces, a trend that would continue throughout World War II.

88. Heinz J. Nowarra, *50 Jahre Deutsche Luftwaffe (1910–1960),* vol. 3 (Genoa: Intyrama, 1967), 204. The commanders of the anti-aircraft defenses operated from the cities of Hamburg, Emden, Essen, Cologne, Frankfurt am Main, Diedenhofen, Saarbrücken, Freiburg, Stuttgart, Munich, and Mannheim.

89. Höppner, *War in the Air,* 48.

90. Eberhardt, *Luftstreitkräfte,* 456. In addition, flak defenses included 37-mm machine guns and 90-mm guns, with 196 of the former and 542 of the latter.

91. Ritter, *Der Luftkrieg,* 158; see also Kennett, *First Air War,* 212.

92. Wetzell, *Deutsche Wehrmacht,* 571.

93. Lothar Schüttel, *Luftsperren: Sperrballone, Luftminen und Drachen* (Munich: J. F. Lehmanns Verlag, 1939), 11.

94. Georg P. Neumann, ed., *The German Air Force in the Great War,* rev. ed., trans. J. E. Gurdon (Portway Bath, England: Cedric Chivers, 1969), 281.

95. Ritter, *Der Luftkrieg,* 159; see also Neumann, *German Air Force,* 281.

96. Eberhardt, *Luftstreitkräfte,* 454.

97. Höppner, *War in the Air,* 49.

98. Corum, *Luftwaffe,* 43.

99. Eberhardt, *Luftstreitkräfte,* 454.

100. Germany, Kriegswissenschaftliche Abteilung der Luftwaffe, *Der Luftschutz im Weltkrieg* (Berlin: E. S. Mittler und Sohn, 1941), 125.

101. Höppner, *War in the Air,* 92.

102. Neumann, *German Air Force,* 286.

103. Lange, *Gegen Bomber,* 301; see also Delsert, Dubois, and Kowal, *La Flak,* 1: p. 6. The latter state that twenty different calibers and forty types of guns were in use by the end of the war.

104. Renz, *Development of German Anti-aircraft,* K113.107-194, AFHRA. This initial fire director relied on information from the optical distance measuring equipment to compute the necessary lead correction for the firing solution.

105. Lange, *Gegen Bomber,* 301.

106. Horst Boog, Werner Rahn, Reinhard Stumpf, and Bernd Wegner, *Das Deutsche Reich und der zweite Weltkrieg,* vol. 6, *Der globale Krieg* (Stuttgart: Deutsche Verlags-Anstalt, 1990), 438.

107. Lange, *Flakartillerie,* 127.

108. Corum, *Luftwaffe,* 43.

109. Lange, *Flakartillerie,* 127; see also Routledge, *Royal Regiment,* 23–26. Routledge remarks that the British figures "must be treated with caution since it is not clear how or by whom they were obtained."

110. Letter from General of the Flak Artillery Walter von Axthelm to Dr. Heinz Peter Ptak, dated September 27, 1955, N 529 *Nachlass von Axthelm*/Folder 9 II, BA-MA. General von Axthelm was the inspector of the Flak Artillery between January 1942 and March 1945; see also Germany, Reichsluftfahrtministerium, Kriegswissenschaftliche Abteilung der Luftwaffe, *Abwehrschlacht zwischen Somme und Oise,* 224–225.

111. Hunke, *Luftgefahr und Luftschutz,* 19. In comparison, French flak accounted for 500 aircraft destroyed compared with 2,000 shot down by aircraft, or 20 percent of the total destroyed. Italian flak tallied 129 aircraft destroyed versus 540 shot down by aircraft, or 19 percent.

112. Eberhardt, *Luftstreitkräfte,* 459.

113. Germany, Kriegswissenschaftliche Abteilung der Luftwaffe, *Der Luftschutz im Weltkrieg,* 136. In 1918 alone, Germany suffered almost 46 percent of personnel losses and 62 percent of the estimated total financial damages.

114. Harvey B. Tress, *British Strategic Bombing Policy Through 1940: Politics, Attitudes, and the Formation of a Lasting Pattern* (Lewiston, N.Y.: Edwin Mellen Press, 1988), 42. According to Tress, 600 persons perished in the attacks against London alone.

115. Mason, *Centennial Appraisal,* 38. It was exactly this psychological element that in many respects shaped the formulations of strategic bombing theory espoused by early airpower advocates such as Hugh Trenchard and Giulio Douhet.

2. A Theory for Air Defense, 1919–1932

1. Renz, *Development of German Anti-aircraft,* 58, K113.107-194, AFHRA.

2. Charles I. Bevans, ed., *Treaties and Other International Agreements of the United States of America, 1776–1949* (Washington, D.C.: Department of State Publication, 1969), 115, 118, 123. The final treaty agreement also allowed the Germans to acquire one 88-mm gun every two years and one 105-mm gun and one motorized 76.2-mm or 77-mm motorized gun every five years. However, these low levels of acquisition in effect excluded domestic production of these guns based on the exorbitant per unit cost. See also Renz, *Development of German Anti-aircraft,* 59, K113.107-194, AFHRA.

3. Koch, *Flak,* 16; see also Militärgeschichtliches Forschungsamt, ed., *Die Generalstäbe in Deutschland 1871–1945. Aufgaben in der Armee und Stellung im Staate,* vol. 3, *Die Entwicklung der militärischen Luftfahrt in Deutschland 1920–1933. Planung und Maßnahmen zur Schaffung einer Fliegertruppe in der Reichswehr* (Stuttgart: Deutsche Verlags-Anstalt, 1962), 236. The Inter-Allied Military Control Commission agreed to allow the gun emplacements at Königsberg on March 20, 1920.

4. Routledge, *Royal Regiment,* 39–40.

5. Examples of the participation of civilian strategists include Alexander Axel, *Die Schlacht über Berlin* (Berlin: Verlag Offene Worte, 1933); and Major Holders (pseudonym for Dr. Robert Knauss), *Luftkrieg 1936: Die Zertrümmerung von Paris* (Berlin: Verlag Tradition Wilhelm Kolk, 1932). In addition to their German

counterparts, other well-known airpower and armor strategists of the period include the Italian Giulio Douhet and the Englishmen Basil Liddell Hart and J. F. C. Fuller.

6. Erich Ludendorff, *Ludendorff's Own Story, August 1914–November 1918,* vol. 1 (New York: Harper and Brothers, 1919), 457. No translator is identified for this edition.

7. Ibid.

8. Ursula von Gersdorff, *Frauen im Kriegsdienst, 1914–1945,* Beiträge zur Militär- und Kriegsgeschichte (Stuttgart: Deutsche Verlags-Anstalt, 1969), 31, 239.

9. Ibid., 33.

10. Tress, *Bombing Policy,* 43. H. A. Jones, in the official British history dealing with the war in the air, concluded that the primary impact of German bombing was the diversion of fighters and anti-aircraft guns from the front to home defense. Likewise, Jones characterized German diversion of resources to the defense of urban areas as the third most important achievement of the British bombing effort.

11. Höppner, *War in the Air,* 114.

12. Routledge, *Royal Regiment,* 39.

13. Militärgeschichtliches Forschungsamt, *Entwicklung der militärischen Luftfahrt,* 126–127.

14. Corum, *Luftwaffe,* 59; see also Corum's footnote 20 on page 299.

15. Ibid., 52–55. Corum provides a detailed discussion of von Seeckt's views on aviation and air defense issues.

16. Ibid., 59.

17. James S. Corum, *The Roots of Blitzkrieg: Hans von Seeckt and German Military Reform Between the World Wars* (Lawrence: University Press of Kansas, 1992), 144–145.

18. Corum, *Luftwaffe,* 63. Seydel commanded Flakgruppe XX during World War I.

19. Neumann, *Germany's War,* 282–283. See also Höppner, *War in the Air,* 89. In fact, during the Battle of the Somme in 1916 and at Cambrai in 1917, German flak crews employed their guns with good effect against British tanks. Höppner claims that the Seventh Anti-Aircraft Battery destroyed eight British tanks at Cambrai on November 23, 1917.

20. Hauptmann a.D. Seydel, "Organisation der Flugabwehr in den fremden Staaten," *Luftschutz-Nachrichtenblatt des Flak-Vereins e.V.* (March 1930): 26; periodical holding of the BA-MA.

21. Oberstleutnant von Keller, *Die heutige Wehrlosigkeit Deutschlands im Lichte seiner Verteidigung gegen die Fliegerangriffe im Kriege 1914/18* (Berlin: Verlag Offene Worte, n.d.), 39. This work appears to have been published in the mid-1920s.

22. Corum, *Luftwaffe,* 64.

23. Ibid., 66.

24. David N. Spires, *Image and Reality: The Making of the German Officer, 1921–1933* (Westport, Conn.: Greenwood Press, 1984), 163–164. In comparison, six hours of theoretical discussion per week were devoted to the subject of "tactics" and three hours each to "military science" and the "engineering service."

25. Ibid., 107, 176–178.

26. Ibid., 251–252, 254.

27. Renz, *Development of German Anti-aircraft,* 60, K113.107–194, AFHRA.

28. Ibid., 60–67; see also Spires, *Image and Reality,* 116–117.

29. "Sammlung ausländischer Aufsätze über Luftkriegsfragen [March 1, 1937]," T-321, *Records of the German Air Force High Command*/Reel 2/Frames 4736812–4736861, NARA. The German armed forces' penchant for evaluating foreign military developments in their professional literature found its ultimate expression in a 1938 Air Ministry collection concerning foreign ground-based air defense. This section alone was divided into ninety-eight subareas covering topics such as training, organization, doctrine, and weapons systems.

30. Corum, *Roots of Blitzkrieg,* 158.

31. *Militärwochenblatt* (Berlin), September 11, 1925.

32. Ritter, *Der Luftkrieg,* 162.

33. Hunke, *Luftgefahr und Luftschutz,* 17, 24–25.

34. Höppner, *War in the Air,* 59.

35. Generalleutnant a.D. Hugo Grimme, "Militärischer Luftschutz," *Luftschutz-Nachrichtenblatt* (Potsdam), January 1933, 10.

36. *Militärwochenblatt* (Berlin), March 4, 1926. This article was written in rebuttal to one that appeared in *La France Militaire* on January 13, 1926. As is customary in the newspapers of the time, only the author's last name is given.

37. *Mitteilungsblatt des Flakvereins e.V.,* no. 3 (March 1926), 53.

38. *Militärwochenblatt* (Berlin), April 4, 1926.

39. Corum, *Luftwaffe,* 105.

40. Peter Fritzsche, *A Nation of Fliers: German Aviation and the Popular Imagination* (Cambridge: Harvard University Press, 1992), 182.

41. Ibid., 254; see also Corum, *Luftwaffe,* 105.

42. Fritzsche, *Fliers,* 205–207.

43. Friedemann Bedürftig, ed., *Das große Lexikon des Dritten Reiches* (Munich: Südwest Verlag, 1985), 365. See also Fritzsche, *Fliers,* 179. Fritzsche contends, "Beginning in the late 1920s, Germany . . . became increasingly concerned with the possibility of air war. Although it was the Nazis who really mobilized Germans around air defense."

44. Suchenwirth, *Development of the German Air Force,* 108. See also Corum, *Luftwaffe,* 105; and Bedürftig, *Lexikon des Dritten Reiches*, 365.

45. Lore Walb, *Ich, die Alte—ich, die Junge: Konfrontation mit meinen Tagebüchern 1933–1945* (Berlin: Aufbau Verlag, 1997), 61.

46. Corum, *Luftwaffe*, 81–83.

47. Richard D. Challener, ed., *United States Military Intelligence*, vol. 25, *Weekly Summaries 1926* (New York: Garland, 1979), 11,406. This report came from a U.S. military attaché and also provided details on the German army's emphasis on passive defense measures to include camouflage and dispersion.

48. Herbert Molloy Mason Jr., *The Rise of the Luftwaffe: Forging the Secret Air Weapon, 1918–1940* (New York: Dial Press, 1973), 96.

49. Challener, *Weekly Summaries,* 11,418–11,421.

50. Warren B. Morris Jr., *The Weimar Republic and Nazi Germany* (Chicago: Nelson Hall, 1982), 85.

51. Hans W. Gatzke, "Russo-German Military Cooperation During the Weimar Republic," *American Historical Review* 63 (April 1958): 567.

52. Harvey Leonard Dyck, *Weimar Germany and Soviet Russia: A Study in Diplomatic Instability* (New York: Columbia University Press, 1966), 21. See also Gatzke, "Military Cooperation," 580. German and Soviet military cooperation also included officer exchanges at field maneuvers, as well as attendance at professional military education courses sponsored by the Truppenamt.

53. Morris, *Weimar Republic,* 86. See also Dyck, *Germany and Soviet Russia,* 20–22. The Reichswehr officers participating in this training were not "officially" serving in the German army because they were required to resign from active service as a precondition for participation.

54. Edward L. Homze, *Arming the Luftwaffe: The Reich Air Ministry and the German Aircraft Industry, 1919–1939* (Lincoln: University of Nebraska Press, 1976), 20–21. The numbers of German pilots and observers trained at Lipetsk between 1925 and 1933 were 120 and 100, respectively. Despite the low number of trainees, many of these men went on to become senior leaders in the Luftwaffe.

55. Sebastian Haffner, *Der Teufelspakt: Fünfzig Jahre deutsch-russische Beziehungen* (Hamburg: Rowohlt Taschenbuch Verlag, 1968), 70.

56. Gatzke, "Military Cooperation," 589–592.

57. "Luftwaffen-Beute-Flak aus dem Feldzug im Osten," T-321/Folder 9/Frame 4745717, NARA. This report prepared by the Luftwaffe's captured weapons unit for the eastern campaign notes that Rheinmetall modified a 75-mm flak gun as a 76.2-mm flak gun for the Russians. These modified guns were subsequently exported to the Soviet Union, with German engineers providing on-site technical expertise. In addition, the captured weapons unit also recovered older models of German fire directors and auxiliary fire directors from Soviet forces. By 1941, the vast majority of the captured weapons and equipment were of simple design and good quality, but well behind the technical standards of the latest Luftwaffe systems.

58. Gatzke, "Military Cooperation," 592, 594.

59. The concept of "differential development" appears especially appropriate when considering the asymmetrical evolution of ground-based versus interceptor air defense. Gerhard Weinberg suggested this term in a conversation with the author.

60. Koch, *Flak,* 16.

61. Hogg, *Anti-Aircraft,* 75.

62. Renz, *Development of German Anti-aircraft,* 99, K113.107-194, AFHRA.

63. "Part I. AA Program 1930–1931 of Appendix C to Interrogation Report General der Flakartillery [*sic*] von Axthelm," 519.601A-12, AFHRA; see also Renz, *Development of German Anti-aircraft,* 100, K113.107-194, AFHRA. In 1927–1928, Zeiss also began work on an additional automatic fire control system, the so-called Tabulator. The Tabulator underwent initial developmental testing in 1932, and Zeiss tested an improved version in 1934. However, the results proved disappointing, and the project was abandoned.

64. Militärgeschichtliches Forschungsamt, *Entwicklung der militärischen Luftfahrt,* 166. The German title of the plan was "Aufstellungsplan einer Kriegswehrmacht."

65. Homze, *Arming the Luftwaffe,* 24. Mittelberger's rank as a brigadier general was an important step in increasing the influence of aviation proponents in the competition for resources and funding.

66. Koch, *Flak,* 17.

67. Militärgeschichtliches Forschungsamt, *Entwicklung der militärischen Luftfahrt,* 168–169.

68. Ibid., 170.

69. Corum, *Luftwaffe,* 119–120.

70. Mason, *Rise of the Luftwaffe,* 215. For example, Mason writes that along with Wever "were buried the Luftwaffe's chances of winning a war spread beyond the narrow frontiers of continental Europe."

71. *Militärwochenblatt* (Berlin), October 18, 1929; October 25, 1929; December 25, 1929; January 18, 1930; and March 18, 1930.

72. *Militärwochenblatt* (Berlin), October 18, 1929.

73. Ibid.

74. *Militärwochenblatt* (Berlin), October 25, 1929.

75. For a review of du Picq's theory of war, see Ardant du Picq, *Battle Studies: Ancient and Modern,* 8th ed., trans. John N. Greely and Robert C. Cotton (New York: Macmillan, 1921).

76. *Militärwochenblatt* (Berlin), October 25, 1929.

77. Ibid.

78. *Militärwochenblatt* (Berlin), January 18, 1930.

79. Corum, *Luftwaffe,* 119.

80. *Militärwochenblatt* (Berlin), December 25, 1929.

81. *Militärwochenblatt* (Berlin), March 18, 1930.

82. Corum, *Luftwaffe,* 119.

83. Michael Geyer, "Das Zweite Rüstungsprogramm (1930–1934)," *Militärgeschichtliche Mitteilungen,* 1 (1975): 125, 145–146.

84. Ibid., 145–146.

85. Corum, *Luftwaffe,* 121. The dollar amount is based on the official exchange rate of 23.8 cents per reichsmark in 1930. See E. Eastman Irvine, *The World Almanac and Book of Facts* (New York: New York World-Telegram, 1942), 515.

86. Karl Friederich Hildebrand, *Die Generale der deutschen Luftwaffe, 1935–1945,* vol. 3 (Osnabrück: Biblio Verlag, 1992), 146.

87. "Entwicklungsprogramm 13.12.30," RL 4 *Chef des Ausbildungswesens/General der Fliegerausbildung und Luftwaffen-Inspektionen/Waffengenerale*/Folder 257, BA-MA.

88. Suchenwirth, *German Air Force,* 106.

89. "Part I. AA Program 1930–1931 of Appendix C to Interrogation Report General der Flakartillery [*sic*] von Axthelm," 519.601A-12, AFHRA; emphasis in the original.

90. "Entwicklungsprogramm 13.12.30," RL 4/Folder 257, BA-MA.

91. "Part I. AA Program 1930–1931 of Appendix C to Interrogation Report General der Flakartillery [*sic*] von Axthelm," 519.601A-12, AFHRA.

92. Renz, *Development of German Anti-aircraft,* K113.107-194, AFHRA.

93. "Part I. AA Program 1930–1931 of Appendix C to Interrogation Report General der Flakartillery [*sic*] von Axthelm," 519.601A-12, AFHRA.

94. Suchenwirth, *Development of the German Air Force,* 106.

95. Militärgeschichtliches Forschungsamt, *Entwicklung der militärischen Luftfahrt,* 172.

96. Hogg, *Anti-Aircraft,* 75.

97. Militärgeschichtliches Forschungsamt, *Entwicklung der militärischen Luftfahrt,* 177.

98. "Entwicklungsprogramm der Fla. Waffen des Heeres [June 12, 1932]," RL 4/Folder 257, BA-MA.

99. "Part II, AA Program 1932–1936 of Appendix 'C' to Interrogation Report General der Flakartillery [*sic*] von Axthelm," 519.601A-12, AFHRA.

100. Ibid. Barrage rockets were to be of two types. One was to have a high-explosive timed warhead capable of reaching up to 23,000 feet, and the second was to have a warhead with a built-in parachute and cable barrier apparently designed to foul propellers and inflict structural damage to attacking aircraft.

101. Michael J. Neufeld, *The Rocket and the Reich: Peenemünde and the Coming of the Ballistic Missile Era* (Cambridge: Harvard University Press, 1995), 23.

102. Ralf Schabel, *Die Illusion der Wunderwaffen: Die Rolle der Düsenflugzeuge und Flugabwehrraketen in der Rüstungspolitik des Dritten Reiches,* Beiträge zur Militärgeschichte (Munich: R. Oldenbourg Verlag, 1994), 261.

103. "Part II, AA Program 1932–1936 of Appendix 'C' to Interrogation Report General der Flakartillery [*sic*] von Axthelm," 519.601A-12, AFHRA.

104. "Richtlinien für die Gefechts- und Schießübungen der Kw.-Batterien 1931," T-405/Reel 1/Frames 4827245–47, NARA.

105. Günter Solltau, *Die Flakabteilung I./12: Geschichte und Schicksal 1914–1945* (Berlin: Kameradschaft des ehem. Flakregiments 12, 1989), 13.

106. Militärgeschichtliches Forschungsamt, *Entwicklung der militärischen Luftfahrt,* 229.

3. Converting Theory into Practice, 1933–1938

1. Wilhelm Deist, *The Wehrmacht and German Rearmament* (Toronto: University of Toronto Press, 1981), 21.

2. Gerhard Weinberg, ed., *Hitlers zweites Buch: Ein Dokument aus dem Jahr 1928,* vol. 7, Quellen und Darstellungen zur Zeitgeschichte (Stuttgart: Deutsche Verlags-Anstalt, 1961), 111.

3. Ibid., 148.

4. Interrogation transcript of Field Marshal Erhard Milch by Royal Air Force of May 23, 1945, 512.61c-6d, AFHRA.

5. Weinberg, *Zweites Buch,* 148.

6. Deist, *German Rearmament,* 28–29.

7. Georg Tessin, *Deutsche Verbände und Truppen, 1918–1939* (Osnabrück: Biblio Verlag, 1974), 273–274.

8. Routledge, *Royal Regiment,* 40, 42.

9. Larry Bland, ed., *The Papers of George Catlett Marshall,* vol. 1, *"The Soldierly Spirit"* (Baltimore: Johns Hopkins University Press, 1981), 464.

10. Solltau, *Flakabteilung I./12,* 13.

11. Ibid., 13–15.

12. "Bemerkungen zur Ausbildung 1933," T-405 *German Air Force Records: Luftgaukommandos, Flak, Deutsche Luftwaffenmission in Rumänien*/Reel 1/Frames 4827259–65, NARA.

13. "Ausbildung der Schw.Battr. in den Monaten März, April u. Mai [February 23, 1933]," T-405/Reel 1/Frames 4827962–63, NARA.

14. "Horchlehrgang der K.A.S [July 1, 1933]," T-405/Reel 1/ Frames 4827867–68, NARA.

15. Ibid., Frame 4827869.

16. "3.(Preuß.) Fahrabteilung. Berlin-Lankwitz, den 21.8.33," T-405/Reel 1/ Frames 4827931–32, NARA.

17. "Taktische Ausbildung der Offiziere im Winter 1933/34 [October 10, 1933]," T-405/Reel 1/Frame 4827952, NARA.

18. "Ausbildungsplan für das Winterhalbjahr 1.11.33 bis 31.3.34 [September 20, 1933]," T-405/Reel 1/Frames 4827776–77, 4827784–85, NARA.

19. See Walter Görlitz, *The German General Staff: History and Structure, 1657–1945,* trans. Brian Battershaw (London: Hollis and Carter, 1953), passim.

20. "Erfahrungs-Bericht [September 1933]," T-405/Reel 2/Frame 4828365, NARA.

21. Karl-Heinz Völker, *Die Deutsche Luftwaffe, 1933–1939: Aufbau, Führung und Rüstung der Luftwaffe sowie die Entwicklung der deutschen Luftkriegstheorie* (Stuttgart: Deutsche Verlags-Anstalt, 1967), 17.

22. "Bemerkungen für die Ausbildung 1934 [November 1934]," T-405/Reel 1/ Frame 4827981, NARA.

23. Ian V. Hogg, *German Artillery of World War Two* (London: Arms and Armour Press, 1975), 150–151, 162–163.

24. It should be noted that normally the designation 88 Flak/36 referred to the caliber and type of weapon and the year of its development or, in this case, 88-mm caliber flak gun developed in 1936. However, in the case of the 37 Flak/18 and 88 Flak/18, the number 18 was used in an attempt to disguise the fact that these weapons had been developed in the 1930s in contravention of the Versailles treaty restrictions and the oath senior officers had taken. See Renz, *Development of German Anti-aircraft,* 102–103, K113.107–194, AFHRA.

25. "Ausbildung ehem.Flak.Offz. und der Leiter des Lehrkdos. Döberitz bei F3 [December 1933]," T-405/Reel 1/Frame 4827839, NARA.

26. Renz, *Development of German Anti-aircraft,* 105, K113.107-194, AFHRA.

27. Völker, *Deutsche Luftwaffe,* 49. The new units were established at Seerapen in the vicinity of Königsberg, Döberitz, Wurzen, and Brandenburg a.d. Havel.

28. "Bemerkungen zur Ausbildung 1934 [November 1934]," T-405/Reel 1/Frame 4827280, NARA.

29. "Werbung von Offizieranwärtern [August 15, 1934]," T-405/Reel 2/Frame 4828531; see also letter from the Inspector of the Air Defense Office of August 13, 1934, T-405/Reel 2/Frame 4828503.

30. "Bemerkungen zur Ausbildung 1934 [November 1934]," T-405/Reel 1/ Frames 4827276–81, NARA.

31. Ibid., Frame 4827289.

32. For a more detailed discussion of these efforts, see Militärgeschichtliches Forschungsamt, *Entwicklung der militärischen Luftfahrt,* 174–179.

33. Homze, *Arming the Luftwaffe,* 53. Göring made this boast in *Aufbau einer Nation,* a propaganda piece published in 1934.

34. Ibid., 49–50.

35. Militärgeschichtliches Forschungsamt, *Entwicklung der militärischen Luftfahrt,* 204–206; see also Homze, *Arming the Luftwaffe,* 57.

36. "Unterstellung der L.S. Truppen [September 16, 1933]," T-405/Reel 1/Frames 4828144–46, NARA.

37. "Rüstungsprogramm L.S. [August 20, 1934]," T-321/Reel 3/Frames 4737810–11, NARA.

38. Rudolf Absolon, ed., *Rangliste der Generale der deutschen Luftwaffe nach dem Stand vom 20. April 1945* (Friedberg: Podzun-Pallas-Verlag, 1984), 130–131.

39. Ibid., 132.

40. James S. Corum and Richard R. Muller, *The Luftwaffe's Way of War: German Air Force Doctrine, 1911–1945* (Baltimore: Nautical and Aviation Publishing Company of America, 1998), 118. All translations for these citations provided by Corum and Muller.

41. Ibid., 119.

42. The German historian Horst Boog went so far as to describe the Luftwaffe's obsession with offensive operations as a "perversion of the concept of the offensive" *(Pervertierung des Angriffgedankens).* See Boog, *Luftwaffenführung,* 133.

43. Hermann Adler, ed., *Ein Buch von der neuen Luftwaffe* (Stuttgart: Franck'sche Verlagshandlung, 1938), 109. As in World War I, observation posts were organized in lines along Germany's borders, as well as in circles around major cities and industrial areas. The introduction of radar greatly reduced the need for such posts during the course of World War II.

44. Corum and Muller, *Luftwaffe's Way of War,* 151–156. Helmuth Wilberg was the primary author of *Regulation 16,* but Corum and Muller contend that Hugo Sperrle, Helmuth Felmy, Wilhelm Wimmer, and Hans Jeschonnek also contributed to the work.

45. "Winter-Kriegsspiel 1934–35," RL 2 II *Generalstab der Luftwaffe/Luftwaffe-Führungsstab*/Folder 76, BA-MA.

46. Ibid.

47. Deist, *German Rearmament,* 61.

48. Der Reichsminister der Luftfahrt und Oberbefehlshaber der Luftwaffe, *Bemerkungen des Oberbefehlshabers der Luftwaffe zur Ausbildung und zu den Übungen im Jahre 1935* (Berlin: Reichsdruckerei, 1936), collection of the German Military History Research Office, 18–19, 27–28.

49. Homze, *Arming the Luftwaffe,* 73.

50. "Vorläufiger Haushaltsvoranschlag für die Weiterentwicklung und Erprobung von Waffen, Munition und Gerät für Flak 1935 [October 1, 1934]," T-321/Reel 3/Frames 4737801–3, NARA. The official exchange rate in 1935 was forty cents per reichsmark. See Irvine, *World Almanac,* 515.

51. Letter from von Axthelm to Field Marshal Kesselring, dated October 13, 1955, N 529/Folder 9, BA-MA.

52. "Luftsperren mit Raketenauftrieb [December 3, 1936]," T-405/Reel 6/Frame 4834628, NARA.

53. "Vorläufiger Haushaltsvoranschlag für die fabrikatorischen Maßnahmen zur Herstellung von 1) Flak 2) Flakmuniton 3) Flakgerät im Jahre 1935," T-321/Reel 3/Frame 4737773, NARA.

54. "Geldmittel für 8,8 cm Flak [June 7, 1935]," T-321/Reel 3/Frame 4737834; and "Fabrikatorische Mittel für 2 cm M.G. 30 [June 14, 1935]," T-321/Reel 3/Frame 4737833, NARA.

55. "Reichsminister der Luftfahrt, Amt L.C. [May 22, 1935]," T-321/Reel 3/Frames 4737836–37, NARA.

56. "Der Reichsminister der Luftfahrt, An Ämter, Abteilungsleiter [March 30, 1935]," T-321/Reel 3/Frames 4737757–58, NARA.

57. "Reichsluftfahrtministerium, LC III, An In. Flak. [August 10, 1935]," T-321/Reel 3/Frame 4737820, NARA.

58. Homze, *Arming the Luftwaffe,* 74–75; see also Irvine, *World Almanac,* 515. Currency conversion based on rate of thirty cents per reichsmark in 1933.

59. Corum, *Luftwaffe,* 125.

60. David Irving, *The Rise and Fall of the Luftwaffe: The Life of Field Marshal Erhard Milch* (Boston: Little, Brown, 1973), 28, 35–36. A product of lessons drawn from the experience of World War I, the essence of the Italian general Guilio Douhet's theory was his belief that large numbers of bombers attacking cities with incendiary devices, high-explosive bombs, and gas could quickly break the morale of the civilian population, leading to the fall of the government.

61. Ibid., 38. Hitler's plan concerning these flak towers was later realized with the construction of immense concrete flak towers in the cities of Berlin, Hamburg, and Vienna. The Luftwaffe also constructed smaller concrete and wooden structures, especially for light flak guns. For a more in-depth discussion of the flak towers, see Michael Foedrowitz, *Die Flaktürme in Berlin, Hamburg und Wien, 1940–1950* (Wölfersheim-Berstadt: Podzun-Pallas-Verlag, 1996).

62. "Organisationsprogramm der Flakartillerie [November 11, 1935]," T-321/Reel 3/Frames 4737712, 4737718–4737721, NARA.

63. Ibid., Frames 4737712, 4737719–20; see also "Friedens-Gliederung eines Flak-Regimentes [1935]," T-321/Reel 3/Frame 4737733, NARA.

64. "Organisationsprogramm der Flakartillerie [November 11, 1935]," T-321/Reel 3/Frame 4737718; NARA.

65. Suchenwirth, *German Air Force,* 110; see also Koch, *Flak,* 19.

66. "Stärkenachweisung einer schweren Flakstammbatterie [February 1, 1937]," T-321/Reel 1/Frames 4734798–801, NARA.

67. "Organisationsprogramm der Flakartillerie [November 11, 1935]," T-321/Reel 3/Frames 4737722–23, NARA. The rule of thumb for selecting men from specific recruiting districts was that they should be able to reach their mobilization points within three hours of notification.

68. "Beweglichmachung der Res.-Flakabteilungen [July 8, 1936]," T-321/Reel 1/Frames 4734943–45; see also "Aufstellungsübersicht der Flakartillerie für die Zeit vom 1.10.36 bis 31.3.37," T-321/Reel 3/Frames 4737673–74, NARA.

69. "Organisationsprogramm der Flakartillerie [July 13, 1936]," T-321/Roll 1/Frames 4734886–87, NARA.

70. "Aufstellung einer Erg. Flak Batterie für Sperrballonausbildung [February 24,

1936]"; and "Aufstellung einer Erg. Flakbattr. für Sperrballonausbildung [March 14, 1936]," T-405/Reel 6/Frames 4833908, 4833915, NARA.

71. "Merkblatt über den Einsatz von Luftsperrverbänden [n.d.]," T-405/Reel 6/ Frame 4834420, NARA. This document is not dated; however, it is among a group of documents from the mid-1930s.

72. "Vorbildung und Weiterbildung der Erg.-Mannsch. der Luftsperr-Waffe [October 8, 1936]"; and "Verbot der Aufstiege von Ballonen und Drachen [July 7, 1936]," T-405/Reel 6/Frames 4834436–37, 4834608–12, NARA.

73. Renz, *Development of German Anti-aircraft,* 146, K113.107-194, AFHRA.

74. Homze, *Arming the Luftwaffe,* 89, 155; see also Deist, *German Rearmament,* 67.

75. "L.A. Nr. 5836/35 g.Kdos. A II, 5 A [November 27, 1935]," T-321/Reel 3/ Frames 4737692–93, NARA.

76. "Beschaffung von Scheinwerfergerät auf Grund des Flak-Programmes," T-321/Reel 3/Frame 4737683, NARA. The proposed delivery date was March 31, 1937.

77. "Notizen für die Kommandeurbesprechung am 6.10.36 (Nachschub) [October 12, 1936]," T-405/Reel 6/Frames 4834394–99, NARA. A document from the Air Ministry of October 10, 1936, noted that the Luftwaffe had 1,058 88-mm/Model 18 flak guns, 197 37-mm/Model 18 flak guns, and 672 20-mm/Model 30 flak guns as of this date. See T-321/Reel 1/Frame 4734665, NARA.

78. "Beschaffungsprogramm für Flakartl. [February 10, 1938]," T-321/Reel 3/ Frame 4737112; and "Beschaffungsprogramm für Flakartillerie [June 10, 1938]," T-321/Reel 3/Frame 4737026, NARA.

79. "Übersicht über den Stand der Beschaffungen für R.d.L [March 31, 1938]," T-321/Reel 3/Frame 4737041, NARA.

80. "LC III 7d [April 1938]," T-321/Reel 3/Frame 4737051, NARA.

81. "Zusammenstellung für den Generalfeldmarschall [December 8, 1937]," T-321/Reel 3/Frame 4737131, NARA. The reserve estimate was based on a daily usage rate of eighty rounds for each 20-mm gun, sixty rounds for each 37-mm gun, and twenty-five rounds for each 88-mm gun.

82. "Entwicklungsprogramm der Flakartillerie 1937," RL 4/Folder 257, BA-MA.

83. Otto A. Teetzmann, *Der Luftschutz: Leitfaden für alle* (Berlin: Verlag des Reichsluftschutzbundes, n.d.), 66–67. Based on its description of available weapons systems, the handbook appears to have been published sometime between 1935 and 1937.

84. Ibid., 67.

85. Wolfgang Pickert, *Unsere Flakartillerie: Einführung in ihre Grundlagen für Soldaten und Laien* (Berlin: E. S. Mittler und Sohn, 1937), 2, 27.

86. "Entwicklungsprogramm der Flakartillerie 1937," RL 4/Folder 257, BA-MA.

87. The term "service ceiling" applies to the aircraft's highest attainable altitude for normal operations.

88. *Jane's Aircraft of World War II* (Glasgow: HarperCollins, 1995), 167, 175, 185, 209, 215. During World War II, the RAF did develop the Meteor jet with a maximum speed of 410 mph, but it did not conduct operational flights over the Continent until early 1945.

89. Roger A. Freeman, *Mighty Eighth War Manual* (London: Jane's, 1984), 21. The weight of the bombs was one factor that limited operational ceilings. In addition, formation flying for the B-17s became increasingly difficult above 27,000 feet because

of the increased instability of the bombers and sluggish control response at high altitudes.

90. John Comer, *Combat Crew: A True Story of Flying and Fighting in World War II* (New York: William Morrow, 1988), 197.

91. Perret, *Winged Victory,* 290. This is only one of numerous examples concerning the ability of both the B-17 and the B-24 to absorb extensive damage.

92. "Das Entwicklungsprogramm der Fla.Waffen [November 22, 1933]," RL 4/Folder 257, BA-MA.

93. Hogg, *German Artillery,* 167, 175.

94. Curtis E. LeMay and MacKinlay Kantor, *Mission with LeMay: My Story* (Garden City, N.Y.: Doubleday, 1965), 178.

95. *Die Sirene* 24 (November 1937): front cover.

96. Hogg, *German Artillery,* 177–182.

97. "Besprechung über 12,8 und 15 cm [January 29, 1936]," RL 4/Folder 257, BA-MA.

98. "Entwicklungsprogramm der Flakartillerie 1937," RL 4/Folder 257, BA-MA. Rüdel used the German term *Blindflug* to identify aircraft operating without visual reference to the ground and flying only in reference to their onboard instruments. Aircraft operating in or above the clouds were therefore impossible to locate using optical systems.

99. "Förderung der Ortung und Kennung von Flugzeugen mittels Ultrakurzwellen-(Dezimeter)—Strahlen oder Infrarot- (Wärme)—Strahlen [1939]," RL 4/Folder 269/Page 61, BA-MA.

100. Werner Niehaus, *Die Radarschlacht, 1939–1945: Die Geschichte des Hochfrequenzkrieges* (Stuttgart: Motorbuch Verlag, 1977), 28–29, 32.

101. "Förderung der Ortung und Kennung von Flugzeugen mittels Ultrakurzwellen-(Dezimeter)—Strahlen oder Infrarot-(Wärme)—Strahlen [1939]," RL 4/Folder 269/Page 61, BA-MA.

102. Renz, *Development of German Anti-aircraft,* 304–305, K113.107–194, AFHRA.

103. "Entwicklungsprogramm der Flakartillerie 1937," RL 4/Folder 257, BA-MA.

104. "Vortrag Major d.Genst.Deichmann [October 29, 1936]," T-405/Reel 6/Frames 4834546–50, NARA.

105. Ibid., Frames 4834555–56.

106. Koch, *Flak,* 19.

107. "Vortrag Major d.Genst.Deichmann [October 29, 1936]," T-405/Reel 6/Frames 4834556–57, NARA; emphasis in the original.

108. Ibid., Frames 4834560–61, 4834563.

109. Suchenwirth, *Development of the German Air Force,* 110.

110. Corum, *Luftwaffe,* 234.

111. "Lehrübung Greifswald [October 23, 1936]," T-405/Reel 6/Frames 4834623–27, NARA.

112. Der Reichsminister der Luftfahrt und Oberbefehlshaber der Luftwaffe, *Bemerkungen des Oberbefehlshabers der Luftwaffe zu den Übungen im Jahre 1936* (Berlin: Reichsdruckerei, 1937), collection of the German Military History Research Office, 20–21, 27–29.

113. Corum, *Luftwaffe,* 234.

114. Irving, *Rise and Fall,* 58.

115. "Bericht der Wehrmachtmanoever (Luftwaffe) 1937," RL 2 II/Folder 159, BA-MA.

116. Corum, *Luftwaffe,* 235.

117. Hajo Herrmann, *Eagle's Wings: The Autobiography of a Luftwaffe Pilot,* trans. Peter Hinchliffe (Osceola, Wis.: Motorbooks International, 1991), 31–32.

118. Raymond L. Proctor, *Hitler's Luftwaffe in the Spanish Civil War* (Westport, Conn.: Greenwood Press, 1983), 60. By the end of the conflict, over 19,000 Luftwaffe personnel had served in Spain.

119. Dr. Eichelbaum, *Jahrbuch der deutschen Luftwaffe 1940* (Leipzig: Breitkopf & Härtel, 1940), 35.

120. "Bereitstellung und Einsatz deutscher Flakartillerie in Spanien [January 15, 1956]," K113.302, AFHRA. This paper was written by Oberst (retired) Aldinger, a member of the Luftwaffe in Spain during the civil war.

121. Proctor, *Civil War,* 134, 259.

122. Eichelbaum, *Jahrbuch,* 40. This is a propaganda text, and as such this claim must be viewed with a certain degree of skepticism. However, such results were possible under ideal conditions against low-flying aircraft.

123. Proctor, *Civil War,* 253.

124. Eichelbaum, *Jahrbuch 1940,* 38.

125. Karl Ries and Hans Ring, *The Legion Condor: A History of the Luftwaffe in the Spanish Civil War, 1936–1939,* trans. David Johnston (West Chester, Pa.: Schiffer Military Aviation, 1992), 234–236.

126. Werner Müller, *German Flak in World War II* (Atglen, Pa.: Schiffer Military/Aviation History, 1998), 6. This is a pictorial history of the German flak forces.

127. Koch, *Flak,* 20.

128. Lutz Hübner, "Die französische Flakartillerie," *Die Sirene* 22 (October 1937): 590.

129. Völker, *Deutsche Luftwaffe,* 110, 112.

130. Koch, *Flak,* 152.

131. "Verteilung von Übungs- und Schiessplätzen für die Flakartillerie, Teilnahme an Übungen des Heeres [March 25, 1936]," T-321/Reel 1/Frame 4734972, NARA.

132. Suchenwirth, *Development of the German Air Force,* 110.

133. Deist, *German Rearmament,* passim; see also Georg Thomas, *Geschichte der deutschen Wehr- und Rüstungswirtschaft (1918–1943/45)* (Boppard am Rhein: Harald Boldt Verlag, 1966), 63. Deist provides an excellent description of the bureaucratic infighting that typified interservice relationships within the Wehrmacht.

134. Letter from von Axthelm to von Renz dated January 15, 1958, N 529/Folder 9II, BA-MA; see also Völker, *Deutsche Luftwaffe,* 110.

135. Koch, *Flak,* 25.

136. Karl-Heinz Hummel, "Die Kommandostrukturen in der Reichsluftverteidigung, 1939–1945," in *Deutsches Soldatenjahrbuch 1987,* ed. H. Dameran (Munich: Schild Verlag, 1986), 432.

137. Gerhard Weinberg, *Germany, Hitler and World War II* (New York: Cambridge University Press, 1995), 68–82.

138. Brereton Greenhous, Stephen J. Harris, William C. Johnston, and William

G. P. Rawling, *The Official History of the Royal Canadian Air Force*, vol. 3, *The Crucible of War, 1939–1945* (Toronto: University of Toronto Press, 1994), 528.

139. Lee, *Goering*, 141.

4. First Lessons in the School of War, 1939–1940

1. The term "Maginot mentality" referred to a series of military border installations built during the interwar period and designed to protect France's eastern border in the event of a war with Germany. The term later became associated with a attribute of "defense-mindedness," the psychological antithesis of the pre–World War I French emphasis on the offensive.

2. Irving, *Rise and Fall*, 62.

3. Heinz Bongartz, *Luftmacht Deutschland: Luftwaffe-Industrie-Luftfahrt* (Essen: Essener Verlagsanstalt, 1939), 86.

4. Suchenwirth, *Development of the German Air Force*, 111–112.

5. Gerhard Granier, "Die Luftverteidigungszone-West," *Jahrbuch für westdeutsche Landesgeschichte* 19 (1993): 546.

6. Gerhard Weinberg, *A World at Arms: A Global History of World War II* (New York: Cambridge University Press, 1994), 28–33.

7. RH 2 *Oberkommando des Heeres/Generalstab des Heeres*/Folder 766/Pages 152–153, BA-MA.

8. "Die Luftverteidigungszone West [March 20, 1956]," N 529/Folder 13, BA-MA.

9. H. Orlovius, ed., *Schwert am Himmel: Fünf Jahre deutsche Luftwaffe* (Berlin: Verlag Scherl, 1940), 161; and Granier, "Luftverteidigungszone," 549.

10. "Die Luftverteidigungszone West [March 20, 1956]," N 529/Folder 13, BA-MA. The dollar conversion is based on the official 1939 exchange rate of forty cents per reichsmark. See Irvine, *World Almanac*, 515.

11. Orlovius, *Schwert*, 160–162.

12. Granier, "Luftverteidigungszone," 542.

13. Werner Baumbach, *The Life and Death of the Luftwaffe*, trans. Frederick Holt (New York: Ballantine Books, 1960), 11.

14. "Die Luftverteidigungszone West [March 20, 1956]," N 529/Folder 13, BA-MA.

15. Greenhous et al., *Crucible*, 531–532.

16. Perret, *Winged Victory*, 28. The Air Corps Tactical School taught airpower doctrine to army fliers during the late 1920s and throughout the 1930s.

17. "Dienstanweisung für den Präsidenten der Luftwaffen-Kommission," RL 4/Folder 269, BA-MA.

18. "Interrogation of General von Axthelm and Lt. Col. Sieber (USSBS Interview No. 68)," 524.606, AFHRA.

19. "Dienstanweisung für den Präsidenten der Luftwaffen-Kommission," RL 4/Folder 269, BA-MA.

20. "Beschaffung von Großgeräten für die Flakartillerie [March 18, 1938]," T-321/Reel 3/Frame 4736999, NARA.

21. Boog, *Luftwaffenführung*, 205.

22. "Fertigung von Flakmunition im Rahmen des Beschaffungsprogramms [August 3, 1939]," T-321/Reel 7/Frame 4742570, NARA.

23. Letter from von Renz to von Axthelm of February 28, 1954, N 529/Folder 7, BA-MA. This is von Renz's estimation of the strength of the ground-based air defense force at the start of the war. See also Müller, *German Flak,* 10. Müller cites the figure of 657 heavy gun batteries in contrast to von Renz's figure of 650.

24. Boog et al., *Der globale Krieg,* 445. The railroad flak battalions included 88-mm and 20-mm gun batteries. The naval flak battalions consisted of one heavy and two light flak companies each.

25. Routledge, *Royal Regiment,* 66–67.

26. Maurer Maurer, *Aviation in the U.S. Army, 1919–1939* (Washington, D.C.: Office of Air Force History, 1987), 414–420. The most notable of these exercises was conducted at Fort Knox in May 1933 and included observers from the German army.

27. Bland, *George Catlett Marshall,* 1:622–623.

28. Lucien Robineau, "French Interwar Air Policy and Air War, 1939–1940," in *The Conduct of the Air War in World War II: An International Comparison,* ed. Horst Boog (New York: Berg, 1992), 641.

29. USSBS, Morale Division, *The United States Strategic Bombing Survey,* vol. 1, *The Effects of Strategic Bombing on German Morale* (Washington, D.C.: GPO, 1947), 66. The survey noted, "At the outbreak of the war Germany had this excellent ARP [air raid protection] system."

30. *Die Sirene* 10 (December 1938): 703.

31. David MacIsaac, ed., *The United States Strategic Bombing Survey,* vol. 2, *Civilian Defense Division Final Report* (New York: Garland, 1976), 43.

32. *Die Sirene,* Special Issue (1940): no page number.

33. *Weltkrieg, 1939–1945: Ehrenbuch der deutschen Wehrmacht* (Stuttgart: Buch- und Zeitschriften-Verlag Dr. Hans Riegler, 1954), 39.

34. Boog et al., *Der globale Krieg,* 447.

35. Boog, *Luftwaffenführung,* 205.

36. Kesselring, *Gedanken zum zweiten Weltkrieg,* 157, 177.

37. "Stellungnahme zur Nachtjagd," RL 4/Folder 269/Page 85, BA-MA; emphasis in the original.

38. Ibid., 85–86.

39. "Vortrag über Technik, Organisation und Einsatz der Jagdkräfte [October 22, 1936]," T-405/Reel 6/Frame 4834485, NARA.

40. The Bf-109 was a single-seat fighter and the Luftwaffe's best fighter aircraft in 1939.

41. Kennett, *First Air War,* 78.

42. Hinchliffe, *Other Battle,* 30–31, 39–40. The organizational terms associated with German flying units were somewhat confusing. The *Staffel* was the Luftwaffe's basic operational unit, consisting of nine aircraft, and was roughly equivalent to an Anglo-American squadron. A *Gruppe* was made up of three *Staffeln* and was equivalent to an American group. Finally, a *Geschwader* was normally composed of three *Gruppen* and was equivalent to an American wing.

43. "Bemerkungen zum Erfahrungsbericht des Gen. d. Lw. beim Ob.d.H. über den Feldzug in Polen [November 30, 1939]," RL 4/Folder 269/Page 87, BA-MA.

44. "Abschlussmeldung über Flakartillerie im Bereich des Gen.d.Lw.Ob.d.H [February 28, 1942]," N 529/Folder 7, BA-MA.

45. Lee, *German Air Force,* 48–50. Lee cites one Luftwaffe report in which several days' worth of combat had resulted in the destruction of 74 Polish aircraft, 28 in the air and 46 on the ground.

46. "Abschlussmeldung über Flakartillerie im Bereich des Gen.d.Lw.Ob.d.H [February 28, 1942]," N 529/Folder 7, BA-MA.

47. "Bemerkungen zum Erfahrungsbericht des Gen. d. Lw. beim Ob.d.H. über den Feldzug in Polen [November 30, 1939]," RL 4/Folder 269/Pages 87–89, BA-MA.

48. Letter from von Axthelm to von Renz of August 15, 1955, N 529/Folder 9 II, BA-MA.

49. Webster and Frankland, *Strategic Air Offensive,* 1:192.

50. Overy, *The Air War,* 37; see also Arthur Harris, *Bomber Offensive* (London: Collins, 1947; reprint, London: Greenhill Books, 1990), 53.

51. Robineau, "French Interwar Air Policy," 646–647.

52. Webster and Frankland, *Strategic Air Offensive,* 1:192–197; see also Alan Beyerchen, "From Radio to Radar: Interwar Military Adaptation to Technological Change in Germany, the United Kingdom, and the United States," in *Military Innovation in the Interwar Period,* ed. Williamson Murray and Allan R. Millett (New York: Cambridge University Press, 1996), 274–275.

53. Webster and Frankland, *Strategic Air Offensive,* 1:200–201.

54. "Abschlussmeldung über Flakartillerie im Bereich des Gen.d.Lw.Ob.d.H [February 28, 1942]," N 529/Folder 7, BA-MA.

55. Denis Richards, *The Hardest Victory: RAF Bomber Command in the Second World War* (New York: Norton, 1994), 341.

56. Letter from Air Marshal Sir Charles Portal to Air Marshal Sir Sholto Douglas of May 19, 1940, AIR 14/Folder 1930, PRO.

57. Laurence Deane, *A Pathfinder's War and Peace* (Braunton, Devon: Merlin Books, 1993), 35–36.

58. Greenhous et al., *Crucible,* 533.

59. "Kriegstagebuch des Luftgaukommandos VII vom 26.8.39-7.6.40," RL 19 *Luftgaukommandos-Luftgaustäbe*/Folder 77/Page 2, BA-MA.

60. Ibid., 4.

61. Letter from von Renz to von Axthelm, dated February 28, 1954, N 529/Folder 7, BA-MA.

62. "Vorstudien zur Luftkriegsgeschichte, Heft 8, Reichsluftverteidigung [1944]," T-971/Reel 69, NARA.

63. "Kriegstagebuch des Luftgaukommandos VII vom 26.8.39–7.6.40," RL 19/ Folder 77/Page 4, BA-MA.

64. "Vorstudien zur Luftkriegsgeschichte, Heft 8, Reichsluftverteidigung [1944]," T-971/Reel 69, NARA.

65. Hogg, *Anti-Aircraft,* 77.

66. "Munitionslage," T-321/Reel 7/Frames 4742443, 4742454–55, NARA.

67. "3,7 cm Sprgr.Patr. für Pak [October 25, 1939]," T-321/Reel 7/Frame 4742512, NARA.

68. "Munitionserzeugungsplan [September 20, 1939]," T-321/Reel 7/Frames 4742461–62, NARA.

69. "Besprechung über Engpässe der Flakmunition bei LE 4 am 4.9.39," T-321/Reel 7/Frame 4742547; "Vortragsnotizen für den Herrn Generalluftzeugmeister [November 13, 1939]," T-321/Reel 7/Frame 4742496, NARA. Two of the primary bottlenecks included the manufacture of the timed fuses and the production of steel shell casings.

70. "Kriegstagebuch des Luftgaukommandos VII vom 26.8.39–7.6.40," RL 19/Folder 77/Page 50, BA-MA.

71. "Vortrag vor dem Herrn Chef der Luftwehr [March 28, 1940]," RL 19/Folder 306, BA-MA.

72. Boog et al., *Der globale Krieg*, 447.

73. "Kriegstagebuch des Luftgaukommandos VII vom 26.8.39–7.6.40," RL 19/Folder 77/Pages 4, 30, 48, BA-MA.

74. Ibid., 54.

75. "Abschlussmeldung über Flakartillerie im Bereich des Gen.d.Lw.Ob.d.H [February 28, 1942]," N 529/Folder 7, BA-MA; "Tagesbefehl des Flakregiments 102 [July 8, 1940]," RL 12 *Verbände und Einheiten der Flakartillerie*/Folder 457, B.A.-M.A; see also Koch, *Flak*, 42–44. Koch states that flak forces brought down 854 aircraft in the west, whereas fighters accounted for 1,525. This disparity most likely reflects Koch's use of both "probable" and "confirmed" kills together.

76. Dr. Eichelbaum, ed., *Jahrbuch der deutschen Luftwaffe 1941* (Leipzig: Breitkopf & Härtel, 1940), 33.

77. "Kriegstagebuch des Luftgaukommandos VII [June 7, 9, 20, 21, 1940]," RL 19/Folder 78/Pages 8, 10, 36, 42, 44, BA-MA.

78. "Tagesbefehl des Flakregiments 102 [July 8, 1940]," RL 12/Folder 457, BA-MA.

79. "Kriegstagebuch des Luftgaukommandos VII," RL 19/Folder 78/Page 72, BA-MA. By 1943, Hitler apparently dropped this prohibition. A book containing the experiences of a number of air defense personnel in the campaign in the west appeared in print. See Hans Georg von Puttkamer, ed., *Flakkorps "I" im Westen* (Berlin: Volk und Reich Verlag, 1943).

80. "Vorstudien zur Luftkriegsgeschichte, Heft 8, Reichsluftverteidigung [1944]," T-971/Reel 69, NARA.

81. "Kriegstagebuch des Luftgaukommandos VII [June 7, 1940]," RL 19/Folder 77/Page 76, BA-MA.

82. Ibid., 78.

83. Ibid.

84. "Vortrag vor dem Chef der Luftwehr [March 28, 1940]," RL 19/Folder 306, BA-MA.

85. Webster and Frankland, *Strategic Air Offensive*, 1:397.

86. "Kriegstagebuch des Luftgaukommandos VII [June 7, 1940]," RL 19/Folder 77/Page 70, BA-MA.

87. Deane, *Pathfinder's War*, 39. The German military quickly recognized this tactic. See "Kriegstagebuch [of Flak Regiment 25]," RL 12/Folder 11/Pages 46, 61, BA-MA. Entries are from December 21, 1940, and February 2, 1941.

88. Dr. Eichelbaum, *Das Buch von der Luftwaffe* (Berlin: Verlagshaus Bong, 1940), 89. Eichelbaum was a major in the Air Ministry at the time that this book was published.

89. Niehaus, *Radarschlacht*, 33; see also Beyerchen, "Radio to Radar," 274–275.

90. "Förderung der Ortung und Kennung von Flugzeugen mittels Ultrakurzwellen-(Dezimeter)—Strahlen oder Infrarot-(Wärme)—Strahlen [1939]," RL 4/Folder 269/Page 61, BA-MA.

91. Renz, *Development of German Anti-aircraft*, 306, K113.107-194, AFHRA.

92. Thomas, *Wehr- und Rüstungswirtschaft*, 413.

93. Ibid., 307–309. The Würzburg went through a number of modifications and model numbers. The initial system was designated *Funkmeßgerät* 62 (FuMG 62); as improvements were made, later systems carried the designations FuMG 39 L, FuMG 39 T (A), and FuMG T (C).

94. Ibid., 310.

95. Control Commission for Germany, Air Division, *Notes on Flak and Searchlight Radar (G.A.F.)* (n.p.: Air Division, C.C.G., 1946), 51, collection of the library of the Imperial War Museum.

96. "Entwicklungsprogramm der Flakartillerie 1937," RL 4/Folder 257, BA-MA.

97. "Förderung der Ortung und Kennung von Flugzeugen mittels Ultrakurzwellen-(Dezimeter)—Strahlen oder Infrarot-(Wärme)—Strahlen [1939]," RL 4/Folder 269/Page 61, BA-MA; see also Irving, *Rise and Fall*, 74–75. On July 3, 1939, the test base at Rechlin provided an exhibition of the Luftwaffe's most advanced technology for Hitler, including rocket-assisted takeoff, a rocket-propelled interceptor aircraft, and a new 30-mm aircraft cannon. In the coming years, both Hitler and Göring complained bitterly that the Technical Office had oversold these capabilities and led them into thinking that these systems would soon be ready for production. In 1942, Göring sarcastically remarked, "'Do you know, I once witnessed a display before the war at Rechlin, compared with which I can only say—what bunglers all our professional magicians are! Because the world has never before and never will again see the likes of what was conjured up before my—and far worse, the Führer's—eyes at Rechlin'" (Irving, *Rise and Fall*, 75).

98. R. J. Overy, *Goering: The "Iron Man"* (London: Routledge and Kegan Paul, 1984), 173, 179. One of the most glaring examples of Göring's technical ineptitude involved his appointment of Ernst Udet as *Generalluftzeugmeister* in charge of technical developments, a disastrous choice that crippled air force development projects and led to Udet's suicide in the face of numerous monumental failures.

99. Adolf Galland, *The First and the Last: The Rise and Fall of the German Fighter Forces, 1938–1945*, trans, Mervyn Savill (New York: Ballantine Books, 1954), 11.

100. Beyerchen, "Radio to Radar," 272–273.

101. "Adjutantur der Wehrmacht beim Führer und Reichskanzler, Br.B.Nr.18a/40 g.Kdos [July 28, 1940]," T-321/Reel 7/Frame 4743251; see also Frames 4743238, 4743243, 4743246–48, NARA.

102. Boog, *Luftwaffenführung*, 205.

103. USSBS, Economic Effects Division, *The United States Strategic Bombing Survey: The Effects of Strategic Bombing on the German War Economy*, 285.

104. "Anl. L.C. 6 Nr.406/40 g.Kdos., Waffen und Gerät Luftwaffe [July 9, 1940]," T-321/Reel 7/Frame 4743275, NARA.

105. "Anl. zu L.C. 6 Nr. 406/40 g.Kdos., Munition Luftwaffe [July 7, 1940]," T-321/Reel 7/Frame 4743273, NARA.

106. USSBS, *United States Strategic Bombing Survey: Report on the German Flak Effort Throughout the War* (n.p., 1945), 4, 137.310-4, AFHRA.

107. For the Luftwaffe Commission forecast, see "Dienstanweisung für den Präsidenten der Luftwaffen-Kommission," RL 4/Folder 269, BA-MA.

108. "Vorstudien zur Luftkriegsgeschichte, Heft 8, Reichsluftverteidigung [1944]," T-971/Reel 69, NARA.

109. Optically directed fire refers to the use of a fire director to compute targeting solutions based on optical measurements.

110. USSBS, Economic Effects Division, *The United States Strategic Bombing Survey: The Effects of Strategic Bombing on the German War Economy,* 284.

111. "Kriegstagebuch des Luftgaukommandos VII [June 7–October 8, 1940]," RL 19/Folder 78/Page 78, entry from July 8, 1940, BA-MA.

112. Germany, Kriegswissenschaftliche Abteilung der Luftwaffe, *Luftschutz im Weltkrieg,* 119; see also "Winter-Kriegsspiel 1934–35," RL 2 II/Folder 76, BA-MA.

113. "Kriegstagebuch des Luftgaukommandos VII [July 17, 1940]," RL 19/Folder 78/Page 86, BA-MA.

114. "Richtlinien für die Kampfführung in der Flakgruppe Vorfeld-West [December 6, 1940]," RL 12/Folder 39/Page 28, BA-MA.

115. "Kriegstagebuch des Luftgaukommandos VII [August 3, 1940]," RL 19/Folder 78/Page 108, BA-MA.

116. Norbert Hoffmann, "Der Luftangriff auf Lauffen am 13. April 1944," *Lauffener Heimatblätter* 8 (April 1994): 8.

117. "Kriegstagebuch des Luftgaukommandos VII [July 19, 1940]," RL 19/Folder 78/Page 90, BA-MA.

118. Ibid. [August 6, 1940], 112.

119. Ibid. [August 1940], 106.

120. Ibid. [August 17, 1940], 128.

121. Ibid. [September 1940], 190, 204.

122. Ibid. [August 1940], 112, 154.

123. Ibid. [October 1, 1940], 258.

124. Elke Fröhlich, *Die Tagebücher von Joseph Goebbels: Sämtliche Fragmente,* part I, vol. 4 (Munich: K. G. Saur, 1987), 395; diary entry of November 14, 1940.

125. "Kriegstagebuch des Luftgaukommandos VII [November, 1940]," RL 19/Folder 79/Page 117, BA-MA.

126. Ibid. [November 11, 1940], 109.

127. Ibid. [December 1, 1940], 135.

128. Military Intelligence 15, *Handbook of German Anti-Aircraft Artillery (Flak),* vol. 5, *Deployment Siting and Emplacements* (London: War Office, 1946), 19, IWM; see also P. D. R. Hunt and Z. Bieniawski, *Air Photographic Analysis of German A.A. Defences* (In the field: Mediterranean Allied Photographic Reconnaissance Wing, 1944), 19, IWM.

129. U.S. War Department, *Handbook on German Military Forces* (reprint, Baton Rouge: Louisiana State University Press, 1990), 357.

130. Hogg, *Anti-Aircraft*, 108; see also Koch, *Flak*, 187–188; and USSBS, *The United States Strategic Bombing Survey: Report on the German Flak Effort Throughout the War*, 6, 137.310–4, AFHRA. The average barrage balloon battalion consisted of four batteries of eighteen balloons each, with almost 700 persons per battalion.

131. The term "coned" referred to aircraft caught and held in the cone of light cast by a searchlight.

132. "Kriegstagebuch des Luftgaukommandos VII [August 1940]," RL 19/Folder 78/Page 120, BA-MA.

133. Ibid. [August 23, 1940], 140.

134. "Kriegstagebuch des Luftgaukommandos VII [October 11, 1940]," RL 19/Folder 79/Page 13, BA-MA.

135. "Richtlinien für die Kampfführung in der Flakgruppe Vorfeld-West [December 6, 1940]," RL 12/Folder 39/Page 2, BA-MA.

136. "Kriegstagebuch des Luftgaukommandos VII [November 9, 1940]," RL 19/Folder 79/Page 103, BA-MA. The "beer hall putsch" involved Hitler's failed attempt to seize control of the Bavarian government in November 1923.

137. "Kriegstagebuch des Luftgaukommandos VII [August 15, 1940]," RL 19/Folder 78/Page 126; see also "Kriegstagebuch des Luftgaukommandos VII [October 14, 1940]," RL 19/Folder 79/Page 17, BA-MA.

138. "Kriegstagebuch [of Flak Regiment 25]," RL 12/Folder 11/Page 79, BA-MA. This information is contained in an overview entry for the period between November 1940 and February 1941. More than 42 percent of the regiment's members were over thirty years old.

139. "Kriegstagebuch des Luftgaukommandos VII [August 31, 1940]," RL 19/Folder 78/Page 170, BA-MA.

140. Ibid. [October 1, 1940], 258–260.

141. "Kriegstagebuch des Luftgaukommandos VII [November 24, 1940]," RL 19/Folder 79/Page 129, BA-MA.

142. Ibid. The new procedure known as "akustische Ortung im Zweistandsverfahren" was demonstrated for the first time on November 28, 1940, in Munich-Freimann. See also "Richtlinien für die Kampfführung in der Flakgruppe Vorfeld-West [December 6, 1940]," RL 12/Folder 39/Page 4, BA-MA.

143. "Kriegstagebuch des Luftgaukommandos VII [November/December 1940]," RL 19/Folder 79/Pages 143–145, 149, BA-MA.

144. Ibid. [December 20, 1940], 155.

145. Lee, *Goering*, 141.

146. "Kriegstagebuch des Luftgaukommandos VII [August 26, 1940]," RL 19/Folder 78/Page 150, BA-MA.

147. Olaf Groehler, *Kampf um die Luftherrschaft*, 2nd ed. (Berlin [East]: Militärverlag der DDR, 1988), 184; see also Koch, *Flak*, 52–53.

148. Groehler, *Luftherrschaft*, 184.

149. Fröhlich, *Tagebücher*, part I, vol. 4, p. 384; diary entry of November 2, 1940.

150. Koch, *Flak*, 52–53. The RAF had conducted small "nuisance" raids against Berlin at the end of August 1940; however, the attacks in October and November

involved up to thirty aircraft; see also Groehler, *Kampf,* 188; and William R. Chorley, ed., *Royal Air Force Bomber Command Losses of World War II*, vol. 1, *Aircraft and Crews Lost During 1939–1940* (Earl Shilton, Leicester: Midland Counties Publication, 1992), 129–131. Groehler states that gun-laying radar were available for use by twelve batteries in the vicinity of Berlin by the end of 1940.

151. "*Flak Nachrichtenblatt,* Herausgegeben vom Oberbefehlshaber der Luftwaffe, L. Inspektion der Flakartillerie, 1-XII/40 g. [December 1940]," RL 4/Folder 262, BA-MA. This is in part to be expected because those shot down would naturally have a high estimation of the area's air defenses; however, increased numbers of aircraft shot down in a specific area would also cause returning crews to view the area with increased respect.

152. "*Flak Nachrichtenblatt,* Herausgegeben vom Oberbefehlshaber der Luftwaffe, L. Inspektion der Flakartillerie, Nr.2–I/41 g. [February 1941]," RL 4/Folder 262, BA-MA.

153. "Flugzeugabschüsse und Munitionsverbrauch durch Flakartillerie im Dezember [January 13, 1941]," T-321/Reel 7/Frames 4742638–41, NARA.

154. Ibid. The report lists five aircraft destroyed through a combination of assisted fire (using an auxiliary predictor) and barrier fire procedures. In Air District VII, a prototype of a gun-laying radar assisted in the destruction of one aircraft at night with the expenditure of only thirty-nine rounds.

155. After the defeat of France, Flak Corps II remained in the west to protect Wehrmacht forces preparing for Operation Sea Lion, the invasion of Great Britain. See Koch, *Flak,* 45.

156. Chorley, *Bomber Command Losses,* 1: 136–143.

157. David Scholes, *Air War Diary: An Australian in Bomber Command* (Kenthurst, New South Wales: Kangaroo Press, 1997), 82. This is a mission description of a raid conducted on July 24, 1944, by a force of Lancasters, but it provides a representative view of the dangers associated with the attack of port and harbor facilities in the west.

158. Hinchliffe, *Other Battle,* 45–49. The Kammhuber line was essentially completed by the summer of 1941. In addition, the Luftwaffe created a similar air defense system to the north and west of Berlin.

159. James D. Crabtree, *On Air Defense* (Westport, Conn.: Praeger, 1994), 72–74.

160. Deane, *Pathfinder's War,* 35–36.

161. Letter from Air Vice Marshal Sir Richard Peirse to Air Marshal Sir Sholto Douglas of October 28, 1940, AIR 14/Folder 1930, PRO.

162. USSBS, Civil Defense Division, *The United States Strategic Bombing Survey: Civilian Defense Division Report,* 2.

163. "Kriegstagebuch des Luftgaukommandos VII [October 9, 1940]," RL 19/Folder 79/Page 3, BA-MA.

164. Denis Richards, *Portal of Hungerford: The Life of Marshal of the Royal Air Force Viscount Portal of Hungerford* (London: William Heinemann, 1977), 188.

165. Josef Pöchlinger, ed., *Front in der Heimat: Das Buch des deutschen Rüstungsarbeiters* (Berlin: Otto Elsner Verlagsgesellschaft, 1942), 14.

166. Koch, *Flak,* 51, 177.

167. Boog, *Luftwaffenführung,* 205. Hitler made this remark in a meeting with Mussolini in January 1941.

5. Winning the Battle, 1941

1. Absolon, *Rangliste,* 152.

2. Lee, *Goering,* 144.

3. Hinchliffe, *Other Battle,* 52.

4. "Kriegstagebuch [of Flak Regiment 25]," RL 12 *Verbände und Einheiten der Flakartillerie*/Folder 11/Pages 49–50, BA-MA; war diary entries of January 2–3, 1941.

5. "*Flak Nachrichtenblatt,* Herausgegeben vom Oberbefehlshaber der Luftwaffe L.Inspektion der Flakartillerie 1-XII/40 g.," RL 4/Folder 262, BA-MA.

6. "Kriegstagebuch [of Flak Regiment 25]," RL 12/Folder 11/Pages 57–58, BA-MA; war diary entries of January 23 and January 27, 1941.

7. Renz, *Development of German Anti-aircraft,* 300–301, 303, K113.107-194, AFHRA.

8. "Beitrag zur kriegswissenschaftlichen Arbeit von Generalfeldmarschall Kesselring," N 529/Folder 12, BA-MA. Because the speed of sound through air remains relatively constant, increased aircraft speeds meant that sound-detector crews had less time to pinpoint their targets in an environment in which initial detection range remains constant. See also "Kriegstagebuch [of Flak Regiment 25]," RL 12/Folder 11/Page 56, BA-MA; war diary entry of January 19, 1941.

9. Renz, *Development of German Anti-aircraft,* 304, K113.107-194, AFHRA.

10. "Kriegstagebuch [of Flak Regiment 25]," RL 12/Folder 11/Page 63, BA-MA; war diary entry of February 10, 1941.

11. Ibid., 74; summary entry for the period between November 1940 and February 1941.

12. "Flak-Munition 8,8 cm [March 25, 1941]," T-321/Reel 7/Frame 4743038, NARA.

13. "8.8 cm Flak-Munition [April 1, 1941]," T-321/Reel 7/Frame 4743028, NARA.

14. "Fertigen von 8,8 cm Flakmunition [May 26, 1941]," T-321/Reel 7/Frame 4742795; see also "8.8 vm Flak-Munition [April 1, 1941]," T-321/Reel 7/Frame 4743029, NARA.

15. Richard Suchenwirth, *Historical Turning Points in the German Air Force War Effort* (Maxwell AFB, Ala.: USAF Historical Division, 1968), 55.

16. "Überblick über den Rüstungsstand 1. Pulver 2. Sprengstoffe [April 24, 1941]," T-321/Reel 7/Frames 4742838–39, NARA.

17. "Fertigen von 8,8 cm Flakmunition [May 26, 1941]," T-321/Reel 7/Frames 4742796–97; see also "8.8 vm Flak-Munition [April 1, 1941]," T-321/Reel 7/Frames 4743030–31, NARA.

18. USSBS, Economic Effects Division, *The United States Strategic Bombing Survey: The Effects of Strategic Bombing on the German War Economy,* 285.

19. Ibid.

20. "Kriegstagebuch [of Flak Regiment 25]," RL 12/Folder 11/Pages 58, 66, BA-MA; war diary entries of January 28 and February 13, 1941.

21. "*Flak-Nachrichtenblatt,* Herausgegeben vom Oberbefehlshaber der Luftwaffe, L. Inspektion der Flakartillerie, Nr.3–III/41 g., [March 1941]," RL 4/Folder 262, BA-MA.

22. "Rohrkrepierer bei 8,8 cm und 10,5 cm Flak [June 10, 1941]," T-321/Reel 7/Frames 4742756–57, NARA.

23. "Rohrkrepierer [June 6, 1941]," T-321/Reel 7/Frames 4742758–59, NARA.
24. Boog, *Luftwaffenführung,* 207.
25. "Der General der Flakartillerie beim R.d.L u. Ob.d.L. [March 28,1941]," RL 4/Folder 257, BA-MA.
26. Schabel, *Illusion,* 262.
27. Neufeld, *Rocket and the Reich,* 150–152.
28. Schabel, *Illusion,* 262.
29. "Flugzeugabschüsse und Munitonsverbrauch durch Flakartl.d.Luftw. [January–April 1941]," T-321/Reel 7/Frames 4742623, 4742627, 4742631, 4742635, NARA.
30. Richards, *Hardest Victory,* 77. The weather was so bad, in fact, that RAF bombers could only attack oil sites, their primary target set, on three nights in the opening two months of the year.
31. Renz, *Development of German Anti-aircraft,* 309–310, K113.107-194, AFHRA.
32. Harris, *Bomber Offensive,* 68.
33. Letter from Air Marshal Sir Richard Peirse to Air Chief Marshal Sir Charles Portal of April 15, 1941, AIR 14/Folder 1927, PRO.
34. Gerhard Wagner, ed., *Lagevorträge des Oberbefehlhabers der Kriegsmarine vor Hitler, 1939–1945* (Munich: J. F. Lehmanns Verlag, 1972), 343; this excerpt is from a meeting of January 12, 1942.
35. "Flugzeugabschüsse und Munitonsverbrauch durch Flakartl.d.Luftw. [January–April 1941]," T-321/Reel 7/Frames 4742624–25, 4742628–29, 4742632–33, 4742636–37, NARA.
36. Chorley, *Bomber Command Losses,* 2:18–19, 29. The aircraft sent to Bremen encountered extremely poor weather, which prevented a number of crews from finding the target.
37. "Vorstudien zur Luftkriegsgeschichte, Heft 8, Reichsluftverteidigung [1944]," T-971/Reel 69, NARA.
38. Ibid.
39. Letter from Air Marshal Sir Richard Peirse to Air Chief Marshal Sir Charles Portal of April 6, 1941, AIR 14/Folder 1927, PRO.
40. Letter from Air Chief Marshal Sir Charles Portal to Air Marshal Sir Richard Peirse of April 22, 1941, AIR 14/Folder 1927, PRO.
41. Letter from Air Marshal Sir Richard Peirse to Air Chief Marshal Sir Charles Portal of April 23, 1941, AIR 14/Folder 1927, PRO.
42. Letter from Air Commodore J. W. Baker to Air Marshal Sir Richard Peirse of April 23, 1941, AIR 14/Folder 1934, PRO.
43. "Interceptions/Tactics Report No.12/42 [January 1942]," *Bomber Command Damage Summaries, 1944–1945,* AHB; see also Hogg, *German Artillery,* 151. In contrast, the 37-mm/Model 43 had an effective ceiling of almost 14,000 feet.
44. "*Flak-Nachrichtenblatt,* Herausgegeben vom Oberbefehlshaber der Luftwaffe, L.Inspektion der Flakartillerie, Nr.4–VI/41 g." RL 4/Folder 262, BA-MA.
45. Suchenwirth, *Historical Turning Points,* 114–115.
46. Letter from Air Marshal Sir Richard Peirse to Air Chief Marshal Sir Charles Portal of February 28, 1941, AIR 14/Folder 1927, PRO.
47. "Vorstudien zur Luftkriegsgeschichte, Heft 8, Reichsluftverteidigung [1944]," T-971/Reel 69, NARA.

48. Ibid. This position was a modification of the office of the commander, center, that had been created on March 3, 1941.

49. Hildebrand, *Generale,* 1:497.

50. Hummel, "Kommandostrukturen," 432; see also "Vorstudien zur Luftkriegsgeschichte, Heft 8, Reichsluftverteidigung [1944]," T-971/Reel 69, NARA.

51. Hummel, "Kommandostrukturen," 432.

52. Friedhelm Golücke, *Schweinfurt und der strategische Luftkrieg, 1943: Der Angriff der US Air Force vom 14. Oktober gegen die Schweinfurter Kugellagerindustrie* (Paderborn: Ferdinand Schönigh, 1980), 108.

53. Feuchter, *Geschichte des Luftkriegs,* 301–302.

54. Karl-Heinz Hummel, "Die Kommandostrukturen in der Reichsluftverteidigung, 1939–1945," in *Deutsches Soldatenjahrbuch 1988,* ed. H. Dameran (Munich: Schild Verlag, 1987), 237.

55. Boog, *Luftwaffenführung,* 132; see also "Vorstudien zur Luftkriegsgeschichte, Heft 8, Reichsluftverteidigung [1944]," T-971/Reel 69, NARA. It was not until November 1943 that the commander of Air Region, Center, gained administrative control over these forces.

56. "Vorstudien zur Luftkriegsgeschichte, Heft 8, Reichsluftverteidigung [1944]," T-971/Reel 69, NARA.

57. Letter from Rüdel to Jeschonnek, dated January 5, 1941, RL 4/Folder 257, BA-MA.

58. "Stellungnahme der Inspektion der Flakartillerie zur Aufstellung von Heeres-Flakartillerie-Abteilungen [April 30, 1941]," RL 4/Folder 260/Page 15, BA-MA.

59. Ibid.

60. "Aufstellung von Heeres-Flakartillerieabteilungen [June 20, 1941]," RL 4/Folder 260/Page 2, BA-MA.

61. Heinrich Steinacker, *Fla-Btl (mot) 22: Seine Geschichte* (Siegen: Bonn und Fries, 1984), 5.

62. George F. Nafziger, *German Order of Battle, World War II,* vol. 3, *German Artillery: Independent Battalions, Railroad, Coastal, Flak, and Sturmgeschütz* (West Chester, Ohio: By the author, 1994), 38.

63. Koch, *Flak,* 96–98.

64. J. Engelmann, *Das Buch der Artillerie, 1939–1945* (Friedberg: Podzun-Pallas-Verlag, 1983), 84. Each of the heavy batteries consisted of between four and six 88–mm guns and three 20-mm guns, while the light battery consisted of six 37-mm guns, three four-barreled 20-mm guns, and four 60-cm searchlights.

65. "Abschlussmeldung über Flakartillerie im Bereich des Gen.d.Lw.Ob.d.H [February 28, 1942]," N 529/Folder 7, BA-MA. In addition to the success of the Luftwaffe's flak forces, a German propaganda piece claimed that army flak units had shot down 250 Soviet aircraft and destroyed "numerous" enemy armored vehicles in the opening months of the campaign. See Emil Sauter, *Fla-nach vorn: Kampf der Fliegerabwehr Bataillone u. Kompanien des Heeres* (Mülhausen in Thüringia: Verlag von G. Danner, 1942), 7–8.

66. Ibid.

67. For a history of the flak units of the Waffen-SS, see Hans Stöber, *Die Flugabwehrverbände der Waffen-SS* (Preußisch Oldendorf: Verlag K. W. Schütz,

1984), 44. The SS Leibstandarte "Adolf Hitler" was the first SS formation to receive a heavy flak battery of four 88-mm flak guns in August 1940.

68. *Weltkrieg,* 42–43.

69. Koch, *Flak,* 64.

70. "Bezug: Gen.Qu. Genst.6.Abt.Nr. 6268/41 geh. (IV T) [May 23, 1941]," RL 4/Folder 257, BA-MA.

71. Letter from Rüdel to Jeschonnek, dated January 5, 1941, RL 4/Folder 257, BA-MA.

72. "Zeitfolge [June 28–July 7, 1941]," RL 4/Folder 257, BA-MA.

73. Letter from Rüdel to von Axthelm, dated October 7, 1942, RL 4/Folder 258, BA-MA.

74. Greenhous et al., *Crucible,* 544.

75. Chorley, *Bomber Command Losses,* 2:49.

76. "*Flak-Nachrichtenblatt,* Herausgegeben vom Oberbefehlshaber der Luftwaffe, L.Inspektion der Flakartillerie, Nr.5–VII/41 g." RL 4/Folder 262, BA-MA.

77. Ibid.

78. "Vorstudien zur Luftkriegsgeschichte, Heft 8, Reichsluftverteidigung [1944]," T-971/Reel 69, NARA.

79. Hinchliffe, *Other Battle,* 66.

80. Suchenwirth, *Historical Turning Points,* 109.

81. Lee, *German Air Force,* 229–230.

82. Hinchliffe, *Other Battle,* 65–66, 69–70.

83. "*Flak-Nachrichtenblatt,* Herausgegeben vom Oberbefehlshaber der Luft-waffe, L.Inspektion der Flakartillerie, Nr.5–VII/41 g.," RL 4/Folder 262; "*Flak-Nachrichtenblatt,* Herausgegeben vom Oberbefehlshaber der Luftwaffe, L.Inspektion der Flakartillerie, Nr.6–VIII/41 g.," RL 4/Folder 262; "*Flak-Nachrichtenblatt,* Herausgegeben vom Oberbefehlshaber der Luftwaffe, L.Inspektion der Flakartillerie, NB 7–X/41 g," RL 4/Folder 262; "*Flak Nachrichtenblatt,* Herausgegeben vom Oberbefehlshaber der Luftwaffe, L.In.4, NB. 8–XI/41g.," RL 4/Folder 262; BA-MA. The totals for aircraft shot down (without USSR losses) for July and August are taken from NB 8–XI/41 and are only for Germany proper and the western territories.

84. "*Flak-Nachrichtenblatt,* Herausgegeben vom Oberbefehlshaber der Luft-waffe, L.Inspektion der Flakartillerie, Nr.5–VII/41 g.," RL 4/Folder 262; "*Flak-Nachrichtenblatt,* Herausgegeben vom Oberbefehlshaber der Luftwaffe, L.Inspektion der Flakartillerie, Nr.6–VIII/41 g.," RL 4/Folder 262; "*Flak-Nachrichtenblatt,* Herausgegeben vom Oberbefehlshaber der Luftwaffe, L.Inspektion der Flakartillerie, NB 7–X/41 g," RL 4/Folder 262, BA-MA.

85. BBSU, *The Strategic Air War Against Germany, 1939–1945: Report of the British Bombing Survey Unit,* 5.

86. Webster and Frankland, *Strategic Air Offensive,* 4:205. The entire Butt report is reproduced in this volume (pp. 205–213). If one takes into account only aircraft that attacked the target, as opposed to all aircraft dispatched, the total ratio of crews that dropped their bombs within the five-mile target area was one in three.

87. Ibid., 211.

88. Chorley, *Bomber Command Losses,* 2:129.

89. "Kriegstagebuch des Luftgaukommandos VII [August–September 1941]," RL 19/Folder 81/Pages 39, 83, BA-MA.

90. "Vorstudien zur Luftkriegsgeschichte, Heft 8, Reichsluftverteidigung [1944]," T-971/Reel 69, NARA.

91. Fröhlich, *Tagebücher,* part II, vol. 1, p. 452; diary entry of September 19, 1941.

92. Letter from Air Chief Marshal Sir Charles Portal to Air Marshal Sir Richard Peirse of October 19, 1941, AIR 14/Folder 1928, PRO. Portal forwarded Peirse a copy of his report to the prime minister.

93. "Kriegstagebuch des Luftgaukommandos VII [September 1, 1941]," RL 19/Folder 81/Page 81, BA-MA.

94. Ibid. [October–December 1941], 129, 183, 233.

95. Ibid. [November 1941], 183.

96. Greenhous et al., *Crucible,* 552.

97. Werner Wolf, *Luftangriffe auf die deutsche Industrie, 1942–45* (Munich: Universitas Verlag, 1985), 129–130.

98. Herrmann, *Eagle's Wings,* 186.

99. Fröhlich, *Tagebücher,* part I, vol. 4, p. 734; diary entry of July 4, 1941.

100. Ibid., part II, vol. 1, p. 32; diary entry of September 7, 1941.

101. "Vorstudien zur Luftkriegsgeschichte, Heft 8, Reichsluftverteidigung [1944]," T-971/Reel 69, NARA.

102. USSBS, Morale Division, *The United States Strategic Bombing Survey,* vol. 1, *The Effects of Strategic Bombing on German Morale,* 66.

103. Earl R. Beck, *Under the Bombs: The German Home Front, 1942–1945* (Lexington: University Press of Kentucky, 1986), 46.

104. Herrmann, *Eagle's Wings,* 203–204.

105. Martin Middlebrook, *The Berlin Raids: RAF Bomber Command Winter, 1943–1944* (New York: Viking, 1988), 337.

106. "*Flak-Nachrichtenblatt,* Herausgegeben vom Oberbefehlshaber der Luftwaffe, L.In.4, NB. 8-XI/41 g.," RL 4/Folder 262, BA-MA.

107. "Stellungnahme der Inspektion der Flakartillerie zur Aufstellung von Heeres-Flakartillerie-Abteilungen [April 30, 1941]," RL 4/Folder 260/Page 17, BA-MA.

108. Beck, *Under the Bombs,* 46.

109. USSBS, Morale Division, *The United States Strategic Bombing Survey,* vol. 1, *The Effects of Strategic Bombing on German Morale,* 67.

110. Koch, *Flak,* 177.

111. Boog, *Luftwaffenführung,* 205.

112. "Vorstudien zur Luftkriegsgeschichte, Heft 8, Reichsluftverteidigung [1944]," T-971/Reel 69, NARA.

113. Boog, *Luftwaffenführung,* 205.

114. Ian Kershaw, *Hitler: 1936–1945, Nemesis* (New York: Norton, 2000), 277, 535.

115. Irving, *Rise and Fall,* 149, 156, 165.

116. "Luftwaffen-Beute-Flak aus dem Feldzug im Osten 1941," T-321/Reel 9/Frames 4745685, 4745853, NARA.

117. "Kriegstagebuch des Luftgaukommandos VII [July 5, 1941]," RL 19/Folder 81/Page 7, BA-MA. In this particular case involving the formation of twenty barrier fire batteries, approximately half were slated for use at dummy installations.

118. "Vorstudien zur Luftkriegsgeschichte, Heft 8, Reichsluftverteidigung [1944]," T-971/Reel 69, NARA.

119. "Die Entwicklung der 'Grossbatterie' in der Luftverteidigung des Heimatkriegsgebietes von 1940–1945 [April 2, 1947]," N 529/Folder 13, BA-MA.

120. Hogg, *German Artillery,* 170–171. The three-piece construction did harbor some technical difficulties. The steel cartridge cases expanded upon firing and became stuck in the barrel at the seam where the bottom two sections joined, a problem that led to the requirement for brass casings. Later versions incorporated a two-piece barrel to alleviate this problem. I would like to thank Jack Atwater for his assistance with a query on this point.

121. Renz, *Development of German Anti-aircraft,* 239, K113.107–194, AFHRA.

122. For comparisons of the various models of the 88-mm and 105-mm flak guns, see Hogg, *German Artillery,* 167, 175. The Model 41 offered a 6 percent increase in effective altitude and a 13 percent increase in muzzle velocity over the 105-mm flak gun.

123. Lee, *Goering,* 148.

124. Alfred Price, *Luftwaffe Handbook, 1939–1945* (New York: Scribner's, 1977), 75.

125. "Die Entwicklung der 'Grossbatterie' in der Luftverteidigung des Heimatkriegsgebietes von 1940–1945 [April 2, 1947]," N 529/Folder 13, BA-MA.

126. Price, *Luftwaffe Handbook,* 75.

127. "Kriegstagebuch des Luftgaukommandos VII [December 10, 1941]," RL 19/Folder 81/Page 245, BA-MA.

128. "Planspiele-Einsatz in der Reichsverteidigung [December 11, 1941]," T-971/Reel 69, NARA.

129. *Weltkrieg,* 43.

130. Lee, *Goering,* 148.

131. "*Flak Nachrichtenblatt,* Herausgegeben vom Oberbefehlshaber der Luftwaffe, L.In.4, NB. 8-XI/41 g. [November 1941]," RL 4/Folder 262, BA-MA. The total number of night raids in this period was 12,994, while the number of daylight raids was 6,488. It should also be noted that the majority of the daylight raids were conducted along the French coast or against targets within the occupied western territories.

132. "*Flak Nachrichtenblatt,* Herausgegeben vom Oberbefehlshaber der Luftwaffe, L.In.4, NB. 9-I/42 g. [January 1942]," RL 4/Folder 262, BA-MA.

133. Groehler, *Luftherrschaft,* 189–190. After the initial raids in 1941, Soviet bombers would not return to the capital until 1944. See also Fröhlich, *Tagebücher,* part II, vol. 1, pp. 197–198; diary entries of September 8 and September 9, 1941.

134. "*Flak Nachrichtenblatt,* Herausgegeben vom Oberbefehlshaber der Luftwaffe, L.In.4, NB. 8-XI/41 g. [November 1941]," RL 4/Folder 262; "*Flak Nachrichtenblatt,* Herausgegeben vom Oberbefehlshaber der Luftwaffe, L.In.4, NB. 9-I/42 g. [January 1942]," RL 4/Folder 262, BA-MA. Unfortunately, there are no British estimates for aircraft losses due to German flak and fighter engagements for this period.

135. Ibid. These percentages are based on Luftwaffe records of the numbers of British aircraft penetrating airspace in the occupied western territories and the Reich proper.

136. Hinchliffe, *Other Battle,* 107.

137. "*Flak Nachrichtenblatt,* Herausgegeben vom Oberbefehlshaber der Luftwaffe, L.In.4, NB. 8-XI/41 g. [November 1941]," RL 4/Folder 262; "*Flak Nachrichtenblatt,*

Herausgegeben vom Oberbefehlshaber der Luftwaffe, L.In.4, NB. 9-I/42 g. [January 1942]," RL 4/Folder 262, BA-MA.

138. Letter from Air Marshal Sir Richard Peirse to Air Chief Marshal Sir Charles Portal of September 23, 1941, AIR 14/Folder 1927, PRO.

139. Letter from Air Chief Marshal Sir Charles Portal to Air Marshal Sir Richard Peirse of September 30, 1941, AIR 14/Folder 1927, PRO.

140. Lee, *Goering,* 148.

141. Ibid., 149.

142. Richards, *Hardest Victory,* 100. Another 133 aircraft bombed Cologne, Boulogne, and Ostend without suffering any losses.

143. Greenhous et al., *Crucible,* 562.

144. Letter from Air Marshal Sir Richard Peirse to Air Chief Marshal Sir Charles Portal of December 2, 1941, AIR 14/Folder 1928, PRO.

145. Chorley, *Bomber Command Losses,* 2:179–197.

146. USSBS, Economic Effects Division, *The United States Strategic Bombing Survey: The Effects of Strategic Bombing on the German War Economy,* 284.

147. Boog, *Luftwaffenführung,* 213; see also McFarland and Newton, *To Command the Sky*, 120; and Murray, *Strategy for Defeat,* 132. Boog provides the most sophisticated discussion of this point by correctly noting that such trade-offs should not be seen as an "either-or" decision. He contends that a more balanced distribution would have been more appropriate.

148. USSBS, Economic Effects Division, *The United States Strategic Bombing Survey,* 187.

149. Fröhlich, *Tagebücher,* part II, vol. 2, p. 579; diary entry of December 25, 1941.

6. Raising the Stakes, 1942

1. Werner Jochmann, ed., *Adolf Hitler: Monologe im Führerhauptquartier, 1941–1944* (Hamburg: Albrecht Knaus, 1980), 179.

2. USSBS, Economic Effects Division, *The United States Strategic Bombing Survey: The Effects of Strategic Bombing on the German War Economy,* 284.

3. Gerhard Förster and Olaf Groehler, eds., *Der zweite Weltkrieg* (Berlin [East]: Militärverlag der Deutschen Demokratischen Republik, 1974), 148, 151.

4. Hildebrand, *Generale,* 1:32.

5. Letter from Rüdel to von Axthelm, dated October 7, 1942, RL 4/Folder 258, BA-MA.

6. Koch, *Flak,* 63; see also Hildebrand, *Generale,* 1:31.

7. Herhudt von Rhoden, *European Contributions to the History of World War II,* vol. 4, *The Battle for Air Supremacy over Germany, 1939–1945* (n.p., [1947]), 101. The numbers for the Western Front included air defense forces in France, Belgium, and Holland.

8. *Bomber Command Operational Research Section Memoranda, "M" Series,* M-73, "A Note on the Use of Countermeasures Against Enemy Defences [November 3, 1942]," AHB.

9. *Bomber Command Operational Research Section Reports, "S" Series,* S-91, "Night-Bomber Losses on German Targets, 1942 [April 12, 1943]," AHB.

10. "Besprechungsnotiz Nr. 67/42 [April 26, 1942]," RL 3/Folder 60/Page 38, BA-MA.

11. "Zu Bericht Nr. 3 über die Flak Besprechung am 23.10.1942 [November 3, 1942]," RL 3/Folder 57/Page 175, BA-MA..

12. Dietrich Eichholtz, *Geschichte der deutschen Kriegswirtschaft, 1939–1945,* vol. 2 (Berlin [East]: Akademie-Verlag, 1985), 660.

13. Martin Middlebrook, *The Battle of Hamburg: Allied Bomber Forces Against a German City in 1943* (New York: Scribner's, 1980), 64.

14. Greenhous et al., *Crucible,* 566.

15. *Bomber Command Operational Research Section Reports, "G" Series,* Report G-27, "Statement on Aircraft Casualties Due to Flak According to Target Attacked [January 20, 1942]," AHB.

16. Webster and Frankland, *Strategic Air Offensive,* 1:399.

17. *Bomber Command Operational Research Section Reports, "S" Series,* S-91, "Night-Bomber Losses on German Targets, 1942 [April 12, 1943]," AHB.

18. *Bomber Command Operational Research Section Reports, "S" Series,* Report S-77, "Casualties Among Aircrew Directly Due to Enemy Action on Night Operations," AHB. The proportion of critical (dangerous) injuries inflicted by flak was 10.5 percent, and the proportion resulting from fighter attacks was 8.3 percent.

19. *Bomber Command Operational Research Section Memoranda, "M" Series,* Memo-25, "A Comparison of Various Types of Day Bombing Operations [February 28, 1943]," AHB.

20. Musgrove, *Operation Gomorrah,* 77.

21. "Tactical Counter-measures to Combat Enemy A.A. Searchlights and Guns," *Air Tactics Box 2,* AHB.

22. Musgrove, *Operation Gomorrah,* 22.

23. *Bomber Command Operational Research Section Reports, "S" Series,* S-91, "Night-Bomber Losses on German Targets, 1942 [April 12, 1943]," AHB.

24. *Bomber Command Damage Summaries,* "Interceptions/Tactics Report No. 11/42" and "Interceptions/Tactics Report No. 15/42," AHB.

25. Middlebrook, *Battle of Hamburg,* 64.

26. "Vorstudien zur Luftkriegsgeschichte, Heft 8, Reichsluftverteidigung [1944]," T-971/Reel 69, NARA.

27. Renz, *Development of German Anti-aircraft,* 310, K113.107-194, AFHRA.

28. "Vorstudien zur Luftkriegsgeschichte, Heft 8, Reichsluftverteidigung [1944]," T-971/Reel 69/NARA.

29. Military Intelligence 15, *Handbook of German Anti-aircraft Artillery (Flak),* vol. 9, *Instruments* (London: War Office, 1946), 17, IWM.

30. Koch, *Flak,* 128.

31. "Besprechungsnotiz Nr. 199/42 [October 14, 1942]," RL 3/Folder 60/Pages 162–164, BA-MA.

32. "Bericht Nr. 3 über die Flakbeschaffungs-Besprechung am 23.10.1942 [October 27, 1942]," RL 3/Folder 57/Page 172, BA-MA.

33. *Bomber Command Damage Summaries,* "Interceptions/Tactics Report No. 12/42" and "Interceptions/Tactics Report No. 19/42," AHB.

34. Greenhous et al., *Crucible,* 780; see also Herrmann, *Eagle's Wings,* 222.

35. Webster and Frankland, *Strategic Air Offensive,* 1:398.

36. "Verfügungen, Erfahrungen und Richtlinien (VER-FLAK) des General der Flakwaffe [October 1942]," RL 4/Folder 264, BA-MA. The number of sound detectors was reduced from three to two, including the associated personnel. This measure had the added benefit of freeing more personnel within the flak arm for other military duties.

37. Webster and Frankland, *Strategic Air Offensive,* 1:398.

38. Lee, *German Air Force,* 231–232.

39. *Bomber Command Operational Research Section Memoranda, "M" Series* [November 4, 1942], Memo-137, "An Examination of Two Special Sources of Information on the Causes of Our Losses," AHB.

40. Webster and Frankland, *Strategic Air Offensive,* 4:432. The official history does not list the estimated cause of loss for February through June 1942. However, in July and August alone, Bomber Command lost an estimated ninety-three aircraft to night fighters and eighty-seven aircraft to flak during night raids, a ratio of 1.07 to 1.

41. "Tactical Counter-measures to Combat Enemy A.A. Searchlights and Guns [April 14, 1942]," *Air Tactics Box 2,* AHB.

42. "Vorstudien zur Luftkriegsgeschichte, Heft 8, Reichsluftverteidigung [1944]," T-971/Reel 69/NARA.

43. Economic Effects Division, *The United States Strategic Bombing Survey: The Effects of Strategic Bombing on the German War Economy,* 284.

44. Interrogation transcript of Field Marshal Erhard Milch by the Royal Air Force on May 23, 1945, 512.619c-6d, AFHRA.

45. "Besprechungsnotiz Nr. 46/42 [March 6, 1942]," RL 3/Folder 60/Page 10, BA-MA.

46. Eichholtz, *Kriegswirtschaft,* 3:191.

47. Jeremy Noakes, ed., *Nazism, 1919–1945,* vol. 4, *The German Home Front in World War II* (Exeter, Devon: University of Exeter Press, 1998), 214. Thomas wrote this in a letter to Keitel, dated June 29, 1941.

48. Irving, *Rise and Fall,* 69, 138–139, 147–148.

49. Ibid., 149–150.

50. "Besprechungsnotiz Nr 109/42 g.Kdos. [June 29, 1942]," RL 3/Folder 60/Page 78, BA-MA.

51. Interrogation transcript of Field Marshal Erhard Milch by the Royal Air Force on May 23, 1945, 512.619c-6d, AFHRA.

52. "Besprechungsnotiz Nr. 46/42 [March 6, 1942]," RL 3/Folder 60/Page 9, BA-MA.

53. Ibid.

54. Burton H. Klein, *Germany's Economic Preparations for War* (Cambridge: Harvard University Press, 1959), 112.

55. "Besprechungsnotiz Nr. 46/42 [March 6, 1942]," RL 3/Folder 60/Page 10, BA-MA.

56. Interrogation transcript of Field Marshal Erhard Milch by the Royal Air Force on May 27, 1945, 512.619c-6d, AFHRA.

57. Berenice A. Carroll, *A Design for Total War: Arms and Economics in the Third Reich* (The Hague: Mouton, 1968), 254.

58. Irving, *Rise and Fall,* 157.

59. Greenhous et al., *Crucible,* 576.

60. Richards, *Hardest Victory,* 113.

61. Harris, *Bomber Offensive,* 95.

62. Richards, *Hardest Victory,* 114–115.

63. Webster and Frankland, *Strategic Air Offensive,* 4:144. This information comes from the bombing directive of February 14, 1942. It is important to note that the emphasis on the use of incendiary attacks preceded Harris's arrival at Bomber Command. Ironically, one German report noted the increasing use of incendiaries in 1941 but attributed this to a shortage of high-explosive bombs in the RAF.

64. Greenhous et al., *Crucible,* 576.

65. Chorley, *Bomber Command Losses,* 3:39.

66. Greenhous et al., *Crucible,* 578, 611–612; see also Musgrove, *Operation Gomorrah,* 33.

67. Greenhous et al., *Crucible,* 578–579.

68. Ibid., 580.

69. "Kriegstagebuch des Luftgaukommandos VII [August 29, September 5, and December 7, 1942]," RL 19/Folder 83/Pages 53, 65, 169, BA-MA.

70. Greenhous et al., *Crucible,* 584.

71. *Bomber Command Operational Research Section Reports, "S" Series,* S-224, "Report on Decoy Sites in the Mannheim and Frankfurt Areas with Particular Reference to Decoy T.I. Devices [July 5, 1945]," AHB.

72. USSBS, *United States Strategic Bombing Survey: Report on the German Flak Effort Throughout the War* (n.p., 1945), 21, 137.310-4, AFHRA.

73. Wagner, *Lagevorträge,* 305. This discussion took place during a conference with Hitler on November 13, 1941.

74. USSBS, *United States Strategic Bombing Survey: Report on the German Flak Effort Throughout the War* (n.p., 1945), 22, 137.310-4, AFHRA.

75. Harris, *Bomber Offensive,* 105.

76. Lee, *Goering,* 151; see also Chorley, *Bomber Command Losses,* 3:39.

77. Fröhlich, *Tagebücher,* part II, vol. 3, p. 582; diary entry of March 30, 1942.

78. Harris, *Bomber Offensive,* 105.

79. "Tactical Counter-measures to Combat Enemy A.A. Searchlights and Guns [April 14, 1942]," *Air Tactics Box 2,* AHB.

80. Harris, *Bomber Offensive,* 108.

81. Ibid., 108–110.

82. Greenhous et al., *Crucible,* 593.

83. Fröhlich, *Tagebücher,* part II, vol. 4, p. 416. This entry is dated May 31, 1942; however, it is important to note that many of the entries were dictated and transcribed the day after the events occurred, as is clearly the case here.

84. Webster and Frankland, *Strategic Air Offensive,* 1:408.

85. Greenhous et al., *Crucible,* 595–596.

86. Kershaw, *Nemesis,* 524.

87. Fröhlich, *Tagebücher,* part II, vol. 4, pp. 422, 431, 435; entries dated June 1, June 2, and June 3, 1942, respectively.

88. Greenhous et al., *Crucible,* 596–597. The RAF launched a subsequent raid consisting of 956 aircraft against Essen on the night of June 1 and a later raid of over 1,000 aircraft against Bremen on the night of June 25. Both raids proved only moderately successful, and in the case of the latter attack, German civilian defense officials estimated the size of the bomber force at merely 80 aircraft.

89. Ibid., 587.

90. Feuchter, *Geschichte des Luftkriegs,* 305.

91. "M.I. 15 Periodical AA Intelligence Summary No. 19 [April 14, 1945]," AIR 40/Folder 1151, PRO; see also Middlebrook, *Battle of Hamburg,* 65.

92. USSBS, *United States Strategic Bombing Survey: Report on the German Flak Effort Throughout the War* (n.p., 1945), 21, 137.310-4, AFHRA.

93. "Vorstudien zur Luftkriegsgeschichte, Heft 8, Reichsluftverteidigung [1944]," T-971/Reel 69/NARA; see also Koch, *Flak,* 70.

94. "Die Entwicklung der 'Grossbatterie' in der Luftverteidigung des Heimatkriegsgebietes von 1940–1945 [April 2, 1947]," N 529/Folder 13, BA-MA; see also Price, *Luftwaffe Handbook,* 75–76.

95. "Die Entwicklung der 'Grossbatterie' in der Luftverteidigung des Heimatkriegsgebietes von 1940–1945 [April 2, 1947]," N 529/Folder 13, BA-MA.

96. Ibid.

97. Hogg, *German Artillery,* 170. Driving bands help to provide a gas seal in the breech, as well as imparting rotation to the projectile to enhance stability.

98. "Besprechungsnotiz Nr. 46/42 [March 6, 1942]," RL 3/Folder 60/Pages 9–10, BA-MA.

99. Renz, *Development of German Anti-aircraft,* 239–242, K113.107–194, AFHRA.

100. Eichholtz, *Kriegswirtschaft,* 2:658.

101. Hogg, *German Artillery,* 177.

102. Eichholtz, *Kriegswirtschaft,* 2:658.

103. Price, *Luftwaffe Handbook,* 75; see also Foedrowitz, *Die Flaktürme,* 3–4. The flak towers were constructed in pairs, with one tower used for gun-laying radar and fire direction devices and the second tower for the flak guns.

104. David Mondey, ed., *The Luftwaffe at War, 1939–1945* (Chicago: Henry Regnery, 1972), 247.

105. Jochmann, *Monologe,* 372.

106. Hogg, *German Artillery,* 177.

107. "Besprechungsnotiz Nr. 46/42 [March 6, 1942]," RL 3/Folder 60/Page 9; "Besprechungsnotiz Nr. 109/42 [June 29, 1942]," RL 3/Folder 60/Page 78, BA-MA.

108. "Besprechungsnotiz Nr. 156/42 [August 27, 1942]," RL 3/Folder 60/Page 100, BA-MA.

109. "AA Intelligence Summary No. 17 [February 11, 1945]," AIR 40/Folder 1151, PRO.

110. Letter from von Axthelm to Dr. Heinz Peter Ptak, dated September 27, 1955, N 529/Folder 9 II, BA-MA.

111. USSBS, *United States Strategic Bombing Survey: Report on the German Flak Effort Throughout the War* (n.p., 1945), 8, 137.310–4, AFHRA.

112. "AA Intelligence Summary No. 17 [February 11, 1945]," AIR 40/Folder 1151, PRO. In contrast, a motorized heavy gun battery employed 196 persons, while the number of persons needed for a motorized light flak battery ranged between 209 and 218. In all cases these are units at full strength. The larger number of personnel for the light flak batteries resulted from the greater number of guns, ranging from two to three times as many as in a heavy battery. See also Golücke, *Schweinfurt,* 180. Golücke states that the personnel strength of a heavy battery consisted of 120 men.

113. "Besprechungsnotiz Nr. 58/42 [March 21, 1942]," RL 3/Folder 60/Page 28, BA-MA.

114. Schumann and Bleyer, *Zusammenbruch der Defensivstrategie,* 146.

115. Germany, Kriegswissenschaftliche Abteilung der Luftwaffe, *Luftschutz im Weltkrieg,* 116–117.

116. "Vorstudien zur Luftkriegsgeschichte, Heft 8, Reichsluftverteidigung [1944]," T-971/Reel 69/NARA.

117. "Besprechungsnotiz Nr. 162/42 [September 1, 1942]," RL 3/Folder 60/Page 106, BA-MA.

118. "Kriegstagebuch des Luftgaukommandos VII [July 30–31, 1942]," RL 19/Folder 83/Pages 25–26, BA-MA; see also "Vorstudien zur Luftkriegsgeschichte, Heft 8, Reichsluftverteidigung [1944]," T-971/Reel 69/NARA.

119. Military Intelligence 15, *Handbook of German Anti-aircraft Artillery (Flak),* vol. 4, *Strength* (London: War Office, 1946), 46, IWM.

120. "Kriegstagebuch des Luftgaukommandos VII [July 30–31, 1942]," RL 19/Folder 83/Pages 25–26, BA-MA.

121. Military Intelligence 15, *Handbook,* 4:46.

122. Jochmann, *Monologe,* 372.

123. "Heimatflak (Home Flak) [January 8, 1943]," AIR 40/Folder 1151, PRO. In this report, British intelligence noted the "tremendous strain on manpower" within Germany as a result of the activities of the field army. The report then continued, "It is not surprising therefore to find that an attempt is being made to ease this strain by the adoption of the policy of employing factory and office workers as part-time Flak personnel."

124. "Vorstudien zur Luftkriegsgeschichte, Heft 8, Reichsluftverteidigung [1944]," T-971/Reel 69/NARA.

125. Military Intelligence 15, *Handbook,* 4:46, IWM; see also "M.I. 15 Periodical AA Intelligence Summary No. 19 [April 14, 1945]," AIR 40/Folder 1151, PRO. The organization Todt was named after the minister of armaments, Fritz Todt, and was responsible for numerous large-scale construction projects in the occupied western and eastern territories.

126. "Verfügungen, Erfahrungen und Richtlinien *(VER FLAK)* des General der Flakwaffe [November 1942]," RL 4/Folder 264, BA-MA.

127. "Besprechungsnotiz Nr. 162/42 [September 1, 1942]," RL 3/Folder 60/Page 105, BA-MA.

128. Gersdorff, *Frauen im Kriegsdienst,* 31–34.

129. Franz W. Seidler, *Frauen zu den Waffen? Marketenderinnen, Helferinnen, Soldatinnen* (Koblenz: Wehr & Wissen, 1978), 63–65, 78.

130. Franz W. Seidler, *Blitzmädchen: Die Geschichte der Helferinnen der deutschen Wehrmacht* (Bonn: Bernard & Graefe Verlag, 1998), 75–103.

131. "Besprechungsnotiz Nr. 162/42 [September 1, 1942]," RL 3/Folder 60/Page 105, BA-MA.

132. These young women received this nickname because of the lightning bolt insignia on their uniforms.

133. Werner Niehaus, *Die Nachrichtentruppe: 1914 bis heute* (Stuttgart: Motorbuch Verlag, 1980), 286–287.

134. "Kriegstagebuch des Luftgaukommandos VII [November 9 and December 31, 1942]," RL 19/Folder 83/Pages 135, 206, BA-MA.

135. Military Intelligence 15, *Handbook,* 4:50.

136. "Übersicht über den Entwicklungsstand und die Entwicklungsabsichten der Flakartillerie [June 22, 1942]," RL 4/Folder 258, BA-MA.

137. Ibid; emphasis in the original.

138. Letter from von Axthelm to Kesselring, dated October 13, 1955, N 529/Folder 9 II, BA-MA. In this letter, von Axthelm informs Kesselring that a variety of active homing measures were being considered, including electrical, optical, and acoustic means.

139. Schabel, *Illusion,* 261, 264.

140. Neufeld, *Rocket and the Reich,* 153.

141. Karl-Heinz Ludwig, "Die deutschen Flakraketen im Zweiten Weltkrieg," *Militärgeschichtliche Mitteilungen* 1 (1969): 89–90.

142. Schabel, *Illusion,* 263; see also Neufeld, *Rocket and the Reich,* 154.

143. Albert Speer, *Inside the Third Reich: Memoirs by Albert Speer,* trans. Richard Winston and Clara Winston (New York: Macmillan, 1970), 435–436.

144. "Übersicht über den Entwicklungsstand und die Entwicklungsabsichten der Flakartillerie [June 22, 1942]," RL 4/Folder 258, BA-MA.

145. David Donald, ed., *The Complete Encyclopedia of World Aircraft* (New York: Barnes and Noble Books, 1997), 157. The B-47 became the first bomber to exceed a speed of 600 mph and a service ceiling of 40,000 feet, but it was not available for operational duty until the middle of 1950.

146. "Übersicht über den Entwicklungsstand und die Entwicklungsabsichten der Flakartillerie [June 22, 1942]," RL 4/Folder 258, BA-MA.

147. "Stenographischer Bericht über die Flak-E-Besprechung [December 7, 1942]," RL 3/Folder 1362, BA-MA.

148. "Flak E[ntwicklung]-Besprechung [December 7, 1942]," RL 3/Folder 1362, BA-MA.

149. Charles B. Burdick, "Dora: The Germans' Biggest Gun," *Military Review* 41 (November 1961): 72–78.

150. Ian V. Hogg, *British and American Artillery of World War 2* (London: Arms and Armour Press, 1978), 113–115.

151. Hogg, *Anti-Aircraft,* 129. There is no record of these guns ever scoring a shootdown.

152. "Übersicht über den Entwicklungsstand und die Entwicklungsabsichten der Flakartillerie [June 22, 1942]," RL 4/Folder 258, BA-MA.

153. The special equipment mentioned most likely refers to an IFF (identify friend or foe) transmitter. By means of an encoded transmission sent by an aircraft, air defense personnel could determine if the aircraft was "friendly" or an enemy.

154. "Übersicht über den Entwicklungsstand und die Entwicklungsabsichten der Flakartillerie [June 22, 1942]," RL 4/Folder 258, BA-MA. The existing smoke generators produced a grayish white smoke that was viewed as inferior to black smoke for concealing the protected object.

155. Ibid.; emphasis in the original.

156. Neufeld, *Rocket and the Reich,* 153.

157. "Verfügungen, Erfahrungen und Richtlinien (VER-FLAK) des General der Flakwaffe [October 1942]," RL 4/Folder 264, BA-MA. Axthelm's evaluation of the Luftwaffe's aerial barrier force is in direct contradiction to a report released by the flak in October 1942 that praised the "various successes" achieved by aerial wire barriers since the beginning of the war.

158. Letter from von Axthelm to Rüdel, dated September 29, 1942, RL 4/Folder 257, BA-MA.

159. Letter from Rüdel to von Axthelm, dated October 7, 1942, RL 4/Folder 258, BA-MA.

160. "Besprechungsnotiz No. 146/42 [August 8, 1942]," RL 3/Folder 60/Page 98, BA-MA.

161. "Bericht Nr. 1 über die Flakbeschaffungs-Besprechung am 18.8.42 [September 5, 1942]," RL 3/Folder 57/Page 260, BA-MA.

162. Boog, *Luftwaffenführung,* 207.

163. "Besprechungsnotiz Nr. 162/42 [September 1, 1942]," RL 3/Folder 60/Page 106, BA-MA.

164. Bernhard R. Kroener, Rolf-Dieter Müller, and Hans Umbreit, *Das Deutsche Reich und der Zweite Weltkrieg,* vol. 5, *Organisation und Mobilisierung des deutschen Machtbereichs* (Stuttgart: Deutsche Verlags-Anstalt, 1988), 720.

165. "Besprechungsnotiz Nr. 162/42 [September 1, 1942]," RL 3/Folder 60/Page 106, BA-MA.

166. Ibid.

167. "Besprechungsnotiz Nr. 124/42 [July 10, 1942]," RL 3/Folder 60/Pages 82–83, BA-MA.

168. "Besprechungsnotiz Nr. 162/42 [September 1, 1942]," RL 3/Folder 60/Pages 106–107, BA-MA.

169. Ibid., 107.

170. Foedrowitz, *Die Flaktürme,* 3–4.

171. "Besprechungsnotiz Nr. 162/42 [September 1, 1942]," RL 3/Folder 60/Pages 107–108, BA-MA; see also "Vorstudien zur Luftkriegsgeschichte, Heft 8, Reichsluftverteidigung [1944]," T-971/Reel 69/NARA.

172. "Besprechungsnotiz Nr. 162/42 [September 1, 1942]," RL 3/Folder 60/Page 108, BA-MA.

173. Ibid.

174. Ibid.

175. Eichholtz, *Kriegswirtschaft,* 2:658.

176. Ibid., 3:187.

177. USSBS, Economic Effects Division, *The United States Strategic Bombing Survey: The Effects of Strategic Bombing on the German War Economy,* 285. This was a rate over three times greater than that of 1941.

178. "Besprechungsnotiz Nr. 162/42 [September 1, 1942]," RL 3/Folder 60/Pages 108–109, BA-MA.

179. Ibid., 109–110.

180. Ibid.

181. Richards, *Hardest Victory,* 134.

182. Greenhous et al., *Crucible,* 598.

183. Richards, *Hardest Victory,* 134–135.

184. Fröhlich, *Tagebücher,* part II, vol. 4, pp. 447–448; diary entry of June 5, 1942.

185. Ralf Georg Reuth, *Goebbels,* trans. Krishna Winston (New York: Harcourt Brace, 1993), 308.

186. Hinchliffe, *Other Battle,* 97–98.

187. Greenhous et al., *Crucible,* 607.

188. Hinchliffe, *Other Battle,* 69–70.

189. Greenhous et al., *Crucible,* 608.

190. Galland, *First and the Last,* 136–137.

191. Boog, *Luftwaffenführung,* 207.

192. Webster and Frankland, *Strategic Air Offensive,* 4:432.

193. Chorley, *Bomber Command Losses,* 3:245, 276.

194. "Kriegstagebuch des Luftgaukommandos VII [August 31, September 10, and September 18, 1942]," RL 19/Folder 83/Pages 59, 80, 85, BA-MA.

195. Lee, *Goering,* 155.

196. "Besprechungsnotiz Nr. 199/42 [October 14, 1942]," RL 3/Folder 60/Pages 162–163, BA-MA.

197. "Kriegstagebuch des Luftgaukommandos VII [September 20–December 1942]," RL 19/Folder 83/Pages 88–206, BA-MA. Air District VII's war diary for this period provides extensive comments on the increasing availability and successful employment of gun-laying radar in this period.

198. Wesley Frank Craven and James Lea Cate, *The Army Air Forces in World War II,* vol. 2, *Europe: Torch to Pointblank, August 1942 to December 1943* (Chicago: University of Chicago Press, 1948; reprint, Washington, D.C.: GPO, 1983), 209 (page references are to reprint edition).

199. Robert T. Finney, *History of the Air Corps Tactical School, 1920–1940* (Maxwell AFB, Ala.: Research Studies Institute, 1955; reprint, Washington, D.C.: Center for Air Force History, 1992), 62–72 (page references are to the reprint edition). Finney provides an excellent discussion of the emergence of the theory of daylight strategic bombing within the Army Air Corps and the impact of the B-17 on this idea.

200. Richards, *Hardest Victory,* 120.

201. Chorley, *Bomber Command Losses,* 3:40.

202. Richards, *Hardest Victory,* 122.

203. *Bomber Command Operational Research Section Reports, "S" Series,* S-71, "Low Level Operations in Daylight [November 4, 1942]," AHB.

204. Wesley Frank Craven and James Lea Cate, *The Army Air Forces in World War II,* vol. 1, *Plans and Early Operations: January 1939 to August 1942* (Chicago: University

of Chicago Press, 1948; reprint, Washington, D.C.: GPO, 1983), 658–659 (page references are to reprint edition).

205. LeMay and Kantor, *Mission,* 229.

206. Craven and Cate, *Army Air Forces,* 1:663–665.

207. Ibid., 2:220–221, 225–226.

208. LeMay and Kantor, *Mission,* 230.

209. Lee, *Goering,* 158.

210. Craven and Cate, *Army Air Forces,* 2:236.

211. Ibid., 233, 237.

212. Harris, *Bomber Offensive,* 122.

213. *Bomber Command Operational Research Section Report, "S" Series,* Report S-91, "Night-Bomber Losses on German Targets, 1942 [April 12, 1943]," AHB.

214. "Verfügungen, Erfahrungen und Richtlinien (VER-FLAK) des General der Flakwaffe [November 1942]," RL 4/Folder 264, BA-MA.

215. Koch, *Flak,* 71.

216. *Frontnachrichtenblatt der Luftwaffe,* Nr. 45 (December 1942): 646.

217. "Vorstudien zur Luftkriegsgeschichte, Heft 8, Reichsluftverteidigung [1944]," T-971/Reel 69/NARA.

218. Heinz Boberach, ed., *Meldungen aus dem Reich: Die geheimen Lageberichte des Sicherheitsdienstes der SS, 1938–1945,* vol. 10 (Herrsching: Pawlak Verlag, 1984), 3,838–3,839.

7. Bombing around the Clock, 1943

1. Craven and Cate, *Army Air Forces,* 2:305.

2. Ibid., 278, 305.

3. Ibid., 308–309.

4. Greenhous et al., *Crucible,* 640–641.

5. Astor, *Mighty Eighth,* 99.

6. Craven and Cate, *Army Air Forces,* 2:310.

7. Mark K. Wells, *Courage and Air Warfare: The Allied Aircrew Experience in World War II* (London: Frank Cass, 1995), 127.

8. Harris, *Bomber Offensive,* 147.

9. Webster and Frankland, *Strategic Air Offensive,* 4:432.

10. Greenhous et al., *Crucible,* 638.

11. Ibid. Flak and fighters each accounted for a further 5 aircraft damaged beyond repair during the period.

12. Boog, *Luftwaffenführung,* 208.

13. MacIsaac, *The United States Strategic Bombing Survey,* vol. 2, *Civilian Defense Division Final Report,* 2.

14. David MacIsaac, ed., *The United States Strategic Bombing Survey,* vol. 1, *The Effects of Strategic Bombing on the German War Economy* (New York: Garland, 1976), 154.

15. Gersdorff, *Frauen im Kriegsdienst,* 375.

16. Ibid., 376.

17. Franz-Josef Schmeling, *Vom Krieg ein Leben lang geprägt: Ehemalige Luftwaffen- und Marinehelfer antworten 50 Jahre danach* (Osnabrück: H. Th. Wenner, 1997).

18. Leopold Banny, *Dröhnender Himmel, brennendes Land: Der Einsatz der Luftwaffenhelfer in Österreich, 1943–1945* (Vienna: Bundesverlag, 1988), 31; see also Rolf Schörken, *Luftwaffenhelfer und Drittes Reich: Die Entstehung eines politischen Bewußtseins* (Stuttgart: Klett-Cotta, 1984), 101.

19. Hans Vogt and Herbert Brenne, *Krefeld im Luftkrieg, 1939–1945* (Bonn: Ludwig Röhrscheid Verlag, 1986), 118.

20. "Vorstudien zur Luftkriegsgeschichte, Heft 8, Reichsluftverteidigung [1944]," T-971/Reel 69/NARA.

21. Seidler, *Frauen,* 81–82, 86. Crews for observation posts included five soldiers or six women auxiliaries for first-class posts, three soldiers or three women auxiliaries for second-class posts, and two soldiers or two women auxiliaries for third-class posts. In addition, six women auxiliaries served at Würzburg radar sites, and four women auxiliaries served at Freya radar sites. Finally, women serving with the flak gun batteries did not operate the guns in 1943 but were involved with related duties.

22. Military Intelligence 15, *Handbook,* 4:45.

23. Niehaus, *Nachrichtentruppe,* 287.

24. Control Commission for Germany, *Notes on Flak,* 22, IWM.

25. Niehaus, *Nachrichtentruppe,* 287.

26. Absolon, *Rangliste,* 163.

27. Fröhlich, *Tagebücher,* part II, vol. 7, p. 493.

28. Kershaw, *Nemesis,* 563.

29. Absolon, *Rangliste,* 172.

30. Banny, *Dröhnender Himmel,* 45; see also Seidler, *Frauen,* 86. Seidler states that women flak auxiliaries received four weeks of training.

31. Seidler, *Blitzmädchen,* 136.

32. Letter from General Walther von Axthelm to General Wolfgang Pickert, dated September 19, 1955, N 529/Folder 9II, BA-MA.

33. "Stenographische Niederschrift der Besprechung beim Reichsmarschall über Ausbildung am Mittwoch, dem 24. Februar 1943," RL 3/Folder 60/Page 254, BA-MA.

34. "Flakentwicklungsbesprechung [January 18, 1943]," RL 3/Folder 57/Page 148, BA-MA.

35. "Besprechungsnotiz Nr. 6/43 [January 21, 1943]," RL 3/Folder 60/Page 175, BA-MA.

36. "Besprechungsnotiz Nr. 39/43 [April 30, 1943]," RL 3/Folder 60/Pages 399–400, BA-MA; meeting attended by both Göring and Milch at Göring's house in Obersalzberg.

37. Renz, *Development of German Anti-aircraft,* 250, K113.107-194, AFHRA.

38. "Flakbeschaffungsbesprechung [March 12, 1943]," RL 3/Folder 57/Page 234; see also "Flakbeschaffungsbesprechung [April 19, 1943]," RL 3/Folder 57/Page 230, BA-MA.

39. "Vorstudien zur Luftkriegsgeschichte, Heft 8, Reichsluftverteidigung [1944]," T-971/Reel 69/NARA.

40. Ibid.; see also Lee, *German Air Force,* 234.

41. "Einsatzgrundsätze für den Einsatz einer Großbatterie [October 3, 1943]," T-405/Reel 15/Frame 4845794, NARA.

42. "Bericht Nr. 21 über die Entwicklungsbesprechung am 5.3.43 [March 10, 1943]," RL3/Folder 42/Page 190, BA-MA; emphasis in the original.

43. Wagner, *Lagevorträge,* 476; protocol of the conference on April 11, 1943.

44. "Flakbeschaffungsbesprechung [April 19, 1943]," RL 3/Folder 57/Page 230, BA-MA.

45. "Vorstudien zur Luftkriegsgeschichte, Heft 8, Reichsluftverteidigung [1944]," T-971/Reel 69/NARA.

46. U.S. War Department, *Handbook,* 166–168.

47. Renz, *Development of German Anti-aircraft,* 251, K113.107–194, AFHRA.

48. "Interrogation of General von Axthelm and Lt. Col. Sieber (USSBS Interview No. 68)," 524.606, AFHRA.

49. USSBS, *The United States Strategic Bombing Survey: Report on the German Flak Effort Throughout the War* (n.p., 1945), 21, 137.310-4, AFHRA.

50. "Flakbeschaffungsbesprechung [April 19, 1943]," RL 3/Folder 57/Page 230, BA-MA.

51. "Flak-Beschaffungsbesprechung [September 13, 1943]," RL 3/Folder 57/Page 213, BA-MA.

52. Eichholtz, *Kriegswirtschaft,* 3:193.

53. USSBS, Economic Effects Division, *The United States Strategic Bombing Survey: The Effects of Strategic Bombing on the German War Economy,* 284.

54. Ibid.

55. "Teil 6: Heimatflakbatterien" and "Teil 7: Sperrfeuerbatterien," RL 4/Folder 259/Pages 134–177, BA-MA. This folder lists each battery individually by type and unit numerical designation and appears to have been compiled at the end of 1943 or in early 1944. By my count there were approximately 222 Home Guard heavy flak batteries, 219 Home Guard light flak batteries, 24 Home Guard medium flak batteries, and 66 batteries of indeterminate type. In addition, I counted 239 barrier fire batteries, with 11 of these listed as having become Home Guard batteries and 9 listed as having become regular or replacement batteries.

56. Military Intelligence 15, *Handbook,* 4:46, IWM.

57. "Tactical Countermeasures to Combat Enemy Night Fighter, AA Searchlight and Gun Defences," AIR 40/Folder 1135, PRO.

58. E. R. Hooton, *Eagle in Flames: The Fall of the Luftwaffe* (London: Arms and Armour Press, 1997), 253.

59. Eichholtz, *Kriegswirtschaft,* 2:656, 658.

60. "Flakbeschaffungsbesprechung [January 15, 1943]," RL 3/Folder 57/Page 245, BA-MA.

61. Vogt and Brenne, *Krefeld im Luftkrieg,* 102.

62. Boog, *Luftwaffenführung,* 254; see Boog's footnote 264.

63. "Ergebnisse der 51. Sitzung der Zentralen Planung am 17. Dezember 1943 [December 23, 1943]," T-971/Reel 30/Frame 564, NARA; see also Noakes, *Nazism,* 4:236. Monthly production levels at the end of 1942 stood at 20 searchlights but rose to 80 searchlights by the end of 1943 and again to 150 searchlights by the end of 1944.

64. Rhoden, *History of World War II,* 4:101.

65. Fröhlich, *Tagebücher,* part II, vol. 8, pp. 84–85; diary entry of April 10, 1943.

66. USSBS, *The United States Strategic Bombing Survey: Report on the German Flak Effort Throughout the War* (n.p., 1945), 13, 137.310-4, AFHRA.

67. Richards, *Portal of Hungerford,* 164.

68. Richards, *Hardest Victory,* 145.

69. Harris, *Bomber Offensive,* 128.

70. Richards, *Hardest Victory,* 146–154.

71. Harris, *Bomber Offensive,* 124–125. The distinctive curvilinear path flown by these aircraft led the Germans to describe this type of bombing as the "boomerang procedure."

72. Operational Research Branch—Bomber Command, *OBOE: A Complete Survey of Its Operational Use in the 1939–1945 War* (n.p.: 1946?), 2–5, AHB.

73. Harris, *Bomber Offensive,* 144.

74. Webster and Frankland, *Strategic Air Offensive,* 2:258.

75. Richards, *Hardest Victory,* 168–169.

76. Greenhous et al., *Crucible,* 665.

77. "Vorstudien zur Luftkriegsgeschichte, Heft 8, Reichsluftverteidigung [1944]," T-971/Reel 69/NARA.

78. Rhoden, *History of World War II,* vol. 3, no page numbers.

79. Fröhlich, *Tagebücher,* part II, vol. 7, p. 483; diary entry of March 6, 1943.

80. Hans Rosenthal, *Zwei Leben in Deutschland* (Bergisch Gladbach: Gustav Lübbe Verlag, 1980), 70. After the war, Hans Rosenthal became one of West Germany's leading television personalities.

81. Fröhlich, *Tagebücher,* part II, vol. 7, p. 491; diary entry of March 7, 1943.

82. Richards, *Hardest Victory,* 169.

83. Groehler, *Luftherrschaft,* 198.

84. Fröhlich, *Tagebücher,* part II, vol. 7, pp. 461, 476, 491; diary entries of March 3, March 5, and March 7, 1943.

85. Ibid., 660.

86. Richards, *Hardest Victory,* 170.

87. Fröhlich, *Tagebücher,* part II, vol. 7, p. 671; diary entry of March 31, 1943.

88. Richards, *Hardest Victory,* 170–171; see also Ulrich Herbert, *Hitler's Foreign Workers: Enforced Labor in Germany Under the Third Reich,* trans. William Templer (New York: Cambridge University Press, 1997), 392. In his seminal examination of forced labor, Herbert remarked, "From 1943, however, the massive Allied air attacks on German cities became the greatest single threat to the foreign workers."

89. USSBS, Civil Defense Division, *The United States Strategic Bombing Survey: Civil Defense Division Final Report,* 3.

90. Boberach, *Meldungen,* 14:5354–5355.

91. *Bomber Command Operational Research Section Memoranda, "M" Series,* M-31, "A Review of Bombing Operations. Feb.–April 1943 [June 1943]," AHB.

92. Ibid.

93. Richards, *Hardest Victory,* 170.

94. *Bomber Command Operational Research Section Reports, "S" Series,* S-224, "Report on the Decoy Sites in the Mannheim and Frankfurt Areas with Particular Reference to Decoy T.I. Devices [July 5, 1945]," AHB. In some reports, crews reported a slight difference in the red of the target indicators and those of the decoy

markers; however, this might appear to be an academic question for most crews facing German air defenses in the vicinity of the target area.

95. "No. 5 Group Tactical Notes (Provisional) 2nd edition, November 1943," *Air Tactics Box 2,* AHB.

96. *Bomber Command Operational Research Section Memoranda, "M" Series,* M-31, "A Review of Bombing Operations. Feb.–April 1943 [June 1943]," AHB.

97. Hoffmann, "Der Luftangriff auf Lauffen," 8.

98. Fröhlich, *Tagebücher,* part II, vol. 7, pp. 502, 506; diary entry of March 9, 1943.

99. Overy, *Goering,* 194.

100. Boog, *Luftwaffenführung,* 271. An indication of Kammhuber's rising fortunes was his appointment as General of the Night Fighters on May 20, 1943.

101. Karl-Heinz Hummel, "Die Kommandostrukturen in der Reichsluftverteidigung 1939–1945," in *Deutsches Soldatenjahrbuch 1989,* ed. H. Dameran (Munich: Schild Verlag, 1988), 294.

102. Webster and Frankland, *Strategic Air Offensive,* 2:295.

103. Irving, *Rise and Fall,* 218.

104. Hummel, "Kommandostrukturen," 294.

105. Webster and Frankland, *Strategic Air Offensive,* 2:258.

106. Greenhous et al., *Crucible,* 662–663.

107. Hummel, "Kommandostrukturen," 294.

108. Herrmann, *Eagle's Wings,* 160.

109. "No. 5 Group Tactical Notes (Provisional) 2nd edition, November 1943," *Air Tactics Box 2,* AHB. This report notes that "small concentrations of searchlights are spread along the Coastal Defence Belts, co-operating with flak positions and also with the night fighter organisation. These small groups consist of anything from 3 to 10 searchlights. In addition to their primary function of illuminating aircraft, they also act as 'tracking indicating' lights for enemy fighters."

110. Greenhous et al., *Crucible,* 663.

111. Herrmann, *Eagle's Wings,* 160–161.

112. Ibid., 164.

113. Wagner, *Lagevorträge,* 509; protocol from conference of May 31, 1943.

114. Ibid., 512; notes from the meeting between Dönitz and Hitler of June 15, 1943.

115. "Besprechungsnotiz Nr. 58/43 [June 21, 1943]," RL 3/Folder 60/Page 419, BA-MA.

116. Webster and Frankland, *Strategic Air Offensive,* 4:432, 435.

117. Chorley, *Bomber Command Losses,* 4:382.

118. Ibid.

119. *Bomber Command Operational Research Section Reports, "S" Series,* S-98, "The Effect of Window on Bomber Operations [August 19, 1943]," AHB. It is important to note that these percentages were not limited to aircraft that reached the target but included sorties devoted to diversions and aircraft returning after takeoff because of technical or mechanical problems.

120. "Minutes of the meeting held at Headquarters, Bomber Command, 1100 hours, 23rd April, 1943 to discuss Tactical Aspects Arising from Recent Operations," AIR 14/Folder 1222, "Group Conferences at Headquarters Bomber Command," PRO.

121. Greenhous et al., *Crucible,* 660. This inaccuracy was to a certain extent ameliorated by the increasing weight of bombs being dropped on German targets.

122. "Bomber Command Tactical Memorandum. Evasive Action at the Target [May 24, 1943]," *Air Tactics Box 2,* AHB.

123. Crosby, *Wing and a Prayer,* 63–64.

124. LeMay and Kantor, *Mission,* 231.

125. "M[ilitary]. I[ntelligence]. 15 Periodical AA Intelligence Summary No. 19 [April 14, 1945]," AIR 40/Folder 1151, PRO. The German document was dated March 1943.

126. Hummel, "Kommandostrukturen," 296.

127. "M[ilitary]. I[ntelligence]. 15 Periodical AA Intelligence Summary No. 19 [April 19, 1945]," AIR 40/Folder 1151, PRO.

128. LeMay and Kantor, *Mission,* 257–258.

129. "M[ilitary]. I[ntelligence]. 15 Periodical AA Intelligence Summary No. 19 [April 14, 1945]," AIR 40/Folder 1151, PRO.

130. "Flakentwicklungsbesprechung [June 16, 1943]," RL 3/Folder 57/Page 105, BA-MA.

131. Hogg, *German Artillery,* 158, 160.

132. "Flakentwicklungsbesprechung [June 16, 1943]," RL 3/Folder 57/Page 105, BA-MA.

133. Renz, *Development of German Anti-aircraft,* 245, K113.107-194, AFHRA.

134. "Flakentwicklungsbesprechung [September 30, 1943]," RL 3/Folder 57/Page 77, BA-MA; see also Hogg, *German Artillery,* 182, 263.

135. USSBS, *The United States Strategic Bombing Survey: Report on the German Flak Effort Throughout the War* (n.p., 1945), 16–17, 137.310-4, AFHRA. The incendiary munition was supplied to some of the most vital defenses, such as those at the oil facilities located near Hannover, Pölitz, and Leuna. The main drawback to the incendiary pellets was their use of a contact fuse that remained armed upon its fall back to the ground in the event that it did not strike an aircraft.

136. *Target Germany: The Army Air Forces' Official Story of the VIII Bomber Command's First Year over Europe* (New York: Simon and Schuster, 1943), 63.

137. Renz, *Development of German Anti-aircraft,* 257, K113.107-194, AFHRA.

138. Fröhlich, *Tagebücher,* part II, vol. 7, p. 505; diary entry of March 9, 1943.

139. Boberach, *Meldungen,* 14:5357.

140. Neufeld, *Rocket and the Reich,* 190–193.

141. "Besprechungsnotiz Nr. 57/43 [June 18, 1943]," RL 3/Folder 60/Pages 415–416, BA-MA.

142. Letter from von Axthelm to Dr. Ing. F. Gosslau, dated February 7, 1953, N 529/Folder 9, BA-MA.

143. Heinz-Dieter Hölsken, *Die V-Waffen: Entstehung, Propaganda, Kriegseinsatz* (Stuttgart: Deutsche Verlags-Anstalt, 1984), 42, 49, 54, 133, 247.

144. Georg Hentschel, ed., *Die geheimen Konferenzen des Generalluftzeugmeisters: Ausgewählte und kommentierte Dokumente zur Geschichte der deutschen Luftrüstung und des Luftkrieges, 1942–1944,* vol. 1 (Koblenz: Bernard & Graefe Verlag, 1989), 183.

145. Schabel, *Illusion,* 265–266.

146. Karl-Heinz Ludwig, "Die deutschen Flakraketen im Zweiten Weltkrieg," *Militärgeschichtliche Mitteilungen* 1 (1969): 93.

147. Schabel, *Illusion,* 266. Renz estimated that propellant savings would be between five and fourteen tons per shootdown depending on the caliber of the flak artillery.

148. Hölsken, *V-Waffen,* 45–46.

149. Schabel, *Illusion,* 268–269.

150. Renz, *Development of German Anti-aircraft,* 414, K113.107-194, AFHRA.

151. Herrmann, *Eagle's Wings,* 166.

152. Ibid., 166–167.

153. Galland, *First and the Last,* 24.

154. Herrmann, *Eagle's Wings,* 167–168.

155. Greenhous et al., *Crucible,* 687.

156. Herrmann, *Eagle's Wings,* 173, 183–184.

157. Hinchliffe, *Other Battle,* 150–151.

158. Herrmann, *Eagle's Wings,* 187–188.

159. Ibid., 186.

160. Vogt and Brenne, *Krefeld im Luftkrieg,* 114.

161. Murray, *Strategy for Defeat,* 187. The total number of fighter aircraft lost is not available, but it would have exceeded this figure because numerous pilots would have bailed out of or landed their damaged aircraft.

162. McFarland and Newton, *To Command the Sky,* 261.

163. Webster and Frankland, *Strategic Air Offensive,* 4:432. The next highest total was 5,816 night sorties in June.

164. Richards, *Hardest Victory,* 189.

165. Wolfgang Schumann and Wolfgang Bleyer, *Deutschland im zweiten Weltkrieg,* vol. 4, *Das Scheitern der faschistischen Defensivstrategie an der Deutsch-Sowjetischen Front* (Berlin [East]: Akademie-Verlag, 1981), 121.

166. Musgrove, *Operation Gomorrah,* 29.

167. Richards, *Hardest Victory,* 190.

168. Greenhous et al., *Crucible,* 695.

169. Musgrove, *Operation Gomorrah,* 29–30.

170. Richards, *Hardest Victory,* 191.

171. Fröhlich, *Tagebücher,* part II, vol. 9, pp. 162–163; diary entry of July 26, 1943.

172. Weinberg, *World at Arms,* 595. Ironically, the Fascist Grand Council voted to remove Mussolini from power on the very evening of the Hamburg raid.

173. Control Commission for Germany, *Notes on Flak,* 76, IWM.

174. Irving, *Rise and Fall,* 213.

175. Ibid., 214; see also Control Commission for Germany, Air Division, *Notes on Flak and Searchlight Radar (G.A.F.)* (n.p.: Air Division, CCG, 1946), 76, IWM.

176. Craven and Cate, *Army Air Forces,* 2:677.

177. USSBS, *The United States Strategic Bombing Survey: Report on the German Flak Effort Throughout the War* (n.p., 1945), 9, 137.310-4, AFHRA.

178. Musgrove, *Operation Gomorrah,* 76, 153.

179. Irving, *Rise and Fall,* 230.

180. Musgrove, *Operation Gomorrah,* 88. The city's canals proved to be both a refuge and a place of death. The extreme heat burned any exposed body parts, and houses collapsed into the canals, crushing those trying to remain afloat. In addition, numerous persons succumbed to exhaustion and drowned in the city's waterways.

181. Richards, *Hardest Victory,* 192–193.

182. Ibid., 193–194.

183. Harris, *Bomber Offensive,* 175.

184. Richards, *Hardest Victory,* 194.

185. Boberach, *Meldungen,* 14:5515, 5562–5563.

186. Irving, *Rise and Fall,* 231.

187. "Besprechungsnotiz Nr 85/43 [August 27, 1943]," RL 3/Folder 63/Page 12, BA-MA.

188. Hummel, "Kommandostrukturen," Teil IV, 295.

189. Cajus Bekker, *Angriffshöhe 4000: Ein Kriegstagebuch der deutschen Luftwaffe* (Cologne: Naumann & Göbel, 1964), 392.

190. Murray, *Strategy for Defeat,* 183.

191. Schumann and Bleyer, *Deutschland im zweiten Weltkrieg,* 4:123.

192. Wagner, *Lagevorträge,* 530. The minutes of the meeting held between August 1 and August 3 note Hitler's remark that "the pursuit and anti-aircraft programme is functioning well."

193. Galland, *First and the Last,* 167.

194. Schumann and Bleyer, *Deutschland im zweiten Weltkrieg,* 4:125, 127. At this time the Luftwaffe operated 10,541 heavy flak guns, with 18 percent located on the Eastern Front, 11 percent in western Europe, and 5 percent each in Italy and the Balkans, respectively.

195. "Heranziehung des Reichspost-Personals für den kurzfristigen Wehrdienst in den Heimat-Flakbatterien [July 27, 1943]," RL 19/Folder 575/Page 93, BA-MA.

196. "Aufstellung von Hei. Flak in Kärnten [August 3, 1943]," FL 19/Folder 575/Page 30, BA-MA.

197. "Umbenennung der Heimatnebelkompanie 1/XVII [August 5, 1943]," RL 19/Folder 575/Page 44, BA-MA.

198. "Besondere Einsatzerfahrungen der Flakartillerie, Nr. 3 [July 31, 1943]," RL 19/Folder 575/Pages 259–260, BA-MA. These three initiatives were originally proposed to von Axthelm from the 7th Flak Division.

199. Wagner, *Lagevorträge,* 536–537. This excerpt from "Conversations with the Fuehrer at the Fuehrer Headquarters Between August 9 and 11, 1943."

200. "Heranziehung von Lw.-Helfern [August 16, 1943]," RL 19/Folder 575/Page 146, BA-MA.

201. "Vorstudien zur Luftkriegsgeschichte, Heft 8, Reichsluftverteidigung [1944]," T-971/Reel 69/NARA. By 1943, all young men performed a year of mandatory service as agricultural or construction workers after completing their high school education and before entry into the military. By this time, most young women were also required to provide a year of service, normally within the agricultural sector or as additional house help for "overburdened" German mothers. See Bedürftig, *Lexikon des Dritten Reiches,* 472–473.

202. Koch, *Flak,* 101–106.

203. Military Intelligence 15, *Handbook,* 4:50, IWM; Seidler, *Blitzmädchen,* 57. Seidler places the highest number of strictly Labor Service batteries at 420.

204. Ibid.; see also Koch, *Flak,* 106.

205. Greenhous et al., *Crucible,* 641.

206. Webster and Frankland, *Strategic Air Offensive,* 4:432.

207. USSBS, Civil Defense Division, *The United States Strategic Bombing Survey: Civil Defense Division Final Report,* 3. It should be noted that many of those killed in these raids included thousands of foreign forced laborers impressed by the National Socialists into factory work at sites throughout Germany and the occupied territories.

208. Control Commission for Germany, *Notes on Flak,* 78, IWM.

209. Leroy W. Newby, *Target Ploesti: View from a Bombsight* (Novato, Calif.: Presidio Press, 1983), 87–88.

210. "Florosa #3, Army Air Forces Board Project No. (M-2) 29 [September 29, 1943]," 245.64, AFHRA.

211. *Bomber Command Operational Research Section Report, "S" Series,* S-98, "The Effect of Window on Bomber Operations [August 19, 1943]," AHB.

212. Fröhlich, *Tagebücher,* part II, vol. 9, p. 220; diary entry of August 5, 1943.

213. Craven and Cate, *Army Air Forces,* 2:694–695; see also McArthur, *Operations Analysis,* 71.

214. Perret, *Winged Victory,* 215–217; see also Schumann and Bleyer, *Deutschland im zweiten Weltkrieg,* 4:128–129. Since the attack was conducted at low level, it is reasonable to assume that the light flak batteries inflicted the vast majority of the losses experienced by the bomber force.

215. Craven and Cate, *Army Air Forces,* 2:847.

216. Flak Section, Ninth Air Force, *Flak Facts: A Brief History of Flak and Flak Intelligence in the Ninth Air Force* (n.p., 1945), 23, collection of the Air University Library, Maxwell AFB.

217. Craven and Cate, *Army Air Forces,* 2:848.

218. Middlebrook, *Schweinfurt-Regensburg Mission,* 319–328. One aircraft credited to the fighters crash-landed in Switzerland, and one aircraft fell victim to unspecified mechanical difficulties.

219. "Monthly Flak Report—August [September 3, 1943]," 520.3813, AFHRA. The total percentage of the wing's aircraft hit by flak during August was 38.79 percent, or 457 aircraft.

220. Chorley, *Bomber Command Losses,* 4:66–234. In addition, six aircraft fell victim to an unspecified combination of flak and fighters during this period.

221. Webster and Frankland, *Strategic Air Offensive,* 4:432.

222. Craven and Cate, *Army Air Forces,* 2:341–342.

223. Monthly flak report for April from the 1st Bombardment Wing on April 30, 1943, and monthly flak report for June from the 4th Bombardment Wing on July 3, 1943, 520.3813, AFHRA. For individual loss and damage rates due to flak, see monthly reports for the period from January to December 1943 in this collection ordered by individual wing rates.

224. Chorley, *Bomber Command Losses,* 4:118, 120–121, 136, 143–144, 232; see also Middlebrook, *Schweinfurt-Regensburg Mission,* 318.

225. Newby, *Target Ploesti,* 70.

226. Boog, *Luftwaffenführung,* 208.
227. Ibid., 209.
228. Irving, *Rise and Fall,* 235.
229. Webster and Frankland, *Strategic Air Offensive,* 4:306–307.
230. Ibid., 308.
231. Boog, *Luftwaffenführung,* 211.
232. "Besprechungsnotiz Nr. 87/43 [September 2–3, 1943]," RL 3/Folder 60/Pages 430–432, BA-MA.
233. "Besprechungsnotiz Nr. 91/43 [September 22, 1943]," RL 3/Folder 60/Page 441, BA-MA.
234. "Besprechungsnotiz Nr. 93/43 [September 25, 1943]," RL 3/Folder 60/Pages 443–444, BA-MA.
235. Webster and Frankland, *Strategic Air Offensive,* 4:432.
236. "Besprechungsnotiz Nr. 93/43 [September 25, 1943]," RL 3/Folder 60/Pages 445–447, BA-MA.
237. "Stenographische Niederschrift über die Besprechung beim Reichsmarschall [October 7, 1943]," RL 3/Folder 60/Pages 461–462, BA-MA.
238. Ibid., 469, 494–495.
239. Ibid., 546–547, 573.
240. Ibid., 639–640, 667.
241. Ibid., 573.
242. Webster and Frankland, *Strategic Air Offensive,* 4:433. Additionally, fighters damaged ten aircraft beyond repair, while the flak accounted for a further twelve aircraft damaged beyond repair.
243. Ibid., 272–273.
244. Schumann and Bleyer, *Deutschland im zweiten Weltkrieg,* 4:127.
245. Comer, *Combat Crew,* 141.
246. "Monthly Flak Report—October, 1943 [November 1, 1943]" from the 1st Bombardment Division; "Monthly AA Report for October [November 4, 1943]" from the 3rd Bombardment Division; and "Monthly Flak Report—October 1943 [October 31, 1943]" from the 2nd Bombardment Division, 520.3813, AFHRA. On this date, the 2nd Bombardment Division sent forty-one aircraft against the submarine yard at Vegesack near Bremen, suffering flak damage to fourteen bombers without a loss.
247. Golücke, *Schweinfurt,* 171–172.
248. Craven and Cate, *Army Air Forces,* 2:850.
249. Golücke, *Schweinfurt,* 255, 292, 295, 297.
250. Craven and Cate, *Army Air Forces,* 2:704; see also "Monthly Flak Report—October, 1943 [November 1, 1943]" from the 1st Bombardment Division; and "Monthly AA Report for October [November 4, 1943]" from the 3rd Bombardment Division, 520.3813, AFHRA.
251. Craven and Cate, *Army Air Forces,* 2:705–706.
252. Tami Davis Biddle, "Bombing by the Square Yard: Sir Arthur Harris at War, 1942–1945," *International History Review* 21 (September 1999): 643, 646.
253. "Monthly Flak Report for December [January 5, 1944]" from the 1st Bombardment Division, 520.3813, AFHRA.
254. Middlebrook, *Berlin Raids,* 2.

255. Herrmann, *Eagle's Wings,* 164.

256. Fröhlich, *Tagebücher,* part II, vol. 9, pp. 204, 217, 564, 627; diary entries of August 2, August 4, September 23, and September 30, 1943. The Italian government surrendered to the Allies on September 9, 1943. By the end of September, the German army captured almost 1,000 flak guns from Italian forces in Italy and the Balkans.

257. Middlebrook, *Berlin Raids,* 26.

258. Groehler, *Luftherrschaft,* 203.

259. Ibid., 204–205.

260. Fröhlich, *Tagebücher,* part II, vol. 9, p. 216; diary entry of August 4, 1943.

261. Lee, *Goering,* 165.

262. Renz, *Development of German Anti-aircraft,* 379–380, K113.107-194, AFHRA.

263. Greenhous et al., *Crucible,* 651.

264. Albert N. Garland and Howard McGaw Smyth, *Sicily and the Surrender of Italy,* United States Army in World War II (Washington, D.C.: GPO, 1965), 376.

265. *Frontnachrichtenblatt,* Nr. 48 (March 1943): 683; *Frontnachrichtenblatt,* Nr. 50 (May 1943): 699; and *Frontnachrichtenblatt,* Nr. 51 (June 1943): 702–703.

8. Escorts over the Reich, January–May 1944

1. Max Domarus, ed., *Hitler: Reden und Proklamationen, 1932–1945,* vol. 2 (Wiesbaden: R. Löwit, 1973), 2,074–2,076.

2. Middlebrook, *Berlin Raids,* 202–210. Major Heinrich Prinz zu Sayn-Wittgenstein was the pilot who claimed six shootdowns. He was killed shortly thereafter during another night combat operation.

3. Fröhlich, *Tagebücher,* part II, vol. 11, p. 39; diary entry of January 2, 1944.

4. Middlebrook, *Berlin Raids,* 202, 207.

5. Ibid., 210, 215. During this mission, 168 aircrew members were killed, and 31 were captured.

6. Fröhlich, *Tagebücher,* part II, vol. 11, p. 43; diary entry of January 3, 1944.

7. Davis Biddle, "Bombing by the Square Yard," 643.

8. Chorley, *Bomber Command Losses,* 5:14; see also "Air Scientific Intelligence Technical Translation, No. 3, Anti-jamming Procedures for Flak Control Radar [January 12, 1945]," 512.62513-3, AFHRA. This is a translation by British intelligence of a captured Luftwaffe manual entitled "Das Orten mit Funkmeßgeräten (Flak) unter erschwerten Bedingungen," published in February 1944.

9. "Überblick über den jetztigen Stand der Erkenntnisse und die Planung auf dem Gebiet der Zentimeter/Technik [February 8, 1944]," RL 3/Folder 42/Pages 36–37, BA-MA. This device was known as the "Kulmbach Z" radar.

10. Middlebrook, *Berlin Raids,* 221–231. The success of the Luftwaffe's night fighters was in large part based on the introduction of a new aerial radar (SN-2), which was unaffected by Window. In addition, the introduction of an upward-firing cannon *(schräge Musik)* provided the night fighters with an effective and deadly weapon with which to attack the RAF bombers from below the aircraft.

11. Otto Svoboda, "Summary of the Status of German Antiaircraft in the Final Phase of World War II," trans. Klaus G. Liebhold, *Flugwehr und Technik* 7 (July 1950): 2. This article was translated for the Rand Corporation in 1950 and is part of the

collection of the U.S. Army Military History Institute. See also USSBS, *The United States Strategic Bombing Survey: Report on the German Flak Effort Throughout the War* (n.p., 1945), 6, 137.310-4, AFHRA.

12. Rhoden, *History of World War II,* 4:102.

13. Schumann and Bleyer, *Deutschland im zweiten Weltkrieg,* 5:148.

14. Suchenwirth, *Development of the German Air Force,* 237.

15. Boog, *Luftwaffenführung,* 132–133. See Boog's footnote 713.

16. Bedürftig, *Lexikon, des Dritten Reiches,* 487.

17. Golücke, *Schweinfurt,* 108. In fairness to Weise, Kammhuber was clearly a difficult subordinate, and his transfer to the command of Air Region 5 in the fall of 1943 clearly assisted Stumpff in exercising increased control over the Reich's fighter arm.

18. "Vorstudien zur Luftkriegsgeschichte, Heft 8, Reichsluftverteidigung [1944]," T-971/Reel 69, NARA; see also Boog, *Luftwaffenführung,* 132. Boog identifies January 17, 1944, as the date for the activation of Air Region, Reich.

19. Schumann and Bleyer, *Deutschland im zweiten Weltkrieg,* 5:147–148.

20. Boog, *Luftwaffenführung,* 132; see also Rhoden, *History of World War II,* vol. 3, no page number. This work is held by the Air University Library at Maxwell AFB, Alabama.

21. Alfred Price, *The Last Year of the Luftwaffe, May 1944 to May 1945* (Osceola, Wis.: Motorbooks International, 1991), 12; see also von Rhoden, *History of World War II,* 4:106.

22. "Stenographische Niederschrift über die Besprechung beim Reichsmarschall am 24. Mai 1944," RL 3/Folder 62/Page 701, BA-MA.

23. Eichholtz, *Kriegswirtschaft,* 2:656–659.

24. USSBS, Economic Effects Division, *The United States Strategic Bombing Survey: The Effects of Strategic Bombing on the German War Economy,* 285.

25. "Erläuterungen zum Flakprogramm vom 28. Februar 1944 [February 21, 1944]," RL 3/Folder 57/Pages 200–201, BA-MA; see also Military Intelligence 15, *Handbook,* 4:63–64, IWM.

26. Military Intelligence 15, *Handbook,* 4:60, IWM.

27. Eichholtz, *Kriegswirtschaft,* 2:660–661.

28. "Erläuterungen zum Flakprogramm vom 28. Februar 1944 [February 21, 1944]," RL 3/Folder 57/Pages 202, BA-MA.

29. "Besprechungsnotiz Nr. 1/44 Chefsache [January 1, 1944]," RL 3/Folder 62/Pages 257–263, BA-MA.

30. "Bericht über die Funkmeßbesprechung [February 11, 1944]," RL 3/Folder 42/Pages 24–25, BA-MA.

31. A. E. Hoffmann-Heyden, "German Radiolocation in Retrospect," *Interavia* 11 (1951): 625–626.

32. USSBS, *The United States Strategic Bombing Survey: Report on the German Flak Effort Throughout the War* (n.p., 1945), 10, 137.310-4, AFHRA; see also Overy, *Why the Allies Won,* 131. Overy estimates that the percentage was between one-half and two-thirds of all radar and communications equipment.

33. U.S. War Department, *Handbook,* 357.

34. "Flakentwicklungsbesprechung [February 14, 1944]," RL 3/Folder 57/Page 54, BA-MA.

35. USSBS, *The United States Strategic Bombing Survey: Report on the German Flak Effort Throughout the War* (n.p., 1945), 12, 137.310-4, AFHRA.

36. Flak Section, Ninth Air Force, *Flak Facts,* 48.

37. "Vorstudien zur Luftkriegsgeschichte, Heft 8, Reichsluftverteidigung [1944]," T-971/Reel 69, NARA.

38. Ibid.

39. USSBS, Economic Effects Division, *The United States Strategic Bombing Survey: The Effects of Strategic Bombing on the German War Economy,* 284.

40. "Flakbeschaffungsbesprechung [May 8, 1944]," RL 3/Folder 57/Page 89, BA-MA.

41. Schumann, Groehler, and Bleyer, *Deutschland im zweiten Weltkrieg,* vol. 6, no page number; see also Eichholtz, *Kriegswirtschaft,* 3:202. The V-3 was an artillery piece over 400 feet long that was capable of firing a 300-pound projectile approximately 100 miles. The V-4 was a four-stage missile capable of traveling 140 miles.

42. Irving, *Rise and Fall,* 222, 263. The monthly demand on aluminum alone would have fulfilled the aluminum requirements for 1,754,000 rounds of 88-mm per month. See "Erforderlicher Rohstoffbedarf [August 10, 1940]," T-321/Roll 7/Frame 4743260, NARA.

43. Webster and Frankland, *Strategic Air Offensive,* 2:296.

44. Military Intelligence 15, *Handbook,* 4:46, 50, IWM.

45. Beck, *Under the Bombs,* 113.

46. Seidler, *Frauen,* 84.

47. Ibid., 86; see also USSBS, *The United States Strategic Bombing Survey: Report on the German Flak Effort Throughout the War* (n.p., 1945), 11, 137.310-4, AFHRA; and Golücke, *Schweinfurt,* 166.

48. Beck, *Under the Bombs,* 165.

49. Absolon, *Rangliste,* 172.

50. Beck, *Under the Bombs,* 166.

51. Ibid., 113; see also Golücke, *Schweinfurt,* 164.

52. Military Intelligence 15, *Handbook,* 4:46, 50, IWM.

53. Price, *Luftwaffe Handbook,* 66.

54. Jerry Ethell and Alfred Price, *Target Berlin: Mission 250, 6 March 1944* (London: Jane's, 1981), 27.

55. USSBS, *The United States Strategic Bombing Survey: Report on the German Flak Effort Throughout the War* (n.p., 1945), 5, 137.310-4, AFHRA.

56. Middlebrook, *Berlin Raids,* 261.

57. Richards, *Hardest Victory,* 215.

58. Middlebrook, *Berlin Raids,* 263.

59. Fröhlich, *Tagebücher,* part II, vol. 11, p. 299; diary entry of February 17, 1944.

60. Ibid., 354, 389; diary entries of February 26 and March 3, 1944.

61. Ibid., 402, 551; diary entries of March 4 and March 25, 1944.

62. "Besprechungsnotiz Nr 85/43 [August 27, 1943]," RL 3/Folder 63/Pages 12–13, BA-MA. At this meeting, Göring discussed the need for cooperation between the flak and the night fighters, by which he meant restrictions on flak operations. See also Musgrove, *Operation Gomorrah,* 32.

63. Herrmann, *Eagle's Wings,* 215–217.

64. Richards, *Hardest Victory,* 218.

65. Herrmann, *Eagle's Wings,* 216.

66. Middlebrook, *Berlin Raids,* 298.

67. Ibid., 299–301.

68. Ibid.

69. Hinchliffe, *Other Battle,* 252.

70. Chorley, *Bomber Command Losses,* 5:139.

71. Groehler, *Luftherrschaft,* 204–205.

72. Harris, *Bomber Offensive,* 188.

73. Richards, *Hardest Victory,* 219.

74. Webster and Frankland, *Strategic Air Offensive,* 4:433.

75. Fröhlich, *Tagebücher,* part II, vol. 11, p. 575; diary entry of March 29, 1944.

76. "Extracts from Conferences on Problems of Aircraft Production: Milch Documents, March 1943–February 1944," K 512.621 VII/140, AFHRA.

77. *Bomber Command Operational Research Section Reports, "G" Series,* G-103, "Monthly Review of Losses and Interceptions of Bomber Command Aircraft in Night Operations—April 1944 [June 5, 1944]," AHB.

78. Hinchliffe, *Other Battle,* 212, 261.

79. Ibid., 214. It should be noted that the total claims by the wild boar units were much higher. However, confirmation of many of these kills proved especially difficult because of the operations of the fighters in close proximity to the anti-aircraft fire zone.

80. McFarland and Newton, *Command the Sky,* 106, 114, 120.

81. Craven and Cate, *Army Air Forces,* 3:43–46.

82. Ibid., 49.

83. Groehler, *Luftherrschaft,* 209.

84. Galland, *First and the Last,* 195.

85. Ethell and Price, *Target Berlin,* 25.

86. Suchenwirth, *Historical Turning Points,* 117; see also Murray, *Strategy for Defeat,* 243–245.

87. Ardery, *Bomber Pilot,* 174–175.

88. Schumann and Bleyer, *Deutschland im zweiten Weltkrieg,* 5:147.

89. Hoffmann-Heyden, "German Radiolocation," 624–625.

90. "*VER—Flak* 24 (Juli 1944), Oberkommando der Luftwaffe, General der Flakwaffe," RL 4/Folder 267/Page 87, BA-MA.

91. "Monthly Flak Report for October 1944 [1st Bombardment Division, November 1944]," 520.3813, AFHRA.

92. Flak Section, Ninth Air Force, *Flak Facts,* 45.

93. "Enemy Capabilities—Flak [April 12, 1945]," 622.646-2, AFHRA.

94. "Die Entwicklung der 'Großbatterie' in der Luftverteidigung des Heimatkriegsgebietes von 1940–1945 [April 2, 1947]," N 529/Folder 13, BA-MA.

95. "*VER—Flak* 24 (Juli 1944), Oberkommando der Luftwaffe, General der Flakwaffe," RL 4/Folder 267/Pages 86–87, BA-MA.

96. "Vorstudien zur Luftkriegsgeschichte, Heft 8, Reichsluftverteidigung [1944]," T-971/Reel 69, NARA.

97. "Die Entwicklung der 'Großbatterie' in der Luftverteidigung des Heimatkriegsgebietes von 1940–1945 [April 2, 1947]," N 529/Folder 13, BA-MA.

98. Craven and Cate, *Army Air Forces,* 3:56.

99. "Monthly Flak Report for May 1944 [June 6, 1944]," 520.3813, AFHRA.

100. Renz, *Development of German Anti-aircraft,* 316, K113.107–119, AFHRA.

101. "Monthly Flak Report for February, 1944 [March 6, 1944]," 520.3813, AFHRA.

102. "Monthly Flak Report for March, 1944 [April 3, 1944]," 520.3813, AFHRA.

103. "Monthly Flak Report for April 1944 [May 7, 1944]," 520.3813, AFHRA.

104. Monthly flak reports from the 1st, 2nd, and 3rd Bombardment Divisions for the period from January until April 1944, 520.3813; "15 Air Force Flak Losses & Damages [May 10, 1945]," 670.3813-1, AFHRA. The bomber losses to flak included 17 in January, 62 in February, 72.5 in March, and 163 in April.

105. Monthly flak reports from the 1st, 2nd, and 3rd Bombardment Divisions for the period from October until December 1943, 520.3813; "15 Air Force Flak Losses & Damages [May 10, 1945]," 670.3813-1, AFHRA. The Fifteenth Air Force summary does not include totals for October.

106. "Monthly Flak Report—March 1944 [April 6, 1944]," 520.3813, AFHRA.

107. Groehler, *Luftherrschaft,* 212.

108. Ibid., 209.

109. Craven and Cate, *Army Air Forces,* 3:51.

110. Ethell and Price, *Target Berlin,* 179–191. In addition to the sixty-four aircraft lost to flak or fighters, seven bombers fell to unknown causes.

111. Monthly flak reports of the 1st, 2nd, and 3rd Bombardment Divisions for March 1944, 520.3813, AFHRA.

112. Ardery, *Bomber Pilot,* 175.

113. Fröhlich, *Tagebücher,* part II, vol. 11, p. 428; diary entry of March 7, 1944.

114. Perret, *Winged Victory,* 292.

115. Lee, *German Air Force,* 241–242.

116. Middlebrook, *Berlin Raids,* 28.

117. "Summary, German Flak [1945]," 519.601A-1, AFHRA. This report was compiled from the findings of the "Air Defense Investigation" field teams between April 1945 and July 1945.

118. "Summary, German Flak [1945]," 519.601A-1, AFHRA.

119. *Bomber Command Operational Research Memoranda, "M" Series,* Memo-66, "Observations on Enemy Decoy T.I. Markers [April 14, 1944]," AHB.

120. Renz, *Development of German Anti-aircraft,* 334–335, K113.107-194, AFHRA.

121. "2d Bombardment Division Monthly Flak Report—November 1944," 502.3813, AFHRA.

122. Newby, *Target Ploesti,* 56.

123. USSBS, Oil Division, *The United States Strategic Bombing Survey: Ammoniakwerke Merseburg GmbH Leuna, Germany* (Washington, D.C.: GPO, 1946), 19.

124. USSBS, Oil Division, *The United States Strategic Bombing Survey: Oil Division Final Report, Appendix* (Washington, D.C.: GPO, 1945), 34.

125. USSBS, Oil Division, *The United States Strategic Bombing Survey: Meerbeck Rheinpreussen Synthetic Oil Plant* (Washington, D.C.: GPO, 1946), 12, 14.

126. USSBS, Oil Division, *The United States Strategic Bombing Survey: Underground and Dispersal Plants in Greater Germany* (Washington, D.C.: GPO, 1945), 1–4. The movement of factories and facilities involved a number of major disadvantages, including high cost, delays in production, and increased difficulties in transporting resources and materials to these sites.

127. USSBS, Oil Division, *The United States Strategic Bombing Survey: Meerbeck Rheinpreussen Synthetic Oil Plant,* 14.

128. Neufeld, *Rocket and the Reich,* 200–213.

129. "Stenographische Niederschrift über die Besprechung beim Reichsmarschall [May 29, 1944]," RL 3/Folder 62/Page 86, BA-MA.

130. "Organisation, Operation, and Degree of Success of G.A.F. Smoke Units [August 11, 1945]," 506.6314A-40, AFHRA.

131. "Vorstudien zur Luftkriegsgeschichte, Heft 8, Reichsluftverteidigung [1944]," T-971/Reel 69, NARA.

132. Flak Section, Ninth Air Force, *Flak Facts,* 50.

133. Wagner, *Lagevorträge,* 585. These meetings were held from May 4 to 6, 1944.

134. USSBS, Oil Division, *The United States Strategic Bombing Survey: Ammoniakwerke Merseburg GmbH Leuna, Germany,* 17. The number of ovens was later increased to 800.

135. USSBS, Oil Division, *The United States Strategic Bombing Survey: Oil Division Final Report, Appendix,* 34; see also USSBS, Oil Division, *The United States Strategic Bombing Survey: Powder, Explosives, Special Rockets and Jet Propellants, War Gases, and Smoke Acid* (Washington, D.C.: GPO, 1945), 58.

136. Newby, *Target Ploesti,* 103, 160.

137. "Organisation, Operation, and Degree of Success of G.A.F. Smoke Units [August 11, 1945]," 506.6314A-40, AFHRA.

138. Crosby, *Wing and a Prayer,* 21.

139. Golücke, *Schweinfurt,* 283, 293. In this case, a relative humidity of less than 60 percent and a high-pressure system proved the determining factors not to commence smoke operations.

140. "Organisation, Operation, and Degree of Success of G.A.F. Smoke Units [August 11, 1945]," 506.6314A-40, AFHRA; see also USSBS, Oil Division, *The United States Strategic Bombing Survey: Oil Division Final Report, Appendix,* 34. One additional disadvantage associated with the smoke generators was the caustic nature of the smoke. The smoke proved especially corrosive to flak gun batteries and equipment in wet conditions.

141. Fröhlich, *Tagebücher,* part II, vol. 11, p. 67; diary entry of January 8, 1944.

142. Crosby, *Wing and a Prayer,* 238.

143. Newby, *Target Ploesti,* 107.

144. USSBS, *The United States Strategic Bombing Survey: Report on the German Flak Effort Throughout the War* (n.p., 1945), 22, 137.310-4, AFHRA.

145. USSBS, Oil Division, *The United States Strategic Bombing Survey: Oil Division Final Report, Appendix,* 34.

146. "Organisation, Operation, and Degree of Success of G.A.F. Smoke Units [August 11, 1945]," 506.6314A-40, AFHRA.

147. USSBS, *The United States Strategic Bombing Survey: Report on the German Flak Effort Throughout the War* (n.p., 1945), 22, 137.310-4, AFHRA.

148. Walther Hubatsch, ed., *Hitlers Weisungen für die Kriegführung, 1939–1945* (Frankfurt am Main: Bernard & Graefe Verlag für Wehrwissen 1962), 233.

149. David Fraser, *Knight's Cross: A Life of Field Marshal Erwin Rommel* (New York: HarperCollins, 1993), 455–457. Rommel was the commander of Army Group B responsible for defending an area along the French coast.

9. Aerial Götterdämmerung, June 1944–May 1945

1. Richards, *Hardest Victory*, 225.

2. Craven and Cate, *Army Air Forces*, 3:74–79.

3. Stephen E. Ambrose, *D-Day: The Climactic Battle of World War II* (New York: Simon and Schuster, 1994), 96.

4. Chorley, *Bomber Command Losses*, 5:161. The high operations tempo combined with the greater probability of survival in attacks conducted in the occupied western territories reduced operational tour lengths from nine months to six months.

5. Greenhous et al., *Crucible*, 797–799, 803.

6. Webster and Frankland, *Strategic Air Offensive*, 3:39.

7. Craven and Cate, *Army Air Forces*, 3:165–172.

8. Perret, *Winged Victory*, 292.

9. "Monthly Flak Report for May 1944 [June 6, 1944]," 520.3813, AFHRA.

10. Groehler, *Luftherrschaft*, 209.

11. Kenneth P. Werrell, *Archie, Flak, AAA, and SAM: A Short Operational History of Ground-Based Air Defense* (Maxwell AFB, Ala.: Air University Press, 1988), 29.

12. Werner Girbig, . . . *mit Kurs auf Leuna: Die Luftoffensive gegen die Treibstoffindustrie und der deutsche Abwehreinsatz, 1944–1945* (Stuttgart: Motorbuch Verlag, 1980), 13–52, 217.

13. Monthly flak reports for the 1st, 2nd, and 3rd Bombardment Divisions for May 1944, 520.3813, AFHRA.

14. "Betr.: 'Drohende Gefahr West' [December 6, 1943]," T-321/Reel 10/Frames 4746474, 4746480–81, NARA. The Luftwaffe also prepared a similar contingency plan entitled "Drohende Gefahr Nord" in the event of an invasion of Europe via Denmark and/or Norway. See "Anlage zu Der Reichsmarschall des Großdeutschen Reiches und Oberbefehlshaber der Luftwaffe Nr. 9050/44 g. Kdos.Chefs (FüSt. Ia) 2.Ang. vom 3.2.44," T-321/Reel 10/Frames 4746575–76, NARA.

15. "Betr.: 'Drohende Gefahr West' [February 27, 1944]," T-321/Reel 10/Frames 4746619, 4746626–29, NARA. The exact composition of the force planned to be sent to the north included 6 heavy flak battalion staffs, 2 light flak battalion staffs, 22 heavy flak batteries, 12 light flak batteries, and 6 flak combat formations *(Flakkampftrupps)*.

16. Koch, *Flak*, 186–187.

17. "Betr.: 'Drohende Gefahr West' [February 27, 1944]," T-321/Reel 10/Frame 4746628, NARA.

18. Koch, *Flak*, 48; see also Nafziger, *German Order of Battle*, 71–72.

19. William H. Tantum IV and E. J. Hoffschmidt, *The Rise and Fall of the German Air Force* (Old Greenwich, Conn.: WE, 1969), 286.

20. Albert Kesselring, "Die Deutsche Luftwaffe," in *Bilanz des zweiten Weltkrieges: Erkenntnisse und Verpflichtungen für die Zukunft* (Oldenburg: Gerhard Stalling Verlag, 1953), 156. These figures are taken from a statement made by General Andreas Nielsen, chief of staff for Air Region, Reich.

21. Janusz Piekalkiewicz, *Die 8,8 Flak im Erdkampf-Einsatz* (Stuttgart: Motorbuch Verlag, 1999), 135.

22. Koch, *Flak,* 87–88.

23. "Summary No. 14 of Flak Operations in the WEST [August 17, 1944]," AIR 40/Folder 1151, PRO.

24. "Summary No. 15 of Flak Operations in the WEST [August 25, 1944]," AIR 40/Folder 1151, PRO.

25. "Summary No. 14 of Flak Operations in the WEST [August 17, 1944]," AIR 40/Folder 1151, PRO; see also Craven and Cate, *Army Air Forces,* 3:303.

26. USSBS, *The United States Strategic Bombing Survey: Report on the German Flak Effort Throughout the War* (n.p., 1945), 14, 137.310-4, AFHRA.

27. "Vorstudien zur Luftkriegsgeschichte, Heft 8, Reichsluftverteidigung [1944]," T-971/Reel 69, NARA.

28. Tantum and Hoffschmidt, *Rise and Fall,* 286–287, 367; see also Adolf Galland, *Die Ersten und die Letzten: Jagdflieger im Zweiten Weltkrieg* (Munich: Franz Schneekluth Verlag, 1953), 321–322.

29. "Stenographische Niederschrift über die Besprechung beim Reichsmarschall am 24. Mai 1944," RL 3/Folder 62/Page 706, BA-MA.

30. Interrogation transcript of Field Marshal Erhard Milch by British intelligence on May 23, 1945, 512.619c-6d, AFHRA.

31. "Stenographische Niederschrift über die Besprechung beim Reichsmarschall am 24. Mai 1944," RL 3/Folder 62/Page 706, BA-MA.

32. Girbig, *Kurs auf Leuna,* 52.

33. Tantum and Hoffschmidt, *Rise and Fall,* 355–356.

34. Schumann, Groehler, and Bleyer, *Deutschland im zweiten Weltkrieg,* 6:162.

35. Craven and Cate, *Army Air Forces,* 3:281.

36. "Monthly AA Report for June 1944 [3rd Bombardment Division, July 19, 1944]," 520.3813, AFHRA.

37. Craven and Cate, *Army Air Forces,* 3:284.

38. "Monthly Flak Report—June 1944 [2nd Bombardment Division, July 5, 1944]," 520.3813, AFHRA.

39. "Monthly Flak Report for June 1944 [1st Bombardment Division, July 5, 1944]," 520.3813, AFHRA.

40. "Vorstudien zur Luftkriegsgeschichte, Heft 8, Reichsluftverteidigung [1944]," T-971/Reel 69, NARA.

41. Webster and Frankland, *Strategic Air Offensive,* 4:321–325.

42. Wagner, *Lagevorträge,* 597.

43. USSBS, *The United States Strategic Bombing Survey: Report on the German Flak Effort Throughout the War* (n.p., 1945), 14, 137.310-4, AFHRA.

44. USSBS, Oil Division, *The United States Strategic Bombing Survey: Oil Division Final Report, Appendix,* 31.

45. Schumann, Groehler, and Bleyer, *Deutschland im zweiten Weltkrieg,* 6:162.

46. Tantum and Hoffschmidt, *Rise and Fall,* 356.

47. "German Flak Defense as Related to Transportation Targets [October 12, 1944]," 248.712-46, AFHRA.

48. USSBS, Oil Division, *The United States Strategic Bombing Survey: Oil Division Final Report, Appendix,* 31.

49. Crosby, *Wing and a Prayer,* 260.

50. Perret, *Winged Victory,* 327.

51. Newby, *Target Ploesti,* 106–107, 167; emphasis in the original.

52. USSBS, *The United States Strategic Bombing Survey: Report on the German Flak Effort Throughout the War* (n.p., 1945), 13, 137.310-4, AFHRA.

53. Fröhlich, *Tagebücher,* part II, vol. 13, pp. 322–323; diary entry of August 25, 1944.

54. "Vorstudien zur Luftkriegsgeschichte, Heft 8, Reichsluftverteidigung [1944]," T-971/Reel 69, NARA.

55. Corum and Muller, *Luftwaffe's Way of War,* 282, 287. This memorandum was part of a series of memorandums entitled "Tactical Observations of the Luftwaffe High Command" released at the beginning of 1944.

56. Albert Kesselring, *The Memoirs of Field Marshal Kesselring,* trans. William Kimber (Novato, Calif.: Presidio Press, 1988), 240, 243.

57. USSBS, *The United States Strategic Bombing Survey: Report on the German Flak Effort Throughout the War* (n.p., 1945), 13, 137.310-4, AFHRA.

58. "M.I. 15 Periodical A.A. Intelligence Summary No. 19 [April 14, 1945]," AIR 40/Folder 1151, PRO; see also Müller, *German Flak,* 100.

59. USSBS, Oil Division, *The United States Strategic Bombing Survey: Oil Division Final Report, Appendix,* 31.

60. Webster and Frankland, *Strategic Air Offensive,* 4:326–329.

61. "Monthly AA Report for July 1944 [3rd Bombardment Division, August 19, 1944]," 520.3813, AFHRA.

62. "Monthly Flak Report—July 1944 [2nd Bombardment Division, August 8, 1944]," 520.3813, AFHRA. The 2nd Bombardment Division listed the loss of twenty-four bombers in attacks on strategic targets compared with seven bombers on tactical targets.

63. "Low, Fast, and Once [Report of the XVth Fighter Command, April 1945]," 670.3813-1, AFHRA. In August and September, the XVth Fighter Command lost a total of 51 aircraft to flak, for the most part during strafing missions. See also Craven and Cate, *Army Air Forces,* 3:610. During Operation Market Garden, the Allies lost a total of 240 aircraft and 139 gliders, with the vast majority falling to German flak defenses.

64. Craven and Cate, *Army Air Forces,* 3:302–303.

65. Monthly flak reports for the 1st, 2nd, and 3rd Bombardment Divisions [June–August 1944], 520.3813; and "15 Air Force Flak Losses & Damages [May 10, 1945]," 670.3813-1, AFHRA.

66. "15 Air Force Flak Losses & Damages [May 10, 1945]," 670.3813-1; and monthly flak reports for the 1st Bombardment Division [June–August 1944], 520.3813, AFHRA. The 2nd and 3rd Bombardment Division flak reports do not indicate the numbers of aircraft seriously damaged, but the 1st Division results can be assumed to be representative of the overall percentages for all three groups.

67. McArthur, *Operations Analysis,* 133.

68. Webster and Frankland, *Strategic Air Offensive,* 4:343.

69. Galland, *Ersten und die Letzten,* 317. A great deal of caution is necessary when using the memoirs of any of the war's participants. The hidden agendas or selfish motives of both Speer and Galland must be recognized and taken into account. However, Goebbels's diary entries for August 18 and August 24, 1944, provide contemporary support for these accounts. See Fröhlich, *Tagebücher,* part II, vol. 13, pp. 259, 312.

70. Galland, *Ersten und die Letzten,* 318. Speer, *Inside the Third Reich,* 483. In his memoirs, Speer contended that Galland asked him to accompany him to Rastenburg.

71. Speer, *Inside the Third Reich,* 483.

72. Galland, *Ersten und die Letzten,* 319. Speer states that they received the order to report to Hitler on the following day just prior to their departure.

73. Speer, *Inside the Third Reich,* 484.

74. Galland, *Ersten und die Letzten,* 319–320.

75. Speer, *Inside the Third Reich,* 484–485.

76. Murray, *Strategy for Defeat,* 291.

77. Craven and Cate, *Army Air Forces,* 3:660, 663–664.

78. Hildebrand, *Generale,* 1:187. Deßloch subsequently commanded Air Region 4 and Air Region 6 before the war ended.

79. Speer, *Inside the Third Reich,* 482, 484. Speer remarked that rock salt replaced 20 percent of the explosive material in artillery ammunition at this time.

80. Richards, *Hardest Victory,* 234–244.

81. Webster and Frankland, *Strategic Air Offensive,* 4:433.

82. Tantum and Hoffschmidt, *Rise and Fall,* 367.

83. Hinchliffe, *Other Battle,* 294.

84. Harris, *Bomber Offensive,* 218.

85. Chorley, *Bomber Command Losses,* 5:257.

86. Richards, *Hardest Victory,* 236.

87. Chorley, *Bomber Command Losses,* 5:290–298.

88. Hinchliffe, *Other Battle,* 293. The "hunting lodge" radar was one of only three operational devices stationed in Germany. It was a centimeter device and the first radar that provided a 360-degree sweep or panoramic view.

89. Harris, *Bomber Offensive,* 229.

90. Webster and Frankland, *Strategic Air Offensive,* 4:433.

91. Rainer Mennel, *Die Schlussphase des zweiten Weltkrieges im Westen (1944/45)* (Osnabrück: Biblio Verlag, 1981), 27; see also Hinchliffe, *Other Battle,* 313.

92. Schumann, Groehler, and Bleyer, *Deutschland im zweiten Weltkrieg,* 6:159.

93. Koch, *Flak,* 82; see also USSBS, *The United States Strategic Bombing Survey: Report on the German Flak Effort Throughout the War* (n.p., 1945), 5, 137.310-4, AFHRA. The USSBS report cited a strength of 573,000 service personnel and 230,700 auxiliary personnel for November 15, 1944. These figures, however, are most probably limited to persons serving with the flak batteries within the Reich proper.

94. USSBS, *The United States Strategic Bombing Survey: Report on the German Flak Effort Throughout the War* (n.p., 1945), 4, 137.310-4, AFHRA.

95. Rhoden, *History of World War II,* 4:101–102.

96. Renz, *Development of German Anti-aircraft,* 379, K113.107-194, AFHRA.

97. Eichholtz, *Kriegswirtschaft,* 2:656–661. The fourth-quarter total for 150-cm searchlights does not include December production.

98. Weinberg, *World at Arms,* 775.

99. USSBS, Economic Effects Division, *The United States Strategic Bombing Survey: The Effects of Strategic Bombing on the German War Economy,* 284.

100. Rhoden, *History of World War II,* 4:102.

101. USSBS, *The United States Strategic Bombing Survey: Report on the German Flak Effort Throughout the War* (n.p., 1945), 2, 137.310–4, AFHRA; see also USSBS, Oil Division, *The United States Strategic Bombing Survey: Powder, Special Rockets and Jet Propellants, War Gases and Smoke Acid,* no page number (Exhibit O-1).

102. Webster and Frankland, *Strategic Air Offensive,* 4:350.

103. "Monthly Flak Report—September 1944 [2nd Bombardment Division, October 6, 1944]," 520.3813, AFHRA; see also Devon Francis, *Flak Bait: The Story of the Men Who Flew the Martin Marauders* (New York: Duell, Sloan and Pearce, 1948), 115, 121–122.

104. "M.I. 15 Periodical AA Intelligence Summary No. 19 [April 14, 1945]," AIR 40/Folder 1151, PRO.

105. Führer Order of November 4, 1944, T-971/Roll 70, NARA.

106. Boog, *Luftwaffenführung,* 212.

107. Führer Order of November 4, 1944, T-971/Roll 70, NARA.

108. "Monthly Flak Report for September 1944 [1st Bombardment Division, October 5, 1944]," 520.3813, AFHRA.

109. "Monthly Flak Report—September 1944 [2nd Bombardment Division, October 6, 1944]," 520.3813, AFHRA.

110. "Monthly AA Report for October 1944 [3rd Bombardment Division, November 10, 1944]," 520.3813, AFHRA.

111. "Monthly Flak Report for October 1944 [1st Bombardment Division, November 1944]," 520.3813, AFHRA.

112. Ibid.

113. Monthly flak reports for the 1st, 2nd, and 3rd Bombardment Divisions for the period between October and December 1944, 520.3813, AFHRA.

114. "2d Air Division Monthly Flak Report—December 1944 [January 8, 1945]," 520.3813, AFHRA.

115. "15 Air Force Flak Losses & Damages [May 10, 1945]," 670.3813-1, AFHRA.

116. Craven and Cate, *Army Air Forces,* 3:474.

117. "15 Air Force Flak Losses & Damages [May 10, 1945]," 670.3813-1, AFHRA. It should be noted that B-24s constituted the majority of Fifteenth Air Force bombers.

118. Craven and Cate, *Army Air Forces,* 3:642–645.

119. "Enemy Capabilities—Flak [Report by the Mediterranean Allied Air Forces, April 12, 1945]," 670.3813-4, AFHRA.

120. Craven and Cate, *Army Air Forces,* 3:658.

121. "2d Air Division Monthly Flak Report—December 1944 [January 8, 1945]," 520.3813, AFHRA.

122. USSBS, *The United States Strategic Bombing Survey: Report on the German Flak Effort Throughout the War* (n.p., 1945), 14, 137.310-4, AFHRA.

123. Renz, *Development of German Anti-aircraft,* 384–385, K113.107-194, AFHRA;

see also Webster and Frankland, *Strategic Air Offensive,* 4:433. The total number of aircraft damaged by flak includes totals from the Eighth Air Force and Fifteenth Air Force monthly flak reports, as well as the damaged aircraft totals provided by the official RAF history of the air war.

124. "*VER-Flak* 33a [January 1, 1945]," RL 4/Folder 268, BA-MA.

125. Weinberg, *World at Arms,* 798–802, 810–814.

126. Golücke, *Schweinfurt,* 389.

127. USSBS, *The United States Strategic Bombing Survey: Report on the German Flak Effort Throughout the War* (n.p., 1945), 15, 137.310-4, AFHRA.

128. "Kriegstagebuch des Chefs des Luftwaffenführungsstabes [February 12, 1945]," T-321/Reel 10/Frame 4746861, NARA.

129. Percy E. Schramm, *Kriegstagebuch des Oberkommandos der Wehrmacht, 1940–1945,* vol. 8 (Bonn: Bernard & Graefe Verlag, 1965), 1033; diary entry of January 23, 1945.

130. "Kriegstagebuch des Chefs des Luftwaffenführungsstabes [February 2, 1945]," T-321/Reel 10/Frame 4746811, NARA.

131. Ibid., Frame 4746861. This order was given on February 6, 1945.

132. Hooton, *Eagle in Flames,* 253. These percentages are based on the number of flak batteries protecting Germany proper in June 1944. Based on the losses suffered in the last half of 1944, these percentages might actually be somewhat higher in both categories.

133. "Kriegstagebuch des Chefs des Luftwaffenführungsstabes [April 17, 1945]," T-321/Reel 10/Frame 4747068, NARA.

134. Schramm, *Kriegstagebuch,* 8:1033; diary entry of January 23, 1945; see also Seidler, *Blitzmädchen,* 53.

135. Fröhlich, *Tagebücher,* part II, vol. 15, pp. 277–278; diary entry of January 30, 1945.

136. "Kriegstagebuch des Chefs des Luftwaffenführungsstabes [February 19, 1945]," T-321/Reel 10/Frames 4746897–98, NARA. By April 1, this transfer included 383 of the flak guns surrounding the synthetic oil sites in central Germany. See Frame 4746979.

137. "2d Air Division Monthly Flak Report—January 1945 [February 6, 1945]," 520.3813, AFHRA. In December 1944, the Eighth Air Force "bombardment divisions" were redesignated as "air divisions."

138. "Monthly AA Report for January 1945 [3rd Air Division, February 11, 1945]," 520.3813, AFHRA.

139. Hinchliffe, *Other Battle,* 319.

140. "Kriegstagebuch des Chefs des Luftwaffenführungsstabes [February 3, 1945]," T-321/Reel 10/Frame 4746817, NARA.

141. Papers of William Griswold Smith, "Ten Missions over Germany," 4159Z, manuscript collection of the Wilson Library at the University of North Carolina, Chapel Hill.

142. Groehler, *Luftherrschaft,* 216.

143. Craven and Cate, *Army Air Forces,* 3:726.

144. "Flak Attrition Analysis: Comparative Analysis of Attrition to Flak Experienced During the Attacks on Vienna of 7 and 8 February 1945 [Fifteenth Air Force, March 30, 1945]," 670.3813, AFHRA.

145. Richards, *Hardest Victory,* 273. A definitive accounting of the total death toll is not possible because at the time of the bombing the city was filled with thousands of refugees fleeing from the advancing Soviet forces in the east; however, the estimate of 25,000 is supported in part by the records of the Dresden police, which gave a total of 18,375 dead among the city's registered residents.

146. Schramm, *Kriegstagebuch,* 8:1103; diary entry of February 17, 1945.

147. Müller, *German Flak,* 70.

148. "Kriegstagebuch des Chefs des Luftwaffenführungsstabes [February 26, 1945]," T-321/Reel 10/Frame 4746932, NARA; see also Schramm, *Kriegstagebuch,* 8:1158, 1166; diary entries of March 8 and March 11, 1945.

149. Fröhlich, *Tagebücher,* part II, vol. 15, p. 557; diary entry of March 21, 1945.

150. USSBS, *The United States Strategic Bombing Survey: Report on the German Flak Effort Throughout the War* (n.p., 1945), 18, 137.310-4, AFHRA.

151. Kesselring, "Die Deutsche Luftwaffe," 157.

152. Herrmann, *Eagle's Wings,* 254.

153. "Kriegstagebuch des Chefs des Luftwaffenführungsstabes," T-321/Reel 10/Frame 4746951, NARA; war diary entry for March 18, 1945.

154. Fröhlich, *Tagebücher,* part II, vol. 15, p. 569; diary entry of March 22, 1945.

155. Hinchliffe, *Other Battle,* 324.

156. "Kriegstagebuch des Chefs des Luftwaffenführungsstabes," T-321/Reel 10/Frames 4746959, 4747010, NARA; war diary entries of March 31 and April 7, 1945.

157. Ibid., Frame 4747050; war diary entry of April 14, 1945.

158. Ibid., Frame 4747052.

159. Golücke, *Schweinfurt,* 156.

160. Control Commission for Germany, *Notes on Flak,* 50, IWM.

161. "High Altitude Bombing Attacks on Flak Batteries [May 31, 1945]," 670.3813-8, AFHRA.

162. Musgrove, *Operation Gomorrah,* 77.

163. Perret, *Winged Victory,* 329; see also Chuck Yeager and Leo Janos, *Yeager: An Autobiography* (New York: Bantam Books, 1985), 55–56.

164. "Kriegstagebuch des Chefs des Luftwaffenführungsstabes," T-321/Reel 10/Frame 4747051, NARA; war diary entry of April 14, 1945.

165. Karl Koller, *Der Letzte Monat: Die Tagesbuchaufzeichnungen des ehemaligen Chefs des Generalstabs der deutschen Luftwaffe vom 14. April bis zum 27. Mai 1945* (Mannheim: Norbert Wohlgemuth Verlag, 1949); see also Kit Carter and Robert Mueller, *The Army Air Forces in World War II* (New York: Arno Press, 1980), 638, 643. After April 25, the Fifteenth Air Force conducted two days of bombing operations against targets primarily in Austria. On May 1, twenty-seven B-17s attacked marshaling yards at Salzburg for the command's final bombing mission of the war.

Conclusion

1. Webster and Frankland, *Strategic Air Offensive,* 4:437. In addition, Bomber Command listed 2,072 aircraft lost during night sorties as a result of "unknown causes" and 112 aircraft lost "not by enemy action."

2. Ibid., 432–433.

3. McFarland and Newton, *To Command the Sky,* 54; see also Perret, *Winged Victory,* 330. McFarland and Newton do not provide specific numbers but state that "half" of American combat losses were due to flak. This figure most probably refers to heavy bombers alone.

4. USSBS, *The United States Strategic Bombing Survey: Report on the German Flak Effort Throughout the War* (n.p., 1945), 18, 137.310-4, AFHRA.

5. Golücke, *Schweinfurt,* 390. The total number of Eighth Air Force heavy bombers lost to all causes during the war was 5,857 aircraft.

6. "Enemy Capabilities—Flak [April 12, 1945]," 670.3813-4, AFHRA.

7. "15 Air Force Flak Losses & Damages [May 10, 1945]," 670.3813-1, AFHRA. The Fifteenth Air Force's total flak losses for the war were 1,291 aircraft. See also USSBS, *The United States Strategic Bombing Survey: Report on the German Flak Effort Throughout the War* (n.p., 1945), 18, 137.310-4, AFHRA.

8. Newby, *Target Ploesti,* 211. Newby estimates that a total of 277 American heavy bombers were shot down during attacks against Ploesti between August 1943 and August 1944, with the vast majority falling to flak defenses.

9. USSBS, *The United States Strategic Bombing Survey: Report on the German Flak Effort Throughout the War* (n.p., 1945), 18, 137.310-4, AFHRA. These two commands conducted tactical air operations.

10. Boog, *Luftwaffenführung,* 211.

11. McArthur, *Operations Analysis,* 133.

12. Eighth Air Force monthly flak reports for the period between December 1942 and April 1945, 520.3813, AFHRA.

13. "15 Air Force Flak Losses & Damages [May 10, 1945]," 670.3813-1, AFHRA.

14. Monthly flak reports for the 1st Bombardment Division in the period from May 1944 to March 1945, 520.3813, AFHRA. Of the three air divisions, the 1st Air Division was the only command that reported seriously damaged aircraft as a separate category in its monthly reports. The Fifteenth Air Force also reported "major damage" due to flak versus "minor damage" in the period between November 1943 and April 1945. The percentage of "major damage" in this period for the Fifteenth Air Force was approximately 17 percent of all aircraft damaged by the flak.

15. Boog, *Luftwaffenführung,* 211; see also "15 Air Force Flak Losses & Damages [May 10, 1945]," 670.3813-1; and Eighth Air Force monthly flak reports for the period between December 1942 and June 1944, 520.3813, AFHRA.

16. "Abschlussmeldung über Flakartillerie im Bereich des Gen.d.Lw.Ob.d.H. [February 28, 1942]," N529/Folder 7, BA-MA.

17. Renz, *Development of German Anti-aircraft,* 384, K113.107-194, AFHRA.

18. Stöber, *Flugabwehrverbände,* 486.

19. Olaf Groehler, "The Soviet Long-Range Airforces in the Great Patriotic War of the USSR (1941–1945)," *Militarhistorisk Tidskrift 1991,* 144–145. These long-range strategic bombing sorties constituted only 3.1 percent of all flights made by Soviet long-range bombers during the war and included thousands of attacks against targets in Finland and Hungary.

20. LeMay and Kantor, *Mission,* 231.

21. "Conference on Bombing Accuracy, 22–23 March 1945 [USSTAF Armament

Memorandum No. 14-3, April 1, 1945]," Box 76, Carl Spaatz papers, Library of Congress. I would like to thank Tami Davis Biddle for this information.

22. McFarland and Newton, *To Command the Sky,* 262–263. See McFarland and Newton's note 89.

23. Greenhous et al., *Crucible,* 781.

24. "Monthly Flak Report (May) [1st Bombardment Division, June 1, 1943]," 520.3813, AFHRA.

25. McArthur, *Operations Analysis,* 131.

26. Ibid., 78–79, 81.

27. Musgrove, *Operation Gomorrah,* 76–77.

28. Craven and Cate, *Army Air Forces,* 3:307. After hearing allegations that American airmen were purposefully landing in these countries to avoid further bombing missions, Spaatz requested an investigation by neutral officials to determine the validity of these claims. The investigation subsequently determined that the vast majority of the aircraft had been too badly damaged to return to their bases in England.

29. Air Publication 3232, Air Historical Branch Monograph, "Air Sea Rescue" (1952), 150. Obviously, a number of rescued aircrew members were from the fighter arm as well as the bomber force; however, the 5,721 rescued includes only those saved by the Air/Sea Rescue Service and does not include those reached too late to be saved or those rescued by the Royal Navy. I would like to thank Sebastian Cox for his assistance with this query.

30. "Anerkennung von Abschüssen fdl. Flugzeuge und Verleihung des Heeres-Flak-Abzeichens [October 20, 1942]," RL 19/Folder 472, BA-MA. These requirements were loosened somewhat in March 1944.

31. Untitled report from Air Region XI, dated September 14, 1944, RL 19/Folder 471, BA-MA.

32. "Abschußergebnisse [July 7, 1944]," RL 19/Folder 451, BA-MA. Interestingly enough, all 124 of the reported fighter shootdowns are listed as confirmed by the "Shootdown Commission."

33. Comer, *Combat Crew,* 89.

34. Stuart Leuthner and Oliver Jensen, *High Honor* (Washington, D.C.: Smithsonian Institution Press, 1989), 127.

35. Wells, *Courage,* 43; see also Middlebrook, *Battle of Hamburg,* 73.

36. Wells, *Courage,* 204–205.

37. Donald W. Hastings, David G. Wright, and Bernard C. Glueck, *Psychiatric Experiences of the Eighth Air Force* (n.p., 1944), 3, 5, 7. The authors were all members of the U.S. Army Air Forces medical corps. Collection of the Health Sciences Library at the University of North Carolina, Chapel Hill.

38. Hans Brunswig, *Feuersturm über Hamburg* (Stuttgart: Motorbuch Verlag, 1978), 395–396; see also Koch, *Flak,* 72. The currency conversions are based on the official exchange rate of forty cents per reichsmark for 1941. See Irvine, *World Almanac,* 665.

39. Military Intelligence 15, *Handbook,* 4: 59. The ratio of 88-mm/Model 36-37 to the total of all other heavy flak guns favored the former by over 3 to 1.

40. Freeman, *Mighty Eighth War Manual,* 21; see also Hogg, *German Artillery,*

167. In contrast, the normal bombing profile for a B-24 was between 20,000 and 24,000 feet. This in part explains the fact that the Fifteenth Air Force lost almost three times as many B-24s to flak as B-17s between November 1943 and April 1945. See "15 Air Force Flak Losses & Damages [May 10, 1945]," 670.3813-1, AFHRA.

41. "Interrogation of General von Axthelm and Lt. Col. Sieber (USSBS Interview No. 68)," 524.606, AFHRA; see also Roger A. Freeman, *Raiding the Reich: The Allied Strategic Offensive in Europe* (London: Arms and Armour Press, 1997), 61, 96. The B-17 made up the majority of Eighth Air Force heavy bombers, while the number of B-24s in the Fifteenth Air Force exceeded B-17s by more than 2 to 1; see also Perret, *Winged Victory,* 361.

42. Hans Rumpf, *The Bombing of Germany,* trans. Edward Fitzgerald (New York: Holt, Rinehart and Winston, 1963), 147. Barrel wear remained a major problem for flak forces because of the rapid rate at which barrels needed to be replaced. For example, the average number of rounds that could be fired by a 128-mm flak gun was 700. See Hogg, *German Artillery,* 183; and Hogg, *Anti-Aircraft,* 116.

43. USSBS, Economic Effects Division, *The United States Strategic Bombing Survey: The Effects of Strategic Bombing on the German War Economy,* 285.

44. Military Intelligence 15, *Handbook,* 4:46.

45. "2d Air Division Monthly Flak Report—December 1944 [January 8, 1945]," 520.3813, AFHRA.

46. Hogg, *German Artillery,* 180.

47. Ethell and Price, *Target Berlin,* 26; see also Werrell, *Archie,* 26; and Müller, *German Flak,* 146. Müller contends that flak auxiliaries also served on the 128-mm guns, but this appears to have been an exceptional case.

48. Military Intelligence 15, *Handbook,* 4:59.

49. "Flugzeugabschüsse und Munitionsverbrauch durch Flakartillerie im April 1941 [April 13, 1941]," T-321/Roll 7/Frame 4742623, NARA.

50. Renz, *Development of German Anti-aircraft,* 384, K113.107-194, AFHRA.

51. Rumpf, *Bombing of Germany,* 147; see also Koch, *Flak,* 72. Both Koch and Rumpf state that one round of 88-mm ammunition cost 80 RM, whereas the cost of one round of 20-mm ammunition was 7.5 RM.

52. Irving B. Holley Jr., *Buying Aircraft: Matériel Procurement for the Army Air Forces,* United States Army in World War II (Washington, D.C.: GPO, 1964), 142, 560. The costs for both aircraft include $23,261 for "government furnished equipment" (GFE). GFE costs include such items as turrets, armaments, navigation devices, and communications systems. Because of economies of scale and the length of the production run, the total cost for B-17s and B-24s (including GFE) in 1944 fell to approximately $227,000 and $248,000, respectively.

53. Ibid., 560. This number does not include the cost of GFE.

54. Letter from General von Axthlem to Major H. P. Ptak of December 11, 1957, N 529/Folder 9II, BA-MA.

55. USSBS, *The United States Strategic Bombing Survey: Report on the German Flak Effort Throughout the War* (n.p., 1945), 5, 137.310-4, AFHRA.

56. Koch, *Flak,* 164–165. By the end of the war, the Luftwaffe had created a total of six flak corps.

57. Kershaw, *Nemesis,* 563, 598.

58. USSBS, *The United States Strategic Bombing Survey: Report on the German Flak Effort Throughout the War* (n.p., 1945), 1, 137.310-4, AFHRA.

59. Herbert, *Hitler's Foreign Workers,* 1, 295.

60. Speer, *Inside the Third Reich,* 332.

61. Webster and Frankland, *Strategic Air Offensive,* 4:343. This information is from a speech made by Speer to the Fighter Staff on August 1, 1944.

62. MacIsaac, *Bombing Survey,* 1:190.

63. Ibid., 181.

64. USSBS, Munitions Division, *The United States Strategic Bombing Survey: Ordnance Industry Report* (Washington, D.C.: GPO, 1945), B-5, B-7, B-8, B-10.

65. MacIsaac, *Bombing Survey,* 1:187. When one adds tank and antitanks guns to this total, the number of guns above 75-mm in 1944 exceeds the total for mid-1941.

66. Schumann, Groehler, and Bleyer, *Deutschland im zweiten Weltkrieg,* 6:158. In contrast, 94 percent of all 105-mm flak guns and 99 percent of the 128-mm flak guns were stationed within the borders of the Reich at this time. In large part this disparity resulted from the general use of fixed or stationary gun positions for the 105-mm and 128-mm guns.

67. MacIsaac, *Bombing Survey,* 1:187.

68. Jonathan Bailey, *Field Artillery and Firepower* (New York: Military Press, 1989), 209. In comparison, the Red Army's heavy reliance on supporting artillery fire provides the counterpoint to the Wehrmacht's position.

69. USSBS, Oil Division, *The United States Strategic Bombing Survey: Powder, Explosives, Special Rockets and Jet Propellants, War Gases, and Smoke Acid,* 1.

70. USSBS, Economic Effects Division, *The United States Strategic Bombing Survey: The Effects of Strategic Bombing on the German War Economy,* 187.

71. USSBS, Munitions Division, *The United States Strategic Bombing Survey: Ordnance Industry Report,* 18.

72. USSBS, *The United States Strategic Bombing Survey: Report on the German Flak Effort Throughout the War* (n.p., 1945), 18, 137.310-4, AFHRA.

73. USSBS, Economic Effects Division, *The United States Strategic Bombing Survey: The Effects of Strategic Bombing on the German War Economy,* 187.

74. USSBS, Munitions Division, *The United States Strategic Bombing Survey: Ordnance Industry Report,* 18.

75. Price, *Last Year,* 16.

76. Müller, *German Flak,* 159.

Bibliography

Archives and Research Centers

AIR HISTORICAL BRANCH, LONDON, UNITED KINGDOM

Air Tactics Box 2
Bomber Command Damage Summaries
Bomber Command Operational Research Section Memoranda, "M" Series
Bomber Command Operational Research Section Reports, "G" Series
Bomber Command Operational Research Section Reports, "S" Series

PUBLIC RECORDS OFFICE, KEW, UNITED KINGDOM

AIR 14	*Air Ministry: Bomber Command*
AIR 40	*Air Ministry: Directorate of Intelligence*
AIR 41	*Air Ministry and Ministry of Defence: Air Historical Branch, Narratives and Monographs*

BUNDESARCHIV–MILITÄRARCHIV, FREIBURG, FEDERAL REPUBLIC OF GERMANY

N 529	*Nachlass von Axthelm*
PH 9 XX	*Inspektion des Militär-, Luft- und Kraftwesens*
RH 2	*Oberkommando des Heeres/Generalstab des Heeres*
RL 2 II	*Generalstab der Luftwaffe/Luftwaffe-Führungsstab*
RL 3	*Generalluftzeugmeister*
RL 4	*Chef des Ausbildungswesens/General der Fliegerausbildung und Luftwaffen-Inspektionen/Waffengenerale*
RL 12	*Verbände und Einheiten der Flakartillerie*
RL 19	*Luftgaukommandos/Luftgaustäbe*

U.S. AIR FORCE HISTORICAL RESEARCH AGENCY, MAXWELL AFB, ALABAMA

248.712–46	*German Flak Defense as Related to Transportation Targets, October 1944*
506.6314A-40	*Organization, Operation, and Degree of Success of G.A.F. Smoke Units*
512.61C-6D	*Interrogation Transcripts of German Prisoners-of-War*
519.601A-1	*Summary, German Flak, 1945*
519.601A-12	*Interrogation Reports of the General of the Flak Artillery Walther von Axthelm*
520.3813	*Eighth Air Force Monthly Flak Reports, December 1942–April 1945*
524.606	*Interrogation of General von Axthelm and Lt. Col. Sieber*

622.646-2	*Enemy Capabilities-Flak*
670.3813	*Flak Attrition Analysis*
670.3813–1	*Fifteenth Air Force Flak Losses and Damage*
670.3813–8	*High Altitude Bombing Attacks on Flak Batteries*
K113.107–194	*The Development of German Anti-aircraft Weapons and Equipment of All Types Up to 1945*
K113.302	*Bereitstellung und Einsatz deutscher Flakartillerie in Spanien*
K512.621	*Extracts from Conferences on Problems of Aircraft Production*

U.S. NATIONAL ARCHIVES II, COLLEGE PARK, MARYLAND

T-321	*Records of the German Air Force High Command*
T-405	*German Air Force Records: Luftgaukommandos, Flak, Deutsche Luftwaffenmission in Rumänien*
T-971	*The von Rhoden Collection of Research Materials on the Role of the German Air Force in World War II*

Unpublished Documents

The United States Strategic Bombing Survey. *The United States Strategic Bombing Survey: Report on the German Flak Effort Throughout the War.* N.p., 1945. Collection of the Air Force Historical Research Agency.

Published Documents

Anhaltspunkte für den Unterricht bei der Truppe über Luftfahrzeuge und deren Bekämpfung. Berlin: Reichsdruckerei, 1913.

British Bombing Survey Unit. *The Strategic Air War Against Germany, 1939–1945: Report of the British Bombing Survey Unit.* London: Frank Cass, 1998.

Control Commission for Germany, Air Division. *Notes on Flak and Searchlight Radar (G.A.F.).* N.p.: Air Division, CCG, 1946. Collection of the Imperial War Museum.

Flak Section, Ninth Air Force. *Flak Facts: A Brief History of Flak and Flak Intelligence in the Ninth Air Force.* N.p., 1945. Collection of the Air University Library, Maxwell AFB.

Military Intelligence 15. *Handbook of German Anti-aircraft Artillery (Flak).* Vol. 4, *Strength.* London: War Office, 1946. Collection of the Imperial War Museum.

Military Intelligence 15. *Handbook of German Anti-aircraft Artillery (Flak).* Vol. 5, *Deployment Siting and Emplacements.* London: War Office, 1946.

Military Intelligence 15. *Handbook of German Anti-aircraft Artillery (Flak).* Vol. 9, *Instruments.* London: War Office, 1946.

Der Reichsminister der Luftfahrt und Oberbefehlshaber der Luftwaffe. *Bemerkungen des Oberbefehlshabers der Luftwaffe zur Ausbildung und zu den Übungen im Jahre 1935.* Berlin: Reichsdruckerei, 1936. Collection of the German Military History Research Office.

———. *Bemerkungen des Oberbefehlshabers der Luftwaffe zur Ausbildung und zu den*

Übungen im Jahre 1936. Berlin: Reichsdruckerei, 1937. Collection of the German Military History Research Office.

United States Strategic Bombing Survey, Civil Defense Division. *The United States Strategic Bombing Survey: Civil Defense Division Final Report*. Washington, D.C.: GPO, 1945.

United States Strategic Bombing Survey, Economic Effects Division. *The United States Strategic Bombing Survey: The Effects of Strategic Bombing on the German War Economy*. Washington, D.C.: GPO, 1945.

United States Strategic Bombing Survey, Morale Division. *The United States Strategic Bombing Survey*. Vol. 1, *The Effects of Strategic Bombing on German Morale*. Washington, D.C.: GPO, 1947.

United States Strategic Bombing Survey, Munitions Division. *The United States Strategic Bombing Survey: Ordnance Industry Report*. Washington, D.C.: GPO, 1945.

United States Strategic Bombing Survey, Oil Division. *The United States Strategic Bombing Survey: Ammoniakwerke Merseburg GmbH Leuna, Germany*. Washington, D.C.: GPO, 1946.

———. *The United States Strategic Bombing Survey: Oil Division Final Report, Appendix*. Washington, D.C.: GPO, 1945.

———. *The United States Strategic Bombing Survey: Meerbeck Rheinpreussen Synthetic Oil Plant*. Washington, D.C.: GPO, 1946.

———. *The United States Strategic Bombing Survey: Powder, Explosives, Special Rockets and Jet Propellants, War Gases, and Smoke Acid*. Washington, D.C.: GPO, 1945.

United States Strategic Bombing Survey, Strategic Bombing Survey Team. *The United States Strategic Bombing Survey: Summary Report*. Washington, D.C.: GPO, 1945. Reprint, Maxwell AFB, Ala.: Air University Press, 1987.

United States Strategic Bombing Survey, Oil Division. *The United States Strategic Bombing Survey: Underground and Dispersal Plants in Greater Germany*. Washington, D.C.: GPO, 1945.

United States War Department. *Handbook on German Military Forces*. Reprint, Baton Rouge: Louisiana State University Press, 1990.

Newspapers and Magazines

Die Luftwacht (Berlin). January 1927–November 1930.

Die Sirene (Berlin). October 1937–December 1942.

Luftschutznachrichtenblatt des Flak-Vereins e.V. (Potsdam). March 1930–July 1933.

Militärwochenblatt (Berlin). September 11, 1925–April 4, 1926; October 18, 1929–March 18, 1930.

Books and Articles

Absolon, Rudolf, ed. *Rangliste der Generale der deutschen Luftwaffe nach dem Stand vom 20. April 1945*. Friedberg: Podzun-Pallas-Verlag, 1984.

Adler, Hermann, ed. *Ein Buch von der neuen Luftwaffe*. Stuttgart: Franck'sche Verlagshandlung, 1938.

Ambrose, Stephen E. *D-Day: The Climactic Battle of World War II.* New York: Simon and Schuster, 1994.

Ardery, Philip. *Bomber Pilot.* Lexington: University Press of Kentucky, 1978.

Astor, Gerald. *The Mighty Eighth: The Air War in Europe as Told by the Men Who Fought It.* New York: Donald I. Fine Books, 1997.

Axel, Alexander. *Die Schlacht über Berlin.* Berlin: Verlag Offene Worte, 1933.

Bailey, Jonathan. *Field Artillery and Firepower.* New York: Military Press, 1989.

Banny, Lepold. *Dröhnender Himmel, brennendes Land: Der Einsatz der Luftwaffenhelfer in Österreich, 1943–1945.* Vienna: Bundesverlag, 1988.

Baumbach, Werner. *The Life and Death of the Luftwaffe.* Translated by Frederick Holt. New York: Ballantine Books, 1960.

Beck, Earl R. *Under the Bombs: The German Home Front, 1942–1945.* Lexington: University Press of Kentucky, 1986.

Bedürftig, Friedemann, ed. *Das große Lexikon des Dritten Reiches.* Munich: Südwest Verlag, 1985.

Bekker, Cajus. *Angriffshöhe 4000: Ein Kriegstagebuch der deutschen Luftwaffe.* Cologne: Naumann & Göbel, 1964.

Bevans, Charles I., ed., *Treaties and Other International Agreements of the United States of America, 1776–1949.* Washington, D.C.: Department of State Publication, 1969.

Beyerchen, Alan. "From Radio to Radar: Interwar Military Adaptation to Technological Change in Germany, the United Kingdom, and the United States." In *Military Innovation in the Interwar Period,* edited by Williamson Murray and Allan R. Millett, 265–299. New York: Cambridge University Press, 1996.

Bland, Larry, ed. *The Papers of George Catlett Marshall.* Vol. 1, *"The Soldierly Spirit."* Baltimore: Johns Hopkins University Press, 1981.

Boberach, Heinz, ed. *Meldungen aus dem Reich: Die geheimen Lageberichte des Sicherheitsdienstes der SS, 1938–1945.* Vol. 10. Herrsching: Pawlak Verlag, 1984.

———. *Meldungen aus dem Reich: Die geheimen Lageberichte des Sicherheitsdienstes der SS, 1938–1945.* Vol. 14. Herrsching: Pawlak Verlag, 1984.

Boetigger, Wilfred O. *An Aircraft Artilleryman from 1939 to 1970.* Louisville, Ky.: By the author, 26 Southwind Road, 1990.

Bongartz, Heinz. *Luftmacht Deutschland: Luftwaffe-Industrie-Luftfahrt.* Essen: Essener Verlagsanstalt, 1939.

Boog, Horst. *Die Deutsche Luftwaffenführung, 1939–1945: Führungsprobleme, Spitzengliederung, Generalstabsausbildung.* Beiträge zur Militär- und Kriegsgeschichte. Stuttgart: Deutsche Verlags-Anstalt, 1982.

Boog, Horst, Werner Rahn, Reinhard Stumpf, and Bernd Wegner. *Das Deutsche Reich und der zweite Weltkrieg.* Vol. 6, *Der globale Krieg.* Stuttgart: Deutsche Verlags-Anstalt, 1990.

Brunswig, Hans. *Feuersturm über Hamburg.* Stuttgart: Motorbuch Verlag, 1978.

Büdingen, E., ed. *Kriegsgeschichtliche Einzelschriften der Luftwaffe.* Vol. 1, *Entwicklung und Einsatz der deutschen Flakwaffe und des Luftschutzes im Weltkriege.* Berlin: E. S. Mittler und Sohn, 1938.

Burdick, Charles B. "Dora: The Germans' Biggest Gun." *Military Review* 41 (November 1961): 72–78.

Carroll, Berenice A. *A Design for Total War: Arms and Economics in the Third Reich.* The Hague: Mouton, 1968.

Carter, Kit, and Robert Mueller. *The Army Air Forces in World War II.* New York: Arno Press, 1980.

Challener, Richard D., ed. *United States Military Intelligence.* Vol. 25, *Weekly Summaries 1926.* New York: Garland, 1979.

Chorley, William R., ed. *Royal Air Force Bomber Command Losses of the Second World War.* Vol. 1, *Aircraft and Crews Lost During 1939–1940.* Earl Shilton, Leicester: Midland Counties Publication, 1992.

———. *Royal Air Force Bomber Command Losses of the Second World War.* Vol. 2, *Aircraft and Crew Losses, 1941.* Earl Shilton, Leicester: Midland Counties Publication, 1993.

———. *Royal Air Force Bomber Command Losses of the Second World War.* Vol. 3, *Aircraft and Crew Losses, 1942.* Earl Shilton, Leicester: Midland Counties Publication, 1994.

———. *Royal Air Force Bomber Command Losses of the Second World War.* Vol. 4, *Aircraft and Crew Losses, 1943.* Earl Shilton, Leicester: Midland Counties Publication, 1996.

———. *Royal Air Force Bomber Command Losses of the Second World War.* Vol. 5, *Aircraft and Crew Losses during 1944.* Earl Shilton, Leicester: Midland Counties Publication, 1997.

———. *Royal Air Force Bomber Command Losses of the Second World War.* Vol. 6, *Aircraft and Crew Losses, 1945.* Earl Shilton, Leicester: Midland Counties Publication, 1998.

Comer, John. *Combat Crew: A True Story of Flying and Fighting in World War II.* New York: William Morrow, 1988.

Corum, James S. *The Luftwaffe: Creating the Operational Air War, 1918–1940.* Lawrence: University Press of Kansas, 1997.

———. *The Roots of Blitzkrieg: Hans von Seeckt and German Military Reform Between the World Wars.* Lawrence: University Press of Kansas, 1992.

Corum, James S., and Richard R. Muller. *The Luftwaffe's Way of War: German Air Force Doctrine, 1911–1945.* Baltimore: Nautical and Aviation Publishing Company of America, 1998.

Crabtree, James D. *On Air Defense.* Westport, Conn.: Praeger, 1994.

Craven, Wesley Frank, and James Lea Cate. *The Army Air Forces in World War II.* Vol. 1, *Plans and Early Operations: January 1939 to August 1942.* Chicago: University of Chicago Press, 1948. Reprint, Washington, D.C.: GPO, 1983.

———. *The Army Air Forces in World War II.* Vol. 2, *Europe: Torch to Pointblank, August 1942 to December 1943.* Chicago: University of Chicago Press, 1948. Reprint, Washington, D.C.: GPO, 1983.

———. *The Army Air Forces in World War II.* Vol. 3, *Europe: Argument to V-E Day, January 1944 to May 1945.* Chicago: University of Chicago Press, 1948. Reprint, Washington, D.C.: GPO, 1983.

Crosby, Harry. *A Wing and a Prayer: The "Bloody 100th" Bomb Group of the U.S. Eighth Air Force in Action over Europe in World War II.* New York: HarperCollins, 1993.

Davis Biddle, Tami. "Bombing by the Square Yard: Sir Arthur Harris at War, 1942–1945." *International History Review* 21 (September 1999): 626–664.

Deane, Laurence. *A Pathfinder's War and Peace*. Braunton, Devon: Merlin Books, 1993.

Deist, Wilhelm. *The Wehrmacht and German Rearmament*. Toronto: University of Toronto Press, 1981.

Delsert, Bernard, Jean-Jacques Dubois, and Christian Kowal. *La Flak, 1914–1918*. 2 vols. Guilherand Grange: La Plume du Temps, 1999.

Domarus, Max, ed. *Hitler: Reden und Proklamationen, 1932–1945*. Vol. 2. Wiesbaden: R. Löwit, 1973.

Donald, David, ed. *The Complete Encyclopedia of World Aircraft*. New York: Barnes and Noble Books, 1997.

Dyck, Harvey Leonard. *Weimar Germany and Soviet Russia: A Study in Diplomatic Instability*. New York: Columbia University Press, 1966.

Eberhardt, Walter von, ed. *Unsere Luftstreitkräfte, 1914–1918: Ein Denkmal deutschen Heldentums*. Berlin: Vaterländischer Verlag C. A. Weller, 1930.

Eichelbaum, Dr. *Das Buch von der Luftwaffe*. Berlin: Verlagshaus Bong, 1940.

———. *Jahrbuch der deutschen Luftwaffe 1940*. Leipzig: Breitkopf & Härtel, 1940.

———. *Jahrbuch der deutschen Luftwaffe 1941*. Leipzig: Breitkopf & Härtel, 1940.

Eichholtz, Dietrich. *Geschichte der deutschen Kriegswirtschaft, 1939–1945*. Vol. 1. Berlin (East): Akademie-Verlag, 1984.

———. *Geschichte der deutschen Kriegswirtschaft, 1939–1945*. Vol. 2. Berlin (East): Akademie-Verlag, 1985.

———. *Geschichte der deutschen Kriegswirtschaft, 1939–1945*. Vol. 3. Berlin: Akademie Verlag, 1996.

Engelmann, Joachim. *Das Buch der Artillerie, 1939–1945*. Friedberg: Podzun-Pallas-Verlag, 1983.

Ethell, Jerry, and Alfred Price. *Target Berlin: Mission 250, 6 March 1944*. London: Jane's, 1981.

Feuchter, Georg W. *Geschichte des Luftkriegs: Entwicklung und Zukunft*. Bonn: Athenäum-Verlag, 1954.

Finney, Robert T. *History of the Air Corps Tactical School, 1920–1940*. Maxwell AFB, Ala.: Research Studies Institute, 1955; reprint, Washington, D.C.: Center for Air Force History, 1992.

Foedrowitz, Michael. *Die Flaktürme in Berlin, Hamburg und Wien, 1940–1950*. Wölfersheim-Berstadt: Podzun-Pallas-Verlag, 1996.

Förster, Gerhard, and Olaf Groehler, eds. *Der zweite Weltkrieg*. Berlin (East): Militärverlag der Deutschen Demokratischen Republik, 1974.

Francis, Devon. *Flak Bait: The Story of the Men Who Flew the Martin Marauders*. New York: Duell, Sloan and Pearce, 1948.

Fraser, David. *Knight's Cross: A Life of Field Marshal Erwin Rommel*. New York: HarperCollins, 1993.

Freeman, Roger A. *Mighty Eighth War Manual*. London: Jane's, 1984.

———. *Raiding the Reich: The Allied Strategic Offensive in Europe*. London: Arms and Armour Press, 1997.

Fritzsche, Peter. *A Nation of Fliers: German Aviation and the Popular Imagination.* Cambridge: Harvard University Press, 1992.

Fröhlich, Elke. *Die Tagebücher von Joseph Goebbels: Sämtliche Fragmente.* Part I. Vol. 4. Munich: K. G. Saur, 1987.

———. *Die Tagebücher von Joseph Goebbels: Sämtliche Fragmente.* Part II. Vol. 1. Munich: K. G. Saur, 1996.

———. *Die Tagebücher von Joseph Goebbels: Sämtliche Fragmente.* Part II. Vol. 2. Munich: K. G. Saur, 1996.

———. *Die Tagebücher von Joseph Goebbels: Sämtliche Fragmente.* Part II. Vol. 4. Munich: K. G. Saur, 1995.

———. *Die Tagebücher von Joseph Goebbels: Sämtliche Fragmente.* Part II. Vol. 7. Munich: K. G. Saur, 1993.

———. *Die Tagebücher von Joseph Goebbels: Sämtliche Fragmente.* Part II. Vol. 9. Munich: K. G. Saur, 1993.

———. *Die Tagebücher von Joseph Goebbels: Sämtliche Fragmente.* Part II. Vol. 11. Munich: K. G. Saur, 1994.

———. *Die Tagebücher von Joseph Goebbels: Sämtliche Fragmente.* Part II. Vol. 13. Munich: K. G. Saur, 1995.

———. *Die Tagebücher von Joseph Goebbels: Sämtliche Fragmente.* Part II. Vol. 15. Munich: K. G. Saur, 1996.

Galland, Adolf, *Die Ersten und die Letzten: Jagdflieger im Zweiten Weltkrieg.* Munich: Franz Schneekluth Verlag, 1953.

———. *The First and the Last: The Rise and Fall of the German Fighter Forces, 1938–1945.* Translated by Mervyn Savill. New York: Ballantine Books, 1954.

Garland, Albert N., and Howard McGaw Smyth. *Sicily and the Surrender of Italy.* United States Army in World War II. Washington, D.C.: GPO, 1965.

Gatzke, Hans W. "Russo-German Military Cooperation During the Weimar Republic." *The American Historical Review* 63 (April 1958): 565–597.

Germany, Kriegswissenschaftliche Abteilung der Luftwaffe, ed. *Der Luftschutz im Weltkrieg.* Berlin: E. S. Mittler und Sohn, 1941.

Germany, Reichsluftfahrtministerium, Kriegswissenschaftliche Abteilung der Luftwaffe. *Die deutschen Luftstreitkräfte von ihrer Entstehung bis zum Ende des Weltkrieges 1918.* Text-Band, *Die Militärluftfahrt bis zum Beginn des Weltkrieges, 1914, Anlage-Band, Dokumente-Karten-Tabellen.* Berlin: E. S. Mittler und Sohn, 1941.

———. *Die deutschen Luftstreitkräfte von ihrer Entstehung bis zum Ende des Weltkrieges 1918.* Vol. 6, *Die Luftstreitkräfte in der Abwehrschlacht zwischen Somme und Oise vom 8. bis 12. August 1918.* Berlin: E. S. Mittler und Sohn, 1942.

Gersdorff, Ursula von. *Frauen im Kriegsdienst, 1914–1945.* Beiträge zur Militär- und Kriegsgeschichte. Stuttgart: Deutsche Verlags-Anstalt, 1969.

Geyer, Michael. "Das Zweite Rüstungsprogramm (1930–1934)." *Militärgeschichtliche Mitteilungen* 1 (1975): 125–174.

Girbig, Werner. . . . *mit Kurs auf Leuna: Die Luftoffensive gegen die Treibstoffindustrie und der deutsche Abwehreinsatz, 1944–1945.* Stuttgart: Motorbuch Verlag, 1980.

Golücke, Friedhelm. *Schweinfurt und der strategische Luftkrieg, 1943: Der Angriff der*

US Air Force vom 14. Oktober 1943 gegen die Schweinfurter Kugellagerindustrie. Paderborn: Ferdinand Schönigh, 1980.

Görlitz, Walter. *The German General Staff: History and Structure, 1657–1945.* Translated by Brian Battershaw. London: Hollis and Carter, 1953.

Granier, Gerhard. "Die Luftverteidigungszone-West." *Jahrbuch für westdeutsche Landesgeschichte* 19 (1993): 539–553.

Greenhous, Brereton, Stephen J. Harris, William C. Johnston, and William G. P. Rawling. *The Official History of the Royal Canadian Air Force.* Vol. 3, *The Crucible of War, 1939–1945.* Toronto: University of Toronto Press, 1994.

Groehler, Olaf. *Kampf um die Luftherrschaft.* 2nd ed. Berlin (East): Militärverlag der DDR, 1988.

———. "The Soviet Long-Range Airforces in the Great Patriotic War of the USSR (1941–1945)." *Militärhistorisk Tidskrift 1991*: 123–150.

Haffner, Sebastian. *Der Teufelspakt: Fünfzig Jahre deutsch-russische Beziehungen.* Hamburg: Rowohlt Taschenbuch Verlag, 1968.

Harris, Arthur. *Bomber Offensive.* London: Collins, 1947. Reprint, London: Greenhill Books, 1990.

Hastings, Donald W., David G. Wright, and Bernard C. Glueck. *Psychiatric Experiences of the Eighth Air Force.* N.p., 1944.

Hentschel, Georg, ed. *Die geheimen Konferenzen des Generalluftzeugmeisters: Ausgewählte und kommentierte Dokumente zur Geschichte der deutschen Luftrüstung und des Luftkrieges, 1942–1944.* Vol. 1. Koblenz: Bernard & Graefe Verlag, 1989.

Herbert, Ulrich. *Hitler's Foreign Workers: Enforced Labor in Germany Under the Third Reich.* Translated by William Templer. New York: Cambridge University Press, 1997.

Herrmann, Hajo. *Eagle's Wings: The Autobiography of a Luftwaffe Pilot.* Translated by Peter Hinchliffe. Osceola, Wis.: Motorbooks International, 1991.

Hildebrand, Karl Friederich. *Die Generale der deutschen Luftwaffe, 1935–1945.* Vol. 1. Osnabrück: Biblio Verlag, 1990.

———. *Die Generale der deutschen Luftwaffe, 1935–1945.* Vol. 2. Osnabrück: Biblio Verlag, 1991.

———. *Die Generale der deutschen Luftwaffe, 1935–1945.* Vol. 3. Osnabrück: Biblio Verlag, 1992.

Hinchliffe, Peter. *The Other Battle: Luftwaffe Night Aces Versus Bomber Command.* Osceola, Wis.: Motorbooks International, 1996.

Hoffmann, Norbert. "Der Luftangriff auf Lauffen am 13. April 1944." *Lauffener Heimatblätter* 8 (April 1994): 1–24.

Hoffmann-Heyden, A. E. "German Radiolocation in Retrospect." *Interavia* 11 (1951): 625–626.

Hogg, Ian V. *Anti-Aircraft: A History of Air Defence.* London: MacDonald and Jane's Publishers, 1978.

———. *British and American Artillery of World War 2.* London: Arms and Armour Press, 1978.

———. *German Artillery of World War Two.* London: Arms and Armour Press, 1975.

Holley, Irving B., Jr. *Buying Aircraft: Matériel Procurement for the Army Air Forces.* United States Army in World War II. Washington, D.C.: GPO, 1964.

Hölsken, Heinz-Dieter. *Die V-Waffen: Entstehung, Propaganda, Kriegseinsatz.* Stuttgart: Deutsche Verlags-Anstalt, 1984.

Homze, Edward L. *Arming the Luftwaffe: The Reich Air Ministry and the German Aircraft Industry, 1919–1939.* Lincoln: University of Nebraska Press, 1976.

Hooton, E. R. *Eagle in Flames: The Fall of the Luftwaffe.* London: Arms and Armour Press, 1997.

Höppner, Ernst von. *Germany's War in the Air: A Retrospect on the Development and the Work of Our Military Aviation Forces in the World War.* Translated by J. Hawley Larned. Leipzig: A. F. Kochler, 1921.

Hubatsch, Walther, ed. *Hitlers Weisungen für die Kriegführung, 1939–1945.* Frankfurt am Main: Bernard & Graefe Verlag für Wehrwissen, 1962.

Hummel, Karl-Heinz. "Die Kommandostrukturen in der Reichsluftverteidigung, 1939–1945." In *Deutsches Soldatenjahrbuch 1987*, edited by H. Dameran, 428–432. Munich: Schild Verlag, 1986.

———. "Die Kommandostrukturen in der Reichsluftverteidigung 1939–1945." In *Deutsches Soldatenjahrbuch 1988,* edited by H. Dameran, 237. Munich: Schild Verlag, 1987.

———. "Die Kommandostrukturen in der Reichsluftverteidigung, 1939–1945." In *Deutsches Soldatenjahrbuch 1989*, edited by H. Dameran, 294–297. Munich: Schild Verlag, 1988.

Hunke, Heinrich. *Luftgefahr und Luftschutz: Mit besonderer Berücksichtigung des deutschen Luftschutzes.* Berlin: E. S. Mittler und Sohn, 1933.

Hunt, P. D. R., and Z. Bieniawski. *Air Photographic Analysis of German A.A. Defences.* In the field: Mediterranean Allied Photographic Reconnaissance Wing, 1944.

Irvine, E. Eastman. *The World Almanac and Book of Facts.* New York: New York World-Telegram, 1942.

Irving, David. *The Rise and Fall of the Luftwaffe: The Life of Field Marshal Erhard Milch.* Boston: Little, Brown, 1973.

Jane's Aircraft of World War II. Glasgow: HarperCollins, 1995.

Jochmann, Werner, ed. *Adolf Hitler: Monologe im Führerhauptquartier, 1941–1944.* Hamburg: Albrecht Knauss, 1980.

Keller, Oberstleutnant von. *Die heutige Wehrlosigkeit Deutschlands im Lichte seiner Verteidigung gegen die Fliegerangriffe im Kriege 1914/18.* Berlin: Verlag Offene Worte, n.d.

Kennett, Lee. *The First Air War, 1914–1918.* New York: Free Press, 1991.

Kershaw, Ian. *Hitler: 1936–1945, Nemesis.* New York: Norton, 2000.

Kesselring, Albert. "Die Deutsche Luftwaffe." In *Bilanz des zweiten Weltkrieges: Erkenntnisse und Verpflichtungen für die Zukunft.* Oldenburg: Gerhard Stalling Verlag, 1953.

———. *Gedanken zum zweiten Weltkrieg.* Bonn: Athenäum-Verlag, 1955.

———. *The Memoirs of Field Marshal Kesselring.* Translated by Kenneth Macksey. Novato, Calif.: Presidio Press, 1988.

Klein, Burton H. *Germany's Economic Preparations for War.* Cambridge: Harvard University Press, 1959.

Koch, Horst-Adalbert. *Flak: Die Geschichte der deutschen Flakartillerie, 1939–1945.* Bad Nauheim: Verlag Hans-Henning Podzun, 1954.

Koller, Karl. *Der Letzte Monat: Die Tagebuchaufzeichnungen des ehemaligen Chefs des Generalstabs der deutschen Luftwaffe vom 14. April bis zum 27. Mai 1945*. Mannheim: Norbert Wohlgemuth Verlag, 1949.

Kranzberg, Melvin. *The Siege of Paris, 1870–1871: A Political and Social History*. Ithaca, N.Y.: Cornell University Press, 1950.

Kroener, Bernhard R., Rolf-Dieter Müller, and Hans Umbreit. *Das Deutsche Reich und der Zweite Weltkrieg*. Vol. 5, *Organisation und Mobilisierung des deutschen Machtbereichs*. Stuttgart: Deutsche Verlags-Anstalt, 1988.

Lange, Curt von, ed. *Flakartillerie greift an: Tatsachenberichte in Wort und Bild*. Berlin: Verlag Scherl, 1941.

———. *Gegen Bomber, Bunker, Panzer*. Berlin: Verlag Scherl, 1942.

Lee, Asher. *The German Air Force*. New York: Harper and Brothers, 1946.

———. *Goering: Air Leader*. London: Duckworth, 1972.

LeMay, Curtis, E., and MacKinlay Kantor. *Mission with LeMay: My Story*. Garden City, N.Y.: Doubleday, 1965.

Leuthner, Stuart, and Oliver Jensen. *High Honor*. Washington, D.C.: Smithsonian Institution Press, 1989.

Ludendorff, Erich. *Ludendorff's Own Story, August 1914–November 1918*. Translator not identified. Vol. 1. New York: Harper and Brothers, 1919.

Ludwig, Karl-Heinz. "Die deutschen Flakraketen im Zweiten Weltkrieg." *Militärgeschichtliche Mitteilungen* 1 (1969): 87–100.

MacIsaac, David, ed. *The United States Strategic Bombing Survey*. Vol. 1, *The Effects of Strategic Bombing on the German War Economy*. New York: Garland, 1976.

———. *The United States Strategic Bombing Survey*. Vol. 2, *Civil Defense Division Final Report*. New York: Garland, 1976.

Mason, Herbert Molloy, Jr. *The Rise of the Luftwaffe: Forging the Secret Air Weapon, 1918–1940*. New York: Dial Press, 1973.

Mason, Tony. *Air Power: A Centennial Appraisal*. London: Brassey's, 1994.

Maurer, Maurer. *Aviation in the U.S. Army, 1919–1939*. Washington, D.C.: Office of Air Force History, 1987.

McArthur, Charles W. *History of Mathematics*. Vol. 4, *Operations Analysis in the U.S. Army Eighth Air Force in World War II*. Providence, R.I.: American Mathematical Society, 1990.

McFarland, Stephen L., and Wesley P. Newton. *To Command the Sky: The Battle for Air Superiority over Germany, 1942–1944*. Washington, D.C.: Smithsonian Institution Press, 1991.

Mennel, Rainer. *Die Schlussphase des zweiten Weltkrieges im Westen (1944/45)*. Osnabrück: Biblio Verlag, 1981.

Middlebrook, Martin. *The Battle of Hamburg: Allied Bomber Forces Against a German City in 1943*. New York: Scribner's, 1980.

———. *The Berlin Raids: R.A.F. Bomber Command Winter, 1943–1944*. New York: Viking, 1988.

———. *The Schweinfurt-Regensburg Mission*. New York: Scribner's, 1983.

Militärgeschichtliches Forschungsamt, ed. *Die Generalstäbe in Deutschland, 1871–1945: Aufgaben in der Armee und Stellung im Staate*. Vol. 3. *Die Entwicklung der militärischen Luftfahrt in Deutschland, 1920–1933: Planung und Maßnahmen zur*

Schaffung einer Fliegertruppe in der Reichswehr. Stuttgart: Deutsche Verlags-Anstalt, 1962.

Mondey, David, ed. *The Luftwaffe at War, 1939–1945*. Chicago: Henry Regnery, 1972.

Morris, Warren B., Jr. *The Weimar Republic and Nazi Germany*. Chicago: Nelson Hall, 1982.

Morrow, John H., Jr. *The Great War in the Air: Military Aviation from 1909–1921*. Washington, D.C.: Smithsonian Institution Press, 1993.

Müller, Werner. *German Flak in World War II*. Atglen, Pa.: Schiffer Military/Aviation History, 1998.

Murray, Williamson. *Strategy for Defeat: The Luftwaffe, 1933–1945*. Maxwell AFB, Ala.: Air University Press, 1983.

Musgrove, Gordon. *Operation Gomorrah: The Hamburg Firestorm Raids*. London: Jane's, 1981.

Nafziger, George F. *German Order of Battle, World War II*. Vol. 3, *German Artillery: Independent Battalions, Railroad, Coastal, Flak, and Sturmgeschütz*. West Chester, Ohio: By the author, 1994.

Nagel, Fritz. *Fritz: The World War I Memoirs of a German Lieutenant*. Edited by Richard A. Baumgartner. Huntington, W.Va.: Der Angriff Publications, 1981.

Neufeld, Michael J. *The Rocket and the Reich: Peenemünde and the Coming of the Ballistic Missile Era*. Cambridge: Harvard University Press, 1995.

Neumann, Georg Paul. *Die deutschen Luftstreitkräfte im Weltkriege*. Berlin: E. S. Mittler und Sohn, 1920.

———. *The German Air Force in the Great War*. Rev. ed. Translated by J. E. Gurdon. Portway Bath, England: Cedric Chivers, 1969.

Newby, Leroy W. *Target Ploesti: View from a Bombsight*. Novato, Calif.: Presidio Press, 1983.

Nicolaisen, Hans Dietrich. *Die Flakhelfer: Luftwaffenhelfer und Marinehelfer im Zweiten Weltkrieg*. Berlin: Ullstein Verlag, 1981.

Niehaus, Werner. *Die Nachrichtentruppe: 1914 bis heute*. Stuttgart: Motorbuch Verlag, 1980.

———. *Die Radarschlacht, 1939–1945: Die Geschichte des Hochfrequenzkrieges*. Stuttgart: Motorbuch Verlag, 1977.

Noakes, Jeremy, ed. *Nazism, 1919–1945*. Vol. 4, *The German Home Front in World War II*. Exeter, Devon: University of Exeter Press, 1998.

Nowarra, Heinz J. *50 Jahre Deutsche Luftwaffe, 1910–1960*. Vol. 3. Genoa: Intyrama, 1967.

Orlovius, H., ed. *Schwert am Himmel: Fünf Jahre deutsche Luftwaffe*. Berlin: Verlag Scherl, 1940.

Overy, Richard. *The Air War, 1939–1945*. New York: Stein and Day, 1981.

———. *Goering: The "Iron Man."* London: Routledge and Kegan Paul, 1984.

———. *Why the Allies Won*. New York: Norton, 1995.

Perret, Geoffrey. *Winged Victory: The Army Air Forces in World War II*. New York: Random House, 1993.

Pickert, Wolfgang. *Unsere Flakartillerie: Einführung in ihre Grundlagen für Soldaten und Laien*. Berlin: E. S. Mittler und Sohn, 1937.

Pielkalkiewicz, Janusz. *Die 8,8 Flak im Erdkampf-Einsatz.* Stuttgart: Motorbuch Verlag, 1999.

Pöchlinger, Josef, ed. *Front in der Heimat: Das Buch des deutschen Rüstungsarbeiters.* Berlin: Otto Elsner Verlagsgesellschaft, 1942.

Price, Alfred. *The Last Year of the Luftwaffe, May 1944 to May 1945.* Osceola, Wis.: Motorbooks International, 1991.

———. *Luftwaffe Handbook, 1939–1945.* New York: Scribner's, 1977.

Proctor, Raymond L. *Hitler's Luftwaffe in the Spanish Civil War.* Westport, Conn.: Greenwood Press, 1983.

Puttkammer, Hans Georg von, ed. *Flakkorps "I" im Westen.* Berlin: Volk und Reich Verlag, 1943.

Reuth, Ralf Georg. *Goebbels.* Translated by Krishna Winston. New York: Harcourt Brace, 1993.

Rhoden, Herhudt von. *European Contributions to the History of World War II.* Vol. 4, *The Battle for Air Supremacy over Germany, 1939–1945.* N.p., [1947].

———. *European Contributions to the History of World War II.* Vol. 3, *Reich Air Defense, 1939–1945.* N.p., 1946.

Richards, Denis. *The Hardest Victory: RAF Bomber Command in the Second World War.* New York: Norton, 1994.

———. *Portal of Hungerford: The Life of Marshal of the Royal Air Force Viscount Portal of Hungerford.* London: William Heinemann, 1977.

Ries, Karl, and Hans Ring. *The Legion Condor: A History of the Luftwaffe in the Spanish Civil War, 1936–1939.* Translated by David Johnston. West Chester, Pa.: Schiffer Military Aviation, 1992.

Ritter, Hans. *Der Luftkrieg.* Leipzig: von Hase & Koehler Verlag, 1926.

Robineau, Lucien. "French Interwar Air Policy and Air War, 1939–1940." In *The Conduct of the Air War in the Second World War: An International Comparison,* edited by Horst Boog, 627–657. New York: Berg, 1992.

Routledge, N. W. *History of the Royal Regiment of Artillery: Anti-aircraft Artillery, 1914–55.* London: Brassey's, 1994.

Rumpf, Hans. *The Bombing of Germany.* Translated by Edward Fitzgerald. New York: Holt, Rinehart and Winston, 1963.

Sauter, Emil. *Fla-nach vorn: Kampf der Fliegerabwehr Bataillone u. Kompanien des Heeres.* Mülhausen in Thüringia: Verlag von G. Danner, 1942.

Schabel, Ralf. *Die Illusion der Wunderwaffen: Die Rolle der Düsenflugzeuge und Flugabwehrraketen in der Rüstungspolitik des Dritten Reiches.* Beiträge zur Militärgeschichte. Munich: R. Oldenbourg Verlag, 1994.

Schmeling, Franz-Josef. *Vom Krieg ein Leben lang geprägt: Ehemalige Luftwaffen- und Marinehelfer antworten 50 Jahre danach.* Osnabrück: H. Th. Wenner, 1997.

Schnatz, Helmut. *Der Luftkrieg im Raum Koblenz, 1944/45: Eine Darstellung seines Verlaufs, seiner Auswirkungen und Hintergründe.* Boppard am Rhein: Harald Boldt Verlag, 1981.

Scholes, David. *Air War Diary: An Australian in Bomber Command.* Kenthurst, New South Wales: Kangaroo Press, 1997.

Schörken, Rolf. *Luftwaffenhelfer und Drittes Reich: Die Entstehung eines politischen Bewußtseins.* Stuttgart: Klett-Cotta, 1984.

Schramm, Percy E., ed. *Kriegstagebuch des Oberkommandos der Wehrmacht, 1940–1945.* Vol. 8. Bonn: Bernard & Graefe Verlag, 1965.

Schumann, Wolfgang, and Wolfgang Bleyer. *Deutschland im zweiten Weltkrieg.* Vol. 4, *Das Scheitern der faschistischen Defensivstrategie an der Deutsch-Sowjetischen Front.* Berlin (East): Akademie-Verlag, 1981.

———. *Deutschland im zweiten Weltkrieg.* Vol. 5, *Der Zusammenbruch der Defensivstrategie des Hitlerfaschismus an allen Fronten. (Januar bis August 1944).* Cologne: Pahl-Rugenstein Verlag, 1984.

Schumann, Wolfgang, Olaf Groehler, and Wolfgang Bleyer. *Deutschland im zweiten Weltkrieg.* Vol. 6, *Die Zerschlagung des Hitlerfaschismus und die Befreiung des deutschen Volkes.* Cologne: Pahl-Rugenstein Verlag, 1985.

Schüttel, Lothar. *Luftsperren: Sperrballone, Luftminen und Drachen.* Munich: J. F. Lehmanns Verlag, 1939.

Schwarte, Max, ed. *Die militärischen Lehren des Großen Krieges.* Berlin: E. S. Mittler und Sohn, 1920.

———. *Die Technik im Weltkriege.* Berlin: E. S. Mittler und Sohn, 1920.

Seidler, Franz W. *Blitzmädchen: Die Geschichte der Helferinnen der deutschen Wehrmacht.* Bonn: Bernard & Graefe Verlag, 1996.

———. *Frauen zu den Waffen? Marketenderinnen, Helferinnen, Soldatinnen.* Koblenz: Wehr & Wissen, 1978.

Showalter, Dennis. *Railroads and Rifles: Soldiers, Technology, and the Unification of Germany.* Hamden, Conn.: Archon Books, 1975.

Solltau, Günter. *Die Flakabteilung I./12: Geschichte und Schicksal 1914–1945.* Berlin: Privately printed by the Kameradschaft des ehemaligen Flakregiments 12, 1989. Collection of the German Military History Research Office.

Speer, Albert. *Inside the Third Reich: Memoirs by Albert Speer.* Translated by Richard Winston and Clara Winston. New York: Macmillan, 1970.

Spires, David N. *Image and Reality: The Making of the German Officer, 1921–1933.* Westport, Conn.: Greenwood Press, 1984.

Steinacker, Heinrich. *Fla-Btl (mot) 22: Seine Geschichte.* Siegen: Bonn und Fries, 1984.

Stöber, Hans. *Die Flugabwehrverbände der Waffen-SS.* Preußisch Oldendorf: Verlag K. W. Schütz, 1984.

Stokesbury, James L. *A Short History of World War I.* New York: William Morrow, 1981.

Suchenwirth, Richard. *The Development of the German Air Force, 1919–1939.* Maxwell AFB, Ala.: USAF Historical Division, 1968.

———. *Historical Turning Points in the German Air Force War Effort.* Maxwell AFB, Ala.: USAF Historical Division, 1968.

Tantum, William H., IV, and E. J. Hoffschmidt. *The Rise and Fall of the German Air Force.* Old Greenwich, Conn.: WE, 1969.

Target Germany: The Army Air Forces' Official Story of the VIII Bomber Command's First Year over Europe. New York: Simon and Schuster, 1943.

Teetzmann, Otto A. *Der Luftschutz: Leitfaden für alle.* Berlin: Verlag des Reichsluftschutzbundes, n.d.

Tessin, Georg. *Deutsche Verbände und Truppen, 1918–1939.* Osnabrück: Biblio Verlag, 1974.

Thomas, Georg. *Geschichte der deutschen Wehr- und Rüstungswirtschaft (1918–1943/45)*. Boppard am Rhein: Harald Boldt Verlag, 1966.

Tress, Harvey B. *British Strategic Bombing Policy Through 1940: Politics, Attitudes, and the Formation of a Lasting Pattern*. Studies in British History. Lewiston, N.Y.: Edwin Mellen Press, 1988.

United States, Ninth Air Force, Flak Section. *Flak Facts: A Brief History of Flak and Flak Intelligence in the Ninth Air Force*. N.p., 1945.

Vogt, Hans, and Herbert Brenne. *Krefeld im Luftkrieg, 1939–1945*. Bonn: Ludwig Röhrscheid Verlag, 1986.

Völker, Karl-Heinz. *Die Deutsche Luftwaffe, 1933–1939: Aufbau, Führung und Rüstung der Luftwaffe sowie die Entwicklung der deutschen Luftkriegstheorie*. Stuttgart: Deutsche Verlags-Anstalt, 1967.

Wagner, Gerhard, ed. *Lagevorträge des Oberbefehlshabers der Kriegsmarine vor Hitler, 1939–1945*. Munich: J. F. Lehmanns Verlag, 1972.

Walb, Lore. *Ich, die Alte—ich, die Junge: Konfrontation mit meinen Tagebüchern, 1933–1945*. Berlin: Aufbau Verlag, 1997.

Webster, Charles, and Noble Frankland. *The Strategic Air Offensive Against Germany, 1939–1945*. Vol. 1, *Preparation*. London: Her Majesty's Stationery Office, 1961.

———. *The Strategic Air Offensive Against Germany, 1939–1945*. Vol. 2, *Endeavour*. London: Her Majesty's Stationery Office, 1961.

———. *The Strategic Air Offensive Against Germany, 1939–1945*. Vol. 3, *Victory*. London: Her Majesty's Stationery Office, 1961.

———. *The Strategic Air Offensive Against Germany, 1939–1945*. Vol. 4, *Annexes and Appendices*. London: Her Majesty's Stationery Office, 1961.

Weinberg, Gerhard. *Germany, Hitler, and World War II*. New York: Cambridge University Press, 1995.

———, ed. *Hitlers zweites Buch: Ein Dokument aus dem Jahr 1928*. Vol. 7. Quellen und Darstellungen zur Zeitgeschichte. Stuttgart: Deutsche Verlags-Anstalt, 1961.

———. *A World at Arms: A Global History of World War II*. New York: Cambridge University Press, 1994.

Wells, Mark K. *Courage and Air Warfare: The Allied Aircrew Experience in the Second World War*. London: Frank Cass, 1995.

Weltkrieg, 1939–1945: Ehrenbuch der deutschen Wehrmacht. Stuttgart: Buch- und Zeitschriften-Verlag Dr. Hans Riegler, 1954.

Werrell, Kenneth P. *Archie, Flak, AAA, and SAM: A Short Operational History of Ground-Based Air Defense*. Maxwell AFB, Ala.: Air University Press, 1988.

Wetzell, Georg, ed. *Die Deutsche Wehrmacht, 1914–1939*. Berlin: E. S. Mittler und Sohn, 1939.

Wolf, Werner. *Luftangriffe auf die deutsche Industrie, 1942–45*. Munich: Universitas Verlag, 1985.

Yeager, Chuck, and Leo Janos. *Yeager: An Autobiography*. New York: Bantam Books, 1985.

Zeidler, Manfred. *Reichswehr und Rote Armee, 1920–1933*. 2nd ed. Beiträge zur Militärgeschichte. Munich: R. Oldenbourg Verlag, 1994.

Zeppelin, Ferdinand von. *Die Eroberung der Luft*. Stuttgart: Deutsche Verlags-Anstalt, 1908.

Index